Systems Analysis and Design:
An Active Approach

George M. Marakas

Kelley School of Business
Indiana University

Upper Saddle River, New Jersey

Marakas, George M.
 Systems analysis and design: an active approach/George M. Marakas
  p. cm.
 ISBN 0-13-022515-0
 1. System design. 2. System analysis. I. Title

 QA76.9.S88 M362 2000
 004.2'1—dc21

Editors: Robert Horan and David Alexander
Editorial Assistant: Erika Rusnak
Associate Editor: Kyle Hannon
Senior Marketing Manager: Sharon Turkovich
Permissions Coordinator: Suzanne Grappi
Director of Production: Michael Weinstein
Manager, Production: Gail Steier de Acevedo
Production Coordinator: Kelly Warsak
Manufacturing Buyer: Natacha St. Hill Moore
Associate Director, Manufacturing: Vincent Scelta
Cover Design: Janet Slowik
Full Service Composition: Impressions Book and Journal Services, Inc.
Printing and Binding: Courier/Kendallville

10 9 8 7 6 5 4 3 2 1
ISBN 0-13-022515-0

This book is dedicated to my wonderful daughter Stephanie:
Always teach from your heart and
your students will always keep you in theirs.

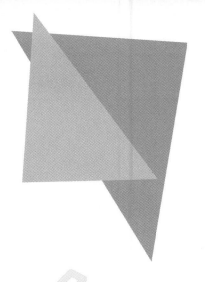

Brief Contents

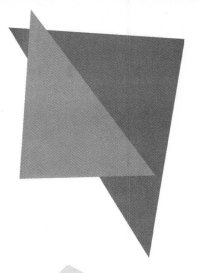

Contents

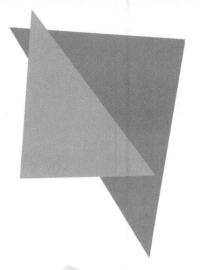

Preface

... twenty-five or thirty years ago, a conference called the "CEO in the Wired World" would not have been possible. And twenty years from now, it will not be necessary.

—PETER DRUCKER, EXCERPT FROM KEYNOTE ADDRESS AT THE FIRST CEO TECHNOLOGY RETREAT IN 1994

We are witnessing the early, turbulent days of a revolution as significant as any other in human history. A new medium of human communication is emerging—one that may surpass the printing press, telephone, and television in its impact on our economic and social lives. Interactive multimedia and the information highway are creating a new economy based on the networking of human intelligence.

—DONALD TAPSCOTT, *THE DIGITAL ECONOMY*

These two epigraphs, when combined in message, serve to define the role of the systems analyst in the twenty-first century. Anything that can become digital will become digital, and this means that all organizations will ultimately become irreversibly dependent on their information and automation systems and the people who design, develop, and maintain them. The core competencies for the information systems (IS) professional in this wired world are built on an understanding of the process by which a business problem or economic opportunity is identified and a successful solution is crafted.

This is exactly what this textbook is about—the core competency for the twenty-first century IS professional—systems analysis and design (SAD). As organizations increase both their awareness of IS as strategic tools and their dependency on them, they are also embracing the structured techniques, developed and refined over the last four decades, used to design and implement those systems. In this new economy, the age-old role of programmer as designer is being replaced by the professional Business Technologist, written with a capital *B* and a capital *T*. Organizations need IS professionals that both understand the intricacies of their business and can skillfully apply a technological solution to their complex problems and strategic initiatives. Although the names and the activities have changed over the last 40 years, this person has been, and will continue to be, the professional systems analyst.

In the coming decades, no stone will be left unturned with regard to the design and deployment of information technologies to capture the narrow windows of economic opportunities that present themselves to wired organizations. For the most part, these "stones" will be turned over by systems analysts who have been trained in structured problem-solving approaches and the crafting of holistic, technology-based solutions. No company of any measurable size will be able to function without a highly valued cadre of systems analysts that are always at the center of their information initiatives. A recent conversation with a bright MBA student of mine may help to make this point. We will call him Jim.

> "Professor Marakas," said Jim. "I am really struggling with where to focus my energies in getting a job when I graduate. It just seems like the really hot technology companies are in such demand that everyone is aiming for them, and I am worried that I will not be able to compete with the rest of the computer geeks."
>
> "This is quite a surprise to me, Jim," I said. "I was under the impression that you received a rather substantial offer from United Parcel Service just last week."
>
> Jim's expression was clearly one of disappointment. "Oh yeah," he said. " The offer from UPS was great, but I was counting on working for a company that was really driven by technology so that I could get involved in some cutting edge stuff. I really do not want to work for someone that delivers boxes all day."
>
> It was clear to me that Jim had missed the most important aspect of the job offer. "Jim, what business do you think UPS is really in?" I queried.
>
> Jim quickly informed me that, "UPS delivers boxes."

The point of this anecdote is that the world is wired and, regardless of the product or service that a company offers, it is most certainly highly dependent on IS. UPS is in more than the box delivery business; it is also a manager, provider, and procurer of reliable information about its deliveries. In a larger sense, everything it does is information—the numbers and letters written on the packages and swirling in the organization's electronic soup are just as critical to achieving the company's mission as the jets and vans that actually transport the packages. All of this information is managed by the team of IS professionals, including a large army of systems analysts, employed at UPS—a company, by the way, that has one of the largest IS budgets in the world!

CONCEPT AND PURPOSE

Teaching systems analysis poses several challenges to the modern business school. Most notably, systems analysis is not something you *know,* it is something you *do.* Because of this, learning how to *do* systems analysis cannot be easily accomplished simply by reading a book. This text and its accompanying curriculum resources were developed using the guiding principle that when students are *doing* systems analysis they develop a richer understanding of the concepts, activities, tools, and techniques that are used daily by the professional systems analyst. Further, given the fierce competition for jobs at the undergraduate and MBA levels, those students, when interviewing, who can say "I have done that" or "I have used that analysis tool" will fair much better than the student who can only say "I have read about that" or "We learned about that tool in our systems class." This is the essence of this book— *an active approach to systems analysis and design.*

WHO SHOULD USE THIS BOOK

This book is directed to business school students who aspire to a career in IS and who want to be an integral part of the strategic initiatives of their organization. The primary targets for this text are upper-level undergraduate or MBA SAD requisites or electives. These types of courses are regularly offered at both four-year universities and many community colleges. Ideally, students should have completed an introductory MIS program and, most likely, a semester of structured programming before moving toward a focus on SAD. In addition, the chapter content and organization also assumes that the student has already completed, or is concurrently completing, a database design course. Finally, the farther the student is in their business curriculum, the more relevant the structured problem-solving perspective of the text becomes. The chapters in this text are written so as to provide a good reference for both students and practitioners to use throughout the course of their daily analysis and design activities.

ELEMENTS OF PEDAGOGY

This text employs a variety of pedagogical techniques intended to create a rich, realistic environment in which the student can actively pursue an understanding of the world of SAD. The combination of the various approaches to learning used in this program of study is also intended to accommodate the widest possible range of cognitive styles for both the instructor and the students.

Chapter Learning Objectives

A statement of learning objectives for each chapter is presented in both performance and behavioral terms. In other words, the objectives state what the student should be capable of *understanding* and *doing* as a result of reading the chapter.

Figures and Tables

Clear and carefully designed figures and tables have been included to aid in the student's understanding of the material. Wherever possible, the diagrams contained in each chapter are not only referenced in the body of the text but are positioned such that they can serve as a repeated visual reference for the detailed explanation that follows.

Key Concepts

Immediately following each chapter summary is a highly detailed outline of the key concepts presented in the chapter in order of their appearance. This section can aid the student in reviewing the material contained in the chapter in preparation for either class discussion or examination.

Questions for Review

Each chapter contains a list of 10 to 20 questions intended to allow students to test their retention and understanding of the material contained in the chapter. Each question is phrased such that the answer can be readily found in the chapter and that a detailed and precise answer can be provided. Sample responses to each question are provided in the Instructor's Manual section of the CD-ROM supplement to this text.

Further Discussion

Following the review questions, several additional questions are provided at the end of each chapter that expand on the material presented. These questions are intended to allow the student to engage in a richer thought process and discussion than would occur using only the review questions. Each of the discussion questions can be used to engage students in an open class discussion, and many of them easily can be expanded into individual or team miniprojects.

Role-Play Case Scenarios

One of the most unique aspects of this approach to *doing* SAD is the use of multimedia-supported role-playing scenarios. Through the use of the access-controlled Web site available when purchased with this text, the students engage in a series of team-oriented, role-play case studies that are intended to simulate the activities, episodes, and encounters typically experienced during the various phases of the systems development life cycle (SDLC). Each case and its associated role-play presentation is designed to create a realistic simulation of the technical, organizational, social, cultural, and behavioral aspects of business problem identification and solving.

Role-play as a pedagogical approach brings with it a number of benefits unavailable in other learning approaches:

> ➤ It allows students to empathize with others in the various roles commonly found in a social setting.

> ➤ Students can experience responsibilities and burdens associated with the role of the expert.

> ➤ The scenarios require students to select, sort, retrieve, link, and prioritize information.

> ➤ The ambiguity of the role-playing scenarios requires the participants to form hypotheses and generalizations from specific evidence.

> ➤ The role-play presentations to the "client" participants require the students to verbally and visually summarize issues relevant to the specific stage of the process.

> ➤ The students are able to reflect on how, what, and why they are learning.

> ➤ The participants are able to experience, firsthand, the chronological order of analysis and design events.

> ➤ Students develop their skills with regard to listening for meaning, purpose, innuendo, and tone as a means of garnering additional information from dialogue.

> ➤ Most important, the students learn to work meaningfully in groups, as a whole class, and individually.

Most would agree that it is not possible to teach SAD experiences. However, students can learn the theories that underlie good analysis and design practice. If they are then given the opportunity to apply these theories to real situations (but without the pressures of failure in an actual work environment), the students can learn how the theories apply in practice. When students are given immediate feedback, asked to reflect on that feedback, and provided an opportunity to put their revised thoughts into practice, they most certainly improve their individual skills in business problem identification and the technology-based crafting of appropriate solutions.

There is a significant amount of empirical evidence in support of the role-play approach to learning found in the academic literature. Kolb's model of experiential learning (Kolb, 1984) provides the educational validity of this approach. The Teach and Govahi (1993) survey found that role-plays were the most effective method of developing conflict resolution and communication skills. Van Ments (1983) identifies negotiation, a common activity in SAD, as one of the specific areas in which role-play is most effective. Petranek, Corey, and Black (1992) provide further advice on how to best use role-plays in higher education.[1]

Interactive Multimedia Web Site
<http://www.prenhall.com/marakas>

All of the materials necessary to conduct the role-playing case studies are delivered and managed through the accompanying Web-based course management system. The site contains the case study materials; streaming-video interview sessions with the client; various software-based analysis tools; a complete course management system, including syllabus generation, presentation scheduling, and course material distribution; and an automated peer evaluation system for grading the role-play presentations by each team.

Details of the setup and use of the Web-based course management systems can be found on instructor accessible sections of the Web site. The instructor accessible sections of the Web site are password protected. To receive your username and password, please contact your local Prentice Hall representative. If you need your representative's name and contact information, call our Faculty and Field Services department at 800-526-0485.

CHAPTER DESCRIPTIONS

Chapter 1—The Systems Development Environment

The opening chapter is intended to provide an overview of the environment of the modern systems analyst, as well as a conceptual understanding of the state of the art. We identify the various roles within the software development process, outline the basic skill set necessary to pursue a career in SAD, and present an initial understanding of the phased development approach.

Chapter 2—So What Is the Problem?

Chapter 2 focuses on developing an understanding of the concepts of problem recognition and problem definition. We present initial problem categorization tools, such as Ishikawa charts and Wetherbe's PIECES framework. Finally, we explain in

---

[1] Kolb, D. 1984. *Experiential Learning: Experience as the Source of Learning and Development.* Upper Saddle River, NJ: Prentice Hall.

Petranek, C., S. Corey, and R. Black. 1992. "Three Levels of Learning in Simulations: Participation, Debriefing, and Journal Writing." *Simulation and Gaming* 23(2): 174–185.

Teach, R., and G. Govahi. 1993. "The Role of Classroom Techniques in Teaching Management Skills," *Simulation and Gaming* 24(4): 429–445.

Van Ments, M. 1983. *The Effective Use of Role-Play.* London: Kogan Page.

detail the individual phases of the SDLC, along with the expected activities and deliverables from each.

Chapter 3—Identification and Selection of Development Projects

Chapter 3 acquaints the student with the processes by which organizations identify and select IS projects. In addition, we present the concept of an IS steering committee and discuss the various roles. Finally, this chapter introduces the logical versus physical building blocks of a modern IS.

Chapter 4—Systems Requirements Determination

The activities associated with gathering and organizing end users' requirements are the focus of chapter 4. Students are introduced to the various traditional and modern data gathering methods, along with examples of when each may be appropriately applied.

Chapter 5—Modeling the Processes and Logic

Chapter 5 covers the concepts, tools, and techniques associated with the construction of both process and logic models. We introduce the data flow diagram (DFD) and several logic modeling tools, including structured English, decision trees and tables, and state-transition diagrams.

Chapter 6—Modeling the Data: Conceptual and Logical Data Modeling

In chapter 6, we turn our attention to the tools and techniques associated with data modeling by introducing the entity-relationship diagram (ERD). To insure that these concepts are well-engrained in the students' understanding, we present in review form several building blocks from their database course, including cardinality, relationship degree, and optionality.

Chapter 7—CASE Tools and Joint and Rapid Application Development

Chapter 7 provides an overview of the evolution of modern CASE tools, as well as coverage of the advantages and disadvantages associated with their deployment in an organization. In addition, we present the process of joint application development in conjunction with an overview of rapid application development as it compares and contrasts to the traditional SDLC approach.

Chapter 8—Moving from Analysis to Design

Chapter 8 begins the shift of focus from the logical design of a system to the physical specifications. We present the various categories of feasibility assessment and economic justification in this chapter.

Chapter 9—Designing Systems for Diverse Environments

Chapter 9 is intended to allow the student to gain an appreciation of the diversity of design and development environments faced by the modern analyst. We discuss design issues related to centralized versus distributed systems, various network topologies, and unique characteristics of systems operating in enterprise resource planning (ERP), data warehouse, collaborative, and intranet environments.

Chapter 10—Designing the Files and Databases

The conversion of the logical data models to physical databases and files is presented in chapter 10. This chapter also serves as a review of the basic concepts taught in the typical database design course.

Chapter 11—Designing the System Output

In chapter 11, we present the basic characteristics of high quality system output and the processes and techniques commonly employed to create such output. In addition, the student is introduced to the concepts associated with the development of control strategies to manage the various types of outputs generated by IS. Finally, we present an overview of various backup and retention strategies.

Chapter 12—Designing the Inputs and User Interface

Chapter 12 covers the various types of common user interfaces and focuses the student on the importance of proper application and design of the interface. We present guidelines for effective interface design, and we continue, from an input control perspective, the presentation of control design issues that began in chapter 11.

Chapter 13—Designing the System Internals

The concepts of structured and modular design are presented in chapter 13. Here, the focus is on the design of high quality program code modules. We present and discuss several concepts, including factoring, coupling, cohesions, and module size.

Chapter 14—Implementing and Maintaining the System

The final chapter of the text allows students to explore the issues and constraints often associated with the activities performed during the implementation and maintenance of a new IS. Topics include selection of an appropriate test strategy, conversion planning and approaches, and development and delivery of various system documentation elements.

Appendix A—Project Management: Process, Techniques, and Tools

Appendix A is intended to be used as a refresher for those students who have had previous training or experience in cross–life cycle activities related to project management. If such training is not a normal part of the curriculum, appendix A can be taught as a separate module within the SAD course.

Appendix B—Object-Oriented Analysis and Design

Appendix B provides an overview of the object-oriented approach to analysis and design. It can be used as a reference, overview, or precursor to a more detailed discussion of the object-oriented methods.

INSTRUCTOR SUPPORT MATERIALS

The Instructor's Resource CD-ROM (0-13-028352-5) features the following support materials:

> ➤ *Instructor's Manual,* by George Marakas, contains teaching suggestions and answers to review and discussion questions. A detailed explanation of the

conduct of each of the ten NOMAS cases, along with sample solutions and deliverables is available on the Marakas Web site.

➤ *Test Item File,* by Nathan Stout, includes true/false, multiple choice, fill-in-the-blank, and essay questions for every chapter.

➤ *Prentice Hall Test Manager* delivers the Test Item File questions in a comprehensive suite of tools for testing and assessment.

➤ *PowerPoint Slides,* by George Marakas, feature key concepts and diagrams from the book.

Both students and faculty have access to the PowerPoint slides on the Marakas Web site <http://www.prenhall.com/marakas>. The Instructor's Manual is also available for download from a secure, password-protected faculty area of the site.

Acknowledgments

Having lived through the humbling, and sometimes arduous, experience of writing my first textbook, I vowed never to do it again. As evidenced by this text, my second, that vow was both short-lived and quickly forgotten. This was, to a large extent, due to my desire to make a positive contribution to the careers of the next generation of systems professionals. This was also due to the unending support and encouragement of my editor, David Alexander. Not being able to take "No" for an answer when he believes strongly in something or someone is one of David's many virtues. Thank you, David, for not giving up.

No project of this magnitude can be accomplished without the constant help of a number of devoted people. Some were charged with correcting my mistakes, others with answering my questions, several with contributing to the vast amount of required labor, and all with reassuring me in the myriad times of self-doubt and frustration. Without them, I do not believe this book would have come to pass. What follows is a brief, but nonetheless heartfelt, expression of my deepest gratitude and dedication to those people who were instrumental in the development of this project.

First and foremost, I must thank my biggest supporters, my parents, George and Joan Marakas. You have made many sacrifices over the years to get me to this point in my life and to allow me, once again, the opportunity to experience the adventure of being a writer. Moreover, you cared enough to actually read my first book and share it with friends and family. I hope this one is equally as lucky.

To my daughter, Stephanie, who is about to embark on her own career as an educator, I also express my thanks. Stephanie has never been shy about expressing her pride in me, and I want it on record that I am proud of her devotion to shaping the future through teaching. I am also just plain proud of her, too!

To Debra Herbenick, my best everything. Once again, through her careful and skillful editing, she transformed my often rambling thoughts into coherent sentences and paragraphs. Without her help, I would be lost. Thank you, LB, for touching feet, hands, and hearts. We could be a whole parade!

To my ever-faithful army of assistants—Yu-Ting "Caisy" Hung, Ji-Tsung "Ben" Wu, Nan Lu, Ya-Lun "Ellen" Huang, and Nate Stout—who invested endless hours in the final compilation of this text and its supporting Web site, thanks. You will be a part of this book, and whatever contribution it makes, forever.

A special thanks to my friend and colleague Carl O. Briggs for his invaluable contribution to the material contained in appendix A. In addition, a very special thanks for my longtime friend, Dr. Peeter Kirs, for allowing me to build on his creative approach to the teaching of systems analysis and to expand on the wonderful list of characters he created in NOMAS. Great projects are much easier to accomplish when they are built on the work of great people. Thanks again, Peeter.

To my mentors, Dan Robey and Joyce Elam: You have given of yourself to teach me how to teach others. Without your wisdom and guidance I would be lost.

I am also indebted to a number of people who reviewed the manuscript, offering their praise and suggestions for improvement:

Dennis Anderson—Pace University

Fred G. Harold—Florida Atlantic University

Richard Johnson—University of Central Florida

Joseph Kasten—Manhattan College

Stan Lewis—University of Southern Mississippi

Vicki McKinney—University of Wisconsin, Milwaukee

David Paper—Utah State University

Sasan Rahmatian—California State University, Fresno

Steven J. Simon—Florida International University

In closing this rather lengthy, but quite necessary, acknowledgment, I must give thanks for my best friends and colleagues Brad Wheeler and Steven Hornik. Both of you continue to give me energy with your friendship and strength with your faith.

Finally, my sincere thanks goes out to all of the student alumni of the NOMAS experience who faithfully attended my classes and assisted in my development of ideas, examples, explanations, and content. You are my true motivation, and I will always remember you.

About the Author

George M. Marakas is an associate professor of information systems and the BAT Faculty Fellow in Global IT Strategy at the Kelley School of Business at Indiana University. His teaching expertise includes systems analysis and design, technology-assisted decision making, electronic commerce, managing IS resources, behavioral IS research methods, and data visualization and decision support. In addition, he is an active researcher in the areas of systems analysis methods, data mining and visualization, creativity enhancement, conceptual data modeling, and computer self-efficacy. He is the recipient of the Center for Teaching Excellence–Lilly Teaching Fellowship and the highly prestigious Krowe Foundation Award for Innovation Excellence in Teaching. His research has appeared in the top journals in his field, including *Management Science, Information Systems Research, International Journal of Human–Computer Studies,* and *European Journal of Information Systems.* In addition, Dr. Marakas is the author of the top-selling textbook *Decision Support in the 21ˢᵗ Century* for Prentice Hall Publishing.

Prior to his academic career, Dr. Marakas enjoyed a successful career as an analyst and systems designer in both the banking and real estate industries. As a result, Dr. Marakas is also an active consultant to a number of organizations, including Citibank-Asia, Nokia Corporation, United Information Systems, Federal National Mortgage Association, Central Intelligence Agency, U.S. Department of Treasury, The National Institute of Drug Abuse, Burger King Corporation, Lotus Development Corporation, and British-American Tobacco, among many others. In addition, Dr. Marakas is considered a leading expert in the area of electronic commerce strategy, and he travels the globe lecturing and consulting on e-business issues for large, multinational corporations.

Dr. Marakas is a Novell Certified Network Engineer and has been involved in the corporate beta testing program for Microsoft Corporation since 1990. He is also an active member of a number of professional IS organizations and is an avid golfer, a PADI-certified divemaster, and a member of Pi Kappa Alpha fraternity.

The Systems Development Environment

Learning Objectives

- Understand the concept of systems analysis and design as a disciplined approach to development
- Become familiar with the evolution of systems analysis and design
- Understand the concepts of data-centricity and process-centricity
- Describe the various roles and responsibilities in systems development
- Explain the types of skills necessary to be a successful systems analyst
- Review the different classes of information systems
- Develop an initial understanding of the phased life-cycle approach to systems development
- Identify two alternative approaches to systems development beyond the life-cycle approach

INTRODUCTION

In 1532, Niccolò Machiavelli, the Italian historian, statesman, and political philosopher posited:

> There is nothing more difficult to take in hand, more perilous to conduct, or more uncertain in its success, than to take the lead in the introduction of a new order of things.

These words may best describe the challenges facing the modern systems analyst. It is hard to imagine a business or organization that has not been materially altered in its processes and daily activities by computer information systems and computer applications. The modern business organization considers its information technology to be an essential element in its ability to gain or secure competitive advantage in the marketplace. This "new order" brings with it an ever-increasing dependence on the technology and a burgeoning demand for new and improved systems on which to depend. As a systems analyst, the variety and opportunity for exploration and discovery in this new world is literally endless and is limited only by your imagination and creativity.

In general, few career paths offer greater opportunity for advancement within a business organization than that of the systems analyst. Analysts are typically high

1

visibility employees that are routinely associated with and involved in those activities within the organization that explore both the depth and breadth of understanding that may otherwise take an individual years to acquire. Further, the analyst can play a variety of organizational roles throughout his or her career, thus allowing for a diverse and exciting set of experiences on which to draw. For our purposes, the analyst will be the center of attention, and the objective is to equip you—the future systems analyst—with the skills and tools necessary to prepare you to work in this exciting and rewarding field. Let me be the first of many to say "Welcome to the world of systems analysis and design!"

DEFINITION

Formally defined, *systems analysis and design* (SAD) is a structured process that is employed in the development of business information systems. Within this process are contained activities that include the identification of business problems; the proposed solution, in the form of an information system (IS), to one or more of the problems identified; and the design and implementation of that proposed solution to achieve the desired and stated goals of the organization.

Often the first thing that comes to mind when one thinks of systems analysis is the writing of computer programs. Certainly activities such as this are commonly found in the world of the systems analyst, but the domain is much more diverse in reality. SAD exists as a vehicle for the design of information systems intended to solve an identified organizational problem. More important is the fact that whereas a great majority of the proposed solutions derived from SAD activities are computer-based, not all SAD solutions incorporate a computer as an essential element. We will see that, in many cases, a good solution attempts to effect change in the processes involved before applying or incorporating technology into the equation.

So what kinds of problems might be faced by a systems analyst?

➤ Suppose a company wants to provide their customers with the opportunity to order products at any time of the day or night regardless of the customer's location. How can this be achieved without incurring additional sales costs in the process?

➤ Consider an organization that needs to know the exact location of every transportation asset they own regardless of whether that asset is stationary or in transit. How can this be achieved such that not only the location of the asset can be determined but its operator can be instructed to proceed to a new location and the instructions on how to proceed can be provided to that operator?

➤ What if the production department of a manufacturing company has limited space resources on the shop floor and needs to carefully and accurately determine the best combination of products to manufacture, at any given time, to make optimal use of the available space?

These are but three examples of the types of problems that a modern systems analyst typically faces and that require a formal SAD approach to solve. Notice that whereas each of the examples will probably require some form of computer programming, none of them can be classified as a programming problem. More accurately, they are complex business problems that require a wide variety of processes, controls, inputs, and relationships to achieve their stated goals. Information systems are designed and implemented to solve business problems, and the analyst uses SAD methods and tools to determine and operationalize those solutions. SAD is not about computers, it is about problems and their solutions, and the modern systems analyst is not as much a computer professional as he or she is an organizational problem solver.

While we are on the subject of definitions, it is important to note that the name *systems analysis and design* implies at least two distinct processes. *Systems analysis* activities are primarily focused on determining the nature and domain of the business problem and, thus, the characteristics of an appropriate solution to solve it. It is here that the analyst is most concerned with issues such as problem identification, solution alternatives, solution requirements, organizational goals, among many others. In contrast, *systems design* activities include the final design specification and the construction, development, and implementation of the solution proposed during analysis and deemed best among any alternatives available.

Think of this type of *analysis* as focusing on two basic questions: (1) What is the problem? (2) What is the best solution to solve it? *Design* focuses on but a single question: How do we transform the solution into a usable IS? Although effective analysis can, and often does, occur without any design activities, the reverse is not often true. Given the complexity of the modern business environment, the importance and value of information as a resource, and the speed at which the environment can change, effective design rarely occurs without a thorough analysis as a precursor. This is not to say that systems are not routinely designed and implemented without formal analysis; unfortunately, they often are. Instead, this is to say that experience has shown that without a thorough, structured analysis as a forerunner, the ultimate and long-term success of a modern IS is less assured. Organizations are beginning to realize that doing it wrong quickly can be many times more costly than doing it right in an appropriate amount of time. This book is all about learning how to do it right the first time rather than how to do it quickly over and over again.

SAD—A DISCIPLINED APPROACH

What sets SAD apart from the process of generalized, day-to-day problem solving is its reliance on a formalized set of elements and its focus on a particular way of viewing the problem domain. The latter characteristic is commonly referred to as the *systems approach,* a perspective originating in the 1950s and exemplified by this quote from normative economist and systems theorist Kenneth Boulding:

> The systems approach is a way of thinking about the job of managing. It provides a framework for visualizing internal and external environmental factors as an integrated whole. It allows for the recognition of subsystems, as well as complex suprasystems within which organizations must operate. . . . It is important to recognize the integrated nature of specific systems. . . . But it is also important to recognize that business systems are part of larger systems—possibly industrywide, or including several, maybe many, companies and/or industries, or even society as a whole. Further, business systems are in a constant state of change—they are created, operated, revised, and often eliminated. (Boulding 1956, 197)

The former characteristic, reliance on a set of formalized elements, can be described in terms of *methodologies, tools,* and *techniques.*

Methodologies

A *methodology* is a multistep approach to the analysis, design, and delivery of an IS. In most cases, the SAD methodology employed by an organization reflects the management style and culture of that organization. Regardless of the methodology adopted (and there are many to choose from), all will reflect a certain degree of formally specified actions and processes by which the analysis of business problems and the operationalization of their solutions occur. This formal specification will address issues such as the step-by-step activities to be performed in each phase of the methodology, the expected deliverables and their associated quality standards, the roles of the various individuals and groups participating, and the various tools and techniques to be employed throughout the project.

The importance of a sound methodology to the success of an organization's IS development projects cannot be understated. A good methodology ensures that a consistent and reproducible approach is applied to the determination and design of business solutions. In addition, a rigorous methodology serves to minimize or eliminate many of the risks and pitfalls commonly associated with taking shortcuts or making common errors. Last, but not least, a sensible methodology results in a consistent and comprehensive documentation of the project such that the knowledge gained from one project can be quickly and easily retrieved by those working on the next.

In this text we will focus attention primarily on the methodology referred to as the *systems development life cycle* (SDLC). We discuss the SDLC in brief later in this chapter and in greater detail in chapter 2. In addition, we discuss three alternative methodologies to the SDLC: *object-oriented analysis and design* (OOAD, appendix B), *joint application development* (JAD), and *rapid application development* (RAD) (chapter 8).

Tools

The *tools* typically used in SAD include those intended to assist in symptom categorization and problem identification, such as the *Ishikawa chart* or the *PIECES Framework* (chapter 2), and the modeling tools used to create graphical representations of processes, data, and logic, such as the *data flow diagram* (DFD), the *entity-relationship diagram* (ERD), and *structured English* and the *decision tree* (chapters 5 and 6). In addition, the tools category includes the various computer programs designed to facilitate the wide variety of techniques and activities to be conducted during a complete analysis and design scenario. These types of tools fall under the general heading of *computer-assisted software engineering* (CASE) applications, and we focus on them in detail in chapter 7.

Techniques

Finally, the *techniques* category includes the various processes and procedures typically employed by an analyst to ensure that the analysis being performed is accurate, comprehensive, and comprehensible to others. Techniques such as *data gathering, requirements determination, project planning,* and the various classes of *feasibility analysis* are discussed in chapters 4, 5, and 9.

The tools and techniques must be consistent with the methodology employed and, in some cases, certain tools or techniques may not be appropriate to use. Collectively, however, these three elements must work together to form a comprehensive organizational approach to the analysis of business problems and the design of appropriate solutions.

MODERN SAD

One of the best ways to understand the current state of something is to become familiar with its evolution. This suggests that we spend some time reviewing the history and evolution of SAD.

A Bit of History

The roots of the analysis and design of information systems were developed as a result of the industrial revolution in which the systems analysts became responsible for the design of an efficient and effective production or manufacturing system. By the early 1950s, the computer was beginning to be seen as a useful tool for certain limited applications in the administration of routine business activities. At that time the development effort was driven by the desire to convert manual processes to automated ones. The most common application of the computer during this decade and the next was the counting and tracking of money. Unlike today, when computing resources such as memory, storage, and power are both plentiful and inexpensive, the emphasis on conservation of computing resources was a strong force with regard to software development. In addition to ensuring that the software application performed the necessary tasks, the systems developer focused on the efficiency of the computer processes with an eye toward conserving as much storage space and computer memory as possible. This early concern over computer resources was one of the major contributing factors to the recent Y2K problems. In the early days of computing, the cost savings associated with storing two digits for a date rather than four digits were substantial. Little did we know that we would be doing the work all over again in the latter part of the century.

During this same period, the software development industry as we know it today was not yet underway. All computer programs had to be written from scratch, with no development tools or platforms to assist the process. In addition, the development languages were limited to low level languages such as machine or assembly language, thus making the process of software development even more tedious and time consuming. The role of the analyst was one of understanding the computer and its languages and possessing the necessary skills to convert common manual processes into more efficient and cost-effective automated ones.

By the 1960s, the first set of procedural programming languages, such as COBOL and FORTRAN, began to emerge.[1] Although computing resources were still considered a premium, technological breakthroughs brought about the beginning of miniaturization that resulted in the development of computers that were not only smaller and faster than their predecessors but also less expensive to operate. Along with these improvements in computer hardware came the first entrants into the modern software industry. Although the majority of software developed during this period was done in-house and from scratch, by the end of the decade the ever-increasing expense of literally reinventing the wheel for each customized application began driving organizations to seek alternatives to in-house development. Standardization in development processes and procedures became a key element in controlling the rising costs of software development.

One of the first of the changes in software development came in the form of an increased discipline. The general consensus was to adopt the perspective of the engineering community, thus moving the activities more toward a scientific approach and away from the artisan or craftsman concepts of the 1950s and early 1960s. At this same time, the development of early database management systems using structured modeling approaches brought a necessary discipline to the concepts behind the storage and retrieval of data. Simultaneously, this new structure changed the focus of application development from a process-first approach to

---

[1] COBOL is an acronym for Common Business Oriented Language and FORTRAN is an abbreviation for Formula Translation Language.

more of a data-centered approach. The role of the systems analyst began to adopt more of a highly technical and structural engineering perspective.

The rapid changes and breakthroughs in computing technologies continued throughout the 1980s, and the birth of the microcomputer brought profound changes to organizations and their processes. The personal computer (PC) became a key element in the conduct of daily business, and the software industry took advantage of its popularity by introducing a vast array of software applications that could perform a wide variety of useful functions. No longer was it necessary to develop every application from scratch, and many of the more generalizable functions, such as payroll and accounting, could actually be automated using off-the-shelf software products. Although this movement away from in-house development to off-the-shelf software was a major impetus for growth in the software development industry, it also brought about an entirely new set of issues with which software developers had to contend. The need to share data and integrate processes became the focus during the late 1980s. Software developers were called on to design interfaces between two or more software applications so that data could be freely exchanged among them. The systems analyst of the period began moving out of the role of software developer and into the role of software and systems integrator.

The systems development environment of today is dramatically more complex than that of the early 1950s. Although the emphasis on systems integration continues, the current focus is on the development of enterprise-wide systems that are designed from a holistic perspective of the organization. The emergence of the client-server concept has allowed for the development of large-scale applications and databases that can facilitate the conduct of activities and processes for an entire organization. Further, the continued growth in the Internet and the World Wide Web (WWW) has spawned an entirely new medium for the conduct of business known as electronic commerce. With all these changes comes the need for new skills and approaches to software development and a burgeoning demand for people who possess those necessary skills and understand the complexity of the development approaches. The modern systems analyst must possess an equal understanding of the technology and the business environment. This dual role is necessary to facilitate the study and identification of complex business problems and the subsequent design and implementation of technology-integrated solutions.

The evolution of software development and application design began with a focus on the process, evolved to a focus on the data, and has now come to an understanding of the need to consider both elements in the design of a modern IS. Although the two perspectives are unique in their characteristics, they are no longer thought to be mutually exclusive. The modern systems analyst must understand the value of the relationships between data and processes, as well as understand the potential disadvantages associated with the strictly data-centric or process-centric approaches of the past.

Process-Centricity

The concept of *process-centricity* was the predominate development approach of the 1950s and early 1960s. During that period, the focus on application development was primarily one of determining what the application was supposed to do. The early transaction processing systems, such as payroll, accounts payable and receivable, or general ledger, were typically designed to accommodate the accounting and administrative practices of each individual business, so an application built by one organization to do payroll would be of little or no use to any other organization. Al-

Table 1-1   Comparison of the Data-Centric and Process-Centric
Development Approaches

Data-Centric Approach	Process-Centric Approach
What data does the system need?	What is the system supposed to do?
Tends to have an enduring design stability due to low volatility in organizational data needs.	Design stability is necessarily limited due to constant changes in business processes.
The file structure is enterprise dependent.	The file structure is application dependent.
Data redundancy is generally limited and controlled.	Data redundancy is generally massive and uncontrolled.

though the data necessary for input to the system was considered important, it was simply assumed that the data requirements could be easily derived if the desired outputs of the proposed system were anticipated and the appropriate processing logic to perform the task were determined. Because of this approach, each application needed its own source of data, and the data had to conform to the structures built into that application. This process-centric approach, although seemingly logical at the time, brought with it several negative outcomes. Table 1-1 compares the process-centric application development approach with its complement, the data-centric approach.

One of the most significant negative characteristics of a process-centric approach is the *limited design stability* associated with an application designed in this manner. Because the entire application is developed to perform a specific set of processes and the data is then gathered and stored in a manner unique to that application, the ability to make changes to the application to accommodate changes in the process or data is limited or possibly untenable. Business processes change constantly, and the need to make changes to the software that support them is critical. The process-centric approach creates a situation in which either applications must be scrapped and new ones developed or the business practices and processes must remain static to conform to the software.

Another negative characteristic of a process-centric approach is a massive *data redundancy* problem, because process-centric development results in a data file structure that is *application specific*. Because each of the data files is unique to a particular application in a process-centric approach, the concepts of data standardization or data integrity are not possible. It is not uncommon for the same data elements to reside in a multitude of data files, sometimes each with a different format or name. Because of this, if the value of a data element in one file, say, a customer's name, changes, that value must be manually updated in every data file where it is stored. This creates a situation of low data integrity and high data redundancy. Despite the extremely high costs of data storage during the early days of computing, it was easier to simply create a new data file for a new application, populate it with what was thought to be accurate data, and then maintain it in isolation from all other applications and data files within the same organization. It became clear, however, that a distinctly process-centric approach was not the best way to design software.

Data-Centricity

In contrast to the process-centric approach just discussed, the *data-centric* approach to software design focuses on the data necessary to operate a given software application rather than on what tasks the application is supposed to perform (see Table 1-1). The goal of the data-centric perspective is to create the ideal structure for the data being stored regardless of how or where the data ultimately will be used by an application. Because of this goal, a data-centric approach results in a design stability that is more enduring than that of the process-centric approach. Generally speaking, the data needs of a business organization are not as volatile and thus do not evolve as rapidly as its various business processes. This means that once the data is efficiently stored, it can be accessed by any number of applications throughout the organization simply by developing the application to access the data in the proper manner. Data redundancy is at a minimum when a data-centric approach is employed, and the data can be organized on an enterprise-wide basis rather than simply for a single application.

As stated previously, the two design perspectives cannot be thought of as either mutually exclusive or competitive. Our increased understanding of the advantages and disadvantages of each perspective has taught us that either approach, by itself, will result in a system that is inadequate to meet the immediate and long-term needs of the modern business organization. Modern systems analysis adopts the practice of considering both the data and the processes, as well as the relationships between them, when designing and constructing a software application. In chapter 5 we focus our attention on the tools and techniques necessary to identify and model the processes within the IS, and in chapter 6 we focus on the tools and techniques necessary to identify and model the data needs of the system. In chapter 9 we direct our attention toward how the two perspectives are integrated into a cohesive and effective software application.

SYSTEMS ANALYSIS AS A PROFESSION

Let us shift the focus a bit to an investigation of SAD as a professional career. We have discussed the systems analyst in terms of a business problem solver and an IS developer. However, many different people within the modern organization perform a portion of these tasks, and the world of a professional systems analysts is, first and foremost, a *team-based environment*. Regardless of the nature of the organization or the structure of its information systems function, multiple organizational members perform systems analysis activities, and the process requires a coordinated team approach. The particular characteristics of the analysis and design project will dictate the composition of the team and the degree of involvement of the various team members, but regardless of the situation, a systems analyst will probably never work alone.

In this section we will look at the systems analysis profession in terms of the present and future job opportunities and professional standards of practice. In the next section we will explore the various job descriptions and roles commonly found in the realm of the systems analyst, and following that, we will identify the various skills necessary to be a successful systems analyst.

Careers and Job Opportunities

In today's wired world, systems analysts can be found working in, or with, organizations of all sizes and industries—from the small start-up business to the Fortune 500 companies to multi- and transnational corporations. Certainly the diversity in these

Table 1-2   Typical Analyst-Organization Relationships

Analyst Role	Relationship to Organization
Programmer/analyst	Employee of the organization
Systems analyst	Employee of the organization
Independent analyst	Contractor to the organization
Outsource provider	Employee of outsourcing contractor
Systems consultant	Contractor to the organization
Software developer	Manufacturer or supplier of software

environments suggests that both the type of technology and the degree of dependence on it will vary a great deal but the basic activities associated with any SAD activities will not. If there are business problems to solve, then there will be a need for systems analysts to solve them.

Another characteristic that is somewhat unique to systems analysis as a profession is that the analyst may perform SAD activities for a particular company in a variety of relationships. Table 1-2 lists the various relationships that a typical systems analyst can have with an organization.

As you can see, there are an equal number of scenarios in which the analyst is employed by the company where the work is being performed as there are in which the analyst may be employed by one company while performing SAD functions for another. Additionally, systems analysts can be found at all levels of the organization. It is just as likely to find a systems analyst working on the shop floor as it is to find one working on a high-level strategy in the executive suites. As you can see, the world of the modern systems analyst can be quite diverse.

Typical Career Paths for Systems Analysts

Often the title *systems analyst* is mistakenly applied to a variety of jobs ranging from an entry-level programmer to a senior manager of all systems development projects. As a result, it is sometimes unclear exactly at what level of the organization a particular systems analyst may reside. Despite this seeming confusion, we can generalize and model the typical career path for a systems analyst to increase our understanding of what lies ahead.

The most common entry-level job for a recent college graduate and aspiring systems analyst is that of an analyst/programmer trainee. This holds true regardless of whether the organization is a corporation or a consulting firm. Although systems analysts are not programmers, they must, nonetheless, learn the systems of the organization from the ground up, and the best place to start is by understanding the basic coding procedures associated with the organization's applications. During the entry-level portion of your career as an analyst, you also may be placed in positions that focus on support activities for end users to increase your understanding of the user's needs within the organization, serve as an information specialist or decision support analyst to learn the development of queries and data analysis routines of the organization, or serve as a trainer, for which you might prepare and conduct seminars or classes on various aspects of information systems and technologies.

As you progress through the various stages of your career, you will begin to align yourself with either the technical or the managerial side of the organization. Depending on your preference, you will advance through job levels that have an increasing focus on technical issues, such as staff or senior-level consultant, or managerial issues, such as project leader or manager. Regardless of the path chosen, however, your role in the organization will, most likely, be both valuable and rewarding.

Professional Societies and Standards of Practice

One of the byproducts of the increased focus on discipline and structure in the SAD profession has been the emergence of standards of practice that include definitions of conduct, training and certification requirements, and accepted standards and guidelines for the analysis and design of a modern IS. These standards are in a constant state of refinement and evolution but are considered to be essential for the long-term viability of any profession.

Although admittedly a relatively new field, SAD is rapidly maturing and evolving due, primarily, to the burgeoning increase in dependence on sophisticated, computer-based information systems and the ever-increasing ubiquity of technology within our society. To date, there are established guidelines and standards in place at the college-level for the design and conduct of a systems analysis curriculum, accepted standards of practice with regard to analysis and design methodologies, and widely adopted codes of conduct and ethics by which the community of systems analysts is governed and judged. In addition, several professional societies, such as the *Association for Computing Machinery* (ACM), exist as clearinghouses for information important to the advancement of systems analysis as a profession.[2]

Suggesting that ethics are an important element in any business endeavor seems intuitive. In systems analysis, however, personal integrity and ethics are often at the center of the conduct of a development effort. The systems analyst commonly has access to data and information that is of a highly sensitive or private nature, information ranging from details of salary and personnel records to highly confidential trade secrets of an organization. The analyst must possess the personal integrity to respect and preserve the private and sensitive nature of such information.

Another potential for unethical behavior is found when one considers the increased exposure to computer-based crime by those individuals with detailed knowledge from a design perspective of an organization's systems. Although unethical behavior can be detrimental in any career, because the stakes are typically quite high even the appearance of impropriety can have a debilitating effect on the career of a systems analyst.

The Current and Future State of the Industry

One need only to make a minimal investigative effort to find that professional systems analysts are in high demand and their current and expected salary levels are among the highest in the computer industry. The prospects for the future are one compelling reason to consider systems analysis as a career choice.

The Bureau of Labor Statistics (1999) estimates systems analysts will be one of the top 3 fastest growing occupations by the year 2006 and among the top 20 in the number of new jobs as computer applications continue to expand throughout the

---

[2] The content of the ACM Code of Ethics and Professional Conduct and the Software Engineering Code of Ethics can be found at the end of this chapter.

economy. Computer scientists, computer engineers, and systems analysts held about 933,000 jobs in 1996, including about 58,000 who were self-employed. Over half of these jobs were held by systems analysts (506,000).

The estimated growth, in excess of 36 percent per year, will be driven primarily by very rapid growth in computer and data processing services, which is projected to be the fastest growing industry. In addition, thousands of job openings will result annually from the need to replace workers who move into managerial positions or other occupations or who leave the labor force.

These estimates appear small when compared to recent studies conducted by the U.S. Department of Commerce (Violino and Mateyaschuk 1999). According to the Commerce Department report, the growth rate for computer systems analysts will have topped 100 percent for the decade ending 2006. That translates into more than 1.3 million new informational technology (IT) workers needed to fill and replace workers leaving the field in that time.

To meet this burgeoning growth an increasing number of companies are trying to attract talented college students with special training programs and other training incentives. As an example, Baltimore Gas and Electric (BG & E) offers a scholarship program that lets students work in IT jobs before graduation while the company pays the student's tuition in job-related coursework while simultaneously paying them an hourly wage. In return, the student agrees to work for BG & E for a certain number of years after graduation.

This astounding demand for systems analysts is not only in the private sector but also occurring in government. According to a 1998 salary survey conducted by the System Administration, Networking, and Security Institute, an educational organization based in Bethesda, Maryland, the average raise for IT professionals in the public-sector was 11.9 percent with a median salary of $60,991 per year (Sawyer 1999).

Figure 1-1 shows salary data from the *1999 InformationWeek Research Salary Survey of 21,398 IT Professionals.* As you can see, regardless of company size, application development and database analysis and development professionals (i.e., systems analysts) are among the highest paid in their field. Pretty compelling, isn't it?

THE ROLES AND RESPONSIBILITIES IN SYSTEMS DEVELOPMENT

Given the collaborative, team approach to SAD, it becomes important to develop an understanding and awareness of the various roles that might be assumed by an individual participating in a design project. Such roles include *client and end users, IS management, systems analysts, application programmers,* and *IS support personnel.* Although the descriptions and nature of these roles may vary across organizations, the basic characteristics will remain similar.

Client and System Users

In many ways, an equally important role to that of the analyst in a typical SAD effort is that of the *client* or *end user.* Although the two roles can be held by the same individuals or group, often they are not. In many cases, the client is defined as the entity who is paying the bill and has formally commissioned the work to be conducted. The user, or *user group,* is usually associated with the client such that the deliverable from the SAD project will be an IS that will be used as a part of his, her, or their daily work. The first general dictum in systems analysis is "the system is always for the user." This concept has been determined to be an essential ingredient in the

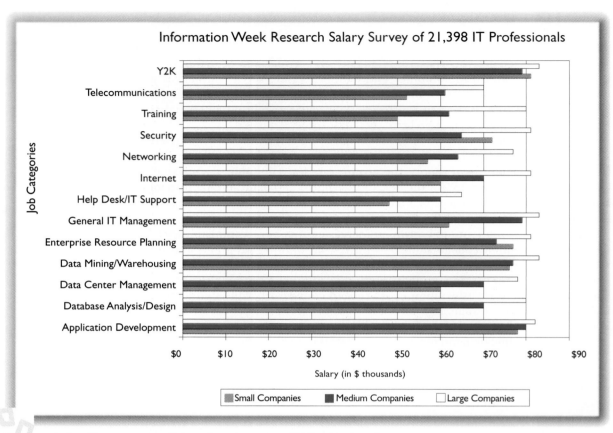

Figure 1-1   Comparative Salary Levels across IT Professionals

ultimate success of a development project, and it is explored in greater detail later in this chapter.

Formally defined, *end users* are those individuals that will ultimately benefit from the development effort and will be directly involved in either the use of the system itself or the information and reports generated by it. The typical end user often possesses detailed, if not expert, knowledge about the job or problem domain for which the system is being designed but lacks the skill, or possibly the time, to directly undertake the development effort. Within the organization, end users can be clerical or staff workers, technical staff, supervisors, members of middle management, and even executives. In addition, depending on the nature of the system, the end users may not ever reside at the same location as the actual system. Regardless, the systems analyst will regularly work closely with all of the end users associated with the system to assist in the determination of requirements for the new system and will incorporate the knowledge of the end user and the problem domain into a usable and supportive IS.

IS Management

The role of *IS management* may be direct or indirect in a typical SAD project. In some cases, particularly in organizations that do not have a large IS staff, the senior IS personnel may be directly involved in the daily activities of the project. In other cases, however, senior IS personnel are typically responsible for the allocation of resources to the project and to oversight activities, rather than participating in the actual development process. Further, IS management is often responsible for the establishment of criteria necessary to determine the success of the development effort. One additional role typically played by IS management is that of representing the organization with regard to career planning and advancement of the systems analysts. In this sense, the IS manager is integral to the long term success of the analyst within the organization and to the sense of growth and personal development felt by analysts at all levels of the organization.

Systems Analysts

Because this entire text is devoted to the details surrounding SAD, we will not dwell on the role of the analyst in too much detail here. In a 1979 ComputerWorld article, Michael Wood offered what is believed to be a classic definition of a systems analyst:

> I submit that systems analysts are people who communicate with management and users at the management/user level; document their experience; understand problems before proposing solutions; think before they speak; facilitate systems development, not originate it; are supportive of the organization in question and understand its goals and objectives; use good tools and approaches to help solve problems; and enjoy working with people. (Wood 1979, 24)

From Wood's definition, it seems clear that the typical analyst's role is quite varied and, actually, not so typical at all. Depending on the circumstances, the analyst can act as a consultant, a staff expert, a project manager, or even a change agent, sometimes simultaneously. In all cases, however, the analyst must be viewed as a facilitator. Figure 1-2 illustrates this constant responsibility to coordinate and facilitate the interactions among the participants in a typical development effort.

Suffice it to say that the key to a successful analysis and design project is the quality and skillfulness of the systems analysts. Becoming a good analyst can take many years of professional study and many more in experience. The development and training of a systems analyst does not end with graduation from college, because virtually all organizations that employ analysts have developed specific career paths and ongoing training programs. This level of attention to analyst development is one reason why so many former analysts can be found in the senior ranks of organizations throughout the world. Systems analysis has been shown to be a good career choice for those individuals seeking senior management status as a career goal.

Application Programmers

In the early years of SAD, the analyst was primarily a *programmer* who collected the initial information necessary to begin developing the application required to address the need. Over time, the roles of analyst and programmer began to separate and become complementary but unique in their focus. Today, computer programming is a separate and distinct career path from that of the systems analyst and, like systems analysis, is one for which years of formal and continuing education are necessary to become skillful.

As applications became more complex and the need for faster, more efficient computer code emerged, the labor-intensive nature of manual programming became untenable and often cost-ineffective. In response to this situation, the modern *code generators* often found within CASE applications were developed. These

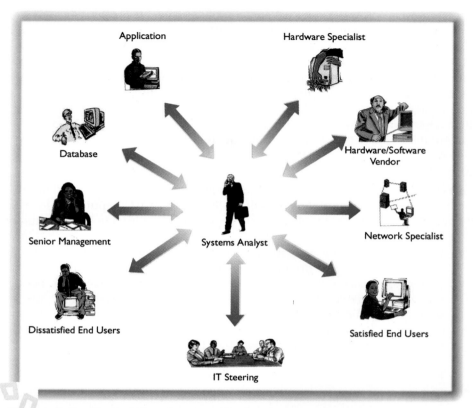

Figure 1-2   Typical Development Project Interactions

specialized computer-based applications can often generate the largest percentage of the application code from the formal specification without any programmer intervention. They are not intended to supplant the role of the programmer, however, but rather to support it. Because of the time and money savings typically associated with the use of code generators, the modern programmer can spend more time on finalization, optimization, and integration of the code into the IS under development. As code generators continue to evolve, so will the role of the programmer in the realm of systems analysis.

IS Support Personnel

Many of the roles within a typical development project are played by vendors, subcontractors, and other members of organizational support functions. Although each will have a highly specialized and often brief role to play, all will be critical to the overall success of the project.

Vendors and Technologists

Given the high cost of acquiring specialized skills and providing highly specialized services in an organization, the use of outside vendors and technologists in development projects is rapidly increasing. In many cases, the complex nature of the IS under development requires significant input from the various technology vendors and suppliers associated with the project. Depending on the size of the project and the extent to which a particular vendor's product is being used, the interaction with the vendor can range from supplying basic technical specification about the project to actually supplying personnel that serve to represent the vendor on the project team. Further, it is often the case that large scale projects employ vendor representatives to work on-site performing maintenance and upgrade activities following the implementation of the system.

Database Administrators

The *database administrator* (DBA) is typically responsible for the oversight and management of the inventory of databases that exist in an organization. The systems analyst will often need to work closely with an organization's DBA to coordinate the access to data that may be necessary for the new system, as well as to insure that the proper data structures and protocols for any new databases or data sources are adhered to. Often, the organization's DBA will be an integral part of the design team and will be responsible for the final designs for any databases resulting from the development project.

Telecom

The need for connectivity and high-speed transfer of a variety of data types makes the role of the *telecommunications expert* an important one to the development effort. This person will support the project with regard to any issues of data or voice communication, connectivity, or integration to existing system networks and will often be a key member of the installation and implementation team.

Audit and Security

Given the extreme dependence on computer-based information systems by the typical organization, combined with the general view of information as a corporate resource, the importance of the role of the *internal auditor* and/or *security officer* is easily seen.

IT Steering Committee

Often, an organization will establish a formal committee intended to coordinate the various IT-related activities of the firm. The analyst will spend a great deal of time working with, and reporting to, the *IT steering committee* of the organization. The steering committee acts as a liaison between senior management, the development team, and the end users. Typically, such committees have both permanent and rotating members and generally meet on a monthly or biweekly basis to review project proposals, discuss the status of current projects, and formulate recommendations to senior management on issues that require a commitment of the organization's resources. In some cases, the steering committee serves as the direct contact to the analyst team during an active development effort. In these situations, the steering committee serves in the role of client, and they represent the primary lines of reporting and approval used by the analysts.

SKILL SET FOR SYSTEMS ANALYSIS

The skill set of successful systems analysts is as varied as the environments in which they might work. Although each analyst will possess certain individual skills and talents, the general skill set can be broken down into four basic categories: (1) *technical,* (2) *analytical,* (3) *managerial,* and (4) *interpersonal.* In the following sections we will explore the fundamental characteristics of each skill category, as well as discuss the importance of each skill to the success of a typical development project. It is important to note that no one set of skills is any more or less important than the others and that, depending on the unique characteristics of the specific development environment, skills other than those identified here may become important from time to time.

Technical Skills

As discussed previously, the realm of the systems analyst is much broader than simply the technical side of information systems. Nonetheless, the technical skill set of an analyst is an important tool. To successfully develop computer-based information systems, a working knowledge of the technology in the areas of *database management, data networks, telecommunications, operating systems, distributed computing architectures, object technology, common programming languages and protocols,* and *automated systems development tools,* among many others, is considered essential.

The primary need for a highly developed technical skill set is so that the needs of the users can be operationalized in the appropriate technology and the new or modified systems can be successfully integrated with the existing technology of the organization. In addition, the technical skill set assists the analyst in effectively communicating with the wide variety of technical domain experts that are common participants in a complex development effort.

A common misconception regarding an analyst's technical skills is that to be successful you must be a skilled programmer as well. In fact, all analysts must know how to program, because they represent the bridge between the nontechnical representation of the system requirements and the highly technical world of the programmer. To make the translation effective, the analyst must be skilled in both worlds. This does not mean, however, all good programmers are naturally good analysts or vice versa. Simply put, a good analyst will also be reasonably skilled in the common programming languages of the organization and should strive to be aware of developments and improvements in the programming community.

The successful analyst also will be highly skilled in the tools and techniques of analysis and software design. Although the basic premises of these techniques remain fairly static, new approaches and refinements to more traditional approaches are constantly being introduced and must, therefore, be constantly reviewed.

The development of the majority of these skills is not a finite activity. To remain successful, a systems analyst must be constantly pursuing a continuing education program and must strive to remain conversant in the latest technological developments within the field. This implies active involvement in reading trade publications, joining and attending the functions of professional societies relevant to the field, attending college-level courses in special technical domains, and regularly seeking opportunities to acquire additional training offered through the organization. The pace of technological change is staggering, and the need to keep up with the latest developments makes technical skill acquisition a career-long activity.

Analytical Skills

First and foremost, a systems analyst is a problem solver. This suggests that the skills associated with problem identification and analysis will be essential to a successful career in development. Although systems analysis solutions can require such personal inputs as creativity, intuition, and judgment, the basic analysis process is a structured and highly programmed one. Generally speaking, the analyst will follow a prescribed method of taking a large and complex business problem and breaking it into its component parts, analyzing the various aspects of each component, and then assembling a new and hopefully improved system as a solution to the identified problem. This divide and conquer approach to problem solving is often referred to as *system thinking*, and we explore it in greater depth in chapter 2.

This ability to examine a complex set of components without losing sight of the bigger picture is essential to an analyst's success. Unlike the highly structured problems typically encountered in the world of mathematics, the prototypical business problem is much less deterministic and can often have multiple feasible solutions. It takes skill and creativity to analyze the various alternatives and their respective tradeoffs and recommend the one most suitable to the organization. Admiral Grace Hopper, the designer of COBOL, was famous for pointing out that the most damaging phrase in the language is "We have always done it that way." Another way to frame this perspective is to note that doing what you have always done will most likely get you only what you have always gotten. The successful systems analyst will always be willing and eager to look beyond the seemingly obvious solution to new and not so obvious ones.

Managerial Skills

A successful analyst is a team player who has developed expertise as both a technical and managerial member of the organization. In many cases the analyst will be called on to lead the development effort and, as such, good management skills will be called into play. Within this skill set are included such areas as *business domain knowledge, resource and project management, assessment and management of risk,* and, as stated previously, *management of change.*

Among these areas of focus, knowledge of the business domain may be the most important. It is no longer simply a matter of having an understanding of the technology or the organization; a good systems analyst must be knowledgeable about the organization, its industry, its competitors, and its processes. The modern systems analyst is expected to be immersed in the business domain and to be able to propose, and justify, solutions that complement the goals and objectives of the organization. Given this importance, the courses commonly found in a college level business school major, such as accounting, finance, marketing, and general management, become good foundations for a career in systems analysis. In addition, an understanding of trends in the conduct of business, such as total quality management, enterprise resource planning, and business process redesign, among many others, is an equally essential skill to develop.

Although some development environments require an expertise in specific aspects of the business or industry, most analysts are expected to be business generalists and to maintain a broad perspective on the business environment. This approach ensures that any technical issues that may arise will be evaluated not only on their technical merits but also on the degree to which they advance the project toward greater support of the organizational mission.

One additional type of managerial skill that is essential for a systems analyst is the ability to manage expectations. The activities associated with the development and implementation of a new IS within an organization can often be confusing, frightening, or even threatening to those who do not understand the goals and objectives of the project. Further, the introduction of a new IS, however valuable to the organization, brings with it the anticipation and stress of change. The analyst will often be called on to insure that the various constituencies within an organization are kept informed as to the nature of the development activities. Further, the expectation levels of the various user groups, often ranging from having few expectations to expecting a miracle, must be carefully managed throughout the project to insure that the end result is both expected and satisfying to those who must use it long after the analyst is no longer involved. Empirical evidence suggests that there is a strong relationship between effective management of user expectations and successful system implementation (Ginzberg 1981).

Interpersonal Skills

Last but not least, the successful systems analyst is a good communicator who can work effectively and easily with all types of people and personalities. In addition to excellent communication skills, the interpersonal skills of an analyst include the *ability to question, listen, and observe; effectively conduct oral and written presentations; facilitate groups;* and *be a team player.*

Communication skills will be called on in a variety of forms. No matter what the activity or issue, the systems analyst will need to communicate information to the other participants in the project environment using verbal, written, or graphical means. In addition, the most effective communicators are also the best listeners and display a noticeable sensitivity to the feelings and viewpoints of others. It is well known that people are naturally resistant to change. In keeping with the need to manage expectations, the persuasive skills of the analyst may be called on to convince the various stakeholders in a development environment of the need for a proposed change. Finally, the team player aspect of the communication skill set suggests that a successful analyst will also be effective in cooperation, conflict resolution, negotiation, and compromise.

One important characteristic of all forms of communication skills is they can be improved through both experience and practice. This suggests that aspiring, as well as experienced, systems analysts should take constant advantage of any opportunity to practice and improve their various communication skills.

TYPES OF INFORMATION SYSTEMS AND SYSTEMS DEVELOPMENT

You have learned about the various types of information systems in previous introductory courses, and therefore we will only briefly review the categories and their common characteristics here. It seems reasonable that just as each organization can have many different business problems, the types of information systems in place to deal with them will also vary. The systems analyst must possess a thorough understanding of the various classes of information systems in terms of their similarities, differences, and appropriate domains of application, because all will be encountered throughout the course of an analyst's career. Further, certain systems types may require specific tools, techniques, and methodological approaches in the course of a development project.

Transaction Processing Systems

The *transaction processing system* (TPS) represents the most prevalent and oldest of the computer-based IS types. The primary purpose of a TPS is to automate the capture and recording of information about the transactions that occur during the course of conducting business. A transaction is quite simply a discrete event, either internal or external, that is of value to the organization or is thought to directly

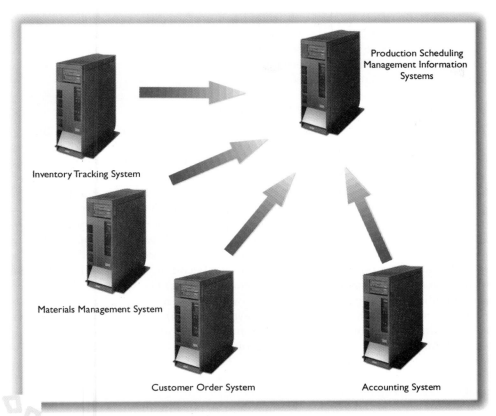

Figure 1-3   Transaction Processing Systems Can Support a Management
Information System

serve the mission of the business. Events such as the specific time of a sale, the
amount of that sale, the day an order was received, the purchase of supplies or materials, and the amount of a payroll check to an employee are all examples of relevant transactions that are typically handled by a TPS. In addition, the TPS will most
likely have the ability to generate reports that provide a variety of detail or summarization of the events captured by the system. These systems generally process a
high volume of data, and the legacy versions (older, less modern systems) were
typically designed from more of a process-centric approach than would be acceptable by today's standards. Nonetheless, the TPS is a mainstay of the modern business
organization, and as these systems are subjected to redesign, many new opportunities for systems analysts will come available.

Management Information Systems

The *management information system* (MIS) is often characterized as an extension of
the TPS in the sense that it accepts as its input the raw data from a TPS and transforms it into meaningful reports or graphs that are intended to assist managers in
the planning and controlling of the business. It is quite common for a single MIS to
collect transaction-level data from several TPSs in the course of report generation.
Figure 1-3 graphically illustrates a typical MIS.

Generally speaking, the early instantiations of the MIS were designed from a primarily data-centric perspective, but the modern MIS design incorporates an equally high degree of focus on both the data and the processes applied to the data. Like the TPS, the MIS is considered an important management resource, and the opportunities for analysis and design in this area are endless.

Decision Support and Expert Systems

The *decision support system* (DSS) is a special type of IS that is designed, built, and used to assist in the activities that it is named for: to provide support to the decision process. Although they are not intended to make the decisions themselves, there are some recent examples of DSS that almost do exactly that. In reality, however, the intention of a DSS is to provide support to the decision maker during the process of making a decision. Formally defined, DSS is *"a system under the control of one or more decision makers that assists in the activity of decision-making by providing an organized set of tools intended to impart structure to portions of the decision-making situation and to improve the ultimate effectiveness of the decision outcome"* (Marakas 1999).

The DSS is a powerful tool and is rapidly becoming an integral component within the realm of organizational information systems. The speed at which the information of today becomes yesterday's news is increasing at a staggering rate. Tomorrow's manager will be faced with an ever-narrowing window of opportunity in which to make effective decisions. Deadlines will be measured in days, hours, or minutes rather than in quarters, months, or years. The leveraging of technology intended to allow for tomorrow's manager to be effective in such a high-speed environment is what decision support is all about. To meet these demands, the modern analyst must be capable of designing and implementing a DSS to provide the decision maker with certain key decision-making elements vital to his or her success.

Closely associated with the DSS is the *expert system* (ES). This type of system is a computer-based application that employs a set of rules based on human knowledge to solve problems that require human expertise. Expert systems imitate reasoning processes based on the concept of information fit used by human experts in solving specific knowledge domain problems. A nonexpert can use an ES to improve their capabilities to solve complex problems by simulating a dialog with experts in a particular field. Experts can use an ES to simulate a highly knowledgeable assistant. Most commonly, an ES is employed to allow for the propagation of scarce expert resources throughout an organization to increase the consistency and quality of problem-solving activities.

The unique characteristics of systems such as a DSS or ES suggest that their development requires certain unique tools and design approaches. Although it is beyond the scope of this text to discuss these issues in detail, we briefly explore some development and design issues that arise in highly specialized and diverse environments in chapter 10.[3]

Executive Information Systems

In basic terms, the *executive information system* (EIS) is a special type of DSS that is uniquely designed to facilitate the analysis of information critical to the overall operation of an organization and to provide an arsenal of tools that can support the strategic decision-making processes conducted by top executives. More specifically, an EIS is a computer-based system intended to facilitate and support the information and

---

[3] For thorough coverage of the design and development characteristics of the DSS and ES, the reader can refer to G. M. Marakas (1999), *Decision Support Systems in the Twenty-First Century.*

decision-making needs of senior executives by providing easy access to both internal and external information relevant to meeting the stated goals of the organization.

An EIS can help a chief executive officer (CEO) get an accurate and almost immediate picture of not only the operations and performance of the organization, but that of its competitors, customers, and suppliers, as well. It performs these functions by constantly monitoring both internal and external events and trends and then making this information available to the top executive in a manner that best suits the needs of the moment. Further, an EIS can provide a wide range of summarization or detail at the convenience of the executive. For example, a CEO can use the EIS to quickly view sales activity categorized by product, region, subregion, month, local market, or any number of other methods of organization. Simultaneous to that, the CEO also can monitor the sales activity of the firm's competitors in much the same way. This high degree of summarization can be used to get a quick, comparative snapshot of what is going on in the company and/or the market. Should this snapshot reveal some discrepancy, unusual variance, or anomaly, the executive can *drill down* into the data to display a greater level of detail. This decomposition process can continue until the individual transaction level is reached, if necessary, to provide the CEO with the information required to explain the variance and to decide on a course of action. Thus, the design of an EIS combines access to a wide variety of information sources with a mechanism for relating and summarizing those sources. It also provides the user with the tools necessary to examine and analyze the gathered information so that a swift, yet well-informed, decision can be made.

Office Automation and Workgroup Management Systems

The *office automation system* (OAS) and the newer concept of *workgroup management system* (WMS) are those systems that facilitate the analysis and dissemination of information throughout the organization. Familiar aspects of an OAS include word processing, spreadsheets, presentation graphics and desktop publishing, electronic scheduling and resource allocation, and common methods of inter- and intraoffice communication such as e-mail, voice mail, and video conferencing. The essence of the OAS class of systems is the concern with getting all of the relevant information to those who need it, when they need it.

The WMS is a newer concept within the modern organization and extends the capabilities of the typical OAS into new functions and purposes. WMS applications include collaborative technologies, such as Lotus Notes, that are used to facilitate and coordinate workgroup access to information relevant to a specific project or task. For example, the workflow associated with the development of a new contract for a client could be facilitated with a WMS by integrating and thus allowing easy access to such diverse applications as secondary databases for research, word processing, spreadsheet analysis, and presentation graphics. More important, the various members of the project team could collaborate and gain access to these diverse resources regardless of whether they were in the same office or geographically dispersed throughout the world.

Web-based Systems

The newest class of information systems has emerged as a result of the burgeoning growth of the Internet and the WWW. These systems are no longer simply Web pages with relevant hypertext links to other sites. *Web-based systems* are complex environments that are designed to facilitate the conduct of business over the Internet, and the areas of application of these systems appears to be endless. Web-based applications supporting business-to-business and business-to-consumer electronic commerce, data management, customer relations, supply chain management, and enterprise resource management are but a few of the many examples in which these systems are in operation. Virtually all major industries are taking advantage of the growth in e-business, and the modern analyst will be increasingly expected to provide Web-based solutions to the business problems of tomorrow.

THE SDLC

Definition

Earlier in this chapter we briefly discussed the concepts of methodologies, tools, and techniques that collectively serve to form a disciplined approach to SAD. In this text, our focus is on a particular methodology that has evolved over the past several decades to be a widely accepted structured approach to the analysis and design of modern information systems: the *systems development life cycle* (SDLC). Over the course of your career as an analyst you will most likely encounter a wide variety of development approaches, but all of them will, in some fashion, be derived from the normative SDLC process we adopt here. We focus on the detailed activities and steps within each phase of the SDLC in chapter 2, but a brief overview of the

Figure 1-4 The Systems Development Life Cycle

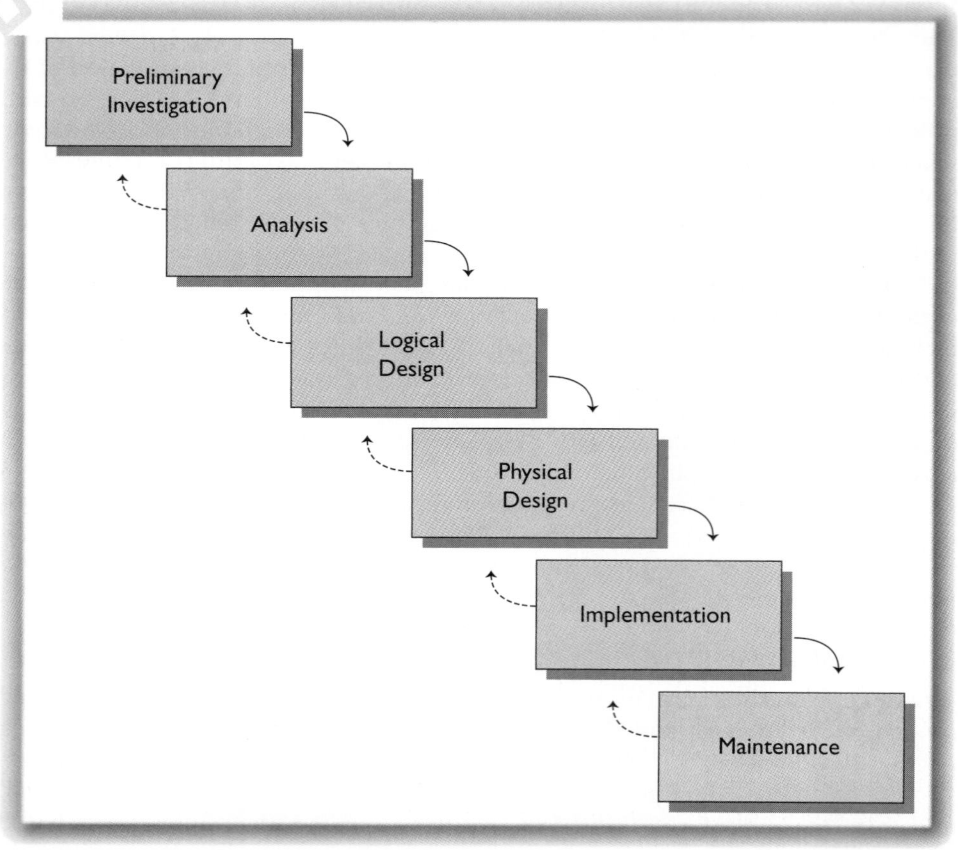

process is presented here to acquaint you with the approach. Figure 1-4 is a graphical illustration of the sequence of phases contained within the SDLC.

At first glance, the SDLC appears to be a sequential process made up of phases that each have a definite beginning and ending point. In reality, however, the SDLC is more of an *iterative* process in which the activities in one phase can, when appropriate, revert back to those of a previous phase to correct or refine the information contained within one or more deliverables for that phase. Similarly, the activities in more than one phase may be conducted in parallel when appropriate. This is why the SDLC is often referred to as a *waterfall model.* Regardless of the name, however, the SDLC is composed of a common set of phases and activities that serve to structure and guide the development process.

Overview of Phases and Activities

The *preliminary investigation* phase is where the process begins. In this phase, a business problem arises because there is an identified need for a new or more modern system or because a situation has been identified that appears to lend itself to improvement through the redesign of one or more existing systems or the creation and integration of an entirely new one. The activities associated with this initial phase are the formal identification and selection of a development project and the formal initiation of a preliminary investigation to determine the feasibility of proceeding with the project. The organization assesses the expected resources for the project by defining its scope and boundaries. In addition, the organization conducts a critical review, of either the identified problem or opportunity that triggered the proposed development, to formally justify the reasons that organizational resources should or should not be committed to this project. Finally, a project team is assembled and a formal project plan developed and presented to management for approval. Chapter 3 focuses on the detailed activities of this first step in the process.

In the *analysis* phase, a thorough study of the organization's related and existing processes, procedures, and systems is conducted. In this phase the initial requirements are determined for the new system, the logical models of the existing system are developed, and the interrelationships among the various systems and data elements are determined. By the end of the analysis phase, a complete picture of the existing environment and the specific definition of the problem to be solved, and its sources, is presented to management. In chapter 4 we focus on the tools and techniques used to assemble and formally determine the requirements for the new system.

The third phase of the SDLC is *logical design.* In this phase the logical models of the existing system are revised and refined to correct the sources of the identified business problem and to determine that the proposed, new system functions as expected and addresses the objectives and requirements determined during the analysis phase. The designs created in this phase are called *implementation-independent,* because they are not yet tied to any specific hardware or software system. Chapters 5 and 6 are devoted to the tools and techniques associated with the development of logical models of the existing and proposed system.

The *physical design* or *development* phase is where the final logical models are converted into physical specifications that include the detailed specification of hardware, software, and programming instructions necessary to turn the system into reality. Issues such as method of data capture, specific processes, and required output are determined and developed in this phase. Chapters 9 through 14 provide a detailed focus on the various activities associated with the conversion from the logical to the physical design.

The second to last phase in the life cycle is *implementation*. In this phase the programmers begin their work, and the assembly and installation of the physical model of the system takes place. Activities in this phase also include the testing and final installation of the hardware and software. Finally, it is in the implementation phase that the end users are trained in the use of the new system. In chapter 14 we focus on the activities and issues associated with system implementation.

The final phase in the SDLC is the *maintenance phase*. Even after a system has been thoroughly analyzed, designed, tested, and installed, the users may sometimes find problems with the new system or discover even better and more refined ways of accomplishing a particular task. Thus, the maintenance phase activities focus on detailed modifications to the new system to either correct a problem not discovered during final testing or to effect modifications to reflect changes in the organization's environment. In many cases, maintenance can be thought of as a repetition of the previous phases of the life cycle. Even the best system requires resources devoted to its maintenance, but as time goes on, it becomes apparent that the maintenance of the system is becoming cost prohibitive, because of either degradation of the technology or significant changes to the business conditions. Regardless of the reasons, this is a clear indication that it is time to begin the process over again and to begin analyzing and designing a replacement for the current system. We explore some of the issues with regard to system maintenance in chapter 14.

Drawbacks to the SDLC

Although the traditional SDLC is clearly the foundation for most, if not all, of the development approaches in use today, it is not without its detractors and criticisms. One primary criticism lies with the organization of the life cycle as a seemingly sequential process. In many cases, the reality of a development effort seems to resist the highly structured and sequential nature of the SDLC. Further, some argue that the time necessary to conduct a development effort using the SDLC has become prohibitive in today's fast paced world where business conditions are in constant flux. Because the analysts would, at some point in the process, have to freeze the logical design and begin creating the physical system to ensure that the project would reach completion, some feel that the SDLC promotes the development of a system that could be obsolete by the time it is completed.

An additional source of criticism about the traditional SDLC is that maintenance costs are often higher than one would expect. This was eventually traced back to what is now believed to be a lack of emphasis on accuracy in the analysis and design phases. Aktas (1987) estimated that the cost of maintenance could represent as much as 70 percent of the total systems development costs. Further, Boehm (1981) pointed out that, for large-scale systems, the cost of repairing or correcting a mistake made in one phase of the life cycle can more than double for each phase of the development process in which it goes undetected. This means that a mistake made in the preliminary analysis phase of a project, that would cost $10.00 to correct if discovered in that same phase, could cost over 100 times that to correct if not discovered until the implementation phase had begun. Although the relationship between cost and correction for smaller systems is somewhat less, any unnecessary cost associated with the development of a sophisticated IS makes its cost justification less tenable. Boehm's work simply reinforced the age-old notion that an ounce of prevention is worth a pound of cure. Figure 1-5 illustrates the relationship between the cost to fix an error when made and the relative increase in cost to fix the error later in the life cycle.

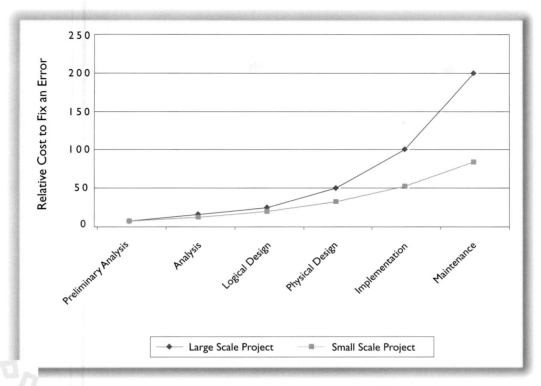

Figure 1-5   Relative Cost to Fix an Error in a Development Project

These criticisms have been responded to in a variety of ways. Yourdon and Constantine (1979) proposed certain modifications to the normative life cycle that increased the focus and structure on the analysis and design activities while simultaneously improving the analyst's ability to revise the initial requirements when deemed necessary due to changing business conditions. Further, improving the level of detail and accuracy associated with the analysis and design activities also served to drastically reduce the high costs typically associated with the maintenance of a competed system. The modifications made to the traditional life cycle became known as *structured analysis and design*. For our purposes, any reference to the SDLC in this text adheres to these structured principles.

ALTERNATIVE APPROACHES TO DEVELOPMENT

Although the majority of our focus in this text is on the structured SDLC approach to systems development, we also look at two more recent methodologies that are becoming increasingly popular: *object-oriented analysis and design* (OOAD) and *rapid application development* (RAD).

OOAD

In contrast to the process- and data-oriented approach found in the SDLC, in OOAD the processes and data are combined into a single entity called an *object*. Each object corresponds to the actual things an IS may be designed to deal with.

Things such as customers, vendors, contracts, employees, trucks, and money can all be considered objects. In fact, anything of importance to a particular IS can be defined as an object, because the essence of the concept recognizes that the combination of processes and data into a single element is in keeping with the fact that there are a limited number of operations that are relevant to any given data structure. By taking this approach to systems development, OOAD attempts to make the various elements within a system more reusable, thus improving the productivity and efficiency of the systems analysis function over time. We compare and contrast the OOAD approach and the structured SDLC approach in appendix B.

RAD

In chapter 7, we focus on a systems development approach, developed by James Martin in 1991, called *rapid application development*. The basic goal behind RAD is to create a more parallel approach to the analysis and design effort than that of the SDLC. A key characteristic of RAD is a heavy reliance on the use of modern CASE tools and the technique of prototyping. We look closely at CASE tools and the various techniques associated with RAD in chapter 7.

CHAPTER SUMMARY

This chapter has provided a general overview of SAD as a profession that is burgeoning with growth and that provides a significant variety of business environments in which to work. The modern systems analyst represents an expert blend of technical, analytical, managerial, and interpersonal skills and is often on the leading edge of IS development practices and situations.

To insure that the significant resources necessary to build a useful IS are not wasted or misused, several structured approaches have been adopted as aids to the development of modern information systems. In the following chapters, we explore in detail the activities, techniques, tools, and skills of the systems analyst with an emphasis on the most common of structured development methodologies, the SDLC.

Once again, let me be the first to say, "Welcome to the world of systems analysis!"

KEY CONCEPTS

➤ Systems analysis and design (SAD) is a structured process that is employed in the development of business information systems. It exists as a vehicle for the design of information systems intended to solve an identified organizational problem. SAD is not about computers; it is about problems and their solutions. The modern systems analyst is not as much a computer professional as he or she is an organizational problem solver.

➤ SAD implies at least two distinct processes:
  • Systems analysis
    Systems analysis activities are primarily focused on determining the nature and domain of the business problem and the characteristics of an appropriate solution for it.
  • Systems design
    Systems design activities include the final design specification and the con-

struction, development, and implementation of the solution proposed during analysis and deemed best among any alternatives available.

➤ SAD is a problem-solving process that relies on a formalized set of elements (methodologies, tools, and techniques) and focuses on a system approach toward viewing the problem domain.

- Methodologies

  A methodology is a multistep approach to the analysis, design, and delivery of an IS. A good methodology

  1. ensures that a consistent and reproducible approach is applied to the determination and design of business solutions
  2. serves to minimize or eliminate many of the risks and pitfalls commonly associated with taking shortcuts or making common errors
  3. results in a consistent and comprehensive documentation of the project such that the knowledge gained from one project can be quickly and easily retrieved by those working on the next

- Tools

  Tools typically used in SAD include

  - Symptom categorization and problem identification tools, for example, PIECES framework
  - Modeling tools, for example, data flow diagram (DFD)
  - Computer facilitating programs, for example, computer-assisted software engineering (CASE)

- Techniques

  Techniques include the various processes and procedures typically employed by an analyst to ensure that the analysis being performed is accurate, comprehensive, and comprehensible to others (e.g., requirement determination).

➤ The evolution of software development and application design began with a focus on the process, evolved to a focus on the data, and has now come to an understanding of the need to consider both elements in the design of a modern IS.

- Process-centric approach
  - What is the system supposed to do?
  - Design stability is necessarily limited due to constant changes in business processes
  - The file structure is application dependent
  - Data redundancy is generally massive and uncontrolled
- Data-centric approach
  - What data does the system need?
  - Tends to have an enduring design stability due to low volatility in organizational data needs
  - The file structure is enterprise dependent
  - Data redundancy is generally limited and controlled

➤ The roles in systems development
  - Client and System Users
  - IS management
  - Systems analysts
  - Application programmers
  - IS support personnel
    - Vendors and technologists
    - Database administrator (DBA)
    - Telecom
    - Audit and security
    - IT steering committee

➤ Skills set for systems analysis
  - Technical skills
  - Analytical skills
  - Managerial skills
  - Interpersonal skills

➤ Types of information systems
  - Transaction processing systems (TPS)
  - Management information systems (MIS)
  - Decision support systems (DSS) and expert systems (ES)
  - Executive information systems (EIS)
  - Office automation systems (OAS) and workgroup management systems (WMS)
  - Web-based systems

➤ The systems development life cycle (SDLC)

  The SDLC is composed of a common set of phases and activities that serve to structure and guide the development process:
  - Preliminary investigation
  - Analysis

- Logical design
- Physical design
- Implementation
- Maintenance

➤ Alternative approaches to development
  - Object-oriented analysis and design (OOAD)

    In the OOAD approach to systems analysis, the processes and data are combined into a single entity called an object. By taking this approach, OOAD attempts to make the various elements within a system more reusable, thus improving the productivity and efficiency of the systems analysis function over time.

  - Rapid application development (RAD)

    A key characteristic of RAD is its heavy reliance on the use of modern CASE tools and the techniques of prototyping.

QUESTIONS FOR REVIEW

1. Define systems analysis and design (SAD) and briefly describe the two distinct processes involved.

2. Why is SAD different from the process of generalized, day-to-day problem solving?

3. Why is a sound methodology important to the success of an organization's IS development projects?

4. What are the tools typically used in SAD?

5. Compare and contrast the process-centric and data-centric approaches to systems development.

6. Describe the importance of ethics and personal integrity in the systems analysis profession.

7. List and briefly describe the various roles and responsibilities in systems development.

8. Define client and end user. Why are end users so important in systems development?

9. Is a systems analyst a computer expert? Why or why not?

10. Briefly describe the general skill set of a successful systems analyst.

11. List and briefly describe the various types of information systems.

12. What are the major differences between a general DSS and an EIS?

13. List and briefly describe the common phases of the SDLC.

14. Why is the SDLC often referred to as a waterfall model?

15. Describe the drawbacks of using the SDLC and how they might be improved.

16. What are the advantages of OOAD to systems analysis and design?

17. What is the major characteristic of the RAD approach to systems development?

FOR FURTHER DISCUSSION

1. You work for a manager who is constantly looking for ways to improve processes, cut costs, and decrease delivery times for new software applications. He has just announced that he wants to stop using the conventional waterfall approach of the SDLC in favor of prototyping. How would you address this issue, and what arguments would you use to dissuade your manager?

2. Using the skills and characteristics essential in a good systems analyst as your guide, evaluate your own skill set and personality characteristics. Are you ready to be a systems analyst? In what areas do you need the most improvement?

3. Given your choice of opportunities, which information systems environment would you prefer to work in: a corporate IS department, an IS consulting firm, a commercial or custom software developer, or an IS services outsourcer? Use what you have learned about the roles and skill set of the modern systems analyst to explain your choice.

4. What if the SDLC did not exist? Try and imagine a situation where no SAD strategy is employed. What would the project look like? What sort of problems would the project face? What would be the outcome?

5. What if systems analysts were not bound by any professional ethical standards? What would be some of the concerns with regard to detailed analysis and logical design activities? Would this change the nature of the role of the systems analyst? Are the codes of professional ethics really necessary? Why or why not?

ACM CODE OF ETHICS AND PROFESSIONAL BEHAVIOR

1. General Moral Imperatives
   As an ACM member I will
   1.1 Contribute to society and human well-being
   1.2 Avoid harm to others
   1.3 Be honest and trustworthy
   1.4 Be fair and take action not to discriminate
   1.5 Honor property rights including copyrights and patents
   1.6 Give proper credit for intellectual property
   1.7 Respect the privacy of others
   1.8 Honor confidentiality

2. More Specific Professional Responsibilities
   As an ACM computing professional I will
   2.1 Strive to achieve the highest quality, effectiveness, and dignity in both the process and products of professional work
   2.2 Acquire and maintain professional competence
   2.3 Know and respect existing laws pertaining to professional work
   2.4 Accept and provide appropriate professional review
   2.5 Give comprehensive and thorough evaluations of computer systems and their impacts, including analysis of possible risks

   2.6 Honor contracts, agreements, and assigned responsibilities
   2.7 Improve public understanding of computing and its consequences
   2.8 Access computing and communication resources only when authorized to do so

3. Organization Leadership Imperatives
   As an ACM member and an organizational leader, I will
   3.1 Articulate social responsibilities of members of an organizational unit and encourage full acceptance of those responsibilities
   3.2 Manage personnel and resources to design and build information systems that enhance the quality of working life
   3.3 Acknowledge and support proper and authorized uses of an organization's computing and communications resources
   3.4 Ensure that users and those who will be affected by a system have their needs clearly articulated during the assessment and design of requirements. Later the system must be validated to meet user requirements
   3.5 Articulate and support policies that protect the dignity of users

and others affected by a computing system

3.6 Create opportunities for members of the organization to learn the principles and limitations of computer systems

4. Compliance With The Code
As an ACM member I will

4.1 Uphold and promote the principles of this Code

4.2 Treat violations of this Code as inconsistent with membership in ACM

SOFTWARE ENGINEERING CODE OF ETHICS AND PROFESSIONAL PRACTICE

(Version 5.1) as recommended by the IEEE-CS/ACM Joint Task Force on Software Engineering Ethics and Professional Practices

SHORT VERSION

Preamble

The short version of the code summarizes aspirations at a high level of abstraction; the clauses that are included in the full version give examples and details of how these aspirations change the way we act as software engineering professionals. Without the aspirations, the details can become legalistic and tedious; without the details, the aspirations can become high sounding but empty; together, the aspirations and the details form a cohesive code.

Software engineers shall commit themselves to making the analysis, specification, design, development, testing, and maintenance of software a beneficial and respected profession. In accordance with their commitment to the health, safety, and welfare of the public, software engineers shall adhere to the following Eight Principles:

1. **PUBLIC**—Software engineers shall act consistently with the public interest.
2. **CLIENT AND EMPLOYER**—Software engineers shall act in a manner that is in the best interests of their client and employer and that is consistent with the public interest.
3. **PRODUCT**—Software engineers shall ensure that their products and related modifications meet the highest professional standards possible.
4. **JUDGMENT**—Software engineers shall maintain integrity and independence in their professional judgment.
5. **MANAGEMENT**—Software engineering managers and leaders shall subscribe to and promote an ethical approach to the management of software development and maintenance.
6. **PROFESSION**—Software engineers shall advance the integrity and reputation of the profession consistent with the public interest.
7. **COLLEAGUES**—Software engineers shall be fair to and supportive of their colleagues.
8. **SELF**—Software engineers shall participate in lifelong learning regarding the practice of their profession and promote an ethical approach to the practice of the profession.

REFERENCES

Aktas, A. Z. 1987. *Structured Analysis and Design of Information Systems.* Englewood Cliffs, NJ: Prentice Hall.

Boehm, B. W. 1981. *Software Engineering Economics.* Englewood Cliffs, NJ: Prentice Hall.

Boulding, K. 1956. "General Systems Theory—The Skeleton of Science." *Management Science* (April): 197–208.

Bureau of Labor Statistics, United States Department of Labor. 1999. *Occupational Outlook Handbook, 1998–1999.* Washington, DC: GPO.

Ginzberg, M. J. 1981. "Early Diagnosis of MIS Implementation Failure: Promising Results and Unanswered Questions." *Management Science* 27: 459–78.

Marakas, G. M. 1999. *Decision Support Systems in the Twenty-First Century.* Upper Saddle River, NJ: Prentice Hall.

Sawyer, P. 1999. "Outsourcing Benefits IT Budgets." *American City and County* 114 (6): 8.

Violino, B., and J. Mateyaschuk. 1999. "Labor Intensive—An Increasing IT Labor Shortage Calls for Creative Ways to Do More with Less." *InformationWeek,* 5 July, 000–00.

Wood, M. 1979. "Systems Analyst Title the Most Abused in the Industry: Redefinition Imperative." *ComputerWorld,* 30 April, 24, 26.

Yourdon, E., and L. L. Constantine. 1979. *Structured Design.* Englewood Cliffs, NJ: Prentice Hall.

So What Is the Problem?

Learning Objectives

■ Develop an understanding of the concepts of problem recognition and problem definition

■ Be able to identify and explain the differences between problems and symptoms

■ Learn to apply two common symptom organization tools: the Ishikawa diagram and the PIECES framework

■ Understand the concept of bounded rationality and its effects on natural problem solving ability

■ Review and explain a system classification approach that can assist in understanding the elements and actions of IS

■ Develop a thorough understanding of the process of functional decomposition and its importance to SAD activities

■ Learn the detailed phases of the SDLC and the typical activities and deliverables associated with each

For either you know what you are looking for and then there is no problem Or you don't know and then you cannot expect to find anything.

—PLATO

INTRODUCTION

Everyone has problems, right? Well, it seems that way in any event. Just turn to the person nearest to you and ask a simple question, "So what is the most important problem you are currently facing?" Although a small number of responses may indicate that the person is facing no problem currently, the majority of responses will indicate that each respondent has at least one problem of importance to deal with, and some will have more than one. There is really only one problem with asking someone about a problem: most people don't know what the problem is. Instead, they are only aware of the symptoms related to the real problem, and they tend to think of a symptom of a problem as synonymous with the actual problem. In this chapter we begin exploring the world of problems as systems and, in the process, develop a greater understanding of the two primary activities of the systems analyst: identifying and solving problems.

PROBLEMS VERSUS SYMPTOMS

The first step in developing this understanding is to define the two most basic elements in problem identification and problem solving: the problem and the symptom.

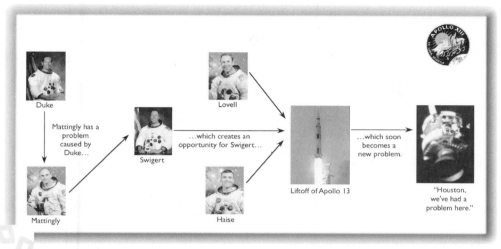

Figure 2-1   One Man's Problem—Another Man's Opportunity

Problems Defined

Definitions for the word *problem* are as widely variant as there are problems. Gause and Weinberg (1990) define a problem as "a difference between things as desired and things as perceived." In a much earlier definition, Pounds (1969) defines a problem as the difference between an existing situation and a desired situation. Using this approach, Pounds suggests that the difference between the output of a model of expected results and the current results is an example of how a typical manager defines the degree to which a problem exists. Yet another offering, this time by Blanchard and Johnson (1997), suggests that "A problem only exists if there is a difference between what is actually happening and what you desire to happen."[1]

Although each of these definitions seems to have commonalities with the others, they all possess the same basic weakness: they are based on desires and perceptions that are inherently subjective because they vary with the observer. One person's problem can be another person's opportunity. Take for example, the crew assignments for the Apollo 13 moon landing mission. Figure 2-1 illustrates the situation.

The original crew was made up of James Lovell, commander, Fred W. Haise, lunar module pilot, and Thomas "Ken" Mattingly, command module pilot. A few days before the scheduled launch date, backup lunar module pilot, Charles Duke, exposed the crew to the measles. Although none of them contracted the disease (before or after launch), Mattingly was the only crewmember who had never had the measles as a child and thus had no natural immunity to the disease. Because the incubation period for the measles was greater than the time left before launch, the worst possible scenario would be for Mattingly to begin to show signs of the disease while somewhere between the earth and the moon. It was decided that rather than postpone the mission, Mattingly would be replaced by the command module pilot

---

[1] Using these definitions we can assume that most of you reading this book have a problem, because you would rather be at the beach or out with your friends (the desired situation) instead of stuck reading this chapter (the actual situation). Given this, I'll do my best to make it enjoyable.

for the backup crew, John L. "Rusty" Swigert. Thus, the crew of Lovell, Haise, and Swigert blasted off for the moon on April 11, 1970.

At the moment the "measles decision" was made, Ken Mattingly clearly had a problem; Rusty Swigert, on the other hand, had an opportunity. Mattingly never did contract the measles (and he later flew to the moon on Apollo 16), but Swigert's opportunity soon turned into a problem. At 55 hours, 55 minutes, and 20 seconds into the mission, (about 200,000 miles from earth) oxygen tanks 1 and 2 exploded and failed, causing Apollo 13 to lose the vast majority of its source for electricity, light, and water. At that moment, Jack Swigert uttered the now famous phrase, "Houston, we've had a problem here." Although the crew returned safely to earth after much drama and creative thinking, the point here is that one person's problem can be another's opportunity. *Problem identification* and *recognition* demand a point of view.

What is most important about this example is the use of the word *problem*. This word is commonly used as a synonym for the word *symptom*. In Swigert's case, his famous phrase would have been more correct if he had said, "Houston, we've had a symptom here." Despite the fact that this sounds funny, we will soon see that it is in fact both accurate and correct.

Symptoms Defined

In contrast to a problem, a *symptom* is an outward or physical manifestation of a problem that usually becomes noticeable as some variance from the norm. Combined with other symptoms, they form a trail back to the problem to which they are related. Think of the symptom as the *effect* and the problem as the *cause*. Although this may seem like a semantic argument, in practice the differences between the two words are very important. Take, for example, the situation in which a person must go visit the doctor because he or she has a headache. Everyone knows that if you have a headache (the perceived condition) and you really do not want one (the desired condition) then you believe you have a problem. So what, then, exactly is a symptom?

As stated previously, the notion of a symptom is rooted in the concepts of cause and effect. The headache is perceived as undesirable and therefore is classified as a problem. We determine the situation to be undesirable and wish to solve the problem by taking action to eliminate the headache. This results in a trip to the doctor. At this point, however, the difference between symptoms and problems begins to become clear.

If the doctor chooses to classify the headache as a problem, he will prescribe some medication, let us say aspirin, and before long the headache goes away. Everything seems OK until we sit down the next day in class and begin taking notes on the material being presented on the blackboard. Suddenly, the headache returns. We have learned of a desirable relationship between the headache and aspirin, so we take some and the headache, once again, goes away. The problem is, the next day it comes back. So, what is the problem?

The problem is that we have become temporarily satisfied with treating the symptom rather than treating the disease. The headache is simply a manifest condition of a more deeply rooted phenomena: we need eyeglasses! Therein lies the distinction between symptoms and problems. A symptom is evidence of a problem but not necessarily the problem itself.

Thinking of a symptom as simply a variance or deviation from the norm also implies that a symptom does not necessarily have to be negative to be a symptom.

For example, if during the review of a periodic budget versus actual report the reviewer notices that costs for a particular item have exceeded estimates, then a perception of a problem immediately manifests itself in the form of an unfavorable variance or symptom. Further, review shows that sales for the product manufactured with that high cost item are way up in a certain region. That sounds good. Would that favorable variance trigger the perception of a potential problem? Probably not, but it should. In both cases, the variance was a deviation from the expected norm. At the very least, these deviations should result in a more detailed review. Although they may seem totally unrelated or rooted in completely different areas, they may also be highly related and serve to point to a deeper problem. Suppose the higher than expected sales in a particular region were due to an overzealous marketing manager reducing the price of the product severely below market simply to increase sales. Without a reasonable short-term strategy for increasing market share or competing with a local vendor, this price reduction is unacceptable. Moreover, this sudden increase in sales also accounts for the sudden increase in costs associated with the material necessary to make the product. If each variance was treated as a core problem, however, the real problem would not be solved. Further, depending on the method used to treat the symptoms, they may actually disappear, thus masking the problem from further investigation.

The difference between a problem and its related symptoms is of extreme importance to successful problem identification and, therefore, problem solving. We can define a symptom as a *manifest effect of an underlying cause*. The real difference lies in the results associated with its elimination. The treatment of a symptom normally results in the elimination of the symptom (effect) but not in the removal of the problem (cause) with which the symptom is associated. The reverse, however, is not true. If we take the time and energy to fully identify and define the root problem, we will be able to craft a solution that results in the elimination not only of the problem but of its associated symptoms as well. More important, if we make the symptoms go away, we may lose track of the problem, because we no longer have any variances to trigger an investigation. In this sense, symptoms are our friends. Later in this chapter we explore several tools that can assist in sorting through, and organizing, the symptoms to get to the problems. For now, just remember that if we get eyeglasses, we see better *and* we do not have a headache. If we simply take aspirin, we get rid of the headache for a little while but never will be able to see clearly.

Problem Recognition and Definition

The reason for all this concern over problems versus symptoms leads us to a dictum of SAD: You cannot solve the problem if you do not know what the real problem is. Problem recognition and definition can be thought of as similar to the process scientists use to develop a hypothesis. Figure 2-2 illustrates this similarity.

First, the scientist observes a phenomenon. From this observation a hypothesis is formulated to test one or more aspects of a theory underlying the phenomenon, and finally, an experiment is designed and conducted to test the hypothesis. Similarly, a systems analyst recognizes one or more variances in the environment, conducts an investigation through interview, observation, and investigation of the current system to test for possible causes, and then proposes a possible root problem that could be cause for these variances. Systems analysts are simply scientists whose laboratory is the organization or business environment.

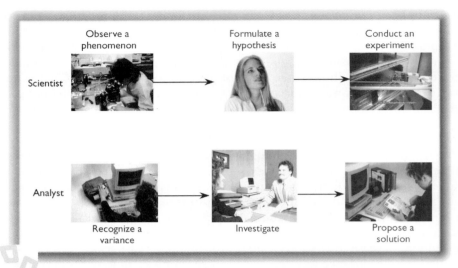

Figure 2-2   Analysts and Scientists Use a Similar Approach

Cause and Effect

One common method, used by scientists and systems analysts alike, to accurately define a problem is to explore the cause and effect trail created by its symptoms. The theory is that if one can discover a common source for the symptoms, then one can assume that he or she has determined the exact nature of the problem. In reality, the actual cause of a problem can be quite elusive. Further, problems and opportunities often vary in their complexity. Although some can be easily identified with a minimal effort, others may require a more comprehensive analysis that makes use of one or more tools designed to assist and structure the investigative process. We review the use of two such tools: the *Ishikawa diagram* and the *PIECES framework*.

Ishikawa Diagram

First developed in 1943 by Dr. Kaoru Ishikawa at the University of Tokyo, the *cause-and-effect diagram,* also known as a *fishbone diagram,* relates the symptom or problem under question to the factors or causes driving it. It accomplishes this through establishing a hierarchical relationship between the problem, the main symptoms of this problem, and any relationships they may have to other symptoms. Originally, Ishikawa developed the technique to assist in brainstorming possible sources of error in a manufacturing scenario. For our purposes, we use it to relate observed variances to a likely problem definition such that a hypothesis can be tested to determine the actual nature of the underlying problem. Although an Ishikawa diagram can be developed by an individual, it is more commonly assembled by a team. Using it in this way allows multiple analysts to record their observations and perceived variances in a manner that helps to organize and coordinate an orderly investigative process.

Figure 2-3 graphically illustrates the concept of an Ishikawa diagram. Structurally, it consists primarily of two parts. The *backbone,* the main horizontal axis, represents the problem under investigation. In other words, think of the backbone as

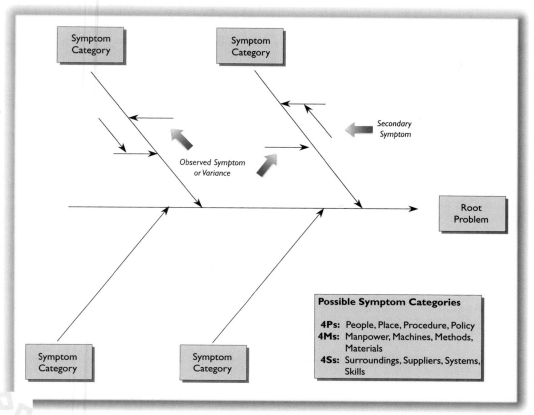

Figure 2-3   Ishikawa "Fishbone" Diagram

being the primary link between all of the observed symptoms. Connected to the backbone are one or more diagonal lines that represent major categories of symptoms. These categories can represent anything the analyst chooses, but there are commonly used sets of categories such as those shown in Figure 2-3. Because the categories are simply intended to assist in organizing the observed symptoms, they may be selected and labeled in any relevant manner.

The first step in constructing a fishbone chart is to select the major categories. Connected to each of the major category lines are shorter horizontal lines that represent the observed symptom or variance. The nature of the symptom determines to which category line you would connect it. For example, if the categories chosen are the "4 Ms" (manpower, machines, methods, materials), and the symptom to be recorded is an unusually high distribution cost, the most likely symptom category to relate it to would be "methods." Although the other three symptom categories could be somehow related to the unusually high distribution costs (and they probably are), the initial categorization that appears most relevant is the methods category.

From each symptom line you may wish to connect a shorter diagonal line that is used to represent a *secondary symptom*. As an example, suppose the observed variance is a high instance of customer walkouts at the various retail locations operated by the organization. This may have been determined through observation or interview.

Using the "4 Ps" (people, place, procedure, policy) approach, this would initially be categorized in the "people" category. Additionally, another analyst observes that there is a relatively low allocation of sales staff to the various retail locations. This may have been determined by comparing industry norms to the actual number of allocated staff or by some commonly accepted algorithm that determines the number of sales staff needed per square foot of retail space. Although this symptom could also be categorized in the people category as a primary symptom, it may be somehow related to the customer walkout symptom. To show this hypothesized relationship, the analyst may choose to represent it as a secondary symptom to the high number of customer walkouts.

The actual process for constructing an Ishikawa diagram is an iterative one that may require a symptom to be repositioned or to be initially represented in one category as a primary symptom and in another category as a secondary symptom. The important element of the process is that as each symptom or subsymptom is classified, the analyst must continually be asking, "Why is this happening?" When enough symptoms that seem to have a common relationship to one another have been observed and classified, a hypothesis as to the root of the problem can be formulated and tested. If supported, at least one of the underlying problems has been identified, and the analyst can proceed to begin thinking of solutions to solve it. Remember, when the root problem is solved and eliminated, the symptoms will go away as well.

PIECES Framework

Another effective tool for symptom categorization and problem recognition, developed by Dr. James C. Wetherbe (Wetherbe and Vitalari 1994), is called the *PIECES framework*. The name is derived from an acronym comprised of the first letter of each of the six categories of the framework: **P**erformance, **I**nformation, **E**conomics, **C**ontrol, **E**fficiency, and **S**ervice. Table 2-1 contains a complete listing of the various characteristics of each category of the PIECES framework.

Although the categories may have some overlap, they are sufficiently different to warrant a separate focus. Further, the categories can sometimes interact, thus allowing for a particular symptom to be assigned to more than one category. For the tool to be effective, however, every attempt should be made to assign a symptom to only one category, and, in no cases should a symptom be assigned to more than two categories.

The *performance* category focuses on symptoms that primarily pertain to the throughput or response time of an organizational process. *Throughput* is the total volume of work performed over a given period of time, and *response time* is the average time between submission of a request and the receipt of the result.

In the *information* category, the focus is on both the quantitative and qualitative aspects of the organization's information and data.

Economics is the category to which symptoms that pertain to costs of a process are assigned. When considering a cost situation, two key variables must be balanced: service level and excess capacity. *Service level* is a measure of the availability of the output of a process or the quality of the product or service offered. *Excess capacity,* or *slack* as it is sometimes referred to, is a measure of the degree to which additional resources exist and can, therefore, be allocated to demands for goods and services. Generally speaking, the higher the service level, the greater the cost due to loss of excess capacity.

Table 2-1   PIECES Problem-Solving Framework and Checklist

The following checklist for symptom identification and categorization uses Wetherbe's PIECES framework. While the categories of PIECES are not mutually exclusive, and therefore some observed variances may show up in more than one column, every effort should be made to assign a variance to one column only and in no case to more than two columns.

The need to improve **Performance**	• Improve throughput: the amount of work performed over some period of time • Improve response time: the average delay between a transaction and a response to that transaction • Throughput and response time should be evaluated separately and collectively

The need to improve
 Information
 and data
	• Improve information (the outputs of the system used for planning, control, and decision making)
	     Too little or too much information
	     Lack of needed or relevant information
	     Lack of relevant information
	     Information that is not in a useful form
	     Information that is not accurate or timely
	     Information that is difficult to produce
	     Illegal information
	 • Data (the inputs to the system)
	     Data is not captured
	     Data is not accurately captured or captured in a timely fashion
	     Data is difficult to capture
	     Data is captured redundantly or too much is captured
	     Illegal data is captured
	 • Stored data
	     Data is stored redundantly
	     Data is not accurate
	     Data is not consistent in multiple stores
	     Data is not secure against accident
	     Data is not secure against sabotage
	     Data is not well organized
	     Data organization is too inflexible to meet information needs
	     Data cannot be easily accessed to produce information

The need to reduce **Economic** **or cost impacts**	• Costs are unknown • Costs are untraceable to source • Costs are excessive • New markets can be explored to generate profit • Marketing can be improved • Opportunities to increase orders exist

The need to improve
 Control
 and security
	• There is too little control
	     Input data is not adequately edited
	     Crimes are committed against data
	         Fraud or Embezzlement

Table 2-1   *(continued)*

The need to improve
 Control
 and security
 (continued)
	Ethics are breached based on data or information
	 Redundantly stored data is inconsistent in different files
	 Privacy of data is being violated
	 Processing or decision making errors are occurring
	 System is deviating from planned performance
	 • There is too little security
	     People get unauthorized access to space or facilities
	     People get unauthorized access to computers
	     People get unauthorized access to data or information
	     (manual or computer)
	     People execute unauthorized updates of data
	 • There is too much control or security
	     Bureaucratic red tape slows the system
	     Controls inconvenience end users or customers
	     Controls cause excessive processing delays or lost
	     transactions

The need to improve
 Efficiency
	• People or machines waste time
	     Data is redundantly input or copied
	     Data is redundantly processed
	     Information is redundantly generated
	 • Machines or processes waste materials and supplies
	 • Effort required for tasks is excessive
	 • Materials required for tasks are excessive

The need to improve
 Service
	• The system produces inaccurate, inconsistent, or
	   unreliable results
	 • The system is not easy to learn or use
	 • The system is too complex or awkward
	 • The system is inflexible to situations and exceptions or
	   new requirements
	 • The system does not interface well to other systems
	 • The system is not coordinated ("left hand does not know
	   what right hand is doing")

In the next category, the focus is on *control* and security. Control is the method by which organizational processes are monitored and regulated. It is achieved by a constant comparison between actual and planned performance. When a variance between the two is detected, some form of control system must be invoked to return the process to a state of acceptable performance level. The concept of control is one of an appropriate balance between risk and cost. Clearly, one can have too little control. In such cases, the system can go out of control, and no easy method exists to remedy the situation. Conversely, however, one can have too much control. A situation for which this is the case can be overly costly or unnecessarily complex and cumbersome ("bureaucratic red tape") or can even invoke dysfunctional behavior from either the system or the entity being controlled. Just try pulling hard on the reins of a horse for too long and you will get an example of what I mean.

Symptom	P	I	E	C	E	S
Management reports are often not received on time.		X				
Production line throughput is below expected standards.	X					
Product rework is high.			X		X	
Inventory control reports are inaccurate.		X				
Exceptions occur frequently and must be processed by hand.						X
Production time is higher than industry average.	X					
Orders are often cancelled due to excessive delivery wait time.	X					
Required information to process an order not available on demand.		X				
Organizational data redundancy is high.		X				
Production lines are often down for repair or maintenance.	X					
Line personnel are often not aware of their production quota.		X				
Data transferred from production system to sales system by hand.					X	X
Several incidents of system sabotage have been recorded.				X		
Totals	4	5	1	1	2	2

Figure 2-4 Example of a Simple PIECES Analysis

The fifth category is *efficiency*. The focus here is on manufacturing a product or providing a service with a minimum of waste. Efficiency can often be expressed as a ratio of work to the energy expended. Mathematically speaking, efficiency is output divided by input.

The final category in the PIECES framework, *service*, is where we categorize symptoms related to the quality of service an organization provides to its customers. Service can also be a measure of the degree to which the customer's needs are being met by the organization or its products.

Preparing a PIECES analysis for an organization begins much like the symptom categorization for an Ishikawa diagram. Figure 2-4 illustrates a simple PIECES analysis.

As a symptom is observed, it is recorded in the first column of the PIECES chart. Then a mark is placed into one, or possibly two, columns indicating an assignment of the symptom to a category of the framework. The symptoms do not have to be recorded in any order, but they should be assigned to a category as quickly as possible if the analysis is being done individually or, if by team consensus, at the beginning or end of each day of the engagement.

As you can see from Figure 2-4, the category assignments can be tallied to create a running frequency distribution of the mapping of symptoms to various categories. Although this distribution of symptoms does not tell where the problem is, it does indicate where the problem probably is not. According to the current state of the analysis shown in Figure 2-4, the problem appears to be centered around *performance* and *information*. As the investigation continues, this distribution may shift, or it may continue to move in the same direction. If it begins to shift, then we either are moving away from the problem of interest or may be investigating multiple problems. The distribution continuing in the same direction, however, is a pretty good indication that we are on the right track. Although not definitive, the PIECES framework can assist an analyst in the allocation of additional resources to further investigate the possible cause of the symptoms and can often expedite the formal definition of a root problem.

Problem Statement

So, let us review the basic process. First, the analyst observes, identifies, and records symptoms in the form of variances from some norm. Then, the recording of these variances is used to analyze either their root cause(s) or the area of the organization in which the root cause(s) is likely to be found. At this point, a hypothesis is formed as to what the root problem is, and it is tested via investigation and interview to determine its support. This process is continued until the analyst feels confident about the identification of the real problem.

It is important to note that this whole process is intended to assist the analyst in finding the cause of the variances not to fix blame somewhere. The various members of an organization under study play a vital role in the success, or failure, of a development effort. As such, the process works best when the users cooperate with it, and that cooperation is not likely to come if you are perceived to be on a witch hunt. Let management worry about fixing blame, if appropriate, while you focus on finding the cause and correcting it.

The problem identified during the preliminary investigation phase is, at best, an informed guess. Proceeding toward design at this stage would be a dangerous choice because much more information about the organization, the nature of the problem, and the current system is still needed to formulate a solution that addresses all of the needs of the organization and truly fixes the problem. What should happen, however, is the generation of a formal *problem statement* as it is currently viewed.

Once initially identified, the root problem must be communicated to a wide variety of interested parties: the users, the managers, the development team, and probably a slew of technical people. The commonly accepted method for making this communication takes the form of a written problem statement. The statement, sometimes referred to as a *statement of scope and objectives,* lists the symptoms, suggests their likely cause or causes, and begins an estimate of the resources necessary to develop an effective solution. As the preliminary investigation phase ends and the detailed analysis activities progress, this problem statement and definition of scope will likely change, maybe even materially. Nonetheless, we cannot edit or refine something that does not exist in tangible form, so we begin the process with a formal problem statement from which we can proceed. Several additional deliverables, including a *preliminary feasibility report,* generally also come out of the preliminary investigation activities. We discuss these deliverables in detail in a later section of this chapter.

BOUNDED RATIONALITY

While we are on the subject of problem recognition, definition, and solution proposing, we need to digress a bit and look at a cognitive phenomenon that can have a material effect on an analyst's ability to correctly identify a root problem. Originally proposed by the 1978 Nobel Prize in economics laureate, Herbert A. Simon, this phenomenon is called *bounded rationality,* and its foundations are actually rooted in the world of economic theory.

Most normative economic theory, such as laws of market equilibrium or supply and demand, were built on the assumption that human beings are distinctly rational in their behavior and therefore always seek the optimal solution to a problem. Despite the apparent attractiveness of this optimization strategy, its practical application in managerial decision-making contexts, particularly structured SAD, is problematic.

Simon can be credited for his demolition of the rational, economic man. In his early work, he questioned the concepts of maximization and optimization as they were applied to normative economic models. Simon suggested that were the concept of human beings as a profit optimizing entity tenable, there would exist no price tags on any of the merchandise in any of the stores. Think about it: if human beings truly wanted to maximize profit, then each transaction would be a negotiation for the highest possible price. Although some buyers would obtain the product at a lower price than other buyers, still others might be willing to pay much higher prices. This would, over time, theoretically result in optimized profits. So why doesn't the economic, so-called optimizing, human do this?

It is much too hard, that is why! Simon argued that the cognitive limitations of human beings make it impractical to consider all possible alternatives to a particular problem. Further, even if all relevant alternatives could be reviewed we would not be able to assimilate all the information such that an appropriate decision could be made. Instead, Simon suggested that we tend to "simplify reality" by focusing our energy on finding a solution that meets our preconceived notion of what an acceptable solution looks like. When we find such a solution, we immediately adopt it and stop looking for a better one. In the case of our price tag example, we decide on an acceptable margin of profit and then openly price our product to reflect that margin. Although this may not result in optimal profits, it does satisfy our criteria of profiting on our sales, and it is a whole lot easier than negotiating each sale into a quantifiable end. Simon used the term *satisficing* to refer to this strategy.

Further, because problem solvers, including systems analysts, are bound by the cognitive limitations inherent in all human beings, they actually do make rational decisions that are bounded by often uncontrollable constraints. Simon referred to this as *bounded rationality.*

Simon's concept of bounded rationality can best be understood by example. Figure 2-5 contains a graphical representation of a typical *problem space.*

Assume that the graphic on the left in Figure 2-5 represents the boundary of the identified problem at hand and all possible solutions to that problem, good ones, bad ones, great ones, OK ones, and so forth. More important, if the concept of optimization is valid, then the problem space contains one best or optimal solution to the identified problem. The rational model of decision making suggests that, in an effort to find that best solution, the problem solver would seek out and test each of the solutions found in the problem space until all of the solutions were tested and compared. At that point, the best solution would be known and, therefore, clearly identifiable.

Simon argued that this is not what really happens in a typical problem-solving scenario. The graphic on the right in Figure 2-5 illustrates Simon's approach. What the problem solver actually does is develop a mental picture of what an acceptable solution to the problem looks like. Then he or she proceeds to search the problem

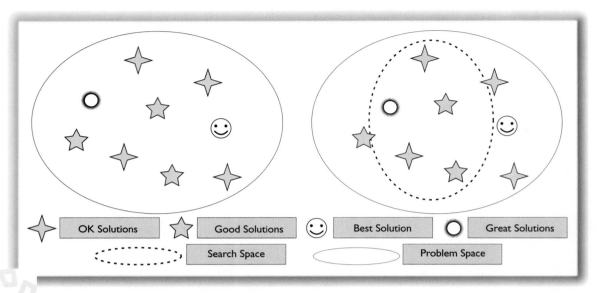

Figure 2-5   Theoretical Problem Space and Bounded Rationality

space for a sufficient match to that preconceived solution model. When such a match is found, the search ends and the solution is implemented. Using this approach, however, the problem solver most likely does not choose the optimal solution, because the narrowed search of the problem space makes it probabilistically unlikely that the best solution will ever be encountered. This suggests that instead of the optimal solution, the problem solver is willing to settle for a satisfactory solution to the given problem and thus avoid the extreme effort necessary to find the best one.

So what does all this have to do with SAD? First, we can see that the typical analyst (being human, of course), is not likely to naturally expend the energy necessary to gather all relevant information available regarding a particular problem. Further, we can assume that even if 100 percent of the symptoms were available, the analyst probably could not assimilate them and thus would not consider all of them. Finally, given the concept of bounded rationality, it appears that, left alone, the typical analyst would instinctively preconceive the structure of a desired solution before the search for the problem was even completed. All this suggests the need for guidance and structure in the identification of a problem and the selection of a satisfactory alternative and thus the need for a structured approach to SAD like the SDLC.

THE CONCEPT OF SYSTEMS

The time has come to focus our attention on one of the two most important parts of systems analysis, that of the *system*. Literally volumes have been written simply in an attempt to fully define the concept, and such coverage is beyond our scope in this text. For our purposes, we need only to acquire and understand a definition that we can use to better understand that which we are charged with the responsibility of analyzing.

One general way to define a system is to think of it as something that is a part of the universe with a limited extension in space and time. Using this definition, it is logical that more, or stronger, correlations exist between one part of a given system and another than between the same part of the given system and parts outside of the given system. Although accurate in its description, using this definition also tends to give one a headache.

Maybe Aristotle's statement of composition will make the concept clearer:

> The whole is more than the sum of its parts, the part is more than a fraction of the whole.

While predating the concept of SAD by a few millennia, Aristotle's perspective does begin to give us a picture of what a system is. When the component elements of a system are working together in some usable fashion, we gain something beyond the mere sum of the component elements when considered individually. We are not there yet, but we are in the ballpark.

According to the most widely used definition, originally offered by Hall and Fagen (1956), a system is *a set of interacting elements that form an integrated whole.* A city, a cell, and a body, then, are systems. So, too, are an automobile, a computer, and a washing machine! For that matter, a problem also can be thought of as a system.

Implicit in this definition is the presence of specific components with specific relationships (interacting elements), a purpose or goal for the system (integrated), and some type of identifiable boundary (whole). So, a system is *a set of interrelated elements, with an identifiable boundary, that function together to achieve a common goal.* Using this definition and drawing from the ones given previously, we can look at the characteristics of the three criteria for a system: *interrelated elements, boundaries,* and *a common goal.*

The concept of interrelatedness suggests that the elements of a system are interdependent. In other words, if one element of a system fails or is malfunctioning, it will affect some or all of the other elements in the system. These elements, often referred to as *subsystems,* work together to achieve the goals or objectives of the system. Going back to Aristotle's conception, we can also conclude that an effective system produces results that could otherwise not be achieved by each element acting individually. This is the concept of *synergy*—the total output of the system is greater in value than the sum of its individual elements.

The concept of a boundary suggests that a system is definable within the context of all other systems and that its limits can be established by virtue of it having a definable boundary. Further, the existence of a boundary implies that the elements of the system must be contained within it and that any element not contained within the defined boundary of the system must, therefore, not be a part of the system. Elements that are not contained within the boundary of a system are said to be a part of the *environment* of the system rather than a part of the system itself. Finally, if we assume that certain systems, particularly IS, are within our span of control, then we can also assume that the elements contained within the system boundary are within our control and those that are a part of the environment are not controllable.

Last, but not least, is the common goal. The goal or purpose of a system is, quite simply, its reason for being. If a system has no reason to be, because it has outlived its usefulness or it no longer can provide the necessary functionality, then the purpose is no longer important and the system is no longer necessary.

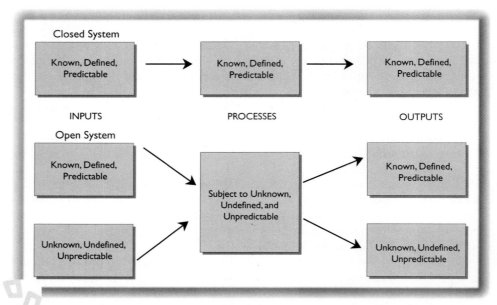

Figure 2-6 Comparison of Characteristics for Open and Closed Systems

System Classifications

Depending on what level of detail or characteristic you choose to focus on, there may be as many ways to classify systems as there are systems. For our purposes, however, we will adopt a common and useful classification scheme consisting of two categories: *open systems* and *closed systems.* Figure 2-6 contains a basic model for the two system types.

Closed-Stable-Mechanistic

A *closed system,* often referred to as a *stable* or *mechanistic* system, has as a distinguishing characteristic a generally self-contained design. This class of systems seldom interacts with the environment to receive input or to generate output. As a consequence, closed systems tend to be both highly structured and routine in operation, and environmental changes tend not to have a material effect on them.

An excellent example of a closed system is a terrarium. Figure 2-7 shows a picture of a typical terrarium. This enclosed glass container contains a stable, self-sustaining world for the plants and animals that live inside. By carefully selecting the proper materials and inhabitants for a terrarium, all of the necessities for the miniature world can be provided by other inhabitants of it. Food, water, moisture, oxygen, and carbon dioxide are produced by some components and used by others, thus sustaining the system.

One important characteristic of a closed system is that, although it is self-sustaining, it is not perpetual. All known systems must eventually interact with the environment in some manner or they will begin to deteriorate and decay. For long term sustainability, a closed system must eventually be replenished with new materials and sources of energy. In other words, a closed system does not have to interact with its environment to exist, but it does eventually have to interact with its environment to survive.

Figure 2-7 A Typical Terrarium—A Closed System

Open-Adaptive-Organic

In contrast to the closed system is the *open system,* often called an *adaptive* or *organic* system. In this category, entities that exist both internally and externally to the system are of importance. Open systems tend to be less structured and routine in operation than closed systems. Further, the interactions of the various components with each other and with the environment, although probabilistic, are constantly changing and much less predictable than those in a closed system.

A distinguishing characteristic of an open system is that it can adapt to changes in both internal and external conditions. The truly perfect open system is considered to be self-organizing in the sense that it can change its organization and structure in direct response to changes in its environment. Although not perfect, two examples of open systems that are of the greatest interest to systems analysts are the *business organization* and the *IS.*

The Subsystem—Functional Decomposition

As given in our definition, one of the characteristics of a system is that it contains interrelated elements. Because of this, we can take a system apart and study each of its individual components. At this point, however, things can get a little confusing, because the elements of a system, called *subsystems,* can also be thought of as systems, and the interrelated elements of the subsystems of the original system can be thought of as systems and . . . well, you get the picture. This confusion is easily resolved by having a specific goal in mind before you begin the process, but we will get back to that in a moment.

The process of breaking a system down into its component elements is called *functional decomposition,* and it is a very important aspect of systems analysis. By using

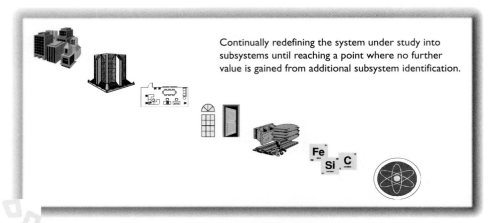

Figure 2-8   The Concept of Functional Decomposition

a structured process of decomposition, an analyst can break a system down into smaller and less complex subsystems that are easier to analyze and understand than the larger, more complex system. Functional decomposition allows us to study a single part of a system and to consider its refinement or modification independently from the larger system. By continuing to decompose subsystems into smaller subsystems we can also learn something about the original system that may not have been apparent prior to the decomposition effort. Figure 2-8 illustrates the concept of functional decomposition by using a city block as the original system under study.

As you can see from Figure 2-8, the original system under study, the city block, is functionally decomposed into its fundamental elements, its buildings. Each of these subsystems can be further decomposed into subsystems, and this process can continue, theoretically at least, *ad infinitum.* So the question becomes "How do we know at what layer of decomposition to stop the process?" The answer depends on what it is we are trying to find out.

For example, let us assume that the reason we are analyzing the city block is because we may want to buy it as an investment. In this case, we would certainly want to look at each building individually, thus decomposing the block into the next layer of component elements. We may want to look at each of the floors and rooms within each building to determine occupancy and possible uses for the space. This would be a decomposition into the next layer of subsystems. If we are really serious we may even look closely at the finish materials, such as doors and windows, to assure ourselves that the building is built and appointed to our standards. This would represent yet another level of decomposition. Would we need to have the doors, windows, and bricks analyzed to determine the raw materials used in their construction? Probably not. In other words, although we could continue to functionally decompose the subsystems into smaller subsystems, we would not gain any useful information at each subsequent layer beyond what we had before. In this case, continuing to decompose the system would not provide any additional benefit, and we therefore choose to stop at the layer of greatest detail that provides beneficial and useful information to us.

Now consider another example. Suppose we were hired to analyze a particular city block because there is an unusually high level of maintenance associated with

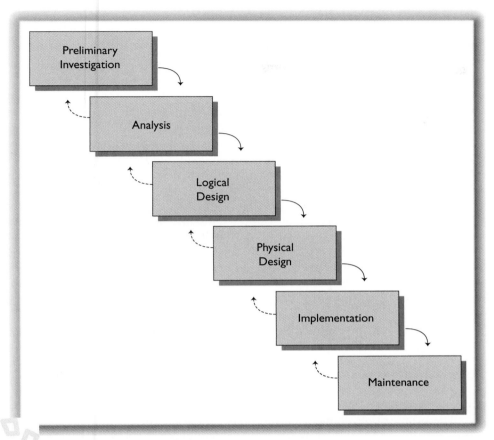

Figure 2-9   The Systems Development Life Cycle

the buildings located there. In this case we would certainly decompose the system into the layers discussed in the previous example, and we might discover the problem. More than likely, however, we would need to continue decomposing the system beyond an inspection of the doors, windows, and bricks into the layer that reveals the raw materials and even possibly to the layer that reveals their chemical composition. We may need this more microscopic perspective to determine the cause of the maintenance problems: substandard building materials. Through functional decomposition we have arrived at the root of the problem and can now turn our attention toward proposing an effective solution to the problem. In chapter 5, we learn about a common tool for systems analysts that allows the concept of functional decomposition to be applied to the analysis of the processes and subprocesses of an IS.

THE SDLC

In chapter 1, you were briefly introduced to the SDLC and its various phases and activities. Now that you have a better understanding of some of the basic concepts in the world of analysis and design, it is time to revisit the SDLC in greater detail and to begin using it to structure the development process. Figure 2-9 shows the sequence of the phases of the SDLC.

DETAILED PHASES AND ACTIVITIES

Preliminary Investigation Phase

The commencement of the preliminary investigation phase of the SDLC can be thought of as the moment the identification of a problem situation has been presented to the analyst team. It is at this point that the formal activities associated with formal problem definition and initial feasibility assessment can begin. As we have discussed previously, it is unlikely that the problem as initially identified by management or a representative of the end users will actually be the root problem that is identified and solved by the analyst team, but the life cycle is officially entered once an analyst is formally engaged to investigate the initial variance identified.

The primary purpose of the *preliminary investigation phase* is to formulate the problem statement in a precise and understandable manner and to investigate the feasibility, in technical, economic, and operational terms, of moving forward with a formal development effort. One of the early deliverables from this phase is the presentation to management of a general statement of the problem and a rough estimate of the resources necessary to solve it. This allows all parties to consider the project before having to commit to an extensive, and often expensive, study of it.

Once approval to continue is given, the analyst continues the preliminary investigation of the organization and the problem environment to begin establishing the initial boundaries and scope of the project. During this phase, as well as throughout the remaining life cycle, the analyst gathers information from a wide variety of sources, including users, management, archival documents, secondary sources, and through observation and testing.

The primary deliverable from this phase of the life cycle is the *preliminary feasibility study,* also referred to as the *baseline project plan.* This report includes an evaluation of the project using several categories of feasibility analysis. In chapter 3 we look at the detailed contents of the preliminary feasibility study, as well as the categories of feasibility analysis.

The temptation exists to continue to advocate for or fund a development project because of the amount of resources already invested. However, a project discontinued for the right reasons is always less costly than a fully implemented disaster. The SDLC provides a safeguard against this temptation to view the sunk cost of a project as a basis for continuing it.

Although not always clearly defined, the end of each phase of the SDLC, and the beginning of the next, can be thought of as formal checkpoints for the project. The structured nature of the SDLC allows for the concept proposed by Gildersleeve (1985), *creeping commitment,* to be used in a formal development effort. This approach suggests that the project can be terminated at any checkpoint if the feasibility of the project comes into question for whatever reason. Under this concept, all costs are considered sunk (unrecoverable) and are, therefore, irrelevant to the go/no go decision at hand. Further, although the information collected and analyzed up to that point may have a finite life in terms of its accuracy, the structured nature of the SDLC often allows the project to be resumed at a later date without the analyst having to start over from the beginning. This allows the steering committee, management, or some other affected party to constantly evaluate the project's feasibility from the standpoint of long-term benefit to the organization without having to feel committed to the completion of the project to do so.

Analysis Phase

As we move into the *analysis phase,* we find that many of the same activities per-formed during the preliminary investigation phase are still being conducted, but now in much greater depth than before. During this phase, the analyst must be-come fully aware of the root problem and must develop enough knowledge about the business environment and the existing systems that an effective solution can be proposed and implemented.

The primary activities in this phase include the gathering of a considerable amount of information intended to facilitate the development of implementation-independent models of the current system from both a data and a process perspec-tive and the determination and documentation of the formal requirements for the proposed system. The first activity, called *logical modeling,* allows the analyst to view the current system by focusing on what it does instead of how it does it. Using this approach, the analyst can see processes and data relationships that may actually be impeding the organization from reaching its stated goals.

The second activity, the assembling of the formal requirements for the pro-posed system, is the result of interviews with users and management, observation of existing processes, review of archival planning and policy documents, review of documentation related to the development and operation of the current system, and gathering of industry-specific best practices data. New analysts often underesti-mate the time, energy, and importance associated with gathering this information and learning as much as possible about the work performed by the user. These ac-tivities are often the most time consuming and human-resource intensive of all SDLC activities. During this phase, the analyst literally becomes an expert on all as-pects of the business that are related to the new system. This includes understand-ing not only what the end users do but the purpose of each activity as well. Further, the flow of information through the current system must be determined and val-idated if the logical models are to be relied on. As all this information gathering takes place, the analyst must be constantly asking whether we have all the infor-mation we need and, if not, where do we go to get it?

The primary deliverable from this phase is the logical models for process (DFD) and data (ERD). Once these logical models of the current system are com-plete and their accuracy verified, they can be used by the analyst to begin the process of designing the proposed solution into the system, as well as any additional features or requirements determined during the information gathering conducted during this phase.

The second deliverable from this phase is the formal requirements definition for the proposed system. This document includes not only those specifications deemed necessary to solve the identified root problem but also any new features or functions requested by the end users. More important, the analyst must review each proposed new feature or requirement with an eye toward prioritizing them for management's approval. It is seldom the case that all desires of the end users can be embodied in a single system. The analyst must begin the expectation management process in this phase by pointing out to management the potential for certain pro-posed features or requirements to be extremely costly or time-consuming to de-velop. Through this prioritization process, management can better define the scope of the new system before the design phase begins. In chapter 4 we focus on the detailed contents of the requirements definition document and the techniques commonly used by analysts to gather the information necessary to prepare the document.

Logical Design Phase

The initiation of the *logical design phase* can be thought of as a major turning point in the SDLC. The activities in this phase are focused on redesigning the existing system to reflect the proposed solution to the root problem and to incorporate any of the new features agreed on during the development of the formal requirements for the system. Here, the analyst focuses on only the logical system, the "what" rather than the "how." Think of logical design as metaphorically similar to the development of a set of final blueprints for a new house. The architect specifies all of the dimensions for the rooms and the locations of switches, lights, and appliances, draws detailed elevations of each side of the house, lays out the roof framing plan, and details the construction of the foundation. In addition, the raw interior finishes, such as dry wall versus plaster and linoleum versus ceramic tile, are considered as part of the blueprints. By using blueprints, final changes can be made to the design of the house without the expense of having to rebuild something that was just built.

In the same manner, the analyst uses a logical design approach to specify the final system. The various processes are mapped out and specified, the data requirements and their relationships are documented, and the entire set of logical models is reviewed and tested to insure that the new system works as intended and meets the needs of the organization. It is at this point that we begin moving from the logical model of what is, developed during the analysis phase to the logical model of what should be, developed in the logical design phase. We discuss this project flow approach in greater detail in chapter 3.

Key deliverables from the logical design phase include the final performance specifications for the new system, the detailed logical models of the new system, and all information necessary to begin the selection of hardware and the development of software necessary to make the system a reality.

Physical Design Phase

Now that a final logical model has been developed, tested, and approved, the focus shifts to the selection of hardware and software for the new system. In essence, we are converting our logical model of what the system should do into a physical model that is committed to a particular way of doing it.

As with all phases in the SDLC, the users are active participants in the *physical design phase* activities that include hardware selection, determination of software with regard to custom versus off-the-shelf applications, the design of user interfaces and data capture devices, the specification of data input and report formats, the media to be used for input and output, and the determination and construction of the structure for the corporate databases to be used by the new system. In addition, the format and design of the test data to be used to test the final system are developed during this phase. Further, the specification and design of the various control mechanisms necessary to regulate the system and its processes are begun. These controls involve how users are authorized to access the system, how the data is protected against loss or damage, and how network communications are conducted to insure against unauthorized interception or system intrusion. Finally, the initial specification and design of training materials for the end users is begun during the physical design phase and completed during the implementation phase.

The key deliverables from the physical design phase include a detailed physical specification of all system elements and a formal feasibility analysis of the proposed system. This analysis includes the technical, operational, human-factor, legal and political, and economic feasibility assessments that management needs to make a decision to proceed with the installation or to revise the scope of the system for economic reasons due to an inability to justify the cost of the proposed solution as specified. In chapter 9, we look in detail at the contents of a feasibility analysis for the proposed system, and the activities necessary to move from the logical model to the physical model are covered in chapters 10 through 14.

Implementation Phase

Using the details specified during the physical design phase, the analyst and technical workers begin the process of assembling and installing the new system during the *implementation phase.* The final hardware installation and testing occurs in this phase, as well as the installation and testing of all software applications.

Probably the two most important activities during implementation are the training of the end users for the new system and the conversion from the current system to the new system. In the latter activity, current data files must be converted to new data formats, a programmed schedule of events must be formalized with regard to when and how the conversion, or *cutover,* to the new system will take place, and all testing of the new system must be completed and any necessary changes made.

The training of end users is probably the single most overlooked and underestimated activity of the entire structured development process. Final system documentation and all end user documentation must be edited, printed, and distributed during implementation. In addition, a formal training program and schedule for its administration must be developed and conducted during this period. This is not an easy task given the typical complexity of a new system combined with the need for the business to continue operating while all of this change is occurring. The issues of implementation and end user training and support are our focus in chapter 14.

Maintenance Phase

The final phase of the SDLC is the *maintenance phase.* Once the system is fully operational within an organization, the end users may find several small problems with how it performs a particular task or the method by which a function is accessed. These issues may not become apparent during the final testing and may remain unnoticed until several months after the system is in full use. Also, after using the system for a while and becoming familiar with its operation, the end user may think of a better or more efficient method of accomplishing some task. Finally, we all are aware that the needs of the business are in a constant state of change and that even the most sophisticated IS requires adaptation to accommodate those changes. These are some of the scenarios that often occur during the maintenance phase.

The activities within this final phase are, in some respects, reminiscent of the combined activities of the entire life cycle. In some cases, the changes necessary will be minor in nature and require little or no analysis. In other cases, however, the necessary changes may be significant enough to represent a formal development effort. How much time and effort is ultimately necessary to devote to the system during the maintenance phase is, in many respects, dependent on the quality of the work performed during the original development effort. Although typically not

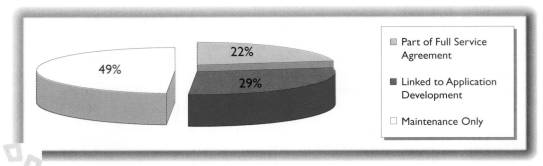

Figure 2-10   Distribution of Types of Maintenance Agreements

directly involved in the maintenance activities, the analyst nonetheless has a signifi-cant influence on the activities in this phase. The better the original analysis and de-sign, the less initial effort needed during maintenance.

Alas, nothing is forever. Regardless of the quality of the system, there even-tually comes a time where the continued cost and effort associated with maintain-ing an application would be better invested in the analysis and design of a new sys-tem to replace it. When this time comes, and it always does, the analyst begins the whole process over again, and a new system comes to life.

Maintenance costs can often represent the bulk of the costs for developing a new system. To alleviate the burden of such costs, organizations are looking to new methods of conducting maintenance activities. Asbrand (1997) reported the results of a poll by the Outsourcing Institute <http://www.outsourcing.com> of New York City, which showed that one in five companies had outsourced its application main-tenance or was considering doing so. The general consensus among the respon-dents was that this was being driven by the increasing cost of conducting mainte-nance activities in-house. Recently, IS budgets have seen steady but unspectacular growth, while development costs have grown significantly. Further, for every dollar spent on application development, more than half is generally allocated to mainte-nance. Figure 2-10 illustrates the relative distribution of maintenance activities across three categories of outsourcing.

Another reason for this increased focus on outsourcing maintenance phase activities is that many IT departments consider application maintenance to be drudgery. Tasks such as version update control and user support are crucial but often undervalued, as many organizations seem to be driven by new development rather than system maintenance. Watching over existing applications means shoul-dering a daunting list of responsibilities, including error correction, testing, quality assurance and measurement, user support, and disaster recovery. Application main-tenance succeeds as a contracted service in part because outside firms can impose new controls on the process. In place of informal requests for support and en-hancements that come via voice mail or hallway chats, outsourcing firms substitute formalized requirements. In fact, outsourcing is less about cost savings than about cost containment. Although many outsourcing firms claim to slash customer costs by 30 percent or more, actual savings are much lower. A recent Coopers and Lybrand study of high-growth firms found that just 60 percent of the companies polled achieved cost savings of 10–20 percent through outsourcing (Caldwell

1997). The Computer Economics 1997 report on IS spending found that only two-thirds of the companies surveyed reported breaking even or realizing a positive return from outsourcing (*Computer Economics* 1998). In other words, one-third of the companies lost money by outsourcing. The point is, just because you outsource does not mean you eliminate costs completely. Outsourcing simply removes the burden of the activity from the staff and transfers it to another location. No matter how they are accomplished, the maintenance phase activities must be performed.

One last issue of importance are those activities that can be classified as *cross–life cycle activities*. These include the basic skills and techniques of project management, such as scheduling, resource allocation and management, conflict resolution, and project automation, among many others. Although these skills and activities are important, they are not easily classified or associated with a specific phase or deliverable within the SDLC. As such, they are conventionally discussed as separate and distinct issues from the SDLC, as we have chosen to do in this text. It is probable that by the time you begin studying systems analysis you will be proficient in the basic tools and skills of project management. If so, then you are already well on your way to being a good analyst. If you are not familiar with these concepts and tools, or would simply like to refresh your memory on the subject, you can find an entire chapter devoted to this topic in appendix A.

Table 2-2 summarizes the phases of the SDLC and the key activities and deliverables associated with each. You should become familiar with these activities, because they serve to define the nature of the work you will do as an analyst throughout your career.

Table 2-2   Activities and Deliverables during the SDLC

Life Cycle Phase	Key Activities	Primary Deliverables
Preliminary investigation	• problem definition • estimate project scope • estimate project feasibility • estimate resource commitment • go/no decision	• preliminary feasibility report • general problem statement
Analysis	• create logical models of current system • refine problem statement via detailed symptom analysis • determine requirements for new system	• DFD of current system • ERD for current system • formal problem statement • formal requirements definition
Logical design	• revise current system logical models to reflect proposed system changes • validate logical model of proposed system against requirements determination	• DFD of proposed system • ERD for proposed system • final performance specifications

Table 2-2   (*continued*)

Life Cycle Phase	Key Activities	Primary Deliverables
Physical design	• determine hardware specifications • determine software specifications • conduct feasibility analysis and cost justification for new system • estimate implementation schedule • design data structures • prepare training guidelines • prepare preliminary testing procedures	• detailed hardware specifications • detailed software specifications • final feasibility report • physical data structures and data dictionary • implementation schedule
Implementation	• acquire hardware and software • determine location requirements • install the new system • create test data and conduct initial system tests • train all end users • verify all system and end user documentation • convert existing data files to new system • conduct final system tests and execute cutover	• final performance test metrics • fully trained end user community • fully installed system • fully converted data files
Maintenance	• conduct postimplementation review • perform requested and necessary changes to new system • monitor performance against established guidelines	• fully functioning system

SYSTEMS DEVELOPMENT PRINCIPLES

As we bring this opening discussion and focus on the challenges facing the modern systems analyst to a close and turn our attention to the detailed skills and tools used during the development process, we need to establish a set of guidelines that can be used to better understand the nature of the process and the importance of its structure. This final section provides an overview of good systems development principles that should be followed regardless of the exact development methodology employed.

Get the Users Involved

If there was ever a fundamental truth to successful systems development, "get the users involved" is it. The analyst must take the lead in making sure that all constituents and affected parties are identified early in the preliminary investigation phase and that effective methods of communication and participation are established for each of them. User involvement is critical to the success of the system, because users represent the real experts in the problem domain. The analyst's job is to extract that expertise and represent it in the new system; if the end users are not involved, that expertise will not be captured.

Equally important to participation is communication. The end users, managers, vendors, steering committee, and other related parties need to know what is going on with the project. The analyst is typically viewed as the frontline source of up-to-date information about all aspects of the project. As a result, the analyst also must be constantly on the lookout for evidence of miscommunication or misunderstanding on the part of the project constituents and must strive to minimize and correct such issues as quickly as possible.

Systems Analysis Is Problem Solving

Regardless of the actual methodology employed within the organization, the common objective for all of them is to identify, define, and solve business problems using computer-based IS. This means that all activities must be focused on this single goal and that the methodology employed should reflect a structured, programmatic approach to problem solving. New or inexperienced systems analysts commonly are tempted to shortcut or skip certain detailed, and often tedious, activities within the life cycle process. When this happens, the organization is exposed to one of three disastrous and costly outcomes: 1) the wrong problem is solved, 2) the symptom is treated and the problem is ignored, or 3) the wrong solution is implemented. When correctly applied and adhered to, these risks are minimized by a sound methodological approach to application development.

IS Are Capital Assets

An organizational IS is not some magical device that defies the basic concepts of business investment. The information is a capital asset just like the production machinery, a new building, a fleet of trucks, or the office furniture. The analyst bears the responsibility of viewing the system as an investment that demands the same level of justification that any other significant asset acquisition would require. Although there are clearly tangible and intangible issues that need to be addressed when considering the feasibility of a new IS, in the end, it must be cost-justified using the same conventions that one would apply to the purchase of a new fleet of trucks or the construction of a new corporate office center.

Good Ideas Can Become Bad Ideas

The concept of the creeping commitment, introduced previously in this chapter, is one of the hallmarks of a phased approach such as the SDLC. The analyst is responsible for controlling the project scope and for accurately informing the client with regard to continued feasibility and changes in costs. Just because a project was a good idea at one point in time does not mean it must be completed at all cost. If the project becomes no longer feasible, it must be reassessed, and a decision to terminate must be made.

Document Now

The typical modern organization has literally thousands of software applications and IS in current use. The common methods associated with the structured development approach set forth in this book help to minimize inconsistencies in the development process from project to project. This minimization of inconsistency becomes critical when you realize that the people who developed the application last time may not be around to develop the next one. People come and go, and IT workers are no exception. This suggests that an additional critical component to insuring long-term consistency is the quality of the documentation associated with the system.

Good documentation is the outcome of a process of documentation during the process as opposed to after it. We must strive to keep the documentation relevant to the system under development at least as current as the present state of the application. In this way, when the project is complete, so is the documentation. Think of documentation as part of the responsibility of the analyst to communicate with the end users. Do not wait until the project is over to start communicating.

Use the Divide-and-Conquer Approach

The systems approach allows for the big problem to be defined as a series of smaller, related ones. Given our cognitive limitations as problem solvers, the smaller the problem, the more likely we are to do a good job at solving it. This same philosophy can be applied to application analysis and development. The analyst must not only become an expert on the system of interest but also understand its relationship to its supersystem as well as the relationships of its various subsystems. You will see this principle appear again and again throughout this book and, hopefully, throughout your career as an analyst.

CHAPTER SUMMARY

As discussed in this chapter, the systems analyst is much like a scientist whose laboratory is found in the business environment. Although analysts perform a variety of functions, in a variety of business settings, the fundamental activity of the modern systems analyst is that of problem identification and solution development.

We have also seen that, regardless of the experience or skill set of systems analyst, they are human and, thus, subject to the frailties and weaknesses of limited information-processing capacity. This bounded rationality can prevent even the best analyst from correctly identifying the underlying problem or proposing a good solution to that problem. Further, we have seen that the urge to treat a symptom as a problem is an inviting one, and the analyst must always guard against this possibility. The methods, tools, and techniques used during the course of systems development are all designed to aid in the prevention of bounded rationality and the treatment of symptoms rather than root problems. The most important of these is the SDLC, and we spend the remainder of this book focusing in detail on its phases, activities, and deliverables. In the next chapter, we begin this detailed focus by looking at the challenges faced by the modern systems analyst in determining the feasibility of a development project.

KEY CONCEPTS

➤ Two basic elements in problem
identification and problem solving are

• Problem (cause)

A problem is a difference between
things as desired and things as perceived. However, because of the inherent subjectivity that exists in all
individuals, problem identification
and recognition demand a point of
view.

• Symptom (effect)

A symptom is an outward, or physical,
manifestation of a problem that
usually becomes noticeable as some
variance from the norm. Combined
with other symptoms, they form a trail
back to the problem to which they are
related.

A symptom is evidence of a problem but
not necessarily the problem itself.

➤ The problem recognition and definition
process

Recognize a variance (observe a phenomenon)

Investigate (formulate a hypothesis)
Propose a solution (conduct an experiment)

➤ Tools designed to assist problem
identification

• Ishikawa diagram (fish bone diagram)

The Ishikawa diagram is a cause-and-
effect diagram that relates the symptom or problem under question to
the factors or causes driving it. It is accomplished through a hierarchical relationship between the problem, the
main symptoms of the problem, and
any relationships they may have to
other symptoms.

• PIECES framework

By assigning the observed symptoms to
the six categories (performance, information, economics, control, efficiency, and service) provided by the
PIECES framework, an analyst can allocate additional resources to further
investigate the possible cause of the
symptoms and can often expedite the
formal definition of a root problem.

➤ Problem statement

The written problem statement should list
the symptoms, suggest their likely cause
or causes, and begin an estimate of the
resources to develop an effective solution.

➤ Bounded rationality

Simon argued that the cognitive limitations of human beings make it impractical to consider all possible alternatives
to a particular problem. Further, even if
all relevant alternatives could be reviewed, people would not be able to assimilate all the information such that an
appropriate decision could be made.
Therefore, problem solvers, including
systems analysts, are willing to settle for
a satisfactory solution to the given problem and avoid the extreme effort necessary to find the optimal solution.

➤ The concept of systems

A system is a set of interrelated elements,
with an identifiable boundary, that
function together to achieve a common
goal:

• Interrelated elements

A set of subsystems works together to
achieve the goals or objectives of the
system. The total output of the system
is greater in value than the sum of its
individual elements.

• Boundaries

A system is definable within the context
of all other systems, and its limits can
be established by virtue of it having a
definable boundary. Elements that
are not contained within the boundary of a system are said to be a part of
the environment of the system (uncontrollable) rather than a part of the
system itself (controllable).

• A common goal

The goal or purpose of a system is its
reason for being.

➤ System classification

• Closed systems

Closed systems have a distinguishing
characteristic of a generally self-
contained design. They tend to be

both highly structured and routine in operation, and environment changes tend not to have a material effect on them. Although they do not have to interact with their environment to exist, they do have to eventually do so to survive.

- Open systems

A distinguishing characteristic of an open system is that it can adapt to changes in both internal and external conditions. Open systems tend to be less structured and routine in operation than closed systems. These systems are self-organizing in the sense that they can change their organization and structure in direct response to changes in their environment.

➤ Functional decomposition

Functional decomposition is the process of breaking a system down into its component elements. It allows us to study a single part of a system and to consider its refinement or modification independently from the larger system.

➤ The system development life cycle (SDLC)

The SDLC is composed of a common set of phases and activities that serve to structure and guide the development process:

- Preliminary investigation

The primary purpose of this phase is to formulate the problem statement in a precise and understandable manner and to investigate the feasibility, in technical, economic, and operational terms, of moving forward with a formal development effort. The primary deliverable is the preliminary feasibility study, also referred to as the baseline project plan.

- Analysis

The primary activities include the gathering of a considerable amount of information intended to facilitate the development of implementation-dependent models of the current system from both a data and process perspective (log-ical modeling) and the determination and documentation of the formal requirements for the proposed system. One primary deliverable is the logical models for process and data, respectively called the data flow diagram (DFD) and the entity-relationship diagram (ERD). A second deliverable is the formal requirements definition for the proposed system.

- Logical design

The activities in this phase are focused on redesigning the existing system to reflect the proposed solution to the root problem and to incorporate any of the new features agreed on during the development of the formal requirements for the system. The analyst focuses on only the logical system, the "what" rather than the "how." Key deliverables from this phase include the final performance specifications for the new system, the detailed logical models of the new system, and all information necessary to begin the selection of hardware and the development of software necessary to make the system a reality.

- Physical design

The focus shifts to the selection of hardware and software for the new system. In essence, the logical model of what the system should do is being converting into a physical model that is committed to a particular way of doing it. The key deliverables include a detailed physical specification of all system elements and a formal feasibility analysis of the proposed system.

- Implementation

The two most important activities during implementation are the training of the end users for the new system and the conversion from the current system to the new system.

- Maintenance

    The activities within this final phase are, in some respect, reminiscent of the combined activities of the entire life cycle. The time and effort necessary to devote to the system during the maintenance phase is dependent on the quality of the work performed during the original development effort.

➤ Systems development principles
  - Get the users involved
  - Systems analysis is problem solving
  - Information systems are capital assets
  - Good ideas can become bad ideas
  - Document now
  - Use the divide and conquer approach

QUESTIONS FOR REVIEW

1. Briefly describe the difference between a problem and a symptom and why this distinction is important in problem identification and problem solving.

2. What is the similarity between the approaches used by analysts and scientists to identify and define a problem?

3. List and briefly describe the six categories defined in the PIECES framework.

4. Why is a written problem statement important?

5. Is it possible to make an optimal decision? Why or why not?

6. Explain the concept of bounded rationality and how this implies the need for a structured approach to SAD.

7. What are the three criteria of a system? Explain their characteristics.

8. Compare and contrast closed versus open systems in terms of input, processes, and output.

9. What is functional decomposition and why is it important to systems analysis?

10. What is the rule of thumb for deciding when to stop decomposing?

11. List and briefly describe the primary activities involved in and the primary deliverables from the analysis, logical design, and physical design phases of the SDLC. What are the major focuses that differentiate them from each other?

12. Explain the reasons why organizations are looking for new methods of conducting the maintenance activities, for example, outsourcing.

13. List and briefly describe the systems development principles.

14. Why is user involvement critical to the success of the system? What is the role of communication in participation?

15. What might happen if the systems analysts take shortcuts or skip certain activities within the life cycle process?

16. What is good documentation? Why is it important?

FOR FURTHER DISCUSSION

1. Use the PIECES framework to evaluate the course registration system at your university. What does the analysis tell you about the current state of affairs? What do you think the root of the problem(s) might be?

2. Pick a problem situation you have encountered recently and analyze it from the perspective of separating the problem from its related symptoms. You should find that many symptoms—some occurring long before you actually

identified the problem—occurred and were identifiable. What does this tell you about the value of monitoring the environment for variances?

3. Pick a non-computer-based system and decompose it to a functional primitive level. Begin by establishing the objective of your decomposition and then demonstrate how the level you stop at serves your needs with regard to informing your investigation.

4. Assume you have been assigned as an analyst to a department that is headed by someone notorious for cutting corners to get projects finished on time or under budget. This typically impatient person is the type that insists on shortcuts to the SDLC and then blames the analysts for failures. How would you discuss the problems associated with skipping various activities or phases of the life cycle? How would you explain the importance of not taking significant shortcuts that compromise the structured approach?

5. Stephanie Essington, staff benefits specialist, has recently completed a thorough training program in employee benefits counseling and is eager to put her new found knowledge to good use in her company. Her company has recently adopted a new medical benefits package that offers several choices with regard to levels of coverage, flexibility of benefits, deductible levels, and range of services and providers.

Stephanie is not new to this type of counseling, but the previous medical benefits program was far less complex than the new one. Since completing her training, Stephanie feels confident that she can explain all of the options available to the employees, but she is finding that most of the employees she has counseled so far have not been excited about the new system. They seem to be struggling with the many options and combinations of benefits, and Stephanie feels she needs to be much more specific with regard to her suggestions to employees.

She is considering developing a computer program that would allow her to develop multiple scenarios ranging from worst-case to best-case for each employee. Shortly after beginning her detailed analysis for this application she runs into several roadblocks. Her requests to the IS department for employee salary and personnel data are taking up to a day to complete. Further, she is finding that much of the data she receives is outdated or even conflicting. Finally, the calculations necessary to perform this scenario analysis are quite complex, and although she is a fairly proficient spreadsheet user, she fears that the development of the application may be a little beyond her programming skills. She knows that a slight flaw in the calculations could have a major negative effect on the decision process.

Evaluate the preceding scenario using the PIECES framework. Analyze the symptom categories carefully, and see if you can think of ways in which Stephanie's problem might be solved.

REFERENCES

Asbrand, D. 1997. "Outsource Your Maintenance Migraines." *PlugIn Datamation* (June) <www.datamation.com>. Accessed July 25, 1997.

Blanchard, K., and S. Johnson. 1997. *The One Minute Manager*. San Francisco: Jossey-Bass.

Caldwell, B. 1997. "No Big Savings." <http://iweek.com/621/21mtout.htm>. Accessed.

The Computer Economics Report on IT Spending. 1998. Vol. 20(4). Carlsbad, CA: Computer Economics, Inc.

Gause, D. C., and G. Weinberg. 1990. *Are Your Lights On? How to Figure Out What the Problem Really Is.* New York: Dorset House.

Gildersleeve, T. 1985. *Successful Data Processing Systems Analysis.* 2d ed. Englewood Cliffs, NJ: Prentice Hall.

Hall, A. D., and R. E. Fagen. 1956. "Definition of a System." *General Systems Yearbook* 1: 18.

Pounds, W. F. 1969. "The Process of Problem-Finding." *Industrial Management Review* (Fall): 1–19.

Wetherbe, J., and N. P. Vitalari. 1994. *Systems Analysis and Design: Traditional, Best Practices.* 4th ed. St. Paul, MN: West Publishing.

Identification and Selection of Development Projects

Learning Objectives

■ Understand the process by which corporate systems development projects are identified and initiated

■ Understand the concepts associated with determining project value to the organization

■ Understand the value chain analysis approach to project selection

■ Explore the concept of creeping commitment

■ Discuss the information systems planning process

■ Identify the deliverables from the ISP

■ Review the contents of a typical baseline plan

■ Discuss the role and composition of a corporate IS steering committee

■ Review the concepts of logical versus physical models of systems

When schemes are laid in advance, it is surprising how often the circumstances fit in with them.

—Sir William Osler, Canadian physician

INTRODUCTION

Regardless of whether a modern IS is ultimately developed to solve the real problem or just a symptom of a problem, one thing is certain: the analysis, development, deployment, and maintenance of a modern IS consume a vast amount of organizational resources. These resources include not only dollars invested but also time, opportunity costs, and knowledge. Solving the wrong problem or choosing to focus the organization's resources on the wrong project is, at the very least, wasteful and can sometimes be disastrous. Just as the actual analysis and development of the system can benefit from a formal, structured approach, so can the identification, evaluation, and selection of potential development projects on which to focus the organization's resources. In the first part of this chapter, we provide an overview of the IS planning process, with our focus being the steps necessary to identify and evaluate potential projects. In the latter part of the chapter, we narrow our focus to those issues and activities associated with conducting the first phase of the SDLC, the *preliminary investigation phase.*

IDENTIFYING POTENTIAL SYSTEMS DEVELOPMENT PROJECTS

The need for a formal systems development effort can manifest itself from a variety of sources and under a variety of conditions. One of the most common ways in which a potential development project is identified is through some perceived organizational need or desire. Perhaps the present system is no longer capable of meeting the changing business needs of the organization or the emergence of new technology suggests that the process could be accomplished better, faster, or more efficiently. Equally familiar is the decision to convert the current applications within the organization to a common operating platform. Finally, there may be a pending crisis, such as a system that is at or near capacity or that expects the merger or addition of a large number of new users that could exceed the original design capabilities of the system. In general, projects are proposed for two basic reasons: (1) the perception of a problem that can be solved with a computer-based solution, or (2) the identification of an opportunity for improvement that can be facilitated by upgrading a current system or designing a new one. Regardless of the source of the need, each potential project must be evaluated and a determination made as to the degree of organizational resources to commit to it.

Evaluating Project Potential

Although no single method has been proved universally successful in evaluating potential development projects, a number of methods have emerged that, when applied in appropriate situations, can assist in the decision process. First it must be understood, however, that the members of the organization who champion a proposed project or stand to benefit most from a new application development effort will be steadfast in their belief that the project is both worthwhile and necessary. In an extreme case, the champion of a proposed development project may see its primary value as the enhancement of his or her personal political power. Despite this sincerity and resolve, however, it is also true that there are usually more necessary projects at any given time than there are resources to commit to them. This suggests that whereas input from the project supporters is necessary in the decision process, the evaluation and selection of development projects should be conducted using as objective and independent a process as possible. To accomplish this, several evaluation criteria that can be universally applied to all projects under consideration must be formally established. Table 3-1 lists evaluation criteria commonly used in the selection of systems development projects.

Potential Organizational Benefits

One of the most common methods for initially evaluating a project or projects is to determine its potential for providing significant, ongoing, and measurable benefits to the organization. Such benefits could take the form of a direct increase in organizational or business unit profits, improved customer service levels, increases in throughput or process efficiencies, or possibly the creation of slack resource or excess capacity over time. The most important characteristic of this evaluation approach is that the criteria adopted must be *measurable.* There is an old saying in

Table 3-1   Examples of Commonly Used Project Evaluation Criteria

Evaluation Criteria	Description of Criteria
Potential organizational benefits	The degree to which the proposed project will improve profits, customer service, organizational performance, etc. and the expected duration of these benefits.
Strategic fit	The degree to which the proposed project will assist the organization in achieving its strategic objectives and other long-term goals.
Level of resource allocation	The various types of resources and their expected levels associated with the proposed project, including time, labor, capital, and identifiable opportunity costs.
Value chain analysis	The degree to which the proposed project contributes value to the manufacture or delivery of goods and services to the marketplace.

business, "If you cannot measure it, then you cannot manage it." Using measurable, quantifiable criteria is essential to making an objective assessment of the benefits associated with one or several competing development proposals. Table 3-2 shows several examples of both measurable and unmeasurable benefits.

Strategic Fit

Another useful evaluation criterion is the degree to which the proposed project fits with the existing or anticipated organizational strategic focus. Commonly, the needs of a particular business unit or department of an organization may not match

Table 3-2   Examples of Measurable Versus Unmeasurable Benefits

Measurable Benefits	Unmeasurable Benefits
Market share will improve to a sustainable minimum of 35%.	We will be one of the leading suppliers in the market.
Line throughput will increase by 7% within the first quarter and by at least 3% each quarter thereafter.	Line throughput will be dramatically increased and will continue this trend over time.
Product quality will increase such that re-work will be reduced more than 12% annually.	Product quality will increase and rework will decrease.
Production costs for the auxiliary power unit will be reduced by at least $3.00 per unit.	Production costs for the auxiliary power unit will go down significantly.

those of the rest of the organization. When this happens, the proposed project must be carefully evaluated to insure that the needs of the few are not subordinating or compromising the needs, and the resources, of the many. In such cases, the project may be deemed to be beyond the core competencies or strategic focus of the organization and may be rejected in favor of a modified proposal that is more in keeping with the organization's direction. An example of this can be found in the decisions facing numerous firms throughout the globe with regard to the Y2K crisis. Many businesses began to realize early on that correcting their Y2K problems was going to be a monumental task that would involve a combination of repairs and modifications to existing systems, as well as replacement of systems with newer, Y2K compliant versions. The real question was how to prioritize the multitude of applications requiring attention so that the maximum gain would be achieved and the minimum exposure on January 1, 2000 would be realized. Every system identified as needing Y2K attention was clearly important, but because of the limited amount of resources combined with the looming deadline, many organizations had to make tough decisions regarding which systems would get attention first. Because of this, some applications were not ready for the millennium, despite their users' view of them as important to the quality of the work. Despite the apparent ease with which the new millennium arrived and with which the many software applications in place functioned, the process of sifting through applications that were not able to be modified in time still continues.

Level of Resource Allocation

The level of resource allocation category of evaluation criteria is probably the most widely employed approach and commonly the most misused. This method looks at the amounts and types of organizational resources that must be committed to the proposed project to reach a successful outcome. Such resources include financial investment, labor, physical plant allocations, time, and opportunity costs, among many others. Commonly, however, the decision to accept or reject a project using this criterion is fraught with error in judgment, because the project has not been cost justified using appropriate estimation techniques for both the true costs of the project and the actual net value of the benefits expected from the investment. Such techniques are commonly employed in the evaluation of a new fleet of trucks or in the decision to invest in a new capital structure, such as another assembly line or a new corporate headquarters. Similarly, sound cost and value estimation techniques must be employed when evaluating the level of resource allocation for a proposed IS development project. We focus on the details surrounding such techniques in chapter 9, but for now, suffice it to say that an inaccurate assessment of the necessary resources for a project can result in misallocation of precious time and money and can often result in an inadequate solution to the problem at hand.

The evaluation of project duration and labor commitment is also an important issue for the level of resource allocation. As we show in chapter 9, both the length of the project and the number of people involved in the project are potential sources of increased risk. The more risk a proposed project presents, the more likely that the resources necessary to manage that risk will increase. In this case, the evaluation of necessary resources and true costs is often inflated to create the proverbial fudge factor that allows for the risks associated with unknowns. However common, this approach is never appropriate and always results in wasted resources. Although a longer project is admittedly a more complex and thus a higher risk project, quantifying that risk is vitally important to the ultimate success of the project. Further, the

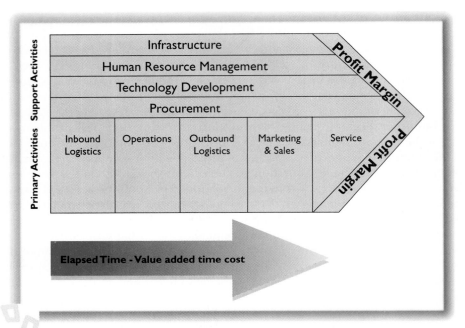

Figure 3-1   Porter's Generic Value Chain

techniques necessary to make an accurate determination of the required resources do exist. At this point, it is important for you to realize that the justification of a proposed IS development project, from a resource perspective, is no different than any other organizational capital investment.

Value Chain Analysis

One valuable approach to the evaluation and assessment of proposed development projects is *value chain analysis*. Originally proposed by Michael Porter (1985), this technique involves the assessment of an organization's overall activities associated with the manufacture and delivery of products and services to the marketplace in terms of the value they add to the enterprise. By gaining a thorough understanding of an organization's value chain, various improvements to both the firm's operations and their overall performance can be achieved. Using this approach, those proposed systems development projects that contribute the greatest benefits to the overall value chain take priority over those with a lesser contribution. Figure 3-1 illustrates the concept of the organizational value chain.

As shown in Figure 3-1, technology (in our case IT) is viewed as an integral part of the support activities in the value chain necessary to produce an acceptable profit margin for the firm. Beyond the support component, however, many organizations have come to realize the value of using their IT to improve all of the activities in the value chain. Figure 3-2 illustrates the potential application of IT to all activities in the value chain.

As you can see, IS can play an integral role in all aspects of the value chain. The support activities can be enhanced by taking advantage of the ability of IS to automate procurement processes, provide rapid information with regard to human

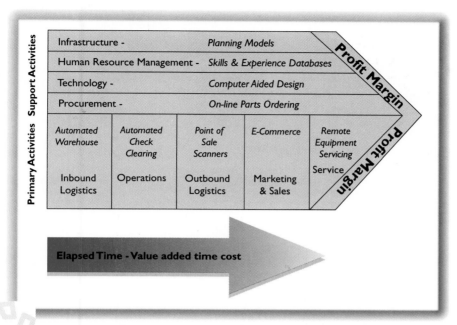

Figure 3-2   Potential IS Contributions to the Value Chain

resource planning activities, and provide support to the various activities in the infrastructure category. Further, each of the primary activities in the value chain model can also be improved with the appropriate application of IT. Everything from automating the warehouse to improve inbound logistics to developing and deploying remote servicing technologies can be used to increase the overall profit margin of the firm. By analyzing the proposed development project in terms of its direct contribution to one or more activities in the value chain, an immediate picture of its contribution, and thus its value to the firm, can be easily determined.

The first step in conducting a value chain analysis for a proposed development project is to envision the organization as a system with definable inputs, processes, and outputs. The inputs are the raw materials and resources necessary to generate the outputs, which are the products and services manufactured and ultimately delivered to the marketplace. The processes are those activities or functions that are necessary to achieve the outputs and where the value is created or should be improved. Once a particular portion of the value chain is focused on, the costs, and the drivers that cause them to vary, can be determined and benchmarked against industry norms or expected levels of performance. The outcome of this comparison identifies specific activities within the value chain that could benefit from the application of IT solutions to improve efficiency or reduce costs or both.

Project Selection

All the analysis in the world does not make the decision regarding which projects to ultimately support and which projects to reject or send back to the drawing board for refinement. That decision rests solely in the hands of the key decision makers within the organization, and it requires a careful blend of those projects

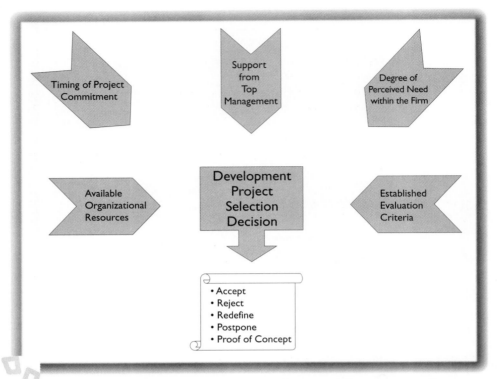

Figure 3-3   Factors Affecting Selection of a Proposed Development Project

that achieve both short-term and long-term goals while maximizing the existing and expected organizational resources. Further, we have already discussed the constantly changing business environment and its impact on development projects and production application systems. Because of this constant change, the process of project evaluation and selection is both a fluid and ongoing activity within the organization.

No single evaluation criterion ultimately drives the decision to accept or reject a development project proposal. Many factors enter into the final decision. Remember that project proposals come in all shapes and sizes and from a wide variety of sources within the organization. Given these conditions, an equally wide variety of justifications are provided in support of a given project. Figure 3-3 illustrates the various factors that must be considered, beyond the objective evaluation criteria, when determining the final disposition of a project proposal.

As shown in Figure 3-3, five general factors, including the objective evaluation criteria, come to bear when deciding on a proposal outcome. In addition, several outcomes can result from the decision process. Probably the most important of these factors, however, is the support of senior management.

Although the project proposal may originate from somewhere other than the senior management level of the organization, nothing will be accomplished unless those who ultimately pay the bill support the initiative. This is not to say that the support of other parties beyond senior management is not important, but the support of top management is an essential ingredient to a successful development project.

Another important factor in the final decision is the overall state of affairs within the organization with regard to ongoing or current projects. Each new project provides an additional drain on existing company resources and may impose untenable situations on certain high demand resources, such as analyst time or specific user expertise. Despite the high marks achieved during the objective evaluation and the strong support shown by senior management, the timing for initiating a proposed project simply may not be right. Under these conditions, the decision to postpone or delay the commencement of the project may be the only workable solution. In instances where such delay may necessitate the revision of the project proposal because of changing cost considerations or environmental conditions, the best decision may be to reject the project with a recommendation to resubmit at a later time. These types of decisions are not easy, and they often result in one or more parties being less than supportive of the final disposition. Nonetheless, the final decision must account for all possible forces and must reflect the most appropriate balance among them.

The Concept of Creeping Commitment

One of the important facts to remember when evaluating proposed development projects is that not all of them will be funded, and if the appropriate selection process is employed, not all of them should be funded either. This fact, however, does not mean that the process of evaluation and selection should not be applied equally to all projects. One of the hallmarks of a structured approach, whether it be the project selection process or the SDLC, is the concept of *creeping commitment* (Gildersleeve 1985). This concept suggests that the process of selection and development is an incremental one that requires a reassessment of the value of the project at each step of the way. At any checkpoint, all costs to date are considered sunk (meaning not recoverable) and, thus, are considered irrelevant to the decision of whether to stop or proceed. By relying on the creeping commitment approach, a project can be placed under constant scrutiny with regard to its ongoing value to the organization and can be modified or terminated, if necessary, should its value diminish. Given the rapidly changing conditions in the typical business environment, this approach is becoming increasingly important to the decision to commit additional resources to a project that no longer meets the original evaluation criteria standards.

INFORMATION SYSTEMS PLANNING

As discussed in the previous section, proposals for IS development projects can come from a wide variety of sources. In some organizations, the primary source for new development projects is the result of a formal, ongoing process called *information systems planning* (ISP). This process is defined as an orderly means of assessing the information needs of an organization and defining the IS, databases, and technologies that best satisfy those needs (Carlson, Gardner, and Ruth 1989). Organizations that embrace an ISP approach take a top-down perspective of the current and future information needs of the organization and develop a set of strategies and formal project plans to move the current state of IT within the organization to the desired state. Much like value chain analysis, ISP must view the organization's information assets in terms of how they contribute to the achievement of business objectives defined by the overall corporate strategy. Successful integration of the information assets of the organization with the stated goals of the firm enables the development of IS that enhance an organization's ability to differentiate itself in the

Table 3-3 Typical Corporate IS Strategy Objectives

A corporate IS strategy is necessary to define
- what IS services will be provided and to whom;
- who is responsible for providing specific IS services;
- how these services will be provided;
- priorities for provision of new facilities and improvement of existing facilities;
- who has access to what information;
- how access to IS services will be distributed and supported;
- what common standards should be applied;
- what resources are required and how resources available should be utilized;
- mechanisms for understanding and mapping current and future business processes;
- a mechanism for maintaining and renewing the strategy.

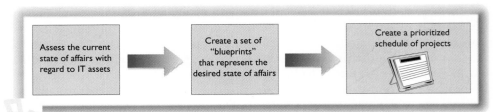

Figure 3-4 Information Systems Planning Process

marketplace. Examples of this approach are numerous and include the Chicago Board of Trade and its 24-hour-a-day automated trading system, Federal Express and its automated package management system, and Phillips Petroleum and its worldwide EIS. Table 3-3 lists the various objectives of a corporate IS strategy, and Figure 3-4 illustrates the three primary steps associated with the ISP approach.

The ISP approach is elegantly simple in structure but is nonetheless extremely effective in organizing the potential IS development projects for an organization into a highly prioritized list. The first step is to assess and document the current state of affairs with regard to IT assets. These include not only the hardware and software but the data, the processes (both manual and automated), and the human assets dedicated to the IT function within the organization. Once this step is complete, a set of "blueprints" is created that represent the desired state of affairs for the organization in terms of the relationships among the various IT-related assets. From this set of blueprints (or models), a series of development projects are scheduled to implement the changes necessary to achieve the desired state. This process is metaphorically similar to the process followed when building a new house. First, the current situation (land, housing needs, budget, etc.) is assessed. Second, a set of blueprints are created to represent the house and its desired configuration. Finally, the designs are approved, and a series of construction projects are scheduled to actually build the house. Also, as you will see, the ISP approach is logically the same method we employ with regard to the analysis and design of a new IS.

Table 3-4   Outline of a Typical Corporate IS Plan

Section of Plan	Description of Section Contents
Organizational mission statement	Describes the objectives and goals of the organization, including both current and future perspectives.
Inventory of information requirements	Contains a summary of both current and future processes, functions, data, and information needs of the organization.
Information systems mission statement	Describes the objectives and goals of the IS organization with regard to its role in the achievement of the stated organizational goals and objectives.
IS development constraints	Itemizes and describes the constraints imposed on current and future development, including technological, financial, human resource, and operational assets and resources.
Long-term IS needs and strategies	Presents the set of long-range (2–5 year) needs and strategies of the IS department prioritized in keeping with the information requirements previously described.
Short-term IS needs and strategies	Provides a prioritized list of current projects and a schedule of all additional projects intended to commence within the current year.
Implications of IS corporate plan	Discusses the various expected impacts on the organization of both the short-term and long-term IS strategies. Additionally, this section can be used to discuss any expected changes in the current business environment.

The Corporate IS Plan

The primary deliverable from the ISP approach is a detailed *corporate IS plan*. This comprehensive plan addresses both the long-range broader issues facing the organization and the more immediate, detailed issues that it must face. These short and long-range issues are expressed within the document as a series of development projects that are logically sequenced such that the long-term projects build a foundation for future needs, whereas the short-term projects respond to specific changes in the business environment. Table 3-4 contains an outline of the component elements typically contained within a comprehensive corporate IS plan.

PROJECT INITIATION AND PROJECT PLANNING

From the corporate IS plan, the prioritized schedule of projects must be put into action. This means that at least one of the projects must begin to move forward into a more formal planning and initiation stage. Appendix A of this text is devoted to a detailed focus on the various cross–life cycle activities associated with the management of a systems development project, and therefore, we do not cover them here. In this section, our primary focus is to discuss the basic concepts of assessing the preliminary feasibility of the project and the techniques and deliverables associated with the conduct of the project initiation and planning process.

Table 3-5   Categories of Project Feasibility Assessment

Feasibility Assessment Category	Description
Technical	Determines the relationship between the present technology resources of the organization and the expected technology needs of the proposed project.
Operational	Determines the degree to which the proposed development project fits with the existing business environment and objectives with regard to development schedule, delivery date, corporate culture, and existing business processes.
Human factors	Determines the relationship between the present human resource base of the organization and the expected human resource needs of the proposed project.
Legal and political	Identifies any potential legal ramifications resulting from the construction and implementation of the new system, including copyright or patent infringements, violation of existing antitrust laws, foreign trade restrictions, or any existing contractual obligations of the organization.
Economic	Assesses the cost-benefit relationship of the proposed project and its net value contribution to the organization.

Preliminary Project Feasibility Analysis

The assessment of project feasibility is an activity that occurs several times throughout the development life cycle. When we adopt the creeping commitment approach to systems development, we are actually reassessing the feasibility of the project, and thus the feasibility of continuing the project, at every milestone in the SDLC. Pressman (1992) points out that given an unlimited resource pool and an infinite amount of time, all projects become feasible. Unfortunately, such situations do not exist in the typical business environment. Most projects face explicit deadlines and limited resource budgets. As such, a categorical approach to the determination of project feasibility must be used to ensure the continued application of corporate resources is both relevant and contributory to the organization's goals. In chapter 9, we focus on the detailed tools and methods used to assess the various categories of project feasibility. For now, we simply introduce those categories and provide a brief overview of their focus and purpose. Table 3-5 contains a list of the five categories of feasibility assessment for a typical development project.

Technical Feasibility

The assessment of *technical feasibility* is focused on gaining an understanding of the present technical resources of the organization and their applicability to the expected needs of the proposed system. The analyst must assess the degree to which the current technical resources, including hardware, software, and operating environments, can be upgraded or added to such that the needs of the proposed system can be met. If the current technology is deemed sufficient, then the technical feasibility of the project is clear. If this is not the case, however, the analyst must determine whether the technology necessary to meet the stated specifications exists. The danger here is that the project may require technology that does not yet exist in a stable form. Despite the claims of vendors that they can supply whatever is required, the analyst must be able to accurately assess the degree to which the needed technology exists in a form suitable for the proposed project.

Operational Feasibility

The *operational feasibility* assessment focuses on the degree to which the proposed development project fits with the existing business environment and objectives with regard to development schedule, delivery date, corporate culture, and existing business processes. Further, this assessment also determines the degree to which the project meets the specific business objectives set forth during the proposal phase. In the early stages of operational feasibility assessment, we are primarily interested in determining whether the identified problem is worth solving or the proposed solution actually solves the problem at hand. In the latter stages of operational feasibility assessment, such as during the physical design phase of the SDLC, we shift our focus to one of *usability analysis*. This is a test of the system's interface, often using a working prototype, to assess how easy the system is to learn and use and whether the user perceives the system to be able to support the desired level of productivity for the task at hand.

Human Factors Feasibility

It is one thing to assess the degree to which a proposed system *can* work and quite another to evaluate whether the system *will* work. The *human factors feasibility* assessment focuses on the most important components of a successful system implementation: the managers and end users. No matter how elegant the technology, the system will not work if the end users and managers do not perceive it to be relevant and, therefore, do not support it. In this category, we assess the degree of resistance to the proposed system, the perceived role of the end users in the development process, the degree of change to the end users' working environment as a result of the new system, and the current state of human resources available to conduct the project and to manage and use the system on completion.

Legal and Political Feasibility

This category of assessment is often overlooked during the early stages of project initiation and analysis. The *legal and political feasibility* of a proposed project includes a thorough analysis of any potential legal ramifications resulting from the construction and implementation of the new system. Such legal issues include copyright or patent infringements, violation of existing antitrust laws (such as in the antitrust suit brought against Microsoft Corporation over Windows and Internet Explorer by the United States Justice Department in 1998), foreign trade restrictions, or any existing contractual obligations of the organization.

The political side of the assessment focuses on gaining an understanding of who the key stakeholders within the organization are and the degree to which the proposed system may positively or negatively affect the distribution of power. Such distribution can have major political repercussions and may cause disruption or failure of an otherwise relevant development effort.

Economic Feasibility

The purpose of the *economic feasibility* assessment is to determine the extent to which the proposed system will provide positive economic benefits to the organization. This determination involves the identification, and quantification, of all benefits expected from the system, as well as the explicit identification of all expected costs of the project. In the early stages of the project, it is impossible to accurately define and assess all of the benefits and costs associated with the new system. Thus, the economic feasibility assessment is an ongoing process in which the definable short-term costs are constantly being weighed against the definable long-term benefits. If a project cannot be accurately judged as economically feasible using hard costs, then the project should not proceed, regardless of the other assessment category outcomes.

By design, the initial feasibility assessment of a project is a very rough analysis of its viability that must be continually refined over time. It is, nonetheless, a necessary first step in making the final commitment of organizational resources to the development of the proposed system. In some cases, however, the need for a preliminary feasibility assessment is a moot one. For extremely small or obvious projects, it may actually represent a waste of valuable time. Also, certain changes in the business environment may dictate the need for change, regardless of the assessed feasibility of such change. If the government changes the tax structure for employee income, an organization has no choice but to make the necessary changes to their payroll system. If a critical program has a major bug in it, the organization has no choice but to address and resolve it. In other words, there is little point in assessing the feasibility of a problem that *must* be solved. In these cases, the feasibility assessment may be better directed to the analysis of alternative approaches to the problem rather than the problem itself. Regardless, however, the conduct of a thorough preliminary feasibility study should be the default standard in the organization, and a decision to eliminate this first step in the process should always be carefully scrutinized and justified.

THE BASELINE PLAN

The deliverable from a successful preliminary feasibility assessment is a formal project proposal for management. This document is called the *baseline plan*. The purpose of this document is to contain the various pieces of relevant information—feasibility assessments, schedules, needs analysis, and so forth—in a single place so that they can be presented to project clients and other related parties, such as vendors or suppliers. Table 3-6 illustrates an example of the typical contents and structure of a baseline plan.

The *plan summary* section of the document contains a brief overview of the project, the formal definition of the problem under consideration, the proposed scope of the project, and a set of explicit recommendations with regard to any subsequent activities related to the project (such as go or no-go). Typically, this section is limited to two or three pages and serves only as an executive summary of the remaining contents of the document. Because of this, although the position of the summary section in a baseline plan is first, its creation in the document building process is usually last. Once the detailed sections of the document are completed, the summary can be created.

Probably the single most important component of this section is the *formal problem definition*, sometimes referred to as the statement of scope and objectives. Although the form and title of this component may vary across organizations, the intent is nonetheless the same. A good problem definition lists the known symptoms in measurable form, the likely causes of the problem, and the likelihood of solving the problem with the proposed solution. It is important to note that the more de-

Table 3-6   Outline of a Typical Project Baseline Plan

Report Section	Description of Contents
I. Plan summary	*Project overview:* specification of the project scope, overall feasibility assessment, expected levels of resources requirements, and proposed schedule.
	Problem statement: formal statement of the identified problem to be solved.
	Summary Recommendations: actions to be taken with regard to the final disposition of this project proposal.
II. System narrative	*System configuration:* specification of the recommended configuration of the system in terms of necessary inputs, processes performed, and output generated.
	Alternative configurations: identification of possible alternative configurations using existing organizational technology assets.
III. Feasibility assessment	*Technical:* technical resources necessary and potential risk factors.
	Operational: degree of fit with existing organizational strategies and scheduling requirements.
	Human factors: assessment of expected human resources needs for the proposed project.
	Legal and political: degree of regulatory or contractual risk or exposure related to the project.
	Economic: economic justification of the project in terms of net benefits to the organization.
IV. Managerial issues	*Team member roles:* description of the proposed project team members, roles, responsibilities, and lines of authority.
	Oversight: method of project management and activity oversight.
	Communication standards: actions to be taken with regard to the final disposition of this project proposal.

tailed and specific the problem statement, the more likely the problem will be appropriately solved.

Another important element of this first section is the discussion of the proposed scope of the project. The purpose of establishing project scope is to define the boundaries of the proposed system as precisely as possible to minimize the impact of a phenomenon called *scope creep*. Creeping scope is a subtle but pervasive increase in the scope of the project over time such that the original estimates of resources necessary and the original problem statement to be resolved become lost and overshadowed by newer requirements and desires. The statement of scope is, however, not intended to eliminate scope creep, because in some cases it can occur for completely legitimate reasons. Instead, the statement of scope is intended to provide a mechanism for documenting and managing the project scope to avoid unanticipated impacts on resources and schedules.

The *system narrative* section contains information related to the proposed system's expected configuration, as well as a discussion of possible alternative approaches. Such alternatives include a consideration of whether the system could be purchased as a *commercial off-the-shelf* (COTS) product, whether the development activities should be conducted in-house or *outsourced* to an external development organization, or whether an existing system configuration within the organization could serve as a platform on which to launch this project. In addition, this section contains an overview description of the proposed functionality of the system, its inputs, tasks performed, and resultant outputs and products.

In the *feasibility assessment* section, the outcomes of the categorical feasibility studies are reported, along with an initial set of proposed high-level project schedules. This report also includes any statements of missing information or expected refinement of the assessments over time, because the initial estimates in this section are necessarily granular and rough. Over time, additional information allows for a more refined analysis and thus the generating of a more accurate set of schedules and cost estimates.

In the final section, *managerial issues,* various cross–life cycle issues are outlined. Such issues include the project team member roles and relationships, the method of project management and oversight, the proposed standards and methods for communicating to management and project stakeholders, the evaluation criteria for all deliverables and outputs, and any necessary deviations from standard life-cycle norms or established organizational operating procedures.

Once the baseline plan document is complete, a formal review of its contents, called a *structured walkthrough,* takes place with all project stakeholders. The focus of this review is for all affected parties to verify the accuracy of the information contained within the baseline plan and to formally make a decision to move forward with the project, reject the project, or table it for further review. In the spirit of the creeping commitment approach to systems development, the structured walkthrough serves as a checkpoint before the formal commencement of SAD activities.

THE ROLE OF THE STEERING COMMITTEE

In many organizations, an increasingly common approach to the approval of proposed projects and the conduct of the formal structured walkthrough of a baseline plan is facilitated by establishing a *steering committee.* This formal governing body is made up of members of senior management, systems managers and analysts, and representatives of various stakeholder groups or departments for the purpose of studying and prioritizing the various competing project proposals. The steering committee analyzes the proposals and determines which projects return the highest value to the organization and, therefore, should be approved for resource allocation and continued development. To make such important decisions, the members of the committee must possess a high degree of business acumen and awareness of the organizational mission and objectives. Given the resource constraints typically found in a business organization, the committee is expected to reject projects that do not meet the necessary criteria for feasibility or organizational value. Such judgments require the steering committee members to have a comprehensive understanding of the organization, its various functions, and its goals.

Although the composition of the steering committee can vary across organizations, and even across projects, the majority of the members should be drawn from non–systems professionals. Admittedly, the analysts and systems managers are important sources of information to the steering committee, but the independent governing nature of the committee suggests that the systems professionals remain as resources to the committee rather than as voting members. This prescription also allows the steering committee to serve as a project liaison between management and the systems analysts once a project has been approved for development.

Additionally, it is important to realize that steering committees, like any other corporate governing body, are often influenced by political pressures and, as such, may need to be approached with a certain degree of political negotiation. No matter how independent the steering committee may be, each representative ultimately has a stake in one or more projects that come before the committee for review. Often, technical professionals view politics as a dirty word and shy away from such activities. Politics is not only acceptable, it is desirable in moderation, for it serves as a socially acceptable method of resolving our conflicts. Effective systems analysts must learn to recognize the political forces that may affect a project proposal and use that knowledge to facilitate a negotiated solution.

THE PROJECT FLOW MODEL

Following completion of the baseline plan, the structured walkthrough, and the formal approval of the project by the steering committee, the project can begin, and the SDLC becomes the governing approach. Formal analysis and modeling commence, and the details of the organization and its current systems must be recorded using a number of tools and techniques. In the following chapters, we focus on the detailed application of each of these analysis and modeling tools. Although we are still focused on the activities prior to formal project commencement, looking at the pending activities in terms of a simple flow model can help us gain a clearer understanding of the events that lie ahead. Figure 3-5 illustrates the flow of

Figure 3-5   Project Process Flow Model

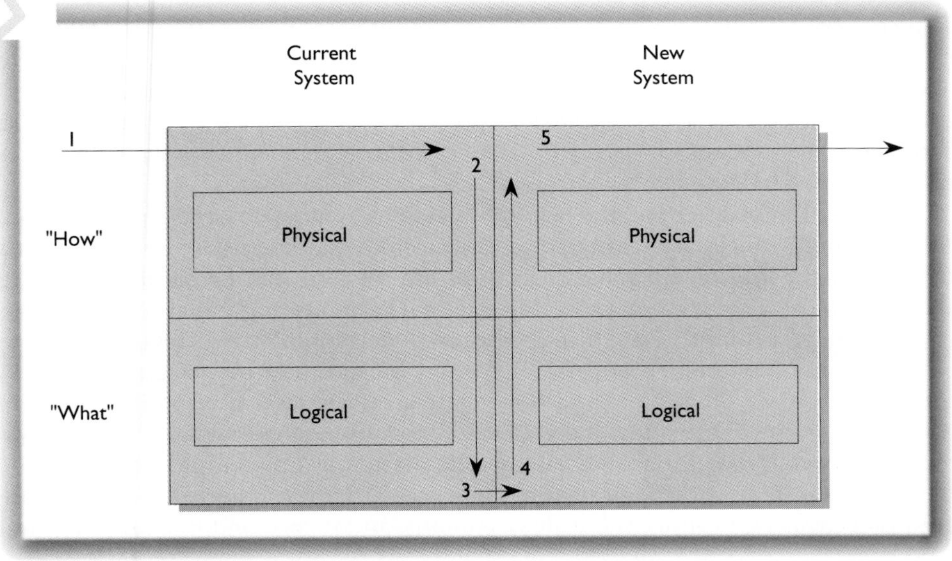

activities within a development project in terms of the primary focus of attention of the analysts.

When we begin our analysis activities, the most common starting point is the current physical system within the organization that presently performs the tasks or functions that are associated with the new system (line 1). This current physical system is not necessarily limited to a computer-based system but may, in fact, be an entirely manual system or some combination of both. Regardless of the actual physical nature of the current system, the first step is for the analyst team to convert it from an implementation-specific system to an implementation-independent model (line 2). This process is called logical modeling, and we focus on the tools and techniques necessary for its conduct in chapters 5 and 6. For now, it is sufficient to understand that our goal is to convert the current physical system, which represents how something is being done, into a logical model of the system that focuses specifically on what is being done, without regard to how it actually is happening.

Once we have an accurate and verified logical model of the current system, we can use the information gained during the problem identification activities and the detailed requirements gathering activities to begin proposing changes to the logical model to effect the solution to the stated problem and bring about the necessary improvements to the current system (line 3). This process normally takes place entirely in a logical modeling environment but may make use of working prototypes or mockups to assist the users in making decisions regarding the functionality of the new system.

When the logical model of the new system is complete and approved by all stakeholders, the models can be used as blueprints from which the new physical system is constructed and implemented (line 4). This process is identical to the process employed at the organizational level during the IS planning process and the formulation of the corporate systems plan. Once the new physical system is in place and completely tested, the maintenance phase of the life cycle for this application can begin, and the organization can begin the process of project selection and development all over again (line 5).

"WHAT" VERSUS "HOW"

The concept of "what" versus "how" deserves a bit more attention before we move on. First, remember that a model is a representation of reality that is constructed to allow for a more thorough and manageable analysis of something that, in its physical form, may be too big or complex to study and manipulate easily. Just as a picture can convey a thousand words, a logical model of a system can convey much richer information than the actual system itself.

Consider, for example, the case of retail credit management systems in which the customer invoices are handwritten, the monthly statements are generated on a typewriter, and the receipts and cash flows are all recorded by hand in a bound journal. As the company matures and grows, the mounting paperwork becomes overwhelming, prompting the firm to approve a development project to investigate and implement automated improvements. To be sure, the new system looks very different from the old system, and how it performs the tasks is very different from how they were performed manually. Despite this measurable physical change, however, every retail credit management system, no matter how simple or technologically sophisticated, works logically the same way. What the system does is generate customer invoices, produce monthly statements, and record and track receipts and cash flows in the various accounting ledgers of the firm. Once we separate how the task is performed from exactly what the essence of the task is, we can more easily see the logic (or lack thereof) of the current system and propose changes to improve the system's ability to reach its intended objectives. As you will see, this concept of logical versus physical, or "what" versus "how," is a key element in understanding and conducting the process of SAD.

CHAPTER SUMMARY

In this chapter, we have established the importance of a formal evaluation and selection process for organizational application development projects. Given the ever-increasing cost of modern IS, making the correct choice among the many candidate projects is tantamount to effective resource utilization and successful application of the technology toward reaching the goals and objectives of the organization.

In addition, it should be clear by now that the same basic structure and process is applied to the development of IS regardless of whether the focus is on selection, prioritization, or individual system development. In the following chapters, we begin a detailed investigation of the development process and the various tools and techniques used by modern analysts to accomplish their goals.

KEY CONCEPTS

➤ In general, systems development projects are proposed for two basic reasons:
  - the perception of a problem that can be solved with a computer-based solution.
  - the identification of an opportunity for improvement that can be facilitated by upgrading a current system or designing a new one.

➤ Common evaluation criteria used in the selection of systems development projects:
  - Potential organizational benefits
    Determination of a project's potential for providing significant, ongoing, and measurable benefits to the organization.
  - Strategic fit
    Evaluation of the degree to which the proposed project fits with the existing or anticipated organizational strategic focus.
  - Level of resource allocation
    Assessment of the amounts and types of organizational resources that must be committed to the proposed project to reach a successful outcome. However,

the decision to accept or reject a project using this criterion is often fraught with error in judgment.

➤ Value chain analysis
Value chain analysis is a technique that involves the assessment of an organization's overall activities associated with IT use in terms of the value it adds to the enterprise. Gaining a thorough understanding of an organization's value chain allows those proposed systems development projects that contribute the greatest benefits to the overall value chain to take priority over those with a lesser contribution.
  - The first step in conducting a value chain analysis for a proposed development project is to envision the organization as a system with definable inputs, processes, and outputs.

➤ Creeping commitment
The concept of creeping commitment suggests that the process of selection and development is an incremental one that requires a reassessment of the value of the project at each step of the way. By relying on a creeping commitment approach, a project can be placed

under constant scrutiny with regard to its ongoing value to the organization and can be modified or terminated, if necessary, should its value diminish.

➤ Information systems planning (ISP)

Information systems planning is an orderly means of assessing the information needs of an organization and defining the IS, databases, and techniques that best satisfy those needs. Through this approach, the successful integration of the information assets of the organization with the stated goals of the firm enables the development of IS that enhance an organization's ability to differentiate itself in the marketplace.

➤ The corporate IS plan

The primary deliverable from the ISP approach is a detailed corporate IS plan. This comprehensive plan addresses both the long-range broader issues facing the organization and the more immediate, detailed issues that must be faced.

➤ Preliminary project feasibility analysis

Preliminary project feasibility analysis takes a categorical approach to the determination of project feasibility to ensure that the continued application of corporate resources is both relevant and contributory to the organization's goals.

• Technical feasibility
• Operational feasibility
• Human factors feasibility
• Legal and political feasibility
• Economic feasibility

➤ The baseline plan

The baseline plan is the deliverable from a successful preliminary feasibility assessment. It is a formal project proposal for management that contains the following sections.

• Summary
• Formal problem definition
• Project scope
• System narrative
• Feasibility assessment
• Managerial issues

➤ Steering committee

A steering committee is made up of members of senior management, systems managers and analysts, and representatives of various stakeholder groups or departments for the purpose of studying and prioritizing the various proposals and determining which projects will return the highest value to the organization and, therefore, should be approved for resource allocation and continued development.

➤ The project flow model

• Physical model of what is
• Logical model of what is
• Logical model of what should be
• Physical model of what should be

QUESTIONS FOR REVIEW

1. What are the two general reasons for systems development projects being proposed?

2. List and briefly describe the criteria commonly used in selecting systems development projects.

3. Why is an appropriate estimation technique for a project's costs and benefits justification important?

4. Depict the role of IS in an organizational value chain.

5. If an organization is a system, what are the definable inputs, processes, and outputs?

6. Why is the process of project evaluation and selection both a fluid and ongoing activity within the organization?

7. What are the five general factors that need to be considered when determining the final disposition of a project proposal?

8. Why is the support of senior management essential to a successful development project?

9. Explain the concept of creeping commitment and why it is an attractive approach.

10. What is information systems planning (ISP) and why is it important to an organization?

11. What are the three primary steps associated with the ISP approach?

12. What is the primary deliverable from the ISP approach? What are the issues needed to be addressed in the plan?

13. List and briefly describe the categorical approach for the preliminary project feasibility analysis.

14. Why is the often tedious feasibility initial assessment of a project crucial to an organization?

15. List and briefly describe the components of a baseline plan.

16. State the importance of the formal problem definition section in a baseline plan.

17. What is the purpose of establishing project scope?

18. What is the purpose of a structured walkthrough after the baseline plan is completed?

19. Describe the role of the steering committee.

20. List and briefly describe the project flow model.

21. What is the difference between the logical and the physical models?

FOR FURTHER DISCUSSION

1. Suppose you are an IS professional in an organization with no corporate planning process of any kind. What would be some of the problems you, or your organization, might face? How would you approach the IS support function for your organization?

2. Using the components of a preliminary feasibility analysis as your guide, try to map out a project you are, or have been recently, involved in. Based on this analysis, is the project feasible?

3. Develop a baseline plan for an upgrade to your university's present student registration system. Once the baseline plan is complete, assess the project using the categories of preliminary feasibility. How does the project look?

REFERENCES

Carlson, C. K., E. P. Gardner, and S. R. Ruth. 1989. "Technology-Driven Long Range Planning." *Journal of Information Systems Management,* 7(4): 9–15.

Gildersleeve, T. 1985. *Successful Data Processing Systems Analysis,* 2d ed. Englewood Cliffs, NJ: Prentice Hall.

Porter, M. 1985. *Competitive Advantage.* New York: Free Press.

Pressman, R. S. 1992. *Software Engineering,* 3d ed. New York: McGraw-Hill.

System Requirements Determination

Learning Objectives

■ Understand the selection criteria for an analysis strategy

■ Learn the three "I"'s of requirements determination

■ Understand the four common mistakes made during requirements determination

■ Identify and understand the characteristics of a good requirement

■ Understand the characteristics and application of both the traditional and modern information-gathering approaches

Truth comes out of error more readily than out of confusion.

—FRANCIS BACON

INTRODUCTION

As we move into the detailed analysis phase of the SDLC, we are faced with the first of many daunting tasks: determining exactly what the system needs to do so that the needs of the users are met and the exact nature of the problem under study is identified and resolved. The gathering of information with regard to *system requirements determination* involves the use of a wide variety of both traditional and modern data-gathering techniques. In this chapter, we explore the various techniques commonly employed during this stage of the process, and we focus on several issues associated with ensuring that the information we collect is both accurate and appropriate for our use.

DEVELOPING AN ANALYSIS STRATEGY

The first decision that must be made is whether the system is conceived of as a collection of processes or a collection of interacting objects. Although both perspectives are focused on what the system does in response to some event, the method by which the system requirements are gathered and modeled and the approach to the logical design process depend on which perspective is adopted.

The more traditional approach to viewing a system is as a collection of *processes,* performed manually by people and in an automated fashion by computers. From this perspective, an event triggers one or more processes that require data as an input and produce data as an output, either for storage or as input to another process. These processes may also interact with end users in a manner that allows for additional data to be provided or specific desired outputs to be generated. This approach to viewing a system is quite common, and it is the perspective we adopt for the majority of the chapters in this text.

A more recent approach to viewing a system is called the *object-oriented perspective*. From this approach, the system is viewed as a collection of *objects* that interact with each other and with the end users of the system. These objects are capable of certain behaviors (referred to as *methods*) that allow them to perform tasks in response to one or more events. For example, one object may request an action from another object by sending it a message, or *request,* to perform that action. The real difference between the process perspective and the object-oriented perspective, however, is that the latter approach makes little or no use of conventional processes or data files. Objects carry out their assigned, or requested, activities independently of other objects, and they internally store the data values necessary to perform the actions. We briefly mentioned the concept of OOAD in chapter 1, and we provide thorough coverage of the approach for those interested in appendix B.

THE THREE "I"'S OF REQUIREMENTS DETERMINATION

Gathering all of the information necessary to determine the many system requirements is metaphorically similar to the process commonly employed by the famous detective Sherlock Holmes and his faithful aide Dr. Watson. Holmes's hallmark was constant attention to detail and a rigorous analysis of the evidence using deductive reasoning. The same basic characteristics found in Holmes's approach can be used to describe the characteristics of a good systems analyst during the requirements determination activities. We refer to these characteristics as the *three "I"'s.*

Impertinence

The first of the three "I"'s is the characteristic of *impertinence.* A good analyst should literally question everything and take nothing for granted during requirements determination. All representations must be verified, and the accuracy of all information must be determined. The key activity of impertinence is asking questions. Is this process always performed at the same time? In the same way? Will we ever want to change the policy associated with this process or transaction? Will this ever be sold at a different price? Are the same people always associated with this type of transaction?

Impartiality

Just as Holmes maintained a constant sense of unbiased investigation into the evidence before him, a good analyst must maintain a posture of complete *impartiality* when gathering information for system requirements determination. Your job is to determine the exact nature of the business problem under study or opportunity at hand and to propose the best solution to that problem or response to the opportunity. This characteristic suggests that the final design of the system reflects what is genuinely needed rather than the whims of the users in terms of what would be nice to have. By maintaining a posture of impartiality, the analyst is able to maximize all of the issues raised by the system stakeholders to provide the best overall solution for the organization.

Insight

The third important characteristic is *insight*. When conducting an analysis of a business environment and gathering information regarding system requirements, the analyst must make the assumption that anything is possible. Insight suggests that traditional methods and practices are not the status quo and the attitude of "We have always done it that way" is not an acceptable reason to assume the continued adoption of a practice.

Another component of insight is a constant and vigilant attention to detail during requirements determination. Recall from chapter 1 that the cost of fixing a mistake grows significantly the longer it remains undetected. Each and every requirement must be carefully thought through, verified, and linked to all others such that a perfect fit is achieved. If such attention to detail is not paid during this stage of the process, the system will be built with one or more flaws that may go undetected for months or years. When they do make their appearance, however, it usually is in the form of a major failure, and it usually means a costly repair.

Finally, the concept of insight suggests the need for creative thinking during requirements determination. The analyst must constantly face the challenge of looking for new ways to do old things and for new opportunities to explore and exploit. Insight requires the analyst to "think outside the box" and to use creative approaches in providing solutions to identified problems.

THE FOUR COMMON MISTAKES IN REQUIREMENTS DETERMINATION

Admittedly, the process of system requirements determination is a complex and often chaotic one, with many opportunities for error along the way. Despite the almost infinite number of systems and requirements that could exist in a modern business environment, the process of requirements determination remains basically the same regardless of the environment. From this, Wetherbe and Vitalari (1994) have identified four common mistakes historically made during the process of requirements determination.

Assuming a Functional System

The first common mistake made in determining requirements is assuming that end users of a system are aware of all of their information requirements. This is not to say that a particular end user does not know his or her job or could not express what he or she would like the system to do. Instead, this suggests that the typical end user is not normally aware of the variety of users of the information he or she generates during the course of performing his or her job. This lack of awareness occurs because most systems are viewed as *functional* rather than as *cross-functional*. By adopting the narrow perspective of a functional system, end users tend to focus only on what information they need to perform their assigned tasks rather than on what information might be needed by secondary users of the system or even by other systems. It is the analyst's responsibility to determine the degree of cross-functional use of the information associated with the system under study and to include those end users in the requirements determination process.

To illustrate the need for a cross-functional perspective, consider a system being developed for the budgeting department of a large organization. This department is responsible for integrating all of the budgets from the functional areas and tracking income and outflows against this budget. To allocate costs, the budgeting department has adopted a policy of tracking all costs by project number and then by revenue or expense category within a given project. Designing the system to accommodate this approach works well for the budgeting department and satisfies the stated requirements of its end users. The problem is that more than just the budgeting department could make valuable use of that system. For example, the marketing manager may want to track costs and revenues by salesperson, customer, and product, as well as by project. Unless the requirements of the marketing department are incorporated into the system requirements, this information need will never be met by the system.

The common argument against adopting the cross-functional perspective is that incorporating the needs of other functional areas increases the cost of developing the system. The flaw in the logic of this argument, however, is that, by failing to incorporate cross-functional information needs into a system, the costs exist anyway. The functional areas must each develop their own system and probably must transfer a great deal of information from one system to the other by hand, thus increasing the costs beyond what they would have been if the system requirements had been determined using a cross-functional approach.

Collecting Requirements from Each End User instead of All End Users

During the course of collecting the information required to specify the exact requirements for a system, it is often necessary to conduct interviews with many, if not all, of the end users of the system. Although there are times when an interview is appropriately conducted in a one-on-one setting, this approach is all too often used inappropriately during requirements determination. Interviewing end users individually can unnecessarily prolong the requirements determination process and can place undue cognitive stress on the interviewee that can actually hinder his or her ability to provide useful or correct responses to the questions asked by the analyst. This suggests the need to gather requirements information from groups rather than individuals whenever feasible.

Consider this example offered by Wetherbe and Vitalari (1994): Someone sits down in your office and asks you to tell them 10 good jokes. Despite the fact that you probably know at least 10 good jokes, you find it extremely difficult to recall them. Most people would.

Now, change the scene to you and a group of your colleagues from the organization being placed in a room and asked to generate at least 10 good jokes. It is quite likely that your group easily generate 100 good jokes. Moreover, most of the group is familiar with the majority of the jokes generated. In other words, each person really knows many good jokes but, when asked to come up with them off the top of their heads, they have difficulty recalling them. The point is that the collective experiences of a group are often more complete than the collective experiences of individuals. When an individual end user is asked about his or her information needs, he or she generally responds with the most recent needs, not everything needed. By pooling the collective memories of the end users, a more thorough coverage of the depth and breadth of the required information takes place.

Asking the Wrong Questions

The third common mistake made by analysts during requirements determination is that they ask the wrong questions and, therefore, get less than useful responses. As stated previously, analysts cannot assume that a typical end user is clear on exactly what his or her information needs are. Unfortunately, however, the typical end user assumes that the analyst knows what he or she is doing. Given this, no matter what question the analyst asks, the end user tries to provide a correct answer. If the wrong question is asked, however, the wrong answer (containing the wrong information) may be given in response.

For example, we know that the goal of the analyst during system requirements determination is to determine the information needs of the end users. Why not begin a focused interview with the question, "What information do you need from the new system?" Though obviously focused on the analyst's objective, the question would not be very helpful to the end user in forming a useful response. This approach is similar to a doctor asking a patient, "What type of treatment do you need?" or a psychiatrist asking a client, "What sort of therapy did you have in mind?"

The problem here is that the analyst rarely is able to reach the objective through a process of direct questioning. Instead, the line of questioning must be indirect, so that the requirements or information needs of the end user are backed into. By asking about the environment in which the end user works and the types of tasks typically performed by that end user, the analyst can effectively determine the information necessary to accomplish those tasks. We focus our attention on the details of constructing a good interview later in this chapter. For now, just remember that asking the end users indirect questions can often get at the objective more quickly and effectively than by asking direct questions.

Failing to Allow Refinement through Trial and Error

The final common mistake identified by Wetherbe and Vitalari (1994) is failing to take advantage of the benefits associated with trial and error. Often referred to as *experiential learning,* trial and error is an important part of system requirements determination. People regularly use trial and error to assist in making a decision, such as when test driving several cars before making a purchase or even having several relationships before getting married. Properly applied, this technique can substantially reduce the amount of time and effort expended to reach a valid set of conclusions.

One of the most common ways in which the trial and error process can be applied to requirements determination is through the use of *iterative prototyping.* This approach allows for a series of sample applications, menus, interfaces, and so forth to be presented to the end user, each representing an inclusion or exclusion of certain characteristics specified by that end user. Over time, the model system begins to take a form and appearance that closely represents what the end user envisions to be the correct solution. We discuss prototyping again later in this chapter, and we focus on it in greater detail in chapter 8.

REQUIREMENTS DETERMINATION DELIVERABLES

The objective of requirements determination is to create a set of deliverables from the requirements gathering process that represents the information necessary to conduct a thorough and detailed analysis within the scope of the system under development. Table 4-1 contains specific examples of the types of information that are gathered during requirements determination activities.

The information gathered during the requirements determination activities forms the basis for the construction of the logical models of the system and is the

Table 4-1   Examples of Information Gathered during
Requirements Determination

Information Gathering Approach	Examples
Interview	• Current system operations • Proposed system requirements • Data needs • Process sequences
Questionnaire	• Confirmation of facts • General user attitudes • End-user demographics
Focus group	• Conflicting system requirements • Synergies across functional areas
Observation	• Implementation of current processes • Confirmation of interview data
Archival document analysis	• Organizational policies and procedures • Examples of data capture and usage • Current system documentation
External research	• Industry best-practices • Technological developments
Joint application design	• Synergistic gathering of system requirements • Identification of conflicting perspectives
Iterative prototyping	• Refined understanding of system configuration • Operationalization of system look and feel

core of the final *system requirements specification.* This document, when completed at the end of the detailed analysis phase, clearly defines the end users' logical requirements and needs in a manner that allows the designers to actually build the system. Given the exponentially increasing cost of fixing a mistake down the line, the more time and effort spent on constructing the requirements specification, the less likely a costly error will be made.

Good Requirement Characteristics

One way to insure that a thorough requirements specification is prepared is to make sure that all requirements in the document conform to certain necessary characteristics. Table 4-2 outlines the six basic characteristics of a well-stated requirement.

Testable and Verifiable

If a stated requirement cannot be effectively tested or verified on completion of the system within a reasonable cost, then the degree to which that requirement has or has not been met cannot be determined. In essence, the requirements of the system must be written such that they represent the acceptance criteria for the new system. A key element in a testable or verifiable requirement is the presence of parameters that can be effectively, and reasonably accurately, measured. Table 4-3 contains several examples of testable and nontestable versions of system requirements.

Table 4-2 Characteristics of a Well-Stated System Requirement

Requirements Characteristic	Description
Testable and verifiable	Requirement must be stated to allow for independent verification that the system meets or exceeds the stated requirement.
Justifiable	Requirement should be necessary rather than simply desirable.
Unambiguous	Requirement should be stated such that multiple interpretations are excluded.
Consistent	Requirement should not be in conflict with any other stated requirement.
Modifiable	Requirement should allow for changes in the business environment.
Hierarchically traceable	Requirement should contain a single system attribute and should be traceable back to a higher level requirement.

Table 4-3 Examples of Testable and Nontestable Requirements

Testable Requirement	Nontestable Requirement
Compute *price extension* by multiplying *quantity* by *unit price*.	*Price extension* is the total cost for each item ordered.
Reorder quantity is computed by multiplying *average daily sales* by 30.	*Reorder quantity* should be equal to a 30 day supply.
Daily inventory levels must be accurate.	Daily inventory levels must be accurate to within 2% for at least 99% of all raw material stores.
The system must increase sales and market share.	The system will increase annual sales by 14% and current market share by 6.5% within the first 12 months of operation.

Justifiable, Accurate, and Correct

It probably should go without saying that all stated requirements should be an accurate reflection of the needs of the end users. All too often, however, whether consciously or unconsciously, unnecessary features or system capabilities find their way into the requirements specification. Although the wants and desires of a small group of end users may be nice, they may not add significantly to the functionality of the system, and they may significantly increase the development cost. It is important to insure that all stated requirements are actually requirements of the system and not simply something that would be nice to have. If the necessity of a requirement cannot be adequately justified by explanation, then perhaps it is not necessary.

Unambiguous

One of the most important characteristics of a good system requirement is that it should be *unambiguous*. This means that each requirement should be stated in enough detail that one and only one interpretation exists. Consider the following stated requirement:

> Sales reports must be mailed at the end of each week.

Although seemingly straightforward, this stated requirement is nonetheless flawed in several ways. To begin, is it a requirement that the sales reports be mailed? If this is the case, then any other form of transmission, such as e-mail, fax, or even voice, is considered not acceptable. Where should the sales reports be mailed to? If a sales report is prepared prior to the end of the week must it be held until the end of the week? Additionally, exactly how is "the end of the week" defined? Is it Friday morning or Saturday morning or before Monday morning? Although a bit exaggerated, this example illustrates the importance of providing a clearly stated requirement in an unambiguous manner. Now consider the same requirement stated with greater clarity:

> All sales reports prepared during a business week must be transmitted to the central office by no later than 4:00 P.M. on the last nonholiday business day of that week.

Consistent

All system requirements should be stated in a manner consistent with all other requirements so that they do not conflict with each other. Because of the ever increasing complexity of modern IS, this characteristic is often one of the most difficult to maintain. Consider the requirement stated previously, and then consider the following:

> The system must be able to generate and transmit all on-demand sales reports within one hour of the request.

Does this mean that there is a difference between a *sales report* and an *on-demand sales report*? If not, then the two requirements are in conflict and must be reconciled.

Understandable and Modifiable

One of the key objectives of the final requirements specification is to communicate the aggregate system requirements to all system stakeholders and interested parties, not just the analysts and programmers. As such, not all readers of the specification possess a technical background. To accommodate this broad audience, all requirements should be written so that they are **understandable** to both technical and non-technical readers.

Additionally, given the often lengthy period of a large systems analysis process, the requirements must be written such that they can be modified to accommodate changes in the business process or the business environment. Rigidly stated and codified requirements can sometimes result in the wrong system being delivered.

Hierarchically Traceable

The final characteristic of a good system requirement is that it be traceable back to a higher-level requirement. This suggests that requirements are structured in some form of **hierarchy.** The concept of traceability is normally achieved by writing each system requirement such that it defines only one system attribute. Consider the following:

> **EXAMPLE 1:**
> The production management system collects throughput data on each production line hourly and uses those data to update the inventory on-hand data store.

> **EXAMPLE 2:**
> 1. The production management system collects throughput data on each production line hourly.
> 2. Hourly throughput data are used to update the inventory on-hand data store.

In these examples, it is quite likely that the collection of throughput data is performed by one process, whereas the updating of the inventory on-hand data store is conducted by a second process. Using example 1, any error in either throughput data or on-hand data could be the result of either process and would be difficult to trace.

In example 2, if the throughput data is incorrect, then the first stated requirement has not been met, and the problem lies with that process. If, on the other hand, the throughput data is correct, then the first requirement is met, and the problem lies clearly with the second requirement. By making system requirements traceable, a test can be devised for each separate requirement, thus facilitating problem identification and resolution.

REQUIREMENTS DETERMINATION METHODS

We can now turn our attention to the various methods and techniques available for the collection of information from end users for the purpose of creating the system requirement specification. A wide variety of approaches to gathering information exists, each with its own unique characteristic advantages and disadvantages. Two general categories for these techniques have been identified based on their relative recency of adoption as information-gathering approaches. The *traditional methods* include interviewing, surveys and questionnaires, observation, archival document research, and forms analysis. The *modern methods* include the application of *JAD* techniques, the use of *CASE* tools, and appropriate use of *iterative prototyping*. In the following sections we focus on each of these methods in detail and discuss the conditions under which they are appropriately chosen and applied.

TRADITIONAL METHODS FOR REQUIREMENTS DETERMINATION

Table 4-4 contains a synopsis of the information-gathering methods associated with the traditional approach category.

Table 4-4   Traditional Information Gathering Methods

Information Gathering Activity	Explanation
Direct interview	Consists of meeting with individuals or small groups to ask questions about their roles, responsibilities, and needs for the current and proposed systems.
Questionnaires and surveys	Consists of submitting written, structured questions to selected individuals to gather information regarding attitudes, perceptions, or population characteristics.
Direct observation	Consists of observing individuals or groups, processes, and events to determine the facts surrounding a particular process or the culture within a business environment.
Archival document analysis	Consists of reviewing recorded organizational documents, such as current system documentation, mission statements, policies and procedures, and recorded memos and reports.
Forms analysis	Consists of analyzing and cataloging the existing data capture forms within the organization to assist in determining the current sources and uses of data.

DIRECT INTERVIEW

Among the variety of information-gathering and fact-finding techniques, the *direct interview* is generally considered to be the most important and most employed. The face-to-face nature of the direct interview allows for a wide range of objectives: exploratory fact gathering, confirmatory analysis, clarification, promotion of user involvement and project buy-in, and brainstorming of new ideas, among many others. Regardless of the objective of the interview, if it is conducted poorly, little or no information—or even inaccurate information—may be the end result. Table 4-5 contains a comparison of the commonly accepted advantages and disadvantages associated with the use of the direct interview technique.

Interview Structure

Direct interviews generally can be classified into one of two categories: *structured* and *unstructured.*

For the *structured interview,* the interviewer prepares a specific set of questions prior to conducting the interview. The goals and objectives of the analyst determine the structure of the interview, but the approach can be successfully employed for both initial fact finding and confirmatory purposes. For this type of approach to be successful, however, everything must be carefully planned out in advance, and the interview plan must be strictly adhered to.

In the *unstructured interview,* the analyst has only a general objective or subject in mind, rather than a specific set of questions. In fact, true to its name, for the unstructured interview the analyst prepares few, if any, specific questions in advance. Under this approach the respondent, rather than the interviewer, provides the structure for the conversation and directs the topical coverage. The purpose of this

Table 4-5   Comparative Advantages and Disadvantages of the Direct Interview Method

Advantages	Disadvantages
• Analyst can motivate the respondent to answer freely and openly.	• The interview process is time-consuming and resource intensive.
• Respondent can more easily develop a sense of active contribution to the proposed system.	• Interview success is highly dependent on the communication skills of the analyst.
• Analyst can probe for additional information and feedback.	• Geographical location of the necessary respondents may make the interview process impractical.
• Questions can be reworded or restated for better clarity or to facilitate mutual understanding.	
• Analyst can easily observe nonverbal communication channels such as body language and facial expressions.	

type of interview is to explore a topic area such that subjects of interest, or those requiring greater detail, are spontaneously addressed in a manner that allows to new ideas and understandings to emerge.

It is important to note, however, that the unstructured interview can easily get off track, and it is the job of the analyst to determine whether the initial objectives of the interview are being met. Although useful under certain exploratory circumstances, the unstructured interview is generally less effective in a SAD setting than its structured counterpart. Table 4-6 contains a comparison of the two interview types on a variety of variables.

Table 4-6   Characteristics of Structured and Unstructured Interviews

Variable	Structured Interview	Unstructured Interview
Required preparation time	High	Low
Required contact time with respondent	Moderate	High
Analyst experience and training required	High	Low
Evaluation of results and responses	Easy	Difficult
Degree of spontaneity of responses	Low	High
Depth and breadth of topic coverage	Moderate	High
Reliability and precision of responses	Moderate to high	Low to moderate
Insight into respondent	Low	High
Overall analyst control of dialogue	High	Low to moderate
Degree of flexibility of interaction	Low	High

Question Types

Along with the decision as to which structure to employ, the analyst needs to understand the two basic forms that questions can take: *open-ended* questions and *closed-ended* questions. Depending on the goal of the question, one form may be more appropriate than the other. Regardless of the interview structure, however, it is important for the analyst to consider the type of question being asked, because each has certain benefits and drawbacks in any given situation.

The *open-ended question* allows the respondent to answer the question in any way he or she deems appropriate. Thus the answer may range from one or two words to several minutes of detailed explanation. Words such as *what, how,* and *why* commonly are good beginnings for these type of questions. The analyst may add additional words of courtesy, such as "would you tell me" or "please explain to me," so as to keep the interview from appearing to be an interrogation. Open-ended questions are usually employed to probe into areas of possible information for which the responses cannot be clearly anticipated or the precise question set is difficult to predetermine. Two examples of this type of question are "Please tell me about the current IS" and "What do you see as the three most important issues facing this department?" One of the most important issues for the analyst when using open-ended questions is to listen carefully to the answer and to quickly determine whether follow-up questions are needed to clarify the points being made or to encourage the respondent to elaborate further.

In contrast, the *closed-ended question* is designed to limit the respondent to a finite set of answers. The most common example of this question type is found on a typical multiple choice examination. Other examples include "How long have you been employed as the department head for production?" and "Who receives the daily sales summary report?" Yet another example of this type is a question that requires respondents to rank a set of listed items or to record their response to an item using some predefined scale, such as *bad* to *good* or *strongly agree* to *strongly disagree.* Closed-ended questions normally have a specific goal or objective associated with them, and the analyst has a preconceived expectation of the possible answers that could be provided.

A special type of closed-ended question is called the *bipolar* question. In this type of question, the respondent is limited to one of two possible answers. The typical yes-no question is an example of a bipolar question. Table 4-7 contains a comparison of the relative advantages and disadvantages associated with the two question types.

It is unlikely that either a structured or unstructured interview contains only open-ended or closed-ended questions. The balance between the two types is often important to the overall success of the interview. Too many closed-ended questions can become unpleasant for the respondent, whereas too many open-ended questions may allow the respondent to get off the track and digress into irrelevant discussion.

Managing the Interview Process

Regardless of the degree of structure or the type of question employed during the interview, several guidelines exist to help ensure a successful outcome to the process.

First, whether a closed-ended or open-ended question is being used, be careful to avoid phrasing it such that a right or wrong answer is suggested or implied. In all cases, respondents should feel comfortable to express their true opinions without feeling as though their answer may place them in a minority or particular class.

Table 4-7   Comparative Advantages and Disadvantages of Open-Ended and Closed-Ended Question Types

Question Type	Advantages	Disadvantages
Open-ended questions	• Increase opportunity for spontaneity. • Are generally easier to phrase. • Allow the analyst to use terms and vocabulary similar to those used by the respondent. • Allow for increased richness in detail of response. • Increase opportunities to explore additional subject areas. • Are generally more interesting to respondents and place them more at ease.	• Can result in responses containing irrelevant detail. • May leave impression that analyst is ill-prepared. • Can result in loss of control of the interview process. • May unnecessarily increase the time needed to gain useful information due to lengthy responses. • Can leave the impression that the analyst is on a "fishing expedition" and has no specific objective.
Closed-ended questions	• Significantly decrease the time necessary to obtain required facts and confirmations. • Allow for increased control over the interview process. • Allow for ease of comparison of responses across multiple interview sessions. • Leave the impression of a clear set of objectives for the interview.	• Can be boring for the respondent. • Tend to reduce rapport between the analyst and the respondent. • Minimize richness in detail of response. • Can allow analyst to overlook or miss important concepts or ideas.

For example, a question such as "Do you believe the system should allow for modification of the supplier classification rating even though most current users believe otherwise?" would not be appropriate, because it signals to the respondent a predetermined socially correct answer.

A second interview guideline to consider is to remember to listen, listen, listen. In addition, notes should be carefully taken, and the entire process should be tape-recorded for further review, if possible. You must approach the interview as a once-in-a-lifetime opportunity to get this information, and you must assume that every piece of information provided is critical to the success of the project. This approach ensures that nothing is missed and that every possible piece of useful information from the respondent is obtained.

A third consideration is to schedule interviews with a variety of users and managers that represent the widest possible set of perspectives. In addition to soliciting requirements from the direct users of the system, information should be solicited from users of other systems that might be affected by proposed changes, IS staff who may be familiar with the current system, and other parties that can provide insight into additional services or functions that might better serve the information needs of the organization. By garnering a wide variety of perspectives, the analyst is able to make a more informed set of recommendations with regard to solving the business problem under study.

Fourth, regardless of the intended purpose of the interview, the analyst must be vigilant in managing the expectations of the respondents. In this regard, care needs to be exercised in setting expectations about possible new functions and features until such time as they have been determined to be a certain addition to the new system. The respondents must understand that their concerns and stated needs are being given careful consideration but that the iterative nature of the requirements determination process makes it difficult to state exactly what the final system will look like.

Finally, once the interview is completed, the analyst should make every attempt to clean up the notes and finalize a report on the interview within the shortest possible time (definitely less than 48 hours). Even the best analysts can forget, and within 48 hours the details of the interview quickly fade if not recorded. In addition, the process of going over the notes and organizing them allows the analyst to discover any points that remain unclear and to generate a set of follow-up questions to eliminate ambiguous information and incomplete responses. Above all, be sure to follow up with the respondents to thank them for their time and to solidify your relationship with them as a potential stakeholder of the new system.

Focus Groups

One additional issue to discuss while on the topic of interviews is the group interview or *focus group*. Commonly, a set of individual interviews turns up inconsistencies and apparent contradictions that require several follow-up telephone calls or meetings to resolve. This process can become quite time-consuming and may not result in all contradictions or inconsistencies being settled. By employing a focus group approach, these inefficiencies commonly can be avoided.

The focus group is simply an interview, structured or unstructured, with a group of respondents rather than with just one. The number of participants in the group can range from two to as many as can be comfortably accommodated. Using this approach has several advantages over the one-on-one method. First, by combining several interviews into a single time frame, more effective use of everyone's time may be realized. Additionally, interviewing several respondents simultaneously allows everyone to discover their inconsistent perspectives and to resolve them through discussion and negotiation. This also creates the possibility of synergies as a result of the interaction. The comments of one respondent may trigger a thought process in another that may have gone undetected in a one-on-one setting. Finally, by observing the interaction, the analyst can see issues on which there is a general consensus and other issues on which there is still a wide divergence in views.

The major drawback to the focus group approach, is in the increased difficulties associated with scheduling. Recently, however, the use of modern collaborative technologies, such as video conferencing, has begun to reduce the complexities associated with scheduling a geographically dispersed group of respondents. The use of the group approach is a core element in the JAD process that we focus on later in this chapter.

QUESTIONNAIRES AND SURVEYS

Another common approach to information gathering and requirements determination is administration of a *questionnaire* or *survey*. Although interviews are clearly an effective method for gathering requirements, they are also time-consuming and

Table 4-8   Comparative Advantages and Disadvantages of the Questionnaire Method

Advantages	Disadvantages
• Questionnaires often can be answered in less time. • Respondents can answer questions at their convenience. • Responses can be easily tabulated and analyzed. • Questionnaires allow for respondents to maintain anonymity.	• Response rate is often low. • Questionnaires allow for less flexibility than other, more direct methods. • No guarantee exists that respondent will answer all questions posed. • No direct observation of the respondent can be conducted during questioning. • Questionnaires are often time-consuming and difficult to prepare. • No opportunity to clarify points or expand on topics covered.

costly to conduct. In contrast, questionnaires are relatively easy to prepare and administer and are much less expensive on a per respondent basis. The instruments can be mass-produced, and the respondents can complete the questionnaire on their own time. Additionally, questionnaires allow the analyst to gather a large amount of information from many respondents in a relatively short period of time and, if properly constructed, result in less bias in the interpretation of the results. The primary disadvantage of questionnaires is that the results obtained are necessarily less rich in depth than those obtained through interviews because of the more passive nature of the technique.

The use of questionnaires by systems analysts has its opponents as well as its supporters. A common criticism of questionnaires is that responses can sometimes lack reliability. Such criticisms of the process, however, commonly can be traced to an inappropriate application of the technique. Properly applied, the questionnaire can be a valuable addition to the analyst's information-gathering tools. Table 4-8 contains a comparison of the advantages and disadvantages commonly associated with questionnaires and surveys.

One important difference between the direct interview and the questionnaire is that the interview permits an interaction between the analyst and respondent that allows for immediate clarification of meanings and redirection of questioning to explore an interesting subtopic. Even a puzzled look from either the respondent or the analyst can result in additional information being gathered during the direct interview process.

None of these opportunities exist when using the questionnaire, however. This places a greater burden on the analyst to construct questions that are clear and logically sequenced. Further, although questionnaires can make use of both open-ended and closed-ended questions, the results may not be as useful as those obtained from a direct interview. Generally speaking, the closed-ended question is the preferred type when employing questionnaires. The open-ended question on a questionnaire normally yields very little response because of the increased cognitive

SECTION B: Working With Information

4. Do you use information resources (e.g. data, statistics, or written material) relating either to social and economic development, natural resource management or environmental concerns in your work?

(Please tick)   Yes   No

If YES, please answer (a), otherwise proceed to Question 5.
(a) Please list up to 6 subject areas in the field of environment, development or human welfare (or 'Agenda 21' subject areas) in which your organization has a particular interest (for example— water supply, public health, forestry, wildlife management, etc.):

1. _____

2. _____

3. _____

4. _____

5. _____

6. _____

5. Are mainframes or minicomputers used within your organization?

(Please tick)   Yes   No

6. If the main office provided a computer to look up part numbers from the shop floor, would you make use of such a computer?

(Please tick)   Yes   No

7. Are PC computers (IBM compatible/Macintosh) used within your organization?

(Please tick)   Yes   No

8. Are geographic information systems (GIS) used within your organization?

(Please tick)   Yes   No

9. Which of the following best describes the use of expert systems within your organization:

(Please tick)   Regularly   Occasionally   Rarely   Never

10. Are computer simulation models used within your organization?

(Please tick)   Yes   No

11. Is email used within your organization?

(Please tick)   Yes   No

Figure 4-1   Example of a Typical Questionnaire

and physical effort associated with writing down a lengthy answer rather than verbalizing it. As such, when a questionnaire is deemed the appropriate tool, its value lies more in gathering fact-based information and generating confirmation of existing facts than in exploring the problem space. Figure 4-1 contains an illustration of a portion of a typical questionnaire.

Survey Design

Several issues become important when designing and administering survey instruments. The preparation of a good questionnaire requires that sufficient time be devoted to the selection of questions, their format (i.e., multiple choice, true-false, ranking or rating, etc.), and their sequencing on the document in a logical and easy to follow manner. In evaluating the quality of construction of proposed survey instrument, three basic characteristics should be used: *reliability, validity, and ease of use.*

The *validity* characteristic focuses on the degree to which the questionnaire obtains the information desired by the analyst in an accurate and interpretable manner. In other words, does the instrument ask the right questions, and are they being asked of the right people? To facilitate the determination of a survey's validity, a series of pilot tests commonly are conducted. These sample administrations are conducted with a small subset of the intended respondent population, and the results and feedback obtained through each test are used to revise and improve the content and flow of the questionnaire. In some cases, certain questions may be found unclear or ambiguous, and they need to be revised or eliminated. In other cases, the results of the pilot study may reveal several key areas for which new questions need to be added. Regardless of the findings, however, the pilot test should be repeated as many times as necessary to ensure that the stated goals and objectives of the study are being met.

One additional issue with regard to the validity characteristic is the perception of *relevance* or *face validity* on the part of the respondent. That is, we are concerned with the degree to which the survey provides the appearance of soliciting information that is valid or relevant. In other words, does the instrument ask the right questions in the right way? Questions that appear meaningless or irrelevant to the respondent may evoke answers given without sufficient thought. Worse, a questionnaire with poor perceived face validity simply may be tossed aside or dismissed entirely as a waste of time. This results in a large expense with little or no useful information being gathered. The judicious use of pilot testing eliminates the potential for this issue to arise.

The second evaluation characteristic for a survey instrument is its degree of *reliability* or *consistency*. Two types of reliability can be assessed: *external* and *internal*. External reliability is a measure of the consistency of results obtained across multiple administrations. Questionnaires that produce similar results when administered multiple times under the same conditions are said to have high external consistency. Internal reliability is determined by the degree of consistency associated with the responses obtained. One method of determining consistency of response is to include more than one question on a key issue or point of interest. These redundant questions should be positioned at different points in the instrument. By comparing the answers obtained from the redundant questions, a decision as to whether the respondents' answers are reliable can be made. Questionnaires that do not display consistency in responses should be deemed unreliable and, therefore, unacceptable for basing decisions regarding a new system.

Finally, a good questionnaire is *easy to use*. This suggests that the typical respondent finds it understandable and easily completed in a reasonable length of time. This also suggests that the answers resulting from its administration should be easy to synthesize into a cogent set of facts or information that can be clearly interpreted by the analyst. In this regard, the overall appearance of the questionnaire can contribute significantly to its relative ease of use. Questions should be grouped logically, and the organization of the instrument should flow smoothly from topic to topic. A good appearance not only contributes to ease of use but also serves to reinforce the perception of face validity.

Fundamentals of Scaling

The process used to assign some value or symbol to a particular characteristic such that it can be measured and further evaluated is called scaling. For example, temperature can be represented using the Fahrenheit scale or the Celsius scale. Further, temperature may be represented by a relative label such as "cold," "warm," or "hot." Although a detailed discussion of the issues associated with instrument scaling are beyond the scope of this text, there are several points we need to consider.

The decision to adopt a particular scaling method for a series of questions is directly related to the objective or goal associated with the asking of those ques-

Table 4-9   Examples of Different Questionnaire Scaling Types

Scale Type	Application	Example
Nominal	Used to classify objects, people, or items	Which of the following do you use most often at work? (1) Word processor (2) Presentation graphics (3) Statistical analysis (4) Spreadsheet
Ordinal	Used to classify objects and provide rank ordering information	How often do you use the Help Desk Services? (1) Never (2) On occasion (3) Regularly
Interval	Used to create scales where intervals between selection options are considered to be equal in distance	How useful is the Help Desk Service to your daily work? 1 2 3 4 5 Not useful Extremely at all useful
Ratio	Used where the need for an absolute zero indicating lack of presence of characteristic is required	How many hours per day do you spend using the expert system? 0 2 4 6 8

tions. Generally speaking, a question is placed on a survey to achieve one of two goals: 1) to measure a specific characteristic or attitude of the respondent, or 2) to solicit a ranking or rating of a particular issue from the respondent. Depending on the goal, a particular scaling method may be more or less appropriate for the task.

In choosing an appropriate scaling method, the analyst has four basic types of measurement scales from which to select. Table 4-9 contains a brief listing of each scale type, its defining characteristic, and an example of a question using the scale.

The *nominal scale* is the most basic and is used to categorize or classify responses. Because it provides no relative or absolute numeric comparison across respondents, the analyst is limited to obtaining totals or frequency distributions for each classification and can conduct little or no analysis of the result beyond that.

The *ordinal scale* is also appropriate for categorizing or classifying. Its main difference from the nominal scale is that it allows the analyst to determine a hierarchy among the items listed and, thus, to determine an average ranking among the respondents with regard to the attitude or characteristic being investigated. Although the usefulness of the ordinal scale lies in its ability to create a rank ordering of items, caution must be exercised in interpreting any results obtained from it, because the degree to which one category is greater or less than another cannot be accurately determined. In other words, item 1 may be greater than item 2, and item 2 may be greater than item 3, but no accurate assumption can be made that the difference between item 1 and item 2 is the same as the difference between item 2 and item 3. We know each item is greater or less than its neighbor, but we do not know by how much.

In the *interval scale,* we solve this problem by establishing an equal distance between each number on the scale. Because of this characteristic, we can conduct basic mathematical operations on results obtained using an interval scale. One extremely common example of the interval scale is how we measure temperature. Both the Fahrenheit and Celsius scales are considered interval measurement scales. Another method of using the interval scale is to anchor the ends of the scale with exact opposites. By making the assumption that the respondent perceives the anchors to be "equally opposite," we can assume that the respondent perceives the intervals between them to be equal as well.

The most powerful scale with regard to performing quantitative analysis is called the *ratio scale.* These scales assume an equal distance between the intervals, but they also have an *absolute zero.* Because of this characteristic, any form of quantitative analysis can be performed on the results. We rely on a common application of the ratio scale whenever we use a ruler to measure something. Because a ruler can determine exact length (or at least as exact as the ruler is calibrated), it can also determine something with a length of zero (no length at all). With an absolute zero, we can measure not only the relative degree of change between two items but also whether the item exists at all.

Deciding which scale to use depends on the objective of the question being asked and the anticipated degree of quantitative analysis to be performed. Table 4-10 offers some general guidelines for selecting an appropriate scaling method.

Sampling

Although the administration of a questionnaire is much less costly on a per respondent basis than the direct interview method, it is not totally without cost. Administering the survey instrument to too many respondents generates unnecessary costs associated with printing, mailing, and tabulating the results. Sending the survey to too few respondents, however, could result in an unacceptably low response rate, certain biases in the results, or possibly inaccurate or unusable results. To prevent these types of problems from occurring, the analyst must under the basic concepts associated with *sampling.*

Sampling is a systematic process by which the analyst can select representative members of a population such that the results obtained from the sample can be assumed to be representative of the population. For example, if the analyst needs to determine the nominal hourly transaction load for a particular process or division, he or she could measure the transactions over several hours and divide by the

Table 4-10   Guidelines for Choosing the Most Appropriate Scaling Method

Scale Type	General Application
Nominal	Classification without need for ranking
Ordinal	Classification with ranking but without need for equal intervals between ranks
Interval	Degree of presence of phenomena using equal intervals without need for absolute zero
Ratio	Degree of presence or absence of a phenomenon

number of hours measured. This result, however, would not be reliable, because it is possible that the transaction load could vary by time of day, or by day of the week, or seasonally. A truly accurate average hourly transaction load could be obtained by reviewing all of the daily recorded transaction loads for, say, the past 12 months, and then dividing that by the total number of hours in the period reviewed. This approach, however, would be far too time-consuming and, therefore, costly. Sampling provides a method of accelerating this process by systematically gathering a sample of the population rather than measuring the entire population.

The topic of sampling is quite complex, and literally volumes have been written on it. For our purposes, however, four basic steps can be followed that allow for an effective and representative sample to be obtained.

Decide on the Scope of the Data

The first step in obtaining a useful sample is to decide on the type and amount of data to be collected. Generally speaking, if the data is scaled using either an interval or ratio scale, a relatively large sample size is desirable. Similarly, the more items being measured on a given survey instrument, the greater the necessity of a relatively large sample size. The good news, however, is that once the scope of the data has been established and a few other decisions made, the determination of the necessary size of the sample is easily calculated.

Identify the Population

Before we can calculate an effective sample size from a population, we need to accurately define that population. If the objective is to sample hard data such as daily transaction loads, the analyst must determine whether a sample taken from the last two months' worth of data will be sufficient or whether the population should be defined as the last year's worth of data or even the last five year's worth. When gathering softer data, either by interview or survey, the analyst must determine what members of the organization represent the population of interest. Is it all employees? Is it just identified system stakeholders? Should the population include all affected parties, including customers? Before a sample can be drawn, the population must be accurately identified.

Determine Sample Characteristics

The characteristics of the sample are an important element in successfully gathering useful data about a population. Four basic types of samples can be identified by their unique set of characteristics. Figure 4-2 illustrates the categorization of sample types based on randomness of selection and the application of specific selection criteria.

Figure 4-2   Categorization of Sample Types

	No Random Selection	Random Selection
No Specific Selection Criteria Applied	Convenience Sample	Simple Random Sample
Specific Selection Criteria Applied	Purposive Sample	Complex Random Sample

The *convenience sample* is just as its name implies. The sample is chosen without regard to either randomness or any specific selection criteria. It is chosen because it is convenient to the analyst. For example, if the analyst chooses to sample his or her subordinates simply because they can be ordered to participate, then a convenience sample is obtained. Further, if an analyst broadcasts an invitation over the company e-mail system for all persons interested in the new system to attend a meeting at a particular date and time, a convenience sample is generated. Although the convenience sample is the easiest type to obtain, it is, because of its lack of representativeness of the population, the least reliable.

The *purposive sample*, like the convenience sample, is selected without regard to randomization of the participants. In contrast to the convenience sample, however, the purposive sample is selected by applying one or more specific selection criteria to the participants. Individuals can be chosen based on a certain affiliation, set of characteristics, or identified knowledge base or skill set. Given that the purposive sample is a nonprobability sample, it is considered only moderately reliable with regard to being a representative sample of the population.

Once we introduce the concept of random selection to the process, the reliability of the sample goes up significantly. In the *simple random sample*, the analyst determines the exact size of the population (total number of relevant documents, total number of items, or total number of people) and then randomly selects the sample by using some method that allows for each member of the population to have an equal chance of being selected. Methods such as generating a random number list or selecting every fifth item can be used to create a simple random sample. This approach is often referred to as *systematic random sampling*. Sometimes, however, determining the exact size of the population is not always practical, particularly when dealing with large numbers of documents or reports. Further, a systematic sample can introduce bias into the sample because of either periodicity (a characteristic that reappears in some predictable time period or sequence) or skewness (such as sampling every fourth element in a list of employees ranked low to high in terms of salary; there are probably more employees at the low end of the list than at the high end, thus skewing the sample).

The *complex random sample* is the most reliable and addresses all of the potential disadvantages of the other sample types. Within this category of samples, two forms can be identified: 1) the *stratified sample*, and 2) the *area sample*.

The *stratified sample* is considered to be the most important of the two forms for the systems analyst. The essence of a stratified sample is that it is selected by identifying *strata*, or subpopulations, within the population and then randomly selecting items or respondents from each strata. If, for example, the analyst needs to measure the attitudes or opinions of the organization on a particular issue, a stratified sample based on the various identified levels of the firm results in a more even distribution of opinions across job types. Using this method, the analyst gets a more representative sample of the population while maintaining the integrity of the randomization process.

In the *area sample*, sometimes referred to as a *cluster sample*, various identifiable units within the population are grouped in clusters such that each area or cluster has a known chance of being selected. Although similar to the stratified sample, the area sample differs from it because the decision to group members of the population into clusters is not made according to any specific criteria but rather simply by geographic assignment. For example, an analyst may choose to use an area sample to sample the school districts within a state or county. By creating a random sample of districts, a random sample of schools and pupils can be created. The area sample is most useful when there is incomplete information on the true composition of the population or when it is desirable to conserve resources by limiting the study to a certain geographical area.

Calculate the Minimum Acceptable Sample Size

The *sample size* refers to the number of objects, items, or people that is ultimately selected for measurement. If everyone thought exactly the same way on a given topic or if all transactions in an organization were identical in every respect, then a sample size of one would be sufficient to determine the characteristics of the population of interest. Because this is probably not the case, the sample size necessary to accurately measure the variable(s) of interest is somewhere between two and the total population. Our problem is to determine the minimum acceptable size for the sample.

The determination of sample size is dependent on a number of variables. First, minimum sample size is determined to be an exact number rather than a percentage of the population. Depending on the situation, a sample size of 30 may be deemed inadequate for a population of 300 items or people but quite sufficient for a population of 300,000. Considerations include the degree of desired precision, what we are measuring, and the degree to which we have specific knowledge about the population under study. In other words, the sample size depends on how representative of the population you want the sample to be. We offer some basic guidelines to consider when calculating the minimum necessary sample size.

Generally speaking, a minimum necessary sample size can be calculated using the following formula:

$$n = p(1 - p)(z/i)^2$$

where n is the minimum necessary sample size, p is the proportion of the population having the measured attribute, z is the confidence coefficient for the level of confidence desired, and i is the percentage of acceptable error (in decimals).

The determination of i, the percentage of acceptable error, is simply based on the degree of precision or confidence you wish to obtain. If you want to be 90 percent sure of the result, then implicitly you are willing to accept an error of 10 percent (0.10). Similarly, if you need a 95 percent level of confidence, then your acceptable error drops to 5 percent (0.05). The greater the desired level of confidence, the larger the minimum necessary sample becomes.

The confidence coefficient, z, can be obtained from virtually any introductory statistics text. Table 4-11 contains a partial listing of a *z-table,* which shows the more commonly used levels of confidence and their associated coefficients.

In estimating p, the proportion of the population having the measured attribute, two approaches can be taken. If through examination of experience it can be determined that a specific proportion of the population possesses the attribute of interest, then the correct minimum necessary sample size is obtained using $p(1 - p)$. If, on the other hand, p cannot be accurately or effectively estimated, then a common heuristic is to replace $p(1 - p)$ with the value 0.25, that is, the maximum possible value of $p(1 - p)$. Using this heuristic, however, commonly always results in the calculation of a sample size larger than necessary, and thus, it should only be used when the determination of the parameter p is deemed too difficult. Consider the following two examples.

We want a 90 percent level of confidence that a given sample of invoices contains a certain measured attribute, and we are unable to accurately

Table 4-11 Partial Table of Confidence Coefficients

Level of Confidence (%)	Confidence Coefficient (z)
99	2.58
98	2.33
97	2.17
96	2.05
95	1.96
90	1.65
80	1.25
50	0.67

determine the proportion of the population of invoices that may contain that attribute.

$$n = 0.25(1.645/0.10)^2 = 68$$

Now suppose that through inspection we determine that the proportion of the population of invoices that contains the measured attribute is only 15 percent.

$$n = 0.15(1 - 0.15)(1.645/0.10)^2 \cong 35$$

By determining the value for p, we can cut our minimum necessary sample size by approximately half.

DIRECT OBSERVATION

So far, the information-gathering methods we have looked at involve getting a person to recall an event, to describe a past action, or to express an attitude or opinion. Despite their best efforts, however, people are often not able to accurately recount their actions or feelings. In some cases, this is due to the fact that the event or feeling may have occurred far enough in the past that the details in their memory are beginning to fade or blur. In other cases, however, people just simply are not aware of the true nature of what they do or the methods by which they do it. This is particularly true with events or feelings that are infrequent or with issues for which the respondent has a strong position or passion. Given these circumstances, the analyst often needs to employ a data-gathering technique that does not require the respondent to verbalize or recall the past.

The technique of *direct observation* can be used to help achieve a wide variety of information-gathering goals. Direct observation is regularly applied in an exploratory, as well as confirmatory, manner, because it can be used to discover what happens and how it happens or to confirm information obtained through recall about an event or process. Properly conducted, direct observation can give the analyst a more objective measure of the true nature of an event or activity. In addition, direct observation can often provide the analyst with information that might otherwise never be obtained using any other data gathering technique.

In a typical direct interview setting, a manager may be asked to describe his or her actions with respect to a particular business process or activity. The manager outlines, as accurately as possible, the flow of his or her actions and the basic decision points that occur along the way. On completion of the interview, the analyst creates a basic flow model of the information gathered and, through inspection, deems it to be logical and complete. During direct observation of the same manager and the same business process, the analyst sees a significantly different picture. Many key actions or decisions are not reflected in the process model, and several actions and decisions that were represented by the manager as occurring simply did not. How can this seemingly contradictory set of circumstances be explained? Why would the manager lie about what he or she does?

The fact is, the manager probably did not lie about the nature of his or her daily activities and decisions. Mintzberg (1973) describes the typical daily activities of a manager as a series of interruptions and crises punctuated by bursts of planned activity or work. In other words, the typical manager works in a somewhat fragmented manner, often distracted from the daily activities by the necessity to solve a problem or to communicate to someone on an issue unrelated to the task at hand. Given this, asking a manager to recall what he or she does most likely results in either the utopian recollection, in which the analyst gets a description of what *should* be happening, or the most significant events recollection, in which the peaks of the daily activities are easily recalled and the less notable valleys are forgotten. Regardless of the reasons behind the lack of accuracy, the analyst must be prepared to use direct observation to insure that the verbal data collection is valid and accurate.

Gathering information using direct observation requires the same level of structuring and planning that the previously discussed techniques demand. Simply going out into a business environment and watching what goes on does not yield a great deal of useful or reliable information. The analyst must decide beforehand what he or she intends to observe and is looking for in order to avoid the observation activity from becoming a "fishing expedition." Further, the direct observation approach is not without its disadvantages or limitations. Unless the analysts agree to work in shifts around the clock, the observation cannot be continuous and, therefore, produces a snapshot of the activity and not necessarily its true nature. Additionally, direct observation is time consuming, thus potentially raising the costs associated with gathering the desired information. Finally, despite its application as a more objective approach than interview or questionnaire, direct observation is not totally unbiased and can, in some cases, yield results significantly different from the norm.

The Hawthorne Effect

The most famous example of this problem can be found in the Hawthorne studies conducted in 1927 at the Chicago Hawthorne Plant of the Western Electric Company (Roethlisberger and Dickson, 1939). Managers at the facility were concerned about large numbers of complaints and high levels of dissatisfaction among workers. Experts using scientific management principles were unable to solve the problem. So, in an attempt to locate the source of productivity problems (and hopefully come up with a solution), a group of people from the production floor were put into a room to work where they could be observed. What happened next was quite unexpected.

Researchers sponsored by the National Academy of Sciences were commissioned to study the effects of lighting on worker productivity. First, they tried increasing the level of lighting in the room, thinking that if the workers could see better, maybe production would go up. Production did increase slightly, so they increased the lighting again, hoping to find the most effective level of lighting for optimal worker performance. Every time they increased the lighting, the production went up. This seemed to suggest that there was a definite relationship between lighting levels and worker productivity. Further, they began to notice that morale and camaraderie were also improving.

Then, the researchers tried decreasing the level of lighting in the room, hoping to confirm their hypothesis. Oddly, production went up again. They continually decreased the light gradually, until at one point it was the equivalent of moonlight. Production just kept going up. The results were so puzzling that the project ended without any useful conclusions.

Further studies by Elton Mayo and others from the Harvard Business School gauged the effects on output of rest pauses, shorter work days and weeks, wage incentives, and supervisory practices. Again, production stayed constant or increased, regardless of the changes the researchers made. Neither physical conditions nor organization structure seemed to affect worker productivity.

Puzzled, the researchers conducted observations and interviews, concluding finally that the workers' on-the-job efforts were the result of the attention they were receiving from the research team, not due to the changes in working conditions. This phenomenon, later termed the "Hawthorne effect," became a foundation for the notion that worker attitudes and feelings, as well as their relationships with others they respected, can significantly influence their behavior. In other words, the productivity would have risen in response to almost any management action that workers interpreted as special attention, including simply being observed.

The Hawthorne effect suggests that direct observation, when known by the person being observed, may yield results that are contradictory to expectations or simply not representative of reality. This is why direct observation should be conducted using both *obtrusive* and *unobtrusive* approaches. The obtrusive approach allows for the subjects under observation to be aware of the fact that they are being observed, such as in the Hawthorne studies. The unobtrusive approach requires that the observer, and the process of observation, go undetected by the subject under observation, such as when watching wild animals in their natural habitat. Although the unobtrusive approach can often yield results more couched in reality and can eliminate the potential biases associated with behavior change while being observed, it also raises certain ethical concerns and obvious privacy issues that must be carefully considered before it is initiated. Nonetheless, when properly conducted, both obtrusive and unobtrusive direct observation can be highly useful information-gathering techniques.

EXTERNAL RESEARCH AND ARCHIVAL DOCUMENT ANALYSIS

One of the primary objectives of requirements determination is to create a detailed system specification that is an accurate reflection of the necessary functions and performance parameters of the proposed system. Regardless of how the requirements are gathered, via interview, survey, or observation, the analyst must be certain that multiple sources of information have been used to confirm each and every requirement for the specification document. To that end, one final traditional method for gathering new information and for enhancing the accuracy of information gathered via interactive techniques can be used: the review of *archival documents* and the use of *external research*.

Organizational Documents

In the following paragraphs, we look at examples of several important archival documents that are commonly used by analysts to better understand the organization and the requirements for a proposed system. It would be impossible in this text to identify and discuss all of the possible archival sources, and thus the examples provided herein are far from exhaustive. In practice, the analyst should make every attempt to locate and review all written documents that may be relevant to both the current and proposed systems. Through analysis of this hard data, the analyst gains a better understanding of where the organization has been and where it is, or needs to be, going.

Mission Statement

The *mission statement* of an organization should be considered the basis for the existence of that organization and should encapsulate the vision for the organization based on internal and external environments, its identified competencies, and the nature of its customers or clients. By reviewing this document, the analyst can gain a high-level understanding of the scope of the business environment in which the new system will reside and the degree to which the proposed system contributes to the stated mission of the organization.

It is important to note, however, that an organizational mission statement does not necessarily dictate the organizational strategies used to achieve the stated strategic objectives. In fact, two radically different organizations can have mission statements that are remarkably similar in their strategic objectives but radically different in operational strategy. To gain an understanding of the latter concept, the analyst must turn to other sources of information within the organization.

Organizational Charts

One source of operational strategy for an organization is the structure with which it chooses to conduct its business. The *organizational chart* of the firm is a schematic drawing of the various positions held within the organization, and it indicates the various levels of authority and reporting lines that have been established. By reviewing the organizational chart, the analyst can envision the flow of decisions throughout the organization and position the proposed system such that it delivers the necessary information to make those decisions to the proper levels of the organization in a timely fashion. One additional benefit of reviewing the organizational chart lies with the need to identify the system stakeholders and their individual position within the organization. By locating the stakeholders on the organizational chart, the analyst can quickly see the degree to which the proposed system crosses functional boundaries and can assess potential political issues or conflicts that may arise as a result.

Job Descriptions

Yet another useful archival document is the job description or work procedure. These documents describe how a particular job or task is intended to be performed and commonly include an overview of the data and information sources deemed necessary to accomplish the task. By reviewing these descriptions, the analyst can gain insight into the expected scope of a particular stakeholder's authority or the intended nature of a particular process within the system. Notice the key words are *expected* and *intended*. It is quite often the case that the description of the job is different from the reality of it. The analyst must look for these discrepancies between intended and actual tasks and processes to reconcile the various stated requirements of the proposed system with the realities of the work environment. In other words, over time, what a person is supposed to be doing and what they actually do may be two entirely different things.

Financials

When relevant to the proposed system project, the various *financial reports* generated by the organization can give the analyst insight into a number of important issues. One important area of insight to be gained is the degree of control imposed by the organization on its operations. Generally speaking, the greater the adherence to budget preparation, financial projection analyses, and established performance ratios, the greater the overall level of control within the organization. Depending on the nature of the system, the financial documents may allow the analyst to create distributions of revenues, costs, or profits that, although not deemed useful to the organization for operating purposes, may provide insight into the financial impact or importance to the organization of the proposed system.

Policies and Procedures

The written *policies and procedures* of an organization serve as a blueprint for decision-making. Most policy statements are standing plans, in that they are designed to cover the limits within which decisions are to be made and the issues that are repeatedly faced by a particular level of the organization. The organizational policies provide the analyst with another indication of the degree of control within the organizational culture. Policies should provide guidelines that are intended to clarify how a particular job is to be done and the type of behavior deemed appropriate within the context of that job. Generally speaking, policies allow for a certain degree of flexibility by employees in their approach to various organizational problems and decisions. This generality, however, commonly tends to make some policies rather vague. Issues of control become much more difficult when employees interpret policy intention and purpose differently. The analyst can gain insight into certain requirements issues through analysis and review of organizational policies.

Organizational procedures are those documents that are intended to guide action rather than thinking. Procedures establish the customary methods by which certain repetitive organizational activities are handled. The major distinguishing characteristic between a procedure and a policy is that the procedure represents a chronological sequencing of events. A good procedure should specify a series of steps that must be taken to accomplish a particular task. By reviewing the stated procedures of the organization that are relevant to the proposed system and then comparing those procedures with what actually is occurring, the analyst gains valuable information with regard to the degree of adherence to *formal* procedures and the degree of development of *informal* ones.

Organizations typically embrace both formal and informal systems. The formal system is embodied in the official documents of the organization. This includes the mission statement, policies, procedures, rules, reporting structures, and so forth. In contrast, the informal system represents the way the organization *actually*

Figure 4-3   Example of a Business Form

does things. Informal systems evolve within an organization because of perceived or real inadequacies of the formal system, individual or collective resistance to control or change, or individual preferences or work habits. For the analyst, the formal system represents what those who conceived the system intended to happen, whereas the informal system is more likely to be associated with information gathered during interview, survey, and direct observation. It is the responsibility of the analyst to identify for management the discrepancies in these two systems so that a reconciliation approach can be determined. Building a system to accommodate the formal system when the informal system is predominant and radically different can bring unexpected results and, often, undesirable consequences.

Forms Analysis

In many ways, the analysis of the *business forms* used within the organization can be the most revealing of all archival document reviews. The forms used by a business are explicit indicators of what data flow into or out of the system and what data are necessary for the proposed system to function properly.

Figure 4-3 contains a typical order form that may be found in a business organization. The review of forms like this can provide critical information about the nature of the system.

For example, by reviewing the form in Figure 4-3, the analyst can see that the business uses a six character all numeric product code, can ship to an address different from the customer to which the goods are sold, bills shipping costs to the customer, accepts checks as payment, allows for COD shipment, has multiple methods for shipment, and allows a discount for prompt payment of an invoice. Forms can also be thought of as data capture mechanisms, and as such, they can be used to get an initial picture of the various entities within an organization's data model and the data elements deemed necessary to associate with those entities. We discuss these concepts in detail in chapter 6 in our focus on the construction of conceptual and logical data models of a system.

Current System Documentation

Last, but not least, an important source of information for requirements determination is those documents that describe the current IS. These include design documentation, data and process models, user reference, configuration maps, and implementation procedures. Although a detailed review of these types of archival documents could prove invaluable in expediting an understanding of the current system and in determining certain critical requirements for the proposed system, typically the analyst finds that many of these documents do not exist. Legacy IS are notorious for having poor documentation, and often what does exist is unclear or outdated. Nonetheless, a thorough requirements determination effort should include a review of whatever documentation about the current system exists.

External Research

When assessing the current business environment and gathering information with regard to the requirements for a proposed IS, the analyst can also turn to *external* sources of information as a guide to best practices or industry norms. Examples of such sources are computer trade journals, technical reference manuals, industry trade associations, and published case studies. References such as these can provide the analyst with a current overview of available technologies, industry practices, and even how others may have approached and solved problems similar to the one at hand.

Probably the greatest single external source for such information is the WWW. From the desktop, the analyst can easily locate and review thousands of sources of information relevant to the study being conducted and can often communicate with experts in a particular topic to gain up-to-the-minute information with regard to emerging technologies and resources available to facilitate the design and implementation of the new system. When used in combination with other information-gathering techniques, the information gained from external research can help to solidify an analyst's understanding of the problem under investigation.

MODERN METHODS FOR REQUIREMENTS DETERMINATION

As we turn our attention to the category of modern methods for gathering system requirements, we should note that the traditional methods just discussed should not be misconstrued as antiquated or old-fashioned in any way. Interviews, questionnaires, observation, and document analysis are still the mainstay techniques of requirements determination and general information gathering. The modern approaches should be thought of simply as recent advancements in the arsenal of requirements determination tools and techniques that, when combined with the traditional approaches, can serve to improve either the quality and accuracy of the information gathered or the efficiency of the process.

JAD

Developed in the late 1970s at IBM, JAD has become a popular information-gathering technique throughout the business world. The main objective of the JAD approach is to bring together the key stakeholders of a proposed system and use that gathering to facilitate and expedite the collection and determination of and consensus on requirements for the new system. Unlike a focus group approach, however, a JAD session is more highly structured with regard to the roles of the participants and the agenda that is followed.

A JAD session is typically conducted in a facility located away from the participants' normal working environment and arranged and equipped specifically for the session. By relocating the participants, the common distractions of the daily business environment can be avoided, and participants can concentrate on the systems analysis activities and addressing the requirements issues and conflicts. Typically, such a session can last from several hours to several days, depending on the complexity of the system under consideration and the number of stakeholders involved in the analysis. Because a JAD session can involve a significant amount of organizational resources, most notably the time of the participants, that session should be very carefully planned and orchestrated to insure that maximum value is realized from the investment in time and resources. Table 4-12 contains a brief list

Table 4-12   Roles and Responsibilities of Typical JAD Participants

JAD Participant	Description of Role
Session leader	• Organizes and runs the actual JAD session • Remains neutral on all issues and does not contribute ideas or opinions • Sets the agenda for the meeting • Concentrates on keeping to agenda, resolving conflicts, and generating dialogue from participants
User	• Represents end users' perspective with regard to proposed system
Manager	• Represents management's perspective with regard to proposed system
Project sponsor	• Represents all parties responsible for funding and supporting the development effort
Analyst	• Analyst participation is limited to observation and listening to better understand the needs of the users and managers
Scribe	• Responsible for taking notes and recording important information and events relevant to the JAD proceedings
IS staff	• Responsible for providing clarification on technical questions and issues • Contribute ideas on technical feasibility and limitations of proposed system components

Figure 4-4   MicroTouch, Inc. IBID Electronic Whiteboard
Source: <http://www.microtouch.com/ibid/ ibid100.htm>

of the various roles of the JAD participants and a description of their typical responsibilities to the process.

A typical arrangement for a JAD facility is a large conference or meeting room with seating arranged in a horseshoe fashion so that all participants have direct line of sight to each other and to the JAD session leader. Numerous audio-visual tools can be employed, including computer projection systems, document cameras, flipcharts, and whiteboards. One increasingly popular tool is the "smart" whiteboard, which can capture whatever is drawn or written on it and store it as an easily retrievable computer graphic. This insures that all notes and sketches can be retrieved for later review and organization. Figure 4-4 contains an example of this relatively new technology.

On completion of a JAD session, the information gathered from all mechanisms is carefully reviewed and organized into a set of documents detailing the current system. In addition, if the agenda for the session was properly structured and executed, an initial set of requirements for the proposed system can also be constructed and used as the basis for detailed information gathering and confirmation using more traditional approaches.

Several benefits can be realized through a successful JAD session. First, the necessarily high degree of interaction among the participants in a typical JAD session serves to promote a sense of common ownership for the new system, because the group is collectively responsible for the initial set of requirements. This cohesiveness among the stakeholders early in a development effort can be invaluable in achieving the stated goals and objectives for the new system. Second, the nature of the JAD approach often reduces the time necessary to gather the information vital to constructing the detailed requirements specification for a new system. Finally, the JAD approach can serve to quickly identify discrepancies in the perspectives of the various stakeholders and facilitate the resolution of conflicting information and requirements.

Iterative Prototyping

An increasingly common technique for requirements determination is the use of *iterative prototypes* as models for evaluation by system stakeholders. A prototype allows the analyst to quickly convert the basic requirements of a system or process into a limited working model that can be viewed and tested by the end users. By allowing the user to see the stated requirements instead of simply reading them, the analyst can often prompt the users to refine their needs and make explicit additional ones that were overlooked during the initial interviews and surveys.

The iterative nature of prototyping means that once the initial working model has been assessed, it is modified to reflect the feedback and information generated by the end users' interactions with the model. This process can continue indefinitely, until a complete set of requirements is developed.

When used properly, iterative prototyping yields several significant benefits. The relatively rapid changes in the system that can be made and reviewed by the users commonly serve to expedite and solidify the necessary changes to the current system very early in the development process. Further, because the users can see early in the process what the proposed system will look like, they are more apt to accept the system when it is actually implemented. Another advantage to using prototypes is that they represent much less of an investment than does the final system, and they commonly can determine the presence or absence of proof-of-concept for various system approaches. Better to know during the requirements determination stage that a conceptual method of delivering a menu of choices or sequencing a series of input screens is not acceptable to the user than during the final stages of systems development.

One caveat to using iterative prototyping as a requirements determination tool is to remember that the goal of the technique is to support the development of a concrete set of system requirements and not to actually build the system. The analyst must guard against the tendency to adopt the final round of prototypes as the completed system. Despite their level of functionality, prototypes are, in fact, only representations of the final system, and they should never be considered for implementation. Think of a prototype as a first draft of a paper. As with a first draft, prototypes are intended to serve as a starting point for discussion and then be thrown away.

CHAPTER SUMMARY

On completing a successful requirements gathering initiative, a complete set of initial system requirements is available to the analyst as a guide for the design and development of a new system. Although the output from requirements determination includes a great deal of valuable information, it most likely is not in a form that allows for a detailed analysis of the current system and the development of a new one. The next step in the process is to structure this information into a more standard format that serves as a common language among the analysts and the end users. A variety of techniques exist with regard to the structuring of requirements and the design of models of the system environment, its processes, and its data. In the next two chapters, we look at the modeling tools of the analyst and discuss a variety of approaches for further structuring the requirements of an IS.

The future is always more cloudy than the past, but a number of developments make prediction with regard to the future of requirements determination a bit easier to make. The continued development and refinement of CASE technologies will improve the requirements determination process by shifting some of the burden of information gathering and organizing from the analyst to the CASE tool. In addition, as the reverse engineering capabilities of modern CASE tools continue to improve, the ease with which a current system can be reduced to first-draft models for analysis also increases. We focus our attention on CASE technologies in chapter 7.

No matter what improvements come forward with regard to requirements determination activities, one thing will remain the same for many years to come. The need for skilled systems analysts who understand how to analyze complex business problems and gather information in an accurate and structured manner will continue to be high. The tools available to assist the analyst in these activities, however, will increase the speed and accuracy with which they are performed.

KEY CONCEPTS

➤ Process-oriented perspective

  A system can be viewed as a collection of processes, performed by people or in an automated fashion by computers.

➤ Object-oriented perspective

  A system alternatively can be viewed as a collection of objects that interact with each other and with the end users of the system.

➤ The three "I"'s of requirement determination
  • Impertinence

    A good analyst should question everything and take nothing for granted during requirements determination.
  • Impartiality

    A good analyst should be able to consider all issues raised by all system stakeholders to provide the best overall solution for the organization.
  • Insight
  • Make the assumption that anything is possible.
  • Pay constant and vigilant attention to detail during requirements determination.
  • Think creatively during requirements determination.

➤ The four common mistakes in requirements determination
  • Assuming a functional system

    Systems must be viewed as cross-functional to insure that all stakeholders and affected parties are identified.
  • Collecting requirements from each end user instead of all end users

    Whenever possible, analysts should collect requirements from user groups rather than individual users.
  • Asking the wrong questions

    Questions must be crafted such that the user can describe his or her work environment rather than prescribe his or her information needs.
  • Failing to allow refinement through trial and error

    Users commonly cannot make firm decisions concerning their information needs without first having an opportunity to explore the possibilities through a period of trial and error, for example, through iterative prototyping.

➤ The objective of requirements determination is to create a set of deliverables from the requirement-gathering process that represents the information necessary to conduct a thorough and detailed analysis within the scope of the system under development.

➤ Good requirement characteristics
  • Testable and verifiable
    Requirement must be stated to allow for independent verification that the system meets or exceeds the stated requirement.
  • Justifiable, accurate, and correct
    Requirement should be necessary rather than simply desirable.
  • Unambiguous
    Requirement should be stated such that multiple interpretations are excluded.
  • Consistent
    Requirement should not be in conflict with any other stated requirement.
  • Understandable and modifiable
    All system requirements should be written such that they are easily understandable by both technical and nontechnical readers and that they can be modified to reflect changes in the business environment.
  • Hierarchically traceable
    Requirement should contain a single system attribute and should be traceable back to a higher-level requirement.

➤ Two general categories for requirements determination techniques have been identified based on their relative recency of adoption as information-gathering approaches: traditional methods and modern methods.

➤ Traditional methods for requirements determination
  • Direct interview
    Consists of meeting with individuals or small groups to ask questions about their roles, responsibilities, and needs for the current and proposed systems.
  • Questionnaires and surveys
    Consists of submitting written, structured questions to selected individuals to gather information regarding attitudes, perceptions, or population characteristics.
  • Direct observation
    Consists of observing individuals or groups, processes, and events to determine the facts surrounding a particular process or the culture within a business environment.
  • Archival document analysis
    Consists of reviewing recorded organizational documents, such as current system documentation, mission statements, policies and procedures, and recorded memos and reports.
  • Forms analysis
    Consists of analyzing and cataloging the existing data capture forms within the organization to assist in determining the current sources and uses of data.

➤ Direct interview generally can be classified as structured or unstructured.
  • Structured interview
    For a structured interview, the interviewer prepares a specific set of questions prior to conducting the interview.
  • Unstructured interview
    In the unstructured interview, the analyst has only a general objective or subject in mind rather than a specific set of questions.

➤ Two basic forms of questions
  • Open-ended questions
    The open-ended question allows the respondents to construct the style and content of their answers.
  • Closed-ended questions
    Closed-ended questions limit the range of possible answers to a finite set.

➤ Interview guidelines
  1. Regardless of whether a closed-ended or open-ended question is being used, be careful to avoid phrasing it such that a right or wrong answer is suggested or implied.
  2. Remember to listen, listen, and listen. Notes should be taken, and the entire process should be tape-recorded for further review, if possible.
  3. Schedule interviews with a variety of users and managers that represent the widest possible set of perspectives.

4. Regardless of the intended purpose of the interview, the analyst must be vigilant with regard to managing the expectations of respondents.

5. Once the interview is completed, the analyst should make every attempt to clean up the notes and finalize a report on the interview within the shortest possible time (within 48 hours).

➤ The focus group can be used to facilitate the information-gathering process and can often serve to minimize or eliminate many inconsistencies in user perspectives.

➤ Self-designed survey instruments must be reliable, valid, and easy to use.
  • Reliability (consistency)
    • *External reliability* is a measure of the consistency of results obtained across multiple administrations.
    • *Internal reliability* is determined by the degree of consistency associated with the responses obtained.
  • Validity
    The validity characteristic focuses on the degree to which the questionnaire obtains the information desired by the analyst in an accurate and interpretable manner. To facilitate the determination of a survey's validity, a series of pilot tests commonly are conducted.
  • Easy to use
    The questionnaire should be understandable and easily completed in a reasonable length of time by the typical respondents.

➤ Questions on a survey instrument can be scaled using a *nominal, ordinal, interval,* or *ratio* scale, depending on the degree of quantitative analysis to be performed.
  • Sampling
    Sampling is a systematic process by which the analyst can select representative members of a population such

that the results obtained from the sample can be assumed to be representative of the population. Four basic steps can be followed for obtaining an effective and representative sample:
    1. Decide on the scope of the data
    2. Identify the population
    3. Determine sample characteristics
    4. Calculate the minimum acceptance sample size

➤ Review of archival documents and the conduct of external research can provide information that is more objective or closer to reality than that provided by other information-gathering approaches.

➤ Modern methods for requirements determination
  • JAD
    The main objective of the JAD approach is to bring together the key stakeholders of a proposed system and use that gathering to facilitate and expedite the collection and determination of and consensus on requirements for the new system. The JAD sessions are typically conducted in a facility located away from the participants' normal working environment and arranged and equipped specifically for the session.
  • Iterative prototyping
    A prototype allows the analyst to quickly convert the basic requirements of a system or process into a limited working model that can be viewed and tested by the end users. The iterative nature of prototyping means that once the initial working model has been assessed, it is modified to reflect the feedback and information generated by the end users' interactions with the model. This process can continue until a complete set of requirements is developed.

QUESTIONS FOR REVIEW

1. Briefly describe the two ways of viewing a system. What is their main difference?

2. List and briefly depict the three "I"'s of requirements determination.

3. What are the four common mistakes made by systems analysts during requirements determination?

4. List and briefly discuss the characteristics of a well-stated system requirement.

5. How can a stated requirement be effectively tested or verified?

6. State the importance of the comprehensibility of the final requirements specification.

7. Describe the pros and cons of the direct interview method.

8. Describe and compare the two common interview structures used by systems analysts.

9. Discuss the importance of balancing between closed-ended and open-ended questions in direct interviews through the comparison of their advantages and disadvantages.

10. How does a good systems analyst manage the interview process?

11. What are the advantages and disadvantages of using focus groups during requirements determination?

12. Compared to direct interview, what are the advantages of using questionnaires and surveys?

13. What are the three basic characteristics that should be used in evaluating the quality of survey instruments?

14. Describe the four basic sample types.

15. What are the advantages and disadvantages of direct observation in collecting system requirements?

16. List and briefly describe the traditional methods for requirements determination.

17. Who are the typical participants in JAD sessions?

18. List the benefits that could be realized through a successful JAD session.

19. What caution needs to be attended to by systems analysts when iterative prototyping is used?

FOR FURTHER DISCUSSION

1. Prepare a direct interview intended to be exploratory in nature about a typical business process. Then prepare the same inquiry using a questionnaire approach. Find several classmates or colleagues to play the role of respondent for each method. What differences in the quality or quantity of responses do you see?

2. Try this experiment: See if you can observe a fellow classmate, worker, or family member performing a common task without them knowing you are watching. After carefully recording your findings, approach the same person and ask if they will let you observe them while they perform the same task. Do not let them know until after the experiment that you have observed them once already. Did they do the same things? What were the differences in your findings from the two observations?

3. Bernie Herbenick runs the Payables Department for a local manufacturer. His company has hired your firm to conduct a thorough study of their current payment system with the intention of updating the processes to increase both efficiency and effectiveness. You have been assigned to solicit basic process flow information from Bernie and his staff. Bernie has begrudgingly agreed to oblige your request for interviews but is distraught over the time it takes him and his workers away from their demanding day. Write a letter to Mr. Herbenick explaining how you intend to go about gathering the necessary information while minimizing the disruption to his department.

4. You have been asked to lead a JAD session for the gathering of requirements associated with a new inventory control system for a large clothing

retailer. Prepare a detailed agenda for your session. What guidelines will you follow as JAD session leader?

5. Eric Gause is the analyst in charge of surveying the sales staff at the Vance Music MegaStore who will be using the new point-of-sales system currently in the early stages of analysis and design. Eric needs to find out the opinions of the various members of the sales staff with regard to the strengths and weaknesses of the current system and what they think should be improved in the new system. The store has over 25,000 square feet of showroom and employs 75 sales staff who work one of three shifts each day. Because Eric needs this information quickly, he has chosen the survey method of information gathering, thinking that it is the fastest way to get at the answers.

Eric assembled his survey instrument carefully and pilot tested it with several Vance Music managers to insure its validity and accuracy. Once his revisions were complete, he placed a copy of the survey in the mailboxes of each of the 75 sales associates. One week later, Eric had three surveys returned to him. By the second week, he had received only two additional completed surveys. Eric's present response rate is only 6.7 percent. In desperation, he comes to you for some suggestions regarding what he might do to improve the response rate. His boss Phil is not that easy to get along with.

REFERENCES

Mintzberg, H. 1973. *The Nature of Managerial Work,* New York: Harper and Row.

Roethlisberger, F. J., and W. J. Dickson. 1939. *Management and the Worker: An Account of a Research Program Conducted by the Western Elec-* *tric Company, Chicago.* Cambridge, MA: Harvard University Press.

Wetherbe, J. C., and N. P. Vitalari. 1994. *Systems Analysis and Design: Best Practices,* 4th ed. St Paul, MN: West Publishing.

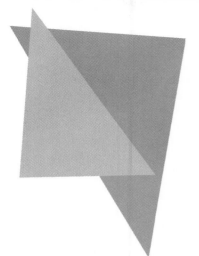

Modeling the Processes and Logic

Learning Objectives

- Understand the basic concepts of logical process modeling
- Draw DFDs using specific rules and components to depict logical process models
- Understand the hierarchy of DFDs using the concept of functional decomposition
- Understand the differences between DFDs and flowcharts.
- Understand the four basic logic modeling techniques of structured English, decision tables, decision trees, and state-transition diagrams and be able to select the appropriate tool for the conditions

I am never content until I have constructed a mechanical model of the subject I am studying. If I succeed in making one, I understand; otherwise I do not.

—LORD KELVIN

INTRODUCTION

In chapter 4, you learned about the activities and tools associated with the gathering of information needs from the various system stakeholders. The objective of these activities was to determine the system requirements such that a clear statement of them could be generated. In the next few chapters, we focus our attention on several tools available to the analyst that are used to articulate the system requirements by representing them as a set of models. In this chapter, we begin this focus with a graphical tool that allows the analyst to represent the various processes and data flows associated with both the current and proposed systems—the DFD.

LOGICAL PROCESS MODELING

As discussed in the beginning of chapter 3, a system can be thought of as a series of processes that respond to various events or triggers within the business environment or within the system itself. Although the data gathered from interviews, questionnaires, and observation provide a comprehensive narrative of these processes, modeling their logical sequence, and the flow of data through them, creates a visual depiction of the system that can serve to solidify our understanding of it.

The concept of modeling something physical to assist in understanding has been around for many centuries. Think of a model as a manageable representation of reality. The complexity of models can range from as simple as a picture (remember, it can be worth a thousand words) to a highly sophisticated, operational, three-dimensional representation of something or to anything in between. The DFD emphasizes the logical perspective of the current or proposed system rather than the physical one. Before we continue, let us look at the distinctions between the two perspectives.

The "What" not the "How"

The *physical model* of a system can be thought of as the system itself. It is the sum of the hardware, software, connections, processes, data flows, policies, procedures, manual activities, and data. By studying the physical model we can see what the system actually does, as well as exactly how it does it. Although the physical system can yield a great deal of information about the processes and data flows, it also has certain significant limitations associated with it. Of primary focus is the fact that the physical system can only inform us as to what is *actually* happening, as opposed to what is *intended* to be happening. In other words, the processes and data flows that can be studied using a physical model are also constrained by the choices of technology used to accomplish them and the limitations associated with those choices. Thus we cannot see what the system is supposed to do independent of how the system does it. For this, we need to separate the "what" from the "how."

In contrast to the physical model, a *logical model* graphically conveys what a system is or does without any of the constraints of how that might be accomplished. Logical models can be thought of as implementation independent, because they depict the system independently from any technical approach or constraint. Thus, they serve to illustrate the essence of the system itself, independent of how it is embodied. By constructing and analyzing a system from its logical, rather than its physical, perspective, an analyst can more easily conceptualize changes to the system's processes, functions, and data flows without having to commit prematurely to their technical realization.

This distinction may be best clarified through a simple example outside the realm of systems development. Suppose we wish to model the activity of peeling an apple. The logical model might look something like the following:

1. Get the apple
2. Get the peeling device
3. Wash the apple
4. Hold the apple
5. Peel the apple with the peeling device
6. Discard peel
7. Process the apple into desired form

Notice that whereas all of the various steps associated with peeling the apple are listed and their sequences are logically correct, we cannot determine anything with regard to how these various activities and steps are carried out. The step *get the apple* tells us what to do but not how to do it. Where is this apple? Should we get it from the tree, or the crate, or from the ground, or the refrigerator? *Wash the apple* tells us what to do but does not convey any information with regard to whether we should stick it under a faucet, scrub it in a vat of liquid, dip it in a tub of water, or stand out in the rain and hold it up in the air. Consider the following physical model of the same set of processes:

1. Get the apple by removing it from the fruit drawer in the refrigerator
2. Get the paring knife from the upper left-hand kitchen drawer
3. Wash the apple under the kitchen faucet using a scrubbing action with your hands
4. Hold the apple in your left hand (use opposite hands if you are left-handed)
5. Peel the apple with the knife with the blade pointing toward you
6. Discard peel in suitable garbage container
7. Eat the apple by biting down on a portion of the apple with your mouth and chewing

Although the preceding physical model makes explicit the methods by which the apple should be peeled, it is also constrained by those methods. In other words, the physical model limits the processes to a particular set of methods and, thus, to a particular environment in which those methods can be reasonably conducted—in the case of our example, the kitchen. The preceding logical model, however, would be equally useful in describing the peeling of an apple in any environment—from the kitchen to an industrial fruit processing plant. By eliminating the physical aspects of a system, the analyst can concentrate on the logic of the processes without worrying about where or how they occur.

Several benefits occur when using a logical modeling approach to the analysis activities of a development project. First, logical models serve to significantly reduce the risk of overlooking or missing important business requirements of the system owing to the analyst becoming preoccupied with the technical elements. We know that such mistakes, if not corrected quickly, can be extremely expensive to fix later on. By eliminating the focus on technical issues, the analyst can concentrate on determining the completeness and accuracy of the system requirements.

Another benefit derived from the use of logical models is the ease with which the analyst can communicate with the end users and system stakeholders with regard to specific system details. The logical model allows for a nontechnical line of communication and the graphical nature of the model puts the end user more at ease with the analysis of it. This can serve to improve the overall communication between analysts and users and can facilitate the determination of the often complex set of requirements associated with a new IS.

Finally, logical models serve to reduce the biases typically associated with the way the current system is implemented. The concept of "that is the only way to do it" is eliminated by using a logical approach to analysis. You probably did not consider the possibility that the preceding logical model of peeling an apple would be equally useful at home or in a factory, did you? This is because the physical model biased you into thinking only about the environment in which it was being applied and not about the process itself.

THE DFD

The DFD is a graphical tool that depicts the sequence of processes and functions contained within a specified system boundary and the flow of data through that system. Using four basic symbols, the analyst can logically represent the data flows, data stores, processes and functions, and the entities that interact with the system but that reside outside the system boundary. Although several representation methods

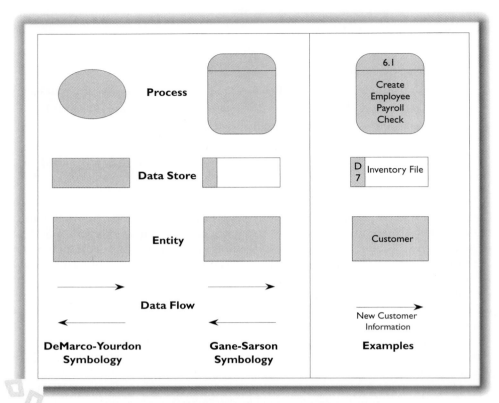

Figure 5-1   Comparison of DFD Symbologies and Examples of Use

have been proposed for DFDs, the two most common are the Gane-Sarson nomenclature (Gane and Sarson 1979) and the DeMarco-Yourdon symbol set (DeMarco 1979). For our purposes, we adopt the Gane-Sarson approach, although both are commonly used in modern business organizations throughout the world. Figure 5-1 illustrates the symbols used in each approach.

DFD Components

The first of the DFD components is the *data flow*. Represented by an arrow indicating direction of flow, together with a noun naming the data contents, the data flow can be best understood as *data in motion*. Because we are looking at the system from a purely logical perspective, a data flow can represent the movement of data in any form possible: data contained on a customer order form, an employee payroll record, the results of a database query or report, or even the flow of goods from a warehouse to a customer. Thus, a single data flow can represent many individual pieces of data that are logically related and flow together to some common destination. However, a single data flow should depict only a single set of related data.

The *data store* represents a repository for data that are either temporarily or permanently recorded within the system, that is, *data at rest* within the system. Like the data flow, a data store is not limited to representing data in a particular physical form but instead can represent any location or method by which data is stored within the system. Thus a data store could be a file on a hard drive, file folder or file cabinet, someone's notebook, an in-box on a desk, or even someone's head. A typical data store can contain data about customers, inventory, orders, students, invoices, payroll checks, or anything else. The direction of a data flow to or from the data store indicates whether the data is being written to or read from the data store. Further, any deletion or modification of a record stored in a computer-based file is depicted as a data flow into the data store, despite the fact that such operations typically require that the data being modified or deleted is first read. This convention is intended to reduce the potential for clutter on the diagram.

A *process* is the means by which the data is transformed into another form, used to create new data, or assembled into some useful output, such as a report or a shipment of goods. When modeling a logical process it does not matter whether that process is performed by a machine, a computer, or a person. Processes are organized on a DFD according to the sequence in which they occur. This sequence is depicted on the diagram by a numerical identifier assigned to each process. Process 1.0 is first, process 2.0 is second, and so forth. Following the concept of functional decomposition introduced in chapter 2, a logical process can be thought of as a subsystem that can be further decomposed into smaller and more detailed subsystems. We show the importance of this later in this chapter.

Four basic types of transformations may occur as a result of a process. First, the data flowing into the process may be used to create a set of data flows that are outputs from that process and may become inputs to another process, data at rest, or output to a sink entity. An example of this transformation would be the input of payroll information into a process resulting in the creation of an employee paycheck (a data flow completely different from the data input to the process).

A second transformation is the gaining of new knowledge from the input data without transforming it and while using it as output in its same basic form. A typical situation in which this occurs is the verification of an account number prior to allowing access to a customer's bank records. The account number input to the process is output in the same form, but because we gained the knowledge necessary to verify its validity, we can use it to trigger additional processes necessary to retrieve the requested information.

Third, a process may reorganize the input data in some manner, such as sorting it, reformatting it, or filtering it. A list of employees sorted alphabetically would be an example of this type of transformation. Finally, the process simply may serve as a routing device or data traffic cop and send the input data to other processes untouched. This routing may occur as the result of one or more characteristics of the data. An example of this type of transformation is the routing of data that indicate a particular job category to one process while all other data is routed to another process.

The fourth data flow component, an *entity*, is someone or something that interacts with the system but resides outside the system boundary and, therefore, outside the control of the system or its users. An entity can take the form of either a *source* or a *sink*. A source entity is one that serves as the origin of data flowing into the system. A customer, for example, could be a source entity for an order processing system by submitting an order for products or services. A sink entity is one that represents a destination for data flowing out from the system. A retail store could be a sink entity for a manufacturing system. Also, a single entity can represent both a source and a sink, such as a customer sending an order to an order processing system and also receiving the goods shipped from that system.

Confusion commonly arises when the analyst attempts to determine whether a particular person is an entity or a process. This decision is not as simple as

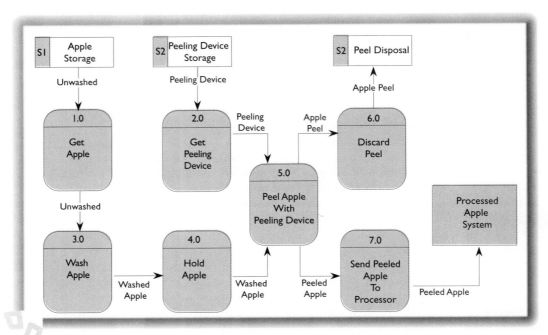

Figure 5-2 Data Flow Diagram for Logical Apple Peeling Process

determining whether the person is an employee of the organization or is external to it. In some cases, a person internal to the organization that owns the system may still reside outside the system boundary and, thus, be an entity with regard to that system. Under the basic test for this, if the person can act independently of the system with regard to the data supplied to the system or received from it, then that person is an entity and not a process. If, on the other hand, the person is bound by the functions defined by the system, then that person represents a process within the system.

Because source and sink entities reside outside the span of control of the system, we are not concerned about them in the same level of detail with which we approach processes contained within the system boundary. For example, we need not be concerned with how an entity functions or exactly what it does in addition to providing data to or receiving data from a system. Further, we are not concerned with any control or redesign issues associated with entities. Finally, because we have no control over the source or sink entities, we cannot allow them to have any direct access to the data stored within the system boundary and, thus, do not need to consider their information needs.

Using these four simple components, the analyst can graphically depict a complex system and can gain detailed understanding into not only the objectives of the system but also the extent to which the system is capable of achieving those objectives. Figure 5-2 contains a simple DFD illustrating our logical process for peeling an apple. Notice that the same diagram can represent the process in your kitchen or in a fruit processing factory.

DFD HIERARCHY

Recall our discussion of functional decomposition from chapter 2. We learned that a system is composed of a decomposable set of subsystems, each of which in turn can be decomposed. We use this concept when creating a set of DFDs to depict

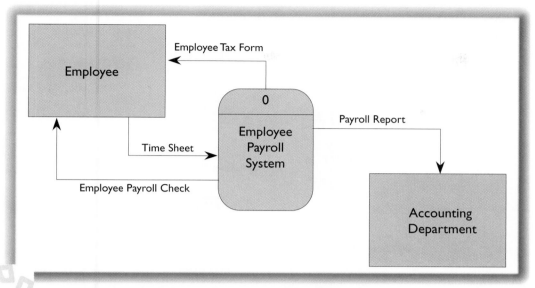

Figure 5-3   Context Level Diagram for Employee Payroll System

various levels of detail regarding the system. By creating a hierarchy of diagrams, each with a greater degree of detail than the last, we can gain understanding about the complexity of the system and analyze it from multiple perspectives. Each layer of a set of DFDs can be thought of as an exploded version of the previous layer.

Context Level Diagram

The first diagram in the set, and the one that displays the least amount of detail, is referred to as the *context level diagram.* The context level diagram is intended to identify the system boundary with regard to its relationship to any source or sink entities that may interact with it. As such, the context diagram contains only one process, labeled with the name of the system and assigned a zero as its identifier. Any source or sink entities that interact with the system are also depicted, along with their respective, labeled data flows. No additional processes beyond the one representing the system and no data stores are shown on the context level diagram, because no processes other than those contained within the system are being depicted and no data stores associated with a given system can reside outside of the system boundary. If it appears that data is stored or supplied from outside the system boundary, the source should be modeled as an external entity. Figure 5-3 shows an example of a context level diagram for a payroll system.

Level-0 DFD

The single process representing the system in the context diagram is represented in greater detail at the next level, the *level-0 diagram.* Using our explosion metaphor, the context level diagram is exploded to the level-0 diagram, which depicts the major processes contained within the system, the sequence of those processes, the data stores accessed by those processes, and the source and sink entities that interact with the system. Each depicted process is given a numeric identifier that corresponds to the sequence in which this process occurs.

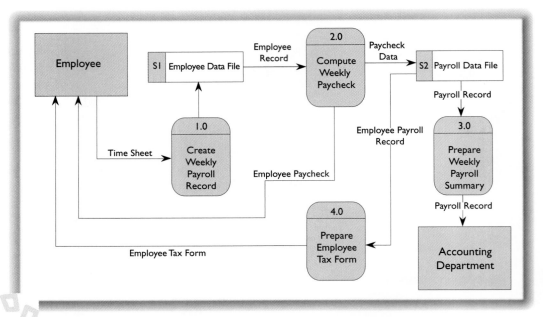

Figure 5-4   Level-0 Data Flow Diagram for Employee Payroll System

The decision as to which processes in the system are major ones and, therefore, should be included at level-0 is a subjective one. Although no hard and fast rules exist with regard to what should or should not be depicted in the level-0 diagram, there are some guidelines that can help the decision process. Generally speaking, the level-0 processes are those that represent one or more of the following:

1. A process that maintains the inflow and/or outflow of a data store
2. A process directly responsible for the production and/or distribution of data to one or more sink entities
3. A process that directly captures data from one or more source entities
4. A process that serves as a high-level descriptor of a multistep data transformation operation

One additional heuristic that is often applied with the modeling of an existing system is using the selection of activities contained on a main menu of the system as the major processes represented at level-0.

An important characteristic of all DFD levels is that anything represented on a previous level must also be represented on all levels that follow. In other words, all source and sink entities on the context level must also appear on level-0 and any subsequent level. All data stores that appear on the level-0 diagram must also appear on all levels that follow. Once a process, data store, or entity is identified, it must be carried through all levels of decomposition. Figure 5-4 illustrates the level-0 diagram for the payroll system identified in Figure 5-3.

Level-1 through Level-n DFD

Once the level-0 diagram is complete and verified to be an accurate representation of the system, the decomposition process continues to the level-1 through level-n stages. This simply means that level-0 is decomposed to level-1 and, if necessary,

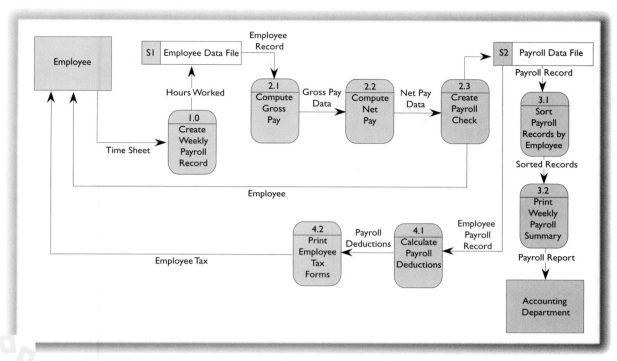

Figure 5-5   Level-1 Data Flow Diagram for Employee Payroll System

level-1 to level-2, and so on until the required level of detail for all processes and their associated subprocesses has been realized. The processes depicted on the level-0 diagram commonly are referred to as *parent processes,* and the resultant exploded subprocesses are called *child processes.* The primary rule for the creation of child processes is that a child process cannot receive any input or produce any output that the parent process does not also receive or produce. In other words, all data flows entering or leaving a parent process must also be shown as entering or leaving the set of child processes. Figure 5-5 shows the level-1 DFD of our payroll system example.

Notice in the level-1 DFD that each child process is linked to its associated parent process by the same sequential numbering system used at level-0. For example, process 2.0 on level-0 is shown on level-1 as the three child processes 2.1, 2.2, and 2.3. Also note that the same data flow entering or leaving each of the parent processes in level-0 is also shown in the level-1 DFD.

So the question becomes, "How many levels of DFDs are enough levels?" This decision is also a subjective one, but the general guideline is that no more than seven levels should be developed, regardless of the complexity of the system. The decomposition process should progress from level-0 until all processes and subprocesses have been exploded to illustrate the necessary level of detail for analysis. When a process has been fully decomposed to the desired level of detail, it is referred to as *functional primitive.* It is possible for some processes to reach the functional primitive stage before others. If this is the case, they are simply treated like the data stores and entities in the previous levels and carried to the next level with no additional explosion or decomposition. When all processes contained in the

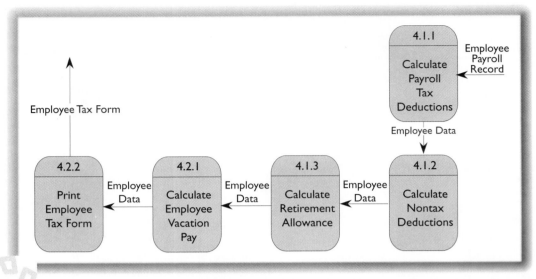

Figure 5-6   Excerpt from Fully Decomposed Data Flow Diagram for Employee Payroll System

level-0 diagram have been decomposed to their functional primitive level, the decomposition process can stop, and the set of DFDs can be considered complete. Figure 5-6 shows process 4 in our payroll system fully decomposed to the primitive level.

The Rules of DFD Construction

Table 5-1 contains a general set of rules that must be followed when constructing a set of DFDs. If any of the rules are violated, the DFD is incorrect, and inaccurate conclusions and decisions may result. It is important to note, however, that simply following the rules for construction does not insure that the system under study is represented accurately. This is the responsibility of the analyst and is achieved by constantly comparing the information gathered during requirements analysis activities with the processes and data flows depicted on the diagrams.

DFDs versus Flowcharts

The DFD has become a de facto standard throughout organizations for the modeling and representation of processes contained within a current or proposed system. Prior to the popularity of the DFD, the tool of choice for analysts was called the *system flowchart.* Although no longer in common use, the system flowchart is an important tool for the analyst to be aware of and understand for two primary reasons. First, a great deal of system documentation for older IS is centered around the use of system flowcharts, and the analyst must be able to read and understand them if any useful information is to be gained. Second, and probably most important, the two approaches to system documentation, although appearing to have similar objectives, are nonetheless significantly different from each other and cannot be used interchangeably. Gaining a basic understanding of the system flowchart should make clear to you why their differences are so important.

Table 5-1   Rules Governing Construction of Data Flow Diagrams

Rule	Incorrect Diagram	Correct Diagram
A process cannot have only outputs. (Miracle)		
A process cannot have only inputs. (Black Hole)		
The inputs to a process must be sufficient to produce the outputs from the process. (Gray Hole)		
All data stores must be connected to at least one process.		
A data store cannot be connected to a source or sink.		
A data flow can have only one direction of flow. Multiple data flows to and/or from the same process and data store must be shown by separate arrows.		
If the exact same data flows to two separate processes, it should be represented by a forked arrow.		

Table 5-1   (continued)

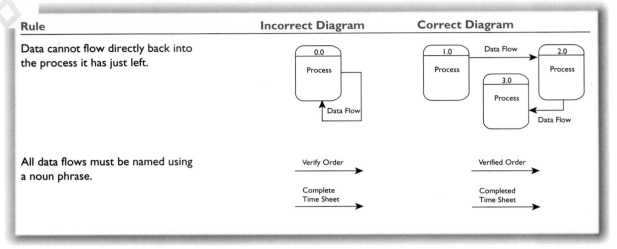

Rule	Incorrect Diagram	Correct Diagram
Data cannot flow directly back into the process it has just left.		
All data flows must be named using a noun phrase.	Verify Order / Complete Time Sheet	Verified Order / Completed Time Sheet

By definition, the system flowchart is a diagram that specifies all programs, inputs, outputs, and data store accesses and retrievals and depicts the specific flow of control through an IS. The American National Standards Institute (ANSI), in an effort to standardize the design of system flowcharts, established a set of symbols that can be used to represent various system functions. Unfortunately, however, although the symbols became standardized, their use did not. Thus most system flowcharts are difficult to comprehend for almost anyone other than the person who originally drew them. Figure 5-7 contains the most commonly used system flowchart

Figure 5-7   ANSI System Flowchart Symbology

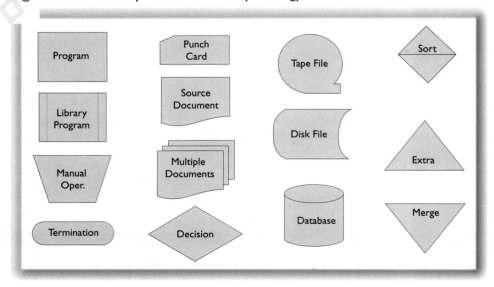

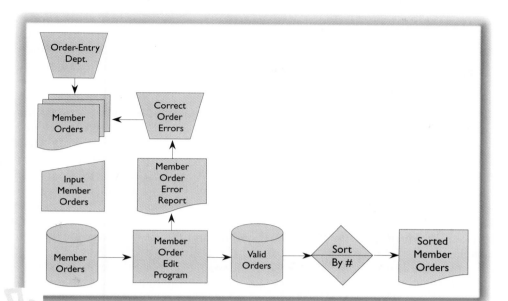

Figure 5-8   System Flowchart Example

symbols and their meanings, and Figure 5-8 illustrates their use in a simple system flowchart for a typical order-entry system.

The differences between the system flowchart and the modern DFD are the primary reason that the DFD has become the favored analysis and design tool. System flowcharts, although appearing to be logical in nature, actually depict the physical details of the system—punch cards, terminals and workstations, disk packs, hard drives, computers, and so forth. Because of this, reliance on the system flowchart can result in a premature commitment to a physical design. Conversely, the DFD avoids any reference to or consideration of a physical representation until such time as it becomes relevant and appropriate to do so. This allows the analyst to focus all of the attention on the objectives of the system, without becoming constrained by technology issues. Although the modern analyst needs to understand both diagramming tools, caution must be exercised to ensure that they are not viewed as synonymous with regard to what they are representing.

Analyzing and Using the DFD

Construction of an accurate set of DFDs is clearly a time-consuming and often tedious exercise. The payoff for the effort, however, can be easily measured in terms of a successful systems design. The old saying made popular by master carpenter Norm Abram is applicable in this regard: "Measure twice, cut once." Quality DFDs require a careful and concerted effort to verify everything contained on the diagram.

Any change to the DFD, no matter how large or small, has a rippling effect throughout the set of diagrams. Thus, constant verification is the key to an accurate set of DFDs. Every data flow should be traced from its destination back to its source. If the source of every data flow can be located, then the internal consistency of the DFD can be considered high. In addition, the DFD should be carefully reviewed with appropriate end users. This often reveals missing data stores, flows, or even entire processes; even if it does not, it serves as yet another source of verification of the DFD's accuracy and completeness. Finally, the DFD should be checked against the stated system objectives to determine the degree to which it can or does meet those objectives. By performing a careful and thorough analysis of the system in its logical form, costly mistakes and errors can be avoided when the system takes its physical form.

Using the DFD as an analysis tool can reveal many areas of improvement in a current or proposed system. Redundant data flows, redundant data updates or storage, and captured but unused data are all easily seen and corrected with the DFD. Additionally, general system inefficiencies, such as excess processing of data, unnecessary approval activities, or bottlenecks in processing, are more easily spotted through the DFD. Finally, the current system can serve as a benchmark against which the proposed system DFD is compared. Processes and data flows that have not changed from one diagram to the next can often be reused in their current form, thus reducing the amount of new coding and design necessary for the new system.

One important point should be remembered: the DFDs probably will be around a great deal longer than the people who drew them. Because of this, careful attention must be given to their accuracy, consistency, and completeness if they are to be considered useful system documentation.

MODELING PROCESS LOGIC

Up to this point, our attention has been on the processes contained within a system boundary and their function as data transformers or routers. By assembling these processes, along with any associated data stores and entities, into a DFD, we are able to visualize the flow of data through the system and the logical progression of events contained within it. Although the DFD is clearly a valuable tool for identifying and sequencing processes, it cannot answer one very important question: "What goes on within a process?" For this, we need to look at the logic contained inside the system processes, and to facilitate our investigation, we need tools that are effective in specifying the detailed instructions for the elementary processes and for modeling the logic associated with those instructions.

Logic Modeling Is Logical but. . . .

The general category of tools that we use to answer the preceding question is called *logic modeling* tools. Although the concept of logic modeling is quite logical in nature, it should not be confused with logical modeling as discussed earlier in the chapter. Logical modeling is the activity associated with creating an implementation-independent model of a system, whereas logic modeling is the technique used to model the sequential or temporal logic contained within the processes. In other words, the former models the sequence of events, and the latter models the instructions within each event.

Logic models are designed to communicate with both the end users and the analysts. They are designed to be independent of any specific programming language and must be stated precisely and unambiguously if they are to be useful. Although a wide variety of logic modeling tools exists, we focus our attention on the four most common ones: (1) *structured English,* (2) *decision tables,* (3) *decision trees,* and (4) *state-transition diagrams.*

Structured English

One of the oldest methods for modeling the logic of a system is *structured English.* By applying certain rules to a subset of the English language vocabulary, an analyst can express detailed and unambiguous process procedures. Although no specific standard for structured English exists, its use generally relies heavily on *action verbs* and *noun phrases* that contain no adjective or adverbs. (Do not worry, this will not become English class.)

Action verbs describe action. *Read, write, sort, merge, move, add, subtract,* and *print* are all examples of action verbs. Noun phrases are used to describe specific data structures or elements such as *customer_name* or *client_id.* By eliminating the use of adjectives or adverbs, structured English avoids much of the potential for ambiguity that can be caused by them. For example, the instruction *multiply quantity_ordered by unit_price* is clear, but *quickly multiply the complete quantity_ordered by each unit_price* is not. Also, structured English uses only strong, imperative verbs and avoids those that may impart ambiguity. For example, if a process needs to delay operations until a particular event has occurred or a specific length of time has passed, the verb *wait* is a better choice than *pause* or *suspend* or *linger.*

Although structured English is not a programming language, the same types of logical constructs that are found in high-level programming languages, such as COBOL or Pascal, are also found in structured English. Using three logical constructs, (1) *repetition,* (2) *decisions,* and (3) *sequentials,* structured English can express the actions of any process contained within the system. Similar to a structured programming approach, structured English requires that each process have only one entrance and only one exit. The requirement of one entrance suggests that the first statement in a structured English representation of a process is where the process begins. Having only one exit suggests that the process must not allow for any statements that route data out of the process until it is complete. A programming example of this would be the GOTO statement, by which control is redirected by one active process to another unrelated process. One exit means the data exits when the process is complete. These two requirements can serve to inform the analyst with regard to the quality of the decomposition on the DFD. If the analyst is having trouble following the one entrance-one exit rule for any particular process, that process probably has not been sufficiently decomposed to its primitive level.

Table 5-2 contains a list of many of the common procedural structures found in an IS and an example representation of each using structured English.

Probably the best way to learn how to use structured English is to see it in action. Recall our DFD for the employee payroll system. Let us look at some examples of how structured English would represent the logic of some of the processes in that model. Figure 5-9 contains a portion of that model for purposes of illustration, and Table 5-3 contains examples of the processes in structured English.

Although structured English is a highly regarded method for text-based process description, it is also a fairly tedious and time-consuming skill to acquire. Learning to follow the guidelines, limit your vocabulary, and still accurately express the process actions is a difficult task. More important, as with any modeling technique, using structured English does not guarantee that the process has been stated correctly or accurately. This still requires verification from the end users and from observation by the analyst. Finally, in cases for which the logic of a process becomes exceedingly complex or lengthy, structured English may not be the best choice for representing the logic. For these cases, we need to turn to other logic modeling

Table 5-2   Structured English Representation of Common Procedural Structures

Procedural Structure	Structured English Model
Nonconditional Sequence—perform an action sequence without conditions.	[**action 1**], [**action 2**], [**action 3**], . . . [**action n**]

Simple conditional sequence—perform an action sequence based on a condition with two possible values. If condition is true, then perform action sequence 1, otherwise perform action sequence 2.	**IF** [condition]
	    THEN
	        [**action sequence**]
	    ELSE
	        [**action sequence**]

Complex conditional sequence—perform an action sequence based on a condition with more than two possible values. If condition is true, then perform action sequence 1, otherwise test each condition until true and perform associated action sequence.	**DO BASED ON** [condition]:
	    IF [condition] = [value] **THEN**
	        [**action sequence**]
	    IF [condition] = [value] **THEN**
	        [**action sequence**]
	    . . .
	    IF [condition] = [value] **THEN**
	        [**action sequence**]

Combinatorial condition sequence—test values for multiple conditions and perform correct action sequence based on those values. A decision table is often used in lieu of nested *if-then-else* conditionals.	Decision Table
	Rule 1
	Rule 2
	Rule 3
	Rule n
	
	[condition 1]
	value
	value
	value
	value
	
	[condition 2]
	value
	value
	value
	value
	
	[condition n]
	value
	value
	value
	value
	
	[**action**]
	
	      X
	      X

Table 5-2   (*continued*)

Procedural Structure	Structured English Model
Combinatorial condition sequence— (*continued*)	[action] X [action] X
Zero-to-many iteration—repeat the action sequence until the condition is false. Used when the action sequence is based upon the initial value of the condition.	**REPEAT UNTIL** [condition]: [action sequence]

One-to-many iteration—repeat the action sequence until the condition is false. Used when the action sequence **must be performed at least once** regardless of the initial value of the condition.	**DO WHILE** [condition]:
	    [action sequence]
	- OR -
	FOR [condition]:
	    [action sequence]

Figure 5-9   Functional Primitive Decomposition for Process 4.0

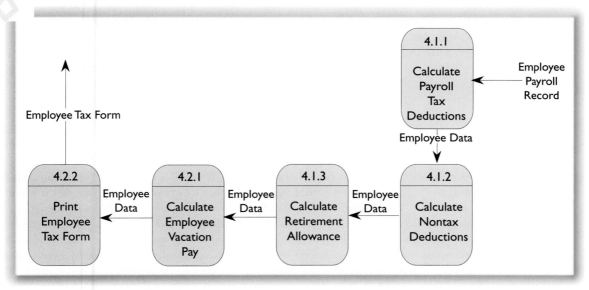

Table 5-3   Structured English Examples for Process 4.0

Process ID	Structured English
4.1.1	Multiply **GROSS_PAY** by **FED_TAX_RATE** and store in **EMP_TAX_DEDUCT**.
4.1.2	**IF EMP_NONTAX_DEDUCT** > 0 **THEN** append **EMP_NONTAX_DEDUCT** to employee data.
4.1.3	Multiply **GROSS_PAY** by .01 and store in **EMP_RETIRE**.
4.1.4	Multiply **CURR_EMP_VACATION** by **EMP_DAY_RATE** and store in **EMP_VACATION_PAY**.

techniques. In the next sections, we look at two common alternatives to structured English: *decision tables* and *decision trees*.

The Decision Table

As stated previously, processes can become quite complex. A single process can contain multiple conditions that dictate which of a set of several actions should be taken. Consider the logic outlined using a structured English approach in Table 5-4.

Under conditions such as those shown in Table 5-4, structured English may be too cumbersome or inadequate to accurately represent the variety of possible actions with any degree of clarity. In these cases, the analyst must turn to logic modeling techniques that are diagram-based or graphical-based rather than text-based. One such method available is the *decision table*.

The decision table is a diagram of all the logic and possible outcomes associated with a particular process. Using this technique, the analyst can easily represent all of the choices and the various conditions on which they depend using a single tabular model. Table 5-5 is an example of a decision table approach to recording the logic for the insurance surcharge rating system shown in Table 5-4.

One of the first things to notice is that when logic becomes complex or decisions become nested, structured English can be fairly cumbersome and confusing. In contrast, the decision table communicates the same information in a more uniform and comprehensible manner.

From a structural perspective, the decision table can be divided into three basic elements: (1) *process rules,* (2) *condition stubs,* and (3) *action stubs.* The process rules, combined with the condition stubs, represent the specific rules that must be followed when making a decision as to which action is appropriate. The action stubs represent all possible courses of action associated with a given set of conditions and rules. In constructing the initial decision table, an exhaustive set of rules must be determined. To determine the number of rules in an exhaustive set, the analyst multiplies the number of values for each condition stub by the number of values for every other condition stub in the table. In Table 5-5, we have six conditions, each with two possible values. To create an exhaustive set of rules we would need 2^6, or 64, rules. If a third condition with three values were added, our exhaustive set would jump to 64×3, or 192, rules. Using this approach, however, it often turns

Table 5-4   Structured English Logic for Insurance Rating System

Structured English Process Description

IF Driver_Age < 25 **THEN**

        IF Accident_Free = "**N**" **THEN**

            Surcharge = 0.20

        ENDIF

    ELSE

        IF Driver_Gender = "**F**" **THEN**

            Surcharge = 0.10

        ENDIF

    ELSE

        IF Driver_Educ = "**N**" **THEN**

            Surcharge = 0.15

        ENDIF

    ELSE

        IF College = "**N**" **THEN**

            Surcharge = 0.12

        ENDIF

    ELSE

        IF HS_GPA < 3.25 **THEN**

            Surcharge = 0.10

        ENDIF

    ELSE

        IF HS_GPA $>= 3.25$ **THEN**

            Surcharge = 0.07

        ENDIF

ELSE

        IF Accident_Free = "**Y**" **THEN**

            Surcharge = 0.00

        ENDIF

    ELSE

        IF Accident_Free = "**N**" **THEN**

            Surcharge = 0.07

        ENDIF

ENDIF

out that many of the rules in the resultant set are either redundant or nonsensical and can be removed from the final table. This determination, however, should not be made until after the exhaustive set of rules has been determined and listed in the table.

Turning back to the decision table presented in Table 5-5, we can see that several rules have at least one condition that has no effect on the action taken (as indicated by a dash at the intersection of the rule and condition). These types of conditions are referred to as *indifferent conditions,* because their value has no influence with regard to the action required. In some cases, indifferent conditions can be either removed or collapsed into a single rule, thus further reducing the complexity of the logic represented in the table.

Table 5-5 Decision Table for Insurance Rating System

Process Rules for Surcharge	A	B	C	D	E	F	G	H
Driver age	25 yrs +	25 yrs +	< 25 yrs	< 25 yrs	< 25 yrs	< 25 yrs	< 25 yrs	< 25 yrs
Accident free	Y	N	N	Y	Y	Y	Y	Y
Driver gender	—	—	—	Female	Male	Male	Male	Male
Driver's education	—	—	—	—	N	Y	Y	Y
College (attending / completed)	—	—	—	—	—	N	Y	Y
High school GPA	—	—	—	—	—	—	< 3.25	3.25+
20% surcharge			X					
15% surcharge					X			
12% surcharge						X		
10% surcharge				X			X	
7% surcharge		X						X
No surcharge	X							

When constructing decision tables, a basic set of procedures should be followed. Table 5-6 contains the steps necessary to successfully construct a useful decision table for a given process.

Although structured English may not be as appropriate as the decision table for expressing complex logic, there is no reason that the analyst cannot make efficient use of both techniques by combining them when describing a single process. For example, a structured English statement in a specification might read:

Determine employee pay using decision table, XYZ Corp. Payroll Policy.

Decision tables are an important and valuable tool when modeling process logic. Their primary advantage over structured English is the ease with which the analyst can check for accuracy and completeness of the logic representation. When used appropriately, a more accurate systems design specification results.

The Decision Tree

In certain cases, process logic can involve a complex web of branching or long sequences of decisions. In these cases, the *decision tree* may be a more appropriate tool than either structured English or a decision table to use to model the logic contained within the process. As its name implies, the decision tree graphically depicts logic in a manner that resembles a tree trunk and its various branches. Unlike a tree from nature, however, the decision tree is constructed as a tree lying on its side, with the trunk on the left side of the diagram and the various branches extending out to the right.

The decision tree used in systems analysis is a derivation of the ones commonly used in management science to depict complex probabilistic events. In systems analysis situations, however, the decision tree is void of any probabilities, because process logic requires all conditions and actions to be structured such that their probability of occurrence does not have any effect on the actions taken. Fig-

Table 5-6   Procedures for Constructing Decision Tables

Rule	Description
Determine all conditions and the values they can assume.	Conditions are the "**IF**" portion of a structured English statement. In most cases, possible values for a condition will be binary (i.e., "yes" or "no"), in other cases values can have many values (i.e., hair or eye color).
Determine all possible actions that need to be taken.	Actions are the "**THEN**" portion of a structured English statement. Actions should be clearly defined so as to avoid any ambiguity.
Calculate and list an exhaustive set of rules.	Multiply the number of possible values for each condition by the number of possible values for all other conditions. For example, 3 conditions with 2 possible values each would yield 8 rules in the exhaustive set—2 x 2 x 2 = 8.
Associate actions with rules.	Each action, as previously determined, should be associated with at least one rule, and each rule should have at least one action.
Simplify the rule set in the decision table.	Remove all redundant or nonsensical rules from the exhaustive set to create a smaller and less complex decision table.

ure 5-10 illustrates the general form of a decision tree in systems analysis, and Figure 5-11 contains an example of a decision tree for our automobile insurance rating system example.

As you can see, a decision tree has two main elements. The *decision points,* also called nodes, are represented by small circles that contain a number corresponding

Figure 5-10   The Basic Structure of a Nonprobabilistic Decision Tree

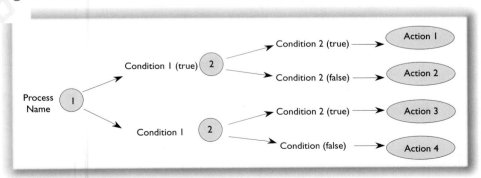

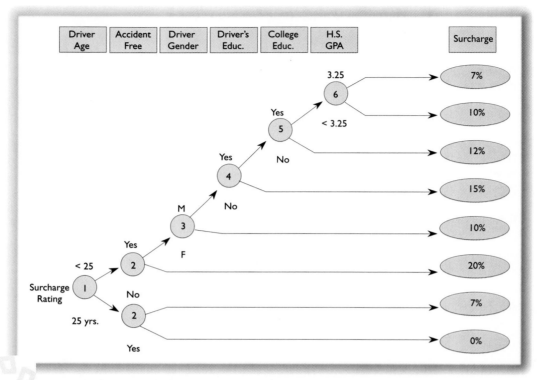

Figure 5-11   Decision Tree for Insurance Rating System

to the sequence in which the decisions are made. The *actions* are represented by ovals that contain a description of the action to be taken and are connected to a node by an arrow. Because a node can have multiple decisions associated with it, it can also be connected to multiple actions. The reverse is not true, however: an action oval can be connected to one, and only one, decision node.

The State-Transition Diagram

The three logic modeling tools discussed previously, although useful for most types of process logic, are not well-suited to logic that is *time-dependent,* or *temporal,* in nature. For these applications, analysts turn to the *state-transition diagram.* A state-transition diagram models how two or more processes are related to each other in time. As its name implies, the state-transition diagram illustrates the various *states* a system component can take in relation to the events or conditions that cause a change from one state to another. Although considered to be an important tool for modeling in an object-oriented environment (see appendix B for more details), state-transition diagrams are equally useful in the process-oriented environment of the SDLC.[1]

To better understand the state-transition diagram, we need to be clear on a couple of definitions. First, a *state* is a condition of existence, or form, that can be taken by a system component. Once in a particular state, an action associated with

[1] A thorough discussion of the state-transition diagram is beyond the scope of this text, but the reader is referred to Harel (1987) for more detailed coverage.

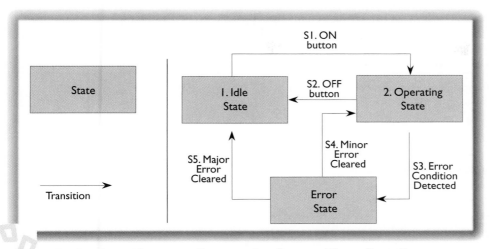

Figure 5-12   State-Transition Diagram for Generic Three-State Event

that state occurs. The *transition* from one state to another occurs as the result of some phenomenon or stimulus referred to as an *event*. When an event occurs, a transition is triggered, and the system component assumes a different state, thus causing an action to occur. The state that the system is in at any moment is called the *current state*. In some cases, a system is designed such that there is always an exit from the current state to an alternate state, such as a light bulb that can switch between "on" and "off." In other cases, however, one or more states may exist from which there is no exit, as, for example, an event that triggers the complete shutdown of a system in an emergency. These states are referred to as *final states*. Figure 5-12 contains the symbols used in constructing state-transition diagrams and an example of a diagram for a generic three-state event.

When constructing state-transition diagrams, it is important to adopt a method that ensures that all possible states, triggers, and actions are accounted for and accurately modeled. Further, do not forget to consider how the system should react if an inappropriate action is taken or some external error occurs. In general, the following steps can be used when constructing state-transition diagrams:

1. Identify the initial state
2. Represent that state by drawing a rectangle on the diagram
3. Connect that state with an arrow to indicate its first transition
4. Each state should lead to at least one other state but can lead to more than one state
5. Label the arrow indicating the transition(s) with a descriptive event name
6. List the appropriate actions to be taken adjacent to each state rectangle
7. Consider system reactions to unexpected events
8. Repeat the process until all possible states are accounted for

When Do I Use What?

You have seen that each of the four logic modeling tools has certain advantages and disadvantages associated with it. The question then becomes, "How do I know which one to use and when?" One approach is to use whichever one you are most

Table 5-7   Criteria for Determining Appropriate Logic Modeling Technique

Primary Criteria 1=Best 2=Better 3= Good	Structured English	Decision Table	Decision Tree	State- Transition
Transformation of conditions or actions into specific sequence	1	3	1	-
Portraying complex logic sequences	3	1	2	-
Portraying simple logic sequences	2	2	1	-
Making basic decisions	3	2	1	-
Determining conditions or actions	2	3	1	-
Checking logic consistency and completeness	3	1	1	-
Ease of manipulation	3	1	2	-
Compactness	3	1	2	-
Portraying temporal logic sequences	-	-	-	1

familiar with and understand the best. Although this may be the easiest way to make the decision, it may not be the best way. The decision as to which logic modeling tool to use is related to the task at hand. Table 5-7 contains a summary of findings conducted by several different researchers (i.e., Vessey and Weber 1986; Subramanian et al. 1992) comparing the four techniques under various settings and conditions.

Generally speaking, no single technique is applicable across all scenarios, and the analyst must be proficient in all of them to ensure that the appropriate technique is applied. As shown in Table 5-7, structured English does not fare as well as either decision tables or decision trees in virtually all scenarios. With the advent of modern software applications, such as CASE tools, to assist the analyst in modeling logic, structured English is becoming less popular. Nonetheless, all the techniques discussed are useful in their own way, and the modern analyst should be adept at using all of them.

CHAPTER SUMMARY

Logical process modeling is an important skill for the analyst that is called on in virtually every design or development scenario. By reducing a complex, physical system into a set of logical models, the analyst can easily view the system in a holistic sense and focus on the intention of the processes independent of the manner in which they are implemented. The logical process models developed during the detailed analysis and logical design activities of the SDLC also serve as valuable documentation during and after the development process.

Systems are a complex set of instructions, controls, and events that, if assembled properly, yield a predictable set of results or outputs. At the root of this predictability is the concept of logic. Using the various logic modeling tools at his or her disposal, the analyst must be able to analyze complex logic sequences and organize them into an exhaustive set of instructions by which the system is governed.

Although the modeling of process and logic for a system plays an essential role in the analysis and development of new or better systems, it does not tell the whole story. In addition to the modeling and understanding of the processes that move the data, we must also understand the data itself. In the next chapter, we focus on the skills and tools available to the analyst to assist in defining and modeling the data used and stored by the system.

KEY CONCEPTS

➤ Logical process modeling

Models are simplified representations of reality. A physical model shows *how* something happens, whereas a logical model graphically conveys *what* a system is or does without any constraints of how that might be accomplished. The DFD, a logical process-modeling tool, emphasizes the *logical perspective* of the current or proposed system rather than the physical perspective.

➤ Benefits of using a logical modeling approach in systems analysis

- Logical models significantly reduce the risk of overlooking or missing important business requirements of the system.
- Logical models make it easier for the analyst to communicate with the end users and system stakeholders.
- Logical models reduce the biases typically associated with the way the current system is implemented.

➤ DFD

The DFD depicts the sequence of processes and functions contained within a specified system boundary and the flow of data through that system.

➤ DFD components

- Data flow
  A data flow represents data in motion.
- Data store
  The data store represents data at rest.
- Process
  A process transforms data into another form, creates new data, or assembles data into some useful output. Four basic types of transformation may occur as a result of a process: creating a set of data flows, gaining new knowledge from the input data, reorganizing the input data, and routing the input data.
- Entity
  An entity interacts with the system but resides outside the system boundary and, therefore, outside the control of the system or its users. An entity can take the form of either a source or a sink. Sometimes a single entity can represent both a source and sink.

➤ DFD hierarchy

Because a system is composed of a decomposable set of subsystems, each of which in turn can be decomposed, systems analysts can gain understanding about the complexity of the system by creating a hierarchy of diagrams and analyzing it from multiple perspectives.

- Context level diagram
  The context level diagram is the least detailed DFD. It identifies the system boundary and its relationship to any source or sink entities that may interact with it.
- Level-0 DFD
  The context level diagram is exploded to the level-0 diagram, which depicts the major processes contained within the system, the sequence of those processes, the data stores accessed by those processes, and the source and sink entities that interact with the system.
- Level-1 to Level-n DFD
  Once the level-0 diagram is complete and verified to be an accurate representation of the system, the decomposition process continues to the level-1 stage and through level-n stages.

➤ The rules of DFD construction
- A process cannot have only outputs (miracle).
- A process cannot have only inputs (black hole).
- The inputs to a process must be sufficient to produce the outputs from the process (gray hole).
- All data stores must be connected to at least one process.
- A data store cannot be connected to a source or sink.
- A data flow can have only one direction of flow. Multiple data flows to and/or from the same process and data store must be shown by separate arrows.
- If the exact same data flows to two separate processes, it should be represented by a forked arrow.
- Data cannot flow directly back into the process it has just left.
- All data flows must be named using a noun phrase.
- System flowcharts graphically depict programs, inputs, outputs, and data storage activities. System flowcharts, although appearing to be logical in nature, actually depict the physical details of the system.
- Constant verification is the key to an accurate set of DFDs.

➤ Logic modeling

Logic modeling is used to model the sequential or temporal logic contained within the processes. Logic models are designed to communicate with both the end users and the analysts.

- Structured English

  Structured English uses action verbs and noun phrases to unambiguously describe logic sequences and events. The three logical constructs used in structured English are, (1) repetition, (2) decisions, and (3) sequentials.

- The decision table

  The decision table is a diagram of all the logic and possible outcomes associated with a particular process. The decision table can be divided into three basic elements: (1) process rules, (2) condition stubs, and (3) action stubs.

- The decision tree

  The decision tree graphically depicts logic in a manner that resembles a tree trunk and its various branches lying on its side. A decision tree has two main elements: decision points (nodes) and actions.

- The state-transition diagram

  State-transition diagrams are useful for modeling logic that is time-dependent or temporal.

QUESTIONS FOR REVIEW

1. Describe the differences between physical models and logical models.

2. What are the benefits of using a logical modeling approach in SAD?

3. What is a DFD?

4. Describe the nature of the four DFD components.

5. What are the four basic types of transformation that may occur as a result of a process?

6. How do you determine whether a particular person is an entity or a process?

7. Why would a systems analyst adopt a DFD hierarchy technique?

8. Explain the concept of DFD hierarchy.

9. When does a process reach the *functional primitive* stage?

10. What is the main difference between a DFD and a system flowchart?

11. List and briefly describe the four most commonly used logic-modeling tools.

12. What are the two requirements of structured English that could serve to inform the analyst with regard to the

quality of the decomposition of the DFD?

13. How does a systems analyst determine whether the number of rules in a decision table represents an exhaustive set?

14. What is an indifferent condition in a decision table?

15. Compare the four logic-modeling techniques and explain the conditions under which they are appropriate.

FOR FURTHER DISCUSSION

1. The senior partner's nephew is home for the summer and he is working as an intern under your supervision. The boss assures you that the nephew has received the finest training possible at Southeastern West North Central Sepulveda A & M University, his home institution. You have him assigned to create a level-0 DFD for the insurance claims system currently under study at one of your biggest clients but you know you need to keep a close eye on his work. He submits the DFD shown in Figure 5-13. Study the diagram and check it carefully for errors (when you find seven of them, you have found them all).

2. Use the following information to create a set of fully decomposed DFDs. Start with a context level diagram and proceed through level-0 to, at least, level-1.

   The purpose of the textbook inventory system at a campus bookstore is to supply textbooks to students for classes at a local university. The university's academic departments submit initial data about courses, instructors, textbooks, and projected enrollments to the bookstore on a textbook master

Figure 5-13   DFD for Problem 1

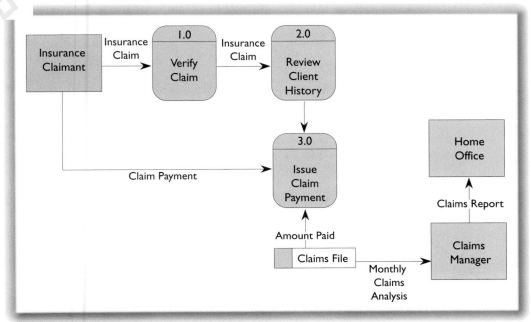

list. The bookstore generates a Form 17: Purchase Order, which is sent to publishing companies supplying textbooks. Book orders arrive at the bookstore accompanied by a packing slip, which is created and verified by the receiving department. Students fill out a Book Request Form that includes course information. When they pay for their books, the students are given a paper tape Cash Register Sales Receipt.

3. Use the following information to create a set of fully decomposed DFDs. Start with a context level diagram and proceed through level-0 to, at least, level-1.

The Music-by-Mail Record Club advertises cassettes and CDs in a variety of magazines. Most orders are submitted by magazine subscribers who complete and send coupons to the mail order company. All mail arrives at the receptionist's desk. The receptionist sorts and distributes the mail to the appropriate departments. Mail orders and letters requesting order cancellations are forwarded to an order-entry clerk in the sales department.

The order-entry clerk initially checks the availability and the price of the ordered items, and, if necessary, mails a back-order notice to the customer. This clerk also takes orders from customers directly by phone and forwards all fillable orders to the credit-clerk.

When the order entry clerk receives a letter requesting an order cancellation (or a cancellation by telephone) the status of the order is first determined. If the customer order has not been invoiced, the order-entry clerk informs the warehouse that the order should be canceled and then informs the customer that the cancellation has been completed.

When fillable orders are received by the credit clerk, the customer's credit status is checked. Orders are approved and an order-confirmation letter is sent to those customers with good credit standing. Customers with bad credit standing are sent a payment-overdue notice requesting prepayment. The credit clerk forwards approved orders to the warehouse.

The warehouse fills the approved order and updates the inventory availability. A packing slip is sent with the packaged order to the customer, and a shipping notice is sent to the accounts receivable department.

Accounts receivable bills the customer for the products shipped. This department also maintains the invoice data files, updating them to reflect charges or payments received. Payments are received in the mail and delivered to accounts receivable by the receptionist. A payment receipt is sent to the customer.

4. Flexible Products Corporation, makers of everything, has established a firm policy with regard to discounts afforded to their customers for various payment scenarios:

If the customer submits their payment within 10 days of the invoice date, then a 5 percent discount is awarded. The customer is also listed as a good credit risk if the amount of the payment exceeds $350 and the payment is received within 30 days from the invoice date. If payment is received within 30 days from the invoice date, then no penalty is applied. If payment is received after 30 days from the invoice date, but within 60 days of the invoice date, then a 3 percent penalty is applied to the amount due. If the customer submits payment after 60 days from the invoice date but within 1 year and they make special arrangements with Dan Hunt, the Chief Credit Officer, then a 6 percent penalty is applied to the amount due. If the balance remains outstanding for more than 1 year, then there is a 20 percent penalty applied to the balance.

Model the logic associated with Flexible Products' payment policy using structured English, a decision table, and a decision tree. Which one do you prefer?

REFERENCES

DeMarco, T. 1979. *Structured Analysis and System Specification.* Englewood Cliffs, NJ: Prentice Hall.

Gane, C., and T. Sarson. 1979. *Structured Systems Analysis.* Englewood Cliffs, NJ: Prentice Hall.

Harel, D. 1987. "Statecharts: A Visual Formalism for Complex Systems." *Science of Computer Programming* 8: 231–74.

Subramanian, G. H., J. Nosek, S. P. Raghunathan, and S. S. Kanitkar. 1992. "A Comparison of the Decision Table and the Decision Tree." *Communications of the ACM* 35: 89–94.

Vessey, I., and R. Weber. 1986. "Structured Tools and Conditional Logic." *Communications of the ACM* 29: 48–57.

Modeling the Data: Conceptual and Logical Data Modeling

Learning Objectives

- Understand the basic objectives of conceptual and logical data modeling
- Be familiar with the components of the ERD
- Understand relationships and the concepts of degree, cardinality, and optionality
- Learn the basic characteristics of a good data model
- Understand the process of data normalization and the concept of functional dependency
- Understand when the normalization process may negatively impact actual system performance

Man is a tool-making animal.
— BENJAMIN FRANKLIN

OBJECTIVES OF DATA MODELING

Despite the best efforts of several inventors, to date there is no such thing as a universal tool, that is, a tool for all tasks. This is because the design of a tool is based on a certain set of assumptions about the context in which it is used, the characteristics of who uses it, and the objectives for its use. Although the systems analyst has available a variety of tools with which to analyze and design applications, relying on the output of any single tool may result in the formation of some very wrong conclusions.

There is a well-known Hindu legend, adapted into a children's poem by John Godfrey Saxe, about six blind men who were asked to provide a description of an elephant (see Figure 6-1). The man who was touching the trunk at the time pro-

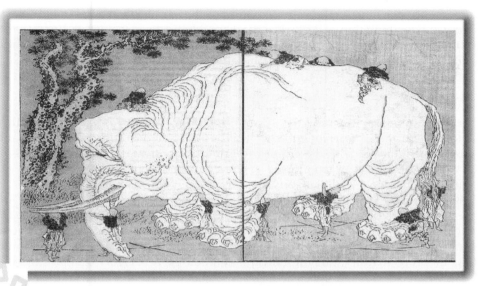

Figure 6-1   Japanese Print of Six Blind Men and the Elephant Parable
Source: <http://tyrone.differnet.com/experience/atlarge
/eleph5b.htm>.

claimed the elephant to be a snake-like creature. The man touching the leg suggested the elephant easily could be compared to a large tree. Yet another, touching the tail of the elephant, described the animal as ropelike in nature. My point is that an analyst with one tool has but one part of the picture and, like the blind men, can draw conclusions on only a portion of the necessary information.

Each tool of systems analysis represents an important perspective on the development project, but none represents a comprehensive picture. In chapter 4, we learned about the wide variety of tools available to gather information and begin the organization of system requirements. In chapter 5, we learned how to use tools that provided a view of the flow of data between the various processes contained within a system, and we learned of other tools that could assist in the determination and organization of the various decisions and logic structures associated with those processes. In this chapter, we focus our attention on tools that assist in the identification and definition of the data themselves. Such tools complete the picture by allowing for the analysis and determination of the structure and relationships within the data moving through our system.

The *data model* represents an important element in the determination of system requirements. All systems exist for data, and the structure and nature of that data often determine the complexity of the processes that must be designed. Although the DFD can answer questions with regard to where the data goes, who receives it, and in what form, its function is limited to describing transient characteristics of the system and the organization. Conversely, the data model focuses on the nature of the data themselves, thus describing the system and the organization in terms of the rules and their relationships by which it operates.

Currently the most widely accepted format for data modeling is the ERD. In the analysis stages of a development project, the ERD is used to represent the conceptual data requirements for the proposed system that identify the rules and interrelationships among data. During the logical design stage, the ERD is transformed into a more detailed, logical representation of the organizational data model such that database definition and physical database design can be achieved. Because the ERD is an essential tool in many stages of the SDLC, the analyst must master the skills associated with its development and interpretation.

THE ERD

Just as its name implies, the ERD details the various data entities associated with a system or business environment, the relationships among those entities, and the specific attributes of both the entities and their relationships. Originally proposed by Chen (1976), the notation used in the construction of an ERD has been extended to include additional constructs (cf. Storey, 1991; Teorey, Yang, and Fry, 1986), and thus a variety of notations and symbologies exist. For our purposes, we adopt the most common notation method currently in use, referred to as the *crow's-foot* approach (Martin and Finkelstein, 1981). If you have had experience in your database class with another form of entity-relationship (ER) notation, you should have no problem translating the concepts between the two. Figure 6-2 illustrates the basic symbols we use in constructing ERDs, and the sections that follow explain each of these symbols in detail.

Entities

Represented by a rectangle on the ERD, an *entity* is anything about which we want to store data. Data describe "things." The entity is used to represent these things, which could be people, places, objects, events, concepts, or whatever else an organization

Figure 6-2   Basic Symbols for Constructing Entity-Relationship Diagrams

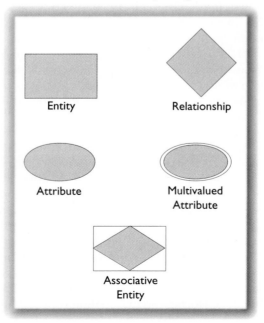

Entity

Relationship

Attribute

Multivalued Attribute

Associative Entity

might wish to maintain data about. An entity must be distinguishable in some manner from all other entities and must occur more than once within the business environment. An example may help to make this clear.

Consider a typical business environment. Contained within it are a number of identifiable things that we may want to store data about. Customers, orders, employees, products ordered, products in stock, and suppliers, among many others, are all typically associated with a business environment. Each of these things has two very important characteristics that serve to make it an entity: 1) it can be distinguished from all of the other entities in the business environment by some set of identifying characteristics or attributes, and 2) it represents a class of things that can occur more than once within the business environment. Given these two characteristics, we can define an entity about which we can store data.

When thinking of entities we must pay attention to several important issues. First, entities in the context of process models and DFDs are somewhat different from entities in the context of ER modeling. In the DFD, an entity, be it a source or sink, lies outside the boundary of the system and is not considered to be within the realm of control. In an ER model, however, no such distinction is made. Whether an entity lies within or outside of the system boundary is not important when modeling data. If we need to store data about it, then it is an entity.

Second, we must distinguish between the concepts of *entity type* and *entity instance* or *occurrence*. An entity type is a collection of entities that all share one or more common properties or attributes. In the ERD, an entity type is given a singular name, such as STUDENT or CUSTOMER, to connote a class or set of entities.

In contrast, an entity instance represents a single, unique occurrence of a member of an entity type. Many occurrences of an entity type can be stored in a database. For example, the entity type STUDENT can represent many thousands of individual and uniquely identifiable students. Similarly, the entity type COURSE can contain all of the unique instances of a particular course offering at a university. Conversely, however, identifying an entity type such as ATHLETIC DIRECTOR would be inappropriate, because there is probably not more than one instance of this proposed entity type. The athletic director would be more appropriately considered an attribute that identifies a unique instance of the entity type EMPLOYEE. From this point on, we refer to entity types as, simply, *entity* and a single, unique occurrence of an entity as an *instance*.

One final issue to address regarding entities on the ERD is to distinguish between an entity and a data flow. A single data flow represented on a DFD, such as a WEEKLY EXPENSE REPORT, can be constructed from several entities and contain an infinite number of instances of those entities. Because of this, a data flow on a DFD should not be confused with an ERD entity. However, because entities generally end up being operationalized in a database system as tables, most data stores on the DFD can be thought of as entities on the ERD.

Attributes

Because we must be able to identify a unique instance of an entity, we must identify one or more specific pieces of data we want to store about each instance. We refer to these pieces of data as *attributes* of an entity.

An attribute is a characteristic or descriptive property of an entity or a relationship. Often attributes are also referred to as *element* or *fields* and are commonly represented on the ERD by an oval or ellipse. Each instance of an entity can have a wide variety of attributes associated with it. The entity STUDENT could be described by attributes such as NAME, ADDRESS, ID NUMBER, DATE OF BIRTH, GENDER,

MAJOR, ETHNICITY, PHONE NUMBER, among many others. Because attributes are the characteristics that serve to uniquely identify an instance, they can take several forms and can play a variety of specific roles.

Key Attribute

To insure that an instance of an entity can be uniquely identified and differentiated from all other possible instances of that entity, we identify a particular type of attribute for each instance called a *key*. The key can be a single attribute, or group of attributes, that assumes a value unique to that entity instance. For example, each instance of the entity PRODUCT might be uniquely identified by a key PRODUCT ID. No two products can have the same PRODUCT ID.

In some cases, more than one attribute is needed to uniquely identify an instance. Consider how we might uniquely identify products in a music store setting. We could use a single attribute such as PRODUCT ID, but this would mean that every instance of an entity, regardless of similarity, would be completely differentiated. In other words, the new release by a particular artist in compact disk is considered to be uniquely different than that same new release in cassette tape. In some cases, this may be a necessary distinction, although in other cases it may not. The store may consider a unique instance of a product entity to be described by the nature of the product itself, as well as what form it is in. In this case, we could not uniquely describe a new release by simply using a PRODUCT ID. Instead, we would use a combination of attributes, such as PRODUCT ID + MEDIA CODE, to insure we can uniquely identify an instance of a new release in compact disk form from that same release in cassette form. When more than one attribute is used to create a key for an instance, we refer to it as a *concatenated* or *combination key*.

In many cases, an entity may have several attributes that, either singularly or in combination, could serve to uniquely identify a singular instance. For example, the entity STUDENT could be uniquely identified by SOCIAL SECURITY NUMBER, STUDENT ID, or even E-MAIL ADDRESS. Any attribute that could serve as key attribute in uniquely identifying an instance is referred to as a *candidate key*.

A candidate key is exactly that: a candidate to become the primary identifier for each instance of an entity. Candidate keys can be either singular or concatenated and are sometimes referred to as *candidate identifiers*. If more than one candidate key exists, the analyst must choose one to serve as the *primary key*. The primary key is the key that is most commonly used to uniquely identify a single instance of an entity. The remaining candidate keys are then referred to as *alternate* keys or *indices* and can be used by the database designer as alternate methods to identify instances. Table 6-1 contains a general set of criteria for selecting a suitable primary key from the set of identified candidate keys.

As shown in Table 6-1, the primary key attribute is represented by underlining the attribute name contained within the oval or ellipse.

Multivalued Attributes

Another special type of attribute is the *multivalued attribute*. This type of attribute can take on multiple values for a single entity instance. Suppose an organization chooses to assign the attribute TRAINING to each instance of the entity EMPLOYEE. If each employee can attend or complete more than one training program, then the attribute TRAINING can have more than one value at any given time. In the early stages of data modeling, such occurrences are represented by a double-lined ellipse to differentiate the multivalued attribute from a single-valued one. When we get to the final stages of data model construction, however, all multi-

Table 6-1   Criteria for Selecting a Primary Key from a List of Candidate Keys

Criteria for Selection	Explanation
Stability	Choose a candidate key that will not likely change its value over time. EXAMPLE: *UNSTABLE* *STABLE* *NAME + ADDRESS* *EMPLOYEE_ID*
Nonnull	Choose a candidate key that is always guaranteed to have a nonnull value. EXAMPLE: *POSSIBLE NULL* *NONNULL* *PHONE_NO* *SSN*
Noninformational	Do not create intelligent keys that attempt to convey information via their structure. EXAMPLE: *INFORMATIONAL* *NONINFORMATIONAL* *99XXX99XX* *123456789* Location Color Shelf Class Code Code Code Code
Simplicity	Wherever feasible, consider using a single attribute primary key instead of a multiattribute primary key. EXAMPLE: *SINGLE ATTRIBUTE* *MULTIATTRIBUTE* *ITEM_NO + COLOR* *ITEM_CODE*

valued attributes must be transformed in a special manner. We discuss this in greater detail when we focus on the concept of data normalization subsequently in this chapter.

Relationships

Because the entities and their attributes do not exist in isolation from one another in a business environment, we must have a method to model the various ways in which they can be related to one another. A *relationship* is an association between one or more entities that is of interest to the organization or business environment. Relationships generally indicate the occurrence of some event or natural association between instances of an entity or entities. Figure 6-3 contains several examples of common relationships found in typical business environments.

Using our previously identified entities of STUDENT and COURSE we can easily envision how the two entities might be related. A STUDENT *may be enrolled in* zero, one, or more COURSES, and a COURSE *may be taken by* zero, one, or more STUDENTS. Note that the relationship is different when viewed from the perspective of the STUDENT entity than when viewed from the COURSE entity. The relationship from the STUDENT is that he or she is *enrolled* in a course, whereas the relationship from the COURSE entity is that it can *be taken*. In some cases this may be nothing more than a semantic difference, and in others the relationship perspectives may be quite divergent. Regardless, all relationships are considered *bidirectional,* meaning they must be defined in both directions. Further, a relationship is

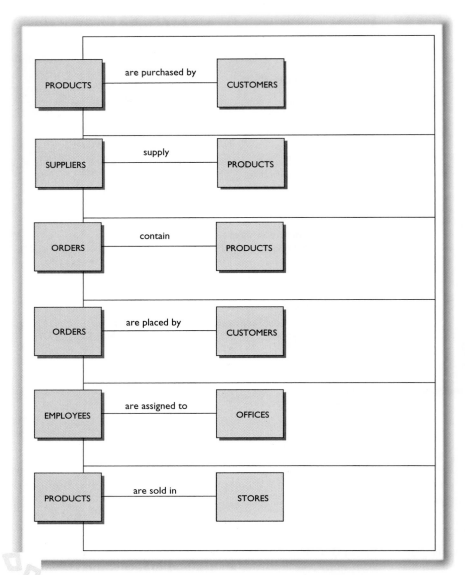

Figure 6-3   Typical Business Relationships between Two Entities

always defined as the number of instances of entity B that are associated with a *single* instance of entity A. In a following section in this chapter, we will learn a simple procedure for analyzing relationships that ensures that this definitional constraint is always met.

Because relationships can take on many forms and entities can be related to each other in many ways, we need to be able to identify the various types of relationships and the conditions under which they can occur. Generally speaking, relationships are identified by three basic characteristics of complexity: (1) *cardinality,* an indication of the number of instances of one entity in a relationship that are associated with each instance of the other entities in that relationship; (2) *optionality,*

an indication of the extent to which a relationship is mandatory or optional; and
(3) *degree,* an indication of the number of entities involved in the relationship.

Cardinality and Optionality

When translating business rules into relationships on a data model, we must be able
to determine the number of instances of one entity that are related to an instance
of another entity. This concept, called *cardinality,* defines the range of the number
of instances of one or more entities to a single instance of another entity.

In addition to the number of instances in a relationship, we must also determine its *optionality,* or the degree to which a particular relationship is mandatory or
optional. Table 6-2 illustrates the notation commonly used in representing both
cardinality and optionality in a relationship, and Figure 6-4 contains examples of
the various combinations of complexity within a given relationship.

Table 6-2   Cardinality and Optionality of Relationships

Cardinality / Optionality	Minimum Instances	Maximum Instances	Notation
Exactly 1 / mandatory	1	1	
One or more / mandatory	1	Many (to n)	
Zero or one / optional	0	1	
Zero, one, or many / optional	0	Many (to n)	

Figure 6-4   Examples of Various Relationship Complexities

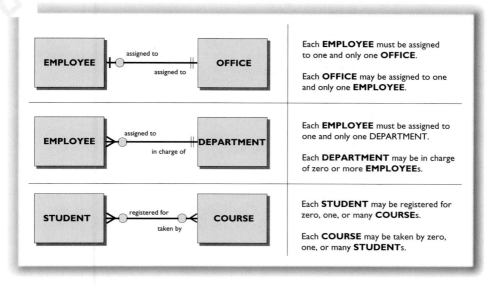

In Figure 6-4 (top), we see the relationship between EMPLOYEE and OF-FICE. The notation suggests that each instance of EMPLOYEE must be assigned to one and only one OFFICE. Further, the bidirectional nature of the relationship suggests that each instance of OFFICE *may* be assigned to one, and only one, EM-PLOYEE. From the perspective of EMPLOYEE, we have a mandatory relationship where every employee in the company has his or her own office. From the perspective of the entity OFFICE, however, we have an optional relationship. There may be an office that has no employee assigned to it, but if assigned, there can be only one employee per office. This is an example of a typical *one-to-one relationship* (1:1).

In Figure 6-4 (middle), we see a relationship between a company EMPLOYEE and a DEPARTMENT within that company. The notation indicates that each instance of EMPLOYEE *must* be assigned to only one DEPARTMENT. This suggests a manda-tory relationship between an employee and a department such that no employee works for this company without being assigned to a department within the company. The reverse, however, is not true. Viewing the relationship from the department's perspective we see that a single instance of DEPARTMENT may have zero, one, or more employees assigned to it. This suggests an optional relationship where, in the-ory at least, a department could exist within a company without having any employees assigned to it, with having only a single employee, or with any number of employees assigned to it. This is an example of a *one-to-many relationship* (1:M).

In Figure 6-4 (bottom), we see an example of a *many-to-many relationship* (M:N). Here, a single instance of STUDENT can take zero, one, or more instances of COURSE, and a single instance of COURSE can be taken by zero, one, or more instances of STUDENT. This relationship is optional in both directions, because a student can elect to take one course, a full load of courses, or take a semester off and still be considered a student. Further, a course can be scheduled and may be taken by many students, one student, or even no students.

Relationship Degree

The final measure of the complexity of a relationship is called its *degree*. The degree of a relationship simply indicates the number of entities that are participating in that relationship. Theoretically speaking, any number of entities can participate in a relationship, but in practice, we rarely encounter more than three basic types: (1) *unary*, (2) *binary*, and (3) *ternary*.

The *unary relationship*, also called a *recursive relationship*, is a relationship be-tween unique instances of a single entity and thus has a degree value equal to 1. Fig-ure 6-5 contains three examples of common unary relationships.

A relationship with a degree value equal to 2 is called a binary relationship. The binary relationship is probably the most common relationship type you en-counter when creating data models. Figure 6-6 contains three examples of typical binary relationships.

Finally, the ternary relationship has a degree value equal to 3, thus describing a simultaneous relationship among instances of three entities. Figure 6-7 contains an example of a ternary relationship.

In the example in Figure 6-7, each student is associated with at least one major and, for each major, there exists at least one student and one advisor for that major. Finally, each student is assigned to at least one advisor associated with his or her major. Remember that a data model represents one or more business rules used by the organization. The accuracy of the data model is what is important, not the qual-ity or rationality of the business rule. In the preceding example, it seems unreason-

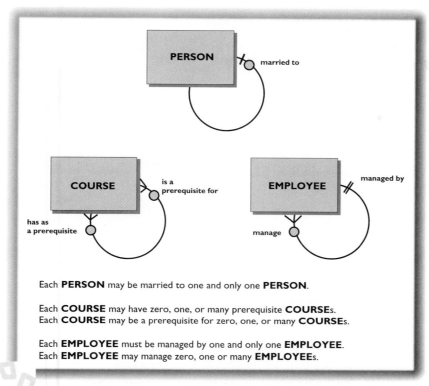

Each **PERSON** may be married to one and only one **PERSON**.

Each **COURSE** may have zero, one, or many prerequisite **COURSE**s.
Each **COURSE** may be a prerequisite for zero, one, or many **COURSE**s.

Each **EMPLOYEE** must be managed by one and only one **EMPLOYEE**.
Each **EMPLOYEE** may manage zero, one or many **EMPLOYEE**s.

Figure 6-5   Examples of Common Unary Relationships

able that a student *must* have a major and an advisor and that all majors *must* have a student assigned to them. Regardless of the seeming irrationality of the business rule, if it exists, then the data model must accurately reflect it.

It is important to note that a true ternary relationship is not equivalent to three distinct binary relationships. Although rare, if a ternary relationship exists, it must be modeled as such if the data model is to accurately reflect the business environment.

Associative Entities

Before we leave our discussion of modeling relationships, we must look at a special entity type. Although a many-to-many relationship can easily exist in a conceptual sense, in practice it becomes a bit more complicated. Commonly, the existence of a many-to-many relationship results in several attributes of the two entity types being closely related as a result. Because of this, it is conceivable that the M:N relationship is, in fact, another entity type related to the other entities in a one-to-many fashion. When this situation occurs, we create what is called an *associative entity* or *gerund*.

In Figure 6-8(a), we see an M:N relationship between the entity PASSENGER and the entity SCHEDULED FLIGHTS. In other words, many passengers may make reservations for many flights. The problem with modeling the relationship this way is that we have difficulty in determining what the exact relationship is between any single instance of PASSENGER and any single instance of SCHEDULED FLIGHT.

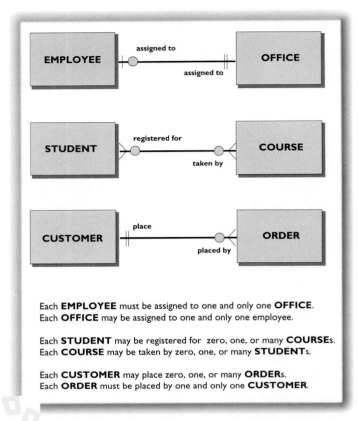

Each **EMPLOYEE** must be assigned to one and only one **OFFICE**.
Each **OFFICE** may be assigned to one and only one employee.

Each **STUDENT** may be registered for zero, one, or many **COURSE**s.
Each **COURSE** may be taken by zero, one, or many **STUDENT**s.

Each **CUSTOMER** may place zero, one, or many **ORDER**s.
Each **ORDER** must be placed by one and only one **CUSTOMER**.

Figure 6-6   Examples of Common Binary Relationships

Figure 6-7   Example of a Ternary Relationship

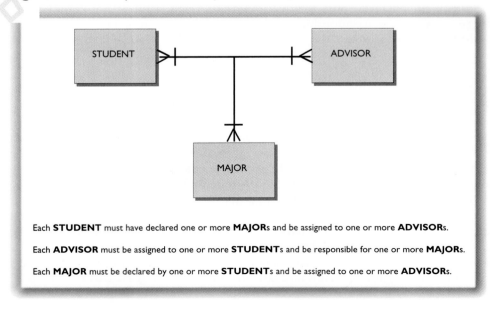

Each **STUDENT** must have declared one or more **MAJOR**s and be assigned to one or more **ADVISOR**s.

Each **ADVISOR** must be assigned to one or more **STUDENT**s and be responsible for one or more **MAJOR**s.

Each **MAJOR** must be declared by one or more **STUDENT**s and be assigned to one or more **ADVISOR**s.

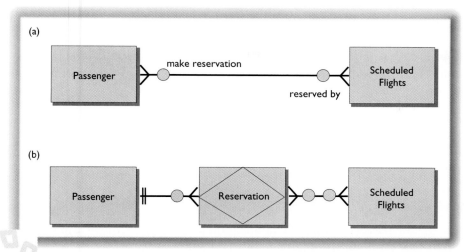

Figure 6-8   Example of an Associative Entity (Gerund)

To clarify this situation, the data modeler has created an associative entity called RESERVATION, shown in Figure 6-8(b). This is an example of a relationship being modeled as an entity, and when you stop and think about it, it makes reasonable sense. The instance of RESERVATION was created as a result of a PASSENGER booking space on one or more SCHEDULED FLIGHTS. By modeling the relationship in this manner, we can now see the exact relationship between any instance of PASSENGER and his or her reservations on SCHEDULED FLIGHTS.

Interpreting and Understanding the ERD

Commonly, the bidirectional nature and cardinal complexity of a relationship can create confusion when the analyst attempts to translate the notation on an ERD into an understandable business rule, or vice versa. To facilitate this translation process, a

Figure 6-9   General Syntax for Reading Relationships

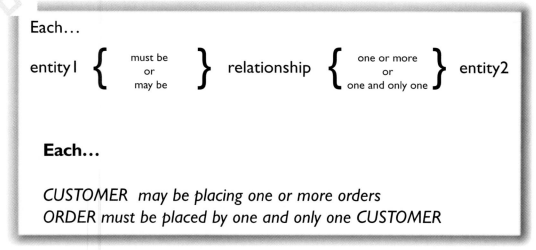

simple set of rules can be applied that insures that all relationships on an ERD are easy to translate into verbal form. Figure 6-9 illustrates this translation approach.

To begin, it is important to realize that regardless of the relationship being depicted, a relationship always begins with a reference to a *single instance* of the first entity. Thus, when reading a relationship, the very first word out of your mouth should be *"Each."*

By following the general syntax for reading relationships, you can be assured that you are correctly verbalizing the depicted relationship. Further, when creating the ERD from your notes, it is much easier if you have first placed the business rules into the general syntax form. From this form, you can easily convert the words into symbols with accuracy.

WHAT DATA?

Now that we have a good handle on the tools used to model the data and various relationships associated with them, the real questions become what data do we model? and where do we start? The answer to the first question is often easier said than done: all of the data associated with the proposed system must be accounted for and accurately modeled. Although the ideal scenario would be to adopt an enterprise approach and model all of the data for the entire organization, most business systems, unfortunately, still exist in some form of isolation from one another, and the analyst's work becomes limited to identifying and modeling the data associated with the system under study. The answer to the second question is the focus of our discussion in this section.

Recall from chapter 4 our discussion of reviewing archival documents and conducting a thorough forms analysis. Though not a completely comprehensive source, probably the single greatest place to start determining what are the various entities, attributes, and relationships within the organization is by gathering up all the forms associated with the system and analyzing their contents. Think of it this way: a form exists to capture data in a manner that allows for their use as input to a process or storage of the data associated with an event. Every form has a scope, meaning it is defined to perform a relatively isolated function, and every form has places to record specific data elements. Viewed from this perspective, a form can be thought of as representing an entity within the organization, and the data elements contained within the form represent the attributes associated with that entity. In creating lists of the data elements contained within the various forms, certain data elements are found to appear in more than one form. Although this could be the result of simple data redundancy, it is more likely an indication that the data on one form are somehow related to the data on another form. This suggests the existence of a relationship between two or more entities and forms the basis for the initial construction of a conceptual data model of the system.

It is important to note that such a *bottom-up approach* to forms analysis is not sufficient to construct an initial conceptual data model. Additional information is required, gained through analysis of the current input screens of the system, descriptions of current and proposed processes contained within the system, and a decomposition of the current and proposed reports and outputs of the system. More important are the results of a *top-down approach,* which identifies and organizes the many business rules that are used by an organization and the system in the conduct of their business processes. Nonetheless, a thorough forms analysis yields a great

Table 6-3   General Procedure for Identifying Entities and Their Relationships

Question Category	Description
Determine system entities	Find out what types of people, business units, things, places, events, materials, or other organizations are associated with, or interact with, the system and about which data must be maintained.
Identify entity attributes	Identify the characteristics by which each entity is associated or identified.
Determine entity keys	Identify the most appropriate characteristic for each entity that uniquely distinguishes an instance of that entity from all other instances of the same entity.
Determine relationships and degrees	Identify the various events, transactions, or other business activities that infer an association between entities.
Determine cardinalities and optionalities	Identify the circumstances under which each of the relationships can occur. This requires an investigation into the various business rules under which the organization operates and the constraints imposed on the events which occur within the business environment.

deal of the data contained within the model and provides a solid foundation from which to complete the process.

Although the process of collecting and identifying the variety of potential entities, attributes, and their relationships associated with the current or proposed system is a daunting and, admittedly, semistructured one, there are some guidelines that can be followed that serve to assist in the endeavor. Table 6-3 contains a list of question categories that may be useful in conducting and completing the conceptual data modeling process.

LOGICAL DATA MODELING

We turn our attention from the initial identification of the component elements of the conceptual data model to the process of refining it into a useful logical model. The process of *logical data modeling* has three basic purposes: (1) formal structuring of the data into a more stable and desirable form through a process called *normalization,* (2) development of a data model in a form that allows for the actual data needs of the organizational system to be accurately reflected, and (3) the development of a data model that allows for the construction of a physical database design.

The process of logical data modeling begins with the formation of the conceptual ERD and ends when we begin actual construction of the physical files and databases. This is because the logical data model must reflect the sum of all data elements contained within and used by the system. To insure a comprehensive and accurate data model of the system, the analyst must account for every data element contained within a system input, output, form, or report, as well as all entities, attributes, and relationships identified during the conceptual modeling process.

Before we begin looking at the logical modeling process, we need to point out that the focus of this topic is developed under the assumption that you have successfully completed an introductory course to database design and data structures. If this is the case, then some of the following material may be a review for you. If not, then any confusion with the concepts being presented should be easily cleared up by looking over any good database text. Because we look at the actual construction of the physical data model in chapter 11, our efforts here are devoted to preparation of the logical data model in a form that allows for its continued refinement and the achievement of the three basic purposes outlined previously.

CHARACTERISTICS OF A GOOD DATA MODEL

Although each data model is unique to the business environment and the system under development, all data models bear certain characteristics that determine their quality and completeness. Table 6-4 contains a listing of the characteristics of a good data model and a brief explanation of each.

As shown in Table 6-4, a good data model has the same characteristics as a well-drawn roadmap. When developing a data model, it may be helpful to think of it as a roadmap to the entities and their relationships within the organization.

THE RELATIONAL DATA MODEL

Although a number of physical data structures have been proposed or adopted over the last several decades, only one has achieved widespread acceptance and adoption: the *relational database model*. Originally proposed by Codd (1970), the relational model organizes data using tables called *relations*. Although a more thorough coverage of the relational model can be found in any current database text, for our purposes we need to become familiar with only a few basic concepts to understand the role that logical modeling plays in its constructions.

Formally defined, a *relation* is a two-dimensional table of data. Each table is composed of *named columns* and *unnamed rows*. The columns in a relation correspond to the various attributes of the entity type represented by the table, and the rows correspond to a unique instance of that entity type. Table 6-5 illustrates a simple example of a relation for the entity STUDENT and the method by which the relational structure can be expressed using a common shorthand notation method.

As you can see, each row of the relation corresponds to a single instance of the entity, and each column of the relation contains a single attribute of the entity. The first column in the table is the most important, because it contains the STUDENT_ID, which is used as the primary key for the entity, thus insuring each instance is unique. We will later see that one or more of the columns in the relation can contain data referencing another table, thus forming the basis for a relationship between two or more tables. By now you should be able to see the correspondence between the elements in a data model and the elements in the final physical database: tables are entities, rows are instances, columns are attributes, and the data contained within a column may create a relationship between two or more tables. It really is that simple.

DATA NORMALIZATION

Once we have a conceptual data model and we have identified the additional data entities, elements, and relationships from a thorough analysis of the various inputs and outputs of the current or proposed system, we must begin transforming it for

Table 6-4   Characteristics of a Good Data Model

Characteristic	Explanation
Pictorial	A good data model should be an accurate graphical depiction of the entities and their relationships.
Rigorous and specific	A good data model should be specific with regard to the identification of all entities and their relationships and rigorous in the identification and specification of the attributes associated with each entity.
Top-down decomposable	A good data model should be decomposable in the sense that the level of detail for each entity and its associated attributes can be investigated at various levels of detail or aggregation.
Provide focus	A good data model should be focused on the data associated with a single system and contained within a single system boundary.
Minimally redundant	A good data model will display minimal redundancy with regard to repeated entity types, data redundancy, and many-to-many relationships.
Transparent	The actual data and the physical structure of the database should be discernable from looking at the graphical data model.
Easily navigated	A good data model should be laid out in an organized fashion to allow for the relationships among the entities to be easily followed.
Predicts the final system	A good data model should be an accurate prediction of the physical implementation of the system.

implementation. The process by which we organize the data attributes contained within the logical data model so that they are grouped in a stable and flexible manner is called *normalization*. This process can be metaphorically thought of as a filtration process for the data such that they are reorganized to conform to a simple set of rules regarding the relationships between various data attributes. The terminology often contributes to making the process sound more difficult than it actually is.

Table 6-5 Example of a Relation for STUDENT

Student_ID	Student_Name	Student_Major	Student_FinAid	Student_Status
279265487	Mark O'Broek	Business	Stafford	Active
301658974	Sam Waterson	Chemistry	None	Active
105455531	Margaret Delaney	Music	None	Graduated
230987413	Susan Santana	Anthropology	Pell	Active
726521324	Christine Lorenzo	Business	BAT fellowship	Inactive

STUDENT(*Student_ID,* Student_Name,Student_Major,Student_FinAid,Student_Status)

By following a simple three-step process with the data, however, the normalization process can be easily conducted and successfully completed.

The Concept of Functional Dependency

The normalization process is based on a concept called *functional dependence,* which refers to a specific relationship between two attributes. Using a formal definition given by Dutka and Hanson (1989), we define functional dependency as follows:

> For any relation R, attribute B is functionally dependent on attribute A if, for every valid instance of A, that value of A uniquely determines the value of B.

In other words, if one attribute can be used to determine the value of one or more other attributes, they are said to be functionally dependent on one another. The process of normalization is designed to create a controlled set of dependencies that conform to specific constraints. On successful completion, we have our data organized such that maintenance is easy and redundancy is minimized. (Sometimes too minimized, but we will get back to that.)

Table 6-6 contains a summary of the three steps in the normalization process and the constraints imposed on the data at each step. The following discussion describes the process in greater detail and provides examples of its application to some familiar data.

Table 6-6 The Three Common Normalized Forms

Normal Form	Description
First normal form (1NF)	A relation is in 1NF if it contains no repeating data elements.
Second normal form (2NF)	A relation is in 2NF if it is in 1NF and contains no partial functional dependencies.
Third normal form (3NF)	A relation is in 3NF if it is in 2NF and contains no transitive dependencies.

First Normal Form

The first step in the normalization process is to place the data into *first normal form* (1NF). A relation is considered to be in 1NF if it contains *no repeating elements*. This suggests that any entity that contains one or more multivalued attributes must be transformed.

Figure 6-10(a) shows the data attributes associated with an order form for a typical CD shop. For our purposes, we assume that this represents the entire set of data for the business (we know, of course, that a typical business has a much larger data model; this just makes it easier to see). Note that all attributes associated with the order form are single-valued, with the exception of those associated with OR-DERED_PRODUCT. These attributes are multivalued, because for each instance of the entity ORDER, they can occur from 1 to *n* times. Our first task is to put this entity in 1NF by removing the repeating elements. The question then becomes, what do we do with the elements we just removed from the entity ORDER?

The presence of repeating elements, or multivalued attributes, in one entity actually describes another entity. In Figure 6-10(b), we see that following the 1NF transformation we have two entities, ORDER and ORDERED_PRODUCT. Also notice that our new entity has a concatenated key made up of PRODUCT_ID and ORDER_NUMBER. This creates a relationship between a single instance of the entity ORDER with one or more instances of the entity ORDERED_PRODUCT (1:M). In other words, one ORDER can contain many PRODUCTS.

Figure 6-10 First Normal Form

(a)

ORDER
ORDER NUMBER
ORDER DATE
CUSTOMER NUMBER
CUSTOMER NAME
CUSTOMER STREET
CUSTOMER CITY
CUSTOMER STATE
CUSTOMER ZIP CODE
CUSTOMER PHONE
ORDERED PRODUCT (repeats 1 – n times)
    PRODUCT ID
    QUANTITY
    DESCRIPTION
    UNIT PRICE
    EXTENDED PRICE
ORDER SUBTOTAL
SALES TAX
SHIPPING
ORDER TOTAL

(b)

ORDER
ORDER NUMBER
ORDER DATE
CUSTOMER NUMBER
CUSTOMER NAME
CUSTOMER STREET
CUSTOMER CITY
CUSTOMER STATE
CUSTOMER ZIP CODE
CUSTOMER PHONE
ORDER SUBTOTAL
SALES TAX
SHIPPING
ORDER TOTAL

ORDERED PRODUCT
PRODUCT ID + ORDER NUMBER
QUANTITY
DESCRIPTION
UNIT PRICE
EXTENDED PRICE

Second Normal Form

Once all of our data have been converted to 1NF, we can move to the next step in the normalization process. A relation is in *second normal form* (2NF) if it is already in 1NF and it contains *no partial functional dependencies*. A partial functional dependency exists when one or more of the *nonkey* attributes can be defined by less than the *full* primary key.

In Figure 6-11(a), we see our 1NF data for the CD shop. We have two entities, ORDER and ORDERED_PRODUCT. Because 2NF is focused only on those attributes that can be described by *less than the full primary key*, we actually only need to look at those relations that have a concatenated key. If a relation has a single-valued key and is in 1NF, then by default, it is already in 2NF. Because of this, we focus our attention on the ORDERED_PRODUCT entity.

To determine if a relation is in 2NF we need to see if the value of any of the attributes in the relation can be derived by using only part of the key rather than all of it. Turning to our ORDERED_PRODUCT relation we see that certain attributes are dependent on the entire key. For example, QUANTITY cannot be derived from less than the entire key. With only the ORDER_NUMBER we would not know which PRODUCT_ID was being referred to, and with only PRODUCT_ID we would be unable to determine which instance of ORDER was being referred to. Turning to DESCRIPTION, however, we see what appears to be a partial functional dependency. We can easily derive the value of DESCRIPTION using only the PRODUCT_ID portion of the key. To resolve this situation, and to complete the transfor-

Figure 6-11   Second Normal Form

(a)

ORDER
ORDER NUMBER
ORDER DATE
CUSTOMER NUMBER
CUSTOMER NAME
CUSTOMER STREET
CUSTOMER CITY
CUSTOMER STATE
CUSTOMER ZIPCODE
CUSTOMER PHONE
ORDER SUBTOTAL
SALES TAX
SHIPPING
ORDER TOTAL

ORDERED PRODUCT
PRODUCT ID + ORDER NUMBER
QUANTITY
DESCRIPTION
UNIT PRICE
EXTENDED PRICE

(b)

ORDER
ORDER NUMBER
ORDER DATE
CUSTOMER NUMBER
CUSTOMER NAME
CUSTOMER STREET
CUSTOMER CITY
CUSTOMER STATE
CUSTOMER ZIPCODE
CUSTOMER PHONE
ORDER SUBTOTAL
SALES TAX
SHIPPING
ORDER TOTAL

ORDERED PRODUCT
PRODUCT ID + ORDER NUMBER
QUANTITY
UNIT PRICE
EXTENDED PRICE

PRODUCT
PRODUCT ID
DESCRIPTION

mation to 2NF, we need to create an entity that has only PRODUCT_ID as its primary key. In Figure 6-11(b), we see our new entity, PRODUCT, with PRODUCT_ID as the primary key and DESCRIPTION as the only nonkey attribute. By making this transformation we have all our data in 2NF, and we can proceed with the process. By the way, notice how we started this process with a single entity derived from a single data capture form, but we now have three related entities.

One additional observation about the entity PRODUCT should be made. It may have occurred to you that the UNIT_PRICE may also be a partial functional dependency, because it could probably be derived from the PRODUCT_ID alone. This is an example of one of the many design tradeoffs that must be faced by a systems analyst. If we move the attribute UNIT_PRICE to the PRODUCT entity, we are faced with a dilemma: What if we want to change the price for a single customer? Although we certainly could do that, we would never be able to retrieve the ORDER with the actual price we sold the item at. This is because UNIT_PRICE would be retrieved from the PRODUCT entity rather than from the ORDERED_PRODUCT entity. To insure that the history of all transactions remains accurate, UNIT_PRICE should be left as an attribute of ORDERED_PRODUCT.

Third Normal Form

The final step in the process is the transformation to *third normal form* (3NF).[1] A relation is considered to be in 3NF if it is already in 2NF and no *transitive dependencies* exist. A transitive dependency is found when one or more *nonkey* attributes can be derived from one or more other nonkey attributes. In other words, the value of a nonkey attribute must be a function of the key, the whole key, and nothing but the key (Davis, 1994). Although not as rigorous as the more formal definition provided first, this second definition expresses the same concept and is a lot easier to remember.

Figure 6-12(a) shows all of the relations and their attributes we have transformed from the beginning of the process. We know all are in 2NF, so we are free to focus on the 3NF transformation. Starting with the ORDER relation, we find that the nonkey attributes of CUSTOMER_NAME, CUSTOMER_STREET, CUSTOMER_CITY, CUSTOMER_STATE, CUSTOMER_ZIPCODE, and CUSTOMER_PHONE all depend on nonkey attribute CUSTOMER_NUMBER but not on the primary key attribute of ORDER_NUMBER. To correct this situation, we must create a new relation, CUSTOMER, and move the appropriate attributes to it. As shown in 12(b), we started with one relation and now we have four.

Another example of a transitive dependency can be found in the ORDERED_PRODUCT relation. The nonkey attribute EXTENDED_PRICE can actually be derived by multiplying QUANTITY times UNIT_PRICE. This type of transitive dependency is called a *calculated value* and must be removed during the 3NF transformation process. Unlike the past steps, however, where we have moved the attribute to another relation, when a calculated value is encountered, we simply remove it altogether. We do not really need to store the value in the database, because anytime we need it, say for a report, we can simply perform the necessary calculations and print the derived value. This eliminates the storage of redundant data and creates a set of relations that are highly stable.

Note that ORDER_TOTAL, although conceivably a value that could be calculated, has not been eliminated. This is because the time it would take to recalculate the individual order totals from their associated transactions might outweigh the

---

[1] To be absolutely correct, there are actually five normal forms. The first three, however, have become the standard for normalization, and the remaining two are rarely used. For the interested reader, a thorough discussion of the five normal forms can be found in Kent (1983).

(a)

ORDER
ORDER NUMBER
ORDER DATE
CUSTOMER NUMBER
CUSTOMER NAME
CUSTOMER STREET
CUSTOMER CITY
CUSTOMER STATE
CUSTOMER ZIPCODE
CUSTOMER PHONE
ORDER SUBTOTAL
SALES TAX
SHIPPING
ORDER TOTAL

ORDERED PRODUCT
PRODUCT ID + ORDER NUMBER
QUANTITY
UNIT PRICE
EXTENDED PRICE

PRODUCT
PRODUCT ID
DESCRIPTION

(b)

ORDER
ORDER NUMBER
ORDER DATE
CUSTOMER NUMBER
ORDER SUBTOTAL
SALES TAX
SHIPPING
ORDER TOTAL

ORDERED PRODUCT
PRODUCT ID + ORDER NUMBER
QUANTITY
UNIT PRICE

PRODUCT
PRODUCT ID
DESCRIPTION

CUSTOMER
CUSTOMER NUMBER
CUSTOMER NAME
CUSTOMER STREET
CUSTOMER CITY
CUSTOMER STATE
CUSTOMER ZIPCODE
CUSTOMER PHONE

Figure 6-12   Third Normal Form

benefits associated with the reduction in data redundancy by eliminating it. In the next section, we look more closely at this special situation in which our normalized set of relations may need to be altered slightly to improve the final performance of our system.

Denormalization

The value of the normalization process lies in the resultant set of organized, non-redundant, and stable relations that are created as a result. Notwithstanding this valuable outcome, however, the normalized set of relations, although technically correct, may actually create certain potential inefficiencies in the final physical database. To facilitate the delicate balance between stability, redundancy, and efficiency in the final set of relations, we may need to consider situations in which we need to *denormalize* the data slightly.

In Figure 6-13(a), we see our normalized relations for ORDER and ORDERED_PRODUCT. From these two relations, we can calculate the value of all transactions for the business on a daily basis. At the end of each day, we can run a report that totals all of the transactions for that day and reports how much we have

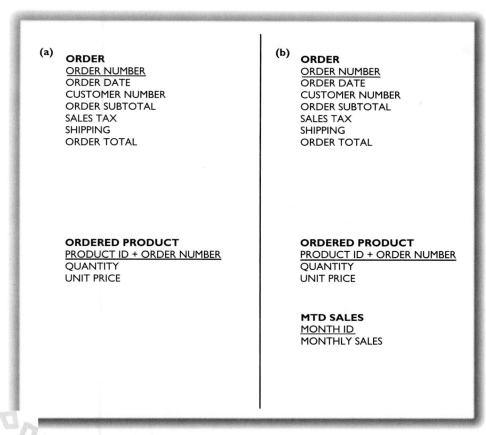

Figure 6-13   Example of Denormalization

sold. Because we have this data available, we could also run reports that give us totals for sales on a monthly or even yearly basis. Here is where the problem begins.

Suppose we want to run a report on year-to-date (YTD) sales at the end of every month. Let us assume the business generates about 1,000 transactions per day and is open seven days a week. From this, we can estimate the need to add up about 31,000 transactions to calculate our YTD sales figure at the end of January. If our system requires 0.001 seconds per transaction to retrieve the data and calculate the total, the report takes approximately 31 seconds to run (31,000 transactions x 0.001 per transaction). Although not instantaneous, this is not an unacceptable figure.

Now suppose we want to run the same YTD sales report on December 31. Not accounting for holiday closings, we have 365,000 transactions to add up to create our total. Using the same multiplier of 0.001 seconds per transaction, our report takes 365 seconds, or 6 minutes and 5 seconds, to run. If the volume of the business should double from the present levels, this same report could take over 12 minutes to run.

In such circumstances, the analyst, in an effort to improve system performance, may decide to violate the strict approach to data normalization and choose to create one or more relations that are not fully normalized according to the rules. Referring to Figure 13(b), the analyst may wish to establish a relation called MTD_SALES, which contains the total sales for each month of the year. Because this relation contains values that could be calculated from other existing data, it cannot be considered to be in 3NF. The effect on performance, however, is easy to see.

By creating a relation that stores MTD sales, we actually only need to look at one transaction for each month of operation when running the YTD sales report. On January 31, our YTD report takes 0.001 seconds to run and on December 31, our YTD report takes 0.012 seconds (12 transactions × 0.001 seconds per transaction). This is an example in which less than fully normalized relations perform better than those that are fully normalized. This decision, however, cannot be made until after all the data have been transformed into 3NF.

The Fully Normalized ERD

Once the normalization process is complete, a fully normalized ERD can be constructed showing all the entities, their attributes, and their relationships to all other entities. From this logical data model, the physical model of the database can be easily constructed. We explore the process of actually building the database from the logical model in chapter 10.

Figure 6-14 illustrates our fully normalized logical data model created from a single order form.

Figure 6-14   Fully Normalized ERD

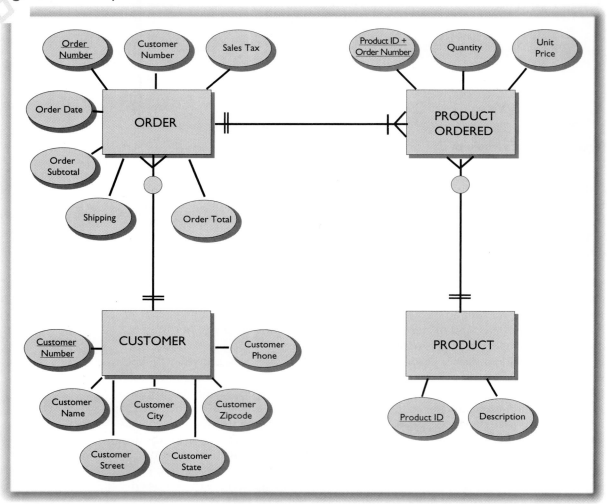

CHAPTER SUMMARY

In this chapter we developed the skills necessary to model the characteristics of the data themselves and the relationships between the various data entities and elements within our IS. As with the DFD, the ERD by itself is not capable of fully defining an IS. It must be used in harmony with the DFD and the logic models to insure that both the process-centric perspective and the data-centric perspective are reflected in the final design.

The skill set for data modeling, as we know it today, is dependent on the need for database technology at the core of a modern IS and the pervasive nature of the relational model as data structure of choice. Despite the rapid advancements in the development of IS, databases will be around for many years to come. As for the relational model, there are two perspectives.

Some maintain that the relational model will ultimately meet its demise at the hands of the object-oriented approach. The argument is that the relational model is incapable of handling the demands for new data storage, such as video, audio, and other large-size data elements. Others, including myself, believe that the relational model is alive and well and will continue to be the predominate choice for database implementation. This belief is based on the fact that whereas the relational model was not originally conceived to handle such unique types of data, there is no physical or logical reason why it cannot. The relational model is already evolving to include object technologies and features and should be quite capable of meeting the increased demands for such design approaches for many years to come. There are application scenarios in which a pure object-oriented approach is the superior choice, but for the majority of database implementations the relational model is still the predominate approach.

KEY CONCEPTS

➤ Data modeling

The data model graphically illustrates the nature of the data used by a system in terms of the rules and their relationships by which it operates.

➤ The ERD

• Entities

An entity is anything about which we want to store data, such as people, places, objects, or events.

• Attributes

An attribute is a characteristic or descriptive property of an entity or a relationship.

• Relationships

A relationship is an association between one or more entities that is of interest to the organization or business environment.

• Associative entities

When an M:N relationship occurs, we create an associative entity, or gerund.

An associative entity inherits its primary key from more than one other entity, with each part of its concatenated key pointing to one, and only one, instance of each connecting entity.

• Multivalued attributes

The multivalued attribute is a special type of attribute that can take on multiple values for a single entity instance.

➤ Two important characteristics of entities

1. They can be distinguished from all of the other entities in the business environment by some set of identifying characteristics or attributes

2. They represent a class of thing that can occur more than once within the business environment

➤ Entity type

An entity type is a collection of entities that all share one or more common properties or attributes.

➤ Entity instance

An entity instance represents a single, unique occurrence of a member of an entity type.

➤ Key attributes

The key attributes are a particular type of attribute that uniquely identifies and differentiates one entity instance from all other possible entity instances of an entity. The key is a single attribute, or group of attributes, that assumes a value unique to that entity instance.

• Candidate key

A candidate key is a candidate to become the primary identifier for each instance of an entity.

• Primary key

The primary key is the candidate key chosen to uniquely identify a single instance of an entity. The criteria for selecting a primary key include

• Stability
• Nonnull
• Noninformational
• Simplicity

➤ Relationships are identified by three basic characteristics of complexity:

• Cardinality

Cardinality indicates the number of instances of one entity in a relationship that are associated with each instance of the other entities in that relationship.

• Optionality

Optionality is the degree to which a particular relationship is mandatory or optional.

• Degree

The degree of a relationship indicates the number of entities that are participating in that relationship.

• Unary (recursive relationship)

A unary relationship contains a single entity and thus has a degree of 1.

• Binary

A binary relationship contains two entities and thus has a degree of 2.

• Ternary

A ternary relationship contains three entities and thus has a degree of 3.

➤ General procedure for identifying entities and their relationships

• Determine system entities
• Identify entity attributes
• Determine entity keys
• Determine relationships and degrees
• Determine cardinalities and optionalities

➤ The process of logical data modeling has three basic purposes

1. Formal structuring of the data into a more stable and desirable form through a process called normalization

2. Development of a data model in a form that allows for the actual data needs of the organizational system to be accurately reflected

3. The development of a data model that allows for the construction of a physical database design

➤ Characteristics of a good data model

• Pictorial
• Rigorous and specific
• Top-down decomposable
• Provides focus
• Minimally redundant
• Transparent
• Easily navigated
• Predicts the final system

➤ The relational data model

The relational data model consists of relations represented as two-dimensional tables of data. Each table is composed of named columns that represent the attributes and unnamed rows that represent unique instances of the entity.

➤ Functional dependency

For a relation R, attribute B is functionally dependent on attribute A if, for every valid instance of A, that value of A uniquely determines the value of B.

➤ Data normalization

Data normalization is the process by which we organize the data attributes contained within the logical data model so that they are grouped in a stable and flexible manner.

• First normal form (1NF)

A relation is considered to be in 1NF if it contains no repeating elements.

- Second normal form (2NF)

A relation is considered to be in 2NF if it is already in 1NF and it contains no partial functional dependencies. A partial functional dependency exists where one or more of the nonkey attributes can be defined by less than the full primary key.

- Third normal form (3NF)

A relation is considered to be in 3NF if it is already in 2NF and no transitive dependencies exist. A transitive depend-

ency is found where one or more non-key attributes can be derived from one or more other nonkey attributes.

➤ Denormalization

In some circumstances the analyst, in an effort to improve system performance, may decide to violate the strict approach to data normalization and choose to create one or more relations that are not fully normalized according to the rule.

QUESTIONS FOR REVIEW

1. Explain the concept of data modeling.

2. List and briefly describe the components of an ERD.

3. What are the two most important characteristics of an entity?

4. Distinguish an entity type and an entity instance.

5. Define key attributes, candidate keys, and primary keys.

6. List and briefly explain the criteria for selecting a primary key from a list of candidate keys.

7. What are the three basic characteristics of complexity that identify relationships?

8. Explain the three basic types of relationships according to their degrees.

9. Under what circumstances should an analyst consider creating an associative entity?

10. Where do we begin the data modeling process? Explain your rationale.

11. List and briefly describe the general procedure for identifying entities and their relationships.

12. What is the purpose of logical data modeling?

13. What are the characteristics of a good data model?

14. Explain what tables, columns, and rows represent in a relational data model.

15. Explain the concept of data normalization.

16. Describe the concept of functional dependency.

17. List and describe the three common normalization forms.

18. Describe the circumstances under which an analyst would consider denormalization.

FOR FURTHER DISCUSSION

1. Lake Lemon University is considering the development of a computer-based system to assist in the process of assigning classrooms for scheduled courses. A classroom is simply a room within a particular building, and all buildings on campus contain at least one classroom. A classroom is scheduled for a particular time and day or days of the week. If a class is listed on the course schedule, then it must have a classroom assigned to it.

   Draw an ERD that accurately models the relationship between the three entities CLASSROOM, BUILDING, and SCHEDULED COURSE.

2. Bubba's Healthy Snacks sells a wide variety of tasty, but healthy, treats. Each of the treats contains several ingredients, each of which is hand picked for quality from a variety of reputable vendors. Bubba is meticulous about quality, and once she finds a vendor that supplies the highest quality ingredient, she always buys that ingredient from that same vendor. In some cases, a vendor may have more than one ingredient that meets Bubba's strict standards. Bubba has several product managers that work with her, and each of the product managers is responsible for more than one product. Bubba is also convinced that she has assigned the best manager to the most appropriate product, so no product is ever managed by more than one product manager.

   Draw an ERD that accurately models the relationships in the preceding scenario.

3. Using your local bank as an example, draw an ERD that models the various relationships that exist among customers, different types of accounts, and typical transactions. Include whatever attributes you believe are appropriate, and identify a primary key for each entity in your model.

4. Don Fraser is the head of a large corporate MIS department. He wants to construct a database to keep track of all of the hardware and software managed by the department. He has assigned you to develop the data model.

   Through your experience with the company, you know that they own network servers, client workstations, and a variety of peripherals. In addition, they own a wide variety of software applications that require management of licenses and renewals. Some of the software licenses are for a single workstation, whereas others allow for a fixed number of users to access them simultaneously. In other words, one network license can authorize a specific number of individual users. Don said he is specifically interested in knowing where all of the licenses are installed. He also pointed out that some licenses have not yet been installed, and he wants to know that, too. In addition, he explained to you that he must be able to verify the currency and legality of any license on demand. Thus, we must be able to trace the source of the license to either a purchase order or a gift. Finally, because we are constantly ordering software and licenses all the time, we need to know what we have coming in with regard to licenses.

   Draw an ERD for DON, and suggest appropriate attributes and keys for each of the identified entities.

5. Try interviewing a family member or friend to elicit the information necessary to construct a data model of a common set of business rules they typically must adhere to at work.

REFERENCES

Chen, P. P-S. 1976. "The Entity-Relationship Model—Toward a Unified View of the Data." *ACM Transactions on Database Systems* 1: 9–36.

Codd, E. F. 1970. "A Relational Model of Data for Large Relational Databases." *Communications of the ACM* 13: 77–87.

Davis, W. S. 1994. *Business Systems Analysis and Design*. Belmont, CA: Wadsworth Publishing.

Dutka, A. F., and H. H. Hanson. 1989. *Fundamentals of Data Normalization*. Reading, MA: Addison-Wesley.

Kent, W. 1983. "A Simple Guide to Five Normal Forms in Relational Database Theory." *Communications of the ACM* 26: 120–25.

Martin, J., and C. Finkelstein. 1981. *Information Engineering*. New York: Savant Institute.

Storey, V. C. 1991. "Relational Database Design Based on the Entity-Relationship Model." *Data and Knowledge Engineering* 7: 47–83.

Teorey, T. J., D. Yang, and J. P. Fry. 1986. "A Logical Design Methodology for Relational Databases Using the Extended Entity-Relationship Model." *Computing Surveys* 18: 197–221.

CASE Tools and Joint and Rapid Application Development

Learning Objectives

■ Understand the history and evolution of CASE tools

■ Understand the motivations to adopt CASE in the modern organization

■ Appreciate the advantages and disadvantages associated with CASE tool adoption and use

■ Learn the components, relationships, and functions contained in a modern CASE tool

■ Understand the processes associated with JAD

■ Learn the various participant roles associated with a JAD session

■ Understand the relationship between the RAD approach and the traditional SDLC

Engineers ... are not superhuman. They make mistakes in their assumptions, in their calculations, in their conclusions. That they make mistakes is forgivable; that they catch them is imperative. Thus it is the essence of modern engineering not only to be able to check one's own work but also to have one's work checked and to be able to check the work of others.

—HENRY PETROSKI, A. S. VESIC PROFESSOR
OF CIVIL ENGINEERING, DUKE UNIVERSITY

INTRODUCTION

The history of SAD has been one of evolution and refinement in the tools and techniques used by the analyst to identify the organizational problems of interest and to provide effective solutions to them. Much of the process, however refined, is nonetheless quite labor intensive and often requires prototyping screens and reports, determining process flows, formulating data definitions, and long hours of tedious drawing and redrawing of models. Once the analysis and design phases are completed, the software must be built and thoroughly tested before it can be successfully implemented. In an effort to streamline and improve the overall efficiency and effectiveness of the analysis and design activities, IS professionals have developed several tools and techniques that serve to automate or speed up certain common activities. This chapter focuses on two such developments: (1) *CASE tools* and (2) *RAD techniques*.

CASE TOOLS

The acronym CASE stands for *computer-aided software engineering*. In simple layman terms, CASE is a tool that aids a software engineer to maintain and develop software. Although numerous formal definitions of CASE can be found throughout the IS literature, to list or attempt to list them would serve only to define confusion and not CASE. The best way to understand CASE is to start with an appreciation of its history and evolution to its present state.

The Evolution and History of CASE Tools

The concept of tools to aid or assist human beings in their activities can be traced back 1,750,000 years ago (after the dinosaurs or possibly a meteor crashed the "big system") to early man. At that time, human beings were at a great physical disadvantage in comparison to their counterpart other carnivores who had tearing claws and long sharp incisors to hunt and get at the meat of their prey. Therefore, to stay in the game (and not become the game) human beings began to intelligently use naturally formed sharp tools, such as rocks and wood. Eventually, human beings began to manufacture tools to aid them in the hunt and to protect them from other hunters.

Human beings since then have adapted their behavior, social structure, and many other attributes—including the concept of using tools to aid in human activities. This is apparent in a whole range of many disciplines varying from medicine to motor mechanics. The latest recruit to this concept is the discipline of software engineering.

One of the first tools used in software development was the humble word processor. The editor or word processor was an excellent tool for holding and manipulating the many documents associated with the specification and design of an IS. The late 1960s and early 1970s saw the introduction of graphical techniques such as hierarchical input-process-output (HIPO) charts and structured DFDs.

The arrival of data flow design and structural analysis led to the concept of the *data dictionary*, a document that contains details of each of the data types and data elements within a system. Eventually, automated graphic tools were integrated with the data dictionary concept to produce powerful design and development tools that could hold complete design cycle documents from specification through to design and finally code. The final step in this evolution was to add tools intended to assist in the validation and cross-checking of the system. Figure 7-1 contains a graphical illustration of the evolution of the modern CASE tool.

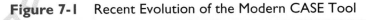

Figure 7-1   Recent Evolution of the Modern CASE Tool

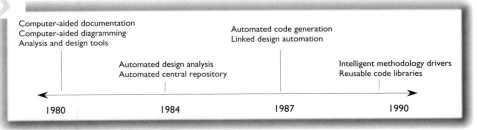

WHY BOTHER WITH CASE ?

It is apparent with today's rapid advancement of technology that the cost of computer hardware is decreasing considerably, whereas, conversely, the cost of software development is escalating. Table 7-1 provides several examples of the cost of developing modern software applications.

The main reason for the high cost of software is that development of software technology is extremely labor intensive, as reflected by Table 7-1. Software projects are often very large, involving a huge number of people and spanning over many years. Further, the development of these systems is often conducted in an ad hoc fashion, resulting in dire consequences.

In 1996, we witnessed the destruction of the space shuttle Ariane, due to errors in the software maintenance. The cost of these errors was in excess of $900 million. Even more recently, the $328 million Mars climate orbiter was lost due to a simple error in the software controlling the spacecraft (NASA 1999a). This error, however, was human, as evidenced by NASA's press conference of September 23, 1999:

> "Early this morning at about 2 A.M. Pacific Daylight Time the orbiter fired its main engine to go into orbit around the planet. All the information coming from the spacecraft leading up to that point looked normal. The engine burn began as planned five minutes before the spacecraft passed behind the planet as seen from Earth. Flight controllers did not detect a signal when the spacecraft was expected to come out from behind the planet.
>
> "We had planned to approach the planet at an altitude of about 150 kilometers (93 miles). We thought we were doing that, but upon review of the last six to eight hours of data leading up to arrival, we saw indications that the actual approach altitude had been much lower. It appears that the actual altitude was about 60 kilometers (37 miles). We are still trying to figure out why that happened," said Richard Cook, project manager for the Mars Surveyor Operations Project at NASA's Jet Propulsion Laboratory. "We believe that the minimum survivable altitude for the spacecraft would have been 85 kilometers (53 miles)." (NASA 1999b)

A major investigation was immediately launched by NASA. The peer review findings indicated that one software development team used English units (e.g., inches, feet, and pounds), whereas another used metric units for the key spacecraft

Table 7-1 Development Costs for Several Modern Software Applications

Product	Cost $	Effort (man years)	Lines of Code
Lotus 1-2-3 V 3.0	22,000,000	263	400,000
NASA space shuttle	1,200,000,000	22,096	25,600
2000 Lincoln Continental	2,800,000	37	93,500
Modern automatic teller machine	13,200,000	150	780,000
IBM retail checkout scanner	3,000,000	58	90,000

altitude stabilization operation. This information was critical to the maneuvers required to place the spacecraft in the proper Mars orbit.

> "Our inability to recognize and correct this simple error has had major implications," said Dr. Edward Stone, director of the Jet Propulsion Laboratory. "We have underway a thorough investigation to understand this issue." (NASA 1999c)

Hence, there is an urgent need for proper and consistent methodologies, techniques, and tools. CASE offers an important opportunity to alleviate these problems of application development and maintenance that can have catastrophic consequences.

The Objectives of CASE

The basic idea behind CASE is to support each phase of the SDLC with a set of laborsaving tools. Some CASE tools concentrate on supporting the early phases of the life cycle by providing automated assistance in the form of diagramming tools, screen design and generation, and accuracy and consistency checking. Such CASE tools are commonly referred to as *Upper CASE*. Others focus only on the implementation phases of the life cycle. They include automated code and test case generators. Intuitively enough, these tools are referred to as *Lower CASE* tools. Most recently, however, CASE tools have evolved into sophisticated applications that can support the entire analysis, design, and implementation process. These *life cycle–spanning CASE tools* (often referred to as *I-CASE* or integrated CASE) are rapidly becoming the standard for computer-assisted software development. Table 7-2 lists some of the common objectives associated with adoption of a life cycle–spanning CASE tool.

The Good News and the Bad News about CASE

The good news about CASE is that many of the objectives associated with the adoption of a modern CASE tool into an organization can, over time, be achieved. The productivity gains derived from developing new applications through the CASE environment are clear. Time to working prototype, time to delivery, and time devoted to system testing and maintenance are all materially decreased when a CASE tool is employed. In addition, the overall quality of the final application is generally better

Table 7-2   Common Objectives for CASE Tool Adoption

- Create development process standards
- Improve overall application quality
- Decrease design time and improve time to market
- Decrease required effort and time in application testing
- Encourage integration of development projects
- Improve effectiveness of project management activities
- Decrease required effort and time in application maintenance activities
- Promote organization-wide reusable program code
- Improve portability of applications across platforms and operating environments

due to the effectiveness of the CASE tool functions, which focus on checking correctness and consistency. Further, the documentation associated with an application developed in a CASE environment is generally of a higher quality. This because the CASE tool makes it much easier for the analyst team to assemble consistent, detailed system documentation. Finally, the enforcement of a consistent set of development standards throughout the organization is more easily realized and achieved when using a CASE tool as the primary vehicle for application development and revision.

There is no such thing as a free lunch, however, and the benefits associated with the adoption of CASE technology are likewise not free. First of all, the acquisition and implementation of a modern CASE tool environment is a relatively expensive proposition. Jones (1993) estimated the cost per workstation to range from $5,000 to $50,000 each, depending on desired functionality. In addition, the training costs for a modern CASE tool installation have been estimated to be between $0.50 and $1.00 for every $1.00 spent on the tool itself. In short, adopting a CASE tool is a major organizational investment.

This leads to another potential barrier to adoption. As we see in the next chapter, there are tools available for evaluating the return on investment associated with the development or acquisition of a software application and its associated hardware. Regardless of the method employed, the evaluation of an investment is based on the amount of money spent versus the amount and timing of the expected returns. Generally speaking, the faster the investment provides a positive return, the better the investment is. That puts CASE tools at a distinct disadvantage when attempting to justify the large cost of acquisition. The benefits, or returns, associated with CASE tools are typically realized in the latter phases of the SDLC and, in many cases, although the overall development time may be reduced through the use of automated code-generators, the time spent in the early stages of a project may actually be increased by as much as 30–40 percent (Stone 1993). Because of this, the return on investment of a modern CASE tool is often longer than the organization would prefer, thus making it a harder sell.

One final potential barrier to adoption is that although most organizations acknowledge the need for a common set of development standards and a formal methodological approach to software development, it is rare that an organization has formal policies and standards in place. The adoption of a CASE tool, although it provides the facility to enforce such standards, is also somewhat of a culture shock to analysts that are not accustomed to operating according to a formal development plan. This learning curve and adaptation period can be quite lengthy, thus further prolonging the realization of benefits from the CASE tool. Table 7-3 summarizes the good and bad news about CASE.

Overall, however, CASE tool adoption is increasing, and the costs are beginning to come down for many of the most sophisticated offerings. As time progresses, the various technologies associated with the development of a modern CASE tool will mature, thus driving the costs down even further. In the near future, CASE technology will emerge as a standard tool in virtually every development environment.

The Components and Functions of Modern CASE Tools

Although every commercial offering of a modern CASE tool is unique in some respect, all *I-CASE* offerings provide a set of integrated tools and functions that are intended to logically support the development life cycle activities. In this section, we discuss the functionality typically associated with a life cycle–spanning CASE tool.

Table 7-3 The Good News and the Bad News about CASE Tool Adoption

The Good News	The Bad News
• Development process productivity and quality increases are realizable	• CASE acquisition costs are extremely high
• Portability of new systems to other platforms is greatly enhanced	• Training of analysts and administrators is costly and time-consuming
• Analyst skill set will improve due to greater understanding of the process	• Most organizations do not have clear standards for application development
• Time to delivery of new applications will decrease	• CASE tools can be viewed as a threat to job security
• Conformity to development standards will increase	• CASE tools do not have a great reputation due to early benefits not being realized

Figure 7-2 illustrates the relationships among the various components of the modern CASE tool.

The Central Repository

The *central repository* of a CASE tool is a sophisticated central database that serves as the nerve center for all CASE tool functions. The repository serves as the central storage and retrieval location for all information related to project management, data specification, diagram components, and report designs and content. In essence, the repository stores all of the information necessary to analyze, create, design, and

Figure 7-2 Component Relationships in Modern I-CASE Tools

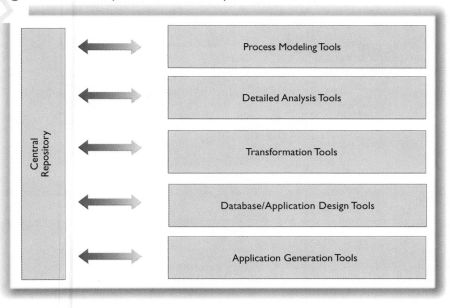

modify a software application from the preliminary feasibility analysis through final implementation and maintenance. Figure 7-3 shows the elements typically stored in the central repository of a modern CASE tool.

One important benefit to having a central repository is the realization of *reusable code.* Throughout the history of software development, a great deal of the functionality of applications has been duplicated because it has been easier to write the code again than to locate and test some previously written code that performed the same function. Think for a moment about the number of times code has been written to create a simple routine for entering and storing a date. This constant reinvention process, over time, contributes to an immense loss of productivity. The advent of the central repository allows for significant portions of prior systems to be

Figure 7-3   Typical Elements Stored in CASE Tool Central Repository

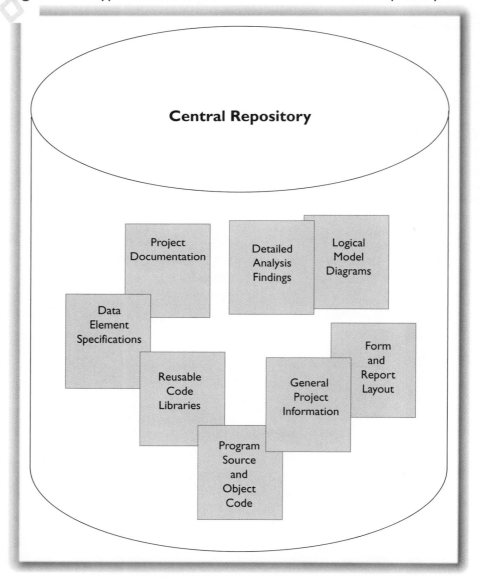

reused in new applications. This results in reduced development time and greatly improved software quality.

Modeling and Diagramming Tools

Much of the work performed by an analyst during the analysis phases of the SDLC involves the development of logical models of processes and data structures. The CASE environment provides several *diagramming tools* to assist in the development and testing of such models.

A *process modeler* can be used to develop a diagram that illustrates the activities within an organization system and the sequence in which they take place. Most businesses are relatively complex, so such a model is likely to consist of a number of steps, each showing part of the overall process.

Modeling business processes creates an understanding of how the organization functions, and it serves to illustrate the various departments, individuals, and organizational resources involved. A process model can illustrate how efficient a particular process is, or it could highlight a process that is overly complicated, cumbersome, or redundant. In the case of a new process under consideration, a process model can help ensure its efficiency from the start.

An effective process modeling tool allows for interaction by both technical and nontechnical participants and can allow for the creation of a model that employs animation, sound, and video components. Properly constructed, the process model can bring life to the analysis of organizational processes and can facilitate the confirmation of process steps early in the detailed analysis stage of the life cycle. Figure 7-4 shows a typical process model created by a CASE tool.

Figure 7-4   Case Tool Process Modeler (Oracle Designer)

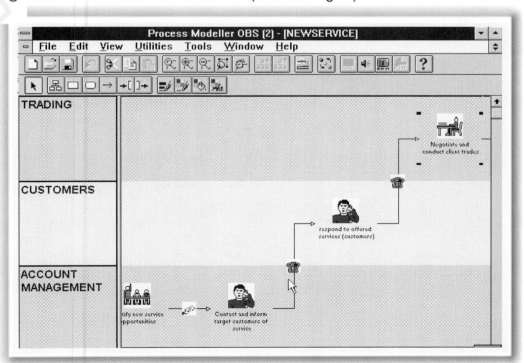

Another common diagramming tool facilitates the modeling of the hierarchies of all the functions that are performed by a business and can assist in identifying which parts of the business are currently, or can be, automated. This type of model is created using a *function hierarchy diagramming* tool. This tool can be used to begin the process of decomposing business functions, identify data needs of those functions, and define the events that trigger them. Figure 7-5 shows a portion of an organization's functional hierarchy diagram.

The diagramming tools devoted to the creation of DFDs and ERDs provide a variety of ways to facilitate the development of logical models for process and data. In addition to providing the basic component shapes for each type of diagram on a simple toolbar, the diagramming tools also allow for the user to have multiple windows open, showing various levels of decomposition for a diagram. When a change is made at one level, all associated levels of the diagram are updated to reflect that change at its proper level of detail. Figures 7.6 and 7.7 provide examples of a context-level data flow and ER diagramming tools in a modern CASE tool.

Prototyping and Transformation Tools

The *transformation tools* enable the rapid conversion of requirements defined during analysis into default database and default application designs. The design created by the transformation tools can be generated as a first-cut implementation of the system and immediately reviewed by the users, thus making for easy prototyping.

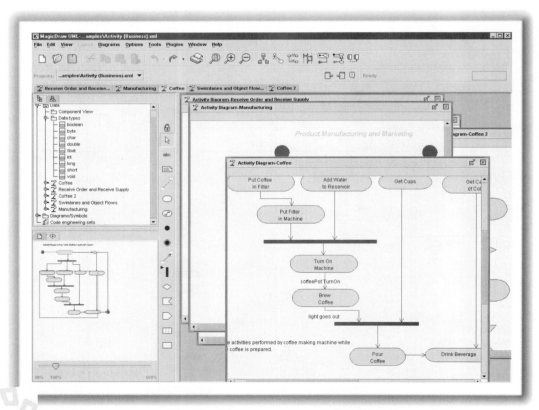

Figure 7-5   CASE Tool Function Hierarchy Diagrammer (Oracle Designer)

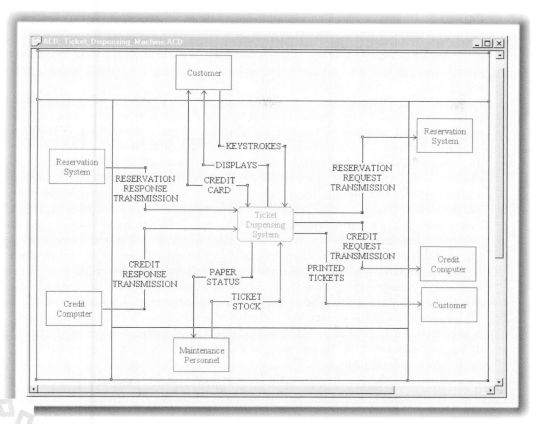

Figure 7-6 Typical Data Flow Diagramming Tool (TurboCASE)

Figure 7-7 CASE Tool Entity-Relationship Modeler (Oracle Designer)

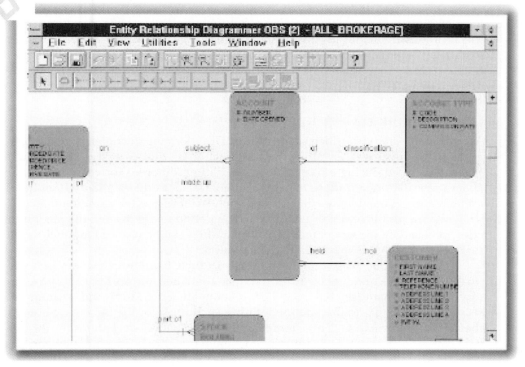

Application transformers create a first-cut application design based on an existing database design and on the functions and business rules placed in the repository during the detailed analysis phase.

The transformation process begins with the conversion of business functions into candidate modules, which can then be implemented as screens, reports, manual procedures, or utilities. The process also converts any relevant data definitions or usages to module-usable data that define how a module uses the tables and columns in the database. The process then converts any module-to-business unit associations into candidate menu modules and structures. These candidate modules are not included in the application design until you choose to accept them. Once the transformation process is complete, the resulting modules and their structures can be used for generating applications using one of the available code generators.

The *database transformer* creates and maintains database designs based on entity models recorded in the central repository. It creates tables to record instances of each entity, columns to store the attributes, and constraints to implement the relationships between entities. It also creates constraints to enforce any unique identifiers that you have defined, as well as indexes to support your foreign keys.

Like the entity model itself, the database design generated by the transformer is stored in the central repository. This model can subsequently be used by other utilities to generate the structured query language (SQL) statements required to create the database itself.

Much like the transformers, the *form and report generators* bring automation to the activities necessary for the analyst to design how the various users interact with the system. Through these generators the analyst can quickly develop on-screen forms and screen or hard-copy reports and can present these prototypes to the user for confirmation or revision. Because the system allows for rapid regeneration of the screens and reports, the analyst can often tailor the interface to the user's specifications in virtually real time. Further, these tools allow the analyst to specify items in the screens and reports that are common to all forms of the interface, such as headers, footers, or specific navigation and function key assignments. Once these specifications are made, all current and future reports and screens inherit them automatically. This allows for a common look and feel to be imparted on the application, thus reducing the time necessary for users to learn the various components of the new system.

Documentation Generators

Ask any good analyst in which phase of the SDLC does the documentation get generated, and the answer is "All of them." The amount and type of documentation that is generated during a particular phase is often different for each application project or each organization, but the common factor is that a good system development effort is one that documents as it goes. Without good documentation, an IS becomes impossible to use or maintain. Hanna (1992) suggests that the amount of effort associated with system maintenance activities can be reduced as much as 400 percent with high quality system documentation.

The *documentation generators* do exactly as their name implies: they generate phase-specific documentation from the data contained within the central repository. One important function of the documentation generator is the creation of a set of master templates that are used during each phase of the life cycle to record the relevant information. These templates provide a set of checkpoints for the analyst team to verify that the appropriate documentation has been generated and that it is complete and accurate. By using a documentation generator, when the system is done, so is the documentation. More important, the documentation is a true representation of the system as built.

Code Generators

The *code generators* contained within a modern CASE tool may represent the most important benefit to adopting CASE technology. These tools produce high-level source code from the various diagrams, models, forms, reports, and data definitions contained within the central repository. The advantage of code generation tools is the flexibility they provide the analyst with regard to what the final platform will be that is used to implement the system. CASE-generated code can be compiled and executed on a wide variety of hardware and operating system platforms with little or no change to the base code. This allows the analyst to avoid being concerned with the final operating platform during the analysis and design stages of the project. Further, the availability of code generators allows for changes required during the maintenance phase of the life cycle to be more quickly put into production. Although the present generation of code generators is still evolving, the goal of 100 percent error-free code is rapidly becoming a reality.

One additional feature of CASE-based code generators is their ability to provide *reverse engineering* and *reengineering functions*. The reverse engineering function allows for the generation of design specifications and models from existing program code and data structures. This literally means that a production application system written in COBOL could be reverse engineered into the CASE tool, modified to allow for new or more effective processes and data structures, and regenerated back out into source code using a completely different programming language, such as C++ or HTML. Given the significant installed base of legacy applications, this functionality could easily pay for itself in a relatively short period of time. Figure 7-8 shows a screenshot from a popular object-oriented reverse engineering tool called Classmapper. Figures 7.9 and 7.10 show a before and after shot of a UNIX-based application regenerated into a Windows environment by a reverse engineering tool from Informix.

Reengineering functions are simply advanced reverse engineering modules that provide a certain level of automation to the redesign process. Their primary distinction is that, in addition to reverse engineering functions, they provide the analyst with a set of tools that can be used to analyze the logic of the program under study and then provide suggested improvements with regard to quality and performance. Figure 7-11 shows an example from a popular reengineering application.

The Future of CASE

The next generation of CASE tools will not only represent refinements to the existing set of common modules but also contain new and more powerful development tools. Code generation and reverse engineering tools will be expanded to include virtually every production language in use. More important, these functions will approach, if not attain, 100 percent error-free code generation, thus reducing preimplementation testing time even further and greatly easing the degree of effort and resources devoted to maintenance activities.

New tools will emerge from the realms of artificial intelligence (AI) and ES. Information-gathering techniques will make use of AI engines that assist the analyst in organizing the volumes of collected data and process specifications into a cohesive set of requirements that generates a foundational set of modules from which to

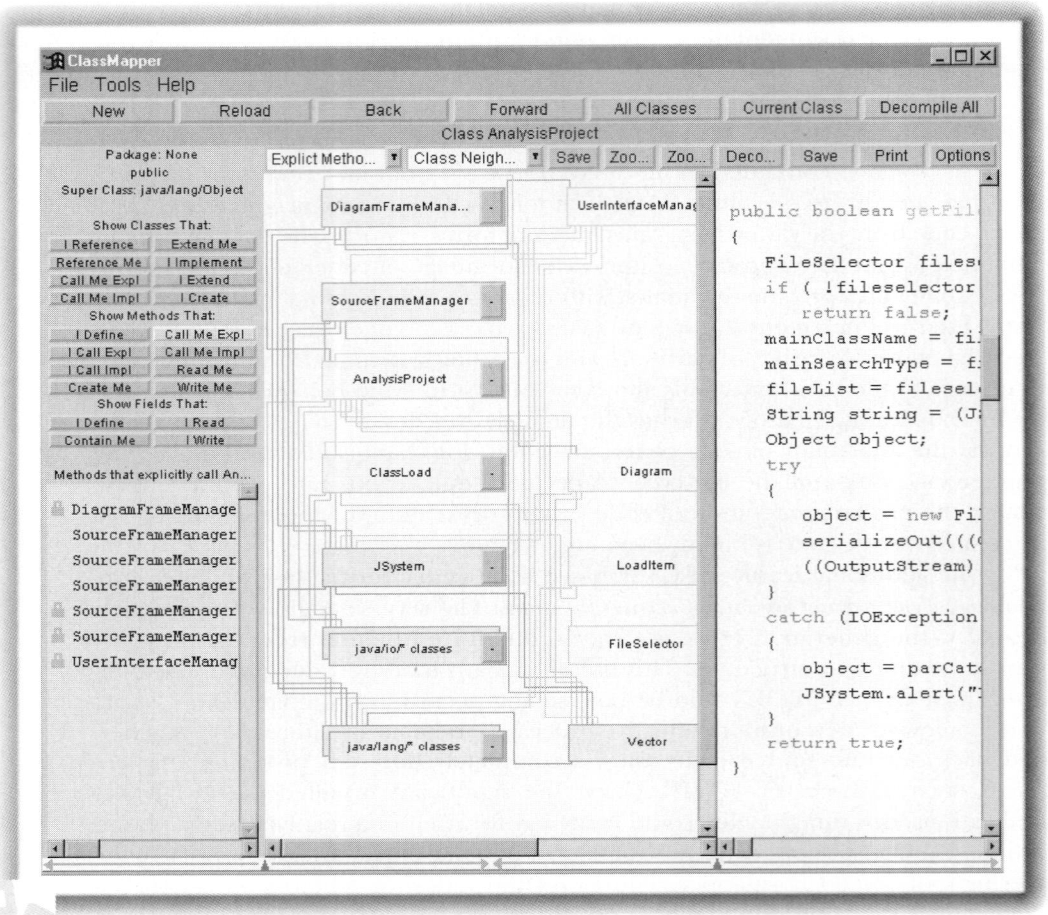

Figure 7-8 Sample Screen from Classmapper Reverse Engineering Tool
Source: MK Software, 1999; <www.classmapper.com>.

start the final design processes. CASE tools will be able to remember past projects and use a concept called *case-based reasoning* to compare the requirements of the current project to those of past projects so that a set of reusable modules can be suggested for use.

It will be a long time before the analyst is able to do his or her job completely through the CASE tool, and the need for strong communication and analytical skills will always be the mainstay in application development. The next generation CASE tools will, however, make the analyst's life a little easier and the quality of the final application significantly better.

JAD and RAD

A camel is a horse designed by a committee.
—SIR ALEC ISSIGONIS, INVENTOR
OF THE ROVER MINICAR

Driven by the need to improve the elicitation and gathering of IS requirements, systems analysts at IBM designed and implemented a new process in the late 1970s called JAD. The motivation for JAD was to bring formal structure and increased ef-

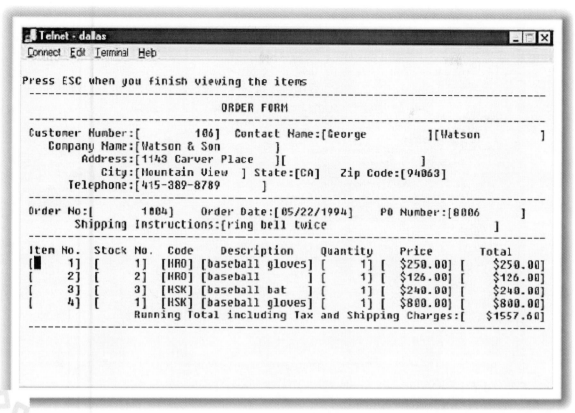

Figure 7-9   UNIX-based Application before Reverse Engineering
Source: Informix Corporation, 2000; <www.informix.com>.

fectiveness to the requirements-gathering activities of the early phases of the SDLC, while simultaneously improving the efficiency of the information-gathering process. JAD has proved to be an effective technique for achieving consensus on requirements, procedures, policies, designs, and other elements of software development. JAD sessions promote cooperation among all parties impacted by the project, resulting in shorter project durations and more satisfied customers.

Complementary to the JAD process, RAD, conceived by James Martin (1991), involves a series of iterative work sessions intended to create a working prototype of the proposed system. Used together and applied properly, these two techniques can serve to dramatically accelerate the design process for many application development projects. We focus on the concept of JAD first and evolve our focus into the broader development technique of RAD later in this chapter.

JAD

Contrary to the more conventional information-gathering techniques originally introduced in chapter 4, a typical JAD session brings together the users, managers, and technical personnel associated with a development project to conduct a series of highly structured intensive information-gathering workshops. Through the proper application of JAD, organizations can improve the quality of their

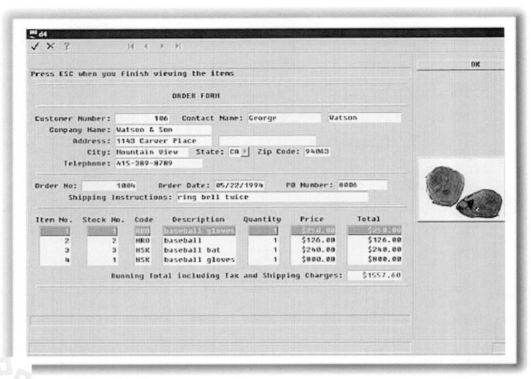

Figure 7-10   Windows Application after Reverse Engineering
Source: Informix Corporation, 2000; <www.informix.com>.

information-gathering activities while managing the time and resources necessary to gather the information in a more efficient manner. In addition, the use of JAD can serve to enhance the development of a shared understanding among the system stakeholders with regard to what the system is intended to do and for whom.

The JAD Session

JAD sessions are often quite energetic and require a great deal of active participation and concentration by all members of the team. As such, JAD sessions are typically held at a location especially designed for the task and, normally, at a location other than the typical workplace to avoid the day-to-day distractions commonly associated with the office. A JAD project can consist of a single session lasting a few hours to several sessions lasting for a week or more.

The facilities necessary for a successful JAD session are not unlike those commonly found in any type of group brainstorming or workgroup meeting environment. The participants need to be arranged such that they can easily view the front of the room and each other. Conversation and participation should be facilitated through clear lines of sight and even sound amplification, if necessary. All available instructional aids, multimedia devices, and other presentation items should be positioned such that they can be easily viewed by all participants and accessed easily when needed. The whole idea is to create an environment where nothing distracts the participants from concentrating on the development of system requirements. Figure 7-12 contains an example of several large-scale JAD session environments.

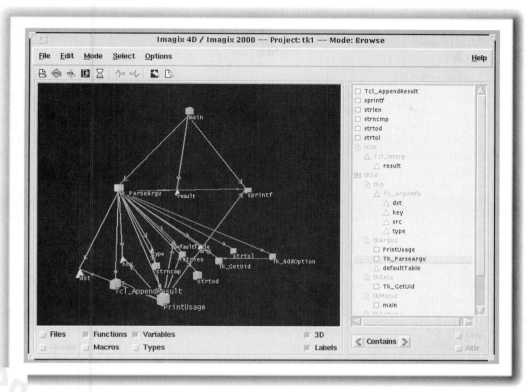

Figure 7-11   Sample Screen from Imagix Reengineering Tool
Source: Imagix Corporation, 2000; <www.imagix.com>.

Preparing for a successful JAD session requires more than basic meeting planning skills. Prior to the session, the analyst team must work closely with the project sponsors to determine the exact scope of the project to be presented and discussed in each JAD session. Further, and probably most important, is the careful preparation of a detailed agenda for each JAD session, including reference documentation intended to brief the participants about the intended scope and objectives of the session. It is important that the agenda lists all activities in their proper order and that a timetable is maintained so that all participants know exactly how much time is remaining in a given activity and what the next topic will be.

The JAD Team

The *JAD team* is the core of the JAD process, and the careful selection and inclusion of appropriate individuals is a critical step toward the overall success of a JAD project.

JAD Facilitator

The key coordinator on the team is the *JAD facilitator,* who is responsible for the planning, execution, and managing of the project. The person chosen to serve in this role should be a respected, skillful leader with a good reputation within the organization. In addition, experience with the JAD process is a necessity. This can be acquired through previous participation in the JAD process or through training. Regardless of the source of JAD experience, the role of JAD facilitator is not one to be entered into lightly, and it is definitely not for the faint of heart. Choosing the wrong JAD facilitator can mean the difference between a successful outcome and a waste of time.

Management Sponsor

As with any computer project, to succeed requires the support of management. As such, it is important to the success of a JAD project to have a highly visible *management sponsor*. This role can be filled by a member of senior management or, in some cases, more appropriately by the divisional head or manager of the business area that the JAD project is addressing. The management sponsor does not have to actively participate in every JAD session; instead, the sponsor should be available throughout the period of the JAD development to solve any serious problems or issues that may arise. It is advisable for the sponsor to attend the first and perhaps the final JAD session to review the results and make comments. During the conduct of the project, the JAD facilitator works closely with the management sponsor to keep him or her fully briefed on progress.

Information Specialists

The role of the *information specialist* is to assist the end users in communicating and developing a design according to their needs. Under the direction of the JAD facilitator, information specialists create prototypes based on the requirements articulated during the early JAD sessions. They can also advise end users on new technology or hardware that can assist in the technical implementation of their project. Information specialists should be good listeners and good communicators. Further, they need a high level of understanding with regard to the organiza-

Figure 7-12   Examples of Large-Scale JAD Environments

Management Deliberation Center
Defense System Management College
Fort Belvoir, VA

Air Force Innovation Center
Pentagon
Washington, DC

Glensidige Insurance
Oslo, Norway

Center for Performance Improvement
Soza and Company, Ltd.
Fairfax, VA

tion and the business area(s) involved. Experienced systems analysts are typically used in this role.

Scribe

The *scribe* has a particularly important role in the JAD team. He or she is responsible for documenting all the activities and important pieces of information generated during the JAD sessions. The scribe works very closely with the JAD facilitator, because the capture of essential information is a rigorously interactive activity and the scribe must learn to quickly identify and capture the important decisions made, who made them, and why. During JAD sessions, it is important to encourage end users to call on the scribe to "make sure that point is documented." The scribe does not have to be a technical person but should possess a logical approach to gathering and documenting information. It is the responsibility of the scribe to organize and distribute the documentation to all participants at the end of each JAD session. The role of a JAD scribe is a challenging one and not to be underestimated.

End Users

The role of the *end user* in specifying requirements and assisting in the design of modern IS is now widely accepted as essential to its ultimate success. In fact, the whole point of JAD is to bring the appropriate end users and technical personnel together in a structured environment.

It is believed that end users rapidly gain a sense of involvement and ownership in systems where JAD is used. As we have discussed previously, this perception is vital to the overall success of a development effort.

JAD Session Tasks and Objectives

No two JAD sessions are ever alike, but most analysts agree that all successful JAD sessions have a similar agenda. Table 7-4 contains a list of tasks commonly found in the typical JAD session agenda.

Table 7-4   Common Tasks in a JAD Session

- Identify all stakeholders and clarify executive goal.
- Scope out the general requirements from each of the users' perspectives.
- Reconcile each user's view of the product with the executive goal into one summary.
- Define the interaction of the product with users, other products or systems, and the organization.
- Concur on business justification, time box, and cost box for project.
- Define the ways in which the users will interact or use the new product. Collect samples of desired inputs and outputs from users. Stick to business processes first, then drill down for data needed and known.
- Prioritize the user interaction scenarios by collective user preference and risk.
- Validate and review the user interaction scenarios.
- Organize the interactions scenarios, constraints, assumptions, and other requirements into a rigorous software requirements specification.
- Design (with technical help) the screen and report layouts. Prototypes are handy for this.

In many cases, a typical JAD session may best be described as controlled chaos; this description is commonly not far from the truth. The analysts make several presentations during each session, facilitate the discussions surrounding the layout and design of screens and reports, answer questions from the various constituents, and make sure the entire proceeding is carefully documented. On regular occasions, however, the analyst facilitator is called on to settle a dispute (at times rather heated) between two or more constituents that have strong opposing views with regard to a particular issue under discussion. It is at this point that all of the communication and conflict resolution skills of the analyst come to bear.

When the JAD session is completed for the day, the work is far from done. The analyst team must meet to further discuss the day's events and reach consensus on what has been determined to date. In addition, the agenda for the following day's JAD session is reviewed and updated to reflect the best possible approach to the investigation given the knowledge obtained to date.

JAD Summary

Although JAD is not an appropriate technique in all environments, where properly applied JAD has been shown to be directly related to dramatic improvements in end-user motivation and performance. Several factors related to the JAD approach have been identified as significant contributors to such improvements, including creating a sense of involvement among the end users in the detailed planning process, the advantages typically associated with group dynamics, and the feeling of instant gratification with regard to obtaining results. Another major advantage of the JAD approach is that it allows for the simultaneous gathering and consolidating of large amounts of information. Moreover, discrepancies are resolved immediately with the aid of the facilitator.

JAD is not without its drawbacks, however. Most important is the extreme commitment of a large number of employees and technical personnel for several days at a time. It is argued that this significant investment in human resources is quickly recovered in the savings associated with reduced frequency of design changes and implementation costs, but this is often a difficult intangible to sell in the early stages of the project. Further, although it has been shown that a JAD approach does contribute positively to creating a sense of ownership among its participants, the number of participants in a typical JAD session is necessarily limited for the sake of practicality and coordination. This could mean that not all of the appropriate participants are included in all JAD sessions and some important personnel may be completely excluded from the process. Finally, although diplomacy and communication skills are always necessary in an information-gathering activity, they become tantamount to success when conducting a JAD session with a group of, sometimes, disparate perspectives and opinions concerning the proposed system.

Despite the drawbacks, JAD has found a place in the modern application development environment and is continuing to increase in popularity and use. In the next section, we explore an alternative approach to the SDLC that makes extensive use of JAD information-gathering techniques.

RAD

From previous chapters, we know that the traditional SDLC is based on a structured step-by-step approach to developing systems. User requirements are identified, a solution is designed, the requirements and design are frozen, and the system is coded, tested, and implemented. Although this approach is the predominant method for application design, it can also be very slow and cumbersome in the face of increasingly shorter delivery times and the constant need to leverage technology to achieve competitive advantage. Arguments against the traditional SDLC approach suggest that end users are primarily involved in the requirements phase with little involvement in subsequent phases and that by the time the system is implemented, it may not meet the current needs of the business.

Although the advent of CASE tools and modern application development platforms has mitigated the situation somewhat, most organizations are still faced with a measurable backlog of new systems to be developed. Further, despite rapid evolution of business dynamics and technology, most organization's mission-critical systems have not changed significantly since they were built 10 to 20 years ago. Organizations faced with upgrading these aging legacy systems or building new applications perceive the traditional SDLC as too slow and rigid to meet business demands that are constantly changing.

So Exactly What Is RAD?

Rapid Application Development is a methodology that promises organizations the ability to develop and deploy strategically important systems more quickly, while simultaneously maintaining quality and reducing development costs. This is achieved by using a series of proven application development techniques within a well-defined methodology. Table 7-5 contains a brief list of the typical application development techniques associated with a RAD approach.

The RAD methodology, although rooted in the defined phases and activities of the SDLC, nonetheless contains several significant departures from the traditional approaches. Active user involvement throughout the RAD life cycle ensures that business requirements and user expectations are clearly understood by all participants. RAD also takes full advantage of powerful application development tools, such as CASE, to rapidly develop high quality applications. Major use of iterative prototyping is employed to help users visualize and request changes to the system as it is being built, allowing applications to evolve rapidly. RAD techniques are also considered desirable in environments with unstable business requirements or those requiring the development of unique, nontraditional applications.

Table 7-5   Application Development Techniques Associated with the RAD Approach

- Use of small, well-trained development teams
- Construction and review of iterative, evolutionary prototypes
- Reliance on integrated development tools that support modeling, prototyping, and component re-usability (CASE)
- Construction and maintenance of a central repository
- Heavy reliance on interactive requirements and design workshops (JAD)
- Adherence to rigid limits on development time frames

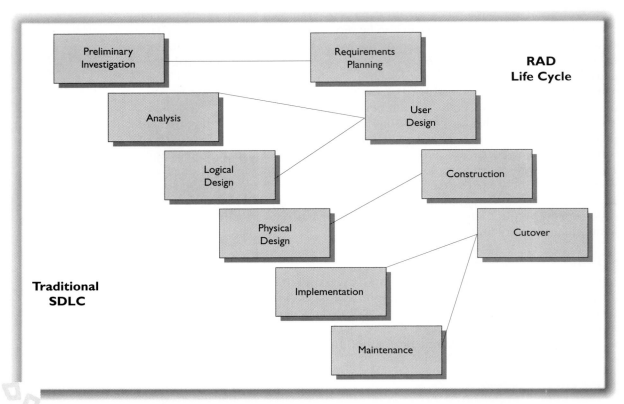

Figure 7-13   Comparison of Phases between SDLC and RAD

RAD Techniques

Up to now, we have actually discussed in detail three of the primary application development techniques used in the RAD approach. The use of iterative prototypes was discussed in chapter 4. The use of integrated software toolsets such as CASE and the conduct of requirements-gathering JAD sessions was covered previously in this chapter. The final, and probably most important, technique used in RAD is the adoption of a timeboxed approach to development.

The *timeboxed* approach is a method applied during the analysis or construction phases to control the scope of a project by imposing an immovable deadline on the completion of a task, activity, stage, or system by strictly controlling functionality. The term *timebox* was first used at DuPont Corporation, and its application allows development teams to quickly build the core of the system and implement refinements in subsequent releases. Although the founders and champions of the RAD approach claim that there are many improvements in RAD over the traditional SDLC approach, a close comparison of the two methods shows the imposition of timeboxes to be the major difference between the two. Figure 7-13 illustrates a comparison of the phases in the traditional SDLC and those contained in the RAD approach.

Comparing RAD to the SDLC

Despite the claims that RAD is an "alternative to the SDLC," one can easily see from Figure 7-13 that RAD actually embraces all of the stages of the traditional SDLC. It includes all the activities and tasks required to scope and define business require-

Table 7-6   Activities and Deliverables in RAD Phases

	Requirements Planning	User Design	Construction	Cutover
Primary Activity	Model and prototype requirements	Model and prototype design	Complete application development	Install application
Data Conversion	Define data requirements	Plan and design data conversion	Develop data conversion modules	Implement conversion plan
Testing		Design application test plan	Conduct user testing	
End-user Training	Define training requirements	Design training plan	Produce training materials	Conduct end-user training

ments and to design, develop, and implement the application system that supports those requirements. The primary difference is that the up-front, and often labor intensive, activities of the SDLC are condensed through parallel actions, the use of JAD information-gathering techniques, and extensive iterative prototyping. Table 7-6 contains a matrix illustration of the various activities and deliverables for each stage in the RAD approach.

Similar to the SDLC, RAD includes the development and refinement of process models, data models, and prototypes. The primary difference here is that in the SDLC these activities are performed in a quasi-sequential manner, whereas in the RAD approach they are performed in an iterative parallel manner. In RAD, user requirements are refined, a solution is designed, the solution is prototyped, the prototype is reviewed, user input is provided, and the process begins again.

Process Model

In the traditional SDLC, the logical process model is used to define requirements and the physical process model is used to define the system design. Using the RAD approach, the prototype serves as the major component of the process model and is used to document user requirements and system design. Functional specifications and design documentation are only required to document critical segments of the system not included in the prototype.

Data Model

Prototyping does not replace the need to analyze and design the system's data. A functional prototype cannot be built without a database; however, in the RAD approach, prototyping is used to help refine data requirements. Although the data models, process models, and prototype evolve in parallel, the data must be designed first, followed by the procedures that use the data.

Parallel Development

One of the major techniques used by RAD to reduce the time necessary for system development is to take extreme advantage of the concept of functional decomposition. We know that a large, complex application system can be divided into subsystems. In

RAD, each subsystem is developed by an independent team. The key to successful parallel development is to subdivide the system into chunks that can be developed and tested independently. The development toolset and standards used by each team must be the same. The data and process models must be interlinked, so that the subsystems are compatible and there is no duplication of effort (e.g., same functions developed twice). The final application system must be tested as a complete, integrated unit.

The Good and Bad News about RAD

A RAD project should be completed in a six to nine month time frame (from initiation to implementation). It is important to note, however, that although the RAD methodology has been designed to achieve speed and flexibility with regard to application development, the methodology does not apply to all systems development projects. Some development projects may not be successful using RAD (e.g., a customer's first client-server project). Remember the geometric truth about system development: if time and cost are the primary drivers of the project, then functionality and quality are likely to suffer. The RAD methodology must be applied carefully if system quality is to be maintained. Figure 7-14 contains a comparison of effort and time between SDLC and RAD, and Table 7-7 contains a comparison of the advantages and disadvantages associated with the RAD approach to application development.

Figure 7-14   Comparison of Effort and Time between SDLC and RAD

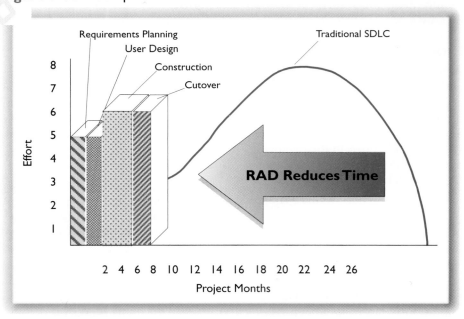

Table 7-7   Comparison of the Advantages and Disadvantages Associated
with the RAD Approach

The Good News	The Bad News
• Time savings in overall project phases are realizable	• Focus on time to delivery and project cost may result in lower system functionality and overall quality
• RAD reduces overall project costs and human resource requirements	• RAD leaves little time to focus on the overall business environment and the expected changes both near and far term
• Works well with development efforts where time is of the essence	
• System design changes can be effected much more rapidly than with the traditional SDLC approach	• Less consistency and integration with other organizational systems
• The user perspective is represented in the final system with regard to both functionality and interface	• Documentation quality and conformity to existing development standards is often decreased
• Creates a strong sense of ownership among all project stakeholders	• System scalability becomes more difficult
	• Requires an extremely high commitment of human resources during the early stages

CHAPTER SUMMARY

This chapter allowed us to look at several methods and techniques intended to expedite the application development process and to improve the quality of the final product. We also saw that, regardless of the approach (CASE, JAD, RAD), the fundamental tenets of structured problem solving as followed by the SDLC still apply and must be adhered to. These modern information-gathering and software development techniques definitely have their place in the analyst's arsenal of tools, but they must be carefully and judiciously applied if they are to positively contribute to the success and quality of the project. Despite the automation available to us, the analyst is still at the center of the process.

KEY CONCEPTS

➤ Reasons for using CASE tools
  • Increasing costs of software development due to the extreme intensive labor required
  • System development is often conducted in an ad hoc fashion
  • Avoid simple human errors in software development
    CASE offers an important opportunity to alleviate the problems of application development and maintenance that can have catastrophic consequences.

➤ Objectives of CASE
  To support each phase of the SDLC with a set of laborsaving tools
  • Upper CASE
    These CASE tools concentrate on supporting the early phases of the life cycle by providing automated assistance in

the form of diagramming tools, screen design and generation, and accuracy and consistency checking.

- Lower CASE

  These CASE tools focus only on the implementation phases of the life cycle. They include automated code and test case generators.

- Life cycle–spanning CASE (I-CASE or integrated CASE)

  These CASE tools are sophisticated applications that can support the entire analysis, design, and implementation process.

➤ Good news and bad news about CASE

- Good news

  - Derive productivity gains
  - Increase the overall quality of the final application
  - Increase the quality of documentation associated with the application
  - Enforce a consistent set of developmental standards throughout the organization
  - Enhance the portability of new systems to other platforms
  - Improve analyst skill set owing to greater understanding of the process
  - Decrease the time to deliver new applications

- Bad news

  - The acquisition and implementation of a modern CASE tool environment is relatively expensive. The justification of the large cost of acquisition of CASE tools is difficult.
  - The return on investment of a modern CASE tool is longer than the organization would prefer.
  - Organizations do not have clear development standards and a formal methodological approach to software development.
  - Training of analysts and administrators is costly and time-consuming.
  - CASE tools can be viewed as a threat to job security.

➤ The components of modern CASE tools

- The central repository

  The central repository of CASE tools serves as the central storage and retrieval location for information nec-

essary to analyze, create, design, and modify a software application development from the beginning to the end. The advent of the central repository allows for the reusability of system codes.

- Modeling and diagramming tools

  - Process modeler

    A process modeler can be used to develop a diagram that illustrates the activities within an organization system and the sequence in which they take place.

  - Function hierarchy diagrammer

    A function hierarchy diagrammer facilitates the modeling of the hierarchies of all the functions that are performed by a business and can assist in identifying which parts of the business are currently, or can be automated.

  - Data flow diagramming tools
  - ER diagramming tools

- Prototyping and transformation tools

  The transformation tools enable the rapid conversion of requirements defined during analysis into default database and default application designs.

  - Application transformers

    The application transformers create a first-cut application design based on an existing database design and on the functions and business rules placed in the repository during the detailed analysis phase.

  - Database transformers

    The database transformer creates and maintains database designs based on entity models recorded in the central repository.

- Form and report generators

  Form and report generators bring automation to the activities necessary for the analyst to design how the various users interact with the system.

- Documentation generators

  The documentation generators generate phase-specific documentation from the data contained within the central repository.

- Code generators
  - Code generators produce high-level code from the various diagrams, models, forms, reports, and data definitions contained in the central repository. They provide the flexibility of choosing future implementation platforms.
  - Reverse engineering and reengineering

    The reverse engineering function allows for the generation of design specifications and models from existing program code and data structures. Reengineering functions are advanced reverse engineering modules that provide a certain level of automation to the redesign process.

➤ JAD

JAD was designed to bring formal structure and increased effectiveness to the requirements-gathering activities of the early phases of the SDLC while simultaneously improving the efficiency of the information-gathering process. A typical JAD session brings together the users, managers, and technical personnel associated with a development project to conduct a series of highly structured intensive information-gathering workshops.

➤ The JAD team
- JAD facilitator
- Management sponsor
- Information specialists
- Scribe
- End users

➤ Benefits of the JAD approach
- Improve the quality of the information-gathering activities while managing the time and resources necessary to gather the information in a more efficient manner
- Enhance the development of a shared understanding among the system stakeholders with regard to what the system is intended to do and for whom

- Improve end-user motivation and performance

➤ Drawbacks of the JAD approach
- Requires extreme commitment of a large number of employees and technical personnel for several days at a time
- The number of participants in a typical JAD session is necessarily limited for the sake of practicality and coordination.
- Requires professional diplomacy and communication skills

➤ RAD

RAD is a methodology that promises organizations the ability to develop and deploy a strategically important system more quickly while simultaneously maintaining quality and reducing development costs. It involves a series of iterative work sessions intended to create a working prototype of the proposed system.

➤ Primary RAD application development techniques
- Use of iterative prototypes
- Use of integrated software toolsets such as CASE
- Conducting requirements-gathering JAD sessions
- Adopting the timeboxed approach to development

  The timeboxed approach is a method applied during the analysis or construction phases to control the scope of a project by imposing an immovable deadline on the completion of a task, activity, stage, or system by strictly controlling functionality.

➤ Major differences between the traditional SDLC and RAD
- The imposition of timeboxes in the RAD approach
- The up-front, and often labor intensive, activities of the SDLC are condensed through parallel actions, the use of JAD information-gathering techniques, and intensive iterative prototyping

➤ Benefits of the RAD approach
- Time savings in overall project phases are realizable
- RAD reduces overall project costs and human resource requirements

- Works well with development efforts where time is of the essence
- System design changes can be affected much more rapidly than with the traditional SDLC approach.
- The user perspective is represented in the final system with regard to both functionality and interface
- Creates a strong sense of ownership among all project stakeholders

➤ Disadvantages of the RAD approach
  - Focus on time to delivery and project cost may result in lower system functionality and overall quality

- RAD leaves little time to focus on the overall business environment and the expected changes both near and far term
- Less consistency and integration with other organizational systems
- Documentation quality and conformity to existing development standards is often decreased
- System scalability becomes more difficult
- Requires an extremely high commitment of human resources during the early stages

QUESTIONS FOR REVIEW

1. Why does there appear to be an urgent need for CASE tools?

2. List and briefly describe the different types of CASE tools and their objectives.

3. What are the benefits CASE tools bring to organizations?

4. What are some of the disadvantages associated with CASE tools?

5. Describe the purpose of the central repository.

6. List and briefly explain the different modeling and diagramming tools found in a modern CASE tool.

7. How can a process modeler assist in the development of an application?

8. List and briefly describe the prototyping and transformation tools provided by modern CASE tools.

9. What are the functions provided by code generators?

10. List the benefits of the JAD approach of information gathering.

11. Who should be included in the JAD team?

12. How do you prepare a successful JAD session?

13. List and briefly describe the role of each type of JAD team members.

14. What are the drawbacks of the JAD approach?

15. List and briefly explain the four primary RAD application development techniques.

16. Compare and contrast the traditional SDLC approach and the RAD approach to application development.

17. Explain the role of prototyping in the RAD approach.

FOR FURTHER DISCUSSION

1. One way to experience the various roles in a JAD session is to play them. Gather several of your classmates together and take turns serving in each of the primary roles of a JAD team. Agree on a development scenario and assign roles to each member of the group. Be sure to have each member serve as JAD facilitator. When you have completed the exercise, discuss with the other team members your feelings and observations while playing the various JAD team member roles.

2. One of the most important goals of the majority of CASE tool vendors is to create a code generator capable of 100 percent error-free code. What effects, both positive and negative, would this achievement have on systems analysis?

3. While attending a planning meeting with several fellow systems analysts, one of the newer additions to the group says, "Why are you guys still insisting on the traditional development methodology? We should get rid of the way we do things and replace the whole process with a CASE tool." How might you respond to your colleague to explain the error in his thinking?

4. Your boss has suddenly "discovered" JAD and wants you to organize and conduct a JAD session to gather requirements for the forthcoming application project. He thinks a great place to hold the session would be the new large conference room in the main office facilities of your company. Write a memo to your boss expressing your concerns with this approach and make the case for an off-site location for the JAD session.

REFERENCES

Hanna, M. 1992. "Using Documentation as a Life-Cycle Tool." *Software Magazine,* 12(12): 41–51.

Jones, T. C. 1993. "Equipping the Software Engineer." *Software Magazine,* 13(1): 100–109.

Martin, J. 1991. *Rapid Application Development.* New York: Macmillan.

NASA. 1999a. <mars.jpl.nasa.gov/msp98/orbiter>. Accessed November 1999.

NASA. 1999b. <mars.jpl.nasa.gov/msp98/news/mco990923.html>. Accessed November 1999.

NASA. 1999c. <mars.jpl.nasa.gov/msp98/news/mco990930.html>. Accessed November 1999.

Stone, J. 1993. *Inside ADW and IEF: The Promise and Reality of CASE.* New York: McGraw-Hill.

Moving from Analysis to Design

Learning Objectives

■ Understand the process of moving from the logical design stages of the SDLC to the physical phases

■ Understand the geometric truth of systems development

■ Discuss the various components of making the decision to adopt a particular design strategy

■ Describe the concept of a feasible solution

■ Understand the role of facts, faith, and fear in the development of a system proposal

■ Describe the various categories of feasibility assessment and their relationship to project risk

There are many hows but only one what. Never tell people how to do things. Tell them what to do and they will surprise you with their ingenuity.
—GENERAL GEORGE S. PATTON

INTRODUCTION

This chapter focuses on an important milestone in your SAD learning experience, as well as in literally all successful IS analysis and design projects: the transition from the world of "what is" to the world of "what should be." We are now at the point where all of the information and requirements gathered, verified, cross-checked, and documented during the preliminary and detailed analysis phases are transformed into a proposed solution to the business problem at hand. The logical requirements and models have allowed us to determine *what* the system must do. The move from analysis to design allows us to determine exactly *how* to meet those requirements. Figure 8-1 illustrates this transition using our project flow model.

At this stage of the process we must carefully assess the solution as it exists in its logical form, because once we begin the conversion of the proposed system into its physical form, the cost of fixing a mistake or changing our minds begins to sky-rocket.

Although some minor ambiguity with regard to the final capabilities of the new system may still exist, because of unresolved perspectives or conflicts among the system stakeholders, the majority of the requirements are ready to be transformed into a proposed physical solution and subjected to a rigorous feasibility as-

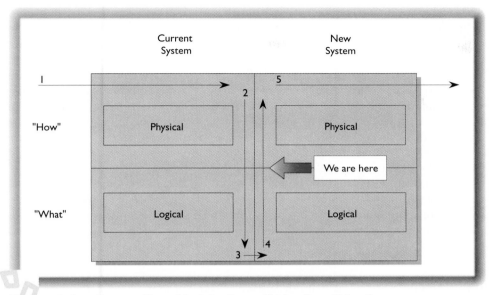

Figure 8-1   Project Flow Model—From "What" to "How"

sessment on all critical dimensions. At this stage also the development process begins to accelerate and move into high gear. Quite soon, many new faces will be looking to the analyst for coordination and guidance, system vendors will be proposing hardware and software, programmers and other technical personnel will become involved and need development resources to support their efforts.

Finally, this point in the process presents a variety of new challenges to the analyst in the form of decisions regarding method of acquisition of the system, hardware and software configuration, data conversion, end-user training, scheduling, and funding. We focus our attention in this chapter on identifying these issues and the methods by which their answers can be determined.

THE GEOMETRIC TRUTH ABOUT SYSTEMS DEVELOPMENT PROJECTS

At the risk of scaring you into remembering high school geometry class, we must take a moment to reflect on the contribution Pythagoras made to the world of SAD. We all know him for his theorem with regard to triangles, and we also know that he was the mathematician that codified most of the properties of the triangle, among other geometric shapes. One of the most common properties of a triangle is that it has 3 angles, the total of which add up to 180 degrees.

It is here that Pythagoras forever changed SAD. We know that if we want to specify the exact number of degrees of the angles in a triangle, we are constrained by certain mathematical truths. The most important constraint is that no matter how much we want to dictate the size of the angles in a triangle, we are limited to specifying the size of only two of the three angles. Any two, mind you, but only two of the three, because the sum of the angles must add up to 180 degrees. If we specify one to be 10 degrees and the second to be 100 degrees then the third angle automatically must be 70 degrees, or we have violated a mathematical truth.

There is an old engineering dictum that states "A project can be delivered right, cheap, and now . . . pick any two." If we consider this dictum in relationship to the triangle, we arrive at the *geometric truth about systems development projects*. Figure 8-2 illustrates this point.

Applying the mathematics of a triangle to the selection of a design strategy, we can see that an emphasis on any one of the project constraints results in a compensating change in at least one of the other two. If we emphasize the minimization of the cost of a project, we must be prepared for a compensatory change in either the quality or the delivery time. Likewise, if we attempt to emphasize two of the three characteristics, say cost and delivery time (cheap and now), we must be prepared to sacrifice the quality of the deliverables.

The point here is that the geometry of a good design strategy dictates that we attempt to maintain a balance between cost, quality, and time to delivery. Failing to acknowledge the truth of the matter normally results in a strategy that does not meet the stated objectives of the development effort or, worse, an analyst doomed

Figure 8-2   The Geometric Truth about Systems Development

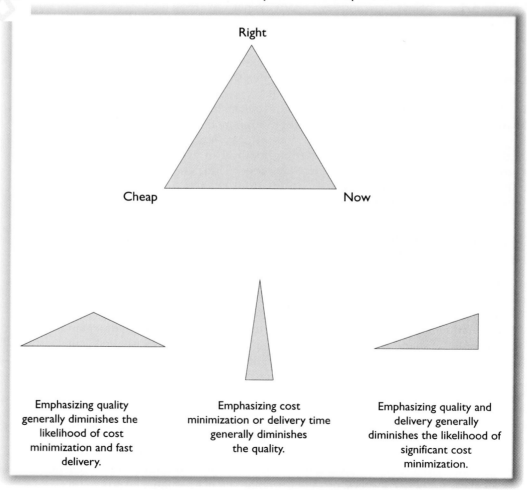

to failure from the start by attempting to successfully accomplish the impossible task of putting more than 180 degrees into a triangle.

SELECTION OF THE DESIGN STRATEGY

Before we can move forward to execute our design strategy and implement our proposed solution, we need to decide what design strategy, among the variety of available alternatives, we are going to pursue. A *design strategy* is simply a formal method for pursuing the physical development of the system. Issues such as method of acquisition of the component elements, system functionality, software development, and implementation schedules are key elements in selecting an appropriate design strategy for the new system. The decisions made regarding each of these issues has a material impact on the final feasibility assessment of the project and the decision of whether to commit to the development and deployment of a physical system solution. Figure 8-3 illustrates the flow of activities for the analyst during this transition from logical to physical design.

Generating Alternative Design Strategies

As with any decision, there are no clear-cut choices but always at least two alternatives from which to choose. Regardless of how much the system appears to be the exact solution to the problem at hand and the obvious choice for implementation, a formal feasibility assessment must be conducted that includes determining the

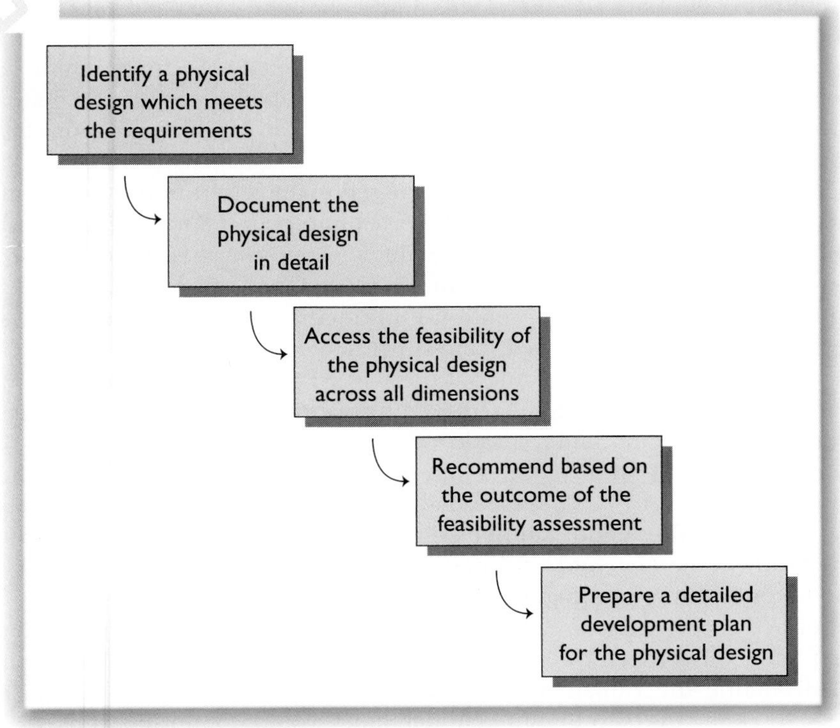

Figure 8-3   Making the Transition from Logical to Physical Design

viability of pursuing the physical system on a number of dimensions. Later in this chapter we focus on each of these dimensions in detail, but at this point we must understand one of the most important alternative strategies available to us in the choice set: *do nothing*.

Do Nothing

At this stage of the development process, the suggestion that the best solution to the problem may be to do nothing may, at first glance, appear to be a ludicrous proposition. Why on earth would we go to all this work to identify the problem and design a logical solution for it and then not follow through with its implementation?

The answer to this question lies with the detailed feasibility analysis. If we are to determine the benefits to be derived from having the system in place as a solution to our problem, we must first be able to compare the solution to the costs and implications of having the problem in the first place. In some cases, be they driven by economic, technical, operational, or even political issues, it may be better to know of the existence of a problem and to fully understand its implications to the organization than it would be to actually implement a solution to that problem. An example may help to make this clearer.

In May 1962, Nikita Khrushchev, then premier of the Soviet Union, conceived the idea of placing intermediate-range nuclear missiles in Cuba as a means of countering an emerging lead of the United States in developing and deploying strategic missiles. He also presented the scheme as a means of protecting Cuba from another United States–sponsored invasion, such as the failed attempt at the Bay of Pigs in 1961.

After seven days of guarded and intense debate in the United States administration, during which Soviet diplomats denied that installations for offensive missiles were being built in Cuba, President John F. Kennedy, in a televised address on October 22, announced the discovery of the installations and proclaimed that any nuclear missile attack from Cuba would be regarded as an attack by the Soviet Union and would be responded to accordingly. He also imposed a naval quarantine on Cuba to prevent further Soviet shipments of offensive military weapons from arriving there.

During the crisis, the two sides exchanged many letters and other communications, both formal and back channel. For example, on October 26, Khrushchev sent Kennedy a long rambling letter seemingly proposing that the missile installations would be dismantled and personnel removed in exchange for United States assurances that it or its proxies would not invade Cuba. On October 27, however, another letter to Kennedy arrived from Khrushchev, suggesting that missile installations in Cuba would be dismantled if the United States dismantled its missile installations in Turkey. These significantly contradictory letters posed a serious problem for Kennedy: which letter should he respond to, the first or the second? If Kennedy responded to the second letter, he must address the issue of trading Russia's missiles in Cuba for U.S. missiles in Turkey, a cost Kennedy was not prepared to pay. If, on the other hand, Kennedy simply chose to ignore the second letter, responded only to the first, and essentially chose to solve the problem created by the second letter by doing nothing, he ran the risk of nuclear war.

Kennedy chose to ignore this second letter and to accept the offer outlined in the first letter of October 26. Khrushchev then announced on October 28 that he would dismantle the Cuban missile installations and return them to the Soviet Union, expressing his trust that the United States would not invade Cuba.

Applying this approach to the development of an IS, we must assess not only the feasibility of implementing our solution but also the costs and consequences associated with not implementing the proposed solution. By taking this perspective, we can remain grounded in the reality of the true value of the solution rather than in simply the desire to effect a solution to an identified problem. When you think of it in this manner, doing nothing is one possible alternative among the set of available solutions to the problem. In President Kennedy's case, it was the most appropriate solution, as well.

Explore All Possible Nonautomated Solutions

Despite the fact that most modern IS have computer hardware and software at their core, it is important for the analyst to give careful attention to the potential for solving the problem in a nonautomated manner. This can be best explained by a brief discussion of the two predominant perspectives with regard to the value of IT.

One predominant perspective is that the advent of the computer has allowed mankind to extend mind and body, advance in realms previously unexplored, and accomplish more than ever before in the history of the species. Although this perspective cannot be credited to any single individual, the pervasiveness of IT in virtually all aspects of our lives suggests that there is more than a casual attraction to this viewpoint.

An opposing perspective to the one cited previously is best exemplified by a now-famous quote by *Digital Media* editor Mitch Radcliffe:

> "The computer allows you to make mistakes faster than any other invention, with the possible exception of handguns and tequila."

Although admittedly comical, the point being made here is that if you automate a poorly designed or executed process, you simply have a bad process traveling at the speed of light. This suggests that before we inject the complexities of automation into the equation, we must first look to those portions of the solution that can be effected without computers. The development of a sound set of written policies and procedures, the effective redesign of paper-based data capture forms, the logical improvement or even elimination of procedures that fail to accurately accomplish their intended objectives, and the education and training of personnel in the overall goals of a process, among many others, can all be considered important and substantive nonautomated solutions. Only when the processes and outcomes make sense when traveling slow should we consider speeding them up through a computer-based solution.

Buy versus Make

Assuming that the best alternative is to proceed with some manner of computer-related or automated solution, the next possible design strategy decision focuses on exactly how to acquire the physical system components, particularly the software applications. In this regard, we must assess the relative benefits and tradeoffs associated with one of three basic approaches: (1) buy a COTS solution and customize it to fit, (2) develop a custom software application in-house, or (3) outsource the project to an external vendor or developer. Each of these approaches carries with it certain advantages and disadvantages that must be considered in the selection of a design strategy.

COTS

Although the typical stakeholder in a systems development effort may assure you that their business needs are unique, the truth is that there are infinite variations of business needs in organizations but a finite number of categories in which they fall. Because of this, many software solutions may already exist in a commercially available form. In the spirit of not reinventing the wheel, the most efficient design strategy with regard to software solutions may be to purchase an existing software application and modify it as necessary to meet the stated requirements of the proposed system. Such COTS solutions can benefit a development effort by providing software that is well tested, proven, and readily available when compared to a custom-developed application.

The most common objection to adopting this design strategy is that rarely, if ever, does a COTS solution exist that meets 100 percent of the stated system requirements. In these cases, the organization must decide whether to restate their requirements so that they conform to the functionality of the available products or determine the degree to which the COTS solution can be successfully modified to meet 100 percent of the business need. Most modern packaged software manufacturers have addressed this issue by allowing for customization of the basic system parameters so that they better conform to the exact requirements of the new system. In many cases, vendors of large-scale packaged software provide technical support to their customers to assist them in making the necessary modifications to their product. Generally speaking, before a decision to build the software from scratch is made, a thorough evaluation of existing COTS solutions should be conducted. Table 8-1 lists several guidelines that should be followed when considering a COTS design strategy for a development project.

Despite the advantages of purchasing an existing product, this approach is not without potential drawbacks. Most notable in this regard is the problem of effectively integrating the COTS solution with other software applications already within the organization or being custom-developed specifically for the new system. The degree to which data may require reformatting or reconfiguring to conform to the COTS solution or the difficulties encountered in exchanging data between the COTS package and organizational legacy systems may be two deciding factors with regard to adopting a prepackaged software solution design strategy.

Custom Software Development

If a feasible COTS solution cannot be found, the alternative design strategy is to build the software from scratch. This approach can be achieved either in-house, where employees of the organization perform the actual software development, or through a third-party software developer, where the analyst and project managers direct the development effort but do not actually cut the code.

The advantages to custom software development are easy to see. The development team has complete control over the look, feel, and functionality of the new system. Further, the degree to which flexibility and contingency for future needs can be incorporated into the initial design is far greater than when using the COTS approach. Finally, building the software from scratch allows for the building and refining of reusable technical skills that allow for a greater understanding of the complexities of the new system and their relationships to existing and future development efforts.

Equally important, however, are the downside risks associated with adopting a custom software development approach. The cost of custom-developed software is

Table 8-1   Guidelines for Evaluating a Proposed COTS Solution

Evaluation Criteria	Characteristics
Application efficiency	• Acceptable response times under actual conditions • Efficient use of a wide variety of data storage solutions • Efficient use of backup and recovery mechanisms
Application effectiveness	• Meets all stated requirements for the present process needs • Expandable and scalable to expected future needs and platform requirements • Logical organization of menus and data capture screens • Capacity for current and expected future user load
Usability	• Functional and logical user interface • Context-sensitive online help system • Appropriate user feedback with regard to application processes and user error • Nondestructive error recovery from command or menu selection errors
Documentation	• Well-organized and comprehensive written user documentation • Complete duplication of all documentation in online form • Comprehensive user tutorials for all application functions
Vendor support	• Telephone technical support with direct access to technicians • Web-based support site with downloadable updates • Searchable Web-based technical support knowledge base for first line solutions

normally significantly greater than a COTS solution, even with substantial modifications. Such a design strategy is costly in terms of time, as well as human and physical resources. Further, because the product is literally a one-of-a-kind application, the amount of testing and risk of failure is significantly increased over the COTS approach. Nevertheless, if the system requirements are such that a COTS solution is unacceptable, then the custom development design strategy is a viable and commonly employed alternative.

Outsourcing

When considering the custom software approach, two additional alternatives become available: (1) outsourcing and (2) a software service provider (SSP).

Outsourcing involves the hiring of an external vendor to provide the necessary expertise and human resources necessary to create the system. This approach is becoming increasing popular, with market revenues expected to exceed $150 billion by 2003.

The benefits associated with the outsourcing approach are quite compelling. A large software development house can bring to bear a significant amount of technical expertise and development tools and resources that would otherwise be too costly for the typical business organization to acquire and maintain. Although often associated with cost reduction, the decision to outsource a software development effort may also be driven by the opportunity to bring increased value to the business. The software developer's core competency can be added to the resources of the organization and integrated into the development effort such that all participants resources are being maximally used.

The disadvantages with selecting the outsourcing alternative lie with the potential increased risk associated with putting a mission critical project in the hands of a third party. In some cases, the development of a software application involves handling information and designing processes of a sensitive or highly confidential nature. In addition, the organization is not benefiting from the development of knowledge and skills that might be used in future development efforts, because the technical expertise associated with the project lies outside the boundaries of the firm. Finally, outsourcing a development effort does not necessarily reduce the amount of time the key stakeholders of the project need to be involved with its development. In fact, outsourcing can actually increase the responsibility of the organization, because constant contact with the development team is critical to the successful completion of the project. Further, outsourcing must be thought of as taking on a strategic partner, and as such, the management of that relationship becomes as critical as the development effort itself. Although these risks can be effectively managed, the analyst must be aware of their existence and give careful consideration to them when assessing the viability of outsourcing a major development effort. Table 8-2 contains a list of guidelines and activities typically associated with the evaluation of an outsourcing design strategy.

Once the decision to enter into an outsourcing design strategy for all, or part, of the development effort has been made, a formal agreement between all parties must be executed. The general terms and conditions of this agreement are intended to set out the majority of the rights and obligations of each party. Table 8-3

Table 8-2   General Guidelines and Activities for Evaluating Outsourcing Design Strategies

Terms of reference document that sets out the objectives, scope, and approach of the evaluation

Strategic business plan (where does the organization want to be?)

Analysis of how outsourcing integrates with the purchaser's strategic plan

Business analysis and feasibility study (the high level requirements and how the process would work)

Human resources impact assessment (may also require the assistance of employment law specialists at an early stage)

Request for information (RFI) (seeking suitable services and indicative costs)

Cost-benefit analysis (what are the economics?)

Risk analysis and business impact (what are the risks?)

Business case and recommendation to management

Specification of requirements (detailed statement of services and service levels required)

Call for proposals from suppliers, known as a request for proposal (RFP)

Evaluation of proposals

Table 8-3   Components of a Typical Outsourcing Agreement

Agreement Components	Component Description
Preamble	A full description of the parties, the processes leading up to the agreement stage, and the essence of the agreement.
Definitions	A precise definition of terms used in the agreement.
Interpretations	Any clarification relating to gender, references, schedules and appendices, other documents, conflicts between documents, etc.
Scope of services	A general description of the services to be supplied. A full definition of the services and service levels should be provided in a schedule. The agreement must also provide a mechanism to enable the specification of services and service levels to be changed at the request of either party.
Term	A definition of the commencement date and the duration of the agreement. Any provision for extending the term of the agreement.
Prices and payments	A reference to the schedules to the agreement which should specify services and applicable fees. The invoicing procedure and terms of payment should be defined.
Responsibilities of the parties	The outsourcer's and purchaser's respective responsibilities during the term of the agreement.
Transition and acceptance	The arrangements for the transition and acceptance of the services from the purchaser and the commencement of services by the outsourcer.
Staffing	The requirement for appropriately skilled and trained personnel and the removal and replacement of personnel. The identification of any personnel whose availability is essential.
Agreement administration	How performance of the services will be monitored and reviewed.
Remedies	Practical remedies for breach of the agreement, including failure by the outsourcer to achieve agreed service levels.
Termination	The basis for termination of the agreement (i.e., where the other party is in breach of its obligations under the agreement).
Consequences of termination	Sets out the consequences of termination—including the basis on which the outsourced services will be handed back to the purchaser or an alternative service provider.
Confidentiality	Requires the parties to keep confidential the information acquired in relation to the other party that is confidential in nature.
Indemnities	Sets out the indemnity that the outsourcer grants the purchaser against claims of infringement arising in relation to services supplied under the agreement. Depending on the nature of the agreement, indemnities against negligent damage and personal injury may also be appropriate.

Table 8-3 *(continued)*

Agreement Components	Component Description
Warranties	Specifies what the supplier warrants with respect to the agreement. This includes conformity to specification and service levels.
Intellectual property	Sets out the rights of each party with respect to any intellectual property associated with the delivery of services.
Limitation of liability	Sets out the extent to which the outsourcer's liability is limited.
Force majeure	Allows a party to be excused from its failure to perform the agreement where it is prevented from doing so by circumstances beyond its control.
Notices	Specifies how and where any formal notices with respect to the agreement must be communicated to the other party.
Assignment and subcontracting	Requires each party to obtain the consent of the other party prior to transferring or subcontracting its rights and obligations under the agreement to any other party.
Amendments	Specifies how any subsequent changes to the agreement, as requested by either party, will be handled. (Change Management.)
Dispute resolution	Defines the processes for both parties to resolve disputes constructively through a defined process. Where possible, this process should involve mediation between the parties.
Entire agreement	Excludes reliance on extraneous material not incorporated in the agreement.

contains a summary list of the necessary components of a typical outsourcing agreement.

As you can see by the level of detail in Table 8-3, a decision to adopt an outsourcing design strategy literally involves entering into what is tantamount to a legal partnership or joint venture with an external organization.

The second alternative outsourcing approach is to contract with an SSP. This concept has been around for several decades and, in its early days, was referred to as the *service bureau.* The SSP generally operates a sophisticated computer facility that houses several specialized software applications that can be used by a wide variety of organizations. One common example of an SSP is Automatic Data Processing (ADP), a multinational company that specializes in accounting and personnel management and support applications, including general ledger, accounts payable and receivable, payroll, human resource and staff planning, and benefits management. By using an SSP, an organization can gain the benefits associated with a large-scale processing operation that would otherwise be too costly to maintain and too large to support the individual organization's volume.

A more recent trend in the SSP concept is being championed by Microsoft Corporation through their *Next Generation Windows Services* (NGWS) initiative, where software applications reside on the Web and organizations simply pay a fee to use them without having to either host the application or manage its operation.

Hardware Design Strategy Issues

The adoption of a design strategy is a complex decision that must carefully consider and resolve the integration of a number of organizational components. Beyond the focus on software development, the analyst must also focus on issues related to hardware, both existing and future, as it relates to the application software under development and the business needs of the organization.

One of the first questions to consider is the degree to which the organization's existing hardware platform supports the new application. Issues such as the operating system platform, age, processing capacity, and expandability must be evaluated with respect to the development of the new software. Although there are clear advantages, most notably in cost savings, to developing the new application to run on the organization's existing hardware, there are several persuasive reasons why this may not be the best approach.

Depending on the type of application being developed and the necessary level of flexibility in its design, it is possible that certain parts of the new software may not run optimally on the existing hardware platform, whereas others might be just fine. This situation dictates upgrading to a platform that allows for both current and future functionality in the software to be realized. Second, developing the new application for a modern hardware platform gives the organization the opportunity to expand its current technology and to upgrade its overall technology holdings. This opportunity may facilitate the restructuring of existing computing operations to effect strategic advantage in other applications areas beyond the development effort. It is important to remember that, although the software is what allows the organization to address the business needs and reach the stated objectives of the development project, the hardware must support that effort as seamlessly as possible if the benefits of the new application are to be realized.

FROM "WHAT" TO "HOW"

Up till now, any decisions we have made with regard to the preliminary design or requirements of the proposed system have been subject to refinement or change with little or no effort or penalty. Now that we have arrived at the transition to the *physical design* phase of the SDLC, the rules have changed. We are now faced with the fact that every recommendation we make to our client with regard to the configuration of the new system is one that, if implemented, is very difficult, if not impossible, to reverse. Although we always have the option of terminating the project rather than continuing to escalate our commitment to a failing effort, the cost of exercising this creeping commitment approach rises significantly over the earlier stages of the SDLC. This suggests that a structured approach to the final determination of the feasibility of the proposed solution must be employed to insure, to the best of our ability, that, when developed, the system meets the stated business needs of the organization in the manner intended. In other words, our solution must be not only capable of solving the problem but also feasible to implement.

The Feasible Solution

For every problem, there are many solutions. Many of those solutions are good ones, and one of them will be determined to be the best one. For that special designation to occur, the implemented solution must have at least one essential characteristic: it must be *feasible.*

Within the context of a proposed solution, the concept of feasibility is defined as a solution that solves the identified problem or maximizes the identified economic opportunity without causing any problems that were not in existence before its implementation. There are many solutions, but only a select few are feasible. Further, we can assume that the solution being proposed is the one that has been deemed ideally suited, from a stated requirements perspective, to solving the problem at hand. Given this, the next question is "Can we actually implement this solution?" The job of the analyst is to assess the feasibility of the proposed solution such that it can be reasonably determined that the solution can be successfully deployed and will work without causing a new set of problems to deal with. Before we focus our attention on the details of assessing system feasibility, however, one important point must be discussed.

Facts, Faith, and Fear

One way to view the assessment of system feasibility is to think of the proposed solution as a business case for a major capital investment by the organization. If we adopt this approach, we can identify three perspectives from which the argument to pursue the investment may be made: (1) facts, (2) faith, or (3) fear.[1] Figure 8-4 provides several examples for each of these perspectives.

In the late 1980s, economic researchers discovered what has come to be called the *productivity paradox*. Despite an immense investment in IT—over a trillion dollars since the beginning of the PC revolution in about 1980—productivity growth in the U.S. has been either stagnant or weak. And growing productivity is what contributes, more than anything else, to expanding opportunity and a better material life. There are clear effects of computerization, such as the speeding up of production and consumption and the ubiquity of computers, but wages and productivity have stalled during the years we have spent most heavily on IT.

Figure 8-4   The Three Perspectives for Making a Business Case

FACTS
- "The system will have a net present value of $753,000."
- "The system will yield a minimum reduction in operating cost of $193,000 annually."
- "The estimated increase in market share is 14.7% within the first 24 months of operation."

FAITH
- "IT is part of the infrastructure, we can't cost justify it like a new fleet of trucks."
- "It seems reasonable to assume that this new system will reduce our costs of servicing this market sector."
- "Trust me. This is why you hired me as the IT Director."

FEAR
- "Our competitors are doing this even as we speak."
- "Our shareholders will view us as technologically behind if we don't do this now."
- "We have a small window of opportunity here and we are wasting precious time trying to decide."

---

[1] I am in debt to my good friend and colleague, Brad Wheeler, for allowing me to use his excellent conceptualization of making the business case.

T. K. Landauer (1995) suggests:

"The information revolution has yet to produce vast and obvious economic benefits or bring widespread and major improvements in the quality of life."

MIT researchers Erik Brynjolfsson and Lorin Hitt (1998), however, recently completed a comprehensive study of productivity in 380 large firms that together generate yearly sales in excess of $1.8 billion. They found that computers were far from unproductive: They were significantly more productive than any other type of investment these companies made. The gross return on investment (ROI) averaged about 60 percent annually for computers, including supercomputers, mainframes, minis, and micros, and IS staffers were more than twice as productive as other workers.

Although there have been many reasons offered as to why the productivity paradox appears to exist or, more recently, why it is a myth, there is one fact that is indisputable: If an investment cannot be justified in fact before it is made, then it can never be justifiable in fact after it is made. One theory behind the inability of researchers and economists to find a justifiable basis for investment in IS is that many of them were never justifiable in the first place.

This brings us to facts, faith, and fear. Many IT investments in the past were made based on faith: "Look, we need to do this if we are to grow as an organization and remain technically competitive with the marketplace. You really have to trust me on this one." Others were made based on fear: "If we do not implement this new system, we will die or our competitors will eat us alive!" The important point here is that the feasibility assessment of an IS, at this point in the development process, must be made purely on fact and must be devoid of faith-based statements or threats of extinction. If the facts support the implementation of the proposed solution, then it is justifiable on all dimensions and should be implemented. If not, then there is no time like the present to realize the potential for failure and deal with it prior to the unwarranted investment of millions of dollars of organizational resources.

THE DIMENSIONS OF SYSTEM FEASIBILITY

To insure that the business case for the development and implementation of the new system is made from a fact-based perspective, the analyst must adopt a rigorous and structured methodology with which to assess the various dimensions of project feasibility. Recall that we performed a more cursory analysis during the first phase of the SDLC, preliminary feasibility analysis. Here, we must perform a much more detailed and dispassionate analysis to insure that the proposed solution works and is a justifiable investment of organizational resources. To facilitate this feasibility analysis, we adopt a categorical approach that focuses on the elements of the project across five primary dimensions: (1) *technical*, (2) *operational*, (3) *human factors*, (4) *legal and political*, and (5) *economic*.

Technical Feasibility

The first dimension of feasibility to be assessed is the *technical feasibility* of the system. The outcome of this assessment dimension is a determination of the practicality of a specific technical solution and the availability of the technology necessary to implement it. Although it is becoming increasingly the case that nothing is impossible from a technological perspective, the immediacy of the need must be met equally by the availability of a given, and proven, technology if the project is to be deemed technically feasible. This suggests that technical feasibility must be constrained by issues of practicality, reasonability, and availability. The assessment of technical feasibility must focus on obtaining the answers to three basic questions:

1. Is the technology necessary for the proposed solution practical to obtain?
2. Do we currently possess the technology necessary to implement the proposed solution?
3. Is the technology necessary to implement the proposed solution available now and has it been tested and proved?

It is in this category of the feasibility analysis that we must be on the look out for *vaporware*. This is a term used to describe technology that, although feasible to develop and obtain, is not yet readily available or mature. Often vaporware takes the form of a product that is announced far in advance of any actual release (which may or may not ever occur). As should be obvious, investing in a technical solution based on vaporware could have disastrous consequences for an organization.

There is an increasing trend in the high-tech industries to announce, in advance, products that may be months or years away from actually reaching the market. Many of these products never reach the market, and few ever have all the features that were advertised. The practice of vaporware has given rise to numerous lawsuits, most notably between Microsoft Corporation and the U.S. Department of Justice, and costs the industry more than a billion dollars a year.

Becoming enamored by vaporware is actually quite easy to do. The velocity of change in our technology almost mandates that software vendors begin marketing their products at the earliest possible moment if they are to build the critical mass necessary to make their application a viable commercial product. Consumers see the value in the features and benefits of the new product and want to incorporate them into their development efforts. The problem with vaporware, from a technical feasibility assessment perspective, is not that it does not exist when it is being considered as a basis for a new application. The problem occurs when one considers what happens when the product cannot be delivered when it is needed to complete the development project. At that moment, your project is now in control of a third-party vendor who has no stake in your success. You would not put a project leader who had not been recruited and hired in charge of your development, and you should not base the success of your development projects on technology that does not exist either.

Operational Feasibility

The dimension of *operational feasibility* assessment is focused on issues related to how well the proposed solution works within the organization and how the end users feel about the new system. In addition, issues of scheduling, testing, deployment, and implementation cutover are assessed in this dimension. We began the assessment of operational feasibility during the preliminary feasibility activities during the first phase of the SDLC. We must return to this dimension in greater detail, however, to assess the additional issues that have come to bear since that time.

The first step in assessing operational feasibility is to reexamine the likelihood that the proposed solution indeed attains the desired organizational goals and objectives. This includes reviewing the degree to which the proposed solution conforms with the existing organizational IS plan. It is important to insure that the new system integrates effectively with the overall IS strategy of the organization and that its target is still the identified business problem, stated organizational goals, or identified economic opportunity as shown in the IS planning documents.

Another important issue to address in this dimension is the proposed development and implementation schedule for the project. The key here is to ascertain the degree to which the proposed schedule is reasonable and has a high likelihood of being executed as described. In some cases, constraints imposed on a project can directly impact the feasibility of the proposed implementation schedule. For example, a deadline for operational cutover of a new human resources management system may be driven by an eminent merger between two companies or a government mandate to adopt certain HR practices by a certain date. In these situations, the schedule must be reviewed such that the critical path for the project milestones is deemed reasonable to insure the required deadlines are met.[2]

Other schedule-related issues include the assessment of the availability of resources at critical stages of the project and the coincidence of project milestones to non-project-related events. The former issues focus on determining the availability of specific organizational resources, including labor, specific technical resources, physical plant space, and any other project-related resource that is critical at a particular stage of the development effort. If the project is to be completed per the schedule, then the necessary resources, at any given stage of the process, must be readily available. If a system is ready to be delivered but the new server room has not yet been completed, then the potential for delay and possible negative economic impact to the project becomes significant.

Related to this is the determination of the degree of fit between the proposed schedule and other known organizational events. Scheduling the final testing and implementation cutover for a new system at the same time as the annual budget preparation and review exercise or a major new product release date may not be the most productive action to take. By reviewing the proposed schedule against other known events, the analyst can make the necessary changes without disrupting the flow of events as they unfold.

A final area of organizational feasibility assessment is to determine the degree of impact on the organization that is likely to result from the implementation and adoption of the new system and its associated business processes. What is the relationship between the existing organizational structure and the new system? What changes in reporting lines or spans of authority need to be made to complement the new system processes? What degree of change is imposed on the typical end user as a result of this system? What actions can be taken now to mitigate any negative impacts associated with its implementation? Recall that a feasible solution is one that addresses the stated problem without causing any new ones that did not exist prior to its implementation. This criteria is at the heart of organizational feasibility assessment and, as such, this dimension represents a critical element in determining the overall feasibility of a proposed solution.

Human Factors Feasibility

Related to the organizational feasibility dimension is the assessment of *human-factors feasibility*. In this dimension, the focus is on issues related to system usability and end-user training. No matter how technically advanced or effective a system may be, if the end users do not adopt it and use it, ultimately the system will fail. User satisfaction with the final system is directly related to its overall *usability*.

---

[2] Issues related to critical path analysis and detailed implementation scheduling are covered in detail in appendix A of this text.

Usability is primarily a measure of various characteristics of the system's user interface with regard to the ease with which it allows the end users to perform their jobs. Although a wide variety of characteristics can be assessed, usability experts generally agree that three basic categories of assessment can be used to determine the overall usability of the proposed system:

1. Ease of use—the degree to which you perceive the system to be easy to use within the context of performing your day-to-day activities. This characteristic also addresses perceptions regarding the ease with which the various system components and skills can be learned or acquired.

2. Perceived usefulness—the degree to which you perceive the system to conform to the needs of your job and its applicability to the task at hand.

3. Overall satisfaction—The degree to which you are pleased with the system interfaces and your overall interaction with the system.

Another human-factors feasibility issue is the determination of the availability of the "right kind" of human resources. The implementation of a new system might bring with it the need to define new roles within the organization or to redefine old ones. The determination of the need and availability of these specific human resources is a critical element in favorably assessing the human-factors dimension. What kind of skill set do we need? Do these skills currently exist within our organization? Can we hire these skills or do we need to train existing personnel?

Once the system is fully tested and installed, we want to begin using it in as efficient and effective manner as possible, so that the benefits associated with its use can be realized by the organization. The training associated with the new system needs to be scheduled and conducted prior to its implementation, so that when the system is ready, so are the end users. Although this seems easy enough to envision, training can often be one of the most complex scheduling decisions to make.

The first question to answer is "When should we begin the training process?" Although we know the training must be completed prior to implementation cutover to the new system, the lead time associated with it is an important issue. If the training is conducted too early in the process, the end users may forget their new skills and thus require additional retraining to get back up to speed. Further, any last minute updates to the interface or processes may not be reflected in the training content if it is initiated too early in the development process. Finally, the training materials must be developed and, in some cases, cannot be developed fully until the system is near completion.

Another training issue to consider is just how to deploy and conduct the training. Do not forget that, although all the end users are being trained in the new system, they must still perform their daily activities on the old one. For example, suppose we have a medium-size retail organization with 200 employees that need to be trained in how to use a new point-of-sale (POS) system at the retail stores. We cannot just gather up all the managers and clerks and put them in a classroom for one or two days; who will run the stores while everyone is being trained? If we stage the training over several weeks, what impact will this time delay have on the early trainees? Should we train on-site or in a controlled facility? What are the resource implications of on-site versus controlled facility training? Who should conduct the training? How can we assess the effectiveness of the training process? Who specifically needs to be trained and on what components? The answers to these questions are essential for the determination of the operational feasibility of the proposed system.

Legal and Political Feasibility

One of the most often overlooked or ignored dimensions of feasibility assessment is the *legal and political feasibility* of the new system. In this area, the analyst needs to gain an understanding of any potential legal issues that may be associated with the new system or any political impacts likely as a result of its deployment. Possible legal issues to consider include violations of patent or copyright, infringement of non-disclosure agreements, antitrust and labor-related laws, foreign trade regulations, and government-mandated reporting standards, among many others. The greatest system in the world, if in violation of existing laws or regulations, can become an organizational nightmare. Just ask Bill Gates and Microsoft.

The political ramifications of the new system must also be carefully considered and assessed during this stage of the development process. This dimension is one that is relatively easy to assess but not so easy to address. The implementation of a new system within the organization most likely brings with it a change in the distribution of, or access to, information for the organization's members. This redistribution of information, and thus redistribution of power, within the organization can have major political implications. Organizational members that are likely to be negatively impacted as a result of the new system might be inclined to oppose, resist, or even disrupt the project. Marakas and Hornik (1996) have suggested that this resistance may even come in a passive form, in which the outward attitude is one of support, whereas the covert approach is one of resistance or subversion. The legal and political ramifications of a new system must be given careful consideration prior to deployment so that any potentially negative outcomes can be addressed in a timely and successful manner.

Economic Feasibility

Last, but not least, we must assess the *economic feasibility* of the proposed system. This dimension focuses on identifying the financial and net economic impacts to the organization of the proposed system. Is it worth doing? Do the benefits outweigh the costs?

Although this activity can be thought of as a cost-benefit analysis, it is actually much more complex, because a great number of the expected benefits from a new IS may appear to be intangible (i.e., improved customer service, improved customer satisfaction, increased employee morale). We will soon see that this complexity can be managed and, using common financial analysis techniques, the true economic value of a system can be determined.

Although economic feasibility assessment may be arguably the most important of the dimensions, it must be performed last if it is to be comprehensive in its analysis. This is because the true economic impact of a system must account for all components, including required changes to the technology and the organization, additional specialized human resources or training, and compliance with, or management of, any material legal or political constraints. Further, the final decision to invest in the proposed system is made primarily on the outcome of the economic analysis rather than on any specific information requirements or favorable feasibility dimension. Thus, to insure that all of the other dimensions of feasibility have been reconciled in favor of the system, we perform the economic assessment last. If it passes this analysis, then it is ready for the next step.

Identifying the Costs and Benefits

It is often said that the good parts of an investment are a lot easier to identify than the bad parts. This is equally true in the identification of the benefits and costs associated with a proposed IS. We begin by focusing our attention on identifying and quantifying the benefits, both tangible and intangible, of the new system.

Table 8-4   Typical Tangible Benefits Associated with a New Information System

Benefit Category	Common Examples
Cost reduction	Reduction in labor or headcount
	Reduction or elimination of overtime
	Consolidation of jobs or employee roles
	Reduction in supply usage
	Less paperwork
	Smaller inventory needs or carrying costs
	Efficiencies in distribution
	Less need for travel
	Efficient use of utilities
	Lower costs of hardware and/or software
	Less maintenance
	Increase in product/process quality
	Improved production throughput or costs
	Reduction in overall cost of funds
	Improved subcontractor or external vendor control
	Reduction in or improved effectiveness of training
Revenue increase	Introduction of new products
	Decreased time to market
	Improved product quality
	Increased efficiency in sales processes
	Product enhancements
	Improved advertising support and target marketing
	Effective bidding tools
	Development of, or access to, new markets

By definition, a *benefit* is something that, either directly or indirectly, increases profit or decreases cost. Benefits are the desirable side of the equation, and the goal is to design a system that has more benefit than cost. The important issue is to identify all the benefits and, as accurately as possible, quantify them in terms of dollars and cents. Benefits can be classified as either tangible or intangible.

A *tangible benefit* is one that can be identified with certainty and that can be easily expressed in terms of dollars and cents. Table 8-4 contains a list of some common tangible benefits associated with a typical IS.

Intangible benefits are those benefits that, although believed to be directly associated with the operation of the new IS, cannot be identified with certainty or easily expressed in dollars and cents. Although difficult to quantify, the intangible benefits nonetheless contribute to the overall economic analysis of the system and can improve the benefit side of the economic feasibility assessment. Table 8-5 summarizes several common intangible benefits associated with a new IS.

Just as with the benefit side of the analysis, the cost side contains both tangibles and intangibles. *Tangible costs* are those costs that can be identified with certainty and easily expressed in dollars and cents. The *intangible costs* are those that are not easily identified with certainty and cannot be readily expressed in terms of dollars and cents. One additional classification of costs is whether they are associ-

Table 8-5   Typical Intangible Benefits Associated with a New Information System

- Improved employee morale
- Improved corporate or public image
- Increase in perceived quality of products or services
- Perceived decrease in time to market by customers
- Improved decision making
- More timely information
- Increased organizational flexibility
- Improved resource allocation and control
- Increased strategic or competitive advantage
- Improved public and community relations
- Improvements in addressing environmental concerns
- Reduced employee turnover
- Increased quality of work for employees
- Proactive attention to ethical issues
- Proactive addressing of legal issues
- Increased workplace and/or community safety

ated with systems development or system operation. *Development costs* are typically incurred once during the development project, whereas *operating costs* are generally incurred following the implementation of the system and are considered to be ongoing. Table 8-6 contains examples of both tangible and intangible costs typically associated with a new IS.

Tangibles and Intangibles

The most difficult problem in performing a thorough economic feasibility assessment lies with the intangibles. They are, admittedly, difficult to identify and even more difficult to quantify. Because of this, there is a tendency to ignore them in the preparation of the assessment. Yielding to this tendency, however, can be the most serious mistake possible in the conduct of a feasibility assessment.

Think of it this way: the intangible benefits are like icing on a cake. They are not the primary reason for pursuing the new system, and their presence or absence in the analysis probably does not make or break the decision to pursue the project. If you are wrong about the intangible benefits, "so what?"

Unfortunately, however, the same cannot be said for the intangible costs. The fact that they can be identified at all suggests that they have the potential to negatively impact the economic assessment. They represent one or more potential "black holes" where money can go in but can never be recovered. Failing to quantify the intangible costs as accurately as possible can be disastrous. If you are wrong about the intangible costs, "then what?" To insure an accurate analysis, all costs and benefits, both tangible and intangible, must be identified and quantified as accurately as possible. The question then becomes, "How do we make that which is intangible tangible?" The answer, in its simplest form, is, we guess.

The validity of an economic assessment that is based on completely unquantified components becomes somewhat difficult to accept. If we are to obtain

Table 8-6   Typical Costs Associated with a New Information System

Cost Category	Common Examples
Tangible development	Development personnel
	Analysis and design consulting fees
	Predevelopment training
	Materials and supplies
	Vendor installation and consulting
	Hiring costs for new operating personnel
	Hardware and software acquisition or development
	Physical plant acquisition and/or conversion
	Documentation preparation and distribution
	Data conversion costs
Tangible operating	Maintenance and upgrades (hardware and software)
	Annual or renewable software licenses
	Repairs (hardware and software)
	Operational personnel
	End-user training
	Connectivity and communication charges
	Materials and supplies
	Equipment lease payments
	Depreciation of system assets
Intangible	Potential disruption to existing productivity and environment
	Loss of customer goodwill
	Reduction in employee morale
	Diversion of attention to daily responsibilities

an accurate assessment of the economic feasibility of the new system, we must take the position that there is no such thing as an intangible cost or benefit. They are all costs and benefits, some of which can be accurately quantified and some that require a reasonable estimation process. To that end, the intangibles must be calculated using a logical set of underlying assumptions that lead to an estimate that, although probably not 100 percent accurate, is nonetheless much closer to reality than simply ignoring the cost or benefit altogether. Let us look at an example.

Suppose the issue is to determine the potential cost of a temporary reduction in employee morale associated with the first six months of implementation for the new system. This intangible cost has been identified through past experience that suggests that a certain number of employees are distressed by the intrusion of new technology into their environment and their productivity will be temporarily reduced as a result of this distress. We have, through a series of surveys and focused interviews, determined that approximately 10 percent of our workforce, based on their concerns expressed during the information-gathering process, experiences this loss of productivity. Further, we know from reviewing other similar projects and by consulting industry professionals that the probability of this reduction in morale occurring is about 60 percent. Our problem is we do not know what a 60 percent chance of a 10 percent reduction in employee morale is worth. What we need is a logical *surrogate measure* for employee morale. In other words, we need something we can quantify to logically represent something we cannot.

Suppose we make the assumption that the overall morale of our workforce is directly related to the profits of our company. In other words, if our employees are unhappy, then we will not sell products or services and we will not make any money. We could argue that morale is directly related to company revenues, but for purposes of illustration, profit becomes a more conservative approach to the problem. Given this assumption, we still do not know what a 10 percent reduction in employee morale is worth, but we now know what a 100 percent reduction in morale would cost: 100 percent of our annual profits!

Consider the following:

100% reduction in employee morale = Nominal annual profits
Nominal annual profits = \$2,000,000
100% reduction in employee morale = \$2,000,000
10% reduction in employee morale = (0.1)(\$2,000,000) = \$200,000
60% probability of a 10% reduction in employee morale =
(0.6)(\$200,000) = \$120,000

By performing the preceding analysis on either intangible costs or benefits, using assumptions that can be agreed on as logical, we have quantified an intangible. Although it can be argued that this approach still does not yield an accurate assessment of the cost or benefit, it nonetheless provides a working boundary for the problem. Other assumptions can be considered and tested until one is found that all agree provides enough reliability to be useful. An estimate is just that: an estimate. The important issue is that a reasonably derived estimate is infinitely more useful in assessing the economic feasibility of a project than no estimate at all. Figures 8.5a through 8.5d provide examples of the various tangible and intangible cost and benefit analyses that must be performed as part of an economic feasibility analysis.

Economic Feasibility Measures

There are many financial methods and approaches to the assessment of economic feasibility, often referred to as a test of *cost-effectiveness*, that can be employed. For our purposes, we examine the use of three common approaches: (1) net present value (NPV), (2) internal rate of return (IRR), and (3) break-even analysis.[3]

All of the preceding assessment approaches share a common concept called the *time value of money*. In essence, this concept suggests that a dollar today is worth more than a dollar in the future. The reasoning behind this concept is that if you have a dollar today, you can invest that dollar in some interest-bearing manner and have more than a dollar in the future. In assessing the economic feasibility of a project, we must consider the time value of money because we must incur cash outflows today, in the form of dollars spent to design, develop, acquire, and implement the proposed system, so that we can enjoy cash inflows in the future through the benefits expected from the new system. To insure we are comparing "apples to apples," we must convert all future dollars in the *present value* of today's dollars. In this way, we can accurately assess the value of the system over its useful life in today's dollars.

---

[3] A detailed coverage of each of these methods is beyond the scope of this text. The explanations provided here are intended to demonstrate the basic use of the assessment approach in a manner that will allow for its application. For more detailed explanations for these methods, the reader is referred to any good financial analysis textbook.

TANGIBLE COSTS

Equipment	Qty	Opt. Buy	Annual Lease	Must Buy	Rec. Buy	Rec. Lease
Dell PC's	44	$ 69,784.00	$ 27,984.00			$ 2,332.00
DirectPOS	45	$134,775.00	$ 54,017.88			$ 4,501.49
Switches	2			$ 5,098.00		
Routers	3			$ 6,585.00		
ISDN Lines	21			$ 4,704.00	$ 101.40	$ 101.40
OC-1 Line	1 (15.3 miles)			$ 80,784.00		
Cat 5 Cable	44			$ 2,640.00		
Network Printers	3	$ 6,207.00	$ 2,639.52			$ 219.96
Retail Printers	21	$ 5,229.00	$ 2,095.80			$ 174.65
Printer Server	2			$ 718.00		
SQL Server	1	$ 4,737.00	$ 1,908.00			$ 159.00
Log On Server	1	$ 3,593.00	$ 1,440.00			$ 120.00
Backup Server	1	$ 3,593.00	$ 1,440.00			$ 120.00
ISDN Modems	21			$ 5,460.00		
Tape Backup	1	$ 24,999.95	$ 10,020.00			$ 835.00
Training Personnel	7			$106,500.00		
Regional Specialist	3				$ 10,000.00	$ 10,000.00
CIO	1				$ 7,083.33	$ 7,083.33
Installation Fee				$ 43,700.00		
Programmers				$ 22,500.00		
BBB Fee				$240,000.00		
NovaNet				$ 799.20		
Peachtree				$ 599.00		
SCAN		$ 17,775.00	$ 10,800.00			$ 900.00
Laptops	6	$ 21,192.00	$ 8,496.00			$ 708.00
Training						
Customer Service Rep.	5			$ 1,200.00		
HQ Line Personnel	8			$ 2,880.00		
HQ Sr. Management	5			$ 3,600.00		
WHSE Personnel	3			$ 720.00		
Regional Managers	3			$ 1,012.00		
Store Managers	21			$ 3,150.00		
Paid Training Retail	158			$ 6,265.00		
WHSE Space	5000 sq ft				$ 4,166.67	$ 4,166.67
WHSE Personnel	3				$ 5,000.00	$ 5,000.00
UPS Cost				$ 780.00	$ 780.00	
		$291,884.95	$120,841.10	$539,694.70	$325,576.80	$437,057.90

Figure 8-5a Example of Tangible Costs Analysis

NPV

Probably the most common technique for assessing the economic feasibility of an investment is the NPV approach. This method allows for the calculation of the present value of a series of cash outflows and expected future cash inflows. The logic behind this technique is very clear. If the net of all current and future outflows and all current and future benefits, using a reasonable cost of capital or rate of

INTANGIBLE COSTS		Year 1
Operational		$311,581.00
Employee turnover		
Fear of technology		
Fear of change		
Probable reduction in morale	[(.6)(.1)(24598500)/6]	$245,985.00
Operational inefficiency		
Errors due to unfamiliarity		
Probable decrease in sales	[(.8)(.02)(24598500)/6]	$65,596.00
Developmental		$28,698.25
Disruption to organization		
Loss of customer goodwill		
Probable decrease in sales	[(.7)(.02)(24598500)/12]	$28,698.25
Total Intangible Costs		$340,279.25

Figure 8-5b   Example of Intangible Costs Analysis

Figure 8-5c   Example of Tangible Benefits Analysis

TANGIBLE BENEFITS					
	Year 1	Year 2	Year 3	Year 4	Year 5
Developmental Benefits					
Salvage of old equipment	$300.00	—			
Salvage of old software	$96.50	—			
Operating Benefits					
UPS Contract	$57,205.82	$58,921.99	$60,689.65	$62,510.34	$64,385.65
Processing error reduction	$39,972.56	$39,972.56	$39,972.56	$39,972.56	$39,972.56
Paperwork reduction	$61,496.25	$61,496.25	$61,496.25	$61,496.25	$61,496.25
Improved response time	$30,748.13	$30,748.13	$30,748.13	$30,748.13	$30,748.13
Fewer stock-outs	$138,366.56	$138,366.56	$138,366.56	$138,366.56	$138,366.56
Improved Cash Flows					
Debt reduction	$17,710.92	$17,888.03	$18,066.91	$18,247.58	$18,430.05
2% net 10	$36,897.75	$37,266.73	$37,639.39	$38,015.79	$38,395.95
Improved credit rating	$12,299.25	$12,299.25	$12,299.25	$12,300.25	$12,301.25
Increased Revenue					
Increased sales	$122,992.5	$123,914.94	$124,844.31	$125,780.64	$126,723.99
Total Tangible Benefits	$518,086.24	$520,874.44	$524,123.01	$527,438.10	$530,820.40

INTANGIBLE BENEFITS					
	Year 1	*Year 2*	*Year 3*	*Year 4*	*Year 5*
Operational Benefits					
Probable increase in morale	$18,448.88	$18,633.36	$18,719.70	$19,007.89	$19,197.97
Competitive Advantage	$106,900.06	$107,969.06	$109,048.75	$110,139.24	$111,240.63
Warehouse savings					
Lower inventory costs					
Lower risk of shrink					
Manager Decision Making	$18,448.88	$18,633.36	$18,819.70	$19,007.89	$19,197.97
Uniform reporting					
Improved information					
Timely information					
Probable increase in sales					
Customer Goodwill	$196,788.00	$198,755.88	$200,743.44	$202,750.87	$204,778.38
Decreased processing delays					
Increased transaction efficiency					
Developmental	$61,496.25	$62,111.21	$62,732.32	$63,359.65	$63,993.24
Increased flexibility					
Improved planning					
Increased organizational learning					
Total Intangible Benefits	$402,082.06	$406,102.88	$410,163.91	$414,265.55	$418,408.20

Figure 8-5d   Example of Intangible Benefits Analysis

return (called the *discount rate*), is positive, then the investment is a good one. If it is negative, then the investment will not yield the necessary returns, and it should be abandoned in favor of one that will. This technique can be used to compare two or more competing investment alternatives, as well. The alternative with the largest NPV is the one that should be chosen, based on the value of its return to the organization. Figure 8-6 illustrates a spreadsheet model used to conduct an NPV analysis of a project.

Note that each of the expected cash outflows and inflows for the project have been calculated and then *discounted* back to today's dollars by applying a factor determined to be an acceptable rate of return for the organization. This factor can be thought of as the *opportunity cost* associated with investing those dollars in other projects, including stock, bonds, or other less risky investments. In many cases, the NPV analysis is conducted using a discount rate that is deemed to be risk-free to determine the relative level of risk in the project. Probably considered to be the most common risk-free rate is the return on a U.S. Treasury Bill. This assumes, of course, that the United States does not go bankrupt or out of business.

It is also important to note that the actual value calculated in an NPV analysis is not an important number. What is important is whether the final calculation is positive or negative. If it is positive, then the investment will yield a return greater

Figure 8-6 Typical NPV Project Analysis

	Year 0	Year 1	Year 2	Year 3	Year 4	Year 5	Totals
Net economic benefit		$ 920,168.30	$ 926,977.32	$ 934,286.92	$ 941,703.65	$ 949,228.60	
Discount rate (8.25%)	1.0000	0.9238	0.8534	0.7883	0.7283	0.6728	
PV of benefits		$ 850,040.00	$ 791,067.06	$ 736,540.37	$ 685,808.14	$ 638,603.49	
NPV of all BENEFITS		$ 850,040.00	$ 1,641,107.06	$ 2,377,647.42	$ 3,063,455.56	$ 3,702,059.05	$ 3,702,059.05
One-Time COSTS	(831,579.65)	(322,659.82)					
PV of Equipment Depreciation		$ (56,086.46)	$ (51,811.97)	$ (47,863.25)	$ (44,215.47)	$ (40,845.70)	
Recurring costs		$ (325,576.80)	$ (341,855.64)	$ (358,948.42)	$ (376,895.84)	$ 395,740.64	
Discount rate (8.25%)	1.0000	0.9238	0.8534	0.7883	0.7283	0.6728	
PV of recurring costs		$ (300,763.79)	$ (291,733.93)	$ (282,975.17)	$ (274,479.38)	$ (266,238.66)	
NPV of all COSTS	$(831,579.65)	$(1,511,089.71)	$(1,854,635.61)	$(2,185,474.03)	$(2,504,168.89)	$(2,811,253.25)	$(2,811,253.25)
Overall NPV							$ 890,805.80
Overall ROI							32%
IRR							38%
Breakeven Analysis							
Yearly NPV cash flow	$(831,579.65)	$ 549,276.21	$ 499,333.13	$ 453,565.19	$ 411,328.75	$ 372,364.83	
Overall NPV cash flow	$(831,579.65)	$ (661,049.71)	$ (213,528.55)	$ 192,173.39	$ 559,286.67	$ 890,805.80	
Project break-even occurs at 2.576 years							

231

than the required return. If it is negative, then the project, at least in its present form, is not economically feasible. It really is that simple.

The present value of a dollar for any period in the future easily can be calculated using the following formula:

$$PV_n = 1/(1 + i)^n$$

where PV_n = present value of $1.00 n years from now, and i = the accepted discount rate or rate of return.

Thus, the present value of a dollar three years from now assuming a discount rate of 10 percent is

$$NPV = PV_1 + PV_2 + PV_3 + ... PV_n$$
$$PV_3 = 1/(1 + 0.10)^3 = 0.751$$

This calculation suggests that a dollar received three years from now is the same as receiving 75.1 cents today if a 10 percent rate of return is required. As shown in these equations and in Figure 8-6, the NPV of an investment is simply the sum of the present value calculations for each period.

Although simple enough to calculate, most financial textbooks contain detailed tables of discount factors for a dollar at various interest rates and for various periods. Table 8-7 contains a partial list of discount factors using common interest rates and discount periods. A more complete list can be obtained from any good financial analysis reference book.

IRR

Another equally popular method of assessing the economic feasibility of a project, and one closely related to the NPV approach, is to calculate the project's IRR. Although mathematically more complicated that calculating an NPV, the IRR is actually the rate of return of the project when the NPV is zero. The result of an IRR calculation is the true net return on the investment expressed as an interest rate. The

Table 8-7   Partial Table of Values for the Present Value of a Dollar

Period	8%	10%	12%	14%
1	0.926	0.909	0.893	0.877
2	0.857	0.826	0.797	0.769
3	0.794	0.751	0.712	0.675
4	0.735	0.683	0.636	0.592
5	0.681	0.621	0.567	0.519
6	0.630	0.564	0.507	0.456
7	0.583	0.513	0.452	0.400
8	0.540	0.467	0.404	0.351

IRR of an investment is mathematically defined as the largest number d that satisfies the equation

$$x = \sum_{t=1}^{T} \frac{R_t}{(1 + d)^t}$$

where T = the expected life of the project in years, X = the total cost of the project, and R_t = the expected net return in year t.

Given the obvious complexity of the preceding calculation, it is much better to use a computer when determining an IRR.[4] Most spreadsheet programs include a simple function for calculating IRR. As shown in Figure 8-6, the calculated IRR of our project is 38 percent.

Break-Even Analysis

The objective of a *break-even analysis* is to determine at what point over the expected life of the project (if ever) the benefits derived from the project equal the costs associated with implementing it. The first step in determining the break-even point is to calculate the NPV of the yearly cash flows for the project. Next, a running total of the overall NPV cash flow during each period of the project must be determined. The year in which the overall NPV cash flow for the project is positive is called the *pay-back period*. To determine the actual break-even point for the project, the following formula can be used:

$$\frac{\text{Pay-Back Period NPV Cash Flow} - \text{Overall NPV Cash Flow}}{\text{Pay-Back Period NPV Cash Flow}}$$

Referring to Figure 8-6, we can see that the project reaches a break-even point in approximately month 7 of year 2.

Another equally effective method for determining the break-even point of a project is simply to plot the expected costs against the expected benefits on a graph. The point at which the two lines intersect is the break-even point. Figure 8-7 contains an illustration of the graphical approach to the assessment.

Risk Assessment

In performing a thorough feasibility analysis for a proposed project, we must also look at the characteristics of the development effort from the perspective of risk. Although related, the dimensions of feasibility and the inherent risks associated with the design strategy are two distinct concepts. In other words, feasibility and risk are complementary concepts, but they are not the same.

All projects have risks, and complete avoidance of risk is usually not a viable strategy from either a cost or simply practical perspective. The important issue with risk is that we must identify the various sources and potential for it in each development effort and then select a design strategy such that the identified risks

---

[4] A related calculation sometimes employed in investment analysis is ROI. While useful as an analysis tool, its applicability in assessing the economic feasibility of a proposed project is limited, because it takes into account only the net results at the endpoints of the investment (i.e., the beginning and the end of the project). Because IRR accounts for the net cash flows during each period, IRR is preferred over ROI.

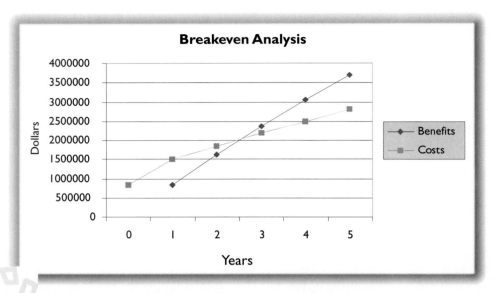

Figure 8-7   Example of Graphical Breakeven Analysis

are minimized to practical levels. In short, risk is something we manage, not necessarily something we avoid.

Cash, McFarlan, McKenney, and Applegate (1992) have identified four general categories of risk inherent in all development efforts: (1) project size, (2) project structure, (3) analysts, and (4) end users. Table 8-8 provides examples of these four basic categories of risk.

Table 8-8   Categories and Examples of Project Risk

Category of Risk	Examples of Risk
Project size	• Length of development schedule • Number of members of development team • Span of involvement across organizational business units • Span of involvement across unrelated organizations • Size of project as measured in number of applications or lines of code
Project structure	• Degree to which development effort is new and/or innovative • Extent of organizational or structural change required • Overall managerial commitment to project
Analysts	• Familiarity with business environment • Familiarity with proposed technologies • Familiarity with similar project scopes and complexities
End-users	• Perception of end-users to necessity or relevance of new system • Familiarity with system development process and change • Familiarity with proposed system application environment

The first category of risk, *project size,* includes not only the size of the project as it relates to cost or delivery time but also size as it relates to the number of stakeholders or people involved. Generally speaking, the larger the development group or the larger the time to delivery of the project, the greater the risk associated with this project. With the velocity of technological change ever increasing, many large development organizations are automatically classifying any project with a delivery window in excess of six months as a high risk project requiring special approvals and management resources.

The *project structure* is a second category of risk in systems development. In general, the more the design and development effort is focused on revising an existing system or developing an application with a clear-cut set of requirements and processes, the less risky the project is. For example, the upgrade of an existing corporate human resources management system would be inherently less risky than the development of a computer-based manufacturing system. The former is, most likely, much more structured and better understood than the latter.

The *analysts* represent a third category of risk to a development project. The degree of familiarity the analysts possess with regard to the business environment, the proposed technology platforms, and the management of a project of a given size all contribute to the overall risk associated with the project.

Finally, the *end users* represent a category of potential risk. If the user community is familiar with the activities of a large-scale development effort and have been actively involved in the design and analysis phases of the project, the project is less likely to pose a risk in this area. If this is the first time a major development effort has been initiated in this organization, however, the risk associated with resistance from the end-user community is greater, and more time effort associated with communicating with and educating the users and involving them directly in the process is required.

CHAPTER SUMMARY

The development and adoption of a successful design strategy is predicated on the outcome of a detailed feasibility and risk assessment process. It is at this stage that all aspects of the logical models and system specifications must be carefully scrutinized as they are translated into a proposed physical form. Although the concept of creeping commitment is still viable during the physical design and implementation stages of the SDLC, the cost of making changes or revising the system becomes significantly greater than during the logical portions of the process. Once the assessments are complete, however, you can make a reasonably clear-cut set of recommendations to the organization with regard to whether to proceed with the next stages of the development process.

In the following chapters, we take a detailed look at each of the major activities associated with the development and implementation of an IS.

KEY CONCEPTS

➤ From "what" to "how"

The transition from logical design to physical design is where the focus of the analyst turns from what the system must do to exactly how the system does it.

➤ The "geometry" of systems development

A good strategy is a strategy that maintains a balance between cost, quality, and time to delivery. An emphasis on any one of the project constraints results in a compensating change in at least one of the other two.

➤ Design strategy

A design strategy describes the approach to be followed in transforming the logical system requirements into a functional, physical IS.

➤ We must assess not only the feasibility of implementing the solution but also the costs and consequences associated with not implementing the proposed system.

➤ Only when the processes and outcomes make sense when traveling slowly should we consider speeding them up through a computer-based solution.

➤ Three basic approaches to the software application side of the development effort

1. Buy a COTS solution and customize it to fit
2. Develop a custom software application in-house
3. Outsource the project of an external vendor or developer

➤ COTS evaluation criteria
- Application efficiency
- Application effectiveness
- Usability
- Documentation
- Vendor support

➤ Outsourcing approaches
- Outsourcing

  Outsourcing involves the hiring of an external vendor to provide the necessary expertise and human resources necessary to create the system.
- Software Service Provider (SSP)

  The second alternative approach is to contract with an SSP. An SSP is an external vendor that sells the use of a large-scale computer facility and its common platform applications to a wide variety of customer organizations.

➤ Hardware considerations
- The degree to which the existing hardware platform supports the new application
- Opportunity for the organization to facilitate the restructuring of existing computing operations to effect strategic advantage in other application areas beyond the development effort

➤ Structured design strategy

A structured approach to the final determination of the feasibility of the proposed solution must be employed to insure that the system meets the stated business need of the organization in the manner intended.

➤ Feasible solutions
- A feasible solution solves the identified problem or maximizes the identified economic opportunity without causing any problems that were not in existence before its implementation.
- If an investment cannot be justified in fact before it is made, then it can never be justified in fact after it is made.

➤ Three perspectives for making a business case:
- Facts
- Faith
- Fear

➤ The dimensions of system feasibility
- Technical

  The outcome of technical feasibility assessment is a determination of the practicality of a specific technical solution and the availability of the necessary technology to implement it. Issues to be considered include:
  - Practicality
  - Reasonableness
  - Availability
- Operational

  Operational feasibility assessment focuses on issues related to how well the proposed solution will work within the organization and how the end users feel about the new system.

- Reexamine the likelihood that the proposed solution attains the desired goals and objectives.
- Assert that the proposed development and implementation schedule for the project is reasonable and executable.
- Assess the availability of resources and the coincidence of project milestones to nonproject events.
- Determine the degree of impact on the organization that results from the implementation and adoption of the new system and its associated business processes.

- Human factors
  - System usability
    Usability is a measure of various characteristics of the system's user interface with regard to the ease with which it allows the end users to perform their jobs. Three basic categories of assessment are
    - Ease of use
    - Perceived ease of use
    - Overall satisfaction
  - End-user training
    - Training schedule
    - Training deployment
- Legal and political
  Gain an understanding of any potential issues that may be associated with the new system or any political impacts likely as a result of its deployment.
- Economic
  Identify the financial and net economic impacts to the organization of the proposed system.

➤ Vaporware
A term used to describe technology that is announced but is not yet readily available to the customer.

➤ Cost and benefit analysis
- Benefits:
  - Tangible benefits
    A tangible benefit is one that can be identified with certainty and that

can be easily expressed in terms of dollars and cents.
  - Intangible benefits
    Intangible benefits are those benefits that, although believed to be directly associated with the operation of the new system, cannot be identified or easily expressed in dollars and cents.
- Costs
  - Tangible costs
    Tangible costs are those costs that can be identified and easily expressed in dollars and cents.
    - Systems development
    - System operation
  - Intangible costs
    Intangible costs are those costs that, although believed to be directly associated with the operation of the new system, cannot be identified or easily expressed in dollars and cents.

➤ Logical estimation
- If we are to obtain an accurate assessment of the economic feasibility of the new system, we must take the position that there is no such thing as an intangible cost or benefit. They are all costs and benefits; some of which can be accurately quantified and some that require a reasonable estimation process.
- Logical estimation is an important method of more accurately assessing the intangible costs and benefits identified during an economic feasibility assessment.

➤ Time value of money
The time value of money concept suggests that a dollar today is worth more than a dollar at some point in the future.

➤ Three common approaches to the test of cost-effectiveness:
- Net present value (NPV)
  Calculate the present value of a series of cash outflows and expected future cash inflows and determine if the final calculation is positive or negative.
- Internal rate of return (IRR)
  Calculate the true net return on the investment expressed as an interest rate.

- Break-even analysis

  Determine at what point over the expected life of the project (if ever) the benefits derived from the project equal the costs associated with implementing it.

➤ Risk assessment

  - Feasibility and risk assessment
    - Feasibility is the determination of the likelihood of success associated with one of the dimensions of a development project.

- Risk is the determination of something going wrong that may be beyond the immediate control of the project participants.
- Potential sources of risk in a development project are
  - Project size
  - Project structure
  - Analysts
  - End users

QUESTIONS FOR REVIEW

1. Explain the concept of the geometry of systems development and its importance.

2. What is the main purpose of a design strategy?

3. What are the two predominant perspectives with regard to the value of IT?

4. Describe the three basic approaches to software development.

5. List and briefly explain the criteria for evaluating a proposed COTS solution.

6. What are the trade-offs of adopting a COTS design strategy?

7. What are the trade-offs of adopting a custom software development design strategy?

8. List and briefly describe the two alternative approaches to outsourcing.

9. List and briefly depict the five dimensions of system feasibility.

10. Explain how the three perspectives of pursuing business investments affect the feasibility assessment.

11. Describe the issues needed to be considered when assessing technical feasibility.

12. What are the key issues of consideration when assessing operational feasibility?

13. List and briefly describe the three basic categories of system usability assessment.

14. Distinguish the main differences between tangible and intangible costs and benefits.

15. How do we ensure the validity of an economic feasibility assessment?

16. Explain the concept of the time value of money.

17. List and briefly explain the three common approaches to the test of cost-effectiveness.

18. Distinguish the concepts of feasibility and risk.

19. Identify the potential sources of risk in a development project.

FOR FURTHER DISCUSSION

1. Using the techniques you have learned in this chapter, conduct a thorough feasibility analysis of the purchase of a new computer system for your personal use. Assume a three year analysis period and use a reasonable rate of return on your investment. Can you justify it from a feasibility analysis perspective? Does it have a positive NPV?

2. Contact a local organization's IT department and see if you can arrange a time to discuss the various processes and activities they are outsourcing. What do these processes have in common? What is the rationale for outsourcing these particular activities and not others? Could an IT department conceivably outsource all activities and just manage the relationships?

3. A large insurance company has hired your firm to consolidate the application software used by their various product divisions into a single, enterprise-wide system. During the initial JAD sessions you compile a list of questions generated by the group as relevant to the development of a new system. One of the questions asked is "Who do we think the next President of the United States will be?" Why would this question be relevant? Under what category of feasibility assessment might this issue fall?

4. Identify three intangible costs and three intangible benefits associated with a software development project. Create a logical approach to converting them to expected values. Be sure to clearly state the logic behind your surrogate measures.

REFERENCES

Brynjolfsson, E., and L. M. Hitt. 1998. "Beyond The Productivity Paradox." *Communications of the ACM* 41 (8): 49–55.

Cash, J. I., F. W. McFarlan, J. L. McKenney, and L. M. Applegate. 1992. *Corporate Information Systems Management*, 3d ed. Boston: Irwin.

Landauer, T. K. 1995. *The Trouble with Computers: Usefulness, Usability, and Productivity.* Cambridge, MA: MIT Press.

Marakas, G. M., and S. Hornik. 1996. "Passive Resistance Misuse: Overt Support and Covert Resistance in IS implementation." *European Journal of Information Systems.*

Designing Systems for Diverse Environments

Learning Objectives

- To gain an appreciation of the diversity of design and development environments faced by the modern analyst
- To understand the advantages and disadvantages of centralized versus distributed data systems
- To learn the differences between the file server and the client–server approaches to networking
- To explore the common network topologies and understand their relative advantages and disadvantages
- To gain an appreciation for development issues within ERP, collaborative, intranet, and data warehousing environments

It is in the nature of the beast (the beast being a distributed information system) that providers of interfaces into the beast have no control over the servers that feed the beast. Which is to say, if NCSA Mosaic locks up trying to access a server in outer Mongolia (or even outer Peoria), don't blame us—somebody's server is down.

—NATIONAL CENTER FOR SUPERCOMPUTING APPLICATIONS,
UNIVERSITY OF ILLINOIS AT CHAMPAIGN-URBANA

Depend on it, nothing is so unnatural as the typical and commonplace.

—SIR ARTHUR CONAN DOYLE

INTRODUCTION

In the last chapter, we made the transition from the logical model to the physical model and learned how to assess the feasibility of a proposed physical solution. We also learned that several strategies must be considered with regard to how the physical solution is defined: COTS? Build in-house? Outsource? Hybrid? In this chapter, we continue our focus on the move from "what" to "how." We concentrate on the issues and complexities associated with the configuration of the processing environment in which our solution resides. The many processing environments in today's wired world preclude us from conducting a thorough investigation of this subject in a single chapter of a textbook. As such, our purpose and scope is necessarily limited to identifying the various environments to be considered and the characteristics that serve to make that environment unique with regard to application design and implementation.

TYPICAL IS NOT SO TYPICAL ANYMORE

Through the evolution of computing, there has always been a "typical" processing architecture and environment. In the late 1960s, typical was easy to define because there was only one technological environment from which to choose: a mainframe computer operated from a central location. The design choices available to the analyst were limited to the type and location of the input devices. This processing environment was considered typical because the application environment was equally monolithic: large-scale batch processing of transactions.

This single computer architecture afforded many advantages to the organization. First, the economies of scale were clear. One large processor serving many users and storing or distributing a wide variety of data was both elegantly simple and cost-effective. In addition, data redundancy was naturally minimal, because all of the applications residing on the central computer made use of only the data that were housed or accessible by that computer. Finally, any controls, security policies, or processing standards were easily enforced at the central processor

As we moved into the 1970s, the central computing environment was still the typical approach, but several new and innovative versions of it were beginning to emerge. New applications and greater volumes of transaction-level data were making the single processor approach untenable. The demands on the capacity of the mainframe made it difficult for a single processor to handle all of the required storage, processing, and retrieval requests. To address these issues, the central computing environment was expanded to allow for multiple, identical, centrally located processors to be clustered together in an effort to harness the sum of their processing capabilities. With this configuration, the common operating system across the computers contained in the central cluster allowed for applications to be run on any processor. Further, new applications were written to monitor the use of the processors in the cluster and divert requests for data storage and retrieval or application processing to the system that was most underused at that moment. Most important, this load-balancing across multiple processors took place invisibly to the user, thus creating the effect of a single supercomputing environment. Figure 9-1 illustrates the clustered central computing approach.

On August 2, 1982, the definition of the typical processing environment changed forever. It was on this date that the PC was born. Shortly after its introduction and rapid acceptance came the desire to link PCs together to share data and processing power in much the same way as the multiple computer concept of the 1970s. Thus was born the local area network (LAN), the wide area network (WAN), and ultimately the Internet and the WWW. The age of distributed computing had begun, and the typical processing environment was not so typical anymore.

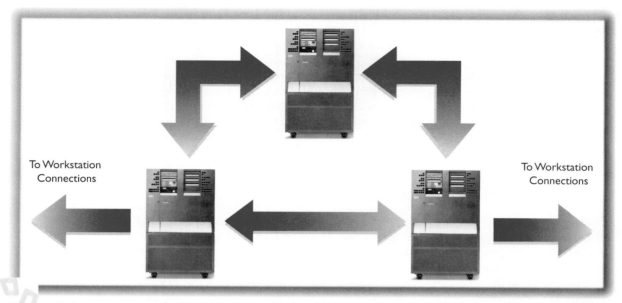

Figure 9-1   Typical Clustered Central Computing System

THE DISTRIBUTED IS

The typical *distributed* IS is composed of relatively independent subsystems, often geographically dispersed, that are tied together within the organizational framework by some method of communication interface. This system of IS can be thought of as a network of subsystems located at, and adapted to, specific areas of need. In such a network, three basic conditions exist: (1) some subsystems need to interact with other subsystems, (2) some subsystems need to share files or data processing facilities with other subsystems, and (3) some subsystems require very little interaction with other subsystems, thus operating in a fairly isolated and self-sufficient manner. In contrast to the monolithic nature of the centralized data processing facility with a common database, the distributed IS is highly modular and employs an aggregation of IS arranged as a network. Figure 9-2 contains an example of a distributed IS architecture.

Although there are a number of similarities with regard to designing for central or distributed computing environments, there are also some important differences. Most important is that the system inherently is distributed over two or more geographically dispersed locations, and additional considerations with regard to both the reliability and the survivability of the system must be carefully considered. The *reliability* of the system suggests that a particular piece of data is available at a given time regardless of the location of the user requesting it. *Survivability* refers to the system's ability to continue to provide service to its users despite the failure of one or more nodes. These issues often require the analyst to consider a number of tradeoffs when designing for a distributed environment.

The Drive to Distribute

A number of forces, both technical and social, are key motivators in favor of distributed computing. First, the cost of desktop computing workstations is dropping rapidly, whereas the interface and computing power of such devices is increasing. The

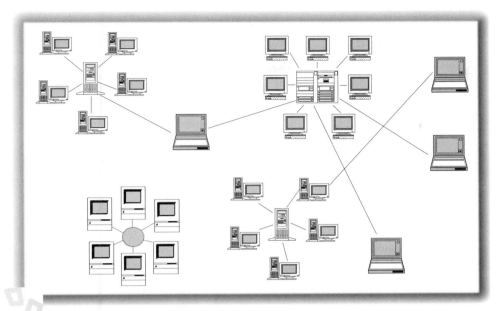

Figure 9-2   Typical Distributed Computer System

desire to share data across multiple computing platforms is being facilitated by increased communications bandwidth and inexpensive storage costs. More important is the fact that the demand for locally specific applications is rising much faster than the ability of any central IS function to respond to that demand. Finally, the Internet and the WWW provide a natural connectivity vehicle to access data and applications from one side of the globe to the other.

The Pros and Cons of Distributed Computing

Although a number of advantages can be identified with regard to adopting a distributed computing environment, probably the single greatest advantage is the ability to design the system to be responsive to the local needs of the end users. This allows the analyst not only to focus on the technical advantages of distributed computing with regard to reliability and survivability but also to pay close attention to the issues of business alignment, scalability, and conformity to existing organizational structures. Table 9-1 contains a brief synopsis of the advantages and disadvantages commonly associated with distributed computing.

As you can see from Table 9-1, distributed computing is not without its downside issues. To begin, the economies of scale found in a centralized approach disappear immediately, and the difficulties associated with management and control of the network rise significantly. Further, although Robert Metcalfe's law suggests that the utility of a given network increases exponentially with the additional of a single node, this concept may be paraphrased to suggest that each additional node in a distributed computing environment also significantly increases the difficulties associated with managing and controlling the network.

Types of Distribution

Although the concept of a distributed computing system lends itself to a variety of configurations and applications, there are basically two types of distributed systems: (1) distributed applications and (2) distributed data. Further, the hardware

Table 9-1   Comparative Pros and Cons of Distributed Computing

Advantages	Disadvantages
• Increased adaptability and responsiveness to local needs	• Increased difficulties in controlling information resources
• Increased availability of resources due to redundant systems	• Potential for massive data redundancy
• Closer alignment with organizational structure	• Increased complexity and cost
• Improved incremental growth and local scalability	• Increased network management resources
• Increased end user empowerment	• Increased difficulty in testing and detecting failures
• Location independence supports development of virtual teams	
• Independence from single vendor solutions	

architecture used to deploy the method of distribution can be categorized by two basic approaches: (1) file server architecture and (2) client–server architecture.

Distributed Applications

In a *distributed application* environment, the focus is on allowing geographically dispersed end users to access and use a variety of software applications. Using this approach, the applications can be stored in a single location and accessed by any processor connected to the system, or a single application can be replicated to multiple locations throughout the network, or different applications can reside at different locations in the network but be made accessible to all end users. This application-server approach is commonly used to reduce the space necessary to store commonly used applications like word processors and spreadsheets that do not lend themselves to multiple user interaction, are generally memory-resident in nature, and are generally limited to the creation of a single access data file.

Distributed Data

The other common type of distribution is the *distributed data* approach. Here, the data can be either replicated across multiple sites for ease of access or partitioned such that a portion of the data resides in several locations throughout the network. We look at the issues associated with distributed data and the concept of data partitioning in detail later in this chapter.

File Server versus Client–Server Approach

One of the most common methods of interconnecting computers to create a distributed processing environment is the LAN. In a typical LAN, the workstations are generally PCs of various configurations, and the server can be a PC or larger computing platform. The workstations are connected to the server via one of several connection topologies and are generally all within 30 meters of each other and within 1 kilometer of the server (as measured in cable length). Networks that go be-

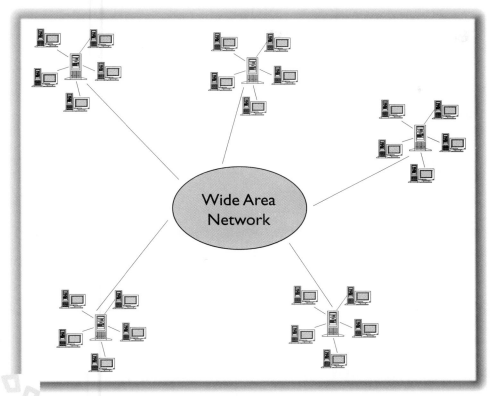

Figure 9-3   Typical LAN/WAN Connectivity

yond the 1 kilometer range are referred to as WAN. Such systems can span buildings, cities, countries, continents, or even the entire globe. Figure 9-3 illustrates a typical network composed of several LANs and a single WAN.

In the typical LAN environment, the processing architecture can be set up using either a *file server* or *client–server* system approach. The *file server* approach manages the various file operations associated with the system and can be thought of as an additional hard drive for each connected PC workstation. Using this method of distribution, the data reside on the file server but all processing must be performed at the workstation level. The software running on the file server is designed to manage the requests for data from the various workstations, but it is the responsibility of the workstation to run the application program necessary to handle all of the data management and manipulation functions. This approach generally means that if a user wishes to look at the information stored for a single customer in a database in a file server environment, the entire customer file is sent to that workstation via the network. Once the workstation has received the file, the query can be executed, and the information can be displayed. Further, all data security checks and record locking functions are performed at the workstation level, thus making the deployment and operation of a multiuser application a highly complex process. Finally, because of the nature of this approach, there is a significant amount of data traffic on the network and the need for very powerful workstations on each connected desktop.

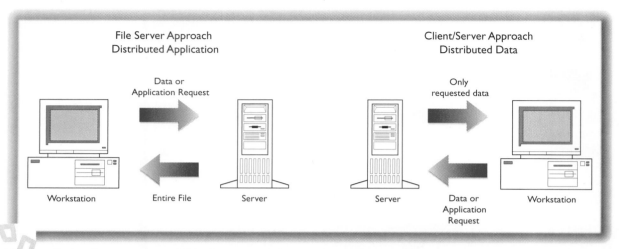

Figure 9-4   Comparison of File Server and Client–Server Approach

A response to the drawbacks associated with the file server approach is the *client–server architecture.* Using this approach, the processing load for a particular application is divided between the client workstation and the server. Although this division of labor is not necessarily equal, it does allow for the various processing activities in a network environment to be handled by the most appropriate and efficient processor.

Under the client–server approach, the workstation is responsible for managing the user interface and the presentation of data, whereas the server is responsible for both the storage of data and the processing of queries to them. This allows the central database server to manage the issues of data recovery, security, and concurrency more efficiently, thus relieving the workstation from having to carry this burden for each connected user. Although the server must be very powerful and larger than that found in a typical LAN environment, the client workstation software is left to concentrate on only the work being done by that user. Figure 9-4 contains an example of both file server and client–server architecture.

Connectivity Diagramming

Prior to the concept of distributed processing and global networks, there was no need to have any formal method of diagramming the location of geographically dispersed users. Although there is still no formal diagramming approach for this activity, several methods have begun to emerge. The *location connectivity diagram* (LCD) suggested by Whitten and Bentley (1998) is the method we use in this text.

The LCD depicts the shape or configuration of a network in terms of the locations of the various users, processes, data, and interfaces residing on the network. Additionally, the LCD identifies the necessary interconnection between the network elements in terms of location. For the purposes of constructing an LCD, the term *location* is defined as "any place at which users exist or interact with the information system or application . . . or any place where business can be transacted or work performed" (Whitten and Bentley 1998, 268). More important, an LCD can depict both logical locations where people do work and physical locations where the various technologies contained within the system reside. Note, however, that an

Table 9-2   Symbology for Location Connectivity Diagrams

Symbol	Description
	Specific location: anyplace where end users exist to use or interact with the information system or application or where business can be conducted and work performed.
	Cluster location: a group of end users who perform the same duties in the same logical or physical location.
	Mobile location: one or more end users who typical perform their work in multiple locations (i.e., sales representatives).
	External location: organizations and agents outside of the company but that interact with or use the information system.

LCD depicts interactivity but not data flow direction. This is because the interconnectivity of the various locations is independent of the direction of data flow. Table 9-2 shows the symbology for constructing an LCD, and Figure 9-5 contains an example of a simple LCD.

Basic Connection Topologies

By decomposing the elements in an LCD we can graphically depict the methods by which the workstations within each LAN are connected to each other and to the servers. Although a thorough discussion of each of the various network topologies and connection standards is better left for a telecommunications text, we visit each of the basic approaches briefly in the following sections.

The Bus Topology

One of the most common connection schemes, and also one of the simplest, is the *bus topology*. Here, a direct point-to-point link for each workstation is provided such that all workstations, shared peripheral devices, and servers can be connected to each other. In the bus approach, only one computer can send data through the bus at any given moment, but this traffic constraint is typically managed at extremely high speeds by one of several available network protocols. The most widely used of these protocols is *Ethernet,* which manages the point-to-point traffic on the bus and resolves any contention that may occur when more than one workstation or device attempts to use the bus for data transmission. Figure 9-6 illustrates a typical bus topology.

The Ring Topology

Another approach to connectivity is the *ring topology*. As its name implies, the workstations, peripherals, and servers on the network are connected via a ringlike structure. Using this approach, each device on the network can communicate with only

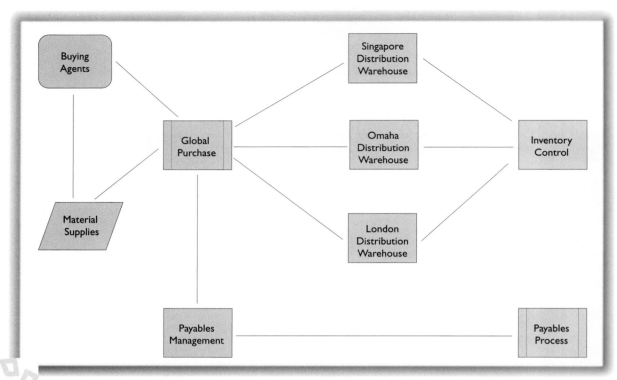

Figure 9-5   Example of a Location Connectivity Diagram
Adapted from Whitten and Bentley 1998

Figure 9-6   Typical Bus Network Topology

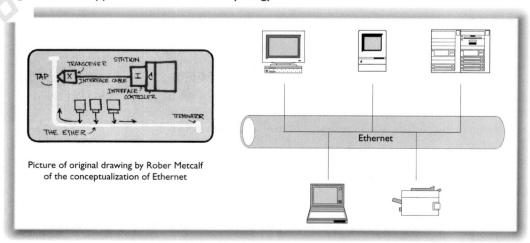

one other device on the network, as the traffic always flows in a single direction. Each communication or request, called a *packet,* sent by a device to its neighbor contains a specific address of the intended recipient device. When a packet is received by a device on the ring, it checks the address. If the device's address matches that of the packet, then the message is processed by that device. If the addresses do not match, the device simply passes the packet on to its neighboring device. Through this process, all packets eventually arrive at their intended destinations. The *token ring* protocol developed by IBM is commonly used with this topology. Figure 9-7 illustrates the ring topology approach.

The Star Topology

One of the first approaches to connectivity was via the *star topology.* In this approach each workstation is connected to a central server via a single hardware connection. Although this may sound like a centralized computing approach, the central server need not be the sole location for either storage or application processing. As shown in Figure 9-8, the center of the star network could be an application server that serves as a traffic manager for queries and requests to a larger mainframe or minicomputer system. Communication from one workstation to another on a star network must first pass through the central server and be routed to the appropriate recipient workstation.

Topology Characteristics and Drawbacks

Although each of the topologies mentioned previously are commonly employed for their unique characteristics, each of the approaches has certain drawbacks that must be considered when selecting a particular approach. Table 9-3 summarizes the characteristics and drawbacks associated with each common connection scheme.

Figure 9-7   Typical Token-Ring Network Topology

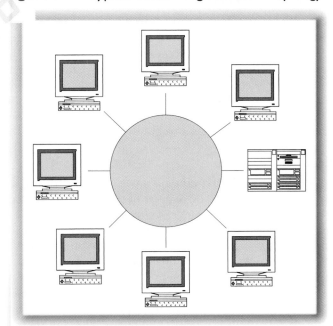

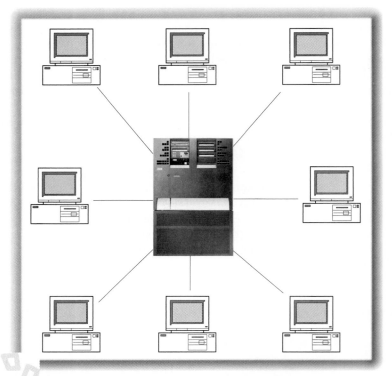

Figure 9-8 Typical Star Network Topology

MANAGING THE DISTRIBUTED DATA

As mentioned earlier in this chapter, geographically dispersed organizations have two alternatives to data storage. One is to store the data in a central location and have each of the dispersed locations access them as needed. The other is to distribute that data among multiple locations throughout the network. The latter choice is rapidly becoming the preferred method due to the advancements in global connectivity and bandwidth. In this next part, we look at the various methods available with regard to distributed data and discuss the various advantages and disadvantages of each from both a design and a usability perspective.

Data Replication

One method of effecting a distributed data environment is through the use of *replication*. This approach creates a copy of each of the databases contained in the system at each workstation or server location throughout the network. Using this method, all users can have access to a database at their location, thus improving throughput and decreasing the processing load on any single database server. The various changes to each of the local database copies are reflected in the other copies via a replication scheme managed by the servers in the network. On either a scheduled or an on-demand basis, the changes in one copy of a database can be inserted into another copy and vice versa. This replication process normally is scheduled to occur during late night hours when database access is low or idle.

Table 9-3   Comparative Advantages and Disadvantages of Common Network Topologies

Topology	Advantages	Disadvantages
Star	• Low complexity with regard to network management • Failure of a node does not disable the network	• Requires significantly more cabling than alternatives • Failure of the central server disables entire network • Throughput can be slowed due to large volumes of requests at the central server
Ring	• Relatively easy to synchronize network connections • Can span greater distances because message is regenerated at each node • Generally high bandwidths can be achieved	• Entire network is disabled if any cable is cut or experiences fault • Relatively high installation costs
Bus	• Low cabling requirements • Relatively inexpensive to install	• All or part of the network may be disabled if cable is cut or experiences fault

The replication approach provides users with the advantage of high reliability of access to the data. If a copy of a database at one of the sites in the network becomes unavailable or fails, a user can simply access a copy stored at another site. Further, the replication approach provides a relatively fast response time to queries, because each site in the network can direct their queries to the local copy of the database.

The disadvantages of the replication method must also be considered when selecting a data distribution approach. Because each site can have a full complement of copies of all databases, the storage requirements for each server, as well as for the network, are significantly increased over other available methods. Further, the processing costs and the complexity associated with managing the database update process across all copies on the network are significantly greater than the more conventional central storage approach. A widely available commercial application that employs the replication approach is the collaborative groupware product Lotus Notes. Figure 9-9 shows an example of the replication control process within a Lotus Notes client.

Data Partitioning

Another approach to data distribution is to partition the data using some logical approach such that the contention for data across workstations or server locations is minimized and, thus, the average throughput of the entire system is increased. Such an approach must allow for access to all data regardless of their physical location and must maintain a *location transparency* to the end user. This means that the end user should not have to be concerned with at what physical location the data actually reside when performing a query. Although an infinite combination of data

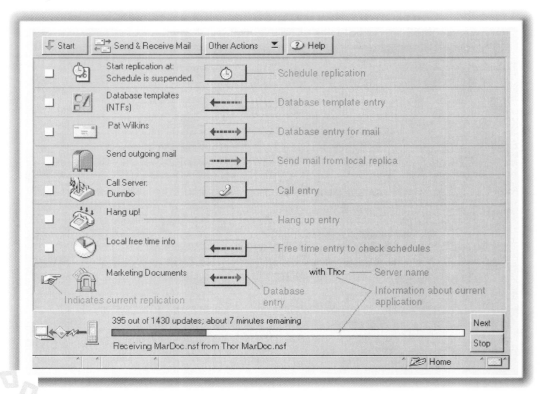

Figure 9-9 Lotus Notes Database Replication Control Screen

partitions can be created, all are based on one of two methods: (1) horizontal partitioning or (2) vertical partitioning. Figure 9-10 illustrates the horizontal partitioning approach, and Figure 9-11 illustrates the vertical partitioning approach.

In the *horizontal partitioning* approach, the data are distributed by partitioning the rows of a data table into separate base relations located at two or more sites. The distribution logic is normally based on locating records (rows) within the database at the same physical location that most frequently accesses them such that maximum throughput is achieved. Because the organization of the fields (columns) at each physical location is the same, the database can be easily reconstructed, if necessary. An example of this approach would be the distribution of customer records across several physical business sites, such as a chain of bank branches. With this approach, any customer's record could be accessed by any bank branch, but it would be stored in the data server located at the customer's assigned home branch.

Conversely, the *vertical partitioning* method relocates certain columns from table and stores them as base relations at two or more physical sites. Using this approach, the new tables must share a common key, so that the master table can be reconstructed if necessary. Vertical partitions allow the data to be separated according to which attributes (fields) are most used by a physical location. As an example, a manufacturing organization may choose to vertically partition a large PARTS file such that the data attributes most used by design are physically located on the design division's system and the attributes most accessed by manufacturing are physi-

Typical Relation for Sales Organization

CUSTOMER NO.	CUSTOMER NAME	DIVISION	STATUS	CURRENT BALANCE
172945	Jordan, Michael	Southeast	Inactive	92154.00
189456	Pippin, Scottie	Northwest	Active	12357.00
721981	O'Neal, Shaquille	West	Active	65879.00
366544	Malone, Karl	West	Active	52987.00
701489	Mourning, Alonso	Southeast	Active	10254.00
252314	Bryant, Kobe	West	Active	11951.00
544479	Walton, Bill	Northwest	Inactive	61234.00

Horizontal Partition for Southeast Division

CUSTOMER NO.	CUSTOMER NAME	DIVISION	STATUS	CURRENT BALANCE
172945	Jordan, Michael	Southeast	Inactive	92154.00
701489	Mourning, Alonso	Southeast	Active	10254.00

Horizontal Partition for West Division

CUSTOMER NO.	CUSTOMER NAME	DIVISION	STATUS	CURRENT BALANCE
721981	O'Neal, Shaquille	West	Active	65879.00
366544	Malone, Karl	West	Active	52987.00
252314	Bryant, Kobe	West	Active	11951.00

Horizontal Partition for Northwest Division

CUSTOMER NO.	CUSTOMER NAME	DIVISION	STATUS	CURRENT BALANCE
189456	Pippin, Scottie	Northwest	Active	12357.00
544479	Walton, Bill	Northwest	Inactive	61234.00

Figure 9-10   Example of Horizontal Partitioning of Data

cally located on their system. As with horizontal partitioning, the local transparency issue must be addressed, so that the end user can issue a query without having to know the physical location of the desired data.

Table 9-4 summarizes the basic approaches to data distribution in terms of their strengths and weaknesses across several dimensions.

Typical Relation for Manufacturing Firm

ITEM NO.	BIN LOCATOR	ITEM DESCRIPTION	ITEM COST	ITEM QTY.	SUPPLIER
72695	A7-S56	Trem spring	.85	924	Century
54132	A9-S62	Ivory bridge	1.65	56	Allparts
95124	C1-S95	Schaller peg	10.23	124	Warmoth
35798	Q6-S52	Tone knob	.65	298	Allparts
67913	R4-S29	5-way switch	4.95	32	Electropart
55231	B3-S87	Strap knob	.25	144	Allparts
84621	T6-S65	Neck plate	3.87	16	StewMac

Vertical Partition for Design Division

ITEM NO.	BIN LOCATOR	ITEM DESCRIPTION	SUPPLIER
72695	A7-S56	Trem spring	Century
54132	A9-S62	Ivory bridge	Allparts
95124	C1-S95	Schaller peg	Warmoth
35798	Q6-S52	Tone knob	Allparts
67913	R4-S29	5-way switch	Electropart
55231	B3-S87	Strap knob	Allparts
84621	T6-S65	Neck plate	StewMac

Vertical Partition for Manufacturing Division

ITEM NO.	ITEM DESCRIPTION	ITEM COST	ITEM QTY.
72695	Trem spring	.85	924
54132	Ivory bridge	1.65	56
95124	Schaller peg	10.23	124
35798	Tone knob	.65	298
67913	5-way switch	4.95	32
55231	Strap knob	.25	144
84621	Neck plate	3.87	16

Figure 9-11   Example of Vertical Partitioning of Data

Table 9-4 Comparative Advantages and Disadvantages of Data Distribution Methods

Distribution Strategy	Reliability	Expandability	Communications Overhead	Manageability	Data Integrity or Consistency
Centralized database Database resides in a single location; data may be distributed to geographically dispersed users for processing at the local level	POOR	POOR	VERY HIGH	VERY GOOD	EXCELLENT
Replicated database Data are replicated and synchronized on demand or by schedule at multiple sites	EXCELLENT	VERY GOOD	MEDIUM due to regular synchronization	MEDIUM	MEDIUM to VERY GOOD depending upon method and timing of synchronization
Partitioned database Horizontal distribution of rows into independent databases that are geographically dispersed but can be accessed by applications on remote computers	GOOD	GOOD	LOW	VERY GOOD	LOW
Partitioned database Vertical distribution of columns which share a common key and span multiple computers and applications	VERY GOOD	VERY GOOD	LOW to MEDIUM if requests are primarily local in nature	DIFFICULT to VERY DIFFICULT	VERY POOR

DESIGNING FOR SPECIALIZED DOMAINS AND ENVIRONMENTS

When moving from the logical to the physical portion of a system design, the characteristics of the environment in which the system operates must be given the same level of scrutiny as the issues surrounding data distribution method and connectivity. Although the domain in which the system operates was given careful attention during the requirements gathering and logical design stages, it must be revisited again from the perspective of the fit between the physical design and the needs of the users working in that specific domain. The remainder of this chapter is, therefore, devoted to an overview of the unique characteristics of various information environments and their relationship to the designs of systems that operate within them. Bear in mind that a detailed discussion of the design considerations for each of the identified environments could easily fill several volumes. As such, we are limited to presenting only the foundational issues to consider in each environment.

DESIGNING FOR COLLABORATION

It is the opinion of many academic researchers and practitioners that the term *advanced collaborative systems* is descriptive of the qualities demanded of the next generation of computer applications. These systems of the future will be *advanced* in that they operate in highly complex and knowledge-rich environments and need to be both intelligent and adept at assisting end users in navigating and exploiting such environments. The systems will be *collaborative* in that they need to provide support for multiple modes of cooperation, both between human beings and between applications. In designing such systems, the analyst must consider several characteristics unique to these collaborative environments.

The System Should Support Individual Work as well as Collaboration

A collaborative system is more successful if end users can using it for their individual work—document production, schedule and plan development, and personal information management—as well as for collaboration. If the system is designed such that the end users can become comfortable using it for their individual work, then their work products will be integrated into the shared, collaborative environment from the early in the process.

In contrast, the current deployment of collaborative systems is such that they are often used only when end users want to communicate with each other. The remainder of the time, other systems that are not integrated with the collaborative system, such as office suites, are employed (e.g., end users who regularly use e-mail systems for daily communication rarely use that mail system to create and revise long documents). In the present situation, end users must face the often significant and tedious hurdle of importing their work into the collaborative system such that it can be shared. The common the result is less collaboration.

If a collaborative system is to be successful, the design must allow end users convenient access to each other's work to interact efficiently. The system must be designed such that the amount of effort required to collaborate with other users is reduced to the point where employees regularly access each other's work.

The common features of the WWW provide two attractive methods for improving the design of collaborative systems. The first concept is to employ several methods of *browsing*. Often, the search for information cannot be easily distilled into a one or two word search string. The design of a collaborative system must allow for the end users to surf the information base and to explore the database using various categorical methods of exploration.

The second Web concept of interest is the use of extensive *hyperlinks*. By integrating the information contained within the knowledge base with other related documents and resources through hyperlinks, the end user can more easily locate the desired information and can interact with its contributor in a much more seamless manner.

The System Must Afford Mutual Intelligibility

Once an end user accesses a colleague's work, he or she must be able to make sense of the stored information. *Mutual intelligibility* is the ability of one user to understand the work stored by another. The design of a collaborative system must support the end users' need to share a common world model such that they can operate in an environment of similar understandings of what knowledge the group possesses, what the goals of the group are, and what work is to be done. The analyst must determine the scope and characteristics of this shared world model during the early stages of analysis and logical design, because it represents a key design element in the final physical system.

The System Must Support Simultaneous, Fine Granularity Access

In any shared database, the degree of simultaneous access by end users is primarily dependent on the granularity of a potential conflict. In other words, how big a chunk of the database must be "locked" when someone edits a piece of information, thus preventing another end user from editing it? As a rule, the finer the granularity of the locked portion of the database, the greater the potential productivity, because there is less turn-taking as end users collaborate on editing and sharing stored documents and other data.

One common collaborative scenario is the coauthoring of a single document or manuscript. The design of the system must allow for one author to send a coauthor or reviewer a link to the document draft, while continuing to allow the authors to independently and collectively work on the draft document. This encourages collaborating authors to give end users early access to their work, even while still under active development.

Yet another granularity issue in designing a collaborative system is the degree to which it supports annotation, or comments, by one end user on the work of others. The design of the system must make it convenient for reviewers to make comments, while simultaneously satisfying the author's need to preserve the integrity of the document. This suggests some form of nondisruptive annotation process should be considered.

In one sense, every collaborative act is some form of communication. Placing an annotation on a document is a way of communicating with its author. Adding a link to a global index so that other end users can access the work is yet another way of communicating with others. The common design metaphor for advanced collaborative systems using a shared database approach is the large-scale construction site, where many workers from multiple organizations make individual contributions to the global structure being built. Using this metaphor for design, the analyst can more easily envision collaboration as the development a large structure (the shared database of documents and data) as a composite of many smaller structures.

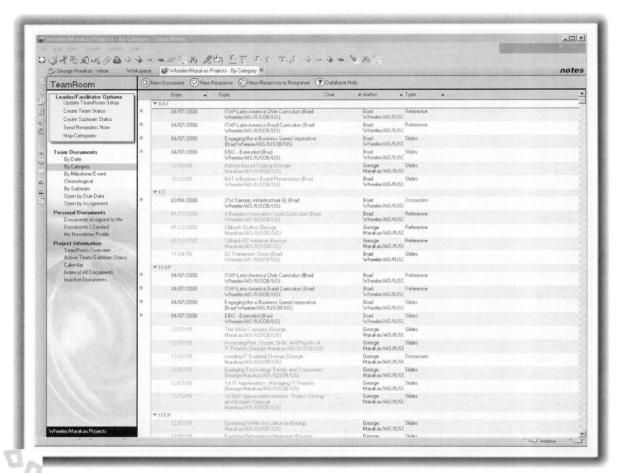

Figure 9-12 Screenshot of Collaborative Work Environment

As mentioned previously, one of the most successful commercially available collaborative systems in today's market is Lotus Notes. Figure 9-12 shows a screenshot from the newest addition to Lotus's collaborative toolset called TeamRoom.

Collaborative Wearable Computers

One additional area of collaborative system design that needs mentioning is the movement toward the development of collaborative systems in common *wearable domains.* In activities associated with maintenance, repair, construction, manufacturing, fire fighting, police and rescue work, and teaching, education, or on-the-job training, among many others, there is an obvious need for need for effective collaboration and communication using systems that are wearable. Currently, most collaborative systems are designed for office use, and few collaborative wearable computers exist. With the continued miniaturization of processors and interfaces, however, this situation is rapidly changing. The modern analyst will be faced with the need to design collaborative systems for wearable environments.

This trend is intuitive, given that wearable collaborative systems could be immediately applied in a variety of day-to-day scenarios, such as those found in time-critical collaboration among field workers where hands-free operation is essential. Such systems could assist a team of workers in readily answering such questions as "Who is close by?" "How far away is the closest member of my team?" "What are individual team members doing?" "Who can assist me with what I am currently doing?" "Who has worked on this equipment before?" Figure 9-13 contains several examples of prototypes being developed to address this growing need for wearable collaborative devices.

Although most physical design issues of common collaborative systems apply equally to wearable systems, the specialized hardware necessary for effective wearable collaboration has many limitations not found in desktop-based collaborative systems: high cpu speed; large memory and storage capacity; increased network bandwidth; reliability; decreased latency or delay characteristics; small screen size combined with high screen resolutions and bit depths; and innovative, hands-free input devices. Designing for the collaborative systems of tomorrow challenges both the knowledge and the creativity of the systems analyst.

DESIGNING FOR ENTERPRISE RESOURCE PLANNING

Tom Davenport first offered a formal definition of an *enterprise resource planning* (ERP) system back in 1998:

> "ERP (Enterprise Resource Planning Systems) is built upon a commercial software package that promises the seamless integration of all the information flowing through the company—financial, accounting, human resources, supply chain and customer information." (121)

Figure 9-13   Examples of Currently Available Wearable Computing Devices

An ERP system is an extension of the manufacturing resource planning (MRP) concept originally proposed by Oliver Wight in 1984 and later standardized by the American Production and Inventory Control Society (APICS). In implementation, ERP systems include several basic features. First, they are installed on a typical database management system. They require initial setup according to the organization's process, but they may be customized according to the organization's unique process requirements through a tool set contained within the ERP application. Using ERP, workflows can be prescribed to automate approval processes through established chains of command. Once installed, the end user only enters data at one point, and the information is then transferred through all relevant processes to other modules. Finally, the typical ERP system includes reporting tools for main, as well as ad hoc, reporting.

How Does ERP Work?

The essence of ERP is the fundamental premise that the whole is greater than the sum of its parts. Traditional application systems treat each transaction separately and are built around the strong boundaries of specific functions that a particular application is intended to provide. In contrast, an ERP no longer considers transactions separately as stand-alone activities but rather considers them to be a part of the integrated processes that make up the organization's business environment.

Typical transaction processing application systems can be thought of as data manipulation tools. They store data, process them, and present them in the appropriate form whenever requested by the end user. Although such applications are clearly one of the foundations on which the modern IS environment is built, it is often the case that no link exists between the application systems used by the various departments within an organization. An ERP system is designed to solve this problem by providing data storage and processing mechanisms that are designed to serve the needs of all departments and functions within the organization. Because of this design approach, the organization's information processing activities become highly integrated.

Figure 9-14 compares the typical organizational information processing environment with an ERP environment.

Implementing ERP Systems

The ultimate success of an ERP solution is, in many ways, dependent on how quickly the benefits can be reaped from it. This suggests the need for rapid implementations that result in significantly shortened ROI periods. One of the methods used to effect this rapid implementation of the ERP system is to conduct concurrent business process reengineering (BPR) sessions simultaneous to the early stages of ERP implementation. This approach is aimed at shortening the total implementation time frame. In applying this implementation method, two distinct scenarios can be identified.

In the *comprehensive implementation* scenario, the focus of the analyst and the design effort is more on business improvement than on technical improvement during the implementation. This approach is most suitable when it is determined that significant improvements in the current business processes are required, thus making customization of the ERP necessary. It is also equally applicable in situations where there exists a relatively high level of integration among existing organizational systems or where multiple sites for the ERP have to be implemented.

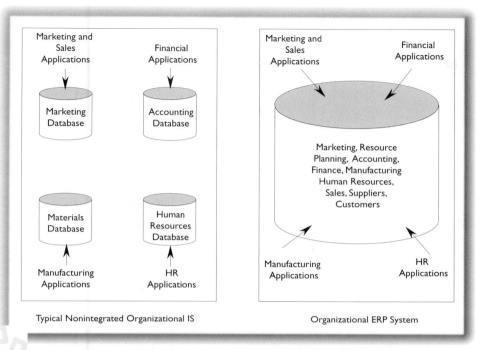

Figure 9-14 Comparison of Typical Organization IS with ERP Approach

In the second basic scenario, called *compact implementation*, the focus is more on making the technical migration to the ERP, with enhancements to the existing business processes coming at a later stage. This approach is most suitable where improvements in the existing business processes are not required immediately because the company operates according to commonly accepted business practices or where a single ERP site is being implemented.

COTS versus Best-in-Class ERP

Increasingly, organizations are embracing ERP systems to fully automate and integrate the traditional back office functions such as accounting, finance, human resources, and manufacturing. Because the functions tend to follow generally accepted business practices with their respective industries, ERP manufacturers are able to offer packaged off-the-shelf solutions. Because most firms now have to consider deploying an ERP solution just to stay on an equal footing with their competitors, these COTS ERP solutions are becoming the de facto standard for ERP implementations. The most successful of these providers is SAP, which offers prepacked business solutions to over 30 vertical market sectors. Figure 9-15 shows several examples from one of SAP's vertical market ERP modules.

Despite the near-term advantages to adopting a prepackaged ERP solution, all of the major ERP vendors have acknowledged that their COTS solutions cannot completely cover the entire range of business activities that a particular organization may require. Because of this, ERP vendors are collectively addressing methods by which a particular organization can select the *best-in-class* applications available

Figure 9-15 Examples of SAP R/3 ERP Application Screens

for specific business requirements and integrate those products into their respective ERP IT backbones.

It is easy to see that the ultimate benefactor of this componentization effort by the major ERP vendors is the end user, as it becomes much easier for ERP components from multiple vendors to cost effectively integrate. Examples of applications that have been considered best-in-class candidates in the past include process manufacturing, materials tracking, order processing, supply chain management, and asset and plant maintenance.

The implementation of ERP is analogous to surgery; there is no such thing as *minor* surgery, and there is no such thing as a *minor* ERP project. The analyst involved in an ERP design and implementation project faces a truly daunting task. The business press and practitioner journals are replete with stories chronicling the experiences of companies who have tried to install monolithic ERP systems in an attempt to reach the nirvana of a truly integrated information environment. Based on these reports, large cost overruns appear to be the norm. Implementation schedules are usually quoted in terms of years when discussing an enterprise scale implementation. Schedule slippages and their primary effect—cancelled ERP projects—are becoming commonplace.

Intuitively enough, the competition to find skilled resources that are knowledgeable in the installation and rollout of ERP systems has become intense. The costs of hiring these resources are now exorbitant and are reaching ever higher. Based on this upward spiraling demand, it is currently not unheard of to pay $400–500 per hour as the lowest rate for ERP-savvy analysts and technicians who most likely are temporary and may disappear before the implementation is complete. These rates generally apply for personnel who are capable of helping a site install and roll out just the core ERP functions, such as financials and human resources modules. It is extremely rare to find resources that are skilled in some of the more specialized functionalities, such as an ERP package's project management features.

In contrast, implementing a *best-in-class* solution from a specialized vendor usually assures availability of skilled implementation resources. The vendor is able to provide a stable complement of personnel who work exclusively on its specific products. These technical support resources typically cost significantly less than core ERP resources, thereby driving the overall total cost of ownership of that system down and consequently driving up the ROI.

It is clear that major business benefits can be realized by implementing an ERP IT backbone. Integrating the data and workflow involved with the standard business and operational systems, such as financials, manufacturing, and human resources, can yield significant improvements and cost savings.

Whereas once the ERP packages were only available as large monoliths that required a company to dedicate years to implementation, now the same ERP vendors are reconfiguring their offerings into a series of components that can be installed piece by piece. Each vendor has also opened its systems up so they can integrate and communicate with legacy systems, older in house systems, and, most important, best-in-class solutions from third party application vendors. As discussed previously, a company can now select an ERP tool as its enterprise data backbone and then, based on its own particular needs, go out to the open market to select the best possible commercial products to plug into that backbone.

Unlike previously, when claims of product interoperation between systems from different vendors were suspect, today's technologies are providing for true, real world integration between these different products. The modern analyst must become conversant in the constantly changing product offerings so that the proper course of action can be taken toward a best-in-class solution for the organization.

DESIGNING FOR THE INTRANET AND THE WEB

The *corporate intranet* has been hailed as the most important business tool since the typewriter, but its track record so far has been mixed. Despite many successes, particularly in cost and time savings, many sponsors of corporate intranets are dissatisfied. They have spent time and money on development, net-enabled desktops, even intranet training, but they still are not enjoying significant enough productivity or cost savings. Why? Although critics often point to technological glitches, the real problems may lie in the design process. Intranets should help employees collaborate on business processes such as product development or order fulfillment, which create value for a company and its customers. Specifically, intranets centralize the business process in an easily accessible, platform-independent virtual space. Successful intranets allow employees from many departments to contribute the different skills necessary to carry out a particular process. Although each department of a company may have its own virtual space, intranets should be organized primarily around the business processes they help employees carry out, rather than around the organizational chart of the company.

Focusing on processes rather than departments is a widely hailed business trend. Recent shifts in corporate structure point to the emergence of *communities of process*. Analysts and intranet designers are helping organizations move away from the typical vertical, hierarchical organizational lines of the past toward more functional horizontal, process-oriented groups that link cross-functional teams focused on the same set of business tasks. The major hurdle is that this change requires significant interaction between departments, functions, even countries. Enter the intranet, the ideal vehicle for creating and empowering process-based corporate communities.

Although successful intranets look and work as differently as the processes they enable, they nonetheless share several common characteristics. First, they focus on tasks rather than documents for simple data capture, and they aim to integrate those tasks into distinct processes. In addition, the best intranets encourage collaboration by creating shared and familiar spaces that reflect the personality of the company and create a common ground for all employees. One example of a highly successful corporate intranet environment can be found at Cisco Systems (Figure 9-16). Virtually every corporate process, from expense reimbursement to employee benefits planning to worldwide recruiting, is conducted through their corporate intranet.

Figure 9-16   Cisco Systems' Worldwide Recruiting via Internet/Intranet Integration

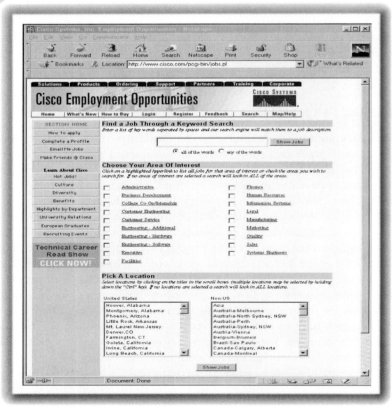

Design is King

Just as physical work spaces rely on architectural plans to optimize efficiency, an intranet needs to be carefully designed to help employees access information and collaborate effectively. Because the public does not see the intranet, information design for intranets often receives scant attention. Unlike customers, employees are assumed to be insiders, able to easily locate company information. So, although the company Web site usually has the input of the marketing department, design and structure of the intranet is often relegated to the IT department.

By default, an organizational chart of the company is often used to organize information on the intranet. Although the seemingly obvious candidate for the structure of the intranet, an organizational chart actually works against the collaboration the intranet is meant to foster. An organizational chart cannot help you have a variety of information and tools at hand. Although a spreadsheet is a calculation tool, and last year's budget is an internal document, both need to be next to each other to develop a new budget. Similarly, on the corporate intranet, the tasks of the users, rather than the classification of documents or tools, should dictate the organization of that intranet. Designed effectively around dynamic tasks rather than static documents, intranets can contribute to dramatic increases in efficiency. Organizing documents within the context of tasks also focuses employees on the function of the documents they are working with. For example, to save employee time while signing up for various retirement plans, information on various retirement plans (including links to financial Web sites) should be placed near the forms actually used to register for those plans.

Even simple processes can become more efficient when incorporated into an intranet. For example, when Ford Motor Company implemented a corporate intranet, the company included an application to help geographically dispersed engineers gain authorization for new projects. What previously was a time-consuming, expensive process, involving the potential for lost documents and delays, is now centralized in an efficient electronic process. More complex processes can also be effectively integrated into an intranet. For example, Cadence Systems created an integrated section of the intranet for its entire sales process. Each phase of the sales process is represented on the intranet with relevant information and tools. So, the section covering an initial stage of the sales process includes links to customer presentations, sample letters, and internal forms. Organizing all steps of the sales process together also allows for easy tracking of each sales effort.

The Intranet Must Support Virtual Workgroups

Intranets can break though departmental walls to help accomplish business processes more efficiently. For example, a customer complaint might involve people and information from the accounting, sales, and marketing departments. Even though the employees necessary to resolve the complaint work in different departments, they are all involved in the process of customer service. By creating spaces for cross-departmental collaboration, the intranet can help employees collaborate to efficiently carry out the central processes of the company and cut costs by avoiding in-person conferences and employee reallocations.

Intranets (and private extranets) can also bring together employees and partners who are geographically dispersed to work on common problems. Travel costs are eliminated, and employees can increase their productivity by sharing knowledge. For example, a pharmaceutical company is using its intranet to allow scientists all over the world to collaborate on research. A major franchise retailer is using bulletin boards on its intranet to coordinate major marketing projects. Caterpillar is developing an extranet application so that experts from around the world can collaborate with employees to design new products. Other applications for intranet collaboration include complex transactions with lawyers and multiple parties, which rely on access to, and modification of, key documents.

The bulk of discussion about collaboration in and between companies centers around security, certainly an important issue to resolve. What receives less attention, but is nonetheless central to the value of an intranet, is the design of virtual spaces that encourage new forms of collaboration. These, in turn, increase the efficiency of key business processes, such as product development, marketing, and customer service.

Intranet Design Myths

As alluded to previously, the corporate intranet is not thought of with the same reverence and value as the corporate Web site where customers get their first impressions of the firm in electronic form. As such, intranets are often thought of as simple, internal, reporting systems that can be relatively easily designed and implemented by a small team of analysts and designers at minimal costs. The following sections briefly address some common design myths associated with the corporate intranet.

Intranets Are Cheap

The initial costs associated with setting up an intranet can actually be quite modest. You find a spare PC lying around, add some memory and disk space, install some Web server software and a network card, and your are on your way. This early ease of implementation, however, is quite misleading. If the corporate intranet is to grow into a useful organizational tool for all end users, be prepared for the increased costs associated with the growth. It is guaranteed that you will soon need a faster server, more memory, increased storage space, more functional application packages, and increased bandwidth. More important, as your intranet grows, you will need to add support staff to manage the system. Intranets are major cost initiatives; plan on it.

Build It and They Will Come

A lot of intranet projects do not take off as expected. One of the most common reasons for this can be described by the cliché "out of sight—out of mind." You may have the greatest corporate intranet in existence, but if your employees do not have a need to use it, then they simply will not. A successful intranet requires the constant application of promotional techniques, not only to get people to visit the intranet but also to keep them coming back. This is one area where the marketing department of the organization can be invaluable in getting the intranet off to a good start.

Intranets Are for REALLY BIG Organizations

Intranets may only have been for really big organizations in the early days of their existence, but today this no longer applies. Even organizations with five to ten employees can use an intranet to their advantage. The success of an intranet is not dependent on the number of end users but rather on the cost savings and increase in productivity realized from its use.

Intranets Require an Internet Connection and Are Not Secure

Nothing could be further from the truth than the statement "intranets require an internet connection and are not secure." A corporate intranet can be up and running by itself without any connection to the outside world. The administrators of the system still use prevailing internet technologies, Web servers, browsers, chat scripts, news and mail servers, and so forth, but there is no need to have the end users connected to the Internet unless the organization wants to allow them access to content from the Internet.

Regarding the security issue, if your intranet is not connected to the Internet and no dial-in access is provided, then there is absolutely no security issue to worry about. Even with an incoming connection, there are a wide variety of effective options to secure the intranet. Firewalls, secure socket layers (SSL), password authentication, Internet protocol (IP) blocking, and many other techniques are all readily available to secure the intranet from intruders.

Intranets Are Low Maintenance Applications

After reading up to this point, if you still believe that intranets are low maintenance applications, you are in for a lot of surprises. The typical intranet can grow very quickly. Even with a well thought out growth strategy in place, be prepared to spend a lot of time on small, routine maintenance tasks. Adding new publishers, adding users, maintaining the user database, keeping the content and technology current, coping with growing demand for bandwidth, applications, and information—these are just a few issues you must deal with. When designing the intranet project, be sure to build plenty of budget in for above-average maintenance.

Intranets Are an IS Thing

Leave the control of your intranet in the hands of the chosen few from the IS support group and you more than likely severely restrict its growth. Admittedly, the IS personnel play an integral role in both the development and the ongoing deployment of the intranet, but the entire organization needs to have a hand in contributing both functionality and content. The IS group is probably best equipped to setup and manage the organizational content publishers, but the various contributors must be empowered to use their own judgment and creativity to come up with new and innovative functions and features.

The corporate intranet is rapidly becoming a mainstay in every wired organization. As an analyst, you most likely will be involved with several large-scale intranet development efforts during your career. As long as you do not design the system around the myths we just discussed, your system will flourish and you will have yet another project to point to with pride.

DESIGNING FOR THE DATA WAREHOUSE

Despite this growing need for more information, organizations large and small every day create billions of bytes of data about all aspects of their business—millions of individual facts about their customers, products, operations, and people—without any formalized initiative beyond the transaction level to organize them. For the most part, these data are literally locked up in many computer systems and are, metaphorically speaking, data in jail.

It is estimated that only a small fraction of the data that are captured, processed, and stored in the enterprise is actually ever made available to executives and decision makers. The concept of the *data warehouse* (DW) is part of the response by IT to meet this identified need. It is an elegantly simple concept that, over time, has the potential to evolve into a significant contributor to the success and stability of an organization in the global marketplace. The essence of the DW concept is a recognition that the characteristics and usage patterns of operational systems used to automate business processes and those of a DSS are fundamentally different but, nonetheless, symbiotically linked (Kelly 1994). The DW provides a facility for integrating the data generated in a world of unintegrated IS. A functional DW organizes and stores all of the available data needed for informational, analytical processing over a historical time perspective. It is the goal of the DW to reintegrate the data generated by many internal and external IS to create a sense of unity about the data without surrendering their natural complexities.

Stores, Warehouses, and Marts

The concept of the DW is brand new and, as such, is in a high state of flux with regard to standardization of terms and definitions. Some definitions focus on data, whereas others refer to people, software, tools, and business processes. The acknowledged father of data warehousing, W. H. Inmon, has provided a clear and useful definition of the DW concept, in terms of measurable attributes, that serves our purposes in this text:

> The data warehouse is a collection of integrated, subject-oriented databases designed to support the DSS (decision support) function, where each unit of data is non-volatile and relevant to some moment in time. (Inmon 1992, 13)

Inmon's definition of a DW makes two implicit assumptions: (1) the DW is physically separated from all other operational systems, and (2) DWs hold aggregated data and transactional (atomic) data for management separate from those used for on-line transaction processing.

This requirement of a separate environment for the DW is an essential element in the concept. In most cases, the systems employed in an operational environment are inadequate, in many respects, with regard to decision making and analysis. Primarily, the type, quantity, and quality of the data contained in such environments are not well-suited to historical analysis. Warehouse data must be consistent, well integrated, well defined, and most important, time stamped. In addition, the need to merge a wide variety of internal and external environments with an equally wide variety of access methods suggests the need for separate DW systems. Table 9-5 contains a comparison between operational and DW characteristics.

Data Warehouse Architecture

A *data warehouse architecture* (DWA) is a method by which the overall structure of data, communication, processing, and presentation that exists for end user computing within the enterprise can be represented. Figure 9-17 graphically illustrates the various interconnected elements that serve to make up the DWA.

The *operational and external database layer* represents the source data for the DW. This layer is composed, primarily, of operational TPS and external secondary databases.

Table 9-5   Operational Data Store and Data Warehouse Characteristics

Characteristic	Operational Data Store	Data Warehouse
How is it built?	One application or subject area at a time	Typically multiple subjects areas at a time
User requirements	Well-defined prior to logical design	Often vague and conflicting
Area of support	Day-to-day business operations	Decision-support for managerial activities
Type of access	Relatively small number of records retrieved via a single query	Large data sets scanned to retrieve results from either single or multiple queries
Frequency of access	Tuned for frequent access to small amounts of data	Tuned for infrequent access to large amounts of data
Volume of data	Similar to typical daily volume of operational transactions	Much larger than typical daily transaction volume
Retention period	Retained as necessary to meet daily operating requirements	Retention period is indeterminate and must support historical reporting, comparison, and analysis
Currency of data	Up-to-the-minute; real time	Typically represents a static point in time
Availability of data	High and immediate availability may be required	Immediate availability is less critical
Typical unit of analysis	Small, manageable, transaction-level units	Large, unpredictable, variable units
Design focus	High performance, limited flexibility	High flexibility, high performance

Adapted from Bischoff 1997.

The *information access layer* of the DWA is the layer that the end user deals with directly. In particular, it represents the tools that the end user normally uses day-to-day to extract and analyze the data contained within the DW. At this layer is where the hardware and software involved in displaying and printing reports, spread-sheets, graphs, and charts for analysis and presentation is found.

As shown in Figure 9-17, the *data access layer* serves as a sort of interface or mid-dleman between the operational and information access layers and the DW itself. This layer spans the various databases contained within the DW and facilitates common access by the DW users. Further, the data access layer not only spans multiple databases and file systems on the same hardware but also spans the wide variety of manufacturers and network protocols.

To provide for universal data access, it is absolutely necessary to maintain some form of data directory or repository of metadata information. This is the job of the *metadata layer*, where data about the data stored within the DW are maintained. Examples of metadata include the directory of where the data are stored, the rules used for summarization and scrubbing, or possibly where the operational data came from.

The *process management layer* focuses on scheduling the various tasks that must be accomplished to build and maintain the DW and data directory information. This layer can be thought of as the scheduler or the high level job control for the many processes (procedures) that must occur to keep the DW up-to-date. Tasks

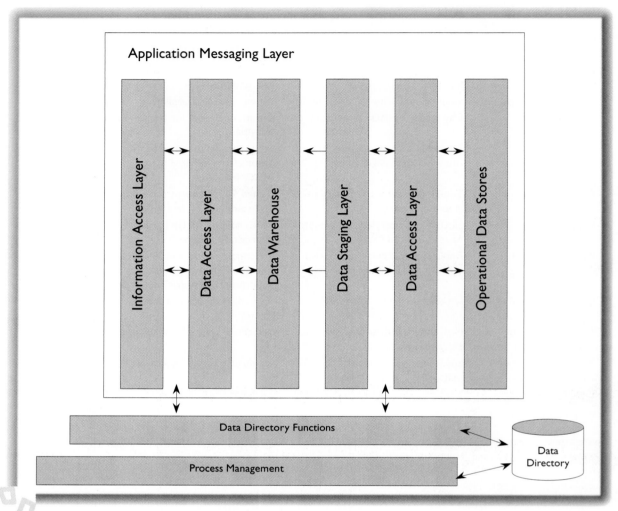

Figure 9-17 Components of the Data Warehouse Architecture

such as periodic download from identified operational data stores, scheduled summarization of operational data, access and download of external data sources, and update of the metadata are typical of those performed at this layer of the DWA.

The *application messaging layer* has to do with transporting information around the enterprise computing network. This layer is also referred to as the *middleware,* but it can typically involve more that just networking protocols and request routing. Application messaging, for example, can be used to isolate applications, operational or informational, from the exact data format on either end, thus facilitating a seamless interface between the uniqueness of a particular data format and the specific format requirements of the analysis tool being used. This layer can also be used to collect transactions or messages and deliver them to a certain location at a certain time. In this sense, the application messaging can be thought of as the transport system underlying the DW.

The physical DW layer is where the actual data used for decision making throughout the organization are located. In some cases, one can think of the DW simply as a logical or virtual view of data, because the DW may not actually involve storing data. As we show in the next section, the physical DW may not ever truly store any of the data accessed through it.

The final component of the DWA is the *data staging layer.* Data staging (sometimes referred to as *copy* or *replication management*) includes all of the processes necessary to select, edit, summarize, combine, and load DW and information access data from operational and external databases.

DW Typology

As mentioned previously, the DW, although appearing to be the source of data for various organizational analysis initiatives and decision-making activities, may not physically be the location of the data being accessed. Although numerous hybrid mechanisms exist in structuring a DW, three basic configurations can be identified: *virtual* or *point-to-point, central,* and *distributed* DWs.

In preface to an overview of each configuration it must be noted that there is no one best approach to configuring a DW schema. Each option fits a specific set of requirements, and a data warehousing strategy may ultimately include all three options.

The Virtual DW

A *virtual* or *point-to-point* data warehousing strategy allows the end users to access the operational data stores directly using tools enabled at the data access layer. This approach, although providing the ultimate in flexibility, as well as the minimum amount of redundant data that must be loaded and maintained, can also put the largest unplanned query load and performance degradation on operational application systems.

Virtual warehousing is often an initial strategy in organizations where there is a broad but largely undefined need to get at operational data from a relatively large class of end users and where the likely frequency of requests is low. Virtual DWs often provide a relatively low-cost starting point for organizations to assess what types of data end users are really looking for.

The Central DW

The central DW is what most people think of when they first are introduced to the concept of DW. The central DW is a single physical database that contains all of the data for a specific functional area, department, division, or enterprise. This warehousing approach is often selected where there is a common need for informational data and there are large numbers of end users already connected to a central computer or network. A central DW may contain data for any specific period of time and usually contains data from multiple operational applications.

The central DW is real. The data stored in the DW are physically located and accessible from one place and must be loaded and maintained on a regular basis. This configuration is the most common of the three basic types and is becoming the de facto standard for DW implementation owing to the wide variety of construction and manipulation tools being offered.

The Distributed DW

A distributed DW is just what its name implies: a data warehouse that has its components distributed across a number of different physical databases. Increasingly, large organizations are pushing decision making down to lower and lower levels of the organization and in turn pushing the data needed for decision making down (or out) to the LAN or local computer serving the local decision maker. Many older DW implementations use the distributed approach because initially it was easier to create several small DW databases than to facilitate one all-encompassing one. The advent of modern DW implementation and management applications, however, has reduced the need for multiple or distributed DWs.

Implementing the DW

The challenge of providing access to the aggregated data of an organization is not a new one. The 1970s saw the advent of the *information center,* an ill-fated concept requiring both a dedicated high-powered computer and a severe resource drain in terms of hardware, software, and personnel. The 1980s brought with it the emphasis on data reengineering using the extended relational model. This, too, was fraught with complexities and severe performance degradation issues. The 1990s answer appears to be the DW. If we are to avoid the problems of the past and realize the successes assumed to be associated with total access to data, IT management and organizational DW champions must understand not only what needs to be done but also just how to do it.

Denis Kozar (1997), vice president of enterprise information architecture for Chase Manhattan Bank, has assembled the "seven deadly sins" of DW implementation. Each of these errors, when committed, can result in a failure of an otherwise valuable DW initiative. Table 9-6 lists the seven deadly sins of DW design and implementation.

Sin #1: "If you build it, they will come."

The first of the seven sins is one of blind faith. It is a failure to recognize the importance of developing a clear set of business objectives for the DW prior to its construction. A successful DW is one in which the needs of the entire enterprise are considered and a documented set of requirements is developed to guide the design, construction, and rollout of the project. The DW cannot simply be built in the hope that someone finds a use for it.

Table 9-6   The Seven Deadly Sins of Data Warehouse Design

- "If you build it, they will come."
- Omission of a data warehouse architectural framework
- Underestimating the importance of documenting all assumptions and potential conflicts
- Abuse of methodology and tools
- Abuse of the data warehouse life cycle
- Ignorance concerning the resolution of data conflicts
- Failure to document the mistakes made during the first DW project

Sin #2: Omission of an Architectural Framework

One of the most important success factors to a DW initiative is the development and maintenance of a comprehensive architectural framework. Such a framework serves as the blueprints for construction and use of the various DW components. Issues such as the expected number of end users, the volume and diversity of data, and the expected data refresh cycle, among many others, must be considered (and reflected) in the DWA.

Sin #3: Underestimating the Importance of Documenting Assumptions

The assumptions and potential data conflicts associated with the DW must be included in the architectural framework for the project. As such, they must be ascertained and codified within the document as early in the project as possible to insure their reflection in the final product. Several questions must be answered during the requirements phase of the project that serve to reveal these important underlying assumptions about the DW. How much data should be loaded into the warehouse? What is the expected level of data granularity? How often do we need to refresh the data? On what platform is the DW to be developed and implemented? The accurate determination of issues such as these is an essential component to the success of a DW project.

Sin #4: Failure to Use the Right Tool for the Job

The design and construction of a DW is, in many ways, very different from the construction of an operational application system. Because of this, a different set of tools must be employed in a DW project than are typically found in an application development effort.

DW tools can be categorized into four discrete groups: (1) *analysis tools,* (2) *development tools,* (3) *implementation tools,* and (4) *delivery tools.* Each of these categories contains specialized tools designed specifically to accommodate the unique design activities associated with DW development.

Analysis Tools

Analysis tools assist in the identification of data requirements, the primary sources of data for the DW, and the construction of the data model for the warehouse. Modern CASE tools are a typical member of this category. Another analysis tool is the *code scanner.* These applications scan source code for file or database definitions and data usage identifiers. This information helps to build the initial data model for the warehouse by determining the data requirements contained within the source operational data store (ODS).

Development Tools

Development tools are responsible for data cleansing, code generation, data integration, and loading of the data into the final warehouse repository. These tools are also the primary generators of metadata for the warehouse.

Implementation Tools

The category of implementation tools contains the data acquisition tools used to gather, process, clean, replicate, and consolidate the data to be contained within the warehouse. In addition, information storage tools from this category may be employed to assist in loading summarized data from external data sources.

Delivery Tools

Delivery tools assist in the data conversion, data derivation, and reporting for the final delivery platform. This category includes specific tools for querying and reporting and the generation and access to data glossaries intended to provide end users with the ability to identify what data are actually contained within the warehouse.

Sin #5: Life Cycle Abuse

The sin of life cycle abuse is the failure of the DW developers to realize the differences between the data warehouse life cycle (DWLC) and the traditional SDLC methodologies. Although similar, these two approaches differ in one critical aspect: the DWLC never ends. The life cycle of a DW project is a continuous, ongoing set of activities that flow from initial investigation of DW requirements through data administration and back again. As each phase of the DW is completed, a new one is typically started owing to new data requirements, additional user groups being identified, and new required sources of data. The DW developers must realize that the project must never end if the warehouse is to remain a viable source of decision-making support.

Sin #6: Ignorance concerning the Resolution of Data Conflicts

The justification for a new DW initiative is often predicated on the need for greater quality of data for decision making within the organization. Although this is a laudable objective for a DW project, it is simply the tip of the iceberg with regard to actually putting the warehouse into operation. There is a natural tendency for people and organizations to be highly protective and territorial when it comes to their data and associated applications. As a result, a great deal of often tedious analysis must be conducted to determine the best data sources available within the organization. Once these systems have been identified, the conflicts associated with disparate naming conventions, file formats and sizes, and value ranges must be resolved. This process may involve working with the data owners to establish an understanding with regard to future planned or unplanned changes to the source data. Failure to allow sufficient time and resources to resolve data conflicts can stall a warehouse initiative and result in an organizational stalemate that can threaten the success of the project.

Sin #7: Failure to Learn From Mistakes

The ongoing nature of the DWLC suggests that one DW project simply begets another. Because of this, the careful documentation of the mistakes made in the first round directly impacts the quality assurance activities of all future projects. By learning from the mistakes of the past, a strong DW with lasting benefits can be built.

CHAPTER SUMMARY

This chapter has covered a lot of ground. Although we have barely scratched the surface of the issues related to designing for the widely diverse environments you will face as an analyst, we have, at least, established the range of diversity you can expect to encounter during your career. It is important for you to realize, however, that despite the diversity of the environment, the basic tenets and foundations of good system design and development still prevail. As technology advances, so does the range of diverse development needs and environments. The one constant in all this is the time-proven structured approach to problem identification and logical solution design.

We continue our focus on physical design issues in the next chapter, where we look at the issues associated with database design and data specifications.

KEY CONCEPTS

➤ Evolution of computing architecture
  - Single computer architecture (mainframe computer)
  - Clustered central computing architecture
  - Distributed computing architecture (LAN, WAN, and WWW)

➤ Advantages of the single computer architecture
  - Economies of scale
  - Minimal data redundancy
  - Easy enforcement of policies and standards

➤ Distributed IS

  The typical distributed IS is composed of relatively independent subsystems, often geographically dispersed, that are tied together within the organizational framework by some method of communication interface. Three basic conditions exist for such systems:

  1. Some subsystems need to interact with other subsystems.
  2. Some subsystems need to share files or data processing facilities with other subsystems.
  3. Some subsystems require very little interaction with other subsystems.

➤ Critical considerations for designing distributed IS
  - Reliability
    The reliability of the system suggests that a particular piece of data is available at a given time regardless of the location of the user requesting it.
  - Survivability
    Survivability refers to the system's ability to continue to provide service to its users despite the failure of one or more nodes.

➤ The drivers to distribute computing
  - The cost of desktop computing workstations is dropping rapidly, whereas the interface and computing power of such devices is increasing.
  - The demand for locally specific applications is rising much faster than the ability of any central IS function to respond to that demand.
  - The Internet and the WWW provide a natural connectivity vehicle to access data and applications from one side of the globe to the other.

➤ Pros and cons of distributed computing
  - Pros
    - Technical advantages
      The ability to design the system to be responsive to the local needs of the end users and to focus on issues of reliability and survivability
    - Business advantages
      The ability to pay attention to the issues of business alignment, scalability, and conformity to existing organizational structure
  - Cons
    - Loss of the economies of scale
    - Increasing difficulties in managing and controlling the network

➤ Types of distribution
  - Software configuration
    - Distributed applications approach
      The focus of a distributed application environment is on allowing geographically dispersed end users to access and use a variety of software applications. The application server approach is commonly used to reduce the space necessary

to store commonly used applications.

- Distributed data approach

  In the distributed data approach, the data either can be replicated across multiple sites for ease of access (data replication) or partitioned such that a portion of the data resides in several locations throughout the network (data partitioning).

- Hardware configuration

  - File server architecture

    The file server approach manages the various file operations associated with the system and can be thought of as an additional hard drive for each connected PC workstation.

    - The software running on the file server serves to manage the requests from workstations.
    - The application programs on each workstation are responsible for data management and manipulation.

  - Client–server architecture

    In client–server architecture, the processing load for a particular application is divided between the client workstation and the server.

    - The workstation is responsible for managing the user interface and the presentation of data.
    - The server is responsible for both the storage of data and the processing of queries to it.

➤ Functions of a location connectivity diagram (LCD)

- The LCD depicts the shape or configuration of a network in terms of the locations of the various users, processes, data, and interfaces residing on the network.
- The LCD identifies the necessary interconnection between the network elements in terms of locations.
- The LCD depicts both logical locations where people do work and physical locations where the various technologies contained within the system reside.

➤ Basic connection topologies

- The bus topology

Each workstation on the network is connected through a direct point-to-point linkage.

- The ring topology

  The workstations, peripherals, and servers on the network are connected via a ringlike structure. Each communication or request (a packet) is labeled with the address of the recipient device.

- The star topology

  Each workstation is connected to a central server via a single hardware connection. However, the central server need not to be the sole location for either storage or application processing. Communication from one workstation to another must first pass through the central server and be routed to the appropriate recipient workstation.

➤ Two alternative data storage approaches

- Data replication

  This approach creates a copy of each of the databases contained in the system at each workstation or server location throughout the network.

  - Advantages
    - Improve throughput
    - Decrease the processing load on any single database server
    - Provide high reliability of access to the data
    - Provide a relatively fast response time
  - Disadvantages
    - Require a large amount of storage space
    - Have greater processing costs and management complexity

- Data partitioning

  This approach partitions the data using some logical approach such that the contention for data across workstations or server locations is minimized, and thus the average throughput of the entire system is increased. Two basic methods are

  - Horizontal partitioning

    Horizontal partitioning locates records (rows) within the database at the same physical location that most frequently accesses them such that maximum throughput is achieved.

- Vertical partitioning

  Vertical partitioning relocates certain columns from tables and stores them as base relations at two or more physical sites.

➤ In designing collaborative systems, the analyst should consider the following characteristics:

- The system should support individual work, as well as collaboration.

  A successful collaborative system must
  - allow end users convenient access to each other's work to interact efficiently
  - require the least amount of effort to collaborate with other users so that employees regularly access each other's work.

- The system must afford mutual intelligibility.

  Mutual intelligibility is the ability of one user to understand the work stored by another. The design should support a common world model.

- The system must support simultaneous, fine granularity access.

  The finer the granularity of the locked portion of the database, the greater the potential productivity.

- Collaborative wearable computers

  There exists an increasing need to design collaborative systems for wearable environments.

➤ Enterprise resource planning (ERP)

- Basic features
  - ERPs are installed on a typical database management system.
  - Once installed, the end user only enters data at one point, and the information is then transferred through all relevant processes to other modules.
  - The typical ERP system includes reporting tools for main, as well as ad hoc, reporting.

- The whole is greater than the sum of its parts.

  An ERP is designed to solve the problem of information islands by providing data storage and processing mechanisms that serve the needs of all departments and functions within the organization.

- Implementation considerations
  - To shorten ROI periods, one should conduct concurrent BPR sessions simultaneous to the early stages of ERP implementation.
    - Identify the implementation scenarios
      - Comprehensive implementation scenario
      - Compact implementation scenario

- COTS versus best-in-class ERP

  ERP manufacturers are able to offer packaged off-the-shelf solutions. However, their solutions cannot completely cover the entire range of business activities that a particular organization may require. Therefore, ERP vendors provide best-in-class applications for specific business requirements and integrate them into their respective ERP IT backbones.

- There is no such thing as a minor ERP project.

➤ Intranet and the Web

Intranets centralize the business process in an easily accessible, platform-independent virtual space.

- Focusing on processes rather than departments

  Intranets should be organized primarily around the business processes they help employees carry out. They help organizations move toward more functional horizontal, process-oriented groups that link cross-functional teams focused on the same set of business tasks.

- Common characteristics shared by successful intranets
  - They focus on tasks, rather than documents, for simple data capture and aim to integrate those tasks into distinct processes.
  - They encourage collaboration by creating shared and familiar spaces that reflect the personality of the company and create a common ground for all employees.

- Design is king

  An intranet needs to be carefully designed to help employees access information and collaborate effectively. The design should be based on *tasks* rather than on *organizational charts*.

- Intranet design myths
  - Intranets are cheap.
  - Built it and they will come.
  - Intranets are for REALLY BIG organizations.
  - Intranets require an Internet connection and are not secure.
  - Intranets are low maintenance applications.
  - Intranets are an IS thing.

➤ Data warehouse (DW)

  A DW provides a facility for integrating the data generated in a world of unintegrated IS. It is the goal of the DW to re-integrate the data generated by many internal and external IS to create a sense of unity about the data without surrendering its natural complexities.

- Definition of the DW concept

  The DW is a collection of integrated, subject-oriented databases designed to support the DSS function, where each unit of data is nonvolatile and relevant to some moment in time (Inmon 1992).

- Two implicit assumptions
  1. The DW is physically separated from all other operational systems.
  2. DWs hold aggregated data and transactional data for management separate from those used for on-line transaction processing.

- Data warehouse architecture (DWA)

  A DWA is a method by which the overall structure of data, communication, processing, and presentation that exists for end-user computing within the enterprise can be presented. The elements of a DWA include

  - Operational (external) database layer

    The operational (external) database layer represents the source data for the DW.

  - Information access layer

    The information access layer of the DWA is the layer that the end users interact with directly.

- Data access layer

  The data access layer serves as a sort of interface between the operational and information access layers and the DW itself.

- Data directory (repository)

  The data dictionary maintains the metadata information (data about the data stored within the DW).

- Process management layer

  The process management layer focuses on scheduling the various tasks that must be accomplished to build and maintain the DW and data directory information.

- Application messaging layer

  The application messaging layer transports information around the enterprise computing network.

- Physical DW layer

  The physical DW layer is where the actual data used for decision making throughout the organization are located. In some cases, the DW is simply a logical or virtual view of data.

- Data staging layer

  The data staging layer serves to manage the processes necessary to select, edit, summarize, combine, and load DW and information access data from operational and external databases.

- Data warehousing typology
  - The virtual DW
  - The central DW
  - The distributed DW

- "Seven deadly sins" of DW design and implementation
  1. "If you build it, they will come"
  2. Omission of an architectural framework

3. Underestimating the importance of documenting all assumptions and potential conflicts
4. Abuse of methodology and tools
5. Abuse of the DWLC
6. Ignorance concerning the resolution of data conflicts

7. Failure to demonstrate the mistakes made during the first DW project
- Data warehouse tools
  - Analysis tools
  - Development tools
  - Implementation tools
  - Delivery tools

QUESTIONS FOR REVIEW

1. What are the two important considerations when designing a distributed IS?

2. What are the main forces of distributed computing?

3. List and briefly describe the pros and cons of distributed computing.

4. Compare the difference between the distributed application approach and the distributed data approach.

5. What is the main difference between a LAN and a WAN?

6. What are the main drawbacks of the file server architecture?

7. Compare and describe the differences between the file server architecture and the client–server architecture.

8. What does "location" mean in a location connectivity diagram (LCD)?

9. List and briefly describe the three basic connection topologies.

10. Describe the logic of the data replication approach and list the pros and cons associated with this approach.

11. Briefly describe the logic of the two basic data partitioning methods.

12. List and describe the critical considerations when designing collaborative systems.

13. Identify the two basic ERP implementation scenarios.

14. Describe the common characteristics shared by successful intranets.

15. Explain why the design of an intranet should be task-oriented rather than functional-oriented or departmental-oriented.

16. List and briefly describe the components of the DWA.

17. List and briefly describe the three basic configurations of a DW.

18. What are the groups of tools available for a DW?

19. What is the main difference between the traditional SDLC and the DWLC?

FOR FURTHER DISCUSSION

1. Consider the circumstances under which you would advocate a file server approach over a client–server approach. What caveats might you convey to your client about each of the two methods?

2. How might you describe the Internet in terms of the various data and application distribution methods in existence? Is there a predominant method being used by the Internet? Which one is it?

3. Write a memo to your boss explaining why the best-of-breed approach to ERP adoption may be superior to adopting a single vendor. Justify your arguments with direct reference to your business environment.

REFERENCES

Bischoff, J., and T. Alexander. 1997. *Data Warehouse: Practical Advice From the Experts.* Upper Saddle River, NJ: Prentice Hall.

Davenport, T. 1998. "Putting the Enterprise into the Enterprise System." *Harvard Business Review* (July-August): 121–133.

Inmon, W. H. 1992. *Building the Data Warehouse.* New York: QED Information Sciences.

Kelly, S. 1994. *Data Warehousing: The Route to Mass Customization.* New York: John Wiley and Sons.

Kozar, D. 1997. "The Seven Deadly Sins." In J. Bischoff J. and T. Alexander, eds., *Data Warehouse: Practical Advice From the Experts.* Upper Saddle River, NJ: Prentice Hall.

Whitten, J. L., and L. D. Bentley. 1998. *Systems Analysis and Design Methods.* Boston: Irwin McGraw-Hill.

Wight, O. 1984. *Manufacturing Resource Planning: MRP II.* Essex Junction, VT: Oliver Wight Limited Publications.

Chapter 10

Designing the Files and Databases

Learning Objectives

■ Discuss the conversion from a logical data model to a physical database schema

■ Understand the issues related to the physical design of fields, records, and files

■ Identify the common file types and their applications

■ Understand the concepts of data integrity and referential integrity and the various methods available as controls

■ Identify the basic characteristics of the four common database architectures

The commercial world is a great reality check for new ideas.
—DR. MICHAEL STONEBRAKER, FOUNDER,
ILLUSTRA INFORMATION TECHNOLOGIES, INC.

INTRODUCTION

We have reached the point in our design process where we can transform the logical data and process models, created during the detailed analysis and logical design phases, into functioning physical databases and software applications. Assuming we constructed our logical designs carefully, the process of converting them into physical form should go smoothly and without any bad surprises. This does not mean that there are not important decisions to made at this stage of the process; there are always decisions to be made. We have yet to determine the storage format, referred to as *data type,* for each data attribute; determine the method by which attributes are grouped into logical records with a database; organize those records such that they can be rapidly retrieved and updated; and specify the options for retrieving specific records from a database. We have many things left to do.

The next four chapters are devoted to the issues associated with the conversion of our logical models into physical form. In chapter 11 we explore the conversion of our logical models into relevant and necessary system output, and in chapters 12 and 13 we continue our logical model conversion into the required system inputs and internals. In this chapter, we begin this conversion process by focusing our attention on the process of physical file and database design.[1]

---

[1] The level of coverage in this chapter is necessarily concise, given that the subject of file and database design can take up an entire text by itself. It is assumed that you have completed a database design

FILE AND DATABASE DESIGN

During the logical design of the data models for our system, we focused on capturing and representing the business requirements of the system as accurately and comprehensively as possible. In the physical design stage, we develop the technical specification for the storage of data within the system. This physical model is referred to as the *database schema,* and it represents the technical implementation of the logical model in terms of its tables, relationships, data domains, and governing business rules. During this phase of the process, we must accomplish two primary goals: (1) the accurate translation of the logical relations into a comprehensive technical specification for the databases and files, including data structures and data access methods; and (2) specifying the storage requirements and technologies for all data to be contained within the system.

Our approach to accomplishing these two goals is a bottom-up perspective. We must start by thoroughly specifying the smallest element in the design, the *field,* and work upward toward the specification of the logical grouping of fields into *records,* the grouping of records into *files,* and the grouping of files into the largest element in the design, the *database.*

DESIGNING AND SPECIFYING FIELDS

When creating the logical data model for the system, the smallest unit of specification is the *data attribute.* In creating a physical data structure the attributes are converted into *fields,* the smallest unit of data specified in the physical model. In most cases, each attribute in the normalized logical model is specified as a field in the physical database, although this is not necessarily always the case. As an example, a logical data attribute such as EMPLOYEE_NAME may be specified as three fields in the physical database: EMP_FIRST_NAME, EMP_MI, and EMP_LAST_NAME. We think of fields as the smallest meaningful unit of data to be stored in a file or database.

Field Types

In any physical database, there are three basic types of fields that may be found: (1) the *primary key,* (2) the *foreign key,* and (3) the *nonkey,* or *descriptive,* element.

The *primary key* is that field that is used to identify a single, unique record contained within the file. In translating from the logical data model to the physical design, the primary key field is that data element that uniquely defines a specific instance of an entity. An example of a primary key field would be the EMPLOYEE_ID field, which contains a unique number assigned to one, and only one, employee. Another example might be the ORDER_NUMBER field, which contains data uniquely associated with a single order record in the database.

A *foreign key* is a field that contains a data element that also serves as a primary key in another file. The foreign key is the field that creates a specific relationship between two or more files in the database. As an example, a record contained within an ORDER file may contain a foreign key field called CUSTOMER_ID, which is the primary key for a record in the CUSTOMER file. This foreign key field links a record in the ORDER file with a specific customer record in the CUSTOMER file, thus creating a relationship between the two files.

---

course prior to beginning your study of SAD. If you have not, then this chapter will serve as a good overview, and any additional information desired can be obtained from one of several good textbooks on the subject.

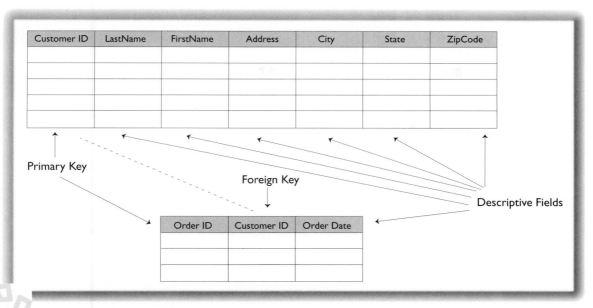

Figure 10-1   Common Field Types

The third field type is the *descriptive field*. These fields contain data describing various attributes of the record but do not serve to uniquely identify that record or to create a relationship between that file and any other file. Figure 10-1 illustrates the three field types.

Data Types

Once the attributes in the logical data model have been converted to fields in the physical model, the process of data typing can begin. A *data type* is a detailed specification of how each field in the file represents the data contained within it. It is, in essence, the definition of the storage format and allowable content for a field. Although the specified data type for a given field is not necessarily how that data are displayed on the screen or in a report, its specification can have a material effect on the space necessary to store the data and the speed with which they can be retrieved.

The *primitive data type* is used to describe data that are supported directly by the system hardware and its low-level programming languages and operating systems. Examples of primitive data types include a memory address or pointer, a short or long integer data element, or single-precision and double-precision numbers. In most cases, the primitive data types are of interest only to the programmers of the actual code necessary to implement the system or database management application.

The *complex data type,* also referred to as a *user-defined data type,* is one that is not directly supported by the hardware or software but is allowable based on a set of specifications supplied by the analyst. Most modern systems for database management have prespecified many of the more commonly used complex data types to make it easier for the records and files to be constructed. Table 10-1 contains several examples of commonly used complex data types.

Table 10-1 Common Data Type Definitions

Data Type	Description
CHAR(*n*)	Alphanumeric character array with a maximum length of *n*
DECIMAL(*m,n*)	Signed numerical data with a total number of digits, *m*, and *n* number of digits to the right of the decimal point
VARCHAR	Alphanumeric character array of variable length
INTEGER	Signed whole number typically up to 11 digits in length
SMALLINT	Signed whole number up to 5 or 6 digits in length
DATE	Date and time including appropriate validity checks (i.e., 4-31 not allowed)
NUMBER	Real number
FLOAT(*m,n*)	Numerical data represented in scientific notation with a total number of digits, *m*, and *n* number of digits to the right of the decimal point
LOGICAL	Binary data (i.e., TRUE/FALSE, YES/NO)
LONG	Variable length alphanumeric character array up to 2Gb
LONGRAW	Binary large object (BLOB)—no assumptions are made about format or content

Field Representation

In addition to determining the data type for each field in the database, certain characteristics about each field must be determined and recorded in the data dictionary for the system. This process is referred to as *data representation,* and it must be performed at the field, record, file, and database levels.

At the field level, several issues must be addressed that relate to both maintenance of the data and the assurance of their integrity. In any field that may be calculated, the formula used to perform that calculation must be performed. Calculated fields are quite common, and although they are technically not in 3NF, they need to be specified in the data dictionary for reference purposes. Generally speaking, there are two methods available to the analyst to specify a calculated or derived data representation: (1) *compute-on-demand* and (2) *recalculate-on-demand.*

Using a *compute-on-demand* approach, the calculated field is represented virtually in the data dictionary but not actually stored in the file. Instead, the formula for its calculation is stored in the data dictionary, and the value of the field is calculated at the time of record retrieval or data element use. Using this approach, no value is actually stored in the database, and, thus, the storage requirements for this approach are minimal. The downside is that each record retrieved, as a result of a query, that contains a calculated field requires additional processing time to perform the calculation. Further, any query based directly on the value of a calculated filed requires a computation of all records contained in the file.

Using the *recalculate-on demand* approach, the field actually contains a value, but it is not recomputed unless there is a change in the one or more of the root values used to calculate it. The formula stored in the data dictionary is only accessed when one or more of the root values used to calculate the field is flagged as

Table 10-2   Common Field Level Data Specifications

Field Specification	Description
Field name	Formal name for the field that uniquely identifies it from all others
Data type	Data type associated with this field
Units	The unit of measure associated with this field (if applicable)
Maintenance	Rules for update, change, or deletion once data is entered (i.e., accounting transaction data cannot be changed once entered)
Missing data	Procedure for handling missing data during multiple record processing (i.e., IGNORE, USE AVERAGE OF OTHER RECORDS)
Check digit	Algorithm for calculating and verifying any check digits used in this field
Formula	Algorithm for computing the value of this field (if calculated)
Coding	Coding conventions or acceptable abbreviations (i.e., 2-character abbreviation for State)
Domain/range	Specification of range limits or default values for the field
Referential integrity	Specification for any referential integrity constraints for the field
Data owner	Identification of the responsible party for identifying the source and meaning of data contained in this field

changed. If the record has not changed since the last access, then no recalculation is necessary.

Other field representation issues that must be determined and listed in the data dictionary include the ownership of the data element, the prescribed coding method for actual data values (i.e., two-character abbreviations for states), and procedures for handling missing data values. Table 10-2 lists several of the data specifications commonly used at the field level.

Data Integrity

It is rare that the user who adds data to a database is the only person who ever uses that data. If this were the case, then any mistakes associated with the entry of that data would affect only the person who made that mistake. The value of a database lies in the fact that many users can deposit elements of the data and others can realize its value by making use of it. This value, however, is predicated on the quality and integrity of the data contained therein. If the data are inaccurate or incomplete, then their value becomes questionable at best and negligible at worst.

The concept of data integrity focuses on processes and procedures that are intended to facilitate an atmosphere of trust with regard to the quality and accuracy of the data in a database. Although no control mechanism is perfect, appropriate implementation of data integrity controls can create a reasonable level of trust and can facilitate confidence in using the data for decision making. Although data integrity controls can take many forms, there are three basic categories in which they occur: (1) *key integrity,* (2) *domain integrity,* and (3) *referential integrity.*

Key Integrity

The key integrity category focuses on insuring that every file has a unique primary key and that controls exist to prevent any two records from having the same primary key value. Although this is true for both single and concatenated primary keys, it is important to note that the individual values of a concatenated key need not be unique. Instead, the combination of those values that make up the key must be. As an example, suppose we have two files, ORDERED_ITEM and PRODUCT, with concatenated primary keys of *orderno+productid+mediacode* and *productid+mediacode*, respectively. It is possible that the value for *productid* or *mediacode* could the same for more than one record in either file, but any combination of *productid+mediacode* would never appear more than once in the PRODUCT file, and any combination of *orderno+productid+mediacode* would appear only once in the ORDERED_ITEM file.

An additional issue with regard to key integrity is the assurance that the primary key field for a given record must never be allowed to have a *null* value. A null value is not the same as a *zero* or a *space*. Zero is value and would be suitable as a primary key for a record. A space character, although normally not visible on a screen or report, nonetheless has a value to the database. If a field is intended to have no value, then it must be set to null. Given the purpose of a primary key to uniquely identify a record, a null value would defeat that purpose.

Domain Integrity

The concept of *domain integrity* focuses on controls to insure that no data element in a file or database takes on a value that is outside its range of legal or relevant values. In this category, a wide variety of controls exists to accomplish this goal, each being dependent upon the nature and context of the data element being controlled. Table 10-3 contains a list and brief explanation of several of the more commonly applied domain controls.

Using the *range control* mechanism as an example, we can see that a field for INTEREST_RATE would benefit from a range control that limits its lower bound value to zero and its upper bound value to some number that reflects either the highest allowable interest rate by law or the highest reasonable value of interest that would be charged or paid for that particular borrowing or lending instrument. Setting the lower bound to zero makes sense because allowing for a negative interest rate does not. Setting the upper boundary to a particular value depends on the context of the data element.

Table 10-3 Common Domain Controls

Domain Control	Description
Default value	Automatic entry of a value commonly found for this field unless other data is entered
Range control	Imposition of acceptable or relecant limits on either alphanumeric or numerical data
Picture control	Imposition of a specific pattern for the data being entered (i.e., DATE=mm/dd/yy or dd-mm-yyyy)
Null value control	Specifications of whether a value in a particular field is required or optional

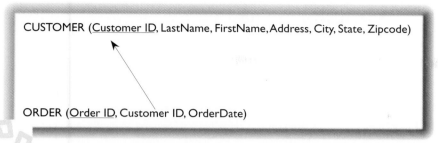

Figure 10-2   Example of Referential Integrity between Files

Referential Integrity

This category of data integrity is intended to insure that the value of a certain field is limited to the range of existing values of another field in another file. The most common example of this constraint is found in the cross-referencing function of a foreign key.

A referential integrity error exists when the foreign key value in one file has no matching primary key value in another related file. Consider the two records shown in Figure 10-2. The relationship between the ORDER file and the CUSTOMER file is such that each record in the ORDER file must be related to only one record in the CUSTOMER file. This infers that an order is placed by a single customer and that any customer can be related one or more than one records in the ORDER file. What happens, however, if a particular customer record is deleted? If this customer has ever placed an order with us, then we have a referential integrity problem: we have records in the ORDER file that do not have any existing customer related to them.

If we look at this scenario from a different angle, we can see the value of enforcing referential integrity controls. When a new record is created for the ORDER file, the value of the field for storing the customer number must be limited to the existing set of primary keys in the CUSTOMER file. Otherwise, we could enter an order for a customer that does not exist.

It must be pointed out that a referential integrity control simply insures that an existing cross-reference value is used. It does not insure that the correct one is used. Having said that, preventing referential integrity errors, such as the example described previously, requires a bit of forethought. One method of maintaining the referential integrity between the ORDER and CUSTOMER files would be to delete all orders associated with a particular customer when deleting that customer's record from the CUSTOMER file. This approach, however, does not make much business sense, because all the order history for that customer would be destroyed and reconstruction of accurate historical sales data would be impossible. More than likely, we would want to prevent deletion of any CUSTOMER file record that is related to any ORDER file record. This suggests that we must have a set of deletion rules to preserve the referential integrity of our database.[2] Table 10-4 contains a list and brief explanation of the various deletion rules used to insure referential integrity.

---

[2] There are also referential integrity rules that apply to insertion and update processes in databases. Although our limited scope prevents detailed coverage of these rules in this text, they are conceptually the same as the deletion rules. A full discussion of these various rules can be found in any good database text.

Table 10-4   Example of Referential Integrity Deletion Rules

Deletion Rule	Explanation
NO RESTRICTION	Any record in the file may be deleted without regard to any other record or file.
DELETE:CASCADE	A deletion of a record must be automatically followed by the deletion of any matching records in any related files.
DELETE:RESTRICT	A deletion of a record in a table must be disallowed until any matching records are deleted from any related files.
DELETE:SET NULL	A deletion of a record must be automatically followed by setting any matching keys in a related file to NULL.

DESIGNING AND SPECIFYING PHYSICAL RECORDS

As we continue with our bottom-up approach to database design, we move from the specification of the data elements and field to the design and specification of the physical records in each file. Recall from our discussion of logical data modeling in chapter 6 that the value of the primary key is to allow for the identification of a single instance of an entity. When we reach the physical database design stage, we can think of a *record* as a group of fields that are used to fully describe a single instance of an entity. Extending this concept to the file level, we can see that a logical entity becomes a physical file and that the collection of files defines the database. It should be clear now why we worked so hard to create a fully normalized set of relations during the logical modeling stage of the SDLC. If we have successfully defined a set of normalized relations in the logical model, they directly translate into fields, records, and files at the physical level.

In designing the physical record, we are concerned with achieving an efficient use of the storage media and the maximization of the processing speed with regard to retrieving and aggregating records from the various files in our database. To that end, we must first determine the sequence of the fields contained in each record of the file. Because of its value in defining a unique record within a file, the primary key field is usually positioned as the first field in the record. After that, the sequencing of the fields is determined by the analyst such that the order of their appearance in the record is logical. For example, although feasible, it is not logical to position the field LASTNAME as the second field in a record and the field FIRSTNAME as the ninth field in a record. The sequencing of fields within a record should be such that a tabular list of records within a file produces a useful format for reading the data. Figure 10-3 graphically illustrates the right and wrong ways to sequence the fields in a typical CUSTOMER file record.

Variable-Length and Fixed-Length Records

In determining the specification for the physical record, we must make a decision regarding the *record length*. There are two approaches to this specification. The first is to adopt a *fixed-length* record. Using this approach, all records contained within a file have exactly the same number of bytes. The advantage of this approach is that the storage requirements for a given file can be easily determined by simply estimating the number of potential records within a file and multiplying that by the

	Customer ID	State	Address	LastName	Zipcode	City	FirstName
WRONG							

	Customer ID	LastName	FirstName	Address	City	State	Zipcode
RIGHT							

Figure 10-3   Examples of Proper and Improper Field Sequencing

specified record length. The disadvantage of this approach, however, lies with the potential for wasting valuable storage space and decreasing processing efficiency. Consider the fixed-length record depicted in Figure 10-4.

Notice that the record has a provision for up to three vendors being listed for a particular product. Although this approach allows for certain flexibility in selecting vendors for a product, it also comes with a cost. For certain products, there may be only one vendor that can supply that product. In such cases, the storage space allocated for the two additional vendors goes unused but, nonetheless, is unavailable for storing any other information. Further, if for some reason a particular product has more than three possible vendors, either the information for the fourth vendor goes unrecorded or the entire physical file and all of the applications that access it need to be rewritten to accommodate the new file structure.

Figure 10-4   Fixed Length Record with Provision For Multiple Vendors

Field Number	Field Identifier	
1	Product ID	
2	Description	
3	Qty On Hand	
4	Qty On Order	
5	Reorder Qty	
6	Vendor ID	
7	Vendor Unit Price	
8	Vendor Price Break Qty	
9	Vendor ID	
10	Vendor Unit Price	Potentially
11	Vendor Price Break Qty	Wasted
12	Vendor ID	Storage
13	Vendor Unit Price	Space
14	Vendor Price Break Qty	

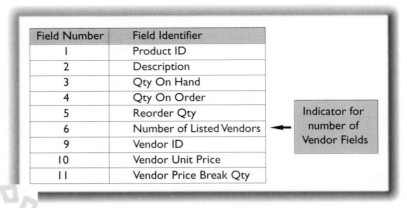

Field Number	Field Identifier
1	Product ID
2	Description
3	Qty On Hand
4	Qty On Order
5	Reorder Qty
6	Number of Listed Vendors
9	Vendor ID
10	Vendor Unit Price
11	Vendor Price Break Qty

Indicator for number of Vendor Fields

Figure 10-5   Variable Length Record with Provision for Multiple Vendors

In contrast to the fixed-length approach, the *variable-length* record allows for each record to contain a variable number of bytes. Although this approach maximizes the use of storage space by not preallocating storage, it also comes with certain tradeoffs. Consider the variable-length record shown in Figure 10-5.

Note that because the length of the record is allowed to vary, there is no easy method of determining where one record ends and another begins. Using the fixed-length approach, the end of a given record can be determined by counting the number of bytes allocated to that record. In the variable-length record, this cannot be done. In situations where the vendor information appears more than once, the record necessarily is longer. Although there are a variety of methods available to indicate the end point for a variable-length record, the most common is to introduce a new field that can store a value that indicates the number of times a recurring group of fields occur within that record. In our example, field 6 contains this information. Although the variable-length approach may be useful in certain situations, it is commonly not employed, owing to the difficulties associated with its processing. Unless there is some compelling reason to adopt a variable-length approach, the fixed-length record should be the default choice.

Paging and Blocking

Beyond the specification of the physical structure of the record, we must consider the method by which the requested information is processed, retrieved, and displayed. To maximize both the efficiency and effectiveness of these operations, several methods are available to the analyst.

When systems programmers design and code an operating system, they must make certain decisions about how best to conserve RAM across the virtually infinite combination of applications that may be in use at any given time. One of these decisions involves setting the sector size for data storage and the page size for data retrieval. A sector is a fixed-length section of a hard disk. Regardless of the actual size of the data requested to be read or written, they are stored or retrieved in sectors. A *page* is defined as the actual amount of data read or written into RAM as the result of a data query or disk read operation. The page size is also a fixed amount of data and is the total amount of RAM allocated regardless of the size of the actual data record(s) retrieved. In most cases, the page size and the sector size are equal in value, or the page is set as a multiple of the sector size. In either case, these two settings can have a material effect on the throughput and speed of a data query and must be considered when designing the record structure.

Let us assume that the sector and page size set by the operating system is 512 bytes. In addition, let us also assume that the operating system has been designed to restrict a physical record from spanning across pages. Under these conditions, a single physical record would be limited in size to no more than 512 bytes. Further, if the physical record size is less than the sector or page size, then wasted space occurs. Figure 10-6 illustrates this example.

To minimize this potential for wasted disk and RAM storage, the analyst can specify both the record length and the *blocking factor*, the number of records stored and/or retrieved for a given query. The idea is to maximize the use of RAM by operating under the assumption that for any given query, the data adjacent to the target record will probably be accessed in a near-term future query. If this record is already in RAM, then no additional disk operation is necessary. Further, if the query involves the retrieval of multiple records, then a record size that is an exact integer multiple (or close to it) of the sector or page size minimizes wasted space.

Referring back to Figure 10-6, we can see that by setting the blocking factor to five, given our record length of 100 bytes, only 12 bytes of disk or RAM storage is wasted.

It may seem intuitive at this point to question why a record could not be allowed to span across sectors, thus making maximum use of the available space. This *spanned records* storage approach is an option available to the analyst and, in some cases, may prove to create additional space efficiency. This method of storage, however, may come with a prohibitive processing cost.

Referring to Figure 10-7, we can see that by using a spanning approach, we could store the five 100-byte records plus the first 12 bytes of the sixth record. The adjacent sector would then contain the remaining 88 bytes of record six, four complete 100-byte records, and the first 24 bytes of record eleven. This would continue until all records were stored. Although storage space is maximized under this approach, processing is not. If a given query requires the data contained in record six, then two disk read operations are required and 1024 bytes of RAM are allocated.

Figure 10-6   Example of Data Stored with and without Blocking

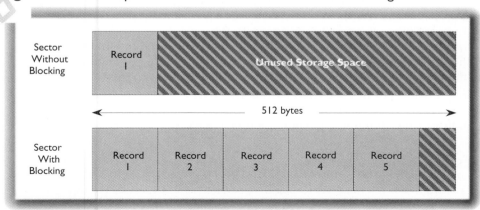

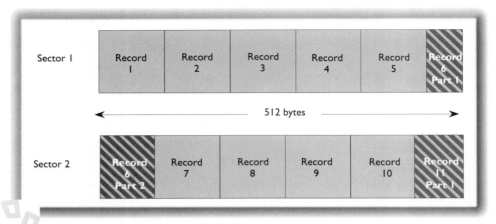

Figure 10-7   Record Spanning Approach

Generally speaking, spanned records sacrifice processing speed for increased efficiency in data storage.

Because the sector or page size and sometimes the blocking factor are beyond the control of the analyst, creative thinking becomes the solution. By investigating ways to adjust the record size to more closely match the constraints imposed by the sector size, the analyst can have a significant positive effect on storage, memory, and processing efficiency.

Let us assume that our sector or page size has been set to 512 bytes as before. We have designed the physical record to be fixed length, totaling 260 bytes. Unless we use a spanning approach, only one record is stored per sector and 252 bytes of storage or RAM are wasted for each record. If, however, we redesign the record slightly by recoding the data in one field to use 4 less bytes, we can now store two complete records per sector or page, and the space required to store the file is literally cut in half.

DESIGNING AND SPECIFYING FILES

Now that we have the fields and records specified, we can move on to the design considerations associated with the files contained in the database. By definition, a *physical file* is a grouping of all occurrences of a given record structure. It is the physical version of an entity in a fully normalized logical data model, and it is often referred to as a *table* because of the way the data are organized into rows and columns. Although the design considerations may vary slightly owing to the intended nature of the file, the general considerations are more our focus in this section. Nonetheless, it is important to realize that the file type may play an important role in the design considerations on the part of the analyst. Table 10-5 contains a list and brief description of the common file types found in a modern IS.

File Access Methods

One issue that must be address in file design is the method used to access a particular record in a file. There are two basic approaches to file access: (1) *sequential access* and (2) *direct* or *random access*.

Table 10-5   Common File Types and Uses

File Type	Description
Master file	Contains records related to business data that is relatively permanent. Once a record is entered, it tends to remain indefinitely. Data values may change (i.e., CUSTOMERS, PRODUCTS, INVOICES, SUPPLIERS).
Transaction file	Contains records that describe business events that can occur on a day-to-day basis. Data tends to have a limited useful life and are usually moved to an archival file after a predetermined period.
Document file	Contains stored copies of historical data in document form such that the overhead associated with recreated or reprocessing the document is eliminated.
Table look-up file	Contains reference data used to validate field values and to maintain consistency throughout the database (INCOME TAX TABLES, POSTAL CODE TABLES).
Audit file	Contains records of updates to other files in the database in case production files are damaged and require reconstruction. Data can be used with records in archival files to recover or restore damaged files or lost data.
Archive file	Contains records that have been deleted from active transaction files but require retention for an indefinite period.
Work file	Contains records stored temporarily or records containing intermediate results in a calculation process. Work files are usually created when needed and deleted upon completion of the task.

Sequential File Access

Using the *sequential access* method, a particular record is accessed by scanning the file from the beginning and checking each record in the file until the desired record is found. This approach is somewhat like searching for a particular word in the dictionary by starting at the first word and reading all words in sequence until the desired word is encountered. During the early days of data processing, where files were stored on magnetic tape, this was the only method available for file access. In using the sequential approach, the records must be organized in ascending order based on the primary key. Further, any additional records to a sequentially accessed file must be inserted at the appropriate point, thus requiring the file to be rewritten each time a record is added. Using the sequential approach, the next record begins one byte after the length of the current record. If the last record of the file is the desired record, the entire file must be read before it can be retrieved.

Direct File Access

Using our preceding dictionary example, the *direct access* method is similar to finding a word in the dictionary by relying on the alphabetical organization of the listing. The word (or primary key) is read, and the file is accessed at the point where this record should exist in the file. With the direct access method, the address of the block containing the record is determined and then that block is retrieved. This approach allows for direct retrieval of the nth record in a file without having to read all records prior to it. Although it is unlikely that the analyst makes direct use of the operating system's file access methods, the file organization approach is used to minimize retrieval times for a particular file type.

Organization Techniques

The concept of *file organization* focuses on the physical arrangement of records within a file on the storage media. Each file type requires separate consideration with regard to file organization, but the goal of fast retrieval and high throughput is generally the key determinant. Hundreds of file organization schemes have been created, but all of them can be categorized into three basic types: (1) *sequential*, (2) *indexed*, and (3) *direct*.

Sequential File Organization

The *sequential file organization* approach is in keeping with our previous explanation of the sequential access approach. The file is organized in ascending order according to the primary key. This method is useful when an entire file needs to be processed, but it is impractical for files where the data need to be accessed randomly. A lookup table is often organized using the sequential method, because its values are relatively static and the size of the file is generally not too large. Figure 10-8 illustrates the sequential file organization method.

Indexed File Organization

Using an *indexed file organization,* the records can be stored in either a sequential or random manner. An index is created that allows the database application software to locate a particular record of interest. This method is somewhat similar to locating a book in the library. First, you find a listing for the book in the card catalog. On that listing is an identification number that corresponds to a particular location in the library. Once you arrive at the designated location, you can easily retrieve the book (if it is there). Figure 10-9 graphically illustrates an indexed file organization scheme.

In Figure 10-9 we see an example of a hierarchical index approach.[3] Three index files have been created with fields containing the highest primary key value found in a particular physical location on the storage media. A *master index* has been

Figure 10-8   Sequential File Organization Method

Physical Record Position in File

Record 1	Record 2	Record 3	Record 4	Record 5	Record 6	...
432751	472982	475631	599874	763216	76327	...

Record Primary Key

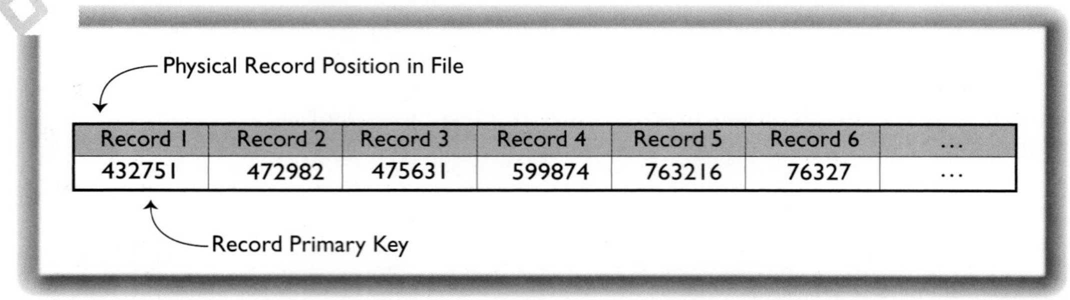

[3] It should be noted that a common indexing scheme is typically much larger and more complex than our example. The presentation of a simplified example, however, better facilitates our understanding of the concept.

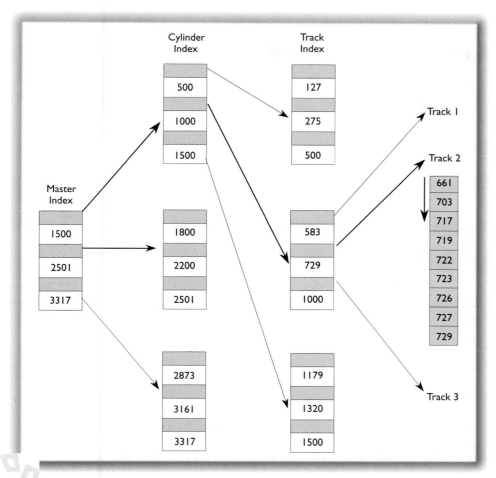

Figure 10-9   Example of Record Lookup Using an Indexed File
Organization Approach
Source: Adapted from McFadden, Hoffer, and Prescott (1999).

created that contains pointers to three cylinders on the storage media. A *pointer* is
simply a field within a record that contains data in the form of a physical storage address that points to a related field or record in another location. Using the master
index pointers, we can find the physical location of the indices for all records up to
a certain primary key value. The *cylinder index* files store the physical locations of the
tracks, and the *track index* contains the pointers to the physical blocks containing
the records on the storage media.

In our example, a request has been placed for a record with primary key 717.
The master index is read, and the requested primary key is compared to the list of
index keys. The value 1500 is the smallest index greater than the requested value,
and, therefore, it is used to locate the cylinder index for that range of records.
Cylinder index value 1000 is the closest greater index value to the requested record,
and it points to the physical location of the track index for the desired record. The
closest greater track index value to the track location for the desired record is 729
points, and a search of that track finds record 717 at the third location in the block.

The general computation for determining a relative storage address slot for a particular record is:

$$\text{Relative slot address} = 1 + \text{Remainder of} \quad \frac{\text{Primary Key Value}}{\text{Total Number of Reserved Address Slots}}$$

Assume a PRODUCT file with 4,500 unique records. The storage allocation for this file is equal to the number of records, therefore 4,500 storage slots will be needed on the media.

The primary key for records in this file is the PRODUCT_ID field.

The location for PRODUCT_ID 734171 can be computed as follows:

$$\text{Relative slot address} = 1 + \text{Remainder of} \quad \frac{734171}{4500} = 1 + 671 = 672$$

Figure 10-10   Division–Remainder Hashing Algorithm

Despite the apparent complexity of this approach and the additional storage space required to store the index pointers, the index file organization method greatly reduces the retrieval time associated with a particular record in a file.

Direct File Organization

The *direct file organization* approach allows for a particular record to be retrieved using a single disk access operation. In certain applications, such as airline reservation systems, there is little need to retrieve multiple records in sequential order or in multiples for analysis of a particular field value. In these situations, minimizing retrieval speed is the primary objective. To accomplish this goal, a system must be able to directly determine the disk address for the block containing the desired record. This is accomplished using a mathematical computation called a *hashing algorithm*. Although a variety of hashing methods are available, the most commonly used approach is the *division-remainder* method. Figure 10-10 contains an example of this method of determining record location.

One disadvantage to the direct file organization approach is the possibility that a particular primary key may hash to a block that is already filled with records. In this case, the home storage block contains a pointer to an overflow block designated to temporarily store overflow records. When space for the overflow record becomes available in the appropriate block, due to record deletion, it is moved from the overflow area to its correct storage location.

File Volumetrics

Often, the analyst must determine the desired storage space for a given file or for all the files in the database. Despite the various file and data organization methods employed to improve retrieval time and use the storage space efficiently, an application may perform poorly if the database server is unable to handle the required volume of data. The concept of *volumetrics* is intended to address the question of exactly how much data the system needs to manage. Generally speaking, the size of a given file is dependent on one or more of the following:

➤ Field data type
➤ Record structure

➤ Storage media employed
➤ Block size
➤ File organization scheme

Although fairly straightforward from a mathematical perspective, volumetric analysis takes into account a wide variety of data storage requirements in reaching the final calculation. Table 10-6 contains an example of a volumetric analysis for a single data file.

Using the calculations in Table 10-6, we can see that our initial storage requirements for this file are approximately 3.6 megabytes (Mb). By applying an agreed upon growth factor based on the expected growth of the business, the future data storage requirements for this file grow to 5.6 Mb by the end of Year 4. Once all files in the database have been analyzed, the totals can be provided to the system designers so that the appropriate technology can be specified to handle the required volume of data.

DESIGNING THE DATABASES

Although the design of the database has, in some respects, been occurring since we began specifying the field types, there are certain decisions that must be made regarding the database itself. It is important to remember that a database is more than simply a collection of files. It is intended to be a coherent and concise source of data for a variety of users and a variety of applications. The central nervous system of a database is the *database management system* (DBMS). By reaching the point where decisions about the DBMS can be made, we have come to the last stage of our physical database design activity.

Table 10-6   Example of Volumetric Analysis
for INVOICE File

Field	Size (bytes)
Invoice_ID	7
Invoice_Date	8
Customer_ID	6
Product_ID	9
Quantity	3
Unit_Price	6
Salesman_ID	4
Record size	43
Record overhead	25%
Total record size	53.75
Total annual record volume	67,000
Expected table volume	3,601,250
Expected annual growth rate	16%
Projected table volume—4 years	5,621,176

Database Architectures

One of the first issues to address at this point is the determination of the structure of the database system, called the *database architecture.* The selection of the appropriate database architecture for the system is really the essence of database design. Four basic architectural approaches are commonly used: (1) *network,* (2) *hierarchical,* (3) *relational,* and (4) *object-oriented.*

The Network Database Model

One of the earliest database architectures to be defined and employed is the *network database model.* In this approach, each file in the database may be associated with any number of subordinate or superior files. The relationships between the files in a network database model are determined simply by data elements that are common to both of the connected files. Another way of describing this approach is that any particular file can be thought of as a child with many parents.

The network database model is very flexible, because any relationship between any number of files can be implemented, but it also requires a significant amount of storage space and maintenance. Once thought of as the workhorse of the data processing industry, remnants of the network database model can still be found in high-powered mainframe installations, where extremely high-volume transaction processing takes place. Figure 10-11 illustrates the network database architecture.

The Hierarchical Database Model

As its name implies, the *hierarchical database model* links the files within the database in the form of a hierarchy. Using this model, a parent file can have many children, but a child file can have only one parent. The hierarchical approach requires that access to the database start at the top of the hierarchy and flow downward to the

Figure 10-11   Example of a Network Database Architecture

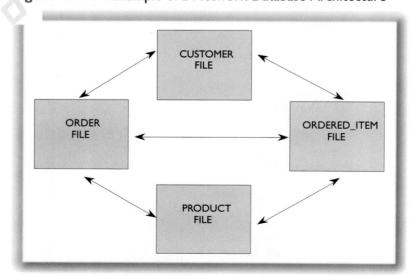

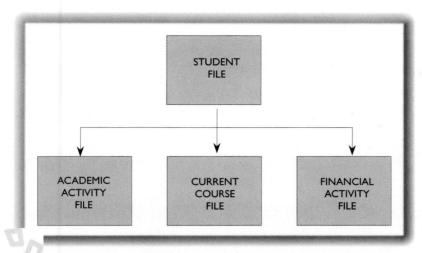

Figure 10-12   Example of Hierarchical Database Architecture

lower levels. This approach is still in existence and is normally applied in high-volume transaction processing environments, where the conceptual data model for the system represents a hierarchy and the access to the various files within the database begins with a single file. Figure 10-12 contains an illustration of a hierarchical database architecture.

The Relational Database Model

E. F. Codd (1970) originated the relational approach to database management in a series of research papers published in the early 1970s. His suggestion that a database could be designed using well-established concepts found in relational mathematics has provided the impetus for widespread research into numerous areas, including database languages, query subsystems, database semantics, locking and recovery, and inferential subsystems.

The *relational database model* is easily visualized as a set of two-dimensional tables or spreadsheets made up of columns and rows. Each column in a table represents a particular data field, and each row in a table represents a single record in that file. Files are linked together by relations formed via attributes shared by two files. The relational approach is the common method for designing new database systems and is the most widely used method in existence. Figure 10-13 illustrates a typical relational database model.

One of the reasons for the widespread adoption of the relational database model is that the data are stored in a manner that both minimizes redundant data and eliminates certain types of processing errors typically associated with the network and hierarchical approaches. In fact, it was once proposed that the relational model was so intuitive that it would allow end users to construct and manipulate databases without the assistance of database design professionals. Although this promise was never fully realized, the relational model has made life easier for the database design professionals and has made access to relevant data more convenient for the end user.

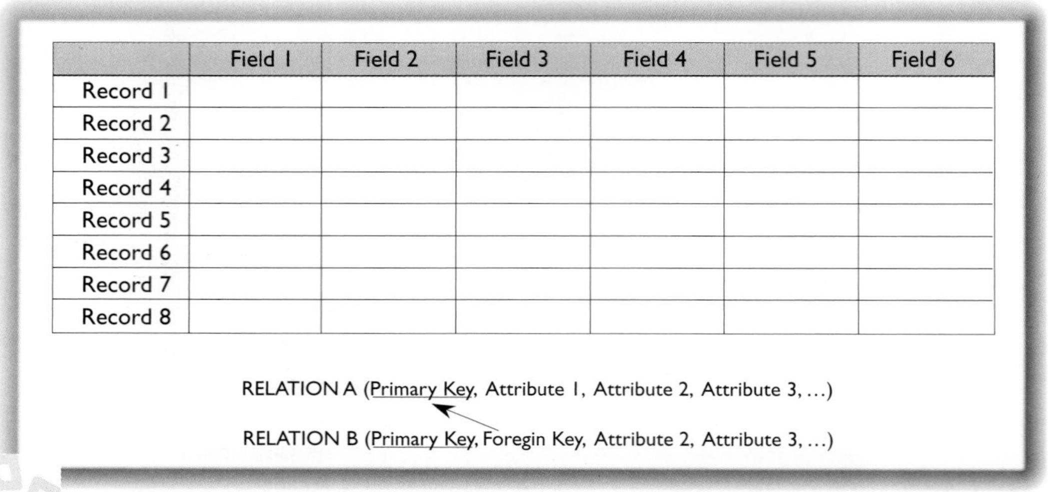

	Field 1	Field 2	Field 3	Field 4	Field 5	Field 6
Record 1						
Record 2						
Record 3						
Record 4						
Record 5						
Record 6						
Record 7						
Record 8						

RELATION A (<u>Primary Key</u>, Attribute 1, Attribute 2, Attribute 3, …)

RELATION B (<u>Primary Key</u>, Foregin Key, Attribute 2, Attribute 3, …)

Figure 10-13   Example of a Relational Database Architecture

The Object-Oriented Database Model

The newest approach to specifying a database architecture is the *object-oriented model*. Unlike the previous database models, where the attributes of a record are stored as fields and used to relate one file to another, the object-oriented model *encapsulates* both the attributes associated with an object and the methods that operate on those objects in a structure referred to as an *object class*. Relationships between object classes are shown by nesting one object class inside another, and, similar to the hierarchical database model, new object classes can be defined from more general ones. The major advantage of this database model is the ability to accommodate complex data types, such as graphics, video, and audio, as well as more common text-based data. Although still in its infancy compared to the relational model, the object-oriented model is gaining popularity in applications requiring the management of complex data types and event-driven programming. We discuss the object-oriented approach to software design in detail in appendix B of this text. Figure 10-14 illustrates the basic concept of objects and relationships in this database architecture.

Figure 10-14   Example of Object-Oriented Database Architecture

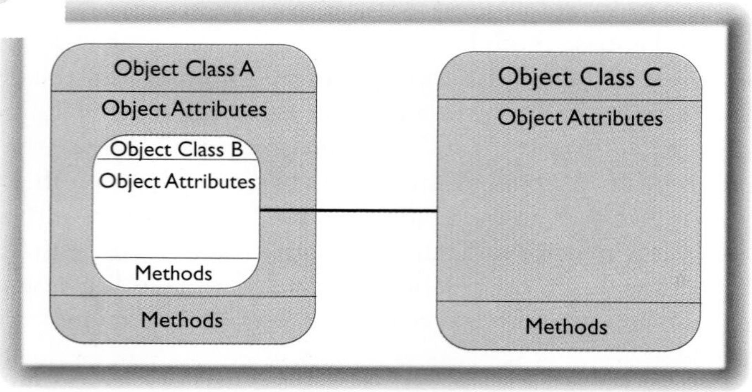

CHAPTER SUMMARY

Despite the comparative brevity of this chapter, a broad range of concepts has been presented for you to consider during the physical modeling of the database structures. The effective design of the physical database is a key element in the successful design and implementation of an organizational IS. The decisions of the world rely on data, and accessibility to that data is the essence of modern management. Properly designed, a physical database can serve many applications and processes. Improperly done, and the data become burdensome and unable to be effectively used.

Although the four types of database architecture can still be found in production installations, the relational is, by far, the most prevalent, and the object-oriented is clearly the fastest growing. Despite this growth, however, the skills associated with the design and implementation of the relational database model will remain viable for many years to come. As a modern systems analyst, you will be expected to understand the appropriate application of each of the data architectures and be able to recommend the appropriate one for the task at hand. Because of the widespread popularity of the relational model, however, you can expect the bulk of your work to be focused in this arena. Because of this popularity, the next three chapters focus on designing the inputs, outputs, and internals assuming a relational approach. The concepts presented, however, can be easily applied in any database architecture environment.

KEY CONCEPTS

➤ Database schema

The physical model of the new system is referred as the database schema, and it represents the technical implementation of the logical model in terms of its tables, relationships, data domains, and governing business rules.

➤ Two primary goals of the data conversion process

1. Accurately translate the logical relations into a comprehensive technical specification for the databases and files, including data structures and data access methods.

2. Specify the storage requirements and technologies for all data to be contained within the system.

➤ The bottom-up approach

The bottom-up approach starts by thoroughly specifying the smallest elements in the design, the *field,* and work upward toward the specification of the logical grouping of fields into *records,* the grouping of records into *files,* and the grouping of files into the largest element in the design, the *database.*

➤ Field types
• Primary key

The primary key is the field used to identify a single, unique record contained within a file. It is the data element that uniquely defines a specific instance of an entity.

• Foreign key

A foreign key is a field that contains a data element that serves as a primary key in another file. It is the field that creates a specific relationship between two or more files in the database.

• Descriptive field (nonkey)

Descriptive fields contain data describing various attributes of the record but do not serve the functions of primary keys and foreign keys.

➤ Data types

A data type is a detailed specification of how each field in the file represents the data contained within it. It is the definition of the storage format and allowable content for a field.

• Primitive data type

Primitive data type is used to describe data that are supported directly by the system hardware and its low-level programming languages and operating systems.

- Complex data type (user-defined data type)

  Complex data type is not directly supported by the hardware or software but is allowable based on a set of specifications supplied by the analyst.

➤ Field-data representation

Field-data representation is a process of determining and recording certain characteristics about each field in the data dictionary for the system. It must be performed at the field, record, file, and database levels.

➤ Field-level data specification

- Calculated fields
  - Compute-on-demand

    Using the compute-on-demand approach, the storage requirements are minimal but additional processing time is required when retrieving a record.

  - Recalculate-on-demand

    Using the recalculate-on-demand approach, the values are stored and are recomputed only when there is a change in one or more of the root values used to calculate them.

- Data element ownership
- Prescribed coding method
- Missing data values handling procedures

➤ Data integrity

The concept of data integrity focuses on processes and procedures that are intended to facilitate an atmosphere of trust with regard to the quality and accuracy of the data in the data. There are three basic categories of data integrity controls:

- Key integrity

  Key integrity focuses on insuring that every file has a unique primary key and that controls exist to prevent any two records from having the same primary key value or to assure a record does not have a null value.

- Domain integrity

  Domain integrity focuses on controls insuring that no data element in a file or database takes on a value that is outside its range of legal or relevant values. Common domain controls include default value, range control, picture control, and null value control.

- Referential integrity

  Referential integrity is intended to insure that the value of a certain field is limited to the range of existing values of another field in another file.

➤ Physical record design and specification

In designing the physical record, we are concerned with achieving an efficient use of the storage media and the maximization of the processing speed with regard to retrieving and aggregating records from the various files in the database.

1. Determine the sequence of the fields contained in each record of the file.
2. Make a decision regarding the record length.
   - Fixed-length approach
   - Variable-length approach
3. Consider the information process, retrieval, and display methods.
   - Paging
   - Blocking

➤ File design and specification

A physical file is a grouping of all occurrences of a given record structure. It is the physical version of an entity in a fully normalized logical data model and is often referred to as a table.

- Common file types
  - Master file
  - Transaction file
  - Document file
  - Table lookup file
  - Audit file
  - Archive file
  - Work file
- File access methods
  - Sequential access

    Using the sequential access method, a particular record is accessed by scanning the file from the beginning and checking each record in the file until the desired record is found.

- Direct (random) access
  Using the direct access method, a particular record is accessed by specifying the primary key of a particular record. The address of the block containing the record is then determined and the block is retrieved. This approach allows for direct retrieval of the nth record in a file without having to read all records prior to it.
- Organization techniques
  The concept of file organization focuses on the physical arrangement of records within a file on the storage media. The organizational schemes can be categorized into three basic types:
  - Sequential file organization
    The files are organized in ascending order according to the primary key.
  - Indexed file organization
    The records can be stored in either a sequential or random manner. An index is created that allows the database application software to locate a particular record of interest.
  - Direct file organization
    The direct file organization approach allows for a particular record to be retrieved using a single disk access operation. In most cases, the objective is to minimize retrieval speed. This is often accomplished using a mathematical computation called a hashing algorithm.
- File volumetrics
  The concept of volumetrics is intended to address the question of exactly how much data the system needs to manage. Generally speaking, the size of a given file is dependent on one or more of the following:
  - Field data type
  - Record structure
  - Storage media employed
  - Block size
  - File organization scheme

➤ Database design
Selecting the appropriate database architecture(the structure of the database(for the system is the essence of database design. Four basic architectural approaches are commonly used:

- The network database model
  In this approach, each file in the database may be associated with any number of subordinate or superior files. The relationships between the files are determined by data elements that are common to both of the connected files.
- The hierarchical database model
  The hierarchical database model links the files within the database in the form of a hierarchy. Using this model, a parent file can have many children but a child file can have only one parent.
- The relational database model
  The relational database model is conceptualized as tables with each column representing a particular data field and each row representing a single record in that file. Files are linked together by relations formed via attributes shared by two files.
- The object-oriented database model
  The object-oriented model encapsulates both the attributes associated with an object and the methods that operate on those objects in a structure referred to as an object class. Relationships between object classes are shown by nesting one object class inside another.

QUESTIONS FOR REVIEW

1. Explain the concept of database schema.

2. What are the two primary goals of the data conversion process?

3. Explain the bottom-up perspective of accomplishing the two goals of the data conversion process.

4. Compare the smallest unit of specification in a logical data model and a physical model. How are they usually related?

5. List and briefly describe the three field types.

6. Explain the main difference between the two data types.

7. List and compare the two approaches of specifying a calculated field.

8. Explain the concept of data integrity.

9. List and briefly describe the three basic categories of data integrity control.

10. Compare and list the pros and cons of the fixed-length records approach and the variable-length records approach.

11. Briefly describe the concepts of paging and blocking.

12. List and briefly compare the two file access approaches.

13. Briefly explain how direct file organization accomplishes locating a particular record of interest.

14. What is file volumetric analysis?

15. List and briefly describe the four basic database architectural approaches.

16. Why is the relational database model the most widely used method in existence?

17. What is the major advantage of the object-oriented database model?

⌦ FOR FURTHER DISCUSSION

1. A new system is being developed for DREA, a major entertainment partnership. A total of six different tables are required and a relational database model has been chosen. The following is a list of the approximate record sizes and expected file sizes for each table.

FILE	RECORD SIZE	FILE SIZE
ARTIST	75 bytes	3,000 records
VENUE	112 bytes	1,100 records
TOUR	76 bytes	1,200 records
ENGINEER	54 bytes	25 records
PROMOTER	127 bytes	1,000 records
TRANSPORT	89 bytes	100 records

Conduct a detailed volumetric analysis on the proposed DREA system. Assume a record overhead of 15 percent and an annual growth rate of 22 percent.

2. Choose a commercial Web site to visit that uses a database of some kind. What database architecture do you envision is being used? What tables would you expect to find in the database? How big do you think the database is?

3. Debra Herbenick is a senior systems analyst for Bizzern Enterprises. In designing the file system for a major client, Debra is faced with a challenge. She is designing the CUSTOMER file using a variable-length record approach. The fixed portion of the record contains basic customer data, and the variable portion of the record contains data describing possible shipping addresses for the customer. In calculating the record size, Debra dis-

covers that the 3,063 byte expected size exceeds the 2,530 block size for the database. What options are available to her to solve this dilemma?

4. Bill is considering the purchase of a DBMS for his desktop computer system. While in college, he took a database course but did not do all that well. He does remember something about files, however, but does not really know the difference between a file and a database. Write Bill a brief note explaining the difference and the advantages and disadvantages of each environment.

REFERENCES

Codd, E. F. 1970. "A Relational Model of Data for Large Shared Data Banks." *Communications of the ACM* 13(6): 377–387.

McFadden, F. R., J. A. Hoffer, and M. B. Prescott. 1999. *Modern Database Management,* 5th ed. Reading, MA: Addison Wesley Longman.

Designing the System Output

Learning Objectives

- Understand the process of designing high quality and effective system output
- Identify the basic characteristics of high quality system output
- Discuss control strategies for system output
- Identify and discuss the various categories of output, media, and output technology
- Understand ways in which unintentional bias can be introduced into system output
- Identify and discuss available backup and retention strategies for data recovery

Computers are useless—they can only give you answers.

—PABLO PICASSO

INTRODUCTION

Output may be the most important aspect of SAD, because it represents the universal goal of all IS—to generate an answer. Every system generates some form of output, some arguably more useful than others, and output can take many forms. In addition to the traditional paper-based report, output can be in the form of a computer screen-based report, audio, video, graphics, film, animation, time code, numerical control data, and even Braille characters on an automated character recognition device. Such output may come from extensive processing of data from a variety of sources or from single-source data requiring very little processing. Regardless of the effort or source, the end users of an IS need output to accomplish their assigned tasks, and the overall satisfaction with, and success of, a system is often measured by the quality of its output. In this chapter, we explore the various types of output and the essential characteristics of high quality system output. Once we know what output we need and the data we need to create it, we can then move on to designing the necessary input and data capture mechanisms to gather the data and submit them for processing. That is the focus of chapter 12. Remember, we first design the output, and then we can design the input.

THE PROCESS OF DESIGNING SYSTEM OUTPUT

Although a certain percentage of the output of a new system can be designed without the direct input of the end user, the majority of the output cannot. Although most, if not all, of the required output was identified during the requirements analysis and logical design stages, output design is very much an end user–centric activity and is often conducted using an iterative prototyping approach. As we continue to move from a logical model to a physical one, we must convert the logical components of the model into their physical counterparts. Just as entities become tables and attributes become fields, in output design, data flows from processes to sinks or even other processes become system output.

The environment in which system output is prototyped is as varied as the output itself. Depending on the nature of the final output, the design can take place using paper and pencil, a simple word processor, a presentations graphics package, an electronic spreadsheet, or a sophisticated CASE tool. The focus is on look and feel rather than the technical requirements for generating the output—that comes during the design of the internal processes. In contrast to the early days of IS, where output was generally designed on a screen coding sheet and limited to 25 lines per screen with 80 characters per line, the advent of graphical operating environments has provided virtually no limit to the variety and type of output that can be designed and generated.

THE CHARACTERISTICS OF SYSTEM OUTPUT

The primary objective of output design is to create output that presents the desired information to the end user in an understandable and usable fashion requiring the least effort on the part of the end user to obtain it. Although easy to describe, this is nonetheless a lofty goal requiring attention to a significant list of critical issues and decisions. Although each output design scenario is different from the last, several generalizable characteristics prevail in all output design activities and products. Table 11-1 contains a brief list of the questions to be answered and the decisions to made in a typical output design scenario. In the following sections we discuss many of them in greater detail.

Table 11-1   Output Design Issues to Be Addressed

Output Design Issue	Description
Purpose	What is the intended use or purpose of the output?
Primary user(s)	Who will be the primary users of the output?
Frequency	How often will the output need to be generated?
Delivery point	Where will the output be used?
Human-machine boundaries	What are the points in the system where the end user must (or can) interact with the system?
Content	What information must be delivered by the output?
Media	In what form will the output be delivered?
Format	How will the content of the output be displayed and formatted?
Controls	What controls are necessary to limit access to the output?

Purpose

Effective output design is dependent on knowing how the output is used. It is not always the case that output is read in its entirety or from top to bottom and left to right. In some cases, the purpose of the output may be to provide quick reference to a variety of data or information such that a process can be controlled or a quick decision can be made. This suggests that the purpose of the output may dictate the order or sequence of the various data elements contained within it. In other cases, the purpose of the output may be to convey certain information to sources external to the organization. Identifying the purpose of a particular output early in the design stage can often dictate or constrain the available options with regard to media type and format of the output.

Recipient

Given that all output eventually is used by someone, knowing who the intended recipients of the output are can serve to inform the design. A typical large-scale IS is intended to serve a variety of end users performing a diverse set of tasks and operations within a single organization. As such, it may be difficult to create personalized output for each user. Nonetheless, the information gathered during requirements analysis interviews and observations must be combined with known cost considerations to design the output to be as close to personalized for each end user as possible. In all cases, the intended recipients of the output should be involved in the design and approval of each system output relevant to their assigned tasks.

Frequency

If a desired output cannot be obtained when it is needed, then its usefulness in assisting a given decision process becomes questionable. One of the single most common complaints among end users is the inability to get the output necessary to make a decision in a timely fashion. Thus, the goal of designing effective output is dependent on design timely output, as well. The frequency of a given output may vary from on demand to hourly, daily, weekly, monthly, quarterly, semiannually, or annually. For those outputs that can be generated directly by the end user, the primary focus is on minimizing the time between the request for the output and the receipt of the output. For those outputs that require assistance in preparation, the required delivery time and frequency combined with the output preparation time dictate when the output must be scheduled. An assisted output required by an end user at 9:00 A.M. on Tuesday may have to be scheduled to run on Monday afternoon to allow for sufficient preparation and processing time.

Distribution

Output is usually generated in one place from data stored in another place. With the increased sophistication of client–server environments and local computer peripherals, the problem of distribution is becoming less and less of an issue. Nonetheless, it remains an issue that must be considered by the analyst when designing output. If great output is not seen by the right end user, its value is reduced to zero very quickly.

Human–Machine Boundary

An additional consideration with regard to output distribution is the identification of the *human–machine boundary* of the IS. This is defined as the points where an end user interacts with the system through the exchange of data or information. Some of the points on this boundary correspond to inputs being provided by the end user, and others represent points of output generation or distribution. Any data flow that crosses the human–machine boundary represents an element of the system that must be physically specified. Figure 11-1 illustrates the identification of the human–machine boundary on a typical DFD.

Data Sources

In most cases, the source for system output is either a data store or a process. In certain situations, however, data from sources external to the organization are necessary in the generation of a given output. When external data are required, the analyst must decide on the best method for accessing and processing that data. If a large volume of external data is needed, the establishment of a formal DW may be the best solution. If the required external data reside on the WWW or some other accessible network, it makes sense to develop a process that simply retrieves the necessary data at the moment they are required, thus treating the external source as a data store. Regardless of the approach, however, before the output can be designed, the data must exist either within the system or accessible to the system. No source data, no output.

Media

When determining the appropriate design for a given output, the various media on which the output is generated must be determined and analyzed. Given the ever-increasing availability of diverse media, some output may be more suited to one

Figure 11-1   Human–Machine Boundary for Employee Payroll System

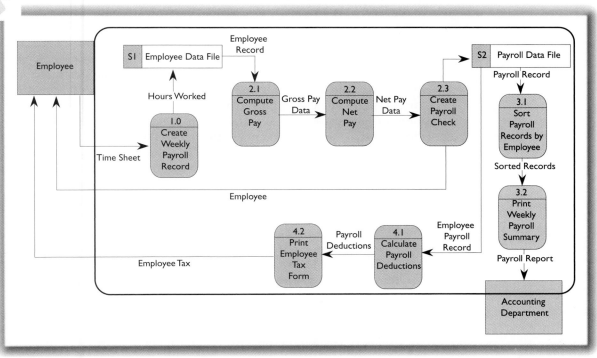

media than another. Moreover, if a given output must be generated using more than one primary media, then additional design constraints may be encountered. We explore the various media types and their characteristics in detail later in this chapter.

Format

No matter how accurate or timely the information contained by the output, its presentation format has a material effect on its usefulness to the end user. In many cases, the context in which the information is used can serve to inform the analyst as to the best format for the task. In other cases, the analyst will want to allow the end user to choose from a variety of output formats or to customize his or her own from a set of templates.

Several issues must be addressed when deciding on output format. First, how will the information be organized: tabular, zoned, narrative, or graphical? The *tabular approach* organizes the information into columns and rows very similar to the organization of the relational data model. In contrast, the *zoned approach* organizes the output into predetermined zones on the paper or screen. This method is similar to the look and feel of a frame-based Web page or a typical newspaper. The zoned approach may often be combined with a tabular approach. An example of this is a typical invoice or customer order form, in which the information for the customer and the shipping address is organized in zones and the information regarding the items to be ordered is organized in a tabular fashion.

If a *narrative approach* is used, then the information is presented using conventional sentences and paragraphs, and in a *graphical format,* the numbers are represented by one of a wide variety of charts or graphs. In some cases, the best method may turn out to be a combination of these approaches. Figure 11-2 illustrates a combination approach to the presentation of a screen-based output.

If the output is to be generated on paper, then what paper size is most appropriate? In the United States, the analyst needs to specify from the common sizes of 8.5 × 11 or 11 × 14 or 8.5 × 14 inches. If the system will be accessed and used by end users in Europe or Asia, however, then the paper standards become A4, A3, A3 nobi, and Super A4. Further, although the standard for computer monitors is rapidly moving toward larger and higher resolution displays that can measure 17 to 21 inches, the analyst must still design the screen output for the lowest common denominator to ensure that all end users have useful access to the output. Therefore, the output must still conform to the standard 640 × 480 pixel screen resolution.

Although the decisions are many and the options available to the analyst often quite varied, there are, nonetheless, some basic characteristics associated with high quality output and guidelines available to achieve those characteristics. Dumas (1988) provides a detailed description of the characteristics of high quality output, and Table 11-2 contains a summary of those recommendations.

Controls

Once output has been generated by a system, it is no longer controllable. This suggests that any control mechanisms associated with the generation and distribution of system output must be enforced prior to the generation of the output. Although a variety of situations exist that require the control of system output, probably the most common is the enforcement or protection of privacy or confidentiality. Information ranging from an organization's customer list to the top-secret design specification for a military weapon must be protected from unauthorized or inappropri-

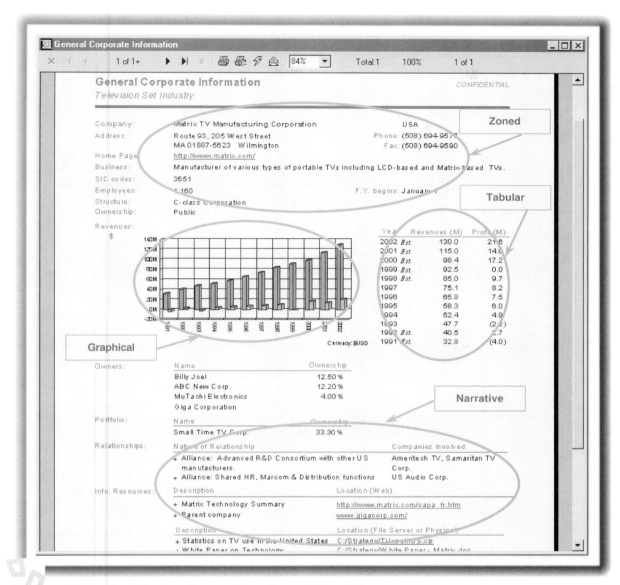

Figure 11-2   Combination Approach to Screen-Based Output

ate distribution. The number of methods available to the analyst to control system output is limited. The analyst must make maximum use of these controls, however, to insure the safety and integrity of the generated output.

One of the most effective output controls available is actually classified as an access control. By securing access to the system itself and limiting it to authorized end users, you are providing some level of control with regard to the system output. Beyond this, however, there are three basic categories of output control available: (1) *distribution control,* (2) *division of labor,* and (3) *completeness controls.*

In the early days of computing, virtually all system output was generated on paper. Distribution of the output was controlled by a central distribution control

Table 11-2   Common Design Guidelines for Output

Output Guideline	Explanation
Clear and meaningful titles	Titles should clearly and specifically describe the content and use of the output.
Relevant content	Only the information necessary to use the output should be included, and the presentation should be such that the output can be used without modification.
Balanced layout	Adequate spacing and margining should be used to allow for a balanced or symmetrical presentation of the output.
Clear navigation	The output should make navigation and location easy for the end user. This includes the use of indicators such as page numbers, section numbers, and end of section or sequence indicators.
Use of highlighting and color	Techniques for emphasizing a particular data value, exception, or section should be used to make it easier for the end user to focus on important items contained within the output. Such techniques include color or intensity differences, multiple size fonts, underlining, bolding or italicizing, and capitalization.
Appropriate formatting of text elements	Text should be presented using mixed upper and lower case with conventional punctuation. Paragraphs should be double-spaced or separated by a blank line when single-spaced. Abbreviation and acronyms should be commonly understood or clearly defined on first use. Words should not be hyphenated between lines.
Appropriate formatting of tabular elements	All columns and rows should be clearly and meaningfully labeled. All labels should be repeated when data extends beyond a single page or screen. Columns and rows should be sorted in a meaningful order. All numerical data should be right-justified with decimal points aligned, and all text data should be left-justified using relatively short line lengths (30 to 40 characters).

desk, where authorized recipients of the output could come and claim their reports. As systems progressed into the client–server era, *distribution control lists* were used to limit access to certain output to a predefined set of end users. For example, the generation of company checks would be limited to a chosen few end users to insure that an unauthorized check would not be generated. As we progress into a less paper-dependent environment, where most system output is generated on screen, we must revert back to the access control method of controlling system output to insure that only authorized individuals can view the proprietary or confidential information contained within the system.

One additional consideration in this category of output control is the extent to which a particular output must be produced using a limited media. Examples of this include employee tax forms, such as a W-2, company checks and purchase orders, and other controlled-media output. In addition to applying controls with regard to who can or cannot access this output, the analyst must make sure that the

Table 11-3   Common Completeness Controls for System Output

- Date and time stamp of output generation
- Data and time stamp for data or information contained in the output
- Time period covered by output contents
- Distribution or routing list
- Cover sheet with output version number and date
- Output header identification and description
- Clear pagination using "page __ of __" format
- Control totals where appropriate
- End of output trailer or indicator

output can only be generated on the proper media, as well. This suggests that the program code used to generate the report must also be written such that a check for the proper form or media on the output device is performed before allowing the output to be generated.

The *division of labor* approach to output control involves the creation of separate activities, performed by separate individuals, such that autonomous control over the creation and generation of output cannot be achieved by a single person. One example of this control mechanism is the limiting of system programmers to programming tasks that do not include data preparation or program execution. The same person who writes the code to generate the output should not be allowed to capture the data for the output or actually generate it. This type of control mechanism is intended to erect barriers to those individuals who may wish to manipulate system output for personal or financial gain.

One additional method of employing a division of labor approach is to rotate personnel through various output generation and/or preparation roles. By dividing the task structure up such that an individual can be randomly assigned to perform a task, the analyst can minimize the opportunity for a single individual to exercise complete control over the process.

Finally, the use of *completeness controls* can help to insure that the output being viewed is both accurate and timely to the extent that the data used to create it are accurate. Table 11-3 contains a brief list of common completeness controls.

TYPES OF OUTPUT

A typical organizational IS produces many outputs, and if the system allows for ad hoc querying and report generation, the number of outputs is virtually infinite. Despite the wide range of output that can be generated, we can easily classify all system output into one of two categories: (1) external or (2) internal.

External Output

As its category name implies, *external output* leaves the boundary of the system and serves to either confirm a system action to the recipient or to trigger an action on the part of a recipient. Common examples of external output include employee paychecks, monthly bills or statements, airline tickets, invoices, and purchase orders, among many others. In many cases, external output is generated on special media, such as preprinted paper or forms. With the advent of high-speed laser printing technology, however, modern IS are being designed to generate not only the required output data but also the form for the data.

A special type of external output that is commonly used is called the *turnaround document*. This type of output is designed to leave the system as output and then trigger an action on the part of the recipient that results in input reentering the system at a later time. In almost all cases, a monthly credit card bill is configured to be a turnaround document that contains not only the invoice and information portion of the bill but also a perforated portion that can be detached and returned along with payment. This portion of the turnaround document normally contains information about the customer and serves to insure that the accompanying payment is applied to the correct account.

Internal Output

The *internal output* of an IS is that output that normally stays within the system boundary and is used to support the organizational responsibilities and activities of the end users. Internal output generally takes the form of management reports and is used as an aid to decision making. Within the internal output category, we can identify three basic types of reports: (1) detailed, (2) summary, and (3) exception.

A *detailed report* is designed to present data or information with only a minimum amount of filtering. Figure 11-3a illustrates an example of a detailed internal output used to review a list of all customer invoices generated on a particular day.

Other examples of common detailed reports include historical lists of past transactions for a given period, a list of all customers sorted by postal code, or a list of paychecks to be generated for a given payroll period.

A *summary report* is generated to allow end users to review information in a filtered or categorized form in situations where the details are too cumbersome to review or are not necessary. In Figure 11-3b we see an example of a summary report that allows the end user to review month-to-date and year-to-date sales by product category. Although a detailed report containing this information could be generated, it would be much larger and would provide no additional useful information to the end user in this situation.

Finally, the *exception report* is an internal output that contains filtered information intended to report events or transactions that require special attention or that fall outside of some preestablished operating guideline or parameter. Figure 11-3c illustrates this type of internal output in the form of a report that contains information related to overdue customer accounts. In contrast to a detailed report listing all of the customer balances, this report allows an end user to more easily focus on those customer accounts that require immediate attention by the collections department. Another common example of an exception report is a list of those items in inventory that have reached their respective reorder points and require additional units to be ordered.

MEDIA TYPE AND OUTPUT TECHNOLOGY

Now that we have a good understanding of the characteristics of high quality output and the various categories to which they may be applied, we must shift our attention to the variety of devices to generate system output and media available for recording the output. In the early days of computing, output was limited to either paper or screen media. Technology has advanced significantly since then, and as a result,

a.

Vance Music Center Customer Invoices
for 05-23-2000

Invoice #	Customer ID	Payment	Type	Total
12780	640	Cash	Merchandise.	$ 121.96
12781	1296	Visa	Merchandise.	$ 17.83
12782	71	Visa	Lessons	$ 56.00
12783	327	Amex	Rental	$ 145.00
12784	509	Cash	Rental	$ 25.00
12785	811	Check	Merchandise.	$ 786.12
12786	687	Amex	Merchandise.	$ 547.89
12787	223	MC	Lessons	$ 28.00
12788	17	Cash	Merchandise.	$ 37.51
12789	53	Cash	Merchandise.	$ 19.75
12790	731	Visa	Spec.Order	$ 3,053.61

b.

Vance Music Center Product Sales Summary
for 06-17-2000

Type	Category	M-T-D	Y-T-D
Merchandise	Guitar	$ 5,789.43	$ 46,323.11
	Piano	$ -	$ 4,650.00
	Keyboard	$ 1,261.87	$ 16,505.79
	Drums	$ 599.00	$ 7,894.65
	Accessories	$ 2,365.41	$ 63,982.45
Rental	Instruments	$ 651.49	$ 5,907.00
	Sound	$ 325.00	$ 3,287.00
Lessons	Guitar	$ 1,975.00	$ 12,477.00
	Drums	$ 657.00	$ 3,702.00

c.

Vance Music Center Delinquent Account Summary
as of 06-30-2000

Customer ID	Name	Telephone	Balance	Past Due	Contacted
603	Harold Markowitz	812-394-0303	$ 311.26	37	X
19	Red Dog Inn	317-455-6500	$ 1,900.00	95	
988	Joan Hampton	812-378-0669	$ 125.00	45	
1217	Charles Irons	812-387-1044	$ 78.06	129	X
641	Lazy J Saloon	812-321-7884	$ 750.00	56	
811	Harper's Garage	812-365-3636	$ 92.75	38	
202	Big Sound Studios	317-487-1000	$ 456.23	96	X
149	Erin Smith	812-344-0159	$ 61.25	57	X

Figure 11-3   Examples of Detail, Summary, and Exception Reports

Table 11-4   Common Output Media and Technologies

Output Technology	Output Media
Printer—impact, page, laser, inkjet, thermal, plotter	Paper, transparency
Computer monitor—CRT, LCD, Plasma	Screen
COM	Microfilm, microfiche
Voice synthesis	Voice synthesizer
Robotic	Mechanical robotic devices
Video	Screen, film, disk, CD-ROM, DVD

an ever-increasing array of output devices and media are emerging. Table 11-4 lists several common output media and devices.

The selection of output media and output technology are necessarily intertwined, as the decision to use a particular output media often dictates what output technology to use. Given this, we focus our discussion on output media and, where appropriate, relate to it the common output technologies.

Hard Copy

Despite the cries for a move toward the paperless society, *hard copy* or *paper-based* output remains the most common output media in use. In some cases, paper is the only viable way to generate output, such as invoices, turnaround documents, or multiple copy forms. Without question, however, paper poses serious problems for the modern organization, and even more so for the environment. As the volume of paper-based output in an organization increases, the problems associated with its storage and retrieval become progressively more difficult. Many organizations are turning to some form of digital scanning and storage for their archived paper documents simply to facilitate more rapid retrieval and workflow. (We discuss scanning technologies in the next chapter when we look at input devices.)

Figure 11-4 contains several examples of common printing technologies that should be familiar to you from your introductory IS course. As you can see, the array of technology available to generate paper-based output is quite broad and can range in price from less than one hundred dollars to over $30,000. The two basic approaches to hard copy output generation are called *impact* and *nonimpact*. The selection of a particular approach is often dependent on the requirements for speed and quality of final output. Impact technologies, although once the de facto standard for printers, have given way to *ink-jet* and *laser* technologies. Even more important, these new printing technologies have brought superior output and color capabilities to the desktop level, while significantly reducing the cost-per-page of high-quality output. The increasingly "wired" world allows many of the paper-based transactions to be replaced with electronic ones, but hard copy output will probably have a significant role in the day-to-day activities of the organization for many years to come.

Screen Output

Once we move beyond the common paper-based output, we have a large selection of media and devices from which to choose. The advent of client–server technology combined with the higher resolution and lower cost of monitors has made *screen-*

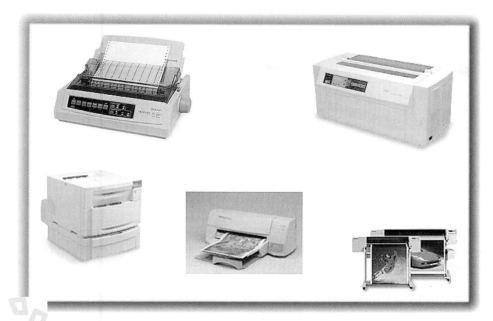

Figure 11-4   Common Printing Technologies

based output an increasingly popular alternative. Screen output offers several distinct advantages over hard copy. First, the output can be viewed from any location that allows access to the database in which it is stored and can also offer real-time editing and modification by the end user where appropriate. Second, the reduction in storage costs alone makes screen output a more desirable alternative for most organizations. Third, a great deal of the output generated in an organization is intended to provide information required at a particular moment in time and does not require long-term storage. Using the screen in these situations avoids unnecessary wasted resources. Finally, by generating screen output, decision makers can access the stored output whenever necessary and can avoid the generation and storage of redundant, and often out of date, printouts.

Audio and Video Output

This category of media and output technology is one of the fastest growing and exciting developments in computing technology. *Audio and video output* offer the potential for richness in the communication of information that no other output media can. Further, these modern media can facilitate previously manual output operations in a manner that can reduce overall costs and provide higher quality interaction with both end users and customers.

One of the fastest growing areas of computer audio output is *speech synthesis*. The implementation of a speech synthesis system begins with the development of a vocabulary. This vocabulary is chosen by a linguist to reflect all of the vowel and consonant sounds (referred to as *phonemes*) that exist in the language being used. In addition, certain inflections are different in male and female voices, so the vocabulary must be established with the gender of the final computer synthesized voice in mind.

Once the vocabulary is complete, a digitized sound library must be created by saying each of the words and phrases contained in the vocabulary into a microphone that is hooked up such that a digital representation of the spoken word is created. Although this process can take a significant amount of time, the good news is that once it is completed, it can be used for both speech synthesis applications and voice recognition input systems (we look more closely at these input devices later in the chapter).

The practical applications for computer audio output are quite varied. Products exist to facilitate the reading of screen content for visually impaired individuals. Another common application is to use a computer system that can generate audio output as "manpower" to staff telephone-based ordering systems that operate 24 hours a day. This allows the vendor to generate sales and take orders that might otherwise be lost without the potentially prohibitive cost of hiring employees to work the late night hours of the day. Still other uses include warnings or enunciators on vehicles ranging from automobiles to jet aircraft. Used in this way, the output serves to notify the operator of an important condition without the operator having to divert attention to a gauge or warning light. When traveling at the speed of sound in a jet fighter aircraft, this feature can become very handy indeed.

Computer video output is used to store and display motion picture or animation-based information. This media can be used to create animated simulations to allow an end user to visualize a complex series of events in a time compressed manner. Another popular use is in the television and motion picture industries, where entire programs are edited and assembled in digital form, using a sophisticated computer workstation, and then output to either film or video tape. Figure 11-5 shows a screenshot from a popular video editing application.

Figure 11-5   Screenshot from Video Editing Software

Video output is still in its infancy with regard to development and widespread use at the consumer level. Its biggest single drawback is the demands it makes on both processing power and storage requirements. A one minute video file running at broadcast quality of 30 frames per second can take up 20 to 30 Mb of storage and RAM. Although several technologies are available to compress and decompress video files, the media is still developing, and it will be a while yet before video output becomes a widespread option for the analyst.

COM Output

Although decreasing somewhat in popularity, owing to the advent of modern digital scanning and storage, a still prevalent output media is *computer output microfilm* or *microfiche* (COM). *Microfilm* is a roll of photographic film that can contain a large volume of paper-based or computer-generated reports and records in miniature form. *Microfiche* stores the output in a single sheet of film rather than a continuous roll. In both methods, a special reading device is used to locate the desired page and magnify it such that it can be easily read or converted into hard copy. The COM method can reduce the storage requirements for paper-based reports by a factor of 1000 or more, and it can decrease the retrieval times 10 to 20 times over conventional printing devices. Figure 11-6 contains several examples of modern COM retrieval and viewing devices.

Robotic Output

One of the most exciting developments in computer output media and technology is in the field of robotics. Literally emerging from the pages of science fiction novels, robots are being used as vehicles for complex output intended to automate production, manufacturing, distribution, and any application requiring precise and accurate handling of physical components. Through the use of robotic output, human beings are able to extend their physical capabilities into realms previously unheard of or unthinkable.

The idea of a robot is not new. For thousands of years human beings have been imagining intelligent mechanized devices that perform humanlike tasks. We have built automatic toys and mechanisms and imagined robots in drawings, books, plays, and science fiction movies. In fact, the term *robot* was first used in 1920 in a play called *R.U.R.* or *Rossum's Universal Robots* written by the Czech writer Karel Capek. The plot was simple: a human being makes a robot then the robot kills the human being! Many movies that followed continued to show robots as harmful, menacing machines.

More recent movies, however, portray robots as human beings' helpers, like C3PO and R2D2 in the 1977 *Star Wars*. "Number Five" in the movie *Short Circuit* and C3PO actually take on a human appearance. These robots that are made to look human are called *androids*.

One ground-breaking application of robotic output is its use in microsurgery and minimally invasive surgery (MIN). Heart surgeons, in particular, are testing robots to help them with new, intricate microsurgery that requires a rock-steady hand. The robots manipulate tiny scissors, needle holders, graspers, and a camera inside the chest cavity through incisions only a few millimeters long. Traditional open-heart surgery involves making a deep incision down the chest, spreading open the rib cage, and working on the heart in the open.

Using a robotic-assisted MIN procedure, a surgeon views the heart via a voice-activated miniature camera and a television screen. He controls the instruments by

Figure 11-6   Examples of COM Output Devices

moving large handles on a console that reads his hand motions, stabilizes them electronically to eliminate tremors, and transmits them to the robotic arms inside the chest.

Fully functioning androids are many years away, owing to the many problems that must be solved. However, real, working, sophisticated robots are in use today, and they are revolutionizing the workplace. These robots do not resemble the romantic android concept of robots. They are industrial manipulators and are really computer-controlled arms and hands. Industrial robots are so different than the popular image that it would be easy for the average person not to recognize one. Figure 11-7 contains several examples of modern devices used to execute robotic output.

Robotic output offers specific benefits to workers, industries, and societies. If introduced correctly, industrial robots can improve the quality of life for certain workers by freeing them from dirty, boring, dangerous, and heavy labor. The benefits of robots to industry include improved management control and productivity and consistently high-quality products. Industrial robots can work tirelessly night and day on an assembly line without any loss in performance. Consequently, they

Figure 11-7   Robotic Output Devices

can greatly reduce the costs of manufactured goods. As a result of these industrial benefits, societies that effectively use robotic output in their industries can gain an economic edge on their competition in world markets.

OUTPUT BIAS ISSUES

We have seen that many characteristics of output must be considered during its design if the goal of transmitting useful information to the end user is to be satisfied. One last issue that needs our attention, however, is the issue of *bias* created by the form in which the output is presented. The analyst needs to be aware that the output from a system is not always viewed as a neutral outcome of an IS by the end user and that certain design elements can actually serve to introduce particular biases that may serve to cloud the decision process. In general, there are three avenues through which unintentional bias may be introduced into system output: (1) *range or value limits,* (2) *sorting or sequence,* and (3) *graphics.*

Range and Value Limits

In most cases, the analysts and programmers have set predetermined ranges of values for certain output or have established specific limits on how values are displayed in a report. In the former case, the range of values displayed can introduce significant bias into exception reports and, in the latter situation, inappropriate limits on displayed values can actually serve to introduce inaccuracies in the information contained in the output.

Recall that exception reports are a form of internal output that contains information intended to report events or transactions that require special attention or that fall outside of some preestablished operating guideline or parameter. The effectiveness of the decisions made as a result of information conveyed through an exception report can be negatively affected if the range of values for inclusion on the report are not appropriate for the intended objective of the output. Ranges that are set too low, too high, too narrow, or too wide can result in exceptions reports that are either of little use or introduce unnecessary biases into the decision process.

For example, consider an exception report intended to report customer balances that are past due. Setting the limit too low, say 2 days past due, results in a past due report of overwhelming proportion. The account managers using this output are presented with a significant amount of data that is irrelevant to their objective of clearing up seriously overdue balances.

Conversely, an inappropriately high limit can also introduce bias into a decision process. Consider an exception report that contains instances of password failure attempts for an organizational IS. If the range for reporting exceptions is set inappropriately high, such as 25 consecutive failed attempts, the security officer of the company will not be aware of someone methodically testing a large number of passwords in an attempt to gain unauthorized access to a secured system.

Similarly, the range of the limits for an exception report can also be a source of unintentional bias. Ranges that are too narrow can produce reports that are of limited use because they are unable to capture enough of the desired information to make an effective evaluation. Ranges set too wide can produce exception reports that bias the end user into thinking there are more exceptions than there actually are.

Sorting and Sequence Bias

In many cases, output is presented in some sorted order based on one or more columns of data contained within the report. Common methods of sorting or sequencing include *alphabetical, chronological, size,* and *cost.* Depending on the situation, a predetermined sorting method may serve to introduce bias or erroneous conclusions on the part of the decision maker.

Generally speaking, humans tend to pay greater attention to those items presented first or those items representing a significant portion of total cost or total size. As such, a predetermined sorting method, such as alphabetical or chronological, may introduce certain biases, because the decision maker tends to pay more attention to the information encountered early in the report rather than later. As such, the A's, B's, and C's or the Januarys and Februarys often get greater attention than the X's, Y's or Z's or Novembers and Decembers. Similarly, items sorted by cost or size serve to focus the end user's attention on the big items. In situations such as analysis of regional spending in certain expense categories, this type of sorting method may be appropriate. In other situations, such as analysis of potential cost savings in manufacturing, this approach may unnecessarily bias the decision maker into focusing on only those items that represent large portions of the cost instead of considering the items that may be unnecessarily adding to the cost.

Graphical Bias

Consider the graph in Figure 11-8a. A cursory analysis reveals that the number of sales for car A exceeds both car B and car C in all four regions. In most cases, the sales units for car C equal approximately 50 to 70 percent of the sales units for car A. Now consider the graph illustrated in Figure 11-8b. The graph depicts exactly the same data, but visually the number of sales for car C appear to be significantly less than 50 to 70 percent of those for car A. Closer inspection reveals the problem. In Figure 11-8a, the scale begins at zero and extends a reasonable amount beyond the highest value in the data set. In Figure 11-8b, however, the scale ends at the same value but begins at 10,000 units rather than at zero. Although both graphs are telling the truth, the difference in the scaling between the two graphs tells a markedly different story to the casual observer.

Inappropriate scaling can serve to introduce an unintended bias into graphical information. Although commonly employed in the advertising industry to

Figure 11-8   Example of Graphical Scaling Bias

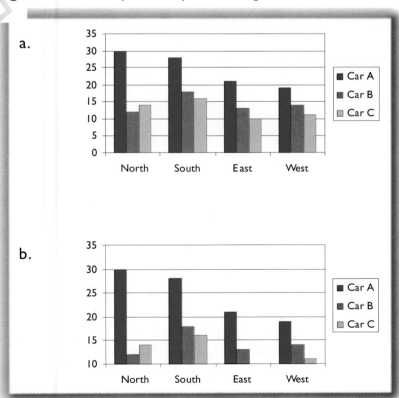

make one product appear more popular or more favorable than the competition, the analyst must be conscious of this problem and seek to avoid it wherever possible. The goal is to specify a scaling that provides an unbiased perspective on the data under investigation.

BACKUP AND RECOVERY

Although not necessarily output in the conventional sense, the backup files of an IS certainly qualify as internal output and require careful attention from the analyst during this stage of the physical design process. A *backup file* is a copy of an entire file, or any changes to that file since the last backup, that is maintained so that any event causing loss of current data can be mitigated by restoring the data from the backup file. Using this approach, the loss of data due to a catastrophic event is limited to only the data entered, updated, or deleted since the last backup was created.

Recent studies have estimated that over 50 percent of end users suffer some material form of data loss each year. Further, studies have concluded that over half of the world's commercial enterprises with no backup procedures in place could go bankrupt within 6 months following a catastrophic loss of data. Finally, the cost of data loss is significant. Here are some typical benchmarks that put the value of data in perspective:

- ➤ $50,000 per Mb to re-create
- ➤ $18,000 per hour in downtime cost for PC LANs
- ➤ $75,000 per hour in downtime cost for UNIX network
- ➤ $17,000 to re-create 20 Mb of sales and marketing data
- ➤ $19,000 to re-create 20 Mb of account data
- ➤ $98,000 to re-create 20 Mb of engineering data

The concept of data backup is one component of a much larger organizational topic called a *disaster recovery plan*. This plan is a comprehensive statement of consistent actions to be taken before, during, and after a disaster to ensure the continuity of operations and availability of critical computing resources in the event of a disaster. Detailed coverage of this topic is beyond the scope of this text, so our focus is limited to only issues of preservation of organizational data. Many excellent resources exist on the topic of disaster recovery, and an organization must be acutely aware of the risks and methods of managing them with regard to losses due to disaster.

Data Backup and Retention Strategies

Although a number of variations exist with regard to backup scheduling and retention, three basic categories of techniques can be identified: (1) *incremental*, (2) *differential*, and (3) *generation*.

The *incremental backup* strategy establishes a repetitive cycle that begins with a full backup of all data files and continues through a series of incremental backups. Table 11-5 illustrates an example of incremental backup strategy. As shown by the schedule in Table 11-5, the need to restore data on Thursday would first require restoration from Monday's full backup, then restoration from Tuesday's incremental backup to add the data modified between Monday and Tuesday, then likewise with Wednesday, and finally, Thursday's backup to reach full recovery.

Table 11-5   Incremental Data Backup Strategy

Monday	Tuesday	Wednesday	Thursday	Friday
Full backup	*Incremental backup*	*Incremental backup*	*Incremental backup*	*Incremental backup*
All files, data, and applications	What has changed since Monday	What has changed since Tuesday	What has changed since Wednesday	What has changed since Thursday

The *differential backup* concept is a variation of the incremental backup strategy. It is based on the backup of all modified files since the previous full backup. Using this approach, data recovery would require less time and effort, because there are fewer incremental files to restore. Restoration would occur from the last full backup and the most recent differential backup.

Finally, the *generation backup,* often referred to as the *grandfather-father-son* (GFS), uses a system of tape rotation via three *storage sets.* The first set is called *grandfather,* the second *father* and the third *son.* Table 11-6 illustrates a typical GFS backup schedule.

The GFS strategy begins with a full "A" backup on a Friday that leaves the whole weekend to carry it out. This storage set is used all week in incremental backups. The following week the same method is employed with the "B" storage set, and the third week with the "C" storage set. Once the cycle is finished, storage set "A" is used to begin the process again. The generational metaphor for this strategy refers to each daily backup as the son, each weekly full backup as the father, and the last full backup of each month as the grandfather. In many cases, the grandfather backup is permanently retired and archived in an offsite location.

Table 11-6   Generation Data Backup and Retention Strategy

	Friday	Monday	Tuesday	Wednesday	Thursday
Storage set A (week 1)	Full backup	Incremental backup	Incremental backup	Incremental backup	Incremental backup
Storage set B (week 2)	Full backup	Incremental backup	Incremental backup	Incremental backup	Incremental backup
Storage set C (week 3)	Full backup	Incremental backup	Incremental backup	Incremental backup	Incremental backup
Storage set A (week 4)	Full backup	Incremental backup	Incremental backup	Incremental backup	Incremental backup
. . .	. . .	. . .	. . .	. . .	. . .

One of the most recent developments in backup and recovery strategies is the *on-line backup system*. Depending on their degree of sophistication, these systems can automatically detect files on an organization's computer network requiring backup, encrypt those files for security, compress the encrypted files, and transmit the data through high-speed point-to-point telecommunications lines to an on-line data vault at a secure facility. The entire process can be completely automated and performed on a predefined, scheduled basis. Further, access to the backup data is available at any time, from any location in the world, to any authorized personnel.

Although it is not possible to completely eliminate internal and external risks to any network environment, the on-line backup and retrieval approach enables an organization to proactively plan for, and guard against, threats that would otherwise have a negative impact on the daily operation, and perhaps even the survival, of the business. In addition, the amount of work necessary to fully protect the data within an organization's network is greatly reduced. Because new files and changes to files are automatically detected, and because all backup operations occur automatically, via a predefined schedule, there is no need for operator attendance for initiating backups or for switching and rotating tapes. Finally, because most automated on-line systems keep track of all file transfers and transactions, the need for indexing and cataloging backup sets is eliminated.

CHAPTER SUMMARY

The goal of a modern IS is to deliver high quality and relevant information to the end users of the system. Regardless of the application, it is the responsibility of the analyst to insure that the desired output is delivered in a timely fashion, with an appropriate format and content, to the right people, using the best available combination of media and technology. The specification of the complete scope of the output for a system is critical, because it not only represents the goals of designing the system in the first place but also serves to identify the inputs necessary for the system to effectively generate the desired output. In the next chapter, we focus our attention on the design and specification of inputs and user interfaces based on the data specified in the data dictionary and through the process of output design.

KEY CONCEPTS

➤ The design and specification of system output precedes the design of input and data capture mechanisms so that the appropriate inputs and interfaces can be determined.

➤ The primary objective of output design is to create output that presents the desired information to the end user in an understandable and usable fashion requiring the least effort on the part of the end user to obtain it.

➤ System output design issues
  • Purpose
  Effective output design is dependent on knowing how the output is used.
  • Recipient
  Knowing who the intended recipients of the output are can serve to inform the design. The information gathered during requirements analysis must be combined with known cost considerations to design the output to be as close to personalized for each end user as possible.

- Frequency

The goal of designing effective output is dependent on design timely output. The frequency of a given output may vary from on demand to hourly, weekly, monthly, quarterly, semiannually, or annually.

- Distribution

Systems analysts need to consider the issue of where the output is used.

- Human–machine boundary

The human–machine boundary is defined as the points where an end user interacts with the system through the exchange of data or information. Any data flow that crosses the human–machine boundary represents an element of the system that must be physically specified.

- Data sources

Before the output can be designed, the data must exist either within the system or accessible to the system.

- Data stores
- Processes
- External sources
- Media

The various media on which the output is generated must be determined and analyzed.

- Format

Output presentation format has a material effect on its usefulness to the end user.

➤ Information organization approaches
- Tabular

Information is organized into columns and rows.

- Zoned

Information is organized into predetermined zones on the paper or screen.

- Narrative

Information is presented using conventional sentences and paragraphs.

- Graphical

In the graphical format, the numbers are presented by one of a wide variety of charts or graphics.

➤ Controls

Output control is limited in scope and must be effected before the output is generated and delivered to the end user. Once in the hands of the end user, no effective control exists. There are three basic categories of output control:

- Distribution control
- Division of labor
- Completeness control

➤ Output design guidelines
- Clear and meaningful titles
- Relevant content
- Balanced layout
- Clear navigation
- Use of highlighting and color
- Appropriate formatting of text elements
- Appropriate formatting of tabular elements

➤ Types of output
- External output

External output leaves the boundary of the system and serves either to confirm a system action to the recipient or to trigger an action on the part of a recipient.

- Internal output

Internal output stays within the system boundary and is used to support the organizational responsibilities and activities of the end users of the system. There are three basic types of internal reports:

- Detailed

A detailed report is designed to present data or information with only a minimum amount of filtering.

- Summary

A summary report is generated to allow end users to review information in a filtered or categorized form in situations where the details are too cumbersome to review or are not necessary.

- Exception

The exception report is an internal output that contains filtered information intended to report events or transactions that require special attention or that fall outside of some preestablished operating guideline or parameter.

➤ Media type and output technology

The selection of output media and output technology are necessarily intertwined, as the decision to use a particular output media often dictates what output technology to use.

- Hard copy

Hard copy or paper-based output is the most common output media in use. The two basic hard copy generations are

  - Impact
  - Nonimpact

- Screen output

Screen output offers several distinct advantages over had copy

  - Increased accessibility
  - Provides real-time editing and modification
  - Reduces storage costs
  - Avoids unnecessary storage resources
  - Avoid redundant and out of date printouts.

- Audio and video output

Audio and video outputs offer the potential for richness in the communication of information that no other output media can. One example of computer audio output is speech synthesis. Computer video output is used to store and display motion picture or animation-based information.

- Computer output microfilm or microfiche (COM) output

Microfilm is a roll of photographic film that can contain a large volume of paper-based or computer-generated reports and records in miniature form. Microfiche store the output in a single sheet of film rather than a continuous roll. The COM method can reduce the storage requirements for paper-based reports by a factor of 1000 or more, and it can decrease the retrieval time by 10 to 20 times over conventional printing devices.

- Robotic output

Robots are being used as vehicles for complex outputs intended to automate production, manufacturing, distribution, and any application requiring precise and accurate handling of physical components.

➤ Output bias issues

Unintended output bias can be introduced through inappropriate range limits, sorting or sequencing conventions, and graphical scaling.

- Range and value limits

The range of values displayed can introduce significant bias into exception reports, and inappropriate limits on displayed values can actually introduce inaccuracies in the information contained in the output.

- Sorting and sequence bias

Common methods of sorting or sequencing include alphabetical, chronological, size, and cost. A predetermined sorting method may serve to introduce bias or erroneous conclusions on the part of a decision maker.

- Graphical bias

Inappropriate scaling can serve to introduce an unintended bias into graphical information.

➤ Backup and recovery

A backup file is a copy of an entire file, or any changes to that file since the last backup, that is maintained so that any event causing loss of current data can be mitigated by restoring the data from the backup file.

- Disaster recovery plan

  The disaster recovery plan is a comprehensive statement of consistent action to be taken before, during, and after a disaster to ensure the continuity of operations and availability of critical computing resources in the event of a disaster.

- Data backup and retention strategies

  - Incremental backup

  The incremental backup strategy establishes a repetitive cycle that begins with a full backup of all data files and continues through a series of incremental backups.

  - Differential backup

  The differential backup concept is a variation of the incremental backup strategy. It is based on the backup of all data files modified since the previous full backup.

  - Generation backup

  Generation backup, often referred to as GFS, uses a system of tape rotation via three storage sets: grand-father, father, and son.

- On-line backup

Depending on their degree of sophistication, on-line backup systems can automatically detect files on an organization's computer network requiring backup, encrypt those files for security, compress the encrypted files, and transmit the data through high-speed point-to-point telecommunication lines to an on-line data vault at a secure facility. The entire process can be completely automated and performed on a predefined, scheduled basis.

QUESTIONS FOR REVIEW

1. State the main objective of system output design.

2. List and briefly describe the critical issues in designing system output.

3. What are the possible data sources of a system output?

4. List and briefly describe the information organization approaches for formatting system outputs.

5. List and briefly explain the common output design guidelines.

6. List and describe the three basic categories of output control.

7. Explain the main purpose of a turn-around document.

8. List and compare the two types of system output with regard to their boundary and main purposes.

9. List and briefly describe the three basic types of internal reports.

10. List and briefly describe the five generally used output media and output technologies.

11. What are the advantages of screen output when compared to hard copy output?

12. List and briefly describe the three avenues through which unintended bias may be introduced into system output.

13. How can range value limits introduce bias into system output?

14. Explain the concept of an organizational disaster recovery plan.

15. List and briefly describe the four commonly used data backup and retention strategies.

FOR FURTHER DISCUSSION

1. You will need a bank ATM card for this small project. If you do not have one, perhaps you can ask a friend who does to assist you. Go to a local ATM for the bank issuing the card and request a transaction to withdraw a small amount of money. It is our intention that this transaction fail, so when asked the account from which to withdraw the money, indicate the wrong type (savings or credit card rather than checking). The transaction will be rejected by the ATM.

    (a) Record the message displayed on the ATM screen. Be sure to retrieve the receipt for the transaction (as well as your ATM card).

    (b) Using the message generated on the screen and the information contained on the receipt, critique the output using the characteristics outlined in this chapter. Were the messages clear and meaningful? Could this output be improved?

2. Find an example of computer-generated, hard copy output. You can choose from a variety of examples: your bank statement, a credit card statement, a subscription renewal reminder, or some other example. Using the guidelines provided in this chapter for high-quality system output, critique the design of the report.

3. Using the WWW as your vehicle, investigate the types and uses of output in different industries. One great example is aviation. How many different output media do they regularly use? How are they used? What, if any, special guidelines for their design can you discover?

4. Given the burgeoning growth in personal data assistants and other hand-held computing devices, what types of outputs and their associated media do we need to provide for? How can we get our information from a device that fits in a shirt pocket?

REFERENCES

Dumas, J. S. 1988. *Designing User Interfaces for Software.* Englewood Cliffs, NJ: Prentice Hall.

Designing the Inputs and User Interface

Learning Objectives

- To become familiar with the various common methods by which end users interact with IS
- To review the common computer input devices and to explore the newer, more sophisticated input technologies
- To understand the three basic metaphors for designing human–computer interaction mechanisms
- To understand and be able to apply the basic design guidelines for high quality and usable data entry screens
- To understand the two categories of input controls, as well as their strengths and limitations

We've all heard that a million monkeys banging on a million type-writers will eventually reproduce the entire works of Shake-speare. Now, thanks to the Internet, we know this is not true.
—ROBERT WILENSKY, PROFESSOR, UNIVERSITY OF CALIFORNIA–BERKLEY

INTRODUCTION

The old computer adage "garbage in equals garbage out" is intended to point out the importance of accurate, high integrity, and comprehensive data capture and input in creating high quality and relevant output. Although most database and systems analysis textbooks (including this one) focus on output and input as separate topics, we must not forget the interrelationships that exist between the design of system output and the inputs necessary to create it.

In this chapter, we discuss issues associated with the capture and input of the data necessary to create the required system outputs. In addition, we focus on the design characteristics of well-designed user interfaces. Finally, we look at the various controls available to the analyst to insure high integrity and accurate input data.

USER INTERACTION METHODS

Just as there are multiple methods available to the end user for generating output, there are a wide variety of methods by which an end user can interact with an IS. Regardless of the method employed, the *interface* is the term used to describe the human–computer interaction (HCI) mechanism. Although some interfaces are hardware-based, others are completely determined by software design. The first step in our focus on quality interface design is to understand the five basic categories of HCI: (1) *command dialogue*, (2) *menus*, (3) *input screens and forms*, (4) *icons and buttons*, and (5) *natural language recognition*.

Command Dialogue

One of the oldest methods available for HCI is the use of a *command dialogue* or *instruction set*. In this approach, the end user initiates all dialogue by issuing instructions to the computer via a structured syntax of commands. Because the syntax of the command dialogue is critical to getting the desired response from the computer, the end user must learn the command language to interact. A wide variety of command structures exist, ranging from quasi-natural language to literally cryptic. Consider the following two commands:

> ➤ A23APRBWISIN1400

> ➤ xcopy manuscript /a /p /s /c /u

The first command may not be familiar to any of you unless you happen to work at an airport that still uses a command dialogue interface to the reservation system. The command, as issued, is a request to display all scheduled flights (A) on April 23 (23APR) from Baltimore-Washington International (BWI) to Singapore (SIN) leaving at or after 2:00 P.M. local time (1400). In this command dialogue, the user must know the abbreviations for the display commands, the sequence in which the component elements of the command must be issued, the many abbreviations for the airports, the correct method for listing a day and month, and international time conventions. Other than that, it is pretty simple!

The second command given previously may be familiar to some of you. It is a command from the disk operating system (DOS) written by Microsoft Corporation for the IBM and compatible PCs. This command syntax is structured as a single command followed by one or more parameters necessary for the command to successfully execute in the desired manner. The command in this example instructs the computer to copy the specified directory or subdirectory (xcopy manuscript) but to limit the copy to only those files that have their archive attributes set (/a) to confirm with the end user the creation of each destination file (/p), to copy all subdirectories unless they are empty (/s), to continue the copy even if an error occurs (/c), and to update any files that already exist in that destination. Piece of cake!

It should be easy to see from these two examples that a command dialogue requires a significant learning curve on the part of the end user if it is to be used with any degree of efficiency and accuracy. The development of computing technology has made the command dialogue approach a thing of the past, although many long-time users still prefer using a command prompt over a graphical interface simply because of comfort developed through years of invested effort in learning the language.

Menus

Moving beyond the command dialogue approach to interaction, the next logical interface method is the *menu*. This approach to interface design presents to the end user a list of available alternatives that are relevant to the task being performed. The user simply selects the desired option, and the command is executed. Figure 12-1 illustrates several approaches to menuing commonly found in system interfaces.

The *single menu approach* displays a text-based set of options that can be individually selected by the end user to perform a command or series of commands. In this approach, the user selects the option from the menu, the command is executed and any necessary output is generated, and the user is returned to the menu. For environments with a limited number of options, this approach is the simplest and easiest to navigate.

In those situations where a series of high-level options exists, each requiring additional decisions or alternatives, a *hierarchical menu approach* is required. Here, the main menu provides the end user with a series of categories of tasks from which to choose, and then, on selection, the user is presented with another menu that contains the task-specific options or selections. This approach allows for a menuing system to be designed in a more logical and less visually complex manner.

With the advent of the *graphical user interface* (GUI), menuing has reached new levels of sophistication and complexity. Commonly found in Windows-based applications is the *menu bar approach,* where categories of command sets are listed horizontally across the top of the screen and subcategories of the command set are displayed as vertical *pull-down menus* when a particular category is selected. As shown in Figure 12-1, the designer can cascade multiple levels of commands and selections under a single menu bar category.

Yet another variation of the menuing approach available in a GUI-based application is the *pop-up menu*. As shown in Figure 12-1, this method allows the designer to embed a context-specific menu under a particular area or text component on the screen. When activated, the pop-up menu appears adjacent to the object selected by the end user, thus allowing the user to select from a list of options relevant to the object without refocusing his or her attention on another part of the screen.

Icons and Buttons

A more recent menuing approach in the GUI-based environment is the use of an *iconic menu* that allows the end user to select and execute commands by pointing and clicking at graphical buttons or icons located on the screen or menu bar. One of the main advantages of the iconic menuing approach is the easy recognition on the part of the end user of an icon that could represent a complex set of commands. The use of a graphical image can assist the user in memorizing the wide variety of functions within an application and can allow the designer to place a large number of complex selections in a relatively small area of the screen. Figure 12-2 illustrates the use of an iconic menu approach in a common software application.

Input Screens and Forms

Probably the most common of all input interactions is the *input screen* or *form*. This method uses a screen-based form that allows end users to fill in the necessary information in the blanks provided such that all data are captured or retrieved in a logical, easy-to-read manner. The form should provide for understandable field

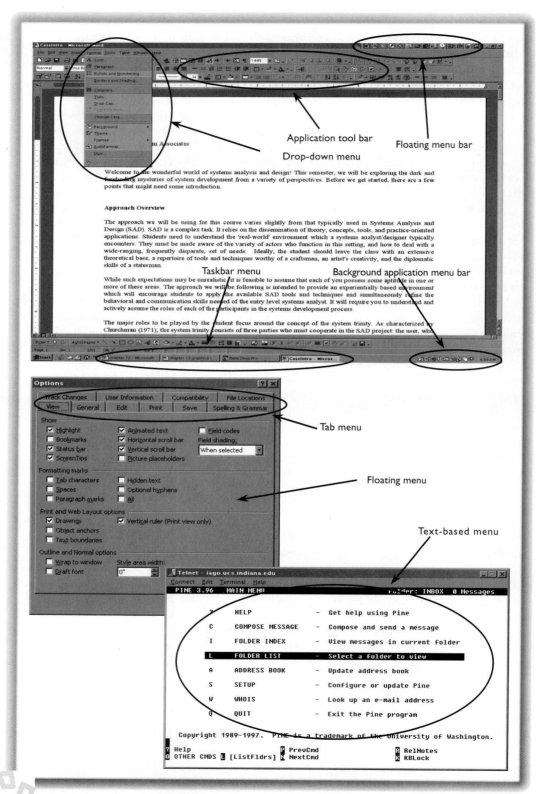

Figure 12-1 Examples of Common Menu Structures

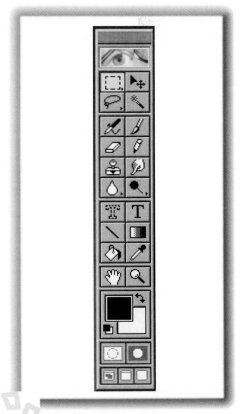

Figure 12-2   Iconic Menu Toolbar

headings and titles and should be logically organized to facilitate entry of data captured in hard copy form or from end user recollection. Further, the navigation method employed should allow the user to move from field to field in a logical, intuitive sequence. Figure 12-3 illustrates a typical input form from a consumer Web site and demonstrates the difference between a logical and counterintuitive navigation sequence.

Voice Recognition

One of the newest and fastest growing developments in computer interaction methods is the use of *voice recognition*. This method makes use of voice synthesis technology (as described in chapter 11) to allow the user to interface with the computing device by using natural language and voice commands. Voice recognition is a technology that has evolved from international efforts to provide computer users with a natural, hands-free human–machine interface. With multiple generations of evolutionary advance and refinement as a foundation, voice recognition technologies are now mature, robust, and "ready for prime-time."

The early commercial offerings of this technology suffered from high error rates and long, tedious training processes. The newest versions of these applications can be trained for in under five minutes and have an error rate less than a professional stenographer. In addition, many commercial voice recognition and

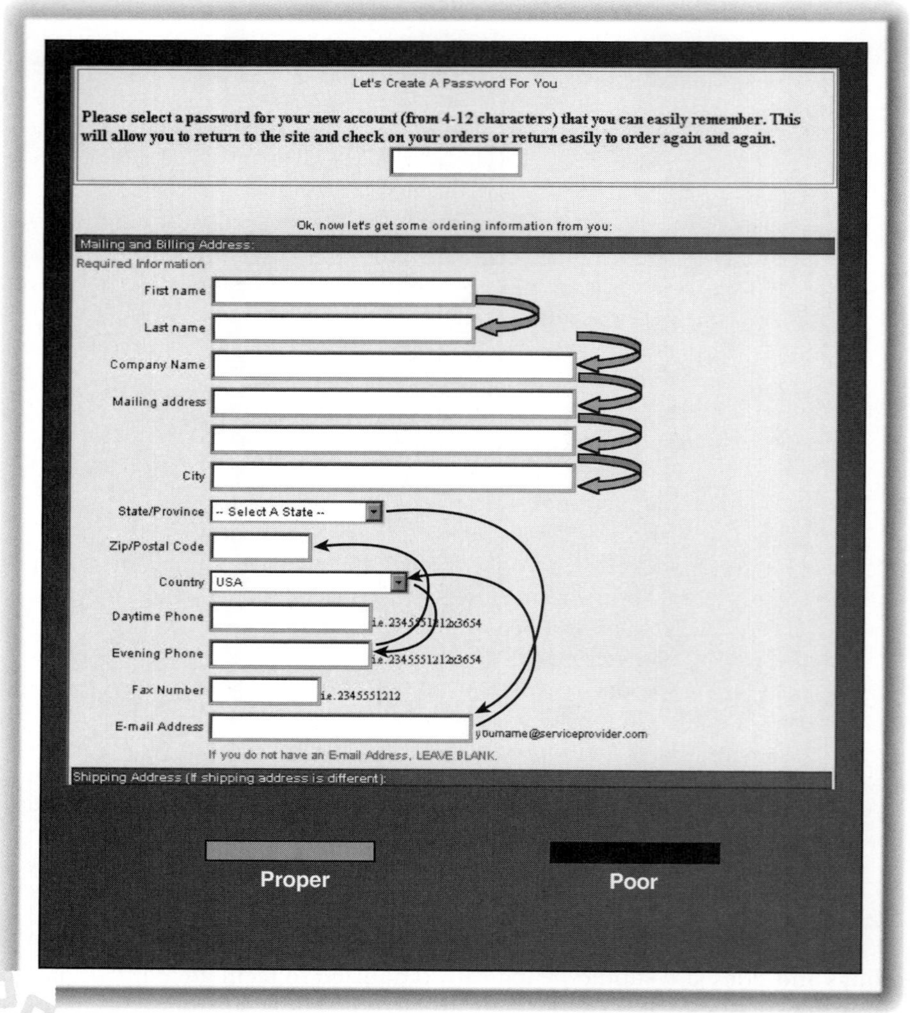

Figure 12-3   Examples of Logical and Counterintuitive Navigation Sequences

input systems allow for the creation of *macro commands* that provide the end user with the option of creating a single voice command that performs several functions or automates complex tasks, such as inserting boilerplate text, filling out forms, or launching applications. Speech technology applications are being applied to areas such as command and control of computers by voice, natural-language database queries with speech input, telephone applications, mobile computing, and speech recognition systems for European and Asian languages. Thus, freed of the constraints posed by keyboard and mouse interfaces, industrial, office, home, and large-screen entertainment PC users can move outside the traditional PC space into a computing world controlled by voice.

Considered a holy grail of computing just a few years ago, natural speech recognition is now within our grasp. We can see the day when interaction with our computers will use the same interface and conventions we use with human beings.

Together with realistic text-to-speech synthesis, computers are inching ever closer toward passing the Turing test, in which a human being cannot distinguish whether he or she is interacting with another human being or a computer.[1]

Continuous speech recognition heralds a revolution in the way we interact with our PCs, but it is hardly the last stop in pursuing the voice interface. First, we must work to overcome the artifacts left over from older forms of voice recognition, having to specify when to insert commas, dashes, new paragraphs, and the like. To overcome this hurdle, computer scientists may need to look carefully for pauses in our voices, or perhaps recognize how certain pitch changes indicate clauses or questions. Such a system might also need to include an effective, real-time grammar checker to guard against dependent clauses.

Another critical step toward the voice interface is speaker independence. Because voice is a more natural input method than using a mouse, users have higher expectations and less tolerance for even the reduced training needed in learning a GUI. Already, many limited speaker-independent applications are in use in voice-response applications accessed via the telephone, but having this feature in a large-vocabulary system is challenging.

Finally, there is the understanding of gestures—shaking, nodding, looking confused or frustrated. Even in a world of perfect voice recognition, users still need to carry on dialogues with a computer. The machine is severely handicapped without the benefit of facial cues and body language that human beings take in unconsciously when having conversations.

The voice-driven computer of tomorrow may dispense with the familiar keyboard and mouse, but will it still have a screen? This likely depends on the application and form factor. For traditional productivity applications, the good news is that a voice-driven interface can function without many of the menu bars and toolbars that dominate today's graphical interfaces. Screens still are practical, however, for viewing documents. Combined with a robust search system, voice-activated filing systems could even shield users from clicking up and down the hierarchies of folders to file and open items.

One extension of the use of voice recognition input systems is the concept of *natural computing*. This approach to user interaction is intended to provide information where we want it, how we want it, and with practically invisible interfaces that adapt to natural human interaction skills. Quite simply, the computer responds to human beings using the time-honored traditions of human interaction: voice and gesture.

Test of applications using this approach to computing use speech recognition software to interpret vocal commands. An embedded camera sends visual information to a machine-vision system that tracks movement and gestures. Special algorithms combine and interpret the users' actions.

Someday, maybe sooner than we think, natural computing technology could be integrated into offices, furniture, household appliances, cars, and so much more. In the areas of science, medicine, and business, users may be able to collaborate remotely with one another in virtual labs, operating rooms, and factories.

---

[1] This test was invented by Alan M. Turing (1912–1954) and first described in a 1950 article on computing machinery and intelligence. The interrogator is connected to one person and one machine via a terminal, and therefore cannot see his or her counterparts. The task is to find out which of the two candidates is the machine and which is the human being only by asking them questions. If the interrogator cannot make a decision within a certain time (Turing proposed five minutes, but the exact amount of time is generally considered irrelevant), the machine is considered intelligent.

COMMON INPUT DEVICES

At one time, the only method of providing input to a computer was through a punched card. In the early 1800s, a French silk weaver called Joseph-Marie Jacquard invented a way of automatically controlling the warp and weft threads on a silk loom by recording patterns of holes in a string of cards. In the late 1800s, the American inventor Herman Hollerith began working on a tabulating system that used the punched card technique developed by Jacquard. Hollerith filed the first of many patents associated with his input device in 1884.

The Hollerith input device was elegantly simple. It was a hand-fed press that sensed the holes in punched cards by pressing a grid of wires against the card. Wherever there was a hole in the card, that wire would pass through into a cup of mercury beneath the card, thus closing an electrical circuit. The card reading process triggered mechanical counters and sorter bins and tabulated the appropriate data. Hollerith's system—including punch, tabulator, and sorter—allowed the official 1890 population count to be tallied in six months, and in another two years all the census data was completed and defined at a cost $5 million less than the forecasts and in more than two years' less time.

Input devices have come a long way since the Hollerith card, and the range of options available for HCI is vast. In this section, we briefly identify the most common input and interaction devices.[2] We then focus our attention on some of the newest input technologies to emerge into commercial use. Figure 12-4 contains several examples of the common input devices found in today's computing environments.

The majority of the devices shown in Figure 12-4 should be familiar to most of you. The *keyboard, mouse, trackball,* and *joystick* have become mainstays in most PC environments. In addition, devices such as *touch-sensitive screens, scanners, laser* and *light pens, graphics tablets,* and even *voice recognition* are readily available input alternatives

Figure 12-4   Common Input Devices

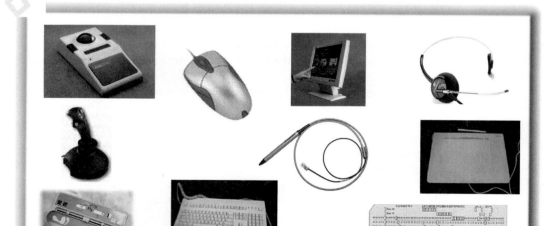

---

[2] A more detailed explanation for each of these devices can be found in any good introductory IS text.

for specific input environments and contexts. With the constant movement toward ever-smaller computing devices, however, new and increasingly sophisticated input devices are emerging.

Biometric Input Devices

Biometrics refers to the automatic identification of a person based on his or her physiological or behavioral characteristics. This method of identification is preferred over current methods involving passwords and PIN numbers, because the person to be identified is required to be physically present at the point-of-identification and identification based on biometric techniques obviates the need to remember a password or personal identification number (PIN). By replacing PINs, biometric techniques can potentially prevent unauthorized access to or fraudulent use of ATMs, cellular phones, smart cards, desktop PCs, workstations, and computer networks. PINs and passwords may be forgotten, and token based methods of identification, such as passports and driver's licenses, may be forged, stolen, or lost. Thus, biometric systems of identification are enjoying a renewed interest. Various types of biometric systems are being used for real-time identification; the most popular are based on face recognition and fingerprint matching. However, there are other biometric systems that use iris and retinal scan, speech, facial thermograms, and hand geometry.

A biometric system is essentially a pattern recognition system that makes a personal identification by determining the authenticity of a specific physiological or behavioral characteristic possessed by the user. An important issue in designing a practical system is determining how an individual is identified. Depending on the context, a biometric system can be either a verification (authentication) system or an identification system. Figure 12-5 contains several examples of current biometric input technologies.

Figure 12-5   Examples of Biometric Input Devices

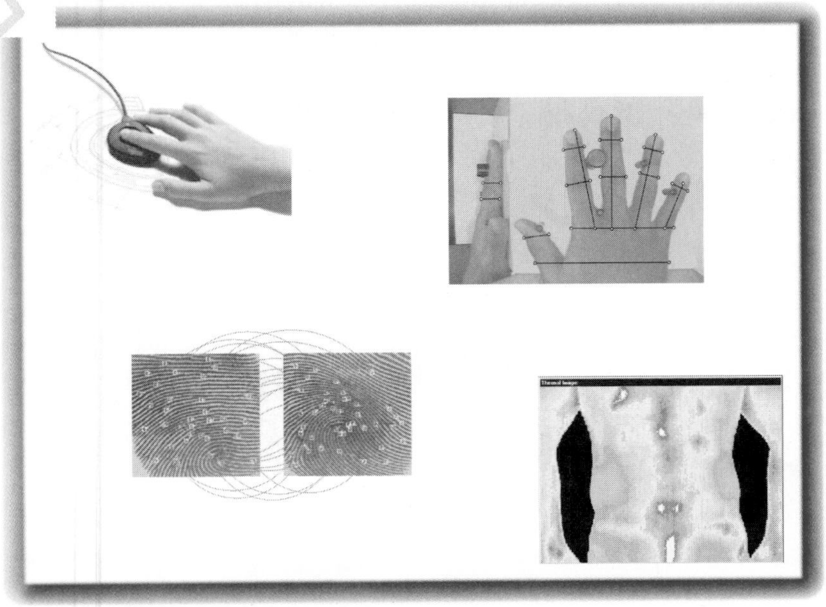

Optical Input Devices

Optical input devices are one of the most pervasive of the new generation of data input devices for IS. Most likely, you have encountered one of the most common optical input devices: *barcodes.*

Barcodes

Barcoding allows data to be collected rapidly and with extreme accuracy. Barcodes provide a simple and easy method of encoding text and numerical information that is easily read by inexpensive electronic laser sensing devices. A barcode consists of a series of parallel, adjacent bars and spaces. Predefined bar and space patterns, or *symbologies,* are used to encode small strings of character data into a printed symbol. Barcodes can be thought of as a printed version of the Morse code, with narrow bars (and spaces) representing dots and wide bars representing dashes. A barcode reader decodes a barcode by scanning a light source across the barcode and measuring the intensity of light reflected back by the white spaces. The pattern of reflected light is detected with a photodiode that produces an electronic signal that exactly matches the printed barcode pattern. This signal is then decoded back to the original data by inexpensive electronic circuits. Owing to the design of most barcode symbologies, it does not make any difference if you scan a barcode from right to left or from left to right. Figure 12-6 contains a picture of a typical barcode scanner and an illustration of the basic structure of a barcode.

A barcode consists of a leading and trailing quiet zone, a start pattern, one or more data characters, optionally one or two check characters, and a stop pattern. There are a variety of different types of barcode encoding schemes, each of which originally developed to fulfill a precise need in a specific industry. Several of these symbologies have matured into de facto standards that are, today, universally used throughout most industries.

OMR and OCR

The last time you took a multiple-choice test, you may have used a separate sheet of paper on which to record your answers. The answers were recorded as pencil marks in a particular block on the form. You also may have been asked to "bubble in" the

Figure 12-6   Barcode Scanner and Barcode Structure

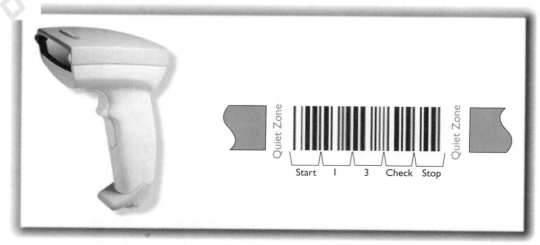

letters in your name by marking a small circle corresponding to each letter. Also, if you reside in the United States, you recently had to fill out a rather detailed set of forms designed to collect information associated with the national census. In both cases, you were using an input technology know as *optical mark reading* (OMR).

An OMR system looks for marks on special forms like the one shown in Figure 12-7. A typical OMR reader uses an array of light-emitting diodes (LEDs) to scan for marks in certain positions (defined by a horizontal line on the left or right border known as a *skunk mark*). Detection is done by measuring the amount of light reflected for each position. The information printed on the form uses a special ink color that does not reflect light. Because of this, any significant mark in a measured position on the form is detected as a reflected image. This image is recorded as a mark in that field and, using a defined key, the total number of marks in each field can be tallied and reported with tremendous speed and accuracy. Typical OMR speeds can be up to 8000 double-sided sheets per hour, with no need for verification. Applications for OMR input technology are quite varied, ranging from questionnaires and objective tests to voter registration, market research, mailing and fulfillment, or any other large scale data capture and entry activity.

In contrast to OMR, which senses only marks in predefined areas of the form, an *optical character recognition* (OCR) system scans virtually any form or document containing numbers, letters, or marks. The system then tries to interpret the content of the document and convert it into electronic form for additional processing or editing. Most printed and handwritten numbers and letters can be recognized, and if in doubt the system flags the characters in question for further review by the user. Tests for numbers and marks can be added (interval check, max marks,

Figure 12-7   Optical Mark Reader Scan Sheet and Auto-Scanner

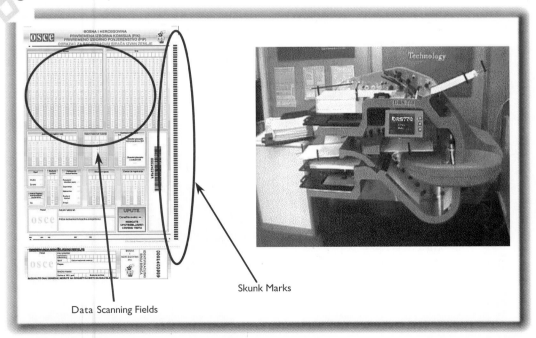

Data Scanning Fields

Skunk Marks

checksums, and more). The speed can be up to 4000 double-sided sheets per hour, depending on scanner and computer speed. The captured data and images may also be exported to files, databases, or electronic archives.

In mid 2000, Photobit Corporation, a leading supplier of image sensors, introduced an optical input sensor for use in an ingestible capsule. This new device, made possible by its ultralow power requirements (less than 3 milliwatts) and ultra-small silicon die size of the sensor, can produce color video of the human gastrointestinal (GI) tract.

The new device is swallowed like a pill and takes images of the stomach and small bowel as it passes through them unaided. An antenna array is attached to the patient, and a wireless recorder, worn on a belt around the patient's waist, records the signals transmitted by the capsule to the array. A computer workstation, equipped with proprietary software, processes the data and produces a 20-minute video clip of the images captured by the optical sensor, in synchronization with the trajectory of the capsule as it passes through the body. Currently, the medical community employs a host of other much more intrusive options for this type of exploration, including endoscopy and radiological imaging. Such procedures can be expensive, produce limited results, or cause discomfort for patients. The capsule, which measures 11 × 30 mm, helps eliminate these drawbacks.

Smart Cards

A *smart card,* shown in Figure 12-8, is a credit-card-size plastic card embedded with an integrated circuit chip that makes it smart. This marriage between a convenient plastic card and a microprocessor allows an immense amount of information to be stored, accessed, and processed either on-line or off-line. Smart cards can store sev-

Figure 12-8   Smart Card Technology

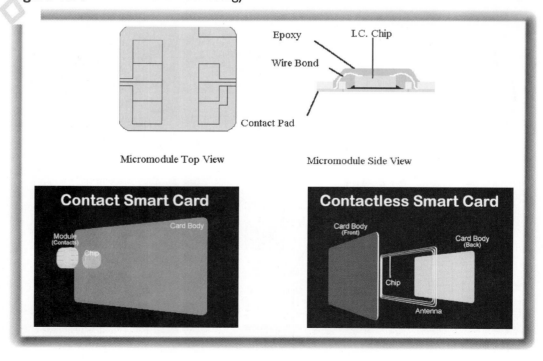

eral hundred times more data than a conventional card with a magnetic stripe. The information or application stored in the IC chip is transferred through an electronic module that interconnects with a terminal or a card reader. A contactless smart card has an antenna coil that communicates with a receiving antenna to transfer information. Depending on the type of the embedded chip, smart cards are either memory cards, which store information, or processor cards, which actually contain limited processing functions.

The ultimate utility of smart cards is in the functions they carry out—payment processing, identification, network computing, health care management, and benefits distribution, among many others. Application programs handle data read by smart card readers and forward them to central computers located at the other end of the smart card infrastructure, such as payment servers in banks, traffic control centers or mobile phone centers, credit card companies, transit authorities, or even governments. Stakeholders in the emerging smart card marketplace include a wide variety of firms and institutions, such as card issuers, content providers, banks, government agencies, security implementers, electronics manufacturers, and other service providers who want to exploit the advantages of smart card technologies.

A prime example of this emerging marketplace is an 18-month pilot project in Southampton, England, that allows citizens to use and pay for leisure, library, and transport services throughout the city without using cash. The new card system, called *SmartCities,* also is used to access services and make payments at Southampton University. This experiment is a portal through which we can see the future, and smart card technology will play an integral part.

GUIDELINES FOR INPUT AND INTERFACE DESIGN

Not all input originates from a system user. Some input is the result of automated gathering of environmental data, tracking and recording domain-related transactions, or even monitoring the performance of another automated process. Although all input might not originate from an end user, all system input is the result of a requirement to capture it imposed by an end user. Because of this global relationship, the design of data capture and input mechanisms must take into consideration the degree to which the end user must interact directly with the data capture and manipulation processes. The multidisciplinary field of HCI is concerned with the application of computer science, psychology, ergonomics, and many other disciplines in industry and commerce. Its goal is to facilitate the design, implementation, and evaluation of information and communications systems that satisfy the needs of those who own and use them. In this next section, we explore the tenets of good input and interface design through the lens of HCI.

HCI Metaphors

HCI has adopted several different perspectives on user design issues that draw on electronic metaphors of common physical interfaces and domains. The research into this area has created a simple three-part classification for these metaphors: (1) desktop or direct manipulation, (2) document, and (3) dialogue.

The Desktop Metaphor

The *desktop* or *direct manipulation* metaphor for HCI builds on the common set of activities and organization schemes associated with a common desktop. This environment can take a wide range of forms and can contain multiple projects, tasks, or activities in various states of completion. The old adage "do not clean my desk or I will not be able to find anything" is a comical way of pointing out that one person's chaos is another person's organization scheme. By transferring this concept into the computing environment, we can create an electronic desktop that provides all of the flexibility and advantages of a physical desktop, as well as many functions not available outside of the electronic environment. The idea is to create an environment that allows for direct manipulation of the multiple items on the desktop and is as close as possible to the real-world environment. By doing this, the end user can apply skills and techniques refined in a physical environment to the electronic metaphor and realize similar and expected results. Figure 12-9 contains an illustration of a typical electronic desktop interface.

The Document Metaphor

The second classification of HCI is the *document metaphor*. Here, the end user interacts with the computer by browsing through or entering data on electronic documents and forms. The advantage of the document metaphor in a computing environment is the use of *hypermedia,* the concept of linking graphics, video, and audio together in a manner that allows the end user to easily navigate between the documents.

The WWW is organized primarily using the document metaphor. Web pages serve as an electronic form of what people have used for a long time to transmit in-

Figure 12-9 Example of Electronic Desktop Metaphor

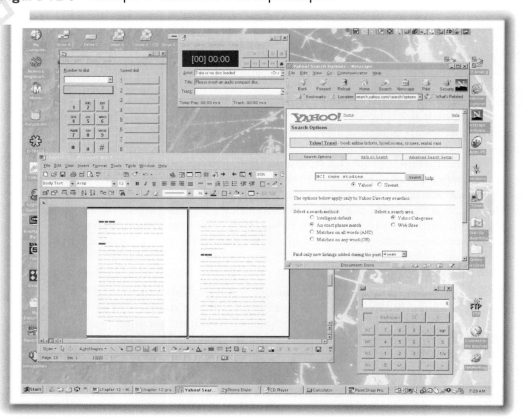

formation: paper documents. In the real world, paper documents come in many shapes and sizes. But whether you are looking at a book, a magazine, a grocery list, a modern yellow sticky, or an ancient scroll, the document is likely to be composed primarily of text and graphics. Similarly, although Web pages can sport interactive applets and flashy animations, most Web pages, like their paper counterparts, are composed primarily of text and graphics. Because people use Web pages in many of the same ways they use paper documents, Web pages evoke a document metaphor.

Web pages are extremely well suited for delivering information to people electronically. Because people are accustomed to getting information from documents in the real world, they understand the document metaphor of Web pages.

One kind of information that Web pages are particularly adept at transmitting to people is links to resources. If you click on a hyperlink, the browser loads the referenced page. People quickly learn to use hyperlinks, in part because "point and click" is easy to understand, but also because hyperlinks bear a strong resemblance to references in paper documents. Hyperlinks and Web browsers merely automate the delivery of such external resources.

Another role a Web page can play is that of a form. Filling in forms on Web pages is reminiscent of filling in forms on paper. The process one goes through to subscribe to a print magazine, for example, is similar to the process visitors to a Web site must go through to subscribe to an electronic newsletter. Because people are generally comfortable with filling out paper forms, filling in text boxes on Web pages is a natural and easy-to-understand way to submit text-based information to the network.

Several new technologies are emerging beyond the WWW that take advantage of our comfort with the document metaphor. Desktops can be very powerful for certain tasks but fall short when doing endless hours of reading for knowledge work. We are accustomed to reading objects that are spatial. It is convenient to read a hardcopy, such as a book or an article. We are able to place the object in any position we desire. We are also able to take that object anywhere we prefer to do our reading. It is tiresome to sit behind a desktop for hours. There are also many health risks that come with sitting behind a desktop. The bottom line behind desktop computer failings is the inconvenience of desktops for certain common reading activities.

There are many practices that come with reading for knowledge work or as it is referred to, *active reading*. It carries far more attributes than reading for pleasure. A reader usually highlights or underlines important documentation. Although this is not much of a problem, because these tasks can already be handled by our current word processors, a researcher also likes to place comments on the page or on its margins. Readers also like to mark certain pages they seem to find relevant to their research. This leads to the strength of hardcopies—the ability to jump to different pages. Many users know where a certain piece of information is by the distance they remember. For example, the reader might know the information he or she is looking for is in the middle of the book or toward the back of the book. Using the document metaphor, several technologies, called *reading machines*, are beginning to emerge. These new technologies encapsulate the physical aspects we are accustomed to when reading from a hard copy.

Desktops do not provide mobility, they are not spatial, and they all vary in software. Paper provides a spatial environment for the reader, an environment in which one can place comments and annotations anywhere on the paper as desired. Desktops typically do not allow this, thus making it difficult to do note-taking knowledge

Figure 12-10   Active Reading Machine

work. The most important information one needs when doing research work is the comments placed on the page by the reader.

Desktops also require many different programs to view all of their resources, which is something readers are not accustomed to when dealing with books. Another major problem with desktops is that every time a user logs off, it takes a couple of minutes to get back to where the reader left off. Because operating systems work around directories and files, it takes too much effort to log on and off. The active reading devices of the future are intended to address these issues. Figure 12-10 contains an example of a popular active reading machine.

The Dialogue Metaphor

In contrast to the desktop and document metaphors, which take advantage of the end user's ability to manipulate objects in an electronic environment, the *dialogue metaphor* attempts to create an electronic version of a conversation using natural language. The key to a successful conversation is that the participants must be able to listen and respond to the comments of all others.

One of the newest uses for the dialogue metaphor is the *electronic personal assistant*. An electronic assistant answers the phone, saves callers' names and numbers, places calls when its subscriber says a name or number, and handles faxes and e-mail. In addition, an assistant can help subscribers handle multiple calls, make conference calls, retrieve voice messages from other systems (including home voice mail boxes), send group messages, and remember follow-up calls and action items. Products such as *Wildfire* can connect a vast network of mobile users to the basic communications resources that previously were limited to the desktop or to multiple, and often cumbersome, devices.

Consider a typical scenario in today's mobile world. An executive is stuck in the Pittsburgh airport. He or she dials a number on a mobile phone and connects to his or her Wildfire assistant by typing in a pass code. Then, simply by conversing with Wildfire, he or she can check messages, return or place calls, conduct a conference call, and leave voice messages for specific people who might call in. If someone phones while the executive is on the system, Wildfire tells him or her who is calling, giving the choice of accepting the call or having a message taken.

A typical interaction with an electronic personal assistant like Wildfire can be as short as 30 seconds or longer than an hour. At every step, the system guides the user along, speaking in a charming, intelligent, and realistic female or male voice.

"Wildfire," says the manager.
"I'm here," answers the computer.
"Make a call."
"Call whom?"

In addition, because of the advanced logic and speech synthesis embedded in an electronic personal assistant, it can be programmed to be quite lifelike in its dialogue. For example, tell Wildfire you are depressed, and it retorts, "Oh, great! Now I'm a therapist?"

Although probably not capable of passing a Turing test, the newest applications based on the HCI dialogue metaphor are rapidly becoming functional elements in the modern business environment.

Data Entry Issues

The vast majority of end user generated input is in the form of raw data entry into a database. The common method for entering this data is via a keyboard, with the data being entered into a screen that is designed to capture the data in some logical manner. If the original data is captured on a paper-based form, such as an order or an application form, the input screen is often designed to replicate the format of the form in a manner that allows the data entry user to easily follow the process of moving the data from the paper to the screen. Because of the electronic environment available to the designer of input screens, a number of common functions should be incorporated when designing and implementing a data entry screen. Table 12-1 contains a list and brief explanation of the common functions to be included in a data entry screen.

Although the screen functions listed in Table 12-1 may seem intuitive, the number of design layouts for data entry in modern IS is often quite daunting. Probably the single most important characteristic of a good data entry screen is *consistency*. In other words, the methods and functions available on one data entry screen should be consistently applied to all entry screens within that application. Further, many organizations are realizing significant benefits associated with standardizing the input screen functions for all applications across the organization. The concept of consistency in design can be extended to all portions of the user interface for the system. By creating a standardized interface, the learning curve for an end user on a new system or screen is significantly reduced, as is the probability of data entry error across screens within an application. Two examples of the significant benefits associated with standardized functions in the user interface are the modern automobile and the Microsoft Windows application environment. In the former, the functions of the interface have become so institutionalized in our global society that virtually anyone trained to drive one make or model of automobile can quickly assume command of another unfamiliar one. This is owing to not only the similarity of the functions but also the positioning of them. In the case of the Windows environment, application designers have adopted a menuing and

Table 12-1   Common Data Entry Screen Functions

Capability Category	Examples
Cursor control	• Move the cursor forward or backward to allowable data fields • Directly move the cursor to the first or last field on the screen • Move the cursor forward or backward by one character within a data field
Editing	• Delete the previous character • Delete the current character • Delete the entire field entry • Clear the entire form of data
Exiting	• Commit the data on the screen to the database or application program • Navigate to a new screen or form • Confirm recent data entry before moving to another screen or form
End user help	• Obtain help with a particular data field definition or entry • Obtain help on the purpose and limitation associated with a particular data entry screen

shortcut-key protocol that makes it easy for a trained user to move from a familiar application to a new one without a significant investment in learning how to navigate the screens. Figure 12-11 illustrates the similarities across interfaces for two commercial software applications.

Data Entry Screen Characteristics

Regardless of the intended application, several guidelines exist with regard to designing effective and efficient data entry screens. Table 12-2 contains a list and brief explanation of the characteristics of a well-designed input screen.

Among the guidelines listed in Table 12-2, the one that is probably most often ignored by screen designers is requiring the user to enter data that are available online or in computed form. How often do we see applications that require the user to enter the date and time? This is easily obtained from the system clock and, if necessary, can be changed by the end user to reflect a transaction that occurred prior to the current date. This suggests that the screen designer should make every attempt to determine default values, where appropriate, such that the common entry for a field can be accepted or altered by the user depending on the situation at hand.

Another often overlooked input screen function is the inclusion of *context-sensitive help*. This function allows the user to obtain additional explanations and guidance that are directly related to the data field being filled or the input function being performed. Several techniques, including pop-up help, hotspots, and tool tips, are available to the designer to facilitate the delivery of context-sensitive help functions to the end user. Figure 12-12 illustrates these techniques.

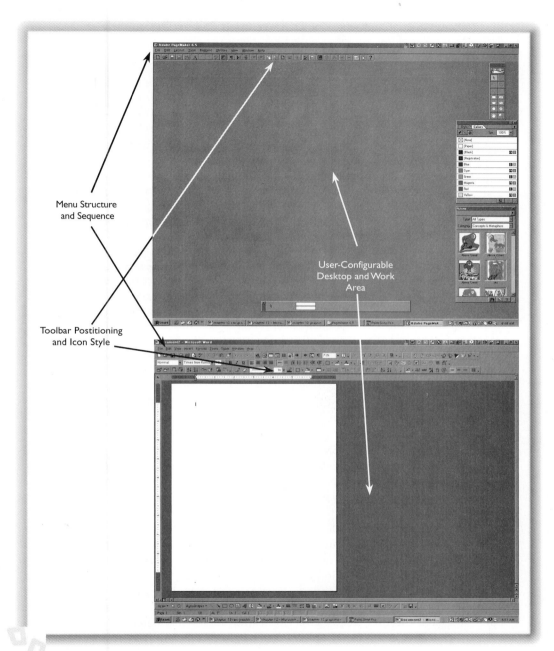

**Menu Structure
and Sequence**

**User-Configurable
Desktop and Work
Area**

**Toolbar Postitioning
and Icon Style**

Figure 12-11   Illustration of Similarity in Interface across Applications

Providing User Feedback

From a control perspective, a feedback loop is defined as *a closed transmission path
that maintains a prescribed relationship between output signals and input signals.* Although
the design of an effective interface is not specifically intended to control anything,
the importance of providing relevant and useful feedback to the end user lies in the
measurable improvement in both the quality of, and satisfaction with, the interaction

Table 12-2 Guidelines for Effective Input Screen Design

Data Entry Activity	Guideline for Effective Design
Data entry	Avoid requiring entry of data that can be computed, derived, or retrieved from an existing on-line source.
Field defaults	Provide relevant field value defaults where appropriate (i.e., assume current date for invoice date field).
Required units	Clearly indicate the desired unit values for data entry fields (i.e., pounds, inches, dollars, tons, etc.).
Data replacement	Provide intelligent character replacement functions by suggesting a completed entry after the user has typed the first few characters.
Field captions	Provide information field captions such that the end user can determine the appropriate data to enter.
Field formatting	Provide explicit formatting examples where relevant to indicate the proper method for entering data with required embedded symbols or a specific sequence (i.e., social security number, 999-99-9999 or date, mm/dd/yyyy).
Data alignment	Provide automatic alignment for data entries using left justification for text and right-justification or decimal justification for numbers.
End user help	Wherever possible, provide context-sensitive help mechanisms and hot-key access to help facilities.

experience. By designing effective feedback mechanisms to relay basic system status information, prompt the user for input or alternative selection, or provide warnings or notification of errors, the success of a user interaction in the form of accuracy and efficiency can be greatly enhanced.

System Status Feedback

There are many occasions during a typical user interaction when the system may be performing a function or process for which there is no need for user input at that moment and no other function can be initiated by the user until completed. In this type of situation, the user needs to be reassured that the intended process is successfully executing. Further, given our ever-decreasing patience with regard to computing speed, the user needs some indication of the estimated length of time for the process to execute or complete. The methods employed to satisfy these needs are referred to as *system status indicators.*

Status feedback can be provided as textual or graphical or some combination of both. In many cases, designers provide status feedback that takes advantage of our comfort level with thinking of the computer as an autonomous being. As such, a process that requires several seconds to open a large file may display a message such as "Please wait while I retrieve the information" or "Please be patient, this could take a few seconds." In other cases, the status of a process such as a file download may be indicated to the user via a graphical device, such as a moving bar or a pie chart indicating the percentage of time remaining or the percentage of the process completed. Figure 12-13 illustrates a combination of text and graphics in providing feedback to the user regarding process status.

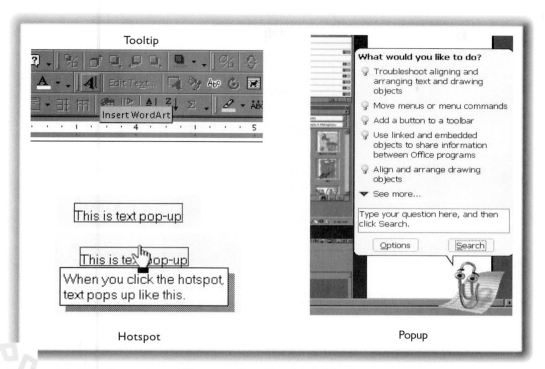

Figure 12-12   Examples of Context-Sensitive Help Mechanisms

User Prompts

User prompts appear virtually everywhere in a typical input screen. If the fields are properly titled, the field names themselves serve as an effective prompt for the user to indicate what input is required. In other cases, the designer may need to communicate information to the user in the form of a statement or, more than likely, a

Figure 12-13   End User Feedback Using both Text
and Graphics

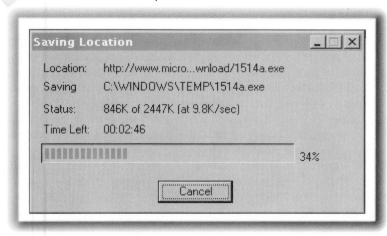

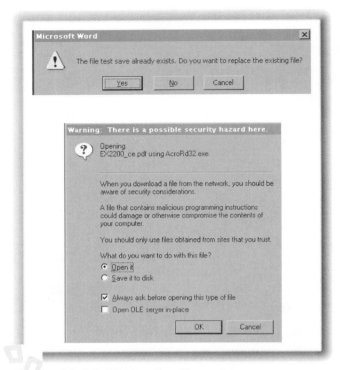

Figure 12-14   Dialog Box Examples

selection that is related to either a process in progress or a possible error condition in effect. A dialogue box, as shown in Figure 12-14, is commonly used for this type of feedback. This dynamic input mechanism allows the user to be informed as to the need for a decision or input and provides the user with a clear-cut cut set of alternatives from which to select.

In some cases, the dialogue is, just as its name implies, simply a mechanism for providing information to the user that they need to acknowledge. In other cases, a dialogue box maybe used as a miniature input screen to capture user input necessary to initiate and execute a requested process.

Dialogue Design

The range of scenarios in which an end user may interact with a computer is virtually limitless. Regardless of the scenario, however, all HCIs are actually "programmed," in the sense that a series of steps have been predetermined by the designer to accomplish the task undertaken by the end user. This sequence of steps and the manner in which information is provided to and received from an end user is called a *dialogue.* For each function or series of functions in the application, the designer must create a dialogue sequence that serves to define the conditions under which input is captured and conveyed. Given the limitless range of possible dialogues that could be initiated, the scope of this subject is quite broad and well beyond our available space and time in this text. Interested readers can find excellent references by Shneiderman (1992), Dumas (1988), and Wagner (1994), among many others, in most libraries. From a general perspective, however, guide-

Table 12-3   Guidelines for the Design of Effective HCI Dialogues

Dialogue Guideline	Explanation
Be consistent	All dialogues should be consistent in action, sequence, required keystrokes, and terminology.
Enable user shortcuts	End users should be allowed to take advantage of shortcut keys or macro commands wherever possible and appropriate.
Provide relevant feedback	Feedback should be provided to the end user for every data entry action.
Allow for closure	All dialogues should have a clear beginning, middle, and end.
Provide error-handling guidance	All possible errors should be captured by the system and reported back to the end user in a manner that allows for correction or provides suggestions as to how to proceed.
Allow reversal of action	Wherever possible, end user actions should be reversible and data deletion should not occur without explicit confirmation from the end user.
Provide user control	The dialogue should allow experienced users to feel in control of the system and should facilitate inexperienced end users by allowing the user to take greater control of the process as experience develops.
Reduce cognitive load	Dialogues must be simple to use and must provide for a minimum cognitive load on the end user.

lines do exist to assist the designer in preparing useful and effective end user dialogues. Table 12-3 contains a summarized list of guidelines that should be followed when conducting dialogue design.

Usability Assessment

The goal of analysts and software designers is to create an application environment that meets the needs and requirements of the users in a manner that makes the application easy and, sometimes, even enjoyable to use. To achieve this goal, analysts often conduct *usability assessments* to determine the effectiveness and efficiency of the various interface structures and components of the application.

To this end, a wide variety of data gathering and assessment techniques is employed. *Surveys* and *questionnaires* can help determine how users perform specific tasks, how they engage interface elements such as icons and menus, how they work with help systems and wizards, and how satisfied they feel about these things. Related to these methods are *focus groups,* widely used in product design of all types, in which a moderator orally questions a group of users. Another type of testing is *field observation,* where the tester watches people use the software in their work environments.

Primarily, however, usability testing is most effective when it attempts to determine how much time a user needs to complete a task or series of tasks and how difficult the tasks seem. This requires a controlled testing environment, because in the case of questionnaires and focus groups, users' memories are unreliable, and in the case of field observation, users face real-world distractions. Controlled tests let designers and developers see how well a program works in and of itself.

A *controlled usability test* typically places a single participant (or on rare occasions, two participants) in a particular location where he or she is given a document, or task list, outlining a set of tasks to perform in a particular order. For example, a task list might ask a participant to save a document or print a document using landscape orientation. The first requires finding a menu item, an icon, or a hot key, then working with the file/save dialogue. The second requires the same, except that the concept of landscape orientation becomes an issue. This test could be designed with visual cues as well, showing the participants an example of a landscape orientation and asking them to print a specific file to resemble it.

The idea is to give program teams highly specific user feedback about their design. Instead of postimplementation user feedback, which tends to be much less focused ("I could not get a graphic to embed in the diagram—it took me an hour!") or completely unfocused ("The new system stinks!"), controlled usability tests show where user satisfaction is likely to suffer unless the application design is altered. If usability testing begins early enough in the development life cycle, these potential problems can be isolated in time to change the finished design and, thus, avoid an undesirable implementation of a new system.

In the major software development companies, in fact, usability personnel work with development teams from the earliest design stages of the product. Still, even in these cases, a great deal of testing takes place after the product is released, and by that point features and interface design are pretty well frozen in place. In that case, the test results affect the next full version or update release of the software.

It is important to keep in mind that usability assessment should not be confused with technical assessment. A feature might work as well as possible from a technical standpoint but still be less friendly than it could be or should be. In other words, the concern is not with technical effectiveness but with whether the application or module is efficient to use. Simultaneously, however, analysts must judge features according to what they were designed to do and not as a particular end user's fancy might remake them. Usability testing is not about discovering missing features but about discovering problems or issues with using the existing features.

DESIGNING THE INPUT CONTROLS

In chapter 11, we discussed the need to control the output of the system before it is generated, because once the output is created, we can no longer control its distribution or use. The same concept of control applies to the input side of the equation, only in reverse. We must apply our controls to input before it is committed to the database, because once it is stored, it becomes very difficult to validate or correct. *Input controls* are intended to ensure that the data input to the system are both accurate and valid to the highest degree possible. Although no system of controls can completely eliminate data entry errors or inaccuracies, a variety of control mechanisms exist to minimize or prevent such occurrences in many instances. We divide our discussion of input controls into two basic categories: (1) data controls and (2) access controls.

Data Controls

Data entry errors can be typically divided into four possible sources of inaccuracy. An *appending error* occurs where a user adds additional characters that are not part of the actual data entry to existing or new data:

Actual Data	Actual Entry
1995 GMC Truck	1995 GMC Truck9g4d

The opposite error source from an appending error is a *truncation error*, where a user drops valid characters from a piece of data during the entry process:

Actual Data	Actual Entry
251s54398x7	251s54398x

The third source of data entry error, the *transcription error*, occurs when invalid data are entered into a data field:

Actual Data	Actual Entry
06–30–2000	06–31–2000

Finally, the *transposition error* occurs when the sequence of one or more characters in a data field is reversed:

Actual Data	Actual Entry
19071 Halstead Street	19701 Halstaed Street

Currently, there are no validation mechanisms available to detect erroneous data. If the customer's last name is "Smith" and the user enters "Smythe," assuming the expected data was alphanumeric, the system accepts the data entry as valid and does not detect the error. In other words, there is a difference between *valid* data and *correct* data. We have to assume that well-trained data entry personnel do not enter erroneous data but may, from time to time, inadvertently enter invalid or inaccurate data. By designing a control mechanism that can validate the data entered into a particular field for each of the four sources of data errors, many inaccuracies can be captured at the source and corrected prior to committing them to the database. Once data is stored in an inaccurate form, it can become virtually impossible to detect or correct the inaccuracy.

To assist the user in detecting invalid data, the analyst can design a control mechanism suitable for the type of data expected in the field and, in some cases, can design control mechanisms that assist the user in detecting certain types of erroneous data. Table 12-4 lists nine common control mechanisms, along with a brief explanation of how and when they can be applied.

Of the nine control mechanisms listed in Table 12-4, the single most complicated but, nonetheless, commonly applied control is the *check digit*. Have you experienced a situation where, when asked to enter your credit card or account number into a system, the system responded with a message indicating that the account number entered was not valid? Assuming the credit card being used was not fraudulent, you most likely simply entered the number wrong. The reason the system was able to detect this error, however, was because of a check digit control embedded in the number itself. A check digit is a digit appended to the actual number that is derived by applying a mathematical algorithm to the actual data. By reapplying the same algorithm to the number being entered, the system can determine whether the data entered are valid. Check digits are used to validate credit card numbers, bank account numbers, ISBN identification numbers, and universal price code (UPC) barcodes, among many other applications. Table 12-5 illustrates how the check digit validation control can detect an invalid entry for a bank account number.

Table 12-4   Input Validation Control Mechanisms

Input Control Mechanism	Explanation
Data typing	Data should be checked for proper type (numeric, alphabetic, or alphanumeric)
Reasonableness	Data should be tested for reasonableness of value given the situation (negative interest rates not allowed, appropriate rate of pay for specific employee category)
Expected value	Data should be checked against some expected value where appropriate (model of automobile should match make of automobile)
Missing or required data	Fields should be checked and flagged for missing data that is deemed necessary to complete the data entry process (has a quantity been provided for every item on the purchase order?)
Check-digit calculation	Check digit calculation should be conducted upon appropriate field entry to insure proper account number or other numerical data accuracy
Data format	Data should be checked against any required format or template to insure proper entry (999-99-9999, (999) 999-9999, 99AAXX9AX)
Value range	Data should be checked against any known or established value range (two-letter state codes should come from acceptable list of codes)
Entry size	The number of expected characters should be checked where appropriate (is the social security number exactly nine digits?)
Allowable entry	Data should be limited to a range of allowable entries and this range of choices should be provided to the end user, where appropriate

Table 12-5   Check Digit Calculation Method

Process	Example
Number each digit of a numeric entry according to place value from either right or left beginning with 2.	Assume account number of 34763: 34763 23456
Multiply each digit in the numeric entry by its assigned place value.	$\begin{array}{rrrrr} 3 & 4 & 7 & 6 & 3 \\ \times\,2 & 3 & 4 & 5 & 6 \\ \hline 6 & 12 & 28 & 30 & 18 \end{array}$
Sum the result of the multiplications.	$6 + 12 + 28 + 30 + 12 = 94$
Divide the sum by the modulus number (usually 10 or 11).	Assume a modulus number of 11: $94/11 = 8$ remainder 6
Subtract remainder from modulus number and append check digit to numerical entry.	$11 - 6 = 5$ (check digit) 347635

Access Controls

As the world becomes more wired and organizations increase their reliance on IS to store and process sensitive proprietary data, the vulnerability of unauthorized access or fraud rises significantly. The U.S. National Center for Computer Crime estimates that 44 percent of all computer-related crime is due to unauthorized access or fraud. The American Bar Association conducted a survey of 1,000 companies in 1998 and found that 48 percent of them experienced computer fraud within the last 5 years, with respondents each reporting losses ranging from $2 to $10 million dollars. The point is that computer fraud is a pervasive crime, and the analyst must design the necessary access controls to prevent unauthorized access to corporate IS.

Several categories of methods currently exist to design authorization and access controls for IS. *Authentication mechanisms* that make use of many of the new technologies, such as biometric readers and smart cards, can be effectively employed to prevent unauthorized access. Despite the recent advances in authorization devices, the most common technique is still the simple user name and password mechanism. The problem with passwords is that they cannot provide any indication of the identity of the person attempting to gain access. It is assumed that if a valid password is presented to the system, access is granted. With the new authorization mechanisms available to the analyst, more sophisticated and reliable authorization schemes can be designed.

An additional form of access control available to the analyst is called an *authorization schema*. This mechanism involves the establishment of access rules that can be applied individually to each user or collectively to all or a subset of users. For example, a mechanism can be put into operation that grants only certain access rights to a particular user. A certain user, or class of users, may be authorized to read data from a particular file but not add, modify, or delete any data in that file. Access limits may be designed to be related to time of day or the day of the week. A particular user's access rights could be limited to 8:00 A.M. to 5:00 P.M. on weekdays only. This would prevent any access to the system on weekends or after business hours.

A third approach to access control is the use of an *encryption mechanism*. Basically, this suggests that the data are encoded on entry and can only be decoded by a user in possession of the appropriate key. Data encryption comes in two basic categories: *public key* and *secret key*. In a secret key setup, the key used to encrypt the data is also used to decrypt it. This works well if the data only need to be read by the same person who encrypted them, or by a small, geographically close group. When necessary, the analyst can create one or more secret keys to facilitate private data encryption. If the data are to be accessed by several people, however, care is needed with regard to distribution of the key in a secure manner. For example, you would not want to send a secret key through Internet mail. Key management issues aside, secret key encryption can still work well, even for large groups.

The more common approach in today's Internet environment is the use of a public key encryption method. Public key encryption involves two keys: one is used to encrypt the data and another is used to decrypt them. The two keys are mathematically related to each other and are called a *key pair*. The key used to encrypt the data is called a *public key*, and the key used to decode the data is called the *private key*. The private key is typically associated with a particular user's ID file or password scheme. Although the two keys are related, it is extremely difficult to figure out the private key, even if you know its public sibling. If you have a spare supercomputer sitting in your basement, you might be able crack a 128 bit key pair before the 22nd century rolls in. Public key encryption bypasses the key management issues present in the secret key method. Everyone already has the keys they need, so there is no need to figure out how to distribute them.

CHAPTER SUMMARY

This chapter provided a detailed overview of the design and control issues facing the analyst with regard to the user interface. In the previous chapter, we explored the design of the outputs necessary to provide effective information to the end users of the system. With these two tasks complete, the system is well on its way to completion and implementation. The final step, the design of the internal program logic, is the activity that serves to marry the inputs and outputs such that the system represents a cohesive and effective IS to its intended users.

KEY CONCEPTS

➤Interface

The interface is the mechanism by which human beings interact with computing devices.

➤ Five basic categories of human–computer interaction

• Command dialogue

In the command dialogue approach, the end user initiates all dialogue by issuing instructions to the computer via a structured syntax of commands. A variety of command structures exist ranging from quasi-natural language to literally cryptic. This approach often requires a significant learning curve on the part of the end user if it is to be used with any degree of efficiency and accuracy.

• Menus

The menu approach presents a list of available alternatives to the end user that are relevant to the task being performed. The user simply selects the desired option and the command is executed.

  • Single menu
  • Hierarchical menu
  • GUI menu bar
  • Pop-up menu

• Icons and buttons

The icon approach uses an iconic menu that allows the end user to select and execute commands by pointing and clicking at graphical buttons or icons located on the screen or menu bar.

• Input screens and forms

The input screen or form method uses a screen-based form that allows end users to fill in the necessary information in the blanks provided such that all data are captured or retrieved in a logical, easy-to-read manner. Issues that have to be taken into consideration when designing the screens and forms are to

  • Provide understandable field headings and titles
  • Organize the fields in a logical manner
  • Allow users to move from field to field in a logical, intuitive sequence.

• Natural language recognition

The natural language recognition method makes use of voice synthesis technology to allow the user to interface with the computing device by using natural language and voice commands.

  • Natural computing

  The natural computing approach to user interaction is intended to provide information where we want it, how we want it, and with practically invisible interfaces that adapt to natural human interaction skills.

➤ Input devices
- Common input devices
  - Keyboard
  - Mouse
  - Trackball
  - Joystick
  - Touch-sensitive screen
  - Scanner
  - Laser and light pen
  - Graphics tablet
  - Voice recognition
- Biometric input devices

  Biometric refers to the automatic identification of a person based on his or her physiological or behavioral characteristics. By using biometric identification and verification systems, unauthorized access to or fraudulent use of systems potentially can be prevented.
- Optical input devices
  - Barcodes

    Barcoding allows data to be collected rapidly and with extreme accuracy. Barcodes provide a simple and easy method of encoding text and numerical information that is easily read by inexpensive electronic laser sensing devices.
  - Optical mark reading (OMR)

    An OMR system senses marks in predefined areas of a special form.
  - Optical character recognition (OCR)

    An OCR system scans virtually any form or document containing number, letters, or marks.
  - Smart cards

    A smart card is a credit-card-size plastic card embedded with an integrated circuit chip that makes it smart. This integration allows an immense amount of information to be stored, accessed, and processed either online or off-line.

➤ Human–computer interaction (HCI)

HCI is a multidisciplinary field concerned with the application of computer science, psychology, ergonomics, and many other disciplines in industry and commerce to facilitate the design, implementation, and evaluation of information and communications systems that satisfy the need of those who own and use them.

➤ Guidelines for input and interface design
- HCI metaphors
  - The desktop metaphor

    The desktop or direct manipulation metaphor for HCI builds on the set of activities and organization schemes associated with a common desktop. The idea is to create an electronic environment that allows for direct manipulation of the multiple items on the desktop and is as close as possible to the real-world environment.
  - The document metaphor

    Following the document metaphor, the end user interacts with the computer by browsing through or entering data on electronic documents and forms. The advantage of the document metaphor in a computing environment is the use of hypermedia, the concept of linking graphics, video, and audio together in a manner that allows the end user to easily navigate between the documents.
  - The dialogue metaphor

    The dialogue metaphor attempts to create an electronic version of a conversation using natural language. The key to a successful conversation is that the participants must be able to listen and respond to the comments of all others.
- Data entry issues
  - Common data entry screen functions
    - Cursor control
    - Editing
    - Exiting
    - End user help
  - Consistency

    The single most important characteristic of a good data entry screen is consistency. In other words, the methods and functions available on one data entry screen should be consistently applied to all entry screens within that application. The concept of consistency in design can be extended to all portions of the user interface for the system.
  - Guidelines for designing effective and efficient data entry screens
    - Avoid data entry that can be computed, derived, or retrieved from an existing on-line source.

- Provide relevant field value defaults where appropriate.
- Clearly indicate the desired unit values for data entry fields.
- Provide intelligent character replacement functions by suggesting a completed entry after the user has typed the first few characters.
- Provide information field captions such that the end user can determine the appropriate data to enter.
- Provide explicit formatting examples.
- Provide automatic alignment for data entries.
- Whenever possible, provide context-sensitive help mechanisms and hot-key access to help facilities.
- Providing user feedback.
- Feedback loop

  From a control perspective, a feedback loop is defined as a closed transmission path that maintains a prescribed relationship between output signals and input signals.
- System status feedback

  System status feedbacks provide the end users reassurance that the intended process is successfully executed or indication of the estimated length of process time in the occasions when the system may be performing a function or process for which there is no need for user input at that moment and no other function can be initiated by the user until completed.
- User prompt

  In some cases, the designer may need to communicate information to the user in the form of a statement or, more than likely, a selection that is related to either a process in progress or possibly an error condition in effect. This dynamic input mechanism allows the user to be informed as to the need for a decision or input and provides the user with a clear-cut set of alternatives from which to select.

- Dialogue design

  All HCIs are actually programmed in the sense that a series of steps have been predetermined by the designer to accomplish the task undertaken by the end user. The sequence of steps and the manner in which information is provided to and received from an end user is called a dialogue. The design of the dialogue sequence should be able to define the conditions under which input is captured and conveyed.
- Usability assessment

  To make sure that the design of an application environment meets the needs and requirements of the user in a manner that makes the application easy and enjoyable to use, analysts conduct usability assessments to determine the effectiveness and efficiency of the various interface structures and components of the application.
  - Survey and questionnaires
  - Focus groups
  - Field observation
  - Controlled usability test

➤ Designing the input controls

Input controls are intended to ensure that the data input to the system are both accurate and valid to the highest degree possible. They accomplish this by validating input and controlling access.

- Data control
  - Data entry errors can be typically divided into four possible sources of inaccuracy:
    - Appending error

      An appending error occurs when a user adds additional characters to existing or new data that are not part of the actual data entry.
    - Truncation error

      A truncation error occurs when a user drops valid characters from a piece of data during the entry process.
    - Transcription error

      A transcription error occurs when invalid data are entered into a data field.

- Transposition error

  A transposition error occurs when the sequence of one or more characters in a data field are reversed.

- By designing a control mechanism that can validate the data entered into a particular field for each of the four sources of data errors, many inaccuracies can be captured at the source and corrected prior to committing them to the database. Common input control mechanisms include

  - Data typing
  - Reasonableness
  - Expected value
  - Missing or required data
  - Check-digit calculation
  - Data format
  - Value range
  - Entry size
  - Allowable entry

- Access control

  Several categories of methods currently exist to design authorization and access controls for IS.

- Authentication mechanisms

  Authentication mechanisms use many of the new technologies, such as biometric readers and smart cards, to prevent unauthorized access.

- Authorization schema

  The authorization schema mechanism involves the establishment of access rules that can be applied individually to each user or collectively to all or a subset of users.

- Encryption mechanism

  Using an encryption mechanism, the data are encoded on entry and can only be decoded by a user in possession of the appropriate key. Data encryption comes in two basic categories: public key and secret key.

QUESTIONS FOR REVIEW

1. List and briefly describe the five basic categories of HCI.

2. What is the main advantage of the iconic menuing approach?

3. List the issues that have to be taken into consideration when designing an input screen or form.

4. Explain the concept of natural computing.

5. Explain how a biometric system works.

6. Describe the main benefits of using barcodes.

7. List and briefly describe the commonly used optical input devices.

8. List and briefly explain the three HCI metaphors.

9. What is the main advantage of using the document metaphor in a computing environment? Use an example to explain this metaphor.

10. List and briefly describe the limitations of the use of the HCI document metaphor.

11. List and briefly describe the commonly used data entry screen functions.

12. Explain the concept of consistency in data entry screen design and state its benefits.

13. List and briefly explain the guidelines for designing effective and efficient data entry screens.

14. Describe the main purpose of designing effective feedback mechanisms.

15. List and briefly describe the design guidelines for effective HCI dialogues.

16. What is the goal of usability assessment?

17. What are the commonly used methods in usability assessment?

18. Compare the difference between usability assessment and technical assessment of a system.

19. List and briefly describe the four possible sources of data errors.

20. What are the commonly used input validation control mechanisms?

21. What are the commonly used access control mechanisms?

FOR FURTHER DISCUSSION

1. The display properties and characteristics available to the designer in a GUI environment are vast, yet certain ones are often either overused or underused. This typically results in a less than effective or desirable interface. In some cases, it may actually serve to impede an end user's performance. Cite some examples from your experiences in which the display properties were appropriately used and others in which they were not.

2. Refer to Figure 12-2. This is a toolbar from a Windows application called *PhotoShop* from Adobe Corporation. Can you look at the toolbar and determine the function of each of the icons? How intuitive is this interface?

3. Using any available repository of icons (plenty are available on the WWW or in common graphics packages), design an iconic toolbar for use in a specific industry, such as banking, healthcare, or food services. Try to design your interface such that one of your classmates can look at it and determine the function of each of the icons.

4. Find an Internet search engine that uses a natural language interface (<http://www.askjeeves.com> is a good one, but there are many others). What are the advantages of a natural language interface over a conventional keyword-based search engine? Is it easier to use a natural language interface?

REFERENCES

Dumas, J. S. 1988. *Designing User Interfaces for Software.* Englewood Cliffs, NJ: Prentice Hall.

Shneiderman, B. 1992. *Designing the User Interface: Strategies for Effective Human-Computer Interaction.* Reading, MA: Addison-Wesley.

Wagner, R. 1994. "A GUI Design Manifesto." *Paradox Informant* 5: 36–42.

Designing the System Internals

Learning Objectives

- Understand the concepts of structured and modular systems design
- Learn the principles and guidelines associated with good systems design practices
- Explain the concepts of factoring, module size, coupling, and cohesion
- Learn to identify and correct for the various types of undesirable cohesion and module coupling
- Understand the concepts behind the hierarchical structure diagram
- Derive a structure diagram from a DFD using either a transform or a transaction analysis approach

Things should be made as simple as possible, but not any simpler.
—ALBERT EINSTEIN

INTRODUCTION

Admittedly, the sequence of design activities associated with IS design appears somewhat counterintuitive and backward. We design the output first and then use that design to inform the design of the inputs, interfaces, and dialogues. Once we have completed the design of the exterior, we begin to work on the interior. The process is not so backward, really, especially when compared to the construction of a house. The exterior first, the interior second. In IS design, once we know what the system needs to generate and how the data for that output are captured, we can focus our attention on designing the internal elements of the system. These elements are the processes that make the interface functional, generate the desired output, and access and store data from both the organizational and external databases necessary for operation.

In this chapter, we direct our attention to the activities associated with internal design of the system. Although one of the primary activities, coding the program logic, is a subject for discussion in another venue, the physical design and preparation of the system's internal specifications is our focus here. Our goal is to apply the tenet of good systems design to the final stages of the project such that the programmers can generate source code that performs as expected.

363

MAKING IT ALL WORK

One of the most widely accepted approaches to software design is called *modular design*. Building on the concept of functional decomposition (from chapter 2), this approach decomposes a large, complex software application into smaller, inter-related components called modules. From the designer's and programmer's perspective, a *module* is defined as a group of executable instructions that has a single point of entry and a single point of exit. In other words, a module is designed to perform its functions independently from all other modules contained within the application. The various functions of the application are executed by either a single module or a series of modules where the currently executing module may call on one or more other modules to perform a particular subtask.

Generally speaking, one of the goals of modular design is to break the system down such that a single module is a relatively short, straightforward group of executable instructions. This is intended to allow for ease in reading and revision of the program code. It is important to realize, however, that the concept of modularization is not simply an issue of size. Modules must also be designed such that they perform a single function. Further, good modularization also strives to minimize the extent to which one module is dependent on one or more additional modules for successful execution. These two concepts, referred to as *cohesion* and *coupling*, are discussed in detail in a following section.

PRINCIPLES OF GOOD INTERNAL DESIGN

Before we begin focusing on the methods by which a good modular design is achieved, it makes sense to briefly discuss what a good design should look like. In other words, the analyst needs to know what the goals of a well-written modular design are such that he or she can keep them foremost in his or her mind when designing the system. In general, the goal of any systems designer is to create a system that is easy to read and understand, easy to code and revise, and easy to maintain. To reach this end, several common guidelines to good systems design should be followed. Table 13-1 contains a list of these guidelines and a brief explanation of each.

System Factoring

The practice of *factoring* is closely related to the concept of functional decomposition. It involves the breaking up of the system in a set of functional modules of manageable size and relationships. System factoring can be envisioned from one of two perspectives: bottom-up or top-down. A *bottom-up* approach identifies the processes that need to be a part of the system and then moves forward to code each identified process as a module that interfaces with all other identified process modules. The problem with this approach is that although each coded module may be functional according to specification, the overall system may still not meet the stated objectives of the organization and its end users.

The more useful and appropriate method of envisioning system factoring is the *top-down* approach. Here, the system is first viewed in the broadest possible sense and then decomposed into subsystems that work together to efficiently and effectively reach the stated objectives for the overall system. This approach is in keeping with the general system approach discussed in chapter 2. Recall the example of functionally decomposing a city block into smaller and smaller subsystems. We eventually identified a subsystem at the atomic and molecular level. Although

Table 13-1   Guidelines for Good System Design

Design Guideline	Explanation
Factor	The system should be *factored,* or decomposed, into small modules that conform to both the size and cohesion guidelines of good design.
Span of Control	No parent module should be given control over more than 5 to 7 child, or subordinate, modules.
Coupling	The extent to which modules are dependent on each other should be minimized such that the amount of communication between dependent modules is also minimized. Ideally, module communication should occur only via passed data elements and informational flags.
Size	A reasonable size for a single module is considered to be between 50 and 100 lines of executable code.
Cohesion	The instructions contained within a module should pertain only to that function. This suggests that a well-factored module should be describable in a few simple words, with no "and" or "or" in the module name.
Shared Use	Wherever possible, a child module should be called by multiple parent modules.

starting with a city block and decomposing it into smaller and smaller levels of analysis appears logical and straightforward, imagine trying to start with atoms and molecules and end up with a functional city block! The top-down approach avoids the potential chaos associated with trying to take a disparate set of functional modules and turn them into a cohesive software application.

Module Span

The concept of *span of control* should be a familiar one to you from your introductory management course. In that context, it is believed that a single manager is limited as to the number of direct report employees he or she can effectively manage. Avoiding an unmanageable span of control scenario usually involves the creation of a hierarchy of authority that divides the management effort and scope of authority of a single senior manager across several direct reports, each with a manageable span of control. Figure 13-1 illustrates this point using a common organizational chart.

In much the same way, *module span* should be limited such that a single module does not have control over more than five to seven subordinate modules. In software design, this condition is referred to as a *low fan-out* design. Figure 13-2 illustrates both high fan-out and low fan-out design for a system module.

Module Cohesion

The concept of *module cohesion* can be thought of as a measure of completeness. Every statement in a module should relate to the identified function of that module. If a module becomes too large or unfocused, it should be decomposed into subsystems that reflect a more focused and cohesive set of objectives.

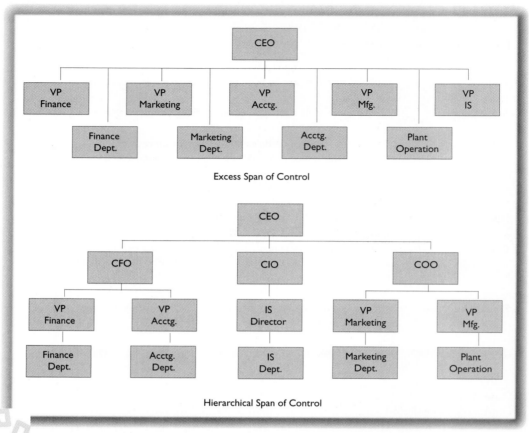

Figure 13-1   Example of Excess and Hierarchical Span of Control

One important benefit to module cohesiveness is that by restricting the functions or operations performed by a module, the analyst also restricts the effects of any modifications or revisions to that module, thus localizing the changes to a single module. In other words, maximally cohesive modules tend to be more loosely coupled to other functional modules, thus they are more loosely coupled, as well.

Types of Cohesion

Page-Jones (1980) developed a taxonomy of types of cohesion that have stood the test of time and are still adhered to today. The seven types identified in this categorization scheme are organized in order of most to least desirable.

Functional cohesion occurs in modules designed such that their instructions work collectively to accomplish a single well-defined task or function. In many cases, the name of the module is indicative of the degree of functional cohesion associated with that module. The more functional cohesion, the more likely the module can be described by a single imperative verb and a concise direct object, such as CALCULATE CREDITS, PRINT REORDER REPORT, or READ INVENTORY DATABASE.

Sequential cohesion is defined as the relationship between one instruction and the next in a given module. Such modules have instructions that are related to each other such that the result, or output, of one instruction becomes the input for the next instruction.

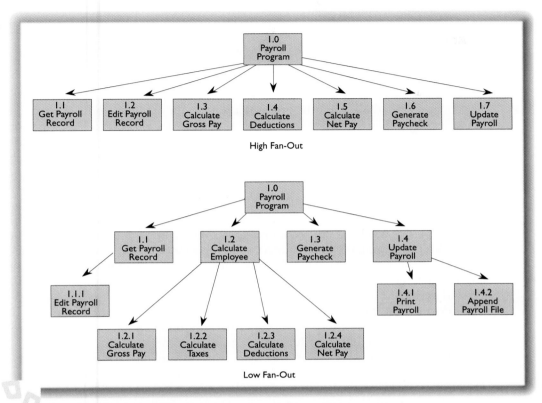

Figure 13-2   Example of High and Low Fan-Out Module Structures

As an example, consider a module designed to perform a series of related tasks: GET INVOICE, EDIT INVOICE, CHECK RECEIPT OF GOODS, PROCESS PAYMENT, TRANSMIT PAYMENT. The invoice serves as the initial input for this set of instructions, and output of the first instruction serves as the input for the second, and so on. Although not posing a major problem with overcoupling or lack of functional cohesion, sequential cohesion necessarily limits the reuse of any given function by other modules in the system and is, thus, considered less than optimal.

When a module is designed such that its instructions accomplish tasks that use the same piece of data but the sequence of those instructions is not critical to a successful outcome, *communicational cohesion* is said to occur. Take, for example, a module consisting of a set of instructions each of which accomplishes a function using inventory data. Functions such as checking the amount of stock for a particular product, adding a new product into inventory, deleting a product from inventory, updating the quantity in inventory, or changing a particular product's reorder point would all use the same data but would not necessarily be related to each other beyond the required data. A module displaying communicational cohesion should be decomposed into multiple modules that accomplish their own separate tasks.

Procedural cohesion occurs when the instruction set in a module performs multiple functions that have a specific sequence in which they must be performed. In such modules, the instructions are generally more related to activities in other modules than they are to each other. Using a nonsystems example to demonstrate procedural cohesion, consider the following set of instructions:

TURN ON FOYER LIGHT

TURN ON PORCH LIGHT

CHECK THAT ALL DOORS AND WINDOWS ARE SECURELY LOCKED

ENTER ALARM CODE TO SET ALARM

EXIT BY REAR DOOR

Such instructions might be given to a household member who is leaving the house at night. The sequence of the instructions is designed such that a person starting at the front entryway would be able to logically progress toward the alarm panel and ultimately out the rear door. Although logical in sequence, procedurally cohesive modules tend to be less maintainable than more functionally cohesive modules.

Modules that have instructions grouped together because of some common relationship based on time are referred to as displaying *temporal cohesion.* In a temporally cohesive module, the sequence of the instructions does not matter. The logic behind grouping the instructions into a single module is because they all need to execute at about the same point in time, such as during program initialization or shut down. Given the high degree of coupling between a temporally cohesive module and various other modules in the application, module maintenance can become extremely difficult. The primary reason for this difficulty is that the timing of the initialization steps cannot be changed because other modules rely on the remaining instructions in the module and may not execute properly.

In modules displaying *logical cohesion,* the instructions are related to each other only because they appear to fall into the same logical class of functions, such as editing or mathematical computation. The *dynamic link library* (DLL) files in Microsoft Windows are, in many cases, designed to be logically cohesive on purpose. A perfect example of this is the file COMMDLG.DLL, which contains the instruction set for the Windows' *File Open, File Save, Search,* and *Print* dialog boxes. The advantage to using this approach is the ease with which all applications can be designed to have the same look and feel without unnecessary duplication of code. The disadvantage is that the designer of a particular application that functions in the Windows environment must either use the limited features of the COMMDLG.DLL file or, if he or she wants to add features, write his or her own. Maintenance of such modules is virtually impossible without disrupting a significant amount of program logic and flow, and DLL files certainly do not meet our goal of functional cohesion. Nonetheless, Microsoft is a good example of how logical cohesion may be used to a designer's advantage when building multiple applications that require identical look and feel.

The least desirable type of cohesion is referred to as *coincidental cohesion.* This occurs in modules that have instructions that bear little or no relationship to each other. Although rare, such modules do exist and normally are the result of the analyst and/or programmer paying insufficient attention to the concept of cohesion at all. Thus, any cohesion that results is based solely on coincidence.

Module Coupling

Module coupling is defined as the extent to which two or more program modules are interdependent. Tightly coupled modules display high interdependence and create a greater probability of program error, because any mistake in a particular module is no longer confined to that module. Further, any changes to the code in one module may have undesirable or unexpected effects in other modules. As you might have surmised, the goal is to create modules that are completely independent or that display *loose coupling*.

Types of Coupling

As with module cohesion, several types of coupling have been identified and are discussed here in order of most to least desirable.

The most desirable form of module coupling is *data coupling*. Here, the dependency between the two modules is limited to the fact that they pass data between each other. Other than communicating data, the modules bear no relationship, thus also suggesting high functional cohesion. A common example of good data-coupled module design can be found in the Microsoft Windows environment in the form of *dynamic data exchange* (DDE), which allows multiple windows programs to share the same data. An end user can store data in his or her word processor and then use that same data in his or her presentation graphics, spreadsheet, or database applications.

Even with a data-coupled module, one particular issue that should be checked by the analyst is the presence of any "tramp" data. This is any data that do not need to be communicated to the other module in order for the function to successfully execute. For example, module A may call module B to calculate employee net pay. In this example, module B does not need to know the tax rate for any employee, because that calculation should have been performed by another functionally cohesive module. By ensuring that no tramp data are being communicated, module dependency is minimized, and any domino effect associated with changes in one module affecting another module that uses the same data stream is minimized.

When data are passed between modules in the form of data structures or entire records, the modules are said to display *stamp coupling*. Such modules tend to display a high degree of tramp data communication, because it is rare that all of the data elements within a record are actually needed by the receiving module. In addition, by passing entire data structures rather than only the necessary data elements, any changes to the data structure or file sequence could also have an adverse effect on module execution.

Control coupling occurs when one module passes control information or flags to another module. Intuitively, control-coupled modules must be significantly interdependent, because the first module must know a great deal about the inner workings of the second to be able to pass control to it. In some cases, control-coupled modules may actually occur because a subordinate module has been designed to pass control to a superordinate module. This condition, referred to as *inversion of authority*, occurs when the subordinate is telling the boss what to do and when to do it.

Two modules are said to be *common coupled* if they both refer to the same global data area. A *global data area* is common in third generation language programming languages such as FORTRAN or COBOL but can be created in programs using many fourth generation languages. This simply means that a single data specification area of a program has been created such that it is global to any module (such as the DATA division being global to any paragraph in the PROCEDURE division in a COBOL program). This type of coupling is extremely undesirable because of the possibility of errors spreading wildly throughout the system due to an error in one module showing up in another module using the same global data area. Common-coupled modules are considered to be highly interdependent.

Finally, when one module actually modifies the procedural content of another module, they are said to display the worst type of coupling, *content coupling*. This condition represents the highest form of interdependency and should be completely avoided in the design. Fortunately, most modern, higher-level languages do not allow for any form of common coupling to occur.

HIERARCHICAL STRUCTURE DIAGRAMS

The top-down approach to systems development using modules, formalized into a workable strategy by Yourdon and Constantine (1979), is called *structured design*. Using a hierarchical, modular approach, the program can be easily evaluated according to certain quality guidelines to ensure the best possible design for the application. The most common design tool for structured design is called the *hierarchical structure diagram* or *structure chart*. This diagram illustrates the relationship of the modules to each other and displays the flow and processing of data between and within the various modules of the system in hierarchical form.

DFDs versus Structure Charts

Even a cursory look at the definition of a structure chart might remind you of an analysis and design tool that we have already constructed: the logical DFD. Our DFD has processes in a given sequence, is organized in a hierarchical manner, and displays the flow of data between processes. So, what is the difference?

The answer to this question lies not in the diagram itself but in its intended user. The DFD and the structure chart do have similar content, and processes appearing on the DFD may directly translate into modules on a structure chart. The difference between them is that the intended audience for the DFD is composed of business managers and end users, whereas the audience for the structure chart is entirely made up of application programmers. It is likely that despite the level of decomposition achieved in the DFD, the level of detail is still insufficient for programmers to effectively do their job. In addition, different symbology is needed to depict certain critical actions to the programmer. Table 13-2 contains a list and brief example of the various elements used to construct a detailed structure chart.

To better understand the differences between the DFD created during analysis and logical design and the structure chart needed for program construction, an example is in order. Figure 13-3 contains a simplified, general form DFD and the structure chart derived from it.

Despite the effort put into development of the DFD in the earlier stages of the life cycle, several factors, essential to final coding, were necessarily omitted from the DFD in the interest of clarity and relevance to the intended audience. Typically, the DFD does not show such elements as *error paths, repetitions* or *loops, control data, data flow decision points, detailed input/output operations,* or *program structure.* Because these elements are critical to the successful coding and implementation of the system, however, the analyst must clearly specify these requisites such that the programmer is not left to determine them by personal discretion.

Referring to Figure 13-3a, we can see from the DFD that the central process is called PROCESS DATA. The two processes preceding the central process are primarily responsible for generating the required input in the appropriate form for the central process. These are referred to as processes contained within the *input stream.* Following execution of the central process, which takes the input stream data and produces the required solution or product, the processes contained

Table 13-2   Elements of a Hierarchical Structure Diagram

Element Name	Element Characteristics	Element Symbol
Module	• Depicts a logical piece of program • Name • ID Number • Can be superordinate or subordinate	2.9 CALCULATE CREDIT HOURS
Library module	• Depicts a logical piece of program that may be repeated within the chart • Name • ID Number	3.2 CALCULATE REORDER POINT
Conditional	• Indicates that subordinate modules are invoked by the superordinate module based on some condition	
Loop	• Indicates that one or more modules are repeated • Symbol is drawn around the lines associated with the repeating modules	
Control couple	• Indicates the passing of a message or system flag being passed from one module to another • Identified by the filled-in circle at its beginning • Names the message or flag being passed • Should always be passed upward	
Data couple	• Indicates the passing of data being passed from one module to another • Identified by the empty circle at its beginning • Names the data type being passed • Can be passed upward or downward	
On-page connector	• Indicates that certain parts of the diagram are continued on another page	Print Reorder Report
Off-page connector	• Indicates that certain parts of the diagram are continued in another location on the same page of the diagram	Print Reorder Report

within the *output stream* take that product and prepare it for display to the end user. Using the symbol set contained in Table 13-2, we can derive the structure chart from the simplified DFD, as shown in Figure 13-3b.

Although the previous example was intentionally simple, it nonetheless serves to illustrate the necessity to transform the DFD into a more suitable diagrammatic form for use by the programmers of the system. In the next section, we explore this

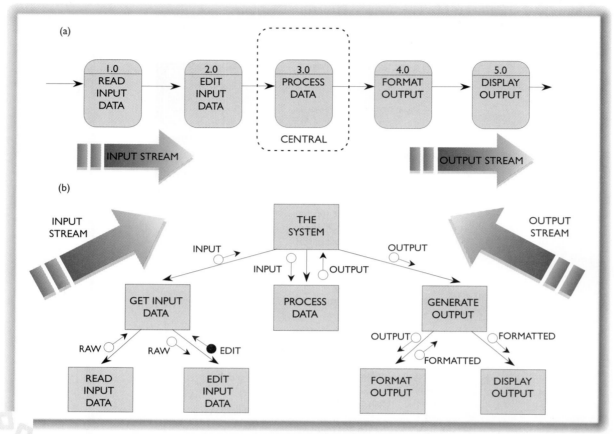

Figure 13-3   Example of a Generalized DFD and Its Associated Hierarchical Structure Diagram

transformation process in greater detail and introduce two approaches to the conversion of a DFD into a usable structure chart.

DERIVING THE HIERARCHICAL STRUCTURE DIAGRAM

As explained in the previous section, the DFD was constructed for an audience different from the one that writes the actual executable code for the program module. Although the programming staff uses the DFD as a reference tool, their primary roadmap for the system is the structure diagram. The first step in constructing the diagram is the preparation of the logical DFDs for transformation.

Preparing the DFDs

The logical DFDs, although accurate and fully validated by now, may nonetheless not be in a form that allows for easy transformation into a structure diagram. To facilitate this transition, several steps may be necessary to prepare the DFDs for easy and accurate conversion.

The first step in the preparation of DFDs for conversion is to insure that all processes contained on the DFD perform only one function. In situations where this is not the case, the elementary processes must be broken into two or more smaller processes to reach the goal of monofunctionality. One method of accomplishing

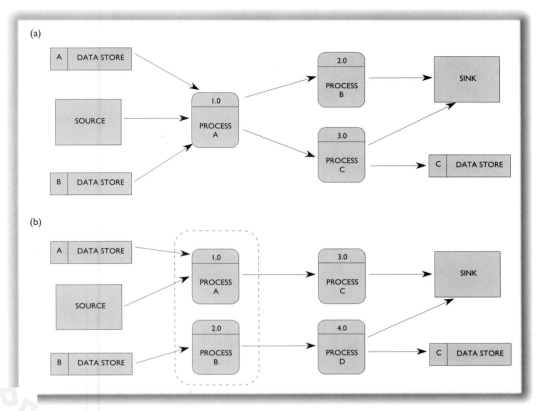

Figure 13-4   Expanding Multifunction Processes on a DFD for Conversion to a Structure Diagram

this goal is to insure that all processes on the DFD have either a single input or a single output. Consider the example in Figure 13-4. As you can see from Figure 13-4a, process 1.0 has three inputs and two outputs associated with it. To transform this process in preparation for creation of the structure chart, we need to create a scenario in which each new process has either a single input with multiple outputs or a single output from multiple inputs. As shown in Figure 13-4b, two new processes were created, each with a single output.

The second step in the transformation process is to add those processes that are associated with reading, modifying, and deleting data from the various data stores on the DFD. To eliminate clutter and confusion, these types of processes are often omitted from the logical DFD during analysis. Now, however, they must be identified and appropriately designed into the DFD. Figure 13-5 illustrates this step in the preparation process.

Finally, several elements necessary for effective program execution were not under consideration during the design and construction of the logical DFD. For the most part, these elements represent processes focused on exceptions, error trapping, and internal control issues. Issues such as input editing and validation controls, exception handling in instances such as missing or incomplete data, and the creation and preservation of an internal audit trail must now be designed into the system so that program code can be written to facilitate their execution.

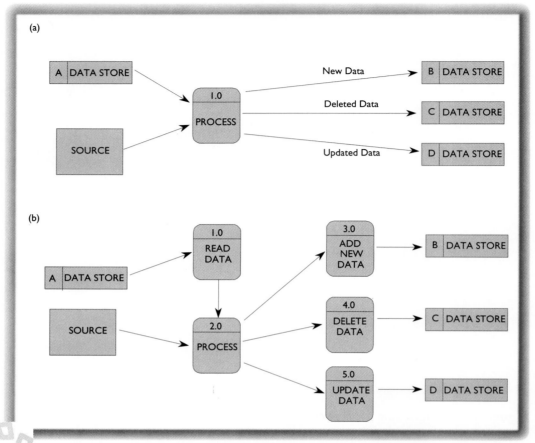

Figure 13-5   Example of Adding Data Access and Maintenance Processes to a DFD

Once the DFD has been prepared for transformation in a structure chart, one of two strategies can be employed to effect the transformation process: (1) transform analysis or (2) transaction analysis.

Transform Analysis

Using a *transform analysis* strategy for conversion, the analyst examines the DFD and divides the various processes into three categories: (1) those that perform either input or input editing functions, (2) those that actually perform calculations or process data, and (3) those that serve to create or finalize system output. Figure 13-6 illustrates this categorization strategy using a simplified DFD.

Following the tenets of the structured design approach, we refer to those processes that are responsible for the input side of the equation as *afferent processes*. The processes responsible for actual transformation of data are referred to as the *central transform*, and the output side processes are called *efferent processes*. Although the categorization of a complex DFD can be both time consuming and somewhat tedious, the process can be organized such that it becomes quickly repetitive. One common way to do this is to trace each afferent process data flow forward through the system until it disappears and to trace each efferent process data flow backward until it also disappears. The point, or points, at which all afferent and efferent data

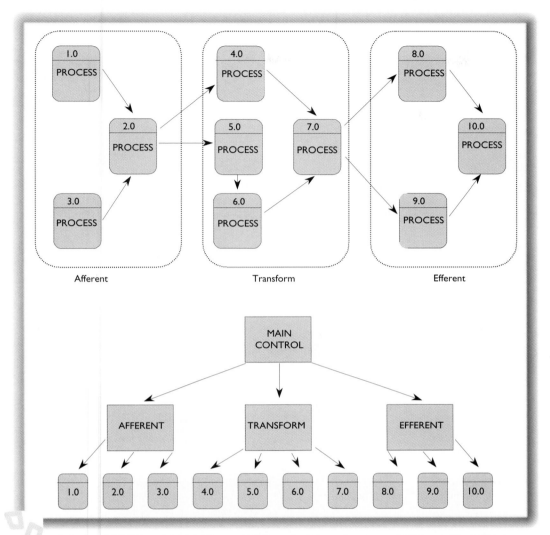

Figure 13-6   The Categorization into Afferent, Transform, and Efferent Processes Implies a Hierarchical Control Structure

flows disappear is the central transform. Once the DFD is partitioned into the three categories, the structure chart can begin to be constructed. Figure 13-7a contains a categorized DFD for a portion of a simple order processing system DFD that we use to illustrate the transformation process. Figure 13-7b illustrates the first-draft structure diagram derived from the DFD.

As you can see by comparing Figures 13.7a and 13.7b, the first-draft structure chart bears a close resemblance to the DFD from which it was derived. Once this conversion has successfully occurred, the analyst must then begin to enhance the structure diagram by adding additional modules and data couples to provide functionality associated with getting input via the user interface; reading, writing, modifying, and deleting to data stores; and generating formatted output data or reports. These additional modules are referred to as *utility modules* and are generally found

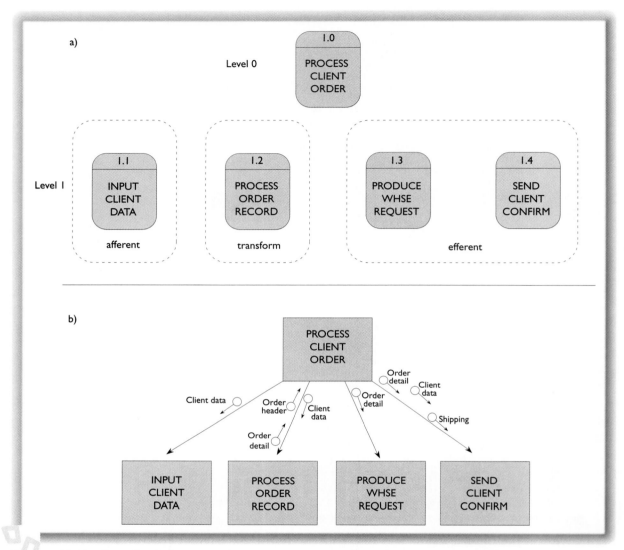

Figure 13-7 First Draft Structure Diagram from a Simple DFD

in the lower-levels of the diagram. Figure 13-8 illustrates our revised structure diagram with the utility modules added.

Once the utility modules and their intermodule relationships have been added to the structure diagram, the analyst can proceed to evaluate the quality of the design using the guidelines discussed earlier in this chapter. Proper coupling, cohesion, span, and factoring insure high-quality executable code is developed and a successful application realized.

Transaction Analysis

The other approach to the development of a structure diagram is called *transaction analysis*. This approach examines the DFD for the purpose of identifying processes that represent transaction centers.

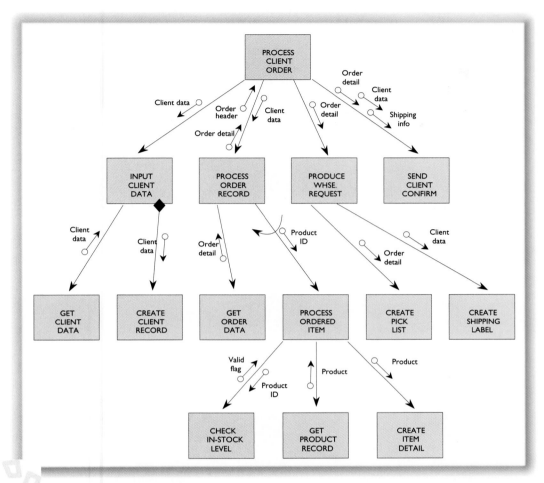

Figure 13-8   Detailed Structure Diagram

Transaction Center

The concept of a *transaction center* is based on the traffic cop metaphor. Although not actually performing any transformation process, the traffic cop directs the flow of cars through the intersection in (hopefully) a logical manner. In much the same way, certain processes on the DFD can be categorized as being directors of the data flow to subordinate processes that actually perform the calculations. It is possible to have a system that contains both transform centers and transaction centers, but generally, the overall application design manifests itself as primarily one or the other. Several common application types, such as file maintenance programs that support functions based on the type of input transaction or on-line systems that are designed to support multiple levels of transactions, are commonly associated with a transaction-centered design. Figure 13-9 illustrates the transaction analysis approach to conversion of a generalized DFD.

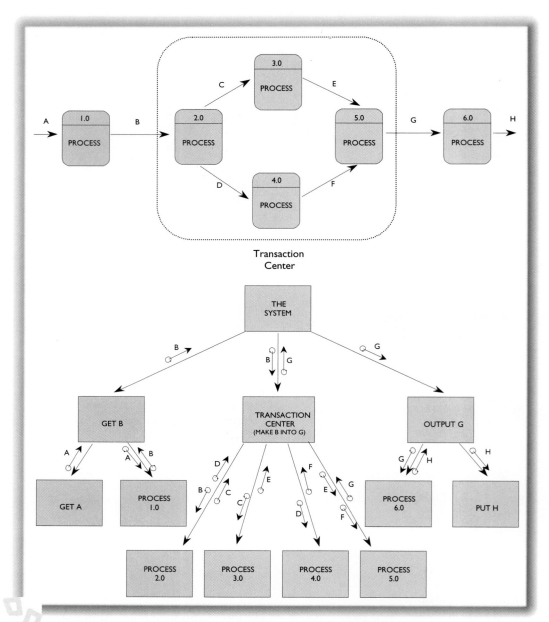

Figure 13-9   Transaction Analysis Approach to Deriving a Structure Diagram
Source: Adapted from Demarco (1979, p. 320).

Advantages and Disadvantages of Hierarchical Structure Diagrams

The development and use of a structure diagram to facilitate the program coding process brings with it several advantages. First, it allows the evolution of the actual program code to occur in the same logical step-by-step manner that was employed in constructing the logical DFD. All of the various system components described by the DFD, data dictionaries, and data models are directly incorporated into a single, logical program design. In addition, by arranging the program into a hierarchical set of modules, the program structure becomes both well-organized and easily manageable. Finally, the structure diagram allows for a detailed quality analysis of the various modules within the system with regard to appropriate coupling and cohesion such that any errors or future upgrade requirements are localized and, thus, easier to correct or add.

The advantages of developing a structure chart do not come without a cost, however. To begin, it must be acknowledged that the development of a good structure chart requires a great deal of effort. The examples provided in this chapter are much more simplified than the typical scenarios you will encounter in actual practice. Nonetheless, the techniques are the same regardless of the complexity of the task, and through practice, an analyst can become quite adept at transforming DFDs into high-quality structure diagrams. In addition, most modern CASE tools do not yet completely facilitate the conversion of a leveled set of DFDs into a finished structure diagram. Because of this, the analyst is faced with manually creating the diagram and thus becomes responsible for its reconciliation to the other logical models of the system. Despite these disadvantages, however, the hierarchical structure chart has become a mainstay tool in the application development process, and you can expect to encounter it regularly throughout your career as a systems analyst.

CHAPTER SUMMARY

We have completed the design of our system from its early conceptual form to its final physical form. The conversion of the logical DFDs into a usable set of structure charts has transformed our system from a logical sequence of processes and data flows into a well-structured set of modules that are related in both an effective and efficient manner. Although we are almost to the end of the life cycle, we still are faced with the phase often thought of by experienced analysts as the most daunting and important set of activities: systems implementation. The final chapter of this text is devoted to discussing strategies and issues associated with moving the system from the programmers to the end users.

KEY CONCEPTS

➤ Modular design

Modular design is a systems design approach that decomposes a large, complex software application into smaller, interrelated components called modules. A module is defined as a group of executable instructions that has a single point of entry and a single point of exit. It is designed to perform its functions independently from all other modules contained within the application.

The goal of a systems designer is to create a system that is easy to read and understand, easy to code and revise, and easy to maintain. Guidelines for good systems design include

• System factoring

The system should be factored, or decomposed, into small modules that conform to both the size and cohesion guidelines of good design.

• Bottom-up approach

A bottom-up approach identifies the processes that need to be a part of the system and then moves forward to code each identified process as a module that interfaces with all other identified process modules.

- Top-down approach
  Following the top-down approach, the system is first viewed in the broadest possible sense and then decomposed into subsystems that work together to efficiently and effectively reach the stated objectives for the overall system.
- Span of control
  No parent module should be given more than 5 to 7 child, or subordinate, modules.
- Module cohesion
  Module cohesion can be thought of as a measure of completeness. The instructions contained within a module should pertain only to that function.
- Module size
  A reasonable size for a single module is considered to be between 50 and 100 lines of executable code.
- Module coupling
  The extent to which modules are dependent on each other should be minimized such that the amount of communication between dependent modules is also minimized. Ideally, module communication should occur only via passed data elements and information flags.
  - Tight coupling
    Tightly coupled modules display high interdependence and create a greater possibility of program error.
  - Loose coupling
    Modules that are completely independent are loosely coupled modules.
- Shared module use
  Wherever possible, a child module should be called by multiple parent modules.

➤ Types of cohesion
- Functional cohesion
  Under functional cohesion the modules are designed such that their instructions work collectively to accomplish a single, well-defined task or function.
- Sequential cohesion
  Sequential cohesion is defined as the relationship between one instruction and the next in a given module.

- Communicational cohesion
  Communicational cohesion occurs when a module is designed such that its instructions accomplish tasks that use the same piece of data but the sequence of those instructions is not critical to a successful outcome.
- Procedural cohesion
  Procedural cohesion occurs when the instruction set in a module performs multiple functions that have a specific sequence in which they must be performed.
- Temporal cohesion
  Modules that have instructions grouped together because of some common relationship based on time are referred to as displaying temporal cohesion.
- Logical cohesion
  In modules displaying logical cohesion, instructions are related to each other only because they appear to fall into the same logical class of function.
- Coincidental cohesion
  Coincidental cohesion occurs in modules that have instructions that bear little or no relationship to each other. Any cohesion resulting is based solely on coincidence.

➤ Types of coupling
- Data coupling
  The dependency between the two modules is limited to the fact that they pass data between each other.
- Stamp coupling
  Data are passed between modules in the form of data structure or entire records.
- Control coupling
  Control information or flags are passed between modules.
- Common coupling
  Two modules are common coupled if they both refer to the same global data area or one module modifies the procedural content of the other module.

➤ Hierarchical structure diagrams
  The top-down approach to systems development using modules is called structured design. The most common design tool for structured design is called the

hierarchical structure diagram or structure chart. This diagram displays the relationships of the modules to each other and displays the flow and processing of data between and within the various modules of the system in a hierarchical form.

➤ Steps in constructing a hierarchical structure diagram

1. Preparing the DFDs

   A. Insure that all processes contained on the DFD perform only one function.

   B. Add the processes that are associated with reading, modifying, and deleting data from the various data stores on the DFD.

   C. Add elements that are necessary for effective program execution but were not under consideration during the design and construction of the logical DFD.

2. Transforming the DFDs into a structure chart

   A. Transform analysis

      (1) Examine the DFD and divide the various processes into three categories.

          (a) Those that perform either input or input editing functions.

          (b) Those that actually perform calculations or process data.

          (c) Those that serve to create or finalize system outputs.

      (2) Construct the structure chart.

      (3) Evaluate the quality of the design.

   B. Transaction analysis

      This approach examines the DFD for the purpose of identifying processes that represent transaction centers.

➤ Afferent processes

Afferent processes are those processes that are responsible for the input side of the equation.

➤ Efferent processes

Efferent processes are processes that are responsible for actual transformation of data.

➤ Pros and cons of hierarchical structure diagrams

• Advantages

   • They allow the evolution of the actual program code to occur in the same logical step-by-step manner that was employed in constructing the logical DFD.

   • By arranging the program into a hierarchical set of modules, the program structure becomes both well-organized and easily manageable.

   • The structure diagram allows for a detailed quality analysis of the various modules within the system such that any errors or future upgrade requirements are localized and easier to correct or add.

• Disadvantages

   • The construction of a good structure chart requires a great deal of effort.

   • Most CASE tools do not yet completely facilitate the conversion of a leveled set of DFDs into a finished structure diagram.

QUESTIONS FOR REVIEW

1. Briefly describe the concept of modular design.

2. How is a module defined in a modular system design?

3. List and briefly describe the guidelines for good systems design.

4. Compare the bottom-up and top-down system factoring approaches. Why is the top-down system factoring approach better than the bottom-up approach?

5. Briefly describe the main benefit of module cohesiveness.

6. List and briefly describe the seven types of module cohesion.

7. Why are loosely coupled modules better than tightly coupled modules in systems design?

8. Use the concept of tramp data to explain how module dependency could be minimized.

9. List and briefly describe the types of module coupling.

10. Explain the main difference between a DFD and a structure diagram.

11. What are the elements that are often omitted from a DFD but are necessary in a structure diagram?

12. List and briefly describe the three steps in preparing the DFDs for transformation into structure charts.

13. Describe afferent processes and efferent processes.

14. Explain the concept of utility modules in a structure diagram.

15. Describe the transformation process of a DFD to a structure diagram using transform analysis.

16. Explain the concept of a transaction center in the transaction analysis.

17. What are the pros and cons of hierarchical structure diagrams?

FOR FURTHER DISCUSSION

1. Draw a hierarchical structure diagram from the DFD specified.
   a) Figure 13-10a contains a DFD of a simple system for managing a cooperative education center at a university. Draw a structure diagram using this DFD.
   b) Figure 13-10b contains a DFD for a simple job scheduling system. Draw a structure diagram using this DFD.

2. Figure 13-11 contains modules that are too closely coupled and possibly lack cohesiveness. Redraw the structure diagram such that the modules are loosely coupled and functionally cohesive.

3. Of what value would an existing hierarchical structure diagram of the current system be to an analyst conducting a detail requirements analysis for a proposed upgrade to the system?

4. Identify the transaction centers in the following description:
   The program allows the end user to conduct inquires with regard to customer accounts, orders, invoices, and products. Using the system, the end user can obtain general information concerning an existing order or information about specific orders that are currently flagged with a back order status. Such inquiries can be made for back orders less than one week old, more than one week old but less than two weeks old, or more than two weeks old. Additionally, end users can query the system with regard to specific parts or back-ordered parts.

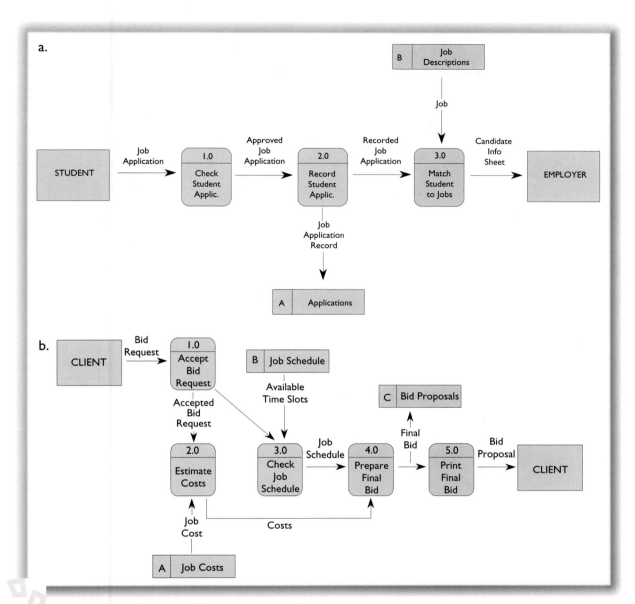

Figure 13-10   a. DFD for Further Discussion Question 1(a)
b. DFD for Further Discussion Question 1(b)

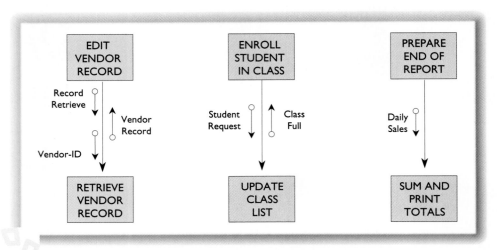

Figure 13-11   Diagrams for Further Discussion Question 2

REFERENCES

Demarco, T. 1979. *Structured Analysis and System Specification*. Englewood Cliffs, NJ: Prentice Hall.

Page-Jones, M. 1980. *The Practical Guide to Structured Systems Design*. New York: Yourdon Press.

Yourdon, E., and Constantine. 1979. *Structured Design*. Englewood Cliffs, NJ: Prentice Hall.

Chapter 14

Implementing and Maintaining the System

Learning Objectives

- Understand the activities associated with the system implementation phase of the SDLC
- Understand the range of appropriate test procedures for a given application
- Identify and select the most suitable conversion strategy for a new application
- Understand the various types of user and system documentation
- Understand the activities and constraints associated with the systems maintenance phase of the SDLC

There are two ways of implementing a software design; one way is to make it so simple that there are obviously no deficiencies, and the other way is to make it so complicated that there are no obvious deficiencies. The first method is far more difficult.
—C. A. R HOARE, JAMES MARTIN PROFESSOR OF COMPUTING, WOLFSON COLLEGE

INTRODUCTION

We have reached the beginning of the end. That is to say that implementation marks the final stage in the systems development process, and on completion, we move into the activities associated with maintaining the system. Shortly after maintenance begins, we also begin the process all over again by developing new systems or updating old ones.

During the implementation phase, the analyst is faced with many, often complex, pressures. At this point, the system has not yet been turned over to the end users, but the date is probably set, and the open anticipation of the new system brings with it a variety of challenges. Some users are excited about the prospect of the system and eagerly await its arrival. Others view the new system with anxiety and dread the day it arrives. Regardless of the perspective, however, none of the end

385

users has ever used the new system in its entirety, and therefore, all must be trained. Further, if the new system is replacing one currently in operation, the method by which the new system is turned on and the old one is turned off can pose a challenge to all participants in the project equal in magnitude to the development process itself. Although implementation officially begins and ends in the latter stages of the development life cycle, the analyst has, in reality, been preparing for it since the first day of the project.

WHAT IS SYSTEM IMPLEMENTATION?

By definition, *system implementation* involves those activities associated with ensuring that the new system is fully functional and operational, as well as those activities associated with turning over control of the new system to the end users. One ongoing debate among systems developers and analysts is with regard to the grammatical category of the word *implementation*. Is it a noun or a verb? In other words, is implementation an event that occurs (noun), or is it a series of actions that must be performed (verb)? The answer is that it is actually both. The implementation of a new system is generally remembered by the end users as the day it actually happened, the day the system was put into actual use. Implementation from the analysts' perspective, however, is generally thought of as the last set of activities that must be performed before the end users can begin to realize the benefits associated with the new system. Both parties look forward to implementation, albeit often for different reasons.

Because our perspective is that of the analyst, we discuss implementation as a series of activities that must be performed prior to turning over the system to the end users and that are essential to the end users successfully enjoying the benefits of the new system. In our world, implementation is definitely a verb.

For our purposes, we divide the process of system implementation into three categories of activities: (1) application testing and user acceptance, (2) user training and final documentation, and (3) system installation and conversion.

APPLICATION TESTING

We can assume that the quality of the application, from a functionality perspective at least, is directly related to the quality of logical design created by the analyst team. This assumption is based, of course, on the assumed skill and acumen of the programmers themselves. No professional programmer is ever going to purposely write unusable or dysfunctional code. Despite these good intentions, however, we are subject to human error, and the complexity of a typical IS makes thorough and comprehensive testing of the final applications an essential element in implementing a new system.

As with the development process itself, the testing activities during implementation must be carefully structured and meticulously conducted to insure that every aspect of the new system has been checked and rechecked. The goal is 100 percent error-free code.

This goal, although lofty, is unfortunately rarely, if ever, achieved. The fact is that all software is faulty. The real question is whether the embedded faults are discoverable through testing or must lie in wait for some unsuspecting end user to initiate the right sequence of events to uncover the latent defect. In an effort to minimize, if not completely remove, the "bugs" in the system, a structured approach to

Table 14-1   Classification of Software Tests

	Manual Test	Automated Test
Static	Inspection	Syntax check
Dynamic	Walkthrough	Unit test
	Desk check	Integration test
		System test

final testing must be followed. Table 14-1 contains one such structured categorization method for system testing proposed by Mosley (1993).

Mosley's classification divides the system testing activities into four categories based on whether the code being tested is actually executed and whether the test is conducted via the computer or manually by the analyst or programmer. Tests in which the code is actually inspected are often referred to as *white-box tests,* because the code being inspected is subject to programmer bias rather than pure, unbiased logic. Further, the order in which the tests are performed can have a material effect on the overall quality of the testing activities. We discuss the various types of tests in the order of most logical sequence.

Code Inspection

The first step in the testing process is to conduct a formal *code inspection.* The participants in this test are normally skilled programmers and analysts, and their objective is to inspect the actual source code for the occurrence of certain types of errors commonly associated with the language in which the program has been written. Figure 14-1 contains an excerpt from a detailed code inspection checklist for applications written in C++.

The more common syntax and grammar errors that may exist are normally checked using an automated inspection application such that the code inspection team can focus on errors that may not be syntactically or grammatically incorrect but may cause the logic of the code to fail nonetheless. Because this is a static test, no attention is given to what the code actually does. Using an inspection team of 5 to 7 members, the focus is limited to purely structural and syntactic issues, and no evaluation of the quality of the code or the design is conducted. Typically, each team member can inspect approximately 70 to 120 lines of code per hour, and each inspection meeting generally lasts no more than 2 to 3 hours. Given these constraints, it is easy to see that a large, complex application may take several days or even weeks to inspect completely.

Fagan (1986) estimates that a formal code inspection can result in the detection of 50 to 70 percent of the software defects contained in a given application. Though tedious in nature, the payoff of a formal code inspection comes in the form of a successful, bug-free application.

Structured Walkthrough

Needless to say, at some point we must turn our attention to testing whether the code actually performs the functions intended by the designers. The first opportunity to conduct such a test comes with the *structured walkthrough.* There is no

C++ Inspection Checklist

I VARIABLE DECLARATIONS
1.1 Arrays
1.1.1 Is an array dimensioned to a hard-coded constant?

```
        int intarray[13];
should be
        int intarray[TOT_MONTHS+1];
```

1.1.2 Is the array dimensioned to the total number of items?

```
        char entry[TOTAL_ENTRIES];
should be
        char entry[LAST_ENTRY+1];
```

The first example is extremely error-prone and often gives rise to off-by-one errors in the code. The preferred (second) method permits the writer to use the LAST_ENTRY identifier to refer to the last item in the array. Instances which require a buffer of a certain size are rarely rendered invalid by this practice, which results in the buffer being one element bigger than absolutely necessary.

1.2 Constants
1.2.1 Does the value of the variable never change?

```
        int months_in_year = 12;
should be
        const unsigned months_in_year = 12;
```

1.2.2 Are constants declared with the preprocessor #define mechanism?

```
        #define MAX_FILES 20
should be
        const unsigned MAX_FILES = 20;
```

1.2.3 Is the usage of the constant limited to only a few (or perhaps only one) class?
If so, is the constant global?

```
        const unsigned MAX_FOOS = 1000;
        const unsigned MAX_FOO_BUFFERS = 40;
should be
        class foo {
        public:
            enum { MAX_INSTANCES = 1000; }
            ...
            private:
            enum { MAX_FOO_BUFFERS = 40; }
            ...
        };
```

If the size of the constant exceeds int, another mechanism is available:

```
        class bar {
          public:
            static const long MAX_INSTS;
            ...
        };

        const long bar::MAX_INSTS = 70000L;
```

The keyword static ensures there is only one instance of the variable for the entire class. Static data items are not permitted to be initialized within the class declaration, so the initialization line must be included in the implementation file for class bar. Static constant members have one drawback: you cannot use them to declare member data arrays of a certain size. This is because the value is not available to the compiler at the point which the array is declared in the class.

1.3 Scalar Variables
1.3.1 Does a negative value of the variable make no sense? If so, is the variable signed?

```
        int age;
should be
        unsigned int age;
```

This is an easy error to make, since the default types are usually signed.

1.3.2 Does the code assume char is either signed or unsigned?

```
        typedef char SmallInt;
        SmallInt mumble = 280; // WRONG on Borland C++ 3.1
        // or MSC/C++ 7.0!
The typedefs should be
        typedef  unsigned  char SmallUInt;
        typedef  signed  char SmallInt;
```

1.3.3 Does the program unnecessarily use float or double ?

```
        double acct_balance;
should be
```

Figure 14-1   Excerpt from a Formal Code Inspection Checklist for C++

substitute for a close examination of the embedded logic in the code. The code walkthrough has been a valued practice since before the birth of software engineering as a concept. Unfortunately, reverence for it is not always matched in practice.

Many organizations believe they are "too busy" for structured code reviews, because the reviews mean that everyone in the team will be too busy trying to track down bugs to make ship dates. This position is, however, evidence of a false economy. The other reason the practice has been neglected is that fast compilers and visual debuggers can convince developers that a quick compile substitutes for a code review, and if a bug shows up the debugger can track it down. The problem with this assumption, however, is that testing does not find as many bugs as a good review, and in particular, it often does not cover the subtle race or run-on conditions that can arise in multithreaded code.

Although the emphasis in a structured walkthrough is on detecting errors with regard to what the code is supposed to do, the reviewers must refrain from making corrections to the code. This is the responsibility of the programmer in charge of that section of code. When the changes have been made, the code is then resubmitted for walkthrough.

The Desk Check

The actual execution of the code is also the focus when conducting a *desk check*. This approach has one or more programmers, not responsible for the actual writing of the code, working through a hardcopy of source code, mentally simulating the control flow. In a sense, the desk check uses the programmer as a human computer to execute each instruction and evaluate the accuracy of the results. No longer common practice in this age of on-screen editing, fast compiles, and sophisticated debuggers, though some veteran programmers maintain stoutly that it ought to be, the desk check is nonetheless a viable debugging technique.

Module Testing

Once the static, white-box inspections have been completed, the testing activities can focus on the use of available dynamic tests to complete the process. The first of these is the *module test*. Sometimes referred to as the *unit test*, module testing focuses on ascertaining the successful execution of each application module prior to integrating it with other tested modules. The goal of module testing is to identify and correct as many errors as possible before integrating the modules into larger, more complex software units in which errors can become more difficult to isolate and fix.

Module testing is also considered to be one of the primary *black-box* tests that must be performed. It is generally believed that when the person who wrote the code also performs the tests, such as in a desk check, an innate bias is present. Because the programmer has intimate knowledge of the module's logic, the tests conducted to insure proper execution may actually be biased in favor of the design. In black-box testing, however, the module is not inspected and is usually not tested by its author. Instead, it is treated like a black-box and fed typical (and sometimes not so typical) input, while the resultant output is evaluated for conformance to expectations. As with the static code tests, module testing should not be viewed as a witch hunt in which the quality of the programmer is being evaluated. Instead, such testing should be viewed as simply another method of ferreting out coding or logic errors that were not discovered during the static testing activities.

Recall from our discussion of module cohesion and factoring in chapter 13 that an ideal module design focuses on the performance of a single function or process step. Further, a hierarchical design that uses parent control modules to call lower-level functional modules should also be employed. Assuming these guidelines are followed and their goals successfully achieved, then the question of how best to test the individual modules must be answered. One approach is to use a *bottom-up* method that tests the lowest-level modules first and then methodically integrates each of them into the next higher level. Because modules are not designed to execute in complete isolation from the rest of the application and are usually called by a higher-level control module, a *test driver* is written to facilitate the test. The test driver simulates the control environment for the module under test by providing simulated input or receiving module output. The main disadvantage to this approach is that each low-level module most likely requires its own, unique test driver for testing. This results in a great deal of additional code being written that ultimately is discarded and that may introduce new avenues of error into the tests.

Stub Testing

The current standards for module testing call for the employment of a *top-down* approach referred to as *stub testing*. In a top-down testing scenario, the highest-level control module is tested first, and the lower-level modules are simulated by a program stub, a two or three line module, containing no logic, that is designed to simply accept control from a high-level module and return it back to that module. In some cases, a stub can output a simple message indicating a successful call to the correct subordinate module. Once the high-level control module has been thoroughly tested, each subordinate module can be individually tested and its corresponding test stub discarded. Figure 14-2 illustrates the use of stub tests in a top-down approach.

Figure 14-2   Stub Testing Using a Top-Down Approach

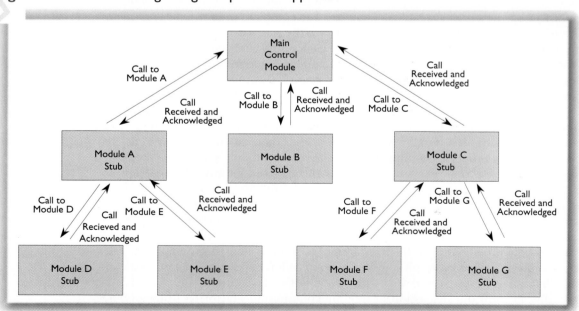

Integration Testing

Following completion of the module testing, the *integration testing* begins. This phase of the testing process focuses on testing the behavior of an entire group of modules to identify errors that either were not or could not be detected at the unit level. One of the most significant aspects of this testing phase is the *integration strategy*. Integration may be performed *all at once* (big-bang), *top-down, bottom-up, critical piece first,* or by first integrating functional subsystems and then integrating the subsystems in separate phases using any of the basic strategies. In general, the larger the project, the more important the integration strategy.

Very small systems are often assembled and tested in one phase. For most real systems, this is impractical for two major reasons. First, the system may fail in so many places at once that the debugging and retesting effort would be impractical. Second, satisfying any white-box testing criterion would be very difficult, because of the vast amount of detail separating the input data from the individual code modules. In fact, most integration testing has been traditionally limited to black-box techniques. Large systems may require many integration phases, beginning with assembling modules into low-level subsystems, then assembling subsystems into larger subsystems, and finally assembling the highest-level subsystems into the complete system.

To be most effective, an integration testing technique should fit well with the overall integration strategy. In a multiphase integration, testing at each phase helps detect errors early and keep the system under control. Performing only cursory testing at early integration phases and then applying a more rigorous criterion for the final stage is really just a variant of the high-risk big-bang approach. However, performing rigorous testing of the entire software involved in each integration phase involves a lot of wasteful duplication of effort across phases. The key is to leverage the overall integration structure to allow rigorous testing at each phase while minimizing duplication of effort.

It is important to understand the relationship between module testing and integration testing. In one view, modules are rigorously tested in isolation using stubs and drivers before any integration is attempted. Then, integration testing concentrates entirely on module interactions, assuming that the details within each module are accurate. At the other extreme, module and integration testing can be combined, verifying the details of each module's implementation in an integration context. Many projects compromise, combining module testing with the lowest level of subsystem integration testing and then performing pure integration testing at higher levels. Each of these views of integration testing may be appropriate for any given project, so an integration testing method should be flexible enough to accommodate them all. Although a thorough discussion of all of the variants associated with integration testing is well beyond the scope of this text, the rest of this section provides an overview of the various integration-level structured testing techniques.

The simplest application of structured testing to integration is to combine module testing with integration testing so that a basis set of paths through each module is executed in an integration context. Although this approach does afford a certain level of efficiency in the testing process, it also brings with it a greater combinatorial problem in locating an error when one arises.

The most obvious combined strategy is pure big-bang integration, in which the entire system is assembled and tested in one step without even prior module testing. As discussed earlier, this strategy is not practical for most real systems.

However, at least in theory, it makes efficient use of testing resources. First, there is no overhead associated with constructing stubs and drivers to perform module testing or partial integration. Second, no additional integration-specific tests are required beyond the module tests as determined by structured testing. Thus, despite its impracticality, this strategy clarifies the benefits of combining module testing with integration testing to the greatest feasible extent.

It is also possible to combine module and integration testing with the bottom-up integration strategy. This strategy begins by performing module-level structured testing on the lowest-level modules using test drivers but not stubs. Then module-level structured testing is performed in a similar fashion at each successive level of the design hierarchy, using test drivers for each new module being tested in integration with all lower-level modules. Figure 14-3 illustrates this technique.

First, the lowest-level modules B and C are tested with drivers. Next, the higher-level module A is tested with a driver in integration with modules B and C. Finally, integration continues until the top-level module of the program is tested (with real input data) in integration with the entire program. As shown in Figure 14-3, the total number of tests required by this technique is the sum of the cyclomatic complexities $(v[X])$[1] of all modules being integrated. Cyclomatic complexity

Figure 14-3   Combined Module and Integration Testing Strategy

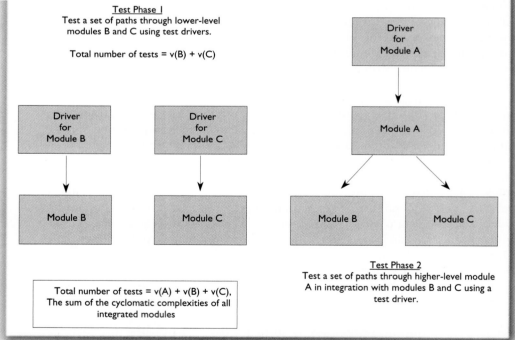

---

[1] Cyclomatic complexity is the most widely used member of a class of static software metrics. Cyclomatic complexity may be considered a broad measure of soundness and confidence for a program. Introduced by Thomas McCabe in 1976, it measures the number of linearly independent paths through a program module. This measure provides a single ordinal number that can be compared to the complexity of other programs. Cyclomatic complexity is often referred to simply as program complexity or as McCabe's complexity. It is often used in concert with other software metrics. As one of the more widely accepted software metrics, it is intended to be independent of language and language format.

is a measure for the complexity of code related to the number of ways there are to traverse a piece of code. It is determined by the minimum number of inputs you need to test all ways to execute the program. In our example, as expected, this is the same number of tests that would be required to perform structured testing on each module in isolation using stubs and drivers.

System Testing

Following integration, it is time for the *system test*. Here the behavior of the entire system is under scrutiny, and the goal is to have no errors or anomalies remaining. Although system testing is similar in nature to integration testing, the difference between them lies in the focus of the test. System testing specifically goes after behaviors and bugs that are properties of the entire system, as distinct from properties attributable to components (unless, of course, the component in question is the entire system). Examples of system testing issues are resource loss bugs, throughput bugs, performance, security, recovery, and transaction synchronization bugs (often misnamed "timing bugs").

Typically, the system test includes all activities to be incorporated into the user acceptance test. In the system test phase, however, the end users are typically not involved. This gives the designers and programmers a dry run period in which to isolate and remove all system-related bugs. One of the most common approaches to system testing is the build and smoke test.

Build and Smoke Test

A typical software development team project involves building an executable program from up to thousands of different files. At Microsoft, for example, software development teams practice the daily *build and smoke test* process in which they compile every file, combine them into a single executable program, and put it through a smoke test to see if it runs. A smoke test exercises the entire system to expose any major problems. The daily build is not valuable unless accompanied by a smoke test. The smoke test can quickly reveal any changes to the code made during integration that, although effective in isolation, cause problems when fully integrated at the system level.

Performing daily build and smoke tests provides a number of important benefits. As discussed, the practice minimizes code integration risk by identifying incompatible code early and allowing the programmers and designers to make debugging or redesign decisions. In addition, the practice supports improved defect diagnosis, making it easier to pinpoint why the product may be broken on any single day. Finally, and probably most important, the practice significantly reduces the risk of a low quality application.

To produce the greatest benefits, the development team must perform the daily build and smoke test each day—not weekly or monthly. The software being built must work, or else the build is viewed as broken and it must be fixed. Performing daily build and smoke tests is like trying to ship a product every day, which enforces a sense of discipline on the team. Standards for daily build and smoke tests vary from project to project, but at a minimum they should include

➤ Compiling all files and components successfully

➤ Linking all files and components successfully

➤ Finding no showstopper bugs that would make the program hazardous to operate or prevent it from launching

➤ Passing the smoke test

USER ACCEPTANCE TESTING

Acceptance testing is the process by which the end user verifies that the delivered and installed product is ready to be put into production use. From the end user's point of view, this means that every user-oriented function should be thoroughly exercised. Acceptance testing proceeds from the user's perspective, so it cannot thoroughly test the exceptional conditions that arise during the operation of a product, such as system failures, timing problems, and so forth. Users can, however, test most user-oriented functions under exceptional cases, for example, ensuring that record locking is operating when two users attempt to modify the same record or handling devices being off-line.

We often distinguish two kinds of acceptance testing. *Alpha testing*, also referred to as *verification testing*, is done by the client at the developer's site, with assistance and monitoring by the developer. In most cases, the alpha test uses simulated data typical of the data types and ranges of values expected. *Beta testing*, also called *validation testing*, is conducted by the end users at their own site, with no analyst or developer on hand. During the beta test, the system is exercised using live data in the actual working environment for the system. An audit of the test is normally conducted by the end user organization's internal audit group or by some other agency independent of the development team.

Typically, the acceptance test is organized as a script. The script is designed to verify that the major functions are properly operating in their most common mode. Then the testing proceeds to minor functions or rarer operating modes. In all cases, certain exceptional condition testing is performed to see how the functions handle error conditions or precondition violations.

A typical acceptance testing script is hierarchically organized by subsystem and function. The top level of the script gives the overall plan for sequencing the tests. It should indicate what tests can be done in parallel and what results from the current test must be achieved to proceed to the next tests. A test can have one of three results:

➤ PASS (P)—the test is passed
➤ RESERVATION (R)—the test is passed except for minor deviations that do not seriously affect functionality
➤ FAIL (F)—the test failed

The minimum acceptable result for each test is specified, and the step in the plan proceeds if all tests achieve the minimum standard. Note that your application might be in a state where certain tests fail, because a feature is not yet ready or has a known bug. In that case, the expected result of the test is the failure.

Although the actual activities associated with user acceptance testing of a specific application or system vary, there are some guidelines that should be adhered to when conducting such a test. Reid (1991) has assembled a list of guidelines in the form of a set of commandments to be followed by both end users and analysts during user acceptance testing. Table 14-2 lists Reid's commandments of acceptance testing.

The 16 Commandments in Table 14-2 provide a methodology, checklist, and hierarchy for planning systems and acceptance policies, processes, and procedures. If followed, the commandments allow and cause developers, users, testers, vendors, and installation managers alike to create, install, and accept systems better able to handle the organization's needs and objectives at a minimum of cost. The price of

Table 14-2   The 16 Commandments of User Acceptance Testing

I. THE REALITIES
1. Thou cannot test everything.
2. Thou shalt let risk point you to the most important errors.
3. Thou shalt not confuse 1000 tests with testing 1000 functions.
4. Thou shalt hunt where the elephants drink—practice creative error guessing.

II. THE ATTITUDES
5. Thou shalt not build on bad specifications and unclear interpretations.
6. Good tests need good code and good design.
7. Let thy enemy design and perform your tests.
8. Honor thy reference checks.

III. THE TECHNOLOGIES
9. Thou shalt control changes.
10. Thou shalt commit to regression testing.
11. Test thy documentation.
12. Test for performance or perish.

IV. THE CORNERSTONES
13. Accept running programs—not working programs (unit testing).
14. Bless off-the-shelf software more carefully than custom software.
15. Thou shalt cultivate and win management and user commitment and understanding.
16. Thou shalt measure progress—and know when to stop.

a failed installation, given the mission-critical use of computers and information resources in today's business environments, simply cannot be tolerated.

INSTALLING THE SYSTEM

We have tested our system, the end users have tested our system, and the auditors have monitored and approved our test results. The time has come that we must turn the system over to the end users so they can begin to realize the benefits that we have worked so long to create for them. Although an exciting time, to be sure, this is often one of the most chaotic and mission-critical stages of the process. This is because we suddenly are faced with three major activities that must occur almost simultaneously, two of which require both the patience and tolerance of literally the entire end user community. At this stage, we are faced with three tasks: (1) system conversion, (2) final documentation, and (3) end user training.

System Conversion

System conversion refers to the activities and processes associated with replacing the existing operational system with the new system. Following this process, all end users, regardless of whether they were directly involved in the design and testing, are now faced with giving up their dependence on the old, familiar system and converting their reliance and allegiance to the new system. This change is by no means easy to accept, and for some, it may be one of the most difficult mental and emotional work-related challenges ever faced. The method by which this change takes place can have a dramatic effect on the successful conversion to the new system and the management of change by the end users. Four basic strategies exist for system conversion, each of which possesses certain characteristics that may be more or less desirable, depending on the complexity of the change and the overall risk aversion of the organization.

Direct Conversion

The simplest conversion strategy, and probably the most disruptive to the organization, is the *direct conversion* approach. This method, sometimes referred to as the *slam dunk* or *cold-turkey* strategy, is as abrupt as its name implies. Using this approach, the old system is simply turned off, and the new system is turned on in its place. Although this method is the least expensive of all available strategies and may be the only viable solution in situations where activating the new system is an emergency or when the two systems cannot coexist under any conditions, it is also the one that poses the greatest risk of failure. Once the new system becomes operational, the end users must cope with any errors or dysfunctions, and depending on the severity of the problem, this approach can have a significant effect on the quality of the work performed. Direct conversion should be considered only in extreme circumstances where no other conversion strategy is viable.

Parallel Conversion

At the opposite end of the risk spectrum is the *parallel conversion* strategy. Here, the old and new systems are run simultaneously until the end users and project coordinators are fully satisfied that the new system is functioning correctly and the old system is no longer necessary. Using this approach, a parallel conversion can be effected with either a *single cutover,* where a predetermined date for stopping the parallel operation is set, or a *phased cutover,* where some predetermined method of phasing in each piece of the new system and turning off a similar piece of the old system is employed.

Although clearly having the advantage of low risk, the parallel approach also brings with it the highest cost. To properly execute a parallel approach, the end users must literally perform all daily functions with both systems, thus creating a massive redundancy in activities and literally double the work. In fact, unless the operational costs of the new system are significantly less than the old system, the cost of parallel operation can be as much as 3 to 4 times greater than the old system alone.

During a parallel conversion, all outputs from both systems are compared for concurrency and accuracy, until it is determined that the new system is functioning at least as good as the one it is replacing. Parallel conversion may be the best choice in situations where an automated system is replacing a manual one. In certain circumstances where end users cannot cope with the often confusing redundancy of two systems, the parallel conversion strategy may not be viable. Also, parallel conversion may not be possible if the organization does not have the available computing resources to operate two systems at the same time.

Pilot Conversion

In some situations, the new system may be installed in multiple locations, such as a series of bank branches or retail outlets. In other cases, the conversion may be able to be planned from a geographic perspective. When these types of scenarios exist, the possibility for using a *pilot conversion strategy* exists. This approach allows for the conversion to the new system, using either a direct or parallel method, at a single location. The advantage to this approach is that a location can be selected that best represents the conditions across the organization but that also may be less risky in terms of any loss of time or delays in processing. Once the installation is complete at the pilot site, the process can be evaluated and any changes to the system made to prevent problems encountered at the pilot site from reoccurring at the remaining installations. This approach may also be required if the individual sites or locations have certain unique characteristics or idiosyncrasies that make either a direct or parallel approach infeasible.

Phased Conversion

A *phased* or *gradual conversion strategy* attempts to take advantage of the best features of both the direct and parallel approaches, while minimizing the risks involved. This incremental approach to conversion allows for the new system to be brought on-line as a series of functional components that are logically ordered so as to minimize disruption to the end users and the flow of business.

Phased conversion is analogous to the release of multiple versions of an application by a software developer. Each version of the software should correct any known bugs and should allow for 100 percent compatibility with data entered into or processed by the previous version. Although having the advantage of lower risk, the phased approach takes the most time and, thus, creates the most disruption to the organization over time.

Figure 14-4 graphically illustrates the four conversion strategies.

Data Conversion

One final issue with regard to conversion is the transfer of data from the old system to the new one. This activity is present regardless of the system conversion strategy selected and can sometimes pose significant logistical problems for the analysts and project coordinators.

During the design phase, the analysts created a data dictionary that not only describes the various data elements contained in the new system but also specifies any necessary conversions from the old system. In some cases, only the name of the data element is changed, as in the old system field CUST_ID becoming CLIENT_ID in the new system. In other cases, the actual format of the data is changed, thus requiring some conversion application to be written to filter the old data and put them into the new format. An example of this might be the creation of a new CUSTOMER_ID format to allow for expansion or to make two merged systems compatible with one another. This type of data element conversion requires additional time to occur, because each element must be passed through the conversion algorithm before being written into the new data files.

Yet another issue is the time necessary to transfer the data from the old data files into the files for the new system. Although it is possible that the new system may have been designed to use the existing data files, this is not normally the case, especially in situations where a new system is replacing a legacy system that is fairly old. The time necessary to transfer the old data can have a material impact on the conversion process and on the strategy that is ultimately selected. Consider the following situation.

Suppose the conversion to the new system requires the transfer of data from 10 different relational files. The average record length across the ten files is 1780 bytes, and the total number of records contained in the ten files is 120 million. With

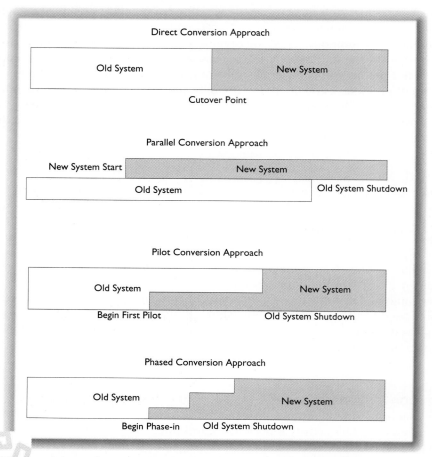

Figure 14-4   Comparison of System Conversion Strategies

this information and an estimate of the transfer time in bytes per minute, the total transfer time can be easily calculated as follows:

Assume a transfer rate of 12.5 megabytes per second (MBps) (Fast Ethernet) with no conversion algorithm.

1780 bytes × 120 million records = 213,600,000,000 bytes
12.5 MBps/213,600,000,000 bytes = 17,088 seconds
17,088 seconds/60 = 284.8 minutes ~ 4.75 hours

Although the preceding calculations appear to be such that the conversion process does not take an inordinate amount of time, we must also be aware that they assume an error-free transfer, no conversion, and 100 percent use of a Fast Ethernet pipe. If the transfer is done using a conventional Ethernet system at 1.25 MBps, the time jumps to 47.47 hours (just under 2 days).

The important consideration here is not simply the time necessary to effect the transfer but the preservation of the integrity of the current system data files during the process. If the transfer turns out to be around 4.5 hours, then it could theoretically occur after business hours and be easily accomplished by the opening of the next day's business. If, however, the process takes two full days, then it would need to begin at the close of business on Friday and would not be complete until late Sunday afternoon. Should any glitches show up in the process, either the transfer would have to wait a week to be rerun or the possibility of disrupting daily operations and losing new data would be very real. The analyst must give careful thought to the logistics associated with data transfer when recommending the most appropriate conversion strategy for the new system.

THE SYSTEM DOCUMENTATION

Ask any engineer or architect about when they start the documentation process for a project and they are likely tell you, "On day number one." However, in systems analysis, the preparation of documentation for a complex IS is one of the most often overlooked activities by designers and analysts. In many cases, this is because the project has adopted a strong prototyping component, and documentation of each iteration of the prototype becomes tedious and overly time-consuming. In other cases, the analyst keeps telling him- or herself, "I will do it later." Regardless of the reasoning behind the delay, failure to maintain proper documentation during the design phases can result in a massive effort to update the documentation at the implementation stage and can further result in documentation that is both incomplete and fraught with errors. The finalization of the documentation must occur during implementation, and the better the record keeping up to that point, the easier and more accurate the final updates are.

The documentation is intended to provide the end users and system administrators with the information they need to successfully operate the new system. Although each development effort is unique in the content of its documentation, the basic structure and deliverables associated with high-quality project documentation remain relatively the same. What has changed over the past several decades is the method by which the documentation is prepared and delivered to the end users. Prior to the mid 1980s, documentation was paper-based and stored in cumbersome binders. In today's environment, however, on-line, context-sensitive documentation is now the standard. Typical on-line documentation includes *electronic user's manuals, hypertext-based help systems, electronic system models,* and *interactive knowledge bases.* Figure 14-5 contains an example of a typical on-line help system in a Microsoft Windows–based software application, and Table 14-3 contains a set of general documentation content guidelines proposed by Bell and Evans (1989).

For the purposes of simplicity, the documentation requirements for any given system can be categorized into two basic types: (1) user documentation and (2) system documentation.

User Documentation

The purpose of the *user documentation* is to provide the end users with a detailed and highly organized description of how to interact with the system in the many scenarios and activities that may be possible. It should clearly describe the range of routine operations associated with system use, including data entry, output creation and generation, and basic troubleshooting.

Although human beings are still working in a primarily paper-based world, the deployment of on-line documentation, particularly for end users, brings with it several advantages. Probably the single most important feature of on-line

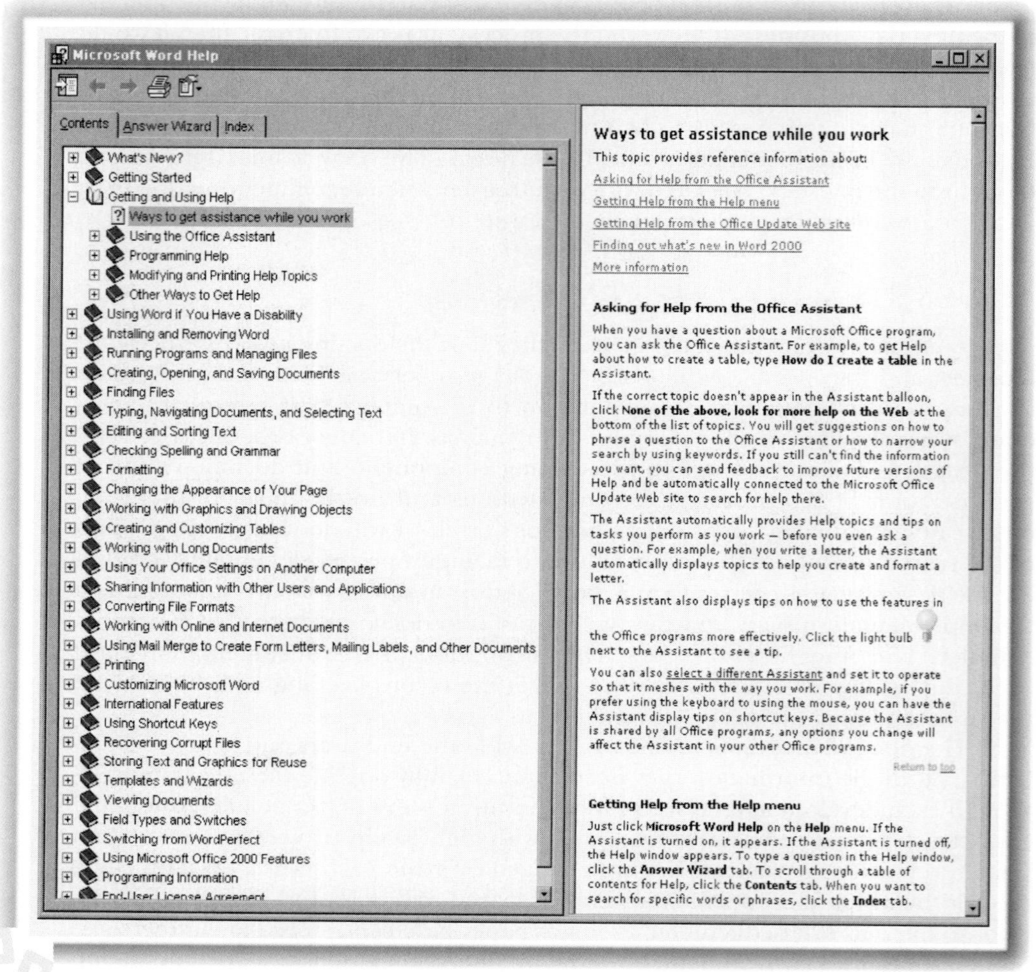

Figure 14-5 Example of an On-Line Help System

documentation is the ability to use *context-sensitive help*. This concept provides the end user with help topics related to the activity being performed at the time the help function is activated. For example, suppose the user needs to perform a somewhat complex formatting function to a paragraph contained in a word processing document. Rather than having to sift through pages and pages of text to find the appropriate steps for the desired function, the user begins the process to the best of his or her ability, and then at the point where additional help is needed, the help function is activated and the information necessary to complete the task is displayed. Figure 14-6 illustrates this example using Microsoft Word.

When preparing the final user documentation for the system, it is common to divide the topics and help functions into three basic categories: (1) procedures, (2) general reference, and (3) tutorials.

The *procedures* help section focuses on providing assistance with performing a particular system task, such as generating a particular report or entering an order. In this type of documentation, the information is organized by task and the content

Table 14-3   General Documentation Deliverable Guidelines for SDLC

Life-Cycle Phase	Documentation
Preliminary investigation	• System requirement specification • Preliminary resource requirement specification
Analysis	• Detailed system requirement specification • Detailed resource requirement specification
Logical Design	• Logical DFD • Logical ERD • State-transition diagrams • Logic analysis
Physical Design	• Detailed physical component specification • Implementation schedule • Detailed feasibility analysis
Implementation	• System test specifications • System test reports • User documentation • Release description • System administration documentation • System reference guide • End user acceptance sign-off

is generally made up of a sequence of instructions to be followed by the user in completing the task. Depending on the complexity of the various system functions, the procedures documentation can be quite lengthy and detailed in nature.

The second category of user documentation, the *general reference,* is normally less complex or lengthy and is intended to provide the end user with a quick reference guide for such things as correct command syntax or available functions. The general reference documents are not intended to teach the end user how to perform a function but rather are a form of dictionary by which the users can look up the correct form of a function or find a command or function that meets their needs for a given situation.

Finally, the *tutorial* is intended to instruct end users in the overall use of the major functions of the system by guiding them through a set of typical tasks or use scenarios. By sequencing the topics in the tutorial according to commonality or complexity, a user can acquire more advanced skills and understanding of the system through practice and repetition.

Regardless of the form, the design of user documentation is a highly specialized skill that requires careful attention to detail and strong written communication skills.

System Documentation

As the name implies, the *system documentation* details the design specifications, the internals of the systems, the as-built program code, and the functionality of all application and utility modules. It is intended to assist and support the personnel responsible for maintaining the final system. Although some portions of the system

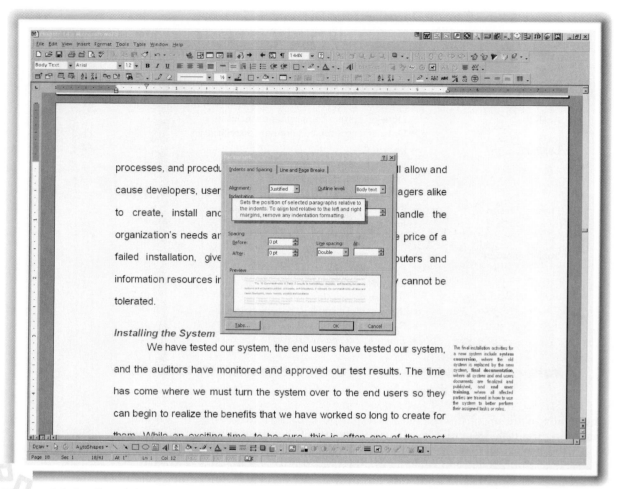

Figure 14-6   Example of a Context-Sensitive Help System

documentation can be considered to be the deliverables associated with the SAD activities, others, such as the program code or the module functionality detail, may not be created until after the design process is complete. This is because the desire is for these particular system documents to reflect conditions *as-built*. This means that the documentation does not reflect what was designed but what was actually coded and compiled. In many cases, these two elements can be quite different. An example using an architectural analogy helps explain this situation.

When an architect constructs a set of blueprints detailing the design of a house, he or she attempts to ascertain the actual conditions under which this house will be constructed. This includes a thorough analysis of the land and it topography, a complete listing of all components and material specifications, and a detailed set of blueprints that articulate exactly the dimensions of every aspect of the house. Despite this care during the design process, however, it is often the case that the actual house is somewhat different than the blueprints. This may be owing to the builder encountering conditions that were unknown by the architect. Say the prints call for wiring to run from the basement to the upstairs through a particular channel in a certain wall. Although the design works on paper, the actual run for the wiring needs to be moved six feet to the left because of some local condition, say an oversized air duct in the way. If the architect's original drawings are filed as the final blueprints, then years later, when the current owners of the house want to remove a wall to allow for more space, they assume that the wiring is where the prints show and are quite surprised to find the wiring right where they want to remove a wall. Thus, the need for *as-built* updated drawings is clear.

These same types of conditions can exist in a systems development project. The original specification by the analyst may pose a problem that could not be seen until the programming stage. If a change is made from the original specification, then the system documentation needs to be updated to reflect the as-built condition. This is important during not only the final implementation activities but also the actual use of the system, where updates and changes may occur. A record of such changes needs to be included in the system documentation in a manner that allows for easy recognition of the current condition of the system.

Maintaining the system documentation for the many applications that can exist in a typical organization can be a daunting task. Many organizations have established a documentation librarian function within the IS department that is responsible for document maintenance and update. With the advent of modern CASE tools and reverse engineering platforms, this process has become much more manageable. Nonetheless, the activity itself remains a critical element in a successful system implementation and postimplementation maintenance and upgrade effort.

User Training and Support

Regardless of the degree of end user involvement during the analysis and design phases of the life cycle, the need for a comprehensive *user training* program is tantamount to a successful system implementation. For some users, the training phase is welcomed as an opportunity to acquire new skills and improve the quality of their work. For others, however, the training process may be the last opportunity for the developers to instill an sense of confidence and trust in the new system. An unsuccessful training effort during implementation can spell doom to a new system down the road. Each individual approaches the onset of change in his or her life differently. Some can readily adapt, others require some time to adjust, and still others view change with anxiety and trepidation. The user training process must be designed to address the needs of all potential end users such that the best possible start to the system can be achieved.

Given the obvious value and importance of the user training activities, it is somewhat paradoxical that user training is often reported to be the most overlooked part of the development process. Commonly, either the design of the user training program is left until the final stages of implementation, thus requiring it to be rushed or abbreviated, or it is assumed that the system is easy enough to learn that no formal training is necessary. Either of these conditions can spell disaster for an otherwise valuable system.

The details associated with the design of an effective user training program are beyond the scope of this text and require the use of professionals skilled in such efforts. Despite this level of complexity, however, two important issues deserve mentioning, because they represent decisions that the analysts most likely participate in making: (1) what training should be provided, and (2) how should the training be delivered?

User Training Design and Content

One common fallacy associated with necessary content for end user training is that the program should be a comprehensive coverage of what the new system can do and how the various functions and modules for the system can, or should, be used. Although this lofty goal seems laudable enough, it is representative of exactly the wrong way to approach user training. The users do not need to be trained on what the system can do, but rather they need to be trained in how to use the system to perform their respective jobs. This implies that a one-size-fits-all training program is not a desirable structure for end user training. Each segment of the training should be targeted to a particular group of end users responsible for a definable set of tasks. The system must be presented to the user within the context of his or her job responsibilities rather than from the perspective of all the marvelous functions the system can perform. Consider your word processor and reflect on how few of the thousands of functions contained within the application you actually use on a daily basis. When was the last time you reconverted Japanese or Chinese language text into Arabic? It can be done, but I suspect very few of you would benefit from being trained in how to do it.

User Training Methods and Delivery

When considering the appropriate pedagogical approach for training a particular class of end users, two important and often conflicting issues arise. The first is associated with the decision regarding which training method is best suited to the topics being covered. A wide variety of teaching approaches are readily available to the training staff. Should the topic be delivered using a *traditional classroom approach* ("chalk and talk")? Would a *one-on-one training* method be more effective? Can the required skills be acquired using a *self-paced* or *computer-based training* method? Should the training be done *off-site* or at the *end user location*? Each of these options may be more or less appropriate for a given class of end users, and a well-designed training program probably makes use of all of the approaches during the training process. Although cost is certainly a valid consideration in designing an end user training program, the effectiveness of the process should be the primary driver when choosing a particular approach.

The second issue that must be considered, and one that can often complicate the process, is the design of the training schedule. In many cases, this decision must be closely linked to the strategy selected for conversion to the new system. If a direct cutover approach is used, then the training for all users must be scheduled such that it is completed prior to the cutover point and conducted close enough to the cutover that it can be retained and immediately applied by the users. If the training occurs too late in the process, it may need to be abbreviated such that it becomes ineffective. If it is done too early in the process, it may be forgotten by the time the system is put into operation.

Similarly, if a phased-in strategy is being followed, the design of the training schedule must complement that approach. Training must be scheduled to coincide with the conversion schedule and must be delivered in a manner that allows for retention by the end users while simultaneously avoiding disruption of the daily activities during the conversion process. Consider how you might have to design a training schedule for medical personnel who work in an emergency room setting at a trauma center. Can they be trained on-the-job? How many separate training sessions need to be schedule to insure that adequate staffing of the trauma center occurs at all times? As you can see, the design of a user training schedule can be quite complex and, thus, requires careful consideration early in the implementation process.

POSTIMPLEMENTATION ACTIVITIES

When all is said and done, the single most costly phase of activity in the life-cycle approach to systems development is the *postimplementation maintenance phase*. The primary objectives associated with systems maintenance are to correct errors or faults in the system, provide changes to effect performance improvement, or adapt the system to changes in the operating or business environment. In a typical organization, more programmers and analysts are assigned to application maintenance activities than to application development. Further, although a new IS can take several months or years to design and build and can cost hundreds of thousands or millions of dollars, the resulting system can operate around the clock and last for five to ten years, or longer. Figure 14-7 illustrates the relative distribution of costs across the various phases of software development.

Although space does not permit a thorough and detailed discussion of the maintenance phase of the life cycle, given the size of the expenditure for maintenance of an organizational IS, several issues deserve mention in this context.[2]

Change Requests

Although it is admittedly an ambitious goal to completely eliminate all software bugs during the implementation testing activities, it is nonetheless reasonable to assume that the vast majority of the errors and faults have been taken care of by the time the system is put into full-scale operation. This suggests, however, that regardless of how thoroughly the software and hardware are tested, some problems will arise during the early stages of actual system operation. Thus, error tracking and correction is one of the primary activities for the maintenance personnel in the first few months following system conversion. Over time, however, the maintenance

Figure 14-7   Relative Distribution of Costs across SDLC Activities

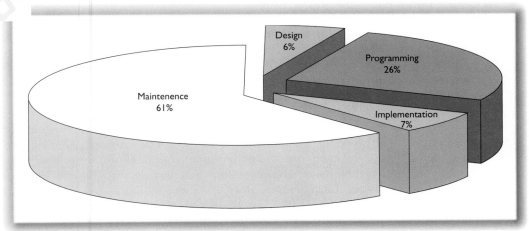

Design 6%

Programming 26%

Implementation 7%

Maintenence 61%

---

[2] An excellent offering that details the activities and issues associated with large-scale software maintenance is Thomas Pigoski's (1996) *Practical Software Maintenance.*

phase activities shift from simply fixing bugs to modifying existing system functions with an eye toward improved performance or to identifying and implementing changes to the system that add or enhance functionality. This latter function is commonly referred to as *change request maintenance*.

We know from discussions in earlier chapters that the typical business environment is one of constant change and evolution. The IS operating within an organization must be able to adapt and respond to this constant change through upgrades and enhancements. These enhancements, however, must not be treated lightly and require the same structured approach to their specification and design that was present during the initial stages of the system itself. To meet this need, systems maintenance personnel must put in place a formal process for submitting and implementing change requests to an existing operational system. Typically, a formal change request process includes a standard method for specifying and submitting requests for change, a review of all requests by a *change control steering committee*, and adherence to structured analysis and design techniques that parallel those performed during the initial construction of the system. Figure 14-8 contains an example of the content typically found in a formal change request form.

Categories of Systems Maintenance

Managing and implementing change requests is only one aspect of the systems maintenance phase activities. In some ways, once the maintenance phase begins, the life-cycle starts over again. New requirements are articulated, analyzed, designed, checked for feasibility, tested, and implemented. Although the range and nature of specific maintenance requests varies from system to system, four basic categories of maintenance have been identified by Andrews and Leventhal (1993): (1) corrective, (2) adaptive, (3) perfective, and (4) preventive.

The activities associated with *corrective maintenance* are those discussed previously with regard to fixing bugs and logic errors that were not detected during the implementation testing period. Although the majority of corrective maintenance activities occur during the first several months of system operation, they never completely go away. The major problem with corrective maintenance demands on the systems maintenance personnel is that they provide no value-added component to the system or the organization. Thus, while corrective maintenance is being performed, new functionality and system enhancements must wait.

The second category, *adaptive maintenance*, refers to those activities associated with modifying existing functions or adding new functionality to accommodate changes in the business or operating environments. This category of maintenance activities is normally not a large one in terms of either cost or time, but it does add value to the organization whenever initiated.

Perfective maintenance activities involve changes made to an existing system that are intended to improve the performance of a function or interface. Although enhancements in this category are often desirable, they are rarely necessary and should be considered bells and whistles rather than necessary upgrades. The more popular and successful the system becomes, the more maintenance personnel are bombarded with requests that fall under the "wouldn't it be nice if . . . " umbrella. The merits of a perfective maintenance request must generally be judged by the change request steering committee and approved before any changes can be made.

The final category of maintenance activities, *preventive maintenance*, involves those activities intended to reduce the chances of a system failure or extend the

1.0 SCI Identification

This section identifies the software change initiative (SCI) for which a change has been requested.

1.1 Name, identification and description of SCI(s)

The name, version/control numbers of the SCI is specified, including page numbers if a document is involved. A brief description is provided.

1.2 Requester

The name of the person requesting the change

1.3 Contact information

How to contact the requester.

1.4 Date, location, and time

When and where the change was requested

2.0 Description of the change

This section presents a brief description of the requested change

2.1 Description

This section presents a detailed description of the circumstances that precipitated the change request and the request desired.

2.2.1 Underlying circumstances

Background information regarding the request.

2.2.2 Examples

Supporting information, e.g., printouts containing an error in a report or an incorrect screen image

2.2.3 The change

A detailed discussion of the change requested.

2.2 Reasons and justification

This section discusses why the change has been requested and the justification for the request.

2.3 Perceived affects

The requester's perception of the affects of the change.

2.4 Alternatives

The requester's perception of any alternatives to the change.

2.5 Requester priority

The priority assigned by the requester to the work generally chosen from a five-value scale.

Figure 14-8   Sample Content for a Software Change Request
Source: Adapted from Pressman (2000).

capacity of a current system's useful life. Preventive maintenance activities are likely to include some or all of the following:

➤ Hardware maintenance to keep electromechanical equipment correctly operating (fans, filters, back up batteries, adjustments, alignments, etc.)

➤ Replacement of hardware components to keep the equipment up to current specifications (i.e., engineering changes)

➤ Updating of system software (bug fixes, new versions, etc.)

➤ Testing and analysis of system reports (error logs, self tests, system parameters, performance measures, etc.)

➤ Maintenance of system documentation

Although often the lowest priority maintenance activity, preventive maintenance is, nonetheless, a high value-adding function and is vital to an organization realizing the full value of its investment in the system.

Systems Maintenance Costs

In 1998, The Standish Group, a leading IT market research organization, published the results of a study that estimated the average cost of a minute of downtime for a mission-critical software application was $10,000 (see Schaider [1999]). There is a direct link between the cost of absolute availability and the cost of downtime. The higher the cost of a lost transaction, the higher the cost of downtime. The more downtime, the greater the cost of ownership. Thus, the question really is not how much maintenance activities cost but rather how much maintenance activities can save.

Pressman (2000) estimates that whereas maintenance costs were as high as 75 to 80 percent of total IS budgets in the late 1980s, through the mid 1990s this number is declining and will continue to drop during the next decade. Although maintenance is still an essential component in overall system success, the biggest single reason for the reduction in maintenance costs as a percentage of total IS budget is the Y2K debacle. Most major organizations focused on upgrading legacy systems to more modern, Y2K-compliant systems, and, as such, the overall need for maintenance is less in the near term. Nonetheless, maintenance can account for a significant portion of the total IS budget and has the potential to be the largest source of cost savings and loss prevention to the organization.

CHAPTER SUMMARY

As I stated at the beginning of this chapter, we are at the beginning of the end. Although this may be true for this textbook, in reality, you are actually at the end of the beginning. By now you have completed your initial study of SAD and have begun to give thought to whether this may be a desirable career choice for you. If it is, then I both welcome you and congratulate you. If it is not, then I know that the concepts you have learned and the skills you have acquired during this experience will

serve you well in whatever career path you follow.

It is important to note that the methodologies and techniques presented in this text were culled from a wide variety of sources. When you actually experience the world of SAD, either as an analyst or as an end user working with one, the details of the methodology in place may differ from what you learned. The important issue, however, is that the underlying concepts, principles, and objectives will most certainly be consistent with what you have learned, and you will be able to adapt easily to the new environment. If you leave this learning experience with an understanding of why each task is performed or each model is created, you will have no trouble functioning effectively in any analysis and design environment.

One final point: Always remember that the SDLC is a general purpose methodology that should be viewed as a tool for assisting the analyst in successfully developing and implementing a useful organizational IS. By itself, the SDLC no more guarantees a successful system than a word processor can guarantee an A on your term paper. The key ingredient in systems analysis has always been, and will always be, you. Good luck!

KEY CONCEPTS

➤ System implementation

System implementation activities focus on ensuring that the new system is fully functional and operational, as well as on the turning over of control of the new system to the end users.

- End users generally view the implementation of a new system as an event.
- From the analysts' point of view, implementation is generally thought of as a series of activities that must be performed.

➤ Implementation activities

- Application testing

Testing activities during implementation must be carefully structured and meticulously conducted to insure that every aspect of the new system has been checked and rechecked. Mosley (1993) divided system-testing activities into four categories based on whether the code being tested is actually executed and whether the test is conducted via the computer or manually by the analyst or programmer:

- Manual test, static: code inspection

The focus of the inspection is limited to purely structural and syntactic issues, and no evaluation of the quality of the code or the design is conducted. It is estimated that a formal code inspection can result in the detection of 50 to 70 percent of the software defects contained in a given application.

- Manual test, dynamic: structured walkthrough

Structured walkthrough is a test that the code actually performs the functions intended by the designers. The reviewers must refrain from making corrections to the codes.

- Automated test, static: the desk check

The desk check uses the programmers as human computers to execute each instruction and evaluate the accuracy of the results.

- Automated test, dynamic
  - Module testing (unit testing)

Module testing focuses on ascertaining the successful execution of each application module prior to integrating it with other tested modules.

  - Bottom-up method

The bottom-up method tests the lowest-level modules first and then methodically integrates each of them into the next higher level.

  - Test driver

The test driver simulates the control environment for the module under test by providing simulated input or receiving module output.

  - Stub testing (top-down approach)

In a top-down testing scenario, the highest-level control module is tested first, and the lower-level modules are simulated by a program stub.

  - Program stub

A program stub is a two or three line module, containing no

logic, that is designed to simply accept control from a high-level module and return it back to that module.

- Integration testing
  This phase of the testing process focuses on testing the behavior of an entire group of modules to identify errors that either were not or could not be detected at the unit level. Integration strategies include
  - All at once (big-bang)
  - Top-down
  - Bottom-up
- System testing
  System testing focuses on testing the entire system in a fully integrated form. End users are typically not involved in this phase of testing. One of the most common approaches to system testing is the build and smoke test.
  - Build and smoke test
    The build and smoke test is a daily system test that focuses on system functionality following any changes or updates made the previous day.
- User acceptance testing
  Acceptance testing is the process by which the end user verifies that the delivered and installed product is ready to be put into production use.
- Alpha testing (verification testing)
  Using simulated data, an alpha testing is done by the client at the developer's site, with assistance and monitoring by the developer.
- Beta testing (validation testing)
  Beta testing is conducted by the end users at their own site, with no analyst or developer on hand. The system is exercised using live data in the actual working environment.
- Acceptance testing script
  An acceptance testing script is designed to verify that the major functions are properly operating in their most common mode. Then,

the testing proceeds to minor functions or rarer operating modes.

- System installation
  - System conversion
    System conversion refers to the activities and processes associated with replacing the existing, operational system with the new system. There are four basic strategies of system conversion:
    - Direct conversion (slam dunk, cold-turkey strategy)
      Under direct conversion, the old system is turned off and the new system is turned on in its place. Due to the high risk involved in this strategy, it should be considered only in extreme circumstances when no other conversion strategy is viable.
    - Parallel conversion
      Under parallel conversion, the old system and new system are run simultaneously until the end users and project coordinators are fully satisfied that the new system is functioning correctly and the old system is no longer necessary. Parallel conversion may be the best choice in situations where an automated system is replacing a manual one.
    - Single cutover
    - Phased cutover
  - Pilot conversion
    Under pilot conversion, the new system may be installed in multiple locations or the conversion may be able to be planned from a geographic perspective. This approach allows for the conversion to the new system, using either a direct or parallel method, at a single location.
  - Phased conversion (gradual conversion)
    A phased or gradual conversion strategy attempts to take advantage of the best features of both the direct and parallel approaches while minimizing the risks involved. It is

analogous to the release of multiple versions of an application by a software developer.

- Data conversion

  Issues related to data conversion include
  - Name and format changes
  - Time necessary to transfer data
  - The preservation of the integrity of the current system data file during the process

- Final documentation

  The final update of the documentation must occur during implementation, and the better the record keeping up to that point, the easier and more accurate the final updates are. The documentation is intended to provide the end users and system administrators with the information they need to successfully operate the new system.

  - User documentation

    The purpose of the user documentation is to provide the end users with a detailed and highly organized description of how to interact with the system in the many scenarios and activities that may be possible.

    - Procedures

      The procedures help section focuses on providing assistance with performing a particular system task.

    - General reference

      General reference is intended to provide the end user with a quick reference guide for such things as correct command syntax or available functions.

    - Tutorials

      The tutorial is intended to instruct end users in the overall use of the major functions of the system by guiding them through a set of typical tasks or use scenarios.

  - System documentation

    The system documentation details the design specifications, the internals of the system, the as-built program code, and the functionality of all application and utility modules.

It is intended to assist and support the personnel responsible for maintaining the final system.

  - As-built system documentation

    As-built system documentation represents what was actually built and implemented rather than what was proposed or designed.

- End user training and support
  - User training design and content

    The users need to be trained in how to use the system to perform their respective jobs, not on what the system can do. This implies that a one-size-fits-all training program is not a desirable structure for end user training.

  - User training methods and delivery
    - Balance between training costs and training effectiveness
    - Closely link the training schedule to the selected system conversion strategy.

➤ Postimplementation activities

  The primary objectives associated with systems maintenance are to correct errors or faults in the system, provide changes to effect performance improvement, or to adapt the system to changes in the operating or business environment.

  - Change requests

    Systems maintenance personnel must put in place a formal process for submitting and implementing change requests to an existing operational system.

  - Categories of systems maintenance
    - Corrective

      Corrective maintenance activities involve fixing bugs and logic errors that were not detected during the implementation testing period.

    - Adaptive

      Adaptive maintenance activities involve modifying existing functions or adding new functionality to accommodate changes in the business or operating environments.

- Perfective

  Perfective maintenance activities involve changes made to an existing system that are intended to improve the performance of a function or interface.

- Preventive

  Preventive maintenance involves those activities intended to reduce the chances of a system failure or to extend the capacity of a current system.

QUESTIONS FOR REVIEW

1. What are the four categories of application tests proposed by Mosley?

2. Explain the concept of "white-box inspection."

3. What are the main reasons that structured walkthrough is generally ignored in system implementation?

4. Explain the concept of "black-box inspection."

5. List and briefly describe the three phases of an automated and dynamic test.

6. Compare and contrast a test driver and a program stub.

7. List and compare the three integration strategies in the systems maintenance phase.

8. Explain how module and integration testing could be combined in a bottom-up manner.

9. What are the benefits of daily build and smoke tests?

10. Explain and compare alpha and beta acceptance testing.

11. List and brief describe the 16 commandments of user acceptance testing.

12. List and compare the three basic system conversion strategies.

13. Briefly state the issues an analyst needs to consider in the stage of data conversion.

14. List and briefly describe the two basic types of documentation.

15. List and briefly describe the basic categories of topics and help functions in user documentation.

16. What is the "as-built system documentation"?

17. Discuss the two main issues in user training and support.

18. List and briefly describe the four basic categories of systems maintenance.

FOR FURTHER DISCUSSION

1. You have used many different IS during your student experience, including on-line class registrations systems, word processors, spreadsheets, airline reservations systems, on-line banking systems, or possibly many others. Choose from the systems you have experienced and imagine you were one of the beta testers for that system. What criteria would you have used to determine when the system was ready for distribution to the end users?

2. User documentation is everywhere. Find an example of documentation from a common software application and look it over. Would you classify it as good or bad? Can you find ways to improve the layout, descriptions, or navigation?

3. Assume that you are the lead analyst in charge of the installation of a new POS system for a major retailer. This organization has stores in 1,500 different locations throughout the United States and employs over 12,000 people

at the retail level. How would you go about training the retail personnel? Develop a training plan that includes a detailed schedule.

4. Rather than go to the time and expense of building a custom inventory system, Phil Gauss, at Vance Music SuperStore, has decided to purchase an off-the-shelf application. The present system is based on manual operation and paper-based forms. What conversion approach do you recommend? Why?

REFERENCES

Andrews, D. C., and N. S. Leventhal. 1993. *Fusion: Integrating IE, CASE, JAD: A Handbook for Reengineering the Systems Organization.* Englewood Cliffs, NJ: Prentice Hall.

Bell, P., and C. Evans. 1989. *Mastering Documentation.* New York: John Wiley and Sons.

Fagan, M. E. 1986. "Advances in Software Inspections." *IEEE Transactions on Software Engineering* SE-12(7): 744–751.

McCabe, T. J., and A. H. Watson. 1994. "Software Complexity." *Crosstalk, Journal of Defense Software Engineering* 7(12): 5–9.

Mosley, D. J. 1993. *The Handbook of MIS Application Software Testing.* Englewood Cliffs, NJ: Yourdon Press.

Pigoski, T. 1996. *Practical Software Maintenance: Best Practices for Managing Your Software Investment.* New York: John Wiley and Sons.

Pressman, R. S. 2000. *Software Engineering: A Practitioner's Approach,* 5th ed. New York: McGraw-Hill.

Reid, W. S. 1991. "The 16 Commandments of Systems/Acceptance Power Testing: A First Hand Account." <http://www.wsrcg.com /testing.htm>. Accessed July 12, 2000.

Schaider, E. D. 1999. "TCO in the Trenches: The Standish Group Study." *SoftwareMag.com* (December) <http://www.softwaremag.com /archive/1999dec/TCO.html>. Accessed July 17, 2000.

Project Management: Process, Techniques, and Tools

Carl Briggs

Department of Operations and Decision Technologies, Indiana University

Learning Objectives

- Understand project prioritization
- Explore the responsibilities of a project manager
- Learn the five phases of the project management process and be able to identify the principle tasks associated with each phase
- Identify the main techniques for identifying, documenting and managing the tasks in any project and be able to assess the value of each for a particular project task
- Identify the fail-proof ways to murder a project

T.C.B. Baby—Taking care of business.

—ELVIS PRESLEY

To have his path made clear for him is the aspiration of every human being in our beclouded and tempestuous existence.

—JOSEPH CONRAD

INTRODUCTION

As a young man I was advised to "make things happen" rather than just sit by and wait for them to happen. Although the wisdom of such advice for one's personal life might be questioned, in business making things happen is critical. Modern project management is a set of processes, tools, and techniques to make things happen. The purpose of this appendix is to introduce the reader to the process, techniques, and tools of project management.

The *project management approach* can provide direction, clarity, and, most important, a plan of action for projects of any scope. Most of these techniques are relatively new, having been developed within the last 40 years. Admiral Hyman Rickover is often cited as one of the earlier pioneers of the modern project management approach. When placed in charge of the U.S. Navy's nuclear submarine initiative, Rickover found himself facing a project with hundreds of thousands of interrelated tasks, resource constraints, and a variety of stakeholders. Because of Rickover's personal resilience and his commitment to a systematic approach toward project management, the Nautilus project was a success. Many of the techniques described in

415

this appendix are descendants of the techniques first applied to the Nautilus project. But do not be misled—your project does not have to be as immense as a nuclear submarine to benefit from the project management approach. In fact, unless your project has a very small number of tasks (say ten or fewer), the techniques of project management can improve the outcomes.

There are two lessons to be learned from the Rickover example: First, modern project management is a process—a way of approaching a problem to achieve a certain outcome—that can be applied to even the largest of projects. Second, excellent project management does not occur in a vacuum. Although his project management skills were outstanding, Rickover's communication style has been characterized as very abrasive, a trait that many attribute as the cause of his relatively minimal success in other aspects of his career. Project management skills are critical for success, but they are never the only success factors that must be considered. For example, there is strong evidence that projects that have executive management support and user involvement have a 50 percent greater chance of success than those projects that do not have these kinds of characteristics (Shillingford 1998).

In this appendix, we discuss the modern project management approach, identify some important aspects of project management that fall outside the realm of the modern project management approach, and point the interested reader to further information and research in the area. For some of you, this may be review. For others, this may be your first exposure to the formal project management approach. In either case, the material in this appendix should prove valuable in your activities as a systems analyst.

The first logical step is to define what is meant by *project*. In general, a project is a finite event (there is a clear beginning and end) that requires resources with some kind of constraints. Using this definition, it becomes clear that, in most cases, an ongoing program is not a project, even though some of the same planning tools may apply.

PRIORITIZATION AND PROJECTS

Before discussing the process of project management, there are a few important topics, usually overlooked by the texts in this area, that deserve some attention. Although the techniques described in this appendix can be used on any project, they do not help you to choose or prioritize any project. These techniques take the same systematic rational approach to every project. Yet in reality, deciding which projects to take (or drop) and prioritizing the projects you have taken can make the difference between long-term career failure and success. Furthermore, project managers (and their bosses) often have pet projects that receive the kind of attention that defies the dictates of a purely rational approach. It is important to be aware of these issues before applying project management techniques. Projects, like the skills required to do them, do not exist in a vacuum. In fact, they exist in a rich social context—to be successful one must understand this context and act appropriately. For example, no project manager should even think about beginning a project without a clear knowledge of the stakeholders and any possible champions. *Stakeholders* are individuals that have something significant to gain (or possibly lose) from a successful project completion. A *champion* is someone in an organization who may not have a clear and immediate stake in the project but has the organizational resources and will to support a project against all internal saboteurs. These metaproject issues deserve more treatment than can be given in this appendix, and the interested reader is directed to Williams (1996) for a solid treatment of many of these issues.

Another area not covered in most articles and books on project management is the responsibilities associated with being a project manager. In addition to competence in basic management tools and techniques, the successful project manager must also have a strong set of communication skills, including the ability to actively listen. Because time is a critical resource in almost every project, it is also important that the successful manager have a good understanding of time management. Although development of these skills is beyond the scope of this appendix, it is strongly suggested that anyone aspiring to project management greatness invest some time in honing these interpersonal skills. A project manager must also be results-oriented. Achieving the desired set of results is the motivation behind the development of the modern project management approach. To understand this approach requires a good working definition of *project*.

WHAT IS A PROJECT?

Although there are many formal definitions of project, for our purposes it will suffice to keep it simple. Unlike some ongoing program, a project is a special set of activities with a clear beginning and end. Every project has a set of goals, objectives, and tasks. Every project must deal with a set of limitations. Furthermore, although content can vary greatly between projects, a comparative analysis of any large number of projects reveals that there are some important similarities in the process. The first, and possibly greatest, contribution of the modern project management approach is to identify this process as a series of phases. The second contribution is the development of a set of techniques to assist and structure the completion of work in each of the phases of the project. These techniques have created a standard for identifying and documenting project activities. Finally, many of these techniques have been incorporated into specific software tools that make it easy to use the techniques and share the results with others. This appendix is organized around these project management ideas: process, techniques, and tools.

THE FIVE PHASES OF THE PROJECT MANAGEMENT PROCESS

The modern project management approach has identified five phases in the project management process. These phases are shown in Table A-1.

Initiating/Defining

The first phase of the project management process serves as a foundation for all that follows. The most important objective to achieve during this phase is the clear and succinct statement of the problem that the project is to solve or the goals that the project is to achieve. Any ambiguity at this point spells doom for even the best executed projects.

What Is the Problem?

The first step in this first phase of project management is identifying the problem that needs to be solved or the goal that needs to be met. Once there is clarity on this issue, decisions about prioritizing the project can be made. Failure to clarify this issue early in the initial phase of the project results in a lack of focus throughout the entire project. The project is susceptible to sabotage, both from within and from external opposition. In addition, when problems and goals are not clearly delineated

Table A-1   Five Phases of the Project Management Process

Project Management Phase	Example Activities
Initiating/defining	• State the problem(s)/goal(s) • Identify the objectives • Secure resources • Explore costs/benefits in feasibility study
Planning	• Identify and sequence activities • Identify the critical path • Estimate time and resources needed for completion • Write a detailed project plan
Executing	• Commit resources to specific tasks • Add additional resources/personnel if necessary • Initiate project work
Controlling	• Establish reporting obligations • Create reporting tools • Compare actual progress with baseline • Initiate control interventions if necessary
Closing	• Install all deliverables • Finalize all obligations/commitments • Meet with stakeholders • Release project resources • Document the project • Issue final report

the problem is highly susceptible to scope creep—the process where the goals and activities of the project continue to slowly grow well into the execution phase, making it impossible to ever complete the work in any satisfactory manner.

What Are the Resources?

Once the problem and goals are clarified, the next question to ask is what resources are available to complete the project. Resources come in a variety of forms, but for our purposes, *resources* refers to staff time, appropriate tools, and capital. There is great optimism during this phase of the project—usually completion times and costs are underestimated and the benefits of the project are overestimated. However, it is important for the project manager to give a sober look at the resources that are available relative to the project tasks. If it is determined that there are insufficient resources available to initiate the project, then the analyst must either identify ways of getting the necessary resources or must decide not to proceed with the project.

What Are the Risks?

As with every endeavor in business, there is a component of uncertainty or risk associated with every project. It is important to calculate the risks that are involved in any project proposal. It may become clear that the value of the project does not outweigh the potential problems that might occur.

Once all of these questions have been asked and successfully answered, the information is oftentimes recorded as part of a feasibility study. This study carefully details the problem, goals, resources, and risks associated with the project, and in most cases the report provides a recommendation for either proceeding with planning the project or not (see chapter 8).

Planning

The second phase of the project management process has, in recent years, received a great deal of attention from the general public. This has resulted in vast improvements in the availability and usefulness of automated planning tools.

Identify the Objectives and the Activities (WBS)

The first step in creating a detailed project plan is to identify every project objective and every activity associated with that objective. It is important to consider every possibility. In fact, it is recommended that several people look at the same list of objectives and activities, just in case one person misses something. Although it is possible to add an objective or set of activities after the planning phase, this can substantially change scheduling, budget, and resource allocation issues and should be avoided at all costs.

The *work breakdown structure* (WBS) is a tool for detailing all project tasks. This tool is described in a later section of this appendix.

Sequence the Activities (Network Diagrams, Gantt)

With an exhaustive list of project activities completed, the next step in the planning phase is to sequence these tasks in the way in which they must be done and that optimizes project results. This sequencing also requires an understanding of the dependencies between tasks.

There are several tools that have been created to help with sequencing. The first set of tools is based on describing a project as a networked set of events and activities. Three types of network diagrams are described in the next section: (1) simple precedence diagrams, program evaluation and review technique (PERT), and critical path method (CPM).

Estimate Time (the Critical Path)

Once the project tasks are appropriately sequenced, it is possible to identify the estimated length of the entire project by identifying the longest path from beginning to end. This path is called *the critical path*. All activities along the critical path are called *critical activities*. This path and tasks are so named because any delay with any critical activity results in the entire project being delayed. We explore the critical path more graphically later in this chapter.

Estimate Cost (Top-Down, Bottom-Up)

The next step in the planning phase, once tasks are identified and sequenced and a critical path is identified, is the estimation of costs. There are two general approaches to budget estimation. The first approach, the *top-down approach*, begins with the entire project in mind. Possibly due to real constraints or because of experience on similar projects, an overall budget is assigned to the project. The task of the project manager in this scenario is to make sure that the project can actually be delivered under these constraints.

The second approach, a *bottom-up approach*, requires that the project be broken down into components and that each component be assigned an estimated cost.

Both approaches are useful under different circumstances and can be helpful in creating an appropriate project budget. Regardless of whether the approach is top-down or bottom-up, there is going to be a good deal of estimation going on during this part of the project planning phase.

The Methodology of Estimation

A methodology is simply a way of doing something. There are three generally accepted methodologies for estimating project parameters. In most instances the parameter is length of time to completion of some objective or activity, though it could also be cost estimation. The three methodologies and associated characteristics are shown in Table A-2.

At first glance, it may seem silly to include *guessing* as an estimation methodology. It is, however, used quite extensively in nearly every project. More important, guessing can be a useful tool—especially if the guesser is experienced, uses meticulous detail, and considers the assumptions on which the guess is dependent. Although guessing can be a powerful methodology, every attempt must be made to anchor the guess. This is usually done by explicit examination of the assumptions on which the guess is founded or by using one of the other methodologies and comparing the results.

The second estimation methodology is *analogy*. This approach can be used whenever there is some known activity that is analogous in some way with the one that is being estimated. This approach is probably the most widely used estimation methodology, but a word of caution is in order. This approach is only as good as the analogy. If there is some important difference between the known activity and the activity whose completion time (or cost) is being estimated, this difference must be taken into account and the estimation revised. It is a rare case indeed when this methodology can be used without making adjustments.

The third estimation methodology is *theory/formula*. This is the most formal of the methodologies. In this approach, the estimation is based on using some theory or formula to calculate the desired project parameter. This can be a powerful methodology and easy to describe and document, but this approach can only be used

Table A-2 Method for Estimating Project Parameters

Estimation Methodology	Characteristic
Guessing	• Used extensively in most projects • Subject to extreme variation, especially when conditions are outside of normal • Can be a powerful tool when the guesser is experienced, uses meticulous detail, and considers all assumptions on which the guess is based
Analogy	• Used whenever there is data on a similar activity • Can be misleading when conditions differ significantly from the analogous activity
Theory/Formula	• Can be a powerful methodology when a relevant theory or formula exists • Only as good as the theoretical assumptions on which the theory or formula is based

when there exists some theory or formula for the specific parameter in question. Of course, caveat emptor—the estimation is only as good as the theory or formula. In many cases the theory or formula was developed in a specific context (i.e., a specific industry, task, or set of economic conditions), and any application outside of those conditions may be substantially distorted.

The good news is that there are many useful formulae available for a wide range of projects. Some are very formal, others are used primarily as a heuristic or rule of thumb. For example, Halstead's Law (1977) was developed in the late 1970s as a way of estimating software completion time. A more general formula, discussed in Weiss and Wysocki (1992), for estimating the average activity completion time (E) for any task is

$$E = (O + 4M + P)/6$$

where E is the average activity completion time, O is the optimistic time, M is the most likely completion time, and P is the pessimistic time (see Littlefield and Randolph [1987] for a discussion of the history and importance of this particular formula).

To demonstrate, suppose a project can be optimistically expected to reach completion in 14 days (assuming everything goes perfectly) and most likely be completed in 20 days (based on past experience). Further, the worst case scenario for project completion is determined to be 30 days (based on logic). Given these estimates, the average activity completion time can easily be calculated:

$$E = (14 + (4 \times 20) + 30)/6$$
$$E = (124)/6 = 20.67 \text{ days}$$

Some formulae have become so commonplace that they are used without question. Others seem just a little suspect. For example, Westheimer's Rule for estimating duration states:

Multiply the original time estimate by two, and then change the unit of measure to the next higher unit. In this way two days will be allotted for a one-hour task.

Another example is this widely quoted quip from a NASA project manager, on estimating costs:

"Then multiply the original cost estimate by pi (3.1416). I have seen this technique used more than once with decent results."

The wisdom to take from these last two examples is that the estimate is only as good as the methodology for reaching the estimate. Choose with care the estimation methodology.

Write the Plan

Once all the planning work has been done, there is a temptation to begin the next phase of the project without writing a comprehensive plan that incorporates all the notes, ideas, and assumptions generated up to this point. This could be a fatal mistake. The formal project plan serves as a blueprint for everything that follows.

When there are questions about sequence, priorities, or scope, a written plan can save the day with much-needed clarification. A written plan also helps managers identify the occurrence of scope creep before it becomes a serious problem. Remember—write the plan!

Executing

Once the detailed plans have been created and approved, the third phase of the project management process can begin. It is in the *execution phase* that the best-laid plans are put into motion. Resources, tasks, and schedules are brought together, and work teams are created. In many respects, this is the most exciting part of the project management process—it is easy, at least early on, to see progress.

Controlling

According to some contemporary writers, the fourth phase, the control phase, is really just a part of the previous execution phase. Although that is an entirely acceptable way of viewing the process, it is also important to give sufficient consideration to techniques for ensuring that project objectives are met.

Reports

The most important tool for project control is the report. There are three types of reports that are especially important to the control phase of the project management process. These are the variance, status, and resource allocation reports.

Variance reports are the most important indicator of the need for some kind of control intervention. Variance reports can refer to the overall project or specific activities within the project. The variance that is reported on is not the variance you learn about in statistics. It is the difference between actual and planned progress. Variance reports focus on outcomes, not on the process that generated those outcomes. So although a variance report is critical in identifying when a project is off track, it is less useful in identifying what is causing the problem.

The second and third types of reports are more helpful to the project manager in determining the source, and possible correction, of project problems. These reports are the *status report* and the *resource allocation report*. The status report is often an open-ended report that details the process that led to current project state. The resource allocation report identifies the resources (in terms of person-hours, equipment, etc.) that are being applied to specific project activities.

These three reports taken together provide the project manager with the information needed to identify and attempt to control departures from the plan.

One caution about relying solely on reports—people often hide, omit, or mask the real problems or issues they are confronting. That is why it is critical that the project manager have face-to-face interaction with the members of the team during this phase of the project management process.

Project Control

When a project begins to significantly veer from the course, it is necessary to address the matter head-on by taking some type of corrective action. Figure A-1 provides a graphical representation of the control activity.

Figure A-1 also presents several important project management concepts. The first is the idea of the *baseline*. The baseline schedule represents the planned course of the project. If everything holds along the critical path, then the project baseline

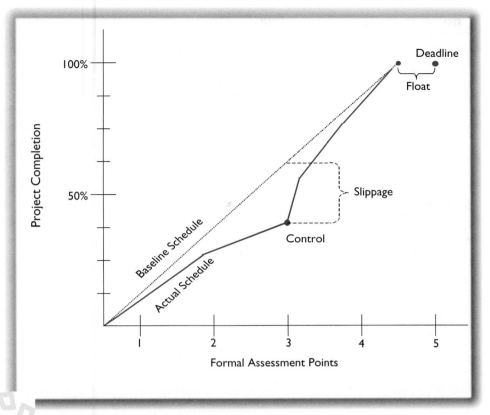

Figure A-1   The Importance of Project Control

is met. In Figure A-1, a dashed line represents this baseline. The solid line represents the actual project schedule. In an ideal world, these two lines would be identical. Of course, this is rarely the case. When the solid line veers above the baseline, the project is said to be *ahead of schedule*. When it veers below the baseline, as it does in Figure A-1, the project is said to be *behind schedule*. The distance between the baseline and the actual in the second instance is called slippage (it is also called variance—not to be confused with the statistical term, variance in this case refers to the difference between planned and actual progress). The project manager becomes aware of slippage as a result of regular scheduled reporting activities. The most basic of these reports is a project, phase, or activity variance report. When slippage becomes a threat to project completion (i.e., it becomes greater than the built-in cushion, or float, allows), it is time to engage in some control activities. There is a wide range of control activities available to the project manager. In most cases, the easiest activity is to reallocate resources that are currently being used in non–critical path activities. This is commonly referred to as *slack management*. However, as Brooks points out in his classic book *The Mythical Man-Month* (1975, 1999), on large technical projects that are behind schedule, adding more resources often makes matters worse. The wise project manager first seeks to determine the cause of the slippage before making any correctives.

Closing

All things (good and bad) must come to an end. The most rewarding or irritating project must, by definition, terminate. The last phase of the project management process deals with bringing a project to a successful end. Many pilots (and passengers for that matter) identify the landing as one of the most critical moments of any flight. It is during this time that even the smoothest flight can come to an undesirable conclusion. Projects are similar in some respects. The most beautifully planned, executed, and controlled project can be deemed a failure if the closing phase is a flop.

The beginning of the end for any project is the installation of all the deliverables. In nearly every instance this involves an iterative process in which deliverables are tweaked once they are placed under the strain of actual operation. With the deliverables satisfactorily in place, it is time to meet with the stakeholders and secure consensus about the status and value of the project results. This step is absolutely critical, and in most organizations can be done informally—prior to the more formal steps of project closure.

The next step in project closure is to release project resources. This rather innocuous statement could mean anything from moving computers from one office to another to firing employees. When this means the former, then do so with all due haste. One of the real pitfalls of project closure is the "ninety-percent stall." This is a well-documented tendency for projects to reach a high completion level (say 90 percent) and then fail to reach closure. When releasing resources means releasing workers, make sure that you have provided your workers with sufficient notice about the process and timing of the release and that every option has been considered for inclusion, integration, or reassignment.

With resources released, it is time to turn attention to the final documenting of project details and the writing and publishing of the final report. Remember that in five years the continued success of your project deliverables may depend on the quality of documentation that was created in the final days of the project. Consider precise, consistent, and thorough documentation to be like an insurance policy on the time, energy, and effort that went into the project. As for the final report, remember that this becomes the official document detailing the process and outcomes of the project. Many who may have known nothing about the project or the deliverables will read the final report and reach some conclusion about the project's value. Your champion is waiting for the final report to justify his or her support for the project and to silence detractors. This is not to imply that the final report should only show the positive and ignore or falsify negative outcomes. In fact, a final report is only accepted and deemed credible when it is clear that it shines a critical eye on all project processes and outcomes. This means that the final report must detail the bad and the ugly—not just the good.

There may be other final requirements that are project-dependent or possibly company-dependent. Make sure that you meet these expectations, whatever they may be.

PROJECT MANAGEMENT TECHNIQUES: IDENTIFYING AND DOCUMENTING PROJECT ACTIVITIES

There are a several project management techniques that can be used at various points during the project to effectively meet the project requirements. These techniques have many variations, ranging from the simple to the extremely technical. At the end of this appendix there are several resources that elaborate on these techniques in great detail. The reader is invited to explore these techniques and their variations, but remember: The technique is a means to an end. Do not get caught up in the form of any given technique and miss the real value—meeting project objectives.

WBS Identifying Tasks

The first project management technique currently in widespread use is the WBS. The purpose of this technique is to detail, in hierarchical fashion, all of the activities that are required to meet project objectives. The steps for creating a WBS are deceptively simple. In reality, it takes a great deal of work to produce a WBS with the kind of detail that is required for most midsize projects.

The steps for creating a WBS are as follows:

1. Identify all the project objectives. List them in sequential order. This list should fully define the project.

2. For each objective, identify all of the activities that must occur if that objective is to be met. List these activities underneath the objective, using a subordinate numbering system.

3. Carefully review each objective and activity, making sure that the list is complete. All project activities should appear in the WBS.

An example WBS is shown in Figure A-2. It is sometimes helpful to represent the WBS in graphical form. The result looks very similar to an organizational chart. The graphical approach is useful for identifying missing activities and for assigning costs to each activity. In fact, the graphical WBS is a useful tool for bottom-up budget estimation.

Simple Precedence Network Diagram

There are several types of important network diagrams used in project management techniques. The most basic of them is the *precedence diagram*. Although the WBS technique is useful for identifying all of the objectives and activities of the

Figure A-2   Example of a Textual Work Breakdown Structure

Work Breakdown Structure (WBS)

1.1   First Project Objective
1.1.1   First activity required to meet objective 1.1
1.1.2   Second activity   "   "   "   "   "
1.1.3   Third activity   "   "   "   "   "
. . .   (Until all 1.1 activities are listed)

1.2   Second Project Objective
1.2.1   First activity required to meet objective 1.2
1.2.2   Second activity   "   "   "   "   "
1.2.3   Third activity   "   "   "   "   "
. . .   (Until all 1.2 activities are listed)

. . .   **Until all Project Objectives are listed**

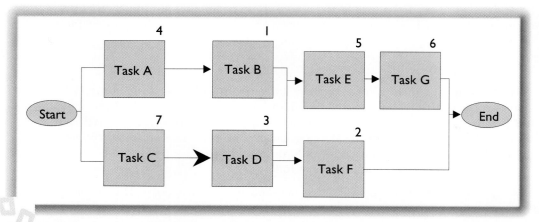

Figure A-3   Example of a Simple Network Diagram

project, it is not very helpful in identifying what should be done first (second, third, and so on). A simple precedence diagram can help establish the appropriate order for the project steps. In its most basic form, a precedence network diagram can be thought of as a set of boxes representing project tasks arranged from left to right in the proposed order of completion. The conventions for a simple precedence network diagram are easy to follow:

➤   Each diagram has a beginning and an end and is read from left to right.

➤   No backward loops are allowed.

➤   Every activity is represented by a labeled box and has some duration attached to it. (See Weiss and Wysocki [1992] for an example of a more elaborate approach to network diagrams that include early and late start and finish dates.)

➤   Milestones may also be included in the diagram, but they are placed in rounded boxes and have no attached duration.

➤   Events that can be worked on simultaneously are connected along parallel paths.

Figure A-3 shows a hypothetical network diagram. In this example, task A must be completed before task B, but tasks A and B can be worked on simultaneously with tasks C and D. Tasks B and D, however, must both be completed before task E can be started.

By ordering project activities in this way, it is possible to begin to estimate the amount of time required to complete the project. The way to do this is to identify the path with the longest duration from start to end. This path has a special name, the *critical path*. It is called critical because any delay to the activities in this path delays the entire project. The activities in this longest path are called *critical activities*. The critical path for the previous hypothetical example is shown in Figure A-4.

Even though a task is not on the critical path, it still must be completed. However, there is some flexibility in the start and finish days of the noncritical task. This flexibility is known as *float* (it is sometimes called slack).

There are two other forms of network diagrams that are important project management techniques, PERT and CPM.

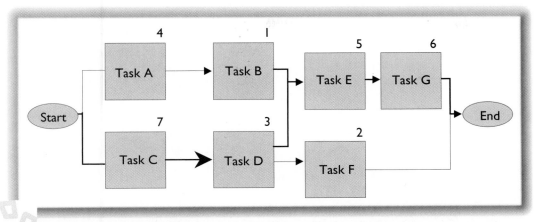

Figure A-4   The Critical Path in a Simple Network Diagram

PERT/CPM

Both of the PERT and CPM network techniques were developed in the late 1950s. The U.S. Navy developed PERT at about the same time that DuPont developed CPM.

The PERT approach is used for most research and development projects, whereas CPM is used more often on construction projects. In practice these techniques are very similar, using nodes (circles) and arcs (arrows) to represent events, activities, and precedence. In fact, for our purposes, it is not worth detailing the differences in these approaches. For the advanced project manager interested in these conventions, please refer to one of the advanced project management texts listed at the end of this appendix.

One distinction, however, that does affect the drawing conventions is whether activities are represented by arcs (arrows) or nodes (circles). The first approach is called the *activity on arc* (AOA) approach. A simple PERT/CPM network diagram using the AOA convention is shown in Figure A-5. One disadvantage of this approach

Figure A-5   PERT/CPM Network Diagram Using Activity on Arc (AOA)

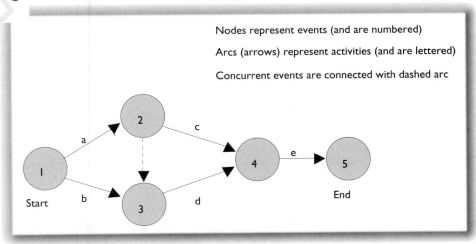

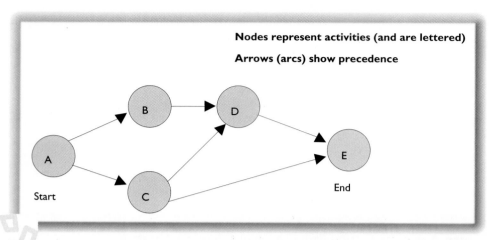

Figure A-6   PERT/CPM Network Diagram Using Activity on Node (AON)

is that it does not easily represent events that must be completed concurrently (this requires the addition of the dummy activity notation). The major advantage of this technique is that it does show events, activities, and their precedence.

The second convention, *activity on node* (AON) is shown in Figure A-6. The AON diagrams use the arcs (or arrows) only to show precedence. All activity is shown in the node. It many ways the AON convention is easier to model with existing spreadsheet tools in those cases where optimization of complex networks is an issue.

Although the PERT/CPM approach can be very useful in those instances when it is necessary to model a very complex project, there are those who contend that this technique does not affect overall project outcomes. The reader interested in mastering the PERT/CPM technique and in exploring the relative value of the technique is referred to the additional reading at the end of this appendix.

Gantt Charting

The most popular technique for planning, executing, and monitoring projects is the *Gantt chart*. Also known as the project bar chart or timeline, this technique is present in nearly all project management texts and is usually the centerpiece of all project management information systems (PMIS). Figure A-7 is one example of a project management Gantt chart.

In this example, all that is shown are the major phases of a project. The project is the development of an on-line instructional system using integration of streaming media into an interactive Web context. A project phase is a collection of related activities that, on completion, represent a significant contribution to the overall project completion.

In Figure A-8, only the details for the first phase of the project are shown. Here we begin to see the real value of the Gantt technique in scheduling activities, identifying dependencies, and visualizing the critical path. The figure has been annotated to draw the viewer's attention to some important elements of the chart. Notice that the phase 1 summary bar is still in place, identifying that all of the activities shown underneath are part of the first phase of the project. Note that the project begins and ends with a milestone. A milestone is an event that does not require any

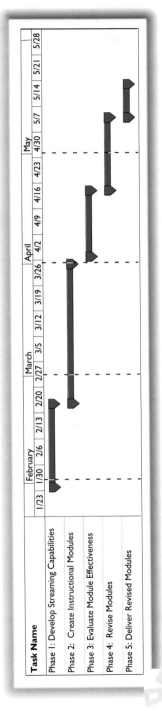

Figure A-7 Project Management Gantt Chart

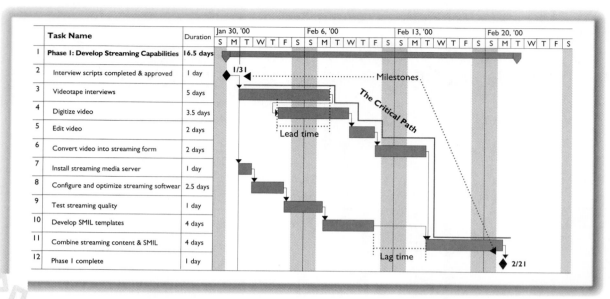

Figure A-8   Detailed Phase 1 Gantt Chart

work and has no time duration. It is used to mark the completion of some important aspect or phase of the project. Each task is graphed as a bar showing the expected duration of the task. Arrows connect dependent tasks, making it possible to show detailed dependencies among the tasks. The most common form of dependency is known as "finish-to-start," where one task starts once the preceding task is completed. However, it is also possible to have two dependent tasks that need not be finish-to-start. When the second task can begin before the first one is completely finished, it is possible to shorten the overall project length by using lead time. In this example, it is not necessary to wait for all interviews to be videotaped before the digitization process begins. Note how the project time would be lengthened by the better part of a week if the relationship was finish-to-start.

In addition to lead time, Gantt charting makes it possible to identify *lag time*, or the time that exists after the finish of one task but before the start of the next. In many cases, lag time represents an underuse of resources that could be addressed by moving resources to an activity along the critical path. As a scheduling tool, Gantt charting makes it possible to begin with a certain end in mind (usually some delivery date) and then work backward until a project plan is complete. This approach to scheduling is commonly called *reverse scheduling* and is a common project management strategy for meeting project deadlines.

Finally, Gantt charting makes it possible to visualize the critical path and identify those activities that, if delayed, delay the entire project (or project phase). In Figure A-8 the critical path is noted. All of the activities along this path are critical activities. Any delay in these areas should be treated seriously.

The project management techniques shown in this appendix, and summarized in Table A-3, are very powerful when properly applied. Unfortunately, there is much more to these techniques than can be covered in this context. The interested reader is directed to the resources at the end of this appendix for further details.

Table A-3   Project Management Techniques

Technique	Description
Work breakdown structure (WBS)	• Hierarchical description of all project objectives and associated tasks • Useful in identifying all project activities
Simple network diagram	• Graphical technique for sequencing project tasks • Easy to create and use • Does not capture complex relationships well
PERT/CPM	• Graphical technique for sequencing project tasks • Also a powerful analytical tool for optimizing outcomes • Requires some practice to create
Gantt chart	• Also called bar chart or project timeline • Useful in sequencing project tasks, identifying critical path, and monitoring progress

PROJECT MANAGEMENT TOOLS: AUTOMATING PROJECT MANAGEMENT

Having identified a rich set of project management techniques, the obvious question becomes "How can I use these tools without having to spend a great deal of time and resources just to draw the pictures?" The answer until just a few years ago was not very satisfactory. The PMIS were prohibitively expensive for all but the largest companies, or when the tools were available, they were substantially limited. Fortunately, that is not the case today. Many of the personal productivity tools available to today's PC user have all the features for easily applying the techniques just described. For example, the popular spreadsheet Excel can be used to create very robust tools for managing projects. The downside, of course, is that the user must create the tools from scratch. A much more attractive alternative is to purchase one of the many PMIS software packages now on the market. In fact, one need not even go that far. There are several powerful PMIS packages that are available for free as part of the growing open source code movement.

The Gantt charts shown previously were all created in Microsoft Project 98. Figure A-9. shows what the screen looks like in this application. Note all of the possible views and reporting tools shown on the left side of the screen. This illustrates the first real advantage of project management software—the ability to input project information once and then generate reports and views using any number of techniques. This can save the project manager literally hundreds of hours and, more important, provides much greater insight into the project progress. The second real advantage of project management software is realized when the tool and the project team are connected over some computer network. The increased communication and tracking offered by this approach represents a significant advance in project management.

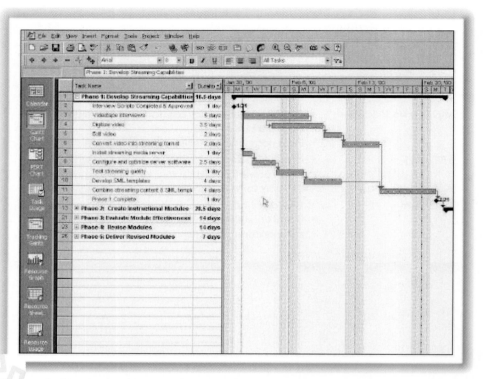

Figure A-9   Typical Microsoft Project Window

What Tools Can Do

Project management software tools come in nearly any size, with a wide range of features and even greater range of prices. Tools are now available for nearly any technology platform. These tools make it possible to streamline the amount of time and energy that goes into project accounting—the actual creating of the charts, graphs, and tables that make it possible for a manager to control a project. More important, many of these new tools are integrated with electronic messaging systems that make it easier than ever to coordinate activities, share progress reports, and locate important project information.

Even with all of these advances, however, a project management tool is only as effective as the users make it. There must be a clear and compelling reason to use the tool, as well as a minimal level of proficiency among team members, if the tool is to add value to the project management process.

What Tools Cannot Do

Although recent years have seen significant advances in the project management tools available to most project managers, there are still some important tasks that the tools cannot accomplish. For example, software tools cannot make decisions or replace a project manager's judgment. Furthermore, although project management tools are very useful in analyzing and holding data, these tools rarely do the kind of data collection that is required. Finally, these software tools cannot correct the results from incorrect or incomplete information being entered into the system. The value of project management software can quickly be undermined if the tool's limitations are not paid proper respect.

FIVE COMMON MISTAKES IN PROJECT MANAGEMENT: WAYS TO INSURE PROJECT FAILURE

There are many paths to a successful project. These paths can often be very complex and quite demanding. On the other hand, the road to project failure is much easier. What follows is a list of five paths that, if followed in their extreme, almost surely result in project failure.

What We Have Here Is a Failure to Communicate

A failure to communicate, and especially a failure to confront conflict, is the surest and quickest route to project hell. Not only are the project team members disgruntled and unhappy about such a state, there is simply no way to produce good long-term results without strong communication.

There are many ways to communicate. Make sure that the method matches the message. Identify the informal, as well as the formal, channels of communication, and use both to get your message across.

Failure to Create a Realistic Plan (Not Too Simple, Complex, or Unrealistic)

The second path to project failure has to do with a planning problem. Notice that this failure to plan is really a failure to plan appropriately. Frankly, some small projects do not require a full battery of project management techniques and tools. If a manager insists on using those tools, either out of habit or ignorance, too many project resources are devoted to overhead costs. A good measure here is if it takes longer to create the Gantt chart than it does to complete the project, then forget the chart.

Of course, the most obvious planning failure is underplanning. Although this error is quite common for a variety of understandable reasons, it is important to remember that planning done early in a project must sustain the project through to completion. Consider appropriate planning to be an investment in all of the resources that are used doing the course of the project.

No Project Buy-In

Many projects are done for less than admirable reasons. In these cases it is often the case that there is little if any commitment on the part of the implementation team or the ultimate consumer for the project. A reasonable level of buy-in is necessary for project success. It helps if there is someone in the organization who is willing to take personal responsibility for the project. Oftentimes this champion helps the project manager when times are at their leanest.

Scope Creep

Another path to failure is to allow the project parameters to increase over time. Although some scope adjustment occurs in nearly every project, this can be kept to a minimum by adopting an appropriate level of planning and by making project goals, objectives, and activities explicit. Whenever a project proceeds into the execution phase without a clear articulation of goals and activities, the result is almost always significant scope creep. The failure that results from scope creep is particularly acrimonious and should be avoided

Throw Resources (Man-Months) at a Project Problem

Finally, the fifth path to project failure is to assume that the solution to any project problem or delay is to add more resources. Brooks (1975, 1999) makes this point painfully clear through anecdotal evidence based on his years of experience as a high-level project manager at IBM. He makes a strong case for the idea that throwing resources (or "man-months," as he puts it) at a complex project usually makes the project even later and much more costly.

MISCELLANEOUS TOPICS

Projects can be very complex. As a result, the ideas of what constitutes project management are equally complex and increasingly involve topics from a variety of disciplines. Two topics that are not covered in this appendix but should be mentioned for the interested reader are time management and communication skills.

Time Management

The personal and organizational skills of time management are a critical for a successful project manager. Fortunately, there are hundreds of books written to help a project manager grow in this area.

Communication Skills

There are at least three types of communication skills that project managers must master to achieve long-term success. The first skill is active listening. When employees, vendors, suppliers, or clients get a sense that the manager does not or cannot really listen to their position, then the project is headed down the pipes.

The second form of communication that project managers must understand is negotiation. This skill is useful in nearly every phase of the project management process. Without proficiency in this area, the project manager is held captive by a variety of external and internal forces.

Finally, the project manager must be adept at conflict resolution. Although it would be nice to believe that professionals can work together harmoniously for the greater good, the reality is much different. The ability to directly face conflict and then receive resolution is invaluable to a project manager.

One critical mistake that is made by many IT project managers is to focus nearly exclusively on the technical issues to the detriment of the human factors. Although technical skills are required—the "table stakes" as one national project manager put it (Alexander 1999)—the real skill of project management is bringing people to results.

CONCLUSION

The purpose of this appendix is to introduce the reader to the process, techniques, and tools of modern project management. With this introduction complete, the burden falls on the reader to assess the utility of this approach in any given project setting, to master techniques, and then to apply the appropriate tools.

APPENDIX SUMMARY

Modern project management is a process for structuring the work of completing a project. This approach identifies five phases of work common to every project: defining, planning, executing, controlling, and closing. Several important techniques have been developed to identify, document, and track project activities. These techniques include the WBS chart, network diagrams (including simple precedence diagrams and PERT and CPM approaches), Gantt charts, and stakeholder analysis. Several software tools, ranging from common personal productivity tools to advanced PMIS, have been developed to automate the implementation of many of the tasks. Although these tools can be very useful, they have important limitations that the successful project manager must always keep in mind.

Although there are many ways to achieve project management success, the road to project failure is much less complicated. Do not communicate, fail to plan appropriately, do not seek buy-in from the team or clients, allow the project scope to grow unfettered, and then throw more resources at any project problem.

Finally, as project management becomes increasing more complex, so do the requirements placed on the project manager. However, do not allow these technical requirements to replace important skills like time management, active listening, conflict resolution, and negotiation.

KEY CONCEPTS

➤ Project management
- Modern project management is a process—a way of approaching a problem to achieve a certain outcome—that can be applied to even the largest of projects.
- Excellent project management does not occur in a vacuum—it exist in a rich social context.
- Responsibilities associated with being a project leader
  - Prioritizing the projects
  - Having a strong set of communication skills, including the ability to actively listen
  - Understanding time management
  - Being result-oriented

➤ Stakeholders
Stakeholders are individuals that have something significant to gain (or possibly lose) from a successful project completion.

➤ Champions
A champion is someone in an organization who may not have a clear and immediate stake in the project but has the organizational resources and will to support a project against all internal saboteurs.

➤ Definition of a project
A project is a special set of activities with a clear beginning and end. Every project has a set of goals, objective, and tasks. Every project must deal with a set of limitations.

➤ Contributions of the modern project management approach
- Process
  Identifying the process as a series of phases
- Techniques
  Developing a set of techniques to assist and structure the completion of work in each of the phases of the project
- Tools
  Incorporating the techniques into specific software tools that make it easy to use the techniques and share the results with others

➤ Five phases of the project management process
- Initiating/defining
  - Identify the problem that the project is to solve or the goals that the project is to achieve.
  - Identify the resources that are available to complete the project.

- Identify the risks associated with project.
- Planning
  - Identify the objective and activities (WBS).
  - Sequence the activities (network diagrams, Gantt).
  - Estimate time (the critical path).
  - Estimate cost (top-down, bottom-up).
  - Write the plan.
- Executing
  - Bring together resources, tasks, and schedules.
  - Create work teams.
- Controlling
  - Reports
  - Project controls
- Closing
  - Install all the deliverables.
  - Release project resources.
  - Document project details and write and publish the final report.

➤ Methods of estimating project parameters
- Guessing
- Analogy
- Theory/formula

➤ Three types of report
- Variance report

  Variance reports report the differences between the actual and planned progress of the overall project or specific activities.
- Status report

  A status report details the process that led to current project state.
- Resources allocation report

  A resource allocation report identifies the resources (in terms of person-hours, equipment, etc.) that are being applied to specific project activities.

➤ Baseline project schedule

The baseline schedule represents the planned course of the project.
- Ahead of schedule

  Ahead of schedule refers to when the actual project schedule is ahead of the baseline schedule.
- Behind schedule

  Behind schedule refers to when the actual project schedule is behind the baseline schedule.

- Slippage

  Slippage is the distance between the baseline and the actual schedule.

➤ Project management techniques
- WBS identifying tasks
  1. Identify all the project objectives.
  2. For each objective, identify all of the activities that must occur if that objective is to be met.
  3. Carefully review each objective and activity, making sure that the list is complete.
- Network diagrams
  - Simple precedence network diagram

    A simple precedence diagram helps establish the appropriate order for the project steps. By ordering project activities in this way it is possible to begin to estimate the amount of time that is required to complete the project.
  - PERT and CPM

    The PERT approach is used for most research and development projects, whereas CPM is used more often on construction projects. Both approaches use nodes (circles) and arcs (arrows) to represent events, activities, and precedence.
- Gantt charting

  Using Gantt charting, each task is graphed as a bar showing the expected duration of the task. Arrows connect dependent tasks, making it possible to show detailed dependencies among the tasks.
  - Lead time

    Lead time occurs when the second task can begin before the first one is completely finished; it is possible to shorten the overall project length by using lead time.
  - Lag time

    A lag time is the time that exists after the one task is finished but before the start of the next.
  - Reverse scheduling

    Reverse scheduling is to begin with a certain end in mind (usually some delivery date) and then work backward until a project plan is completed.

➤ Critical path

The critical path is the path with the longest duration from start to end. The activities in this longest path are called critical activities.

➤ Project phase

A project phase is a collection of related activities that, on completion, represent a significant contribution to the overall project completion.

➤ Milestone

A milestone is an event that does not require any work and has no time duration. It is used to mark the completion of some important aspect or phase of the project.

➤ Project management tools: automating project management
- PMIS
- PC tools (e.g., Excel, Microsoft Project)

➤ Five common mistakes in project management
- Failure to communicate
- Failure to create a realistic plan (not too simple, complex, or unrealistic)
- No project buy-in
- Scope creep
- Throw resources (man-months) at a project problem.

➤ Communication skills
- Three types of communication skills that a project manager must master
  - Listening
  - Negotiation
  - Conflict resolution

QUESTIONS FOR REVIEW

1. What is a project, and how does it differ from a program?

2. What are the five phases of the project management process, and what are the principle activities of each phase?

3. Explain each of the following project management techniques and identify the context in which each might be used: WBS, network diagram, PERT, CPM, and Gantt charting.

4. Define objectives and activities.

5. Explain each of the three methods for estimating project parameters (i.e., cost, time, etc.).

6. Discuss the following project management concepts: lag and lead time, slack management, critical path, slippage, and baseline.

7. Explore the benefits and limitations of using a project management software package or PMIS.

8. Describe and discuss the soft skills that a project manager must have to succeed.

FOR FURTHER DISCUSSION

There are many valuable resources available to the reader interested in learning more about the process, techniques and tools of project management.

PROFESSIONAL ORGANIZATIONS

The Project Management Institute (PMI)

The PMI is the leading nonprofit project management professional association in the world. It was founded in 1969 and has a current international membership in excess of 50,000. The institute works to establish standards for project management skills, provides seminars and courses, and facilitates discussion among project managers around the world. For more information visit the association's Web site at <http://www.pmi.org>.

International Project Management Association (IPMA)

This international association of project managers was established to "improve, on an international level, the ability of people and organizations to work together in managing resources." This organization also publishes the *International Journal of Project Management*. For information about this organization, visit <http://www.ipma.ch>.

BOOKS ABOUT PROJECT MANAGEMENT

The Mythical Man-Month, by Fred P. Brooks Jr. Published in 1975, revised in 1999 by Addison Wesley Publishing Company. ISBN 0201835959

This is one of the most influential books ever written about managing large technical projects. Although some of the technology discussed in the book is out of date, the precepts that Brooks identifies are not. The 1999 version also contains some new essays, like one on the "silver bullet," that make this edition a classic in its own right.

The Fast Forward MBA in Project Management, by Eric Verzuh. Published in 1999 by John Wiley and Sons. ISBN 0471325465

By design, this book packs a lot of information into a minimal amount of space. There is good use of graphs, illustrations, and tables to explore the principles of project management. There is also a good treatment of the relational and political aspects of project management. This is a good source of information for the reader with introductory to intermediate knowledge of project management.

5-Phase Project Management: A Practical Planning and Implementation Guide, by Joseph Weiss and Robert Wysocki. Published in 1992 by Perseus Books. ISBN 0201563169.

This book is a project management classic. Chapters are structured along the phases of the project management process and include useful examples. Written for the practitioner, this book covers most of the major techniques of project management. This book is written with the introductory to intermediate level project manager in mind.

Project Management: Strategic Design and Implementation, by David Cleland. Published in 1994 (2nd edition) by McGraw Hill. ISBN 0070113513.

David Cleland is a recognized expert in the area of project management. In this book, a third edition, the author focuses on teamwork in project management and on project management as a strategic planning tool. This book is written for the intermediate to advanced level project manager.

Project Management: A Systems Approach to Planning, Scheduling, and Controlling, by Harold Kerzner. Published in 1997 (6th edition) by John Wiley and Sons. ISBN 0471288357.

This book, now in its sixth edition, explores resource allocation issues and the relationship of project management techniques and total quality management methods. There is also a section on studying for the PMI Certification exam. This book is written with the experienced project manager in mind.

Applied Project Management: Best Practices on Implementation, by Harold Kerzner. Published in 2000 by John Wiley and Sons. ISBN 0471288357.

This new book from Kerzner has a clear focus on the implementation component of project management. The book has a strong real-world flavor, including over 20 case studies throughout. It is written for advanced level project managers who have mastered the concepts presented in Kerzner's sixth edition *Project Management* text.

Project Management for the 21st Century, by Kathryn Rea and Bennet Lientz. Published in 1998 by Academic Press. ISBN 012449966.

Written in a very readable format, this book focuses on problems commonly encountered in the project management process. The book is written for the introductory to intermediate level project manager.

The Complete Idiot's Guide to Project Management, by Sunny and Kim Baker. Published in 1998 by Alpha. ISBN 0028617452.

If you can get past the offensive title, you will find this text to be a well-written introduction to the basic ideas and techniques of project management. It is written for the introductory level project manager, but more experienced project managers may still find this a useful text.

PROJECT MANAGEMENT RELATED WEB SITES

➤ <http://www.apmgroup.co.uk/theapm.html>—The Web site for the UK-based Association for Project Management.

➤ <http://www.pmi.org>—The Web site for the PMI.

➤ <http://www.computerworld.com/home/online9697.nsf/all /970922projectlinks>—A nice collection of links to project management resources maintained by *Computerworld* magazine.

➤ <http://www.ipma.ch>—Web site for the IPMA.

➤ <http://www.pmforum.org>—The Project Management Forum is a nonprofit organization designed to facilitate exchange among project managers. The Web site includes a list of Internet project management resources and an extensive bibliography.

REFERENCES

Alexander, S. 1999. "Life after Project Management." *Computerworld* (July 12).

Brooks Jr., F. P. 1975, 1999. *The Mythical Man-Month,* 20th anniversary ed. New York: Addison Wesley.

Halstead, M. H. 1977. *Elements of Software Science.* New York: Elsevier North-Holland.

Littlefield Jr., T. K., and P. H. Randolph. 1987. "An Answer to Sasieni's Question on PERT Times." *Management Science* (October).

Shillingford, J. 1998. "USA Discovers Key to Successful Projects." *Computer Weekly* (25 June).

Weiss, J., and R. Wysocki. 1992. *5-Phase Project Management: A Practical Planning and Implementation Guide.* Perseus Books.

Williams, P. 1996. *Getting a Project Done on Time: Managing People, Time, and Results.* New York: AMACOM.

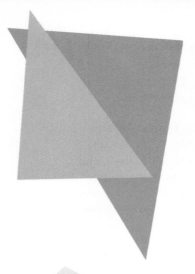

OOAD

Learning Objectives

- Understand the basic characteristics and objectives of the object-oriented approach to software development
- Identify the component elements of object-oriented software design
- Understand the Unified Modeling Language (UML) and its relationship to object-oriented design
- Explore the various diagrams and their applications contained within the UML

C lets you shoot yourself in the foot rather easily. C++ allows you to blow your whole leg off.

—GERALD KARAM, AT&T LABS RESEARCH

Most programmers prefer to use C because it is the easiest language to spell.

—ANONYMOUS

INTRODUCTION

One thing is always certain in the world of SAD: there is always room for improvement. Despite our continued advancement into better techniques, tools, and methods, we are also being faced with larger and more complex systems to design and build. In addition, projects still come in over budget and past deadlines, and they sometimes fail to meet the needs of the end users. The smart analyst learns from both the mistakes and successes of the past and uses that experience to create an atmosphere of continuous improvement. The focus of this appendix is one example of the evolution of approaches in the world of the systems analyst.

One of the most revolutionary changes to occur to the traditional SAD approaches is the development of *object-oriented techniques*. The object-oriented approach to software development views the system as a collection of self-contained modules, or *objects*, that carry with them both the processes necessary to execute their intended role and the data, or the identification of the data, necessary for that execution. Because of their self-contained nature, objects can be built as stand-alone units and then assembled, as needed, to form a functional system. Unlike the traditional approach to software development, objects can be reused over and over in a wide variety of systems without having to modify them in any manner.

In this last appendix we present an overview of the object-oriented approach to analysis and design such that you can develop an understanding of the basic concepts contained within the approach, as well as the differences between traditional software development and object orientation. We begin this process by turning our attention to the core concept in the object-oriented approach: the object model.

THE CONCEPTS OF OBJECT-ORIENTATION

You recall from our earlier work in this text the concept of a model. A model is a representation of a real-world problem or environment that represents what are believed to be the essential elements or features of that problem or environment. The better the model, the closer our understanding to the actual situation. Just as logical modeling is valuable in the analysis stages of the SDLC, the object-oriented approach to analysis and design also embraces the use of detailed models. The difference between the two approaches, however, lies in the component elements of the model. In this section, we identify and define the core concepts and component elements found in the object-oriented model.

Objects

As you might have guessed, the core concept in the object-oriented model is the *object*. An object is any person, place, thing, or event about which we wish to store data or capture its behavior. Just like the objects in your daily environment, objects in analysis and design can be thought of as anything that can be seen, touched, or sensed in some manner, and about which we need to store data. This means objects can be used to represent anything. An object may represent an employee, a customer, a vendor, a student, a truck, a building, a warehouse, a store, a product, a piece of equipment, or even an invoice, a payment, an application, or a dinner reservation. In other words, in the object-oriented model, the centers of attention are the objects of relevance that exist in the system environment.

In some ways, objects are similar to the concept of entities used in the logical data model. In other ways, however, they are quite different. First, like an entity, an object has certain *attributes* that are used to describe the object. As such, the object TRUCK, might have attributes such as *model, serial number, date of operation, mileage, location, size, color,* or *weight,* among many others. In addition, an object can be said to have a current *state,* such as *new, operational, retired,* or possibly *in-repair.*

The primary difference between an object and entity, however, is that objects can also have *behavior.* Behaviors are *methods* or operations that serve to specify what actions the object can perform. As an example, consider an object defined to represent a RESERVATION. Its behaviors may include *scheduling a reservation, deleting an existing reservation, locating the next available time slot,* or *rejecting a request for a reservation.* Figure B-1 graphically illustrates the concept of an object, its attributes, and its associated methods.

Another difference between objects and entities is that whereas entities use primary and foreign keys to identify unique instances, an object instance is assigned a *unique identifier* (UID) by the system when it is first created. The UID of an object instance is often hidden from end users and is typically used by the system to distinguish between two or more instances (potentially with the exact same attributes and methods).

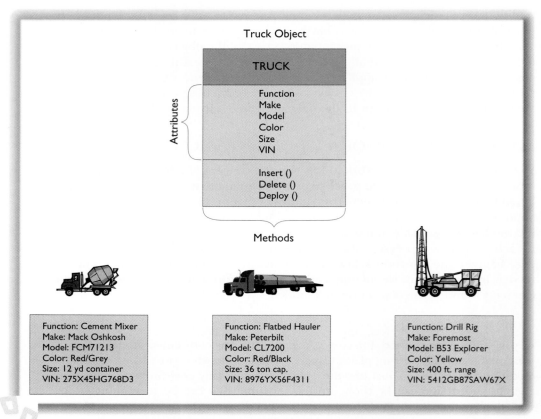

Figure B-1   Objects, Attributes, Methods, and Instances

By applying the concept of objects to software design, we can represent real-world objects with software objects. We might choose to represent a real-world dog as a software object in some animation program. Maybe we want to write an application that controls an electronic exercise bicycle; in this case we would create a bicycle object. Figure B-2 illustrates the component elements that might be contained within a software object designed to represent a real-world bicycle.

Everything that the software object knows (its *state*) and can do (its *behavior*) is expressed by the variables and the methods within that object. A software object modeled after a real-world bicycle would have variables that indicate the bicycle's current state: its speed is 10 mph, its pedal cadence is 90 rpm, and its current gear is the 5th gear. These variables are formally known as *instance variables* because they contain the state for a specific instance of a bicycle object.

In addition to its variables, the bicycle object also contains *methods* to brake, change the pedal cadence, and change gears. Note that our bicycle object does not contain a method for changing the speed of the bicycle. This is because the bicycle's speed is actually just a side effect of what gear it is in, how fast the rider is pedaling, whether the brakes are on, and how steep the hill is. As such, the speed changes as a result of changes to the values of the contained methods. These methods are formally known as *instance methods* because they inspect or change the state of a particular bicycle instance.

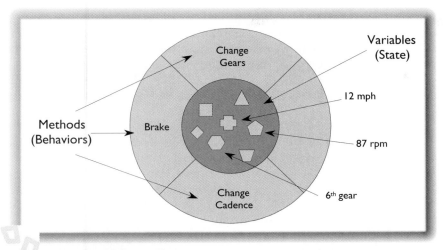

Figure B-2   Software Object Representation of a Bicycle

A typical object diagram, such as the one illustrated in Figure B-2, shows that the object's variables make up the center, or nucleus, of the object. Methods surround and hide the object's nucleus from other objects in the program. This representation is by design and is an accurate depiction of another characteristic of an object. Packaging an object's variables within the protective custody of its methods is called *encapsulation,* or the localization of knowledge within a module. Because objects encapsulate both data and implementation, the user of an object can view the object as a black box that provides services. Instance variables and methods can be added, deleted, or changed, but as long as the services provided by the object remain the same, code that uses the object can continue to use it without being having to be rewritten or revised.

In some cases, however, often for practical reasons, a programmer may wish to expose some of an object's variables or hide some of its methods. In the popular object-oriented programming language JAVA, an object can be set to one of four access levels for each of its variables and methods. The access level determines which other objects and classes can access that variable or method.

The concept of encapsulation of variables and methods into a neat software bundle is a simple yet powerful idea that provides two primary benefits to software developers. First, the developer gains the well-known benefit of *modularity.* The source code for an object can be written and maintained independently of the source code for other objects. Also, just as in the real world, an object can be easily passed around in the system. You can give your bicycle to someone else, and it still works.

The second benefit of encapsulation is *information hiding.* An object has a public interface that other objects can use to communicate with it. Simultaneously, however, that same object can maintain private information and methods that can be changed at any time without affecting the other objects that depend on it. You do not need to understand the physics of gearing ratios and torque to know how to use the gears on your bike.

Class

The *class* of an object refers to some generalized description we create to describe objects that are similar in nature or share many of the same characteristics. A class can be thought of as a blueprint, or prototype, that defines the variables and the methods common to all objects of a certain kind. Every object is associated with at least one class, and in some cases, an object can be a member of many different classes.

In the physical world, we often have one or more objects of the same kind. For example, your bicycle is just one of many bicycles in the world. Using object-oriented terminology, we say that your bicycle object is an *instance of the class* of objects known as BICYCLES. Bicycles have some state (current gear, current cadence, two wheels) and behavior (change gears, brake) in common. However, each bicycle's state is independent of, and therefore can be different from, that of other bicycles. When building bicycles, manufacturers take advantage of the fact that bicycles share characteristics, building many bicycles from the same blueprint. It would be very inefficient to produce a new blueprint for every individual bicycle manufactured.

In the object-oriented world, it is also possible to have many objects of the same kind that share characteristics: rectangles, trucks, employee records, invoices, products, video clips, and so on. Using the same approach as the bicycle manufacturers, you can take advantage of the fact that objects of the same kind are similar, and you can create a blueprint for those objects. Figure B-3 illustrates this blueprint concept for a software object.

The *class* for our bicycle example would declare the instance variables necessary to contain the current gear, the current cadence, and so on, for each BICYCLE object. The class would also declare and provide implementations for the instance methods that allow the rider to change gears, brake, and change the pedaling cadence, as shown in Figure B-4.

Figure B-3   Blueprint Concept of a Software Object

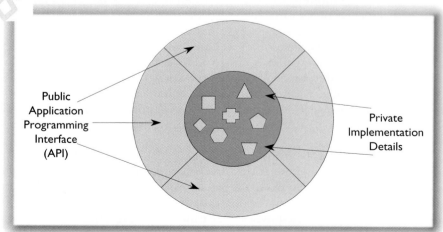

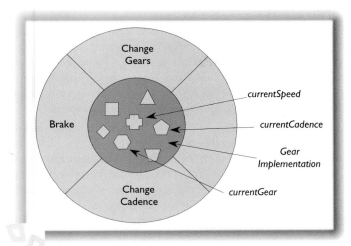

Figure B-4   Example of Object Class
Implementations

After a bicycle class is created, any number of bicycle objects can be created from the class. When an instance of a class is created, the system allocates enough memory for the object and all of its instance variables. As shown in Figure B-5, each instance gets its own copy of all the instance variables defined in the class.

In addition to instance variables, classes can also define *class variables*. A class variable contains information that is shared by all instances of the class. For example, suppose that all bicycles have the same number of gears. In this case, defining an instance variable to hold the number of gears is inefficient and redundant, because

Figure B-5   Instance Objects Created from BICYCLE Class

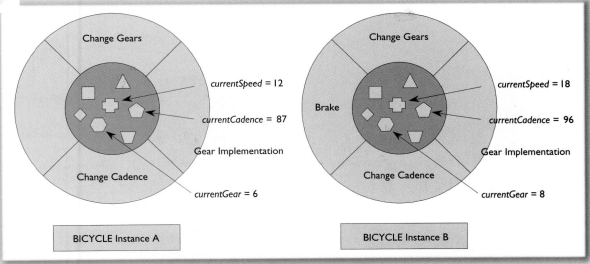

each instance of the object would have to carry its own copy of the variable, with the value being the same for every instance. In such situations, a class variable can be defined that contains the number of gears. All instances share this variable. If one object is allowed to change the variable, it is changed for all other objects of that type. Also, like an object, a class can declare *class methods*. A class method can be invoked directly from the class, whereas instance methods are only invoked on a particular instance. Figure B-6 illustrates the concept of class instance.

Objects versus Classes

If you have looked closely at the examples in Figures B.2 through B.6, you may have noticed that the illustrations of objects and classes look very similar. Indeed, the difference between classes and objects is often the source of some confusion. In the physical world, it is obvious that classes are not themselves the objects they describe: *a picture of a bicycle is not a bicycle.* However, it becomes a bit more difficult to differentiate between classes and objects in software, partially because software objects are simply electronic models of real-world objects or abstract concepts in the first place and also because the term *object* is sometimes used to refer to both classes and instances. Although no particular nomenclature exists to differentiate between an object class and an instance of a class, in most cases the context helps you determine whether the item of interest is a class or simply a member of a class. In other cases, as you will see, it may not matter at all.

Hierarchical Inheritance

Generally speaking, objects are defined in terms of their classes. You can know a lot about an object simply by knowing its class. Many people would not know what a *Marin* is, but if I told you it was a special type of bicycle, you would know that it had two wheels, handle bars, and pedals.

Figure B-6   Example of Instance Derived from Object Class

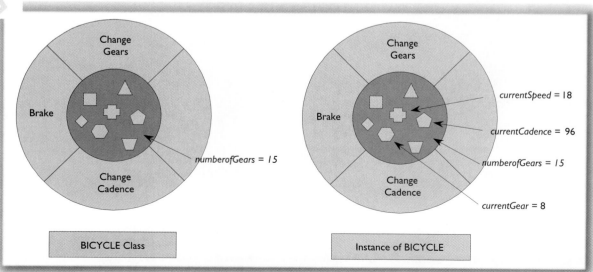

Object-oriented systems take this concept a step further and allow classes to be defined in terms of other classes. For example, mountain bikes, racing bikes, and tandems are all kinds of bicycles. In object-oriented terminology, mountain bikes, racing bikes, and tandems are all *subclasses* of the bicycle class. Similarly, the bicycle class is the *superclass* of mountain bikes, racing bikes, and tandems. This concept of *hierarchical inheritance* is shown in Figure B-7.

Each *subclass inherits state* (in the form of variable declarations) *from the superclass*. Mountain bikes, racing bikes, and tandems share some states: cadence, speed, and the like. Also, each *subclass inherits methods from the superclass*. Mountain bikes, racing bikes, and tandems share some behaviors: braking and changing pedaling speed, for example.

However, subclasses are not limited to the state and behaviors provided to them by their superclass. Subclasses can add variables and methods to the ones they inherit from the superclass. Tandem bicycles have two seats and two sets of handle bars; some mountain bikes have an extra set of gears with a lower gear ratio. Subclasses can also override inherited methods and provide specialized implementations for those methods. For example, if you had a mountain bike with an extra set of gears, you would override the change gears method so that the rider could use those new gears. This concept of inheritance allows an analyst or a programmer to efficiently define the various characteristics of an object by first using those of the superclass and then modifying as needed in the subclass.

This concept is also not limited to just one layer of inheritance. The inheritance tree, or class hierarchy, can be as deep as needed. Methods and variables are inherited down through the levels. Intuitively enough, the farther down in the inheritance hierarchy a class appears, the more specialized its behavior.

The OBJECT class is at the top of class hierarchy, and each class is its *descendant* (directly or indirectly). A variable of type OBJECT can hold a reference to any object, such as an instance of a class or even an array of values. In this way, the OBJECT provides behaviors that are required of all objects running in the application.

Messages

A single object alone is generally not very useful. Instead, an object usually appears as a component of a larger program or application that contains many other objects. Through the interaction of these objects, analysts and programmers can achieve higher-order functionality and more complex behavior. Your bicycle hanging from a hook in the garage is just a bunch of metal, plastic, and rubber; by itself, the bicycle is incapable of any activity. But when another object (you) interacts with it (pedal), your bicycle becomes an effective and enjoyable mode of transportation.

Similarly, software objects interact and communicate with each other by sending *messages*. When OBJECT A wants OBJECT B to perform one of B's methods, OBJECT A sends a message to OBJECT B. Figure B-8 illustrates an example of object messaging.

In certain situations, the receiving object may need more information so that it knows exactly what to do. Using our bicycle example, when you want to change gears on your bicycle, you have to indicate which gear you want. This additional information is passed along with the message as *parameters*.

One of the biggest advantages to object messaging is that because an object's behavior is expressed through its methods, message passing can support all possible interactions between objects. Further, the interacting objects do not need to be a part of the same process or even reside on the same platform to send and receive messages back and forth to each other.

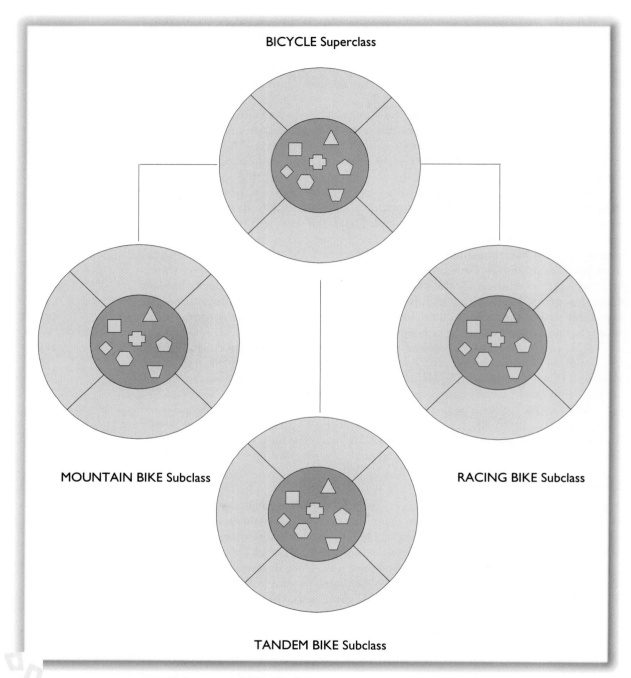

Figure B-7   Hierarchical Inheritance—Superclass and Subclasses

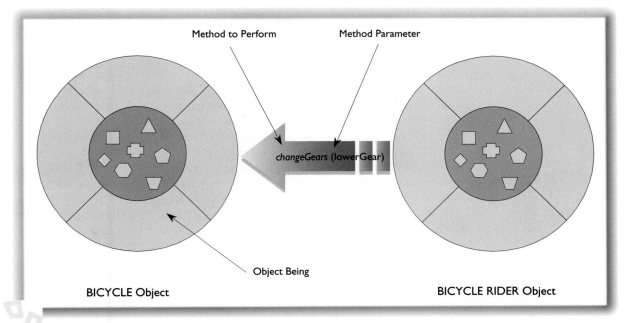

Method to Perform   Method Parameter

changeGears (lowerGear)

Object Being

BICYCLE Object   BICYCLE RIDER Object

Figure B-8   Example of Object Messaging

Polymorphism

A closely related concept to messaging is *polymorphism,* meaning "many forms." This concept allows for a message to one object to invoke different behavior than the same message to a different object or class.

Suppose you send a message to a bicycle object to stop. The bicycle object applies the brakes until the speed variable has reached a value of zero. If that same message is sent to a piece of electrically powered machinery, however, the behavior of the object is quite different. Instead of applying the brakes, as in the bicycle object, the message stop triggers the removal of power from the machine, and it stops. The effect is the same, but the behavior is quite different.

Using this concept of polymorphism in an object-oriented application, an analyst can simply instruct the requesting object to issue a message requesting a certain behavior. The requesting object does not need any information with regard to how that behavior is accomplished. One message—many forms.

THE UNIFIED MODELING LANGUAGE

Now that we have a good understanding of the component elements of the object-oriented model, we can begin to explore its application and use in a development environment. In an effort to develop a set of standards from which the object-oriented approach could grow, the leaders of the field came together to combine the best of all available methods into a single comprehensive development approach.

The *Unified Modeling Language* (UML) is the industry-standard language for specifying, visualizing, constructing, and documenting the artifacts of object-based software systems. It simplifies the complex process of software design, making a blueprint for construction. The UML definition was led by three industry-leading methodologists: Grady Booch, Ivar Jacobson, and Jim Rumbaugh.

The UML emerged from the unification that occurred in the 1990s following the method wars of the 1970s and 1980s. Even though the UML evolved primarily from various second-generation object-oriented methods (at the notation level), the UML is not simply a third-generation object-oriented modeling language. Its scope extends its usability far beyond its predecessors, and it is experience and experimentation with, and gradual adoption of, the standard that reveal its true potential and enable organizations to realize its benefits. Table B-1 contains a list of many of the characteristics that serve to define what the UML is and what it is not.

The key word in describing the UML is the word *unified*. The UML embodies a set of nine unique object modeling and diagramming tools that, when used appropriately, comprehensively define and model an object-oriented system. The common element in these nine tools is that they all use exactly the same syntax and nomenclature, thus making it easy for analysts and programmers to learn and use the UML. Further, the diagramming techniques are used throughout all phases of the development life cycle being used, and they are simply changed and updated as the project moves from the logical design stages to the physical design stages. The UML can even document and facilitate the activities found in the implementation stages of a project. Table B-2 contains a list of the nine UML diagramming techniques, along with a brief description of their intended applications.

Table B-1   Identifying Characteristics of the Unified Modeling Language

The UML is
- **Within a system-intensive process**, a method applied as a process to derive or evolve a system.
- **As a language**, used for communication. That is, it is a means to capture knowledge (semantics) about a subject and express knowledge (syntax) regarding the subject for the purpose of communication. The subject is the system under discussion.
- **As a modeling language**, one that focuses on understanding a subject via the formulation of a model of the subject (and its related context). The model embodies knowledge regarding the subject, and the appropriate application of this knowledge constitutes intelligence.
- **Regarding unification**, a tool that unifies the information systems and technology industry's best engineering practices across types of systems (software and non-software), domains (business versus software), and life-cycle processes.
- **As it applies to specifying systems**, a tool that can be used to communicate "what" is required of a system and "how" a system may be realized.
- **As it applies to visualizing systems**, a tool that can be used to visually depict a system before it is realized.
- **As it applies to constructing systems**, a tool that can be used to guide the realization of a system, similar to a blueprint.
- **As it applies to documenting systems**, a tool that can be used for capturing knowledge about a system throughout its life-cycle.

The UML is not
- **A visual programming language** but a visual modeling language.
- **A tool or repository specification** but a modeling language specification.
- **A process**, but it enables processes.

Table B-2   Diagramming Tools Contained within the Unified Modeling Language

UML Diagram	Diagram Description	Diagram Application	Typical SDLC Phase
Use case	Depicts the interactions between external end users and the system.	Used to describe the system requirements.	Entire SDLC
Class	Displays the system in its static form at the class level.	Used to illustrate the class relationships for a particular use-case.	Logical analysis Logical/physical design
Object	Displays the system in its static form at the object level.	Used to illustrate the object relationships for a particular use-case.	Logical analysis Logical/physical design
Sequence	Depicts the interaction between classes within a particular use-case. Diagram is arranged in temporal sequence.	Models the behavior of the various classes for a particular use-case.	Logical analysis Logical/physical design
Collaboration	Depicts the interaction between classes within a particular use-case. Diagram is *not* arranged in temporal sequence.	Models the behavior of the various classes for a particular use-case.	Logical analysis Logical/physical design
Statechart	Depicts the various sequence of states that a particular object can assume, the events that can cause transition from one state to another, and the actions that can occur as a result of a state change.	Focuses on the behavior of a single class for a particular use-case.	Logical analysis Logical/physical design
Activity	Depicts a specific business process and provides a view of the flows inside a use-case or among several classes.	Provides a graphical representation of the flow of activities for a particular use-case.	Logical analysis Logical/physical design
Component	Displays the physical components (files) in a software application along with their location.	Used to depict the physical structure of a given software application.	Physical design Implementation
Deployment	Depicts the structure of the entire runtime system by identifying how the various code modules are distributed across platforms.	Used to illustrate the associations between the code modules in a software application and the hardware components necessary to support them.	Physical design Implementation

It is important to note that, although the UML does bring structure to the modeling and diagramming processes of a project, it is not a development methodology and does not provide any formal structure with regard to how the diagramming techniques are employed. Many organizations are finding that the tools contained within the UML can be easily adopted in an SDLC environment and can simply replace older structured methodology techniques (such as DFDs and ERDs).

In the following sections, we briefly outline the basic characteristics, applications, and interactions among the nine modeling techniques. The purpose of this appendix is not to prepare you to conduct an object-oriented development effort. For that you need additional training and coursework in object-oriented programming. Our intention here is to provide you with a working knowledge of the tools that exist in the object-oriented world, because you most likely will encounter them during the course of your work. Further, many organizations are adopting several of the UML modeling techniques in their structured analysis and design programs and replacing the more the traditional diagrams with the newer UML-based ones. In any event, you should become familiar with their construction and use, and this is what we accomplish here.

The Use-Case Model

Although each of the nine diagramming techniques in the UML is important, the central building block of the UML is the *use-case diagram*. The intention of this tool is to provide a high-level description of what the system must do. Typically, the analyst creates a use-case diagram for each major function of the system in the early stages of the SDLC during the requirements gathering process and uses the diagram to communicate back to the end users exactly what the proposed system is expected to do. In this way, the use-case diagram can serve to replace the early iterations of a logical DFD.

Several benefits are typically associated with the use-case. First, and foremost, the use-case can serve as a basis for identifying the relevant objects in a system environment, as well as their high-level relationships, roles, and responsibilities.

Second, the use-case, when complete, provides an effective tool for validating system requirements and for providing a view of the system from an external perspective. Finally, because the use-case is modified throughout the development process, in its final form it can serve as the basis for the development of a comprehensive test plan, as well as for structuring the final end user documentation.

Use-Case Components

The use-case diagram consists of 2 main components: *actors* and the *use-cases*. An *actor* is any person, organization, or computer system, external to the system but interacting with it. The actor does not represent a specific end user but rather a role that an end user can play while interacting with the system. Further, remember that, like sources and sinks in a DFD, the actor in a use-case is always external to the system. As such, any end users that would be contained within the system boundaries in a DFD would not be included in a use-case diagram. For example, a data entry clerk in a university registration system would not be considered an actor in a use-case diagram because he or she would normally be found as a process within the system boundary. In addition, an actor can interact with another actor or with the system in a manner that is different from that of a typical actor. In such cases, the actor is referred to as a *specialized actor* and is connected to the more general superclass actor using a line with a hollow triangle at its end. The specialized actor inherits the behaviors and characteristics of the superclass actor but may initially interact with the system in a slightly different manner than normal. For example, a new student initially interacts differently with a university registration system than an existing student does.

The *use-cases* are the interfaces that the system makes visible and available to the outside world through which the actor can interact. One common way of thinking of a use-case is that of a *scenario*. In this sense, the use-case represents a sequence of steps, either manual or automated, that define the completion of a single business task. Actors are illustrated as stick figures, use-cases as ovals, associations (except in specialized cases) as a solid line with no directionality, and the system as a box surrounding the use-case diagram. A simplistic example of a university IS could be described with the following use-cases: *enroll students in courses, input student grades,* and *produce student transcripts.* Figure B-9 graphically illustrates this example. The actors represent the students, the lecturer, and the registrar.

Uses and Extends

There are situations where one use-case either *makes use* of the functionality of another use-case or serves to *extend* the functionality of another use-case. In these situations, the use-cases are connected on the diagram using a hollow arrowhead, as with a specialized actor, but the arrow also contains either the word *uses* or *extends*, surrounded by double brackets, [[ ]], or pointers, $<< >>$.

Class Diagram

The class diagram provides a static structure of all the *classes* that exist within the system. The diagram shows the various classes, each defined through a set of *attributes* and *methods*, and points out the relationship between each of those classes via *associations* or *inheritance*. These associations also include an indication of the class cardinalities but without any temporal information. Table B-3 contains a list of the component elements found in a class diagram, and Figure B-10 analyzes the class

Figure B-9   Simple Use Case Diagram

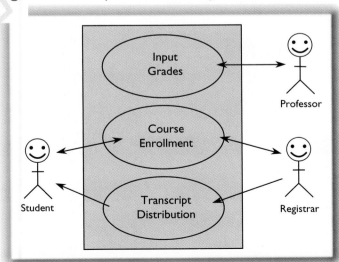

Table B-3   Class Diagram Components

Class Diagram Component	Class Diagram Symbol
CLASS Can represent a person, place, or thing of interest to the system and about which the system must capture and/or store information	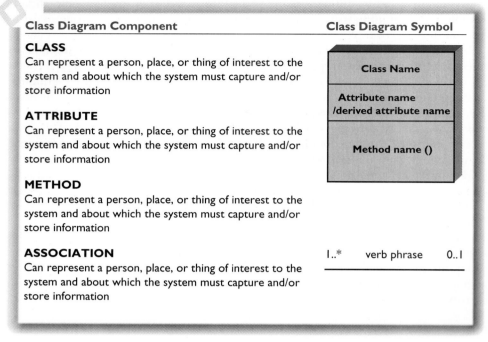
ATTRIBUTE Can represent a person, place, or thing of interest to the system and about which the system must capture and/or store information	
METHOD Can represent a person, place, or thing of interest to the system and about which the system must capture and/or store information	
ASSOCIATION Can represent a person, place, or thing of interest to the system and about which the system must capture and/or store information	1..* verb phrase 0..1

Figure B-10   Example Class Diagram for a Contact Maintenance System

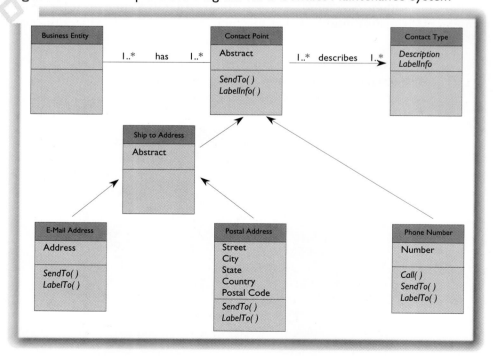

diagram of a contact maintenance system. POSTAL ADDRESS, E-MAIL ADDRESS, PHONE NUMBER, and BUSINESS ENTITY are examples of some of the classes, whereas the lines joining the different classes indicate their relationships.

Before we continue with class diagrams, we need to discuss an important subtlety in the way that people use class diagrams. This subtlety is usually undocumented, but it has, nonetheless, an important impact on the way you interpret a class diagram, for it really concerns what it is you are describing with a model. Although only one class diagram protocol exists, there are actually three perspectives you can use in drawing and interpreting them. (This actually holds true for any model, but our focus here is on class diagrams.)

The first of the three is the *conceptual* perspective. In this case, the diagram is drawn in a manner that represents the concepts in the domain under study. These concepts naturally relate to the classes that implement them, but it is often not a direct mapping. Indeed, the model is drawn with little or no regard for the software that might implement it and therefore is generally language independent.

The second approach is the *specification* perspective. In this perspective we are looking at software, but we are looking at the interfaces of the software rather than the implementation. We are, thus, looking at *types* rather than *classes*. Object-oriented development puts a great emphasis on the difference between type and class, but this is often overlooked in practice. I believe it is important to separate interface (type) and implementation (class). Most object-oriented languages do not do it, and methods, influenced by that, have followed suit. This is changing (JAVA is one example) but not quickly enough. Types represent an interface that may have many implementations, due to the chosen implementation environment, performance characteristics, or vendor. This distinction can be very important in a number of design techniques based on delegation.

The final perspective is one of *implementation*. In this view, we really do have classes, and we are laying the implementation bare. This is probably the perspective used most often, but in many ways the specification perspective is often a better one to take.

Understanding the three perspectives is crucial to both drawing and reading class diagrams. When you are drawing a class diagram, draw it from a single clear perspective; when you read a diagram, make sure you know which perspective the diagram is taking. That knowledge is essential if you are to interpret the diagram properly. Unfortunately, the lines between the perspectives are not sharp, and most modelers do not take care to get their perspective sorted out when they are drawing.

Class diagrams are the backbone of nearly all object-oriented methods, so you will find yourself using them all the time. The trouble is that they are so rich that they can be overwhelming to use. There are some general guidelines to follow, however, that may make their creation and use easier.

To begin, do not try to use all the various notations available. Start with the simple stuff: classes, associations, attributes, and generalization. Introduce other notations only when you need them.

Second, sort out which perspective you are drawing the models from. If you are in analysis, draw conceptual models. When working with software, concentrate on specification models. Draw implementation models only when you are illustrating a particular implementation technique.

Finally, do not draw models for everything; instead, concentrate on the key areas. It is better to have a few diagrams that you use and keep up to date than many forgotten, out-of-date models.

The biggest danger with class diagrams is that you can get bogged down in implementation details far too early. To combat this, use the conceptual or specification perspective. One technique associated with class diagramming that may help you avoid this problem is the *class-responsibility-collaboration (CRC) card*.

CRC Cards

In the late 1980s, one of the biggest centers of object technology was the research labs of Tektronix in Portland, Oregon. These labs were one of the main users of Smalltalk, and many key ideas in object technology were developed there.

Two renowned Smalltalk programmers at Tektronix were Ward Cunningham and Kent Beck. They were, and are, very concerned about how to teach people that same deep knowledge of how to use Smalltalk that they have gained. From this question of how to teach objects came the simple technique of CRC cards.

Rather than using diagrams to develop models, as most methodologists suggest, Cunningham and Beck proposed representing classes on 4 × 6 index cards. Rather than indicating *attributes* and *methods* on the cards, they proposed that *responsibilities* be recorded. So, what is a responsibility? It is really a high level description of the purpose of the class. The idea is to try to get away from a description of bits of data and process and instead capture the purpose of the class in a few sentences. The choice of a card is deliberate—*you are not allowed to write more than what fits on the card*. Figure B-11 illustrates a simple CRC card.

The last letter in CRC refers to collaborators. With each responsibility you indicate which other classes you need to work with to fulfill it. This gives you some idea of the links between classes, although still at a high level.

CRC cards are an aggressively informal technique that encourages discussion among the developers and analysts. In a CRC session, the participants crowd around a table, with each person picking up a card as they describe how the class participates in some use-case.

By giving the developers something to touch that represents the class, you make it easier to talk through the designs. By accenting responsibilities instead of data and methods, you help developers get away from dumb data holders and ease them toward understanding the higher level behavior of the class.

Some people find CRC cards to be wonderful, others find CRC leaves them cold. It is my belief that you should try CRC cards out to see if the team likes working with them. Use them in particular if you find teams are getting bogged down in too many details too early or seem to be identifying classes that are cluttered and do not have clear definitions.

Use class diagrams and interaction diagrams to capture and formalize the results of CRC modeling. If you are using class diagrams, ensure each class has a statement of its responsibilities. Finally, beware of long lists of responsibilities: if it does not fit on a 4 × 6 card, you are missing the point!

Statechart Diagram

The *statechart* diagram is useful when describing a single object that can have different states during its lifetime. This diagram illustrates how the object changes from one *state* to another in response to a given *event*. The attributes define the state of the object at one time, whereas the methods define the transitions that take place.

By definition, an object *state* is a particular condition during the life of the object when the object satisfies some condition, performs a specific behavior, or waits for the onset of a particular event. Each state for an object has a unique *state name*.

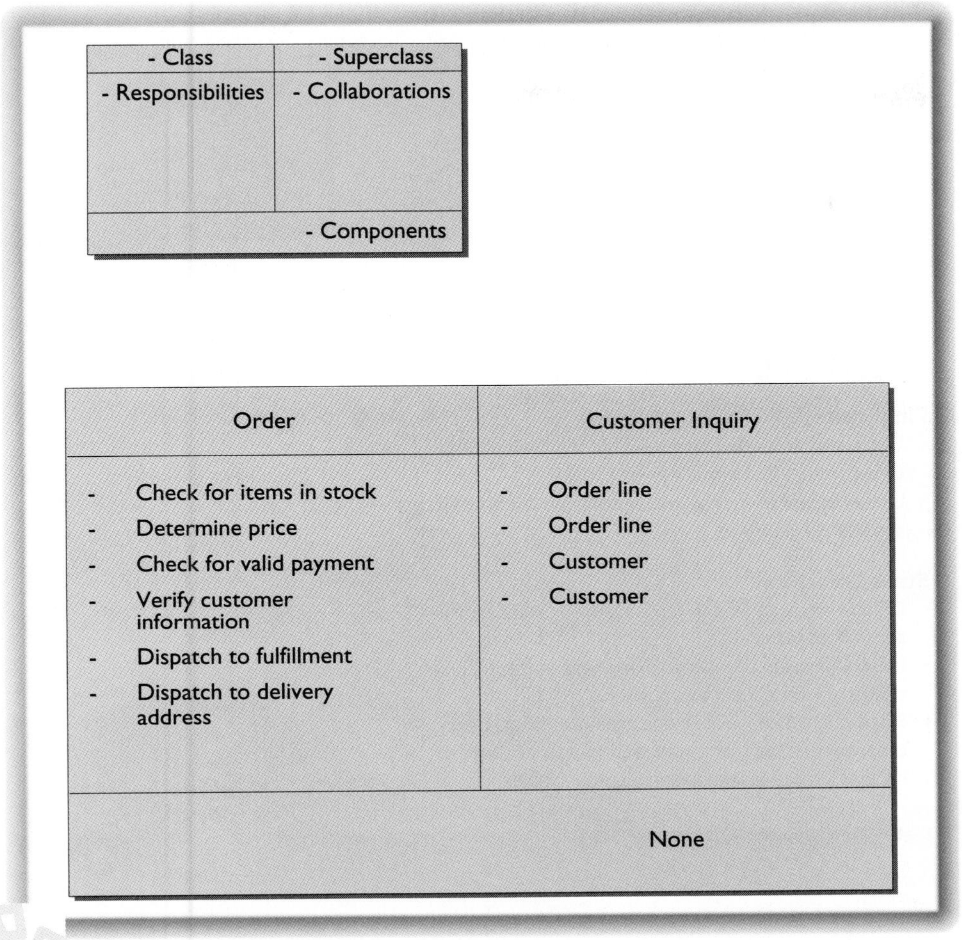

- Class	- Superclass
- Responsibilities	- Collaborations
	- Components

Order	Customer Inquiry
- Check for items in stock	- Order line
- Determine price	- Order line
- Check for valid payment	- Customer
- Verify customer information	- Customer
- Dispatch to fulfillment	
- Dispatch to delivery address	
	None

Figure B-11   Class-Responsibility-Collaboration (CRC) Card

States are considered to be *semipermanent,* in that an object remains in a particular state until some event or trigger causes it to move to another state.

In contrast to a state, an object *action* is some activity the object is performing while in a particular state.

Table B-4 contains a list of the component elements in a statechart diagram, and Figure B-12 provides an example of a statechart diagram for a bank account. The rectangles represent the various states that the account can be in, and the arrows correspond to the transitions due to the call of a method on the object.

Activity Diagram

An *activity diagram* is a special form of a statechart diagram. Transitions in the diagram are mainly triggered by the completion of action by the source state. The diagram focuses on the flow of operations driven by internal processing as opposed to external events. However the diagram does not make explicit which objects execute which activities.

Table B-4　Component Elements of a Statechart Diagram

State
- Displayed as a round-cornered rectangle
- Contains a label identifying the state object

Active

Initial state
- Displayed as a solid circle
- Used to represent the moment at which an object begins to exist

Final state
- Displayed as a solid circle within a larger unfilled circle (much like a bull's eye)
- Used to represent the moment at which an object activity is complete

State transition
- Displayed as an arrow from the first state to the second state
- Label indicates the event that triggers the transition from one state to another
- State change can occur due to a condition becoming true, the passage of a specified length of time, or receipt of a message from another object

For many people looking at the latest version of the UML, the activity diagram is the most unfamiliar. This is because the diagram was not present in the works of either Booch, Jacobson, or Rumbaugh but was added later.

The activity diagram focuses on activities, chunks of process that may or may not correspond to methods or member functions, and the sequencing of these activities. In this sense it is like a flow chart. It differs, however, from a flow chart in that it explicitly supports parallel activities and their synchronization.

In Figure B-13, we see the receive order activity triggers both the authorize payment and the check line item activities. Indeed, the check line item is triggered for each line item on the order. Thus, if an order has three line items, the receive order activity would trigger four activities in parallel, leading (at least conceptually) to four separate threads. These threads, together with other threads started by the receive supplies activity, are synchronized before the order is dispatched.

Note that this diagram does not have an end point. This is typical of activity diagrams that define a business process that synchronizes several external incoming events. You can think of the diagram as defining the reaction to that process, which continues until everything that needs to be done is done.

The biggest disadvantage of activity diagrams is that they do not make explicit which objects execute which activities or what way the messaging works between them. You can label each activity with the responsible object, but that does not make the interactions between the objects clear (that is when you need to use an in-

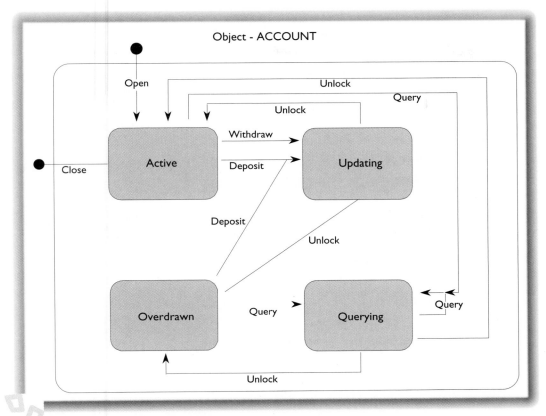

Figure B-12   Statechart Diagram for a Bank Account

teraction diagram). Often, drawing an activity diagram early on in the modeling of a process is useful to help you understand the overall process. Then you can use interaction diagrams to help you allocate activities to classes.

Activity diagrams are useful when you want to describe behaviors that are parallel or when you want to show how behaviors in several use-cases interact. Use interaction diagrams when you want to show how objects collaborate to implement an activity diagram. Use a state transition diagram to show how one object changes during its lifetime.

Interaction Diagram

Interaction diagrams provide models to describe how objects within a set of objects interact with each other. The main components of interaction diagrams are the *objects* and the *messages* that are sent to each other. UML has two forms of interaction diagrams, namely, the *sequence diagram* and the *collaboration diagram*.

Interaction diagrams are models that describe how a group of objects collaborate in some behavior—typically a single use-case. The diagrams show a number of example objects and the messages that are passed between these objects within the use-case.

We can illustrate the approach with the following simple use-case. In this behavior, the order entry window sends a *prepare* message to an order. The order then sends *prepare* to each order line on the order. The order line first checks the stock

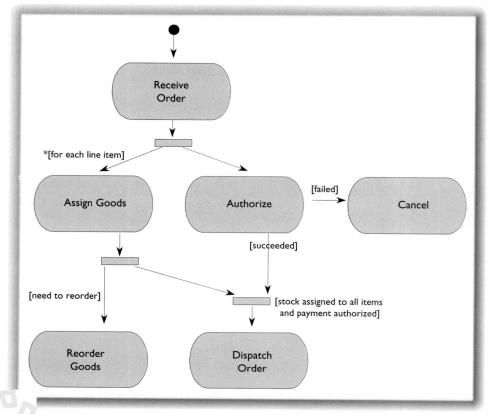

Figure B-13   Activity Diagram for Order Process

item, and if the check returns true, it removes stock from the stock item. If the stock item falls below the reorder level, it requests a new delivery.

Interaction diagrams come in two forms, both present in the UML. The first form is the *sequence diagram.* These are useful in systems that have time-dependent functions, for example, in real-time applications or in those systems where time dependencies play an important role. In this form, objects are shown as vertical lines with the messages as horizontal lines between them. Figure B-14 shows this form in its UML notation. The sequence of messages is indicated by reading down the page.

The second form of the interaction diagram is the *collaboration diagram.* Collaboration diagrams contain the same information as the sequence diagrams but are presented in a different format. They differ from sequence diagrams in that they emphasize the operating context of the objects rather than how they interact over time. The collaboration diagram shows the relationship between the objects but does not show time as a separate dimension, and therefore message sequences are indicated by a numbering scheme.

Figure B-15 shows an example of a collaboration diagram. In it, the example objects are shown as *icons.* Again, arrows indicate the messages sent in the use-case. This time the sequence is indicated by a numbering scheme. Simple collaboration diagrams merely number the messages in sequence. More complex schemes use a decimal numbering approach to indicate if messages are sent as part of the imple-

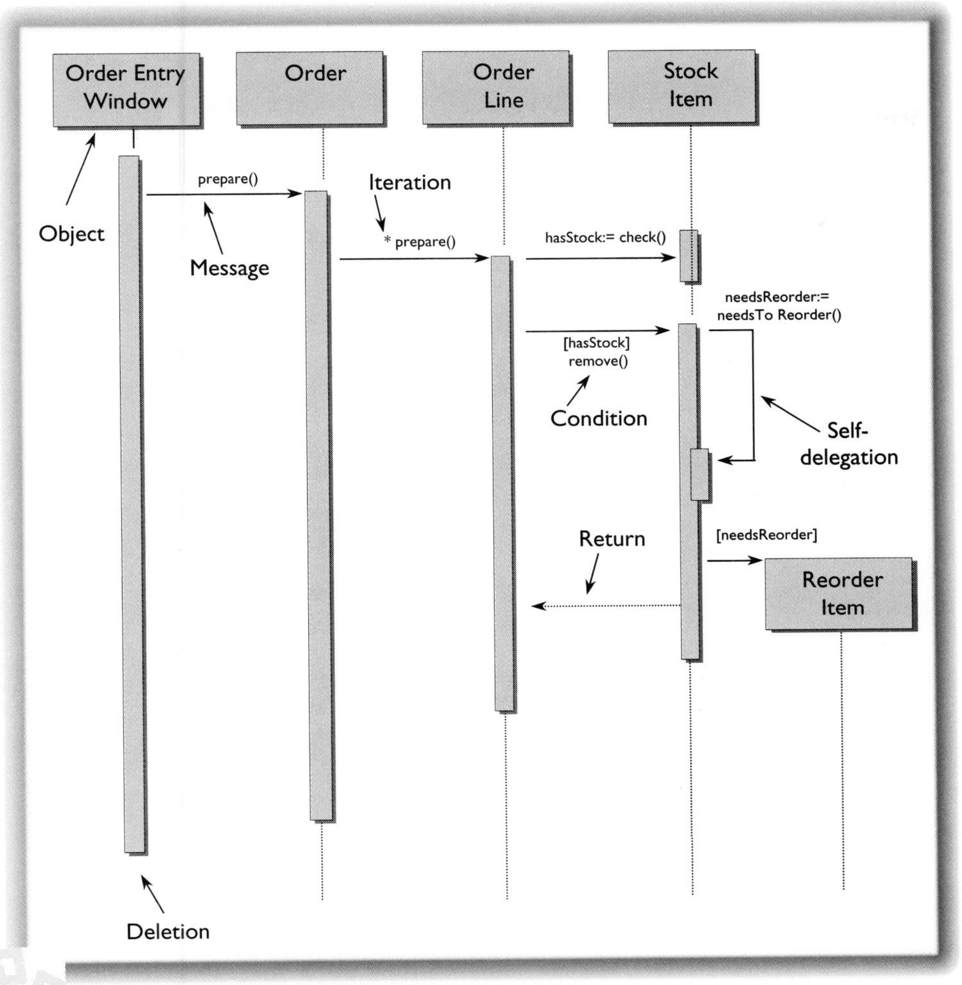

Figure B-14   Sequence Form of Interaction Diagram

mentation of another message. In addition, a letter can be used to show concurrent threads.

One of the great strengths of an interaction diagram is its simplicity. It is difficult to write much about interaction diagrams because they are so simple. They do, however, have weaknesses, the principal one being that although they are good at describing behavior, they do not define it. Interaction diagrams typically do not show all the iteration and control that is needed to give a computationally complete description. Various things have been done to try and remedy this in the UML.

Interaction diagrams should be used when you want to look at the behavior of several objects within a single use-case. They are good at showing the collaborations between the objects; they are not so good at precise definition of the behavior.

Implementation Diagram

UML provides two forms of *implementation diagrams* to support the documentation of implementation issues, including source code structure and runtime implementation issues.

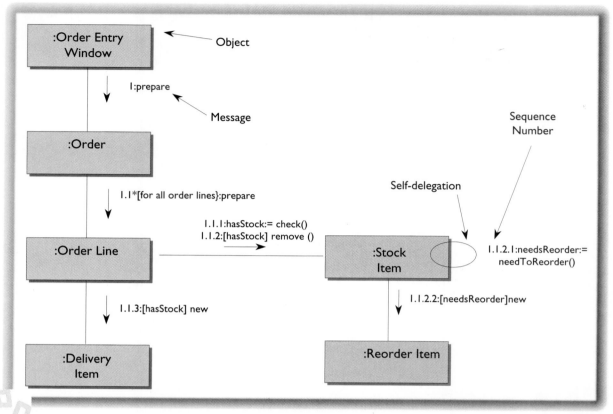

Figure B-15   Collaboration Form of Interaction Diagram

Component Diagram
Component diagrams illustrate the physical structure of the system in terms of actual components (either source code or binary components). They show the dependencies among the software components, including source code components, binary code components, and executable components. Figure B-16 shows a simple component diagram.

Deployment Diagram
Deployment diagrams show the configuration of runtime processing elements and the software components, processes, and objects that live on them. Deployment diagrams represent how the hardware and software units are configured and deployed. For example, they can show which components exist on which machines and how they might be connected together. Figure B-17 illustrates a deployment diagram.

   Each of the modeling diagrams described previously exists for a specific purpose. For example, use-cases are used when defining what the system should do, whereas the class diagram is only built once the overall idea of the internal structure of the system is available. The UML can therefore be used to describe all aspects of a software project—from the user requirements to the actual implementation and distribution.

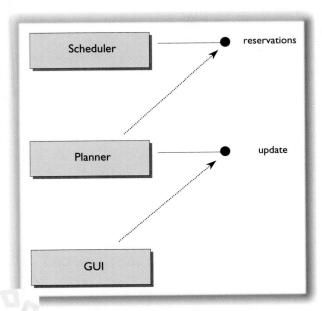

Figure B-16   Example of a Simple Component
Implementation Diagram

Figure B-17   Deployment Implementation Diagram

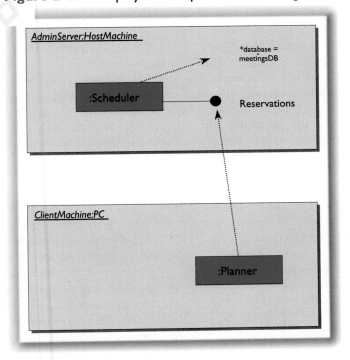

ADVANTAGES AND DISADVANTAGES OF THE OBJECT-ORIENTED APPROACH

Although not yet as widely adopted or accepted as the more traditional relational data and process orientation to software development, the object-oriented approach offers certain advantages over traditional approaches. To begin, it is based on a very intuitive set of concepts. Objects really do exist, events really happen, and the states of real-world objects change as a result of some trigger. Once you understand the relationships between the various objects in the real-world system, modeling them becomes fairly straightforward.

Another advantage of the object-oriented approach lies with its high modularity. Modules can be established to reflect natural classifications and, therefore, can be designed to be completely independent from one another. This independence also insures a highly stable system. Further, the independent nature of object modules makes object-oriented systems easier to change, maintain, and repair.

Yet another advantage to the object-oriented approach is the possibility for reusable code. Because the object modules are independent and fully definable, the dream of reusable code may be closer to reality than ever before. A library of modules could easily be assembled that would allow a programmer to select those modules that best fit the needs for a particular software application. This saves time and money.

One disadvantage associated with the object-oriented approach, however, is a perception of inefficiency. Single processor systems do not yet possess the power to support large-scale object-oriented applications. With the emergence of multiple processor systems and the ever-increasing power of each succeeding generation of chips, this perception may soon be a thing of the past.

APPENDIX SUMMARY

The object-oriented approach to software development is a new and highly promising method that may one day become the standard for designing and developing complex software systems. As stated in the introduction to this appendix, our limited space necessitates a brief coverage of the topic. Given the growth of this method in the modern development environment, however, you should make every effort to pursue your exploration of the topic and plan on becoming skillful in its application. The world of the analyst is constantly evolving, and object-orientation is the next big revolution.

KEY CONCEPTS

➤ Object-oriented approach to software development

The object-oriented approach to software development views the system as a collection of self-contained modules, or objects, that carry with them not only the processes necessary to execute their intended role but also the data, or the identification of the data, necessary for that execution.

➤ The objects can be built as stand-alone units and then assembled, as needed, to form a functional system.

➤ Objects can be reused over and over in a wide variety of systems without having to modify them in any manner.

➤ Objects

An object is any person, place, thing, or event about which we wish to store data or capture its behavior. It can be used to represent anything.

➤ Encapsulation

Packaging an object's variables within the protective custody of its methods is called encapsulation, or the localization of knowledge within a module. Two primary benefits of encapsulation are
  - Modularity
  - Information hiding

➤ Objects versus entities
  - Like an entity, an object has certain attributes that are used to describe the object. In addition, an object can be said to have a current state.
  - The primary difference between an object and an entity is that objects can have behaviors. Behaviors are methods or operations that serve to specify what actions the object can perform.
  - Another difference between objects and entities is that although entities use primary and foreign keys to identify unique instances, an object instance is assigned a UID by the system when it is first created.

➤ Class

The class of an object refers to some generalized description we create to describe objects that are similar in nature or share many of the same characteristics.

➤ A class can define its own instance variables as well as its class variables. A class variable contains information that is shared by instances of the class.

➤ Like an object, a class can declare class methods.

➤ Objects versus classes

The word *object* is sometimes used to refer to both classes and instances. Thus, although no particular nomenclature exists to differentiate between an object class and an instance of a class, in most cases the context helps you determine whether the item of interest is a class or simply a member of a class.

➤ Hierarchical inheritance
  - Each subclass inherits state (in the form of variables declarations) and methods from the superclass. However, subclasses are not limited to the state and behaviors provided to them by their superclass. They can add variables and methods to the ones they inherit from the superclass.
  - This concept is not limited to just one layer of inheritance. The inheritance tree, or class hierarchy, can be as deep as needed. The OBJECT class is at the top of the class hierarchy, and each class is its descendant (directly or indirectly). A variable of type OBJECT can hold a reference to any object. In this way, the OBJECT provides behaviors that are required of all objects running in the application.

➤ Messages

Software objects interact and communicate with each other by sending messages. In certain situations, the receiving object may need more information so that it knows exactly what to do. This additional information is passed along with the message as parameters. Benefits of object messaging include
  - Message passing can support all possible interactions between objects
  - The interacting objects do not need to be a part of the same process or even reside on the same platform to send and receive messages back and forth to each other

➤ Polymorphism

Polymorphism allows a message to one object to invoke a different behavior from the same message to a different object or class. Using this concept of polymorphism in an object-oriented application, an analyst can simply instruct the requesting object to issue a message requesting a certain behavior. The requesting object does not need any information with regard to how that behavior is accomplished.

➤ The Unified Modeling Language (UML)

The UML is the industry-standard language for specifying, visualizing, constructing, and documenting the artifacts of object-based software systems. The UML embodies a set of nine unique object modeling and diagramming tools that, when used appropriately, comprehensively defines and models an object-oriented system:

➤ The use case model

The intention of this tool is to provide a high-level description of what the system must do.

➤ Several benefits are associated with the use-case:

- The use-case can serve as a basis for identifying the relevant objects in a system environment, as well as their high-level relationships, roles, and responsibilities.

- The use-case, when complete, provides an effective tool for validating system requirements and for providing a view of the system from an external perspective.

- In its final form, the use-case can serve as the basis both for the development of a comprehensive test plan and for structuring the final end user documentation.

➤ Use-case components

- Actor

An actor is any person, organization, or computer system external to the system but interacting with it.

- The use cases

The use-cases are the interfaces that the system makes visible and available to the outside world through which the actor can interact. One common way of thinking of a use-case is that of a scenario.

➤ Uses and extends

In the cases where one use-case either makes use of the functionality of another use-case or serves to extend the functionality of another use-case, these use-cases are connected on the diagram using a hollow arrowhead that contains either the word *uses* or *extends*, surrounded by double brackets or pointers.

➤ Class diagram

The class diagram provides a static structure of all the classes that exist within the system. The diagram shows the various classes, each defined as a set of attributes and methods, and points out the relationship between each of those classes via associations or inheritance. There are three perspectives that one can use in drawing and interpreting the class diagrams:

- Conceptual perspective

In this perspective, the diagram is drawn in a manner that represents the concepts in the domain under study.

- Specification perspective

In this perspective, we are looking at the interfaces of the software rather than the implementation. Thus, we are looking at the types rather than classes.

- Implementation perspective

In this perspective, we really do have classes, and we are laying the implementation bare.

➤ One technique associated with class diagramming is the class-responsibility-collaboration (CRC) Card

- Rather than using diagrams to develop models, this technique represents classes on 4 × 6 index cards, and rather than indicating attributes and methods on the cards, this technique records responsibilities, a high-level description of the purpose of the class.

➤ Statechart diagram

A statechart diagram illustrates how the object changes from one state to another in response to a given event. The attributes define the state of the object at one time, whereas the methods define the transaction that occurs.

➤ Activity diagram

An activity diagram is a special form of a statechart diagram. The diagram focuses on the flow of operations driven by internal processing as opposed to external events. It is like a flow chart but differs from a flow chart in that it explicitly supports parallel activities and their synchronization. It is useful when you want to describe a behavior that is parallel or when you want to show behaviors in several use-cases interacting.

➤ Interaction diagram

An interaction diagram provides models to describe how a set of objects interact with each other. The main components of interaction diagrams are the objects and the messages that are sent to each other. The UML has two forms of inter-action diagrams:

- Sequence diagram
  A sequence diagram shows the objects participating in the interaction and the message that they exchange in time sequence. Objects are shown as vertical lines with the message as horizontal lines between them.
- Collaboration diagram
  A collaboration diagram contains the same information as a sequence diagram but is presented in a different format. In this form, the sequence is indicated by a number scheme. Collaboration diagrams emphasize the operating context of the objects rather than how they interact over time.

➤ Implementation diagram
  The UML provides two forms of implementation diagrams to support the documentation of implementation issues:

- Component diagram
  Component diagrams illustrate the physical structure of the system in terms of actual components (either sources code or binary components).
- Deployment diagram
  Deployment diagrams show the configuration of runtime processing elements and the software components, processes, and objects that live on them.

REFERENCES

Booch, G. 1994. *Object-Oriented Analysis and Design with Applications*, 2d ed. Redwood City, CA: Benjamin-Cummings.

Jacobson, I., M. Christerson, P. Jonsson, and G. Overgaard. 1992. *Object-Oriented Software Engineering: A Use-Case Driven Approach.* Reading, MA: Addison-Wesley.

Jacobson, I., G. Booch, and J. Rumbaugh. 1999. *The Unified Software Development Process.* Reading, MA: Addison-Wesley.

Rumbaugh, J., M. Blaha, W. Premerlani, F. Eddy, and W. Lorenson. 1991. *Object-Oriented Modeling and Design.* Englewood Cliffs, NJ: Prentice Hall.

Index

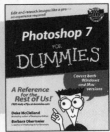